Lecture Notes in Computer Science 14316

Founding Editors

Gerhard Goos

Juris Hartmanis

T0220829

The series Lecture Notes in Computer Science (LNCS), including its subseries Lecture Notes in Artificial Intelligence (LNAI) and Lecture Notes in Bioinformatics (LNBI), has established itself as a medium for the publication of new developments in computer science and information technology research, teaching, and education.

LNCS enjoys close cooperation with the computer science R & D community, the series counts many renowned academics among its volume editors and paper authors, and collaborates with prestigious societies. Its mission is to serve this international community by providing an invaluable service, mainly focused on the publication of conference and workshop proceedings and postproceedings. LNCS commenced publication in 1973.

Marijn Janssen · Luiz Pinheiro ·
Ricardo Matheus · Fernanda Frankenberger ·
Yogesh K. Dwivedi · Ilias O. Pappas ·
Matti Mäntymäki
Editors

New Sustainable Horizons
in Artificial Intelligence
and Digital Solutions

22nd IFIP WG 6.11 Conference on
e-Business, e-Services and e-Society, I3E 2023
Curitiba, Brazil, November 9–11, 2023
Proceedings

 Springer

Editors
Marijn Janssen (iD)
Delft University of Technology
Delft, The Netherlands

Ricardo Matheus (iD)
Delft University of Technology
Delft, The Netherlands

Yogesh K. Dwivedi (iD)
Swansea University
Swansea, UK

Matti Mäntymäki (iD)
University of Turku
Turku, Finland

Luiz Pinheiro (iD)
Positivo University
Curitiba, Paraná, Brazil

Fernanda Frankenberger (iD)
Positivo University
Curitiba, Paraná, Brazil

Ilias O. Pappas (iD)
University of Agder
Kristiansand, Norway

ISSN 0302-9743   ISSN 1611-3349 (electronic)
Lecture Notes in Computer Science
ISBN 978-3-031-50039-8   ISBN 978-3-031-50040-4 (eBook)
https://doi.org/10.1007/978-3-031-50040-4

This Springer imprint is published by the registered company Springer Nature Switzerland AG
The registered company address is: Gewerbestrasse 11, 6330 Cham, Switzerland

Paper in this product is recyclable.

Preface

The IFIP I3E conference, now in its 22nd edition, continues to be a successful forum for discussing digital transformation, e-business, e-services, e-society, e-government, and artificial intelligence and other technology advancements. Researchers worldwide have sought to participate in this conference, recognizing it as an event with a strong reputation and leadership in research related to the adoption of new technologies.

The call for papers invited both full research papers and work in progress in full and short paper formats under the theme "New Sustainable Horizons in Artificial Intelligence and Digital Solutions". The conference also featured panels and keynote sessions with experts. This volume contains 31 articles, comprising 29 full papers and 2 short papers. All submissions underwent a double-blind peer-review process, with a minimum of three reviewers per submission, resulting in an acceptance rate of 45%. The review process this year was completed in 32 days, thanks to the contributions of the many Program Committee members.

The papers included in this volume (vol. 14316) have been categorized into the following topics:

- Artificial Intelligence and Algorithms
- Digital Transformation and New Technologies
- Sustainable Technologies and Smart Cities

The conference committee jointly awarded two prizes. The first prize was given to the best paper, selected from among the top three. The best reviewer was selected from a list of the three best reviewers of the event. The winners in each category were announced during the mandatory awards ceremony at the conference.

The IFIP I3E 2023 conference was hosted by Positivo University in Curitiba, Brazil. Established in 1988, Positivo University (https://www.up.edu.br/) is a for-profit private higher education institution and a large Brazilian higher education institution (uniRank enrollment range: 10,000–14,999 students). The Business School (BSUP) offers courses and programs leading to officially recognized higher education degrees, including bachelor's (B.Sc.), master's (M.Sc.), and doctoral (Ph.D.) degrees in various areas of study. The beautiful location inspired the researchers to have in-depth discussions and to come up with many new research ideas.

We want to express our gratitude to the members of the Program Committee and the reviewers for their significant efforts in evaluating the submitted papers. We also want to thank the local organizers for all their work and dedication to make the conference a success.

We hope that this volume will assist researchers in their studies and contribute to the advancement of new research.

November 2023

Marijn Janssen
Luiz Pinheiro
Ricardo Matheus
Yogesh K. Dwivedi
Ilias O. Pappas
Matti Mäntymäki
Fernanda Frankenberger

Organization

Conference Chairs

Marijn Janssen   TU Delft, The Netherlands
Luiz Pinheiro   Positivo University, Brazil
Fernanda Frankenberger   Positivo University, Brazil
Ricardo Matheus   TU Delft, The Netherlands

Conference Co-chairs

Yogesh K. Dwivedi   Swansea University, UK
Ilias O. Pappas   University of Agder & NTNU, Norway
Matti Mäntymäki   University of Turku, Finland

Program Co-chairs and Local/Regional Supporters

Fernanda Frankenberger   Positivo University, Brazil
Beatriz Lanza   Federal University of Paraná, Brazil
Edimara Luciano   Pontifical Catholic University of Rio Grande do
                                  Sul, Brazil
Maria Alexandra Cunha   Getulio Vargas Foundation, EAESP FGV, Brazil
Taiane Ritta Coelho   Federal University of Paraná, Brazil

Program Committee

Stuti Saxena   Graphic Era University, India
Renan Vieira   University of São Paulo, Brazil
Clarissa Wandscheer   Positivo University, Brazil
Franciany Dugonski   Positivo University, Brazil
Gustavo Salati   University of Campinas, Brazil
Leandro Pykosz   Santa Catarina State University, Brazil
Maryam Hina   LUT University, Finland
Prianka Sarker   Manchester Metropolitan University, UK
Raul Beal Partyka   Getulio Vargas Foundation, Brazil
Thiago Maldonado   Positivo University, Brazil

Contents

Digital Transformation and New Technologies

Sustainable Technologies and Smart Cities

Artificial Intelligence and Algorithm

The Role of Algorithm and Task Familiarity in Algorithm Aversion: An Empirical Study

Hasan Mahmud$^{(\boxtimes)}$ ⓘ and Najmul Islam ⓘ

LUT University, Lappeenranta, Finland
{hasan.mahmud,najmul.islam}@lut.fi

Abstract. Algorithm aversion, characterized by the tendency to distrust algorithmic advice despite its demonstrated superior or identical performance, has become an increasingly concerning issue as it reduces the practical utility of algorithms. To gain insights into this phenomenon, our research centers on individual traits, specifically focusing on familiarity with algorithms and familiarity with the task at hand, and their connections with attitudes toward algorithms. We construct a causal model to delve into these relationships and assess how attitudes, in turn, impact algorithm aversion. Our analysis draws upon data collected through an online survey involving 160 participants, and we employ PLS-SEM for our analysis. The results underscore a noteworthy positive correlation between familiarity with algorithms and attitudes toward algorithms. Interestingly, our findings indicate that familiarity with the task or domain knowledge does not significantly influence attitudes. Moreover, attitudes are demonstrated to have a negative impact on algorithm aversion. These discoveries hold significant implications for comprehending and addressing the issue of algorithm aversion. They shed light on the roles of individual traits and attitudes in shaping people's acceptance of algorithms, ultimately offering valuable insights for mitigating this phenomenon.

Keywords: Algorithmic decision-making · Algorithm Aversion · Familiarity with Algorithms · Familiarity with Task · Attitudes

1 Introduction

Algorithms are becoming increasingly prevalent in our everyday lives, impacting decisions that affect us directly. Algorithms are constantly used by the government, private organizations, and individuals in decision-making, profoundly influencing millions of lives. For example, in the USA, judges rely on COMPAS (Correctional Offender Management Profiling for Alternative Sanctions) algorithms to decide on the likelihood of recidivism. Companies such as Amazon or IBM are using artificial intelligence (AI) algorithms to manage their human resources [1, 2]. Similarly, individuals are increasingly relying on algorithms to decide on what to buy (e.g., Amazon, Ali Express), what to eat (e.g., Uber Eats), where to go (e.g., Tripadvisor), how to go (e.g., Google Maps, Uber), and where to live (Airbnb), to name a few. However, research indicates that in many cases people are reluctant to follow algorithmic advice, despite the superior performance of algorithms, a phenomenon known as algorithm aversion [3, 4]. Such an

© IFIP International Federation for Information Processing 2023
Published by Springer Nature Switzerland AG 2023
M. Janssen et al. (Eds.): I3E 2023, LNCS 14316, pp. 3–13, 2023.
https://doi.org/10.1007/978-3-031-50040-4_1

aversion may lead to serious damage to the overall decision quality, undermining the expected value of the algorithm's utility [5].

Extant literature discovered many factors related to individual characteristics that lead to algorithm aversion. For instance, Mahmud *et al.* [4] found that an individual's familiarity with algorithms, task, and human advisor plays a significant role in algorithm aversion. In algorithmic decision-making, it is intuitive to believe that individuals who are more familiar with the decision task and the general work process of algorithms, are more likely to have positive attitudes toward algorithms. Interestingly, while some research indicates that familiarity with algorithms increases the likelihood of algorithm acceptance [6], others demonstrate that familiarity with the decision task, also known as domain knowledge, has no impact on algorithm adoption [7, 8]. Even, some studies reported that familiarity with task is negatively related to algorithm adoption [9, 10]. Given the divergent results offered by different studies about the impact of different types of familiarity on the utilization of algorithms in decision-making, it is important to investigate these different types of familiarity in a single study for a better understanding of their impact on attitudes toward algorithms. Therefore, considering the desiderata for a greater understanding of how different types of familiarity impact attitudes toward algorithms, we pose the following research question: **RQ1**: How does familiarity with algorithms and tasks influence attitudes toward algorithms? Again, several prior studies [11, 12] demonstrate that people's attitudes affect their behaviors (in our case, algorithm aversion). Therefore, to understand the role of attitudes in algorithmic decision-making, we pose our final research question: **RQ2**: How do attitudes influence algorithm aversion?

To address the above research questions, we conducted an online study with 160 subjects. Collected data were analyzed using the partial least squares structural equation modeling (PLS-SEM). The results indicate that familiarity with algorithms significantly affects attitudes, while familiarity with task has no significant effect on attitudes. Attitudes negatively affect algorithm aversion.

The current study makes two important contributions to algorithmic decision-making literature [3, 4]. First, our study examines the impact of two types of familiarity on attitudes toward algorithms, putting them in a single model to produce a synthesized and holistic body of knowledge about familiarity in the domain of algorithmic decision-making. Second, contrary to previous scholarships [9, 10], our study shows that domain knowledge has no significant impact on attitudes toward algorithms. Our study also provides practical implications for the managers informing what type of familiarity is needed among the individuals to succeed in the implementation of algorithmic decision-making.

2   Theoretical Background

2.1   Algorithmic Decision-making and Algorithm Aversion

Algorithmic decision-making, often referred to simply as 'algorithms' in our study, is an automated process that offers guidance without human involvement. These algorithms can have or lack artificial intelligence (AI) capabilities. The key difference lies in AI-enabled algorithms, also known as AI decisions, which can independently learn from data and make decisions [13].

Algorithm aversion is defined as *a behavior of discounting the decisions of algorithms with respect to one's own decisions or others' decisions, either consciously being aware of the history of high-performance of algorithms or unconsciously out of fundamental distrust toward algorithms* [14, 15]. Several factors influence the aversion of algorithms. In a recent literature review on algorithmic decision-making by Mahmud *et al.* [4], it is found that factors related to algorithms themselves, human characteristics, decision tasks, and various organization, societal, environmental, and cultural factors play critical roles in algorithm aversion. They found that an individual's familiarity with algorithms fosters an individual's acceptance of algorithms while familiarity with task decreases or, in some cases, does not influence the algorithm adoption. However, they do not find any evidence studying both types of familiarity in a single study, highlighting the paradoxical effect of familiarity with algorithms and familiarity with task. Therefore, the current study takes an initial step by investigating the impact of both forms of familiarity on algorithm aversion. In this study, by familiarity with algorithms we refer to the knowledge about the algorithm technology in general such as what are algorithms, how they are designed, what they do, how they do, and what their advantages and limitations. By familiarity with task, we refer to the knowledge and experience pertinent to the task at hand, wherein decision needs to be made.

3 Research Model and Hypotheses Development

This study aims to examine the different types of familiarity: familiarity with algorithms and familiarity with task in the context of decision-making. The model assumes that different types of familiarity might be related to positive attitudes toward algorithms and algorithm aversion the proposed model was controlled for gender, age, education, and employment (Fig. 1).

Familiarity refers to one's understanding of an entity, often based on prior direct and indirect interactions, experience, and knowledge of what, who, how, and when of what is happening [16–18]. Within the realm of algorithmic decision-making, Mahmud *et al.* [4] identified three dimensions of familiarity: (1) familiarity with algorithms, (2) familiarity with the decision task, and (3) familiarity with human decision-makers, whose judgments are compared with those of algorithms. In this study, we focus on the first two dimensions. Familiarity with algorithms arises from direct or indirect exposure to, or knowledge of, algorithms in a general sense. Similarly, familiarity with a task is acquired through direct or indirect involvement with the task, commonly known as domain knowledge.

Past research has shown that an individual's familiarity with algorithms significantly impacts their attitudes toward algorithms [4, 19]. Familiarity increases trust by mitigating uncertainties associated with expectations from and utilization of algorithms through an improved understanding of historical performance [16, 17]. It simplifies the complexities through an understanding of how these algorithms function [16]. Familiarity helps in building confidence in the competence of algorithms [17]. Several prior research on consumer psychology demonstrated that an individual's prior experience with the product fosters positive attitudes toward the product. For example, studying the investors' decision-making behavior in the Islamic stock market, Husin *et al.* [20]

found that investors' familiarity with stock influences their attitudes toward the stock. Furthermore, through an experimental study, Dewar *et al.* [21] confirmed the causal effect of familiarity on brand evaluation. Therefore, we posit that as individuals become more familiar with algorithms, their attitudes toward algorithms are likely to become more positive.

H1a: Familiarity with algorithms positively affects the attitudes toward algorithms.

Familiarity with task pertains to one's experience with the specific task about which decisions, recommendations, or predictions are made. Although experience with the task increases self-efficacy in using algorithms, such experience does not foster attitudes toward algorithms [4]. Prior studies showed that experienced people rely less on algorithms. Experienced people feel more confident in their abilities, leading them to make decisions independently [22]. Experienced people think that they have a greater understanding of the task and the situation, in which they can consider many other things that algorithms might not be capable of doing. Due to this egocentric bias, stemming from the beliefs of a superior understanding of themselves, they trust less in algorithms [10]. Furthermore, due to the black-box nature and lack of explanation of the algorithms, people are unsure about how the decisions are made, making it challenging to follow algorithmic advice blindly. Taking these insights into account, we believe that individual with a high level of familiarity with task displays a lower degree of positive attitudes toward algorithms. Thus, we define our next hypothesis:

H1b: Familiarity with the task negatively affects the attitudes toward algorithms.

Attitude is an individual's favorable and unfavorable evaluation of a given behavior [20, 23]. People's attitudes toward algorithms are strongly connected with algorithm aversion [4, 23]. People tend to hesitate in utilizing algorithms when they perceive them as lacking competence [24, 25]. Negative attitudes discourage individuals not to rely on algorithms [26, 27]. Prior AI adoption literature suggested a positive association between attitudes and the adoption of algorithms [23, 28]. Therefore, we propose:

H3: Attitudes will have a significant negative effect on algorithm aversion.

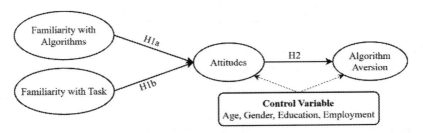

Fig. 1. Proposed research model.

4 Methodology

4.1 Measures and Data Collection

To test the proposed model, data were collected through the crowdsourcing platform Prolific, using a structured survey questionnaire. For the questionnaire, measurement items were adapted from existing literature. Each of the measures of familiarity with algorithms [16, 24, 29], familiarity with task [30], and attitudes [29, 31] contains four items. The construct algorithm aversion [14, 15] consists of five items. However, due to the lack of sufficient loading one item from this construct was dropped from the final analysis. A total of 16 items were measured using a 7-point Likert scale. The developed questionnaire was pre-tested with five experts (three academics and two practitioners) and subsequently made a few modifications according to their suggestions. In the survey, to give a general idea about the algorithms, we provided a short scenario about stock market prediction and asked to predict the index value of the S&P 500 one month from today with and without the help of the algorithm's prediction. After the scenario exercise, we asked the respondents to rate the statements related to measurement items. The survey includes a few attention-check questions to exclude responses that are not given with deliberate thought. Besides measurement items, we also collected information about the demography of the respondents.

A total of 173 participants completed the study, out of which 13 failed to respond to attention check questions correctly. This left us with a final sample of 160. Among the survey population, 52.50% is male, and the average age of the respondents is 28.03. 71.25% of the respondents are employed and all of them are at least undergraduate.

4.2 Data Analysis

Collected data were analyzed using statistical software. In the beginning, SPSS 28.0.0.0 was used to test the normality, multicollinearity, and common method bias (CMB) of the data to ensure the appropriateness of the data for further analysis. In the next stage, we used SmartPLS 4 to examine the reliability and validity of the constructs and to test the proposed hypotheses, following the partial least squares (PLS) approach of structural equation modeling (SEM). A general recommendation for determining the acceptable sample size in PLS is that it should be a minimum of 10 times greater than the largest number of predictors of the most complex multiple regression in the model [32–34]. Our sample size (N = 160) satisfies this condition. To establish the significance of path coefficients, we employed a bootstrapping method involving 5000 bootstrap samples [35]. In bootstrapping, we conducted a one-tailed test since we assumed the relationships toward a particular direction [36].

5 Results

5.1 Measurement Model

We examined the convergent and discriminant validity, following the procedure suggested by Gefen *et al.* [37]. Convergent validity was established by assessing the values of item loadings, composite reliability, and average variance extracted (AVE). We maintained a minimum item loading of 0.70, composite reliability of 0.8, and AVE of 0.5, following the guidelines of Furnell & Locker [38]. To comply with these standards, we removed one item from the algorithm aversion construct. Thus, we confirmed the convergent validity. The descriptive statistics, item loadings, composite reliability, and AVEs are presented in Table 1.

Table 1. Item loadings, VIF, composite reliability, AVEs, and R2 of the constructs.

Construct	Indicators	Loading > 0.7	VIF < 5	CR > 0.7	AVE > 0.5	R2
Familiarity with algorithms (FA)	FA_1	0.887	2.963	0.948	0.792	-
	FA_2	0.856	2.629			
	FA_3	0.902	2.878			
	FA_4	0.914	2.949			
Familiarity with the task (FT)	FT_1	0.888	2.618	0.897	0.734	-
	FT_2	0.815	2.063			
	FT_3	0.894	2.635			
	FT_4	0.828	1.957			
Attitudes	Att_1	0.900	3.405	0.906	0.773	0.452
	Att_2	0.887	3.127			
	Att_3	0.908	3.414			
	Att_4	0.817	2.305			
Algorithm Aversion	AA_1	0.813	1.680	0.816	0.803	0.339
	AA_2	0.785	1.753			
	AA_3	0.766	1.766			
	AA_4	0.799	1.587			

VIF = Variance inflation factor; CR = Composite (Rho) reliability; AVE = Average variance extracted.

Table 2. Inter-construct correlations and the square root of AVEs.

	Algorithm Aversion	Attitude	FA	FT
Algorithm Aversion	**0.791**			
Attitudes	−0.570	**0.879**		
FA	−0.065	0.247	**0.890**	
FT	0.027	0.117	0.523	**0.857**

FA = Familiarity with algorithms; FT = Familiarity with the task.

Discriminant validity denotes whether the items of a construct measure the construct in question [39]. Discriminant validity is assessed by comparing whether the values of square roots of AVEs are higher than the values of inter-construct correlations. In Table 2, we can see that the values of square roots of AVEs, presented diagonally, are higher than the off-diagonal inter-construct correlation values, confirming the discriminant validity between the constructs [38].

5.2 Structural Model

The results (Fig. 2) revealed that familiarity with algorithms had a significant positive impact on attitudes toward algorithms, supporting H1a ($\beta = 0.254$, p < 0.01). However, in contrast to our hypothesis (H1b) that familiarity with task has a negative effect on attitudes toward algorithms, the model found no significant effect of familiarity with task on attitudes toward algorithms ($\beta = -0.005$, ns). Finally, algorithm aversion was found to be influenced negatively by attitudes ($\beta = -0.555$, p < 0.001), thus confirming our hypothesis (H2). Altogether, the model explained a 10.10% variance in attitudes toward algorithms and a 33.80% variance in algorithm aversion. Regarding the control variables, we did not find any significant effect.

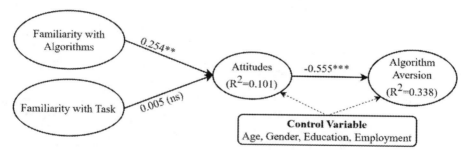

Fig. 2. PLS analysis results (***p < 0.001; **p < 0.01; ns: not significant).

6 Discussion

6.1 Key Findings

Our study delves into different types of familiarity's impact on attitudes toward algorithms and subsequent influence on algorithm aversion. The study aims to explore the contrasting effects of familiarity (algorithms vs. task) on attitudes toward algorithms. First, we examine the influence of familiarity with algorithms and familiarity with task on attitudes toward algorithms. Second, we assess the impact of attitudes on algorithm aversion. The analysis of our research model produces several compelling discoveries.

Familiarity with algorithms demonstrates a significantly positive impact on attitudes toward algorithms, aligning with prior research that has underscored the role of familiarity in fostering positive attitudes toward algorithms [20, 40]. Surprisingly, the hypothesized negative relationship between familiarity with task and attitudes toward algorithms is not supported (H1b). Although extant literature supports the notion that task experience boosts self-confidence, decreasing the reliance on algorithms [8, 9, 41], a few studies reported that there is no significant relationship between task familiarity and attitudes toward algorithms [7, 8]. Our findings corroborated the latter.

Concerning the other relationships that were discovered; we found a significant negative relationship between attitudes and algorithm aversion. This suggests that individuals with a greater degree of positive attitudes toward algorithms are less likely to avert algorithms.

6.2   Implications for Research

The study will have several contributions that could benefit scholars and advance research in information systems.

First, extending prior research on algorithm aversion, we underscore how different types of familiarity influence attitudes toward algorithms. We contribute empirically to algorithm aversion literature by examining the contrasting effects of familiarity with algorithms and familiarity with task in a single study. Although the familiarity with algorithms and familiarity with task are studied in the prior research separately [9, 19], research exploring both in a single study is scarce [8].

Second, we empirically validated the measurement scale of algorithm aversion developed by Mahmud *et al.* [15] in a different context. Although prior research measured algorithm aversion by observing the behavior of individuals in the experimental setting, measuring algorithm aversion using a measurement scale is relatively novel. Thus, we contribute to the advancement of algorithm aversion research.

Third, in terms of practical implication, our study demonstrated a non-significant relationship between familiarity with task and attitude toward algorithms. Hence, it is intuitive to believe that domain knowledge does not predict the acceptance of algorithms. Therefore, in predicting the algorithm use behavior, practitioners may rethink the importance of the user's domain knowledge.

6.3   Limitations and Future Research

Despite the study rigor, the current study has a few limitations that must be acknowledged. First, our study was cross-sectional, which may not capture the changing nature of familiarity and attitudes of individuals. Therefore, longitudinal research may be undertaken in the future to overcome this limitation. Second, the study was conducted in a particular context (stock market), thus limiting the generalizability of the findings. Therefore, we suggest future study validates our findings by replicating our study in different contexts. Third, our model does not introduce any moderator or mediator in the proposed relationships. Future research might be undertaken to understand the moderating and mediating impact of different variables in these relationships.

7   Conclusion

This study examined algorithm aversion and its connection to individual characteristics, namely familiarity with algorithms and familiarity with task. The results suggest that individuals with a greater degree of familiarity with algorithms tend to possess a greater degree of positive attitudes toward algorithmic advice. Interestingly, domain knowledge or familiarity with task was not found to significantly influence attitudes toward algorithms. Additionally, the study explored the influence of overall attitudes toward algorithms on algorithm aversion. These findings bear important implications for both research and practice, highlighting the importance of developing positive attitudes toward algorithms to overcome algorithm aversion.

References

1. Bailey, D., Faraj, S., Hinds, P., von Krogh, G., Leonardi, P.: Special issue of organization science: emerging technologies and organizing. Organ. Sci. **30**(3), 642–646 (2019). https://doi.org/10.1287/orsc.2019.1299
2. Vrontis, D., Christofi, M., Pereira, V., Tarba, S., Makrides, A., Trichina, E.: Artificial intelligence, robotics, advanced technologies and human resource management: a systematic review. Int. J. Hum. Resour. Manag. **33**, 1237–1266 (2022). https://doi.org/10.1080/09585192.2020.1871398
3. Dietvorst, B.J., Simmons, J.P., Massey, C.: Algorithm aversion: people erroneously avoid algorithms after seeing them err. J. Exp. Psychol. Gen. **144**, 114–126 (2015). https://doi.org/10.1037/xge0000033
4. Mahmud, H., Islam, A.K.M.N., Ahmed, S.I., Smolander, K.: What influences algorithmic decision-making? A systematic literature review on algorithm aversion. Technol. Forecast. Soc. Change. **175**, 121390 (2022). https://doi.org/10.1016/j.techfore.2021.121390
5. Filiz, I., René Judek, J., Lorenz, M., Spiwoks, M.: The Tragedy of Algorithm Aversion. Ostfalia Hochschule für Angewandte Wissenschaften, Fakultät Wirtschaft (2021)
6. Fenneman, A., Sickmann, J., Pitz, T., Sanfey, A.G.: Two distinct and separable processes underlie individual differences in algorithm adherence: differences in predictions and differences in trust thresholds. PLOS ONE **16**, e0247084 (2021). https://doi.org/10.1371/journal.pone.0247084
7. Kawaguchi, K.: When will workers follow an algorithm? a field experiment with a retail business. Manag. Sci. **67**, 1670–1695 (2021). https://doi.org/10.1287/mnsc.2020.3599
8. Whitecotton, S.M.: The effects of experience and a decision aid on the slope, scatter, and bias of earnings forecasts. Organ. Behav. Hum. Decis. Process. **66**, 111–121 (1996). https://doi.org/10.1006/OBHD.1996.0042
9. Allen, R.T., Choudhury, P.: Algorithm-augmented work and domain experience: the countervailing forces of ability and aversion. Organ. Sci. **33**, 149–169 (2022). https://doi.org/10.1287/orsc.2021.1554
10. Logg, J.M., Minson, J.A., Moore, D.A.: Algorithm appreciation: people prefer algorithmic to human judgment. Organ. Behav. Hum. Decis. Process. **151**, 90–103 (2019). https://doi.org/10.1016/j.obhdp.2018.12.005
11. Ajzen, I.: The theory of planned behavior. Organ. Behav. Hum. Decis. Process. **50**, 179–211 (1991). https://doi.org/10.1016/0749-5978(91)90020-T
12. Fishbein, M., Ajzen, I.: Belief, attitude, intention, and behavior: an introduction to theory and research. Hilosophy Rhetor. **10**, 130–132 (1977)
13. Wesche, J.S., Langer, M., Sonderegger, A., Landers, R.N.: Editorial to the virtual special issue: human-automation interaction in the workplace: a broadened scope of paradigms. Comput. Human Behav. **134**, 107335 (2022). https://doi.org/10.1016/j.chb.2022.107335
14. Mahmud, H., Islam, A.K.M.N., Mitra, R.K., Hasan, A.R.: The impact of functional and psychological barriers on algorithm aversion – an IRT perspective. In: Papagiannidis, S., Alamanos, E., Gupta, S., Dwivedi, Y.K., Mäntymäki, M., Pappas, I.O. (eds.) The Role of

Digital Technologies in Shaping the Post-Pandemic World: 21st IFIP WG 6.11 Conference on e-Business, e-Services and e-Society, I3E 2022, Newcastle upon Tyne, UK, September 13–14, 2022, Proceedings, pp. 95–108. Springer International Publishing, Cham (2022). https://doi.org/10.1007/978-3-031-15342-6_8

15. Mahmud, H., Islam, A.K.M.N., Mitra, R.K.: What drives managers towards algorithm aversion and how to overcome it? Mitigating the impact of innovation resistance through technology readiness. Technol. Forecast. Soc. Change. **193**, 122641 (2023). https://doi.org/10.1016/j.techfore.2023.122641

16. Gefen, D.: E-commerce: the role of familiarity and trust. Omega **28**, 725–737 (2000). https://doi.org/10.1016/S0305-0483(00)00021-9

17. Komiak, S.Y.X., Benbasat, I.: The effects of personalization and familiarity on trust and adoption of recommendation agents. MIS Q. Manag. Inf. Syst. **30**, 941–960 (2006). https://doi.org/10.2307/25148760

18. Sun, S., Wang, Y.: Familiarity, beliefs, attitudes, and consumer responses toward online advertising in China and the United States. J. Glob. Mark. **23**, 127–138 (2010). https://doi.org/10.1080/08911761003673454

19. Chen, J., Dibb, S.: Consumer trust in the online retail context: exploring the antecedents and consequences. Psychol. Mark. **27**, 323–346 (2010). https://doi.org/10.1002/MAR.20334

20. Husin, M.M., Aziz, S., Bhatti, T.: The impact of brand familiarity, perceived trust and attitude on investors' decision-making in Islamic stock market. J. Islam. Mark. (2022). https://doi.org/10.1108/JIMA-04-2020-0093/FULL/HTML

21. Dawar, N., Lei, J.: Brand crises: The roles of brand familiarity and crisis relevance in determining the impact on brand evaluations. J. Bus. Res. **62**, 509–516 (2009). https://doi.org/10.1016/J.JBUSRES.2008.02.001

22. Sharan, N.N., Romano, D.M.: The effects of personality and locus of control on trust in humans versus artificial intelligence. Heliyon. **6**, e04572 (2020). https://doi.org/10.1016/J.HELIYON.2020.E04572

23. Cao, G., Duan, Y., Edwards, J.S., Dwivedi, Y.K.: Understanding managers' attitudes and behavioral intentions towards using artificial intelligence for organizational decision-making. Technovation **106**, 102312 (2021). https://doi.org/10.1016/J.TECHNOVATION.2021.102312

24. Berger, B., Adam, M., Rühr, A., Benlian, A.: Watch me improve—algorithm aversion and demonstrating the ability to learn. Bus. Inf. Syst. Eng. **63**, 55–68 (2021). https://doi.org/10.1007/s12599-020-00678-5

25. Luo, X., Tong, S., Fang, Z., Qu, Z.: Frontiers: machines vs. humans: the impact of artificial intelligence chatbot disclosure on customer purchases. Mark. Sci. **38**, 913–1084, ii–ii (2019). https://doi.org/10.1287/mksc.2019.1192

26. Gogoll, J., Uhl, M.: Rage against the machine: automation in the moral domain. J. Behav. Exp. Econ. **74**, 97–103 (2018). https://doi.org/10.1016/J.SOCEC.2018.04.003

27. Prahl, A., Swol, L.V.: Out with the humans, in with the machines?: investigating the behavioral and psychological effects of replacing human advisors with a machine. Hum.-Mach. Commun. **2**, 209–234 (2021). https://doi.org/10.30658/hmc.2.11

28. Duan, Y., Edwards, J.S., Dwivedi, Y.K.: Artificial intelligence for decision making in the era of Big Data – evolution, challenges and research agenda. Int. J. Inf. Manag. **48**, 63–71 (2019). https://doi.org/10.1016/J.IJINFOMGT.2019.01.021

29. Breward, M., Hassanein, K., Head, M.: Understanding consumers' attitudes toward controversial information technologies: a contextualization approach. Inf. Syst. Res. **28**, 760–774 (2017). https://doi.org/10.1287/isre.2017.0706

30. Chau, P.Y.K., Lai, V.S.K.: An empirical investigation of the determinants of user acceptance of Internet banking An Empirical Investigation of the Determinants of User Acceptance of Internet Banking. J. Organ. Comput. Electron. Commer. **13**, 123–145 (2003)

31. Morris, M.G., Venkatesh, V.: Age differences in technology adoption decisions: implications for a changing work force. Pers. Psychol. **53**, 375–403 (2000). https://doi.org/10.1111/J.1744-6570.2000.TB00206.X
32. Whelan, E., Islam, A.K.M.N., Brooks, S.: Applying the SOBC paradigm to explain how social media overload affects academic performance. Comput. Educ. **143**, 103692 (2020). https://doi.org/10.1016/J.COMPEDU.2019.103692
33. Barclay, D., Higgins, C., Thompson, R.: The partial least squares (PLS) approach to causal modelling: personal computer adoption and use as an illustration. Technol. Stud. **2**, 285–309 (1995)
34. Hair, J.F., Ringle, C.M., Sarstedt, M.: PLS-SEM: indeed a silver bullet. J. Mark. Theory Pract. **19**, 139–152 (2011). https://doi.org/10.2753/MTP1069-6679190202
35. Hair, J.F., Hult, G.T.M., Ringle, C.M., Sarstedt, M.: A Primer on Partial Least Squares Structural Equation Modeling (PLS-SEM). Sage, Thousand Oaks (2017)
36. Kock, N.: One-tailed or two-tailed P values in PLS-SEM? Int. J. E-Collab. **11**, 1–7 (2015). https://doi.org/10.4018/IJEC.2015040101
37. Gefen, D., Straub, D., Gefen, D., Straub, D.: A practical guide to factorial validity using PLS-Graph: tutorial and annotated example. Commun. Assoc. Inf. Syst. **16**, 91–109 (2005). https://doi.org/10.17705/1CAIS.01605
38. Fornell, C., Larcker, D.F.: Evaluating structural equation models with unobservable variables and measurement error. J. Mark. Res. **18**, 39–50 (1981). https://doi.org/10.1177/002224378101800104
39. Gefen, D., Straub, D.W.: Consumer trust in B2C e-Commerce and the importance of social presence: Experiments in e-Products and e-Services. Omega **32**, 407–424 (2004). https://doi.org/10.1016/J.OMEGA.2004.01.006
40. Copeland, L., Bhaduri, G.: Consumer relationship with pro-environmental apparel brands: effect of knowledge, skepticism and brand familiarity. J. Prod. Brand. Manag. **29**, 1–14 (2020). https://doi.org/10.1108/JPBM-03-2018-1794/FULL/HTML
41. Sieck, W.R., Arkes, H.R.: The recalcitrance of overconfidence and its contribution to decision aid neglect. J. Behav. Decis. Mak. **18**, 29–53 (2005). https://doi.org/10.1002/BDM.486

Investigating Developers' Perception on Success Factors for Research Software Development

Erica Mourão[1]([⊠])(iD), Daniela Trevisan[1](iD), José Viterbo[1](iD),
and Carlos Eduardo Pantoja[1,2](iD)

[1] Institute of Computing, Fluminense Federal University, Niterói, RJ, Brazil
ericamourao@id.uff.br, {daniela,viterbo}@ic.uff.br
[2] Federal Center for Technological Education Celso Suckow da Fonseca,
Rio de Janeiro, RJ, Brazil
pantoja@cefet-rj.br

Abstract. Modern research depends on software libraries, tools, and applications, specially in Artificial Intelligence (AI) to support science, engineering, and business. Research software is often developed in academia by academic researchers in Information and Communication Technology (ICT). However, this software rarely achieves effective success: it is often developed and maintained in an inefficient and unsustainable way, resulting in failure, non-adoption, and abandonment. The goal of this work is to better understand how academic research software developers evaluate success factors in different categories: technical, organizational, and people. A survey with thirty Brazilian academic research software developers was conducted to gather information about the level of importance of the factors. An analysis of the collected data was conducted to identify the importance of these success factors. The results show the ranking of success factors into categories among the research developers. Our study indicates that academic developers can conduct more software development by being aware of the success factors that can provide software sustainability and successfully. The comprehension of the level of importance of each factor will help to improve and guide the support for research software developers on development.

Keywords: Empirical Research · Research Software · ICT · Success Factors · Academia · University · Brazilian Academic Developers

1 Introduction

Modern research in sciences, engineering, and other fields depends on software, specifically, research software [1]. Research software is a software developed by researchers and consists of libraries, tools, and applications or end-user software [2] including Artificial Intelligence (AI), Machine Learning, Analytics and Data Science tools [3], e.g., OpenML, ChatGPT, GitHub, Jupyter, and Overleaf.

© IFIP International Federation for Information Processing 2023
Published by Springer Nature Switzerland AG 2023
M. Janssen et al. (Eds.): I3E 2023, LNCS 14316, pp. 14–26, 2023.
https://doi.org/10.1007/978-3-031-50040-4_2

Researchers in a wide variety of domains develop, maintain, or use research software to conduct or support their research [2,4,5] and such software is most often produced by academic researchers within academia, faculty, and university [1,6].

Research software is essential to several modern research projects in AI and Digital Solutions, and academic researchers are unable to work without it. A comprehensive survey reports that academic faculty and staff at UK universities found that 92% of academics use research software, with 69% saying that their research would not be practical without it [7] and another study expanded the UK data, focusing instead on US universities, and the results were similar [8].

Software engineering researchers have developed several important practices that result in a software overall with higher quality [9,10]. However, in the academy there are a number of factors that result in a software not developed in an efficient or sustainable way. While academic researchers have deep knowledge in their discipline, they generally do not have sufficient training across the software lifecycle and several types of tools [1], and the development of research software is still *ad hoc* and improvised, making such infrastructure fragile and vulnerable to failure [11]. Additionally, best practices that provide academic researchers methods for performing development, ease maintainability, and that encourage sustainability and reproducibility are not widely used, resulting in failure, non-adoption, and abandonment software [1,3,12,13].

In recent decades, several studies about factors determining the success of traditional software projects have been performed in the organizations or industry [12,14–16]. Critical success factors identified in project software were mapped into different categories, such as Technical, Organizational, and People [17–21]. However, the literature investigating success factors in an academic context is scarce, and there is a gap in understanding whether these success factors identified in traditional software projects influence the success of research software from the perspective of academic research software developers in Information and Communication Technology (ICT).

Therefore, the objective of this study is to understand the technical, organizational, and people factors that determine successful research software by developer's perceptions. In this work, we conducted an empirical study [22] using a survey with 30 academic researchers developers to investigate technical, organizational, and people factors of research software in the Brazilian academies. We used the factors identified previously in the literature about successful project software [17,18,23,24] to understand the level of importance of each factor in research software and consequently the sustainability of such software. We used closed questions with a five-point Likert Scale to define the importance of the factors. Finally, we perform descriptive statistics to generate results.

The contributions of this work are: it investigates the developers' perception of success factors for Brazilian research software development, provides a ranking of factors that may guide the development successfully, and it discusses the findings to provide insight into the situation in the academic context.

The paper is organized as follows. In Sect. 2, we provide related works. In Sect. 3, we present the method, including research questions, study design, data collection, and analysis. In Sect. 4, we present the results. In Sect. 5, we discuss the findings. In Sect. 6, we discuss the threats to validity and limitations. Finally, in Sect. 7, the conclusions and future works are presented.

2   Related Works

Success is essential in traditional software development, and projects succeed when enough factors go well to allow a project's objectives to be satisfied [12]. Moreover, the project manager or organization needs to control these factors to drive toward project success [16]. The success factors of software projects can be identified and grouped into categories of a model or framework to provide guidelines and insights that influence the success of software development projects [17–19]. Hence, a successful software project depends on several factors: not only time, quality, scope, and budget but also technical factors, organizational factors, people factors, process factors, and other factors. Therefore, understanding their importance is critical for people who work in software engineering research and information and communication technology.

We performed a search [25] to identify studies related to success factors in the context of research software development and used a hybrid search, which consisted of using *DatabaseSearch* in Scopus to select the set of relevant initial articles followed by parallel *Backward and Forward Snowballing* [26]. We selected the articles that were most similar to our problem in the academic context.

A study examining claims about how scientists develop software reported 33 different claims about 12 software engineering practices [9]. Most of the claims indicated that software engineering practices are useful for scientific software development. Moreover, a recent study reported the use of software engineering practices for scientific application development and their impact on software quality [10]. However, these studies do not present the practices as success factors and do not evaluate a ranking of their importance in academia.

Members of academic research groups or institutions work on research projects. A study presents an organizational structures model for research software development at universities that includes the use of software engineering practices and processes [1]. Three different models for research software development are reported: one traditional Research Software Engineering (RSE) group in the UK at the University of Manchester and two in the US Universities. Moreover, the need for more opportunities and time for developers of research software to receive training in practices is a sustainability challenge faced in developing and using research software [11]. Although these models and challenges are presented and discussed, the success factors of the project were not defined and evaluated.

The occurrence of certain factors can lead to the success of academic research software. Therefore, we did not find studies related to factors that influence academic developers on a research software project, regarding technical, organizational, and people factors, such as traditional software that lead to success.

3   Method

Our research aims to investigate in the academic context the developer's perceptions of success related to factors technical, organizational, and people in research software development. It is an initial step towards understanding the perceptions of these factors that determine the success of software by developers in the context of Brazilian academia. We conducted explanatory survey research, following the guidelines defined by Kitchenham and Pfleeger [27], that is, an empirical research method [22], to understand these factors identified.

According to Goal-Question-Metric (GQM) paradigm [28], our survey aims to *analyze* research software development *with the purpose of* characterizing *with respect to* determining the importance of the technical, organizational and people factors for the success of the research software *from the point of view of* Brazilian academics developers *in the context of* the research software development in academia.

The next step following GQM is to define questions and metrics to address this defined goal. In this phase of the study, we used the following Research Questions (RQs):

RQ1. *What are the technical factors that determine the success of research software developed in academia?* We formulated this research question to investigate the level of importance placed on each technical factor regarding software engineering in research software development by developers. We considered the set of relevant software engineering concepts identified in the literature and SWE-BOK [23,24].

RQ2. *What are the organizational factors that determine the success of research software developed in academia?* We formulated this research question to understand the level of importance placed on each organizational factor in research software development [17,18].

RQ3. *What are the people factors that determine the success of research software developed in academia?* We formulated this research question to understand the level of importance placed on each people factor in research software development [17,18].

To answer those research questions, we planned and conducted an explanatory study using a survey instrument with Brazilian developers of research software. The metrics were based on primarily close-ended questions, some multiple-choice type questions, and some open-ended questions. The survey was conducted between November 2021 and February 2022.

3.1   Study Design

Following the GQM approach, a set of questions addressed to all participants to assess their general knowledge and opinions on the subject was planned with the aim of investigating the success factors in research software development in the academy by academics.

We used a questionnaire to support the participants in answering our questions. We developed the instrument in Google Forms[1], which consisted of the following sections: (i) the objective of the study and term of consent, to participants read and accept the explanatory statement about goals and data privacy of the study; (ii) research profile; (iii) personal and professional background; (iv) questions related to technical, organizational and people in research software development.

The questions primarily consist of closed-type questions with a single choice, some multiple-choice type questions, and a few open-ended questions. Furthermore, in most questions, we use Likert scales on an ordinal scale of 1 to 5, and define for each a minimum value (e.g., "nothing important"), a maximum value (e.g., "very important"), and the middle (e.g.,"median important"). In addition, if the respondent do has no knowledge about the subject of the question, he can select the option (e.g.,"I don't know"), which is assigned a value of 0.

At the beginning of the survey instrument, we included a consent form that inform to the respondents of the study's privacy policies clearly and thoroughly, following ethics guidelines, data anonymity, and participation, the possible benefits and risks, the estimated time to respond to the answers, and the author's e-mails so that the respondent could ask any questions about the research. Thus, the respondents had enough information to make the decision to participate or not, and these actions reduced the risk ethics and increases the validity of our empirical study [22].

Before inviting respondents, we conducted the pilot test of the survey with affiliated researchers to improve its understandability and remove any inconsistencies. Our samples' composition from a target population included Brazilian academic researchers who are developers of the software research. We selected researchers from our affiliation and collaboration network, comprising contextual diversity. Based on these criteria, we invited the participants by e-mail.

3.2   Data Collection

The survey was conducted by invitation to have better control over the distribution into the academy, and our method was convenience sampling [29]. Our samples' composition from a well-defined target population included Brazilian academic researchers who are users and work in research software development. We sent email invitations to (i) academic research developers of the Brazilian Computer Society, (ii) email lists used at the Fluminense Federal University (UFF), which include researchers, (iii) coordinators of research projects and professors teaching Computer Science or Information Systems courses at public and private higher education institutions. Moreover, WhatsApp groups were used to invite.

We sent our survey questionnaire to potential respondents in various institutions, considering federal and state, public and private higher education institutions. The authors' goal was to reach the maximum number of Brazilian academic

---

[1] https://docs.google.com/forms/.

researcher respondents who meet the target audience to answer the survey. We did not restrict ourselves to any particular project size or organizational culture in institutions. Thus, we were able to survey researchers in Computing that are widely geographically distributed across Brazil. In addition, as the survey was online, it was cost-efficient, and the respondents were able to answer the questions more thoughtfully according to their own time allowing.

We used the Google Forms[2] to design, host, and administrate our online survey, which was available for four months from November 2021 to February 2022. Our survey was 30 responses obtained.

3.3 Data Analysis

In the analysis of the results, we adopted assumptions: (i) we anonymized the data, (ii) we cleaned the data, (iii) in the results, the sum of percentages equals one hundred percent for single closed questions with a range of options and the five-point Likert Scale, (iv) all responses have been filled in completely.

Regarding RQ1, RQ2, and RQ3 we perform statistical analysis to explore data and generate results. Thus, we prepared the available data to perform the descriptive statistical analysis.

The first analysis involved frequency counting for questions where respondents could choose one or more options. An example of this would be a question asking about years of experience or duration of use of research software.

The second analysis is related to the importance rating using the five-point Likert scale (I don't know = 0. Nothing important = 1, Little important = 2, Median important = 3, Important = 4, Very important = 5). The median for each category was calculated, and the top ratings were presented. The dataset is available at Zenodo in the link https://doi.org/10.5281/zenodo.8110912.

4 Results

In the following, we summarise our results structured according to the respondents' demographics and research questions defined in Sect. 3.

4.1 Respondents' Demographics

The participant's ages were divided into the following intervals. Of a total of 30 respondents, a majority (33.3%) are between 30 and 39 years old, and the second most representative group (30.0%) are between 18 and 29 years old. Other respondents are (16.67%) between 40 and 49 years old, (13.3%) between 50 and 59 years old, and (6.67%) 60 years or older. Most academics are male 90.00%, and 10% are female, with ages between 30 and 39 years old.

Regarding the frequency of use of research software, which is software to conduct or support your research in an academic context, most of the respondents (30.00%) Often use the research software followed by (46.66%) Always.

---

2 https://docs.google.com/forms/.

Then, (13.33%) the respondent informed Occasionally uses the research software. Therefore, we observed a high usage of such software, as expected.

Regarding the year of use of research software, most respondents (60.00%) had more than six years ago. The other respondents (23.33%) have between three and five years of use, (10.00%) between one and two years of use, and (6.67%) less than one year ago.

Regarding the years of experience in research software, (33.33%) of respondents are between one and five years, and (33.33%) between six and ten years of experience, characterized by more solid expertise in research software. After that, (6.67%) of respondents with experience between eleven and fifteen years of experience, (13.33%) between sixteen and twelve years of experience, and (10.40%) with more than twelve years of experience are presented. Finally, one developer (3.33%) had less than one year and is a beginner in research software development.

Thus, respondents over six years of experience or more (66.67%) are characterized by specialized expertise in research software development. The following subsection describes the results and analysis for the Research Questions.

4.2   What are the Technical Factors that Determine the Success of Research Software Developed in Academia (RQ1)?

This subsection provides the results of RQ1. The factors were sorted in increasing order according to the proportion of the top two ratings Very important (Vi) and Important (I) to obtain an overall understanding of whether research software developers follow. Figure 1 summarizes the results from this question.

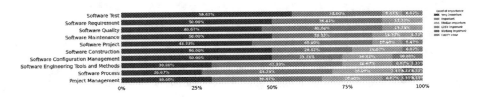

Fig. 1. Importance rating of technical factors that determine the success project

The results show that 86.67% of the participants (56.67% Vi and 30.00% I), (50.00% Vi and 36.67% I) and (46.67% Vi and 40.00% I), respectively, consider the factors "Software Test", "Software Requirement" and "Software Quality" influential in importance, suggesting that they are the top critical success factors impacting the research software development, as they represent the highest median score. This is followed by 83.33% of the participants (50.00% Vi and 33.33% I) and (43.33% Vi and 40.00% I) informed that the factors "Software Maintenance" and "Software Project" are important in the research software. Then, 76.67% of the participants (50.00% Vi and 26.67% I) consider that the factor "Software Construction" is influential in importance. This is followed by

73.33% participants (50.00% Vi and 23.33% I) and (30.00% Vi and 43.33% I) that consider the factors "Software Configuration Management" and "Software Engineering Tools and Methods" have of importance. Finally, 70.00% of the participants (26.67% Vi and 43.33% I) consider that the factor "Software Process" following 66.67% of the participants (30.00% Vi and 36.67% I) consider that the factor "Software Management" are important.

4.3 What are the Organizational Factors that Determine the Success of Research Software Developed in Academia (RQ2)?

This subsection provides the results of RQ2. The factors were also sorted in increasing order according to the proportion of the top two ratings Very important (Vi) and Important (I) to obtain an overall understanding of whether research software developers follow. Figure 2 summarizes the results from this question.

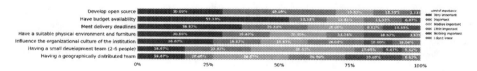

Fig. 2. Importance rating of organizational factors that determine the success project

The results show that 70.00% of the participants (30.00% Vi and 40.00% I) consider the factor "Develop open source" influential in importance, suggesting that it is the top critical success factor impacting the research software development, as it represents the highest median score. This is followed by 66.66% of the participants (53.33% Vi and 13.33% I) informed that the factor "Have budget availability" are important in the research software. Then, 60.00% of the participants (36.67% Vi and 23.33% I) consider that the factor "Meet delivery deadlines" is influential in importance. This is followed by 46.67% participants (30.00% Vi and 16.67% I) and 43.34% participants (26.67% Vi and 16.67% I) that consider the factors "Have a suitable physical environment and furniture" and "Influence the organizational culture of the institution" have of importance. Finally, 40.00% of the participants (16.67% Vi and 23.33% I) consider that the factor "Having a small development team (2–6 people)" following 26.67% of the participants (16.67% Vi and 10.00% I) consider that the factor "Having a geographically distributed team" is important.

4.4 What Are the People Factors that Determine the Success of Research Software Developed in Academia (RQ3)?

This subsection provides the results of RQ3. The factors were finally also sorted in increasing order according to the proportion of the top two ratings Very

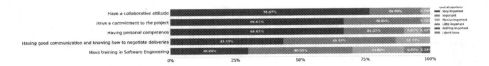

Fig. 3. Importance rating of people factors that determine the success project

important (Vi) and Important (I) to obtain an overall understanding of whether research software developers follow. Figure 3 summarizes the results from this question.

The results show that 96.67% of the participants (76.67% Vi and 20.00% I) and (66.67% Vi and 30.00% I) respectively consider the factor "Have a collaborative attitude" and the factor "Have a commitment to the project" influential in importance, suggesting that they are the top critical success factors impacting the research software development, as they represent the highest median score. This is followed by 90.00% of the participants (66.67% Vi and 23.33% I) informed that the factor "Having personal competence" are important in the research software. Then, 86.66% of the participants (43.33% Vi and 43.33% I) consider that the factor "Having good communication and knowing how to negotiate deliveries" is influential in importance. Finally, this is followed by 70.00% participants (30.00% Vi and 40.00% I) that consider the factor "Have training in Software Engineering" have of importance.

5   Discussion

In this section, we discuss the implications of our study findings in RQ1, RQ2, and RQ3. They suggest gaps between the topics studied in literature and practices applied in the research software. The suggestions to help to fill in this gap include:

Implications of Technical Factors (RQ1). The results show that "software test", "software requirement", and "software quality" factors are at the top of the ranking importance. The importance of software engineering practices has existed more than a decade, and these factors are still among the most important for research developers [23]. Moreover, the ranking shows that factors that influence software projects in organizations to achieve success also influence the research software development [30]. Therefore, the findings of this study suggest that these three factors can be combined into actions that involve of academic users and all stakeholders to generate better and more efficient software predicting success. On the other hand, "software process" and "project management" factors are lower overall. These results show that developers do not give importance to managing a project and following a process, as they are carried out in an ad hoc manner. However, software processes and plan the software development, monitoring, and control can influence the development [4].

Implications of Organizational Factors (RQ2). The results show that "develop open source" has overall high importance. This can suggest that the respondents can be structuring, sharing, and opening research data to promote open source code produced by academic researchers. The second factor "have budget availability" also has a high level of importance. This factor in the need for budget attention affects the software, as well as the context in which it is developed. On the other hand, the factor "having a small team" and "geographically distributed team" is not important for researchers. In the success projects, having a small team is ideal. A larger team might pose great hindrance to fast communication and decision making in projects [18]. Moreover, the centralized organization of the team positively influences the success, and distributed projects are affected by the cultural and political situations in those regions [19].

Implications of People Factors (RQ3). The results of people factor "have a collaborative attitude" is high important. This is a suggestion that researchers and developers collaborate mainly when participating in open source software development. We can observe that "Have personal competence" and "have commitment with the project" has the same level of very importance. This result suggests that research software developers are highly skilled in having a collaborative attitude, sense of responsibility, high competence, and expertise with deliveries of the work in success projects [17]. On the other hand, the factor "having good communication and knowing how to negotiate deliveries" and "have training in Software Engineering" have lower importance. Note that in successful projects, contributions are usually discussed and evaluated with others more quickly and efficiently in good communication [21], and researchers not see the need for formal training in software that is the essential success factor of research software [6,23].

6   Threats to Validity

Although we aimed to reduce the threats to validity of our study methodology, some decisions may have affected the results of the survey. We present the threats to validity [22] regarding (i) *External Validity*: to generalization of our results, the population and sample size of the respondents is based on the number of emails sent to the Brazilian researchers' developers. Our sampling rate can provide representative results of the population we want to generalize in Brazil; (ii) *Internal Validity*: to the causality, we followed the guidelines proposed by Kitchenham and Pfleeger [27] and analyzed other questions similar in surveys to create new questions based on our research. In addition, we invited researchers and volunteers and were therefore motivated to participate; (iii) *Construct Validity*: to the generalization of the study results, a threat is the scenario of the Brazilian academic developers and the construction of the study variables. It is possible that the study participants are not representative of the population. Thus, the results of this study may not be generalizable to all research software developers; (iv) *Conclusion Validity*: the survey received 30 responses from respondents. We ensured that all respondents were aware of software research by asking the first question to check whether they were develop software research. If the answer was no, the survey ended.

7 Conclusions and Future Works

This study provides insight and a ranking into the importance of the factors in understanding software development success by Brazilian academic developer's perception. Other study findings will be discussed and submitted in an extended version. The results from this study will help stakeholders in research software to predict the likelihood of project success, evaluate their ongoing projects, and improve the decision-making towards successful software development. Furthermore, future research can take the findings of this study and quantitatively test them on a large sample, explore future researchers and connect with a literature review to provide gaps and expected new advances, explore how the factors are related using, for example, the linear regression technique, and verify if it influences software adoption and use in the academic context.

Acknowledgement. This study was financed in part by Fundação de Amparo à Pesquisa do Estado do Rio de Janeiro (FAPERJ) and Coordenação de Aperfeiçoamento de Pessoal de Nível Superior - Brasil (CAPES) Finance Code 001.

References

1. Katz, D.S., McHenry, K., Reinking, C., Haines, R.: Research software development & management in universities: case studies from Manchester's RSDS group, Illinois' NCSA, and Notre Dame's CRC. In: IEEE/ACM 14th International Workshop on Software Engineering for Science (SE4Science), pp. 17–24. IEEE 2019 (2019)
2. Eisty, N.U., Thiruvathukal, G.K., Carver, J.C.: A survey of software metric use in research software development. In: IEEE 14th International Conference on e-Science (e-Science), pp. 212–222. IEEE 2018 (2018)
3. Pan, S.L., Nishant, R.: Artificial intelligence for digital sustainability: an insight into domain-specific research and future directions. Int. J. Inf. Manag. **72**, 102668 (2023)
4. Eisty, N.U., Thiruvathukal, G.K., Carver, J.C.: Use of software process in research software development: a survey. In: Proceedings of the Evaluation and Assessment on Software Engineering, pp. 276–282 (2019)
5. Eisty, N.U., Carver, J.C.: Developers perception of peer code review in research software development. Empir. Softw. Eng. **27**(1), 1–26 (2022)
6. Mourão, E., Trevisan, D., Viterbo, J.: Understanding the success factors of research software: interviews with Brazilian computer science academic researchers. In: Rocha, A., Ferras, C., Ibarra, W. (eds.) Information Technology and Systems. ICITS 2023. LNNS, vol. 692, pp. 275–286. Springer, Cham (2023). https://doi.org/10.1007/978-3-031-33261-6_24
7. Hettrick, S.: It's impossible to conduct research without software, say 7 out of 10 uk researchers, Software Sustainability Institute Blog (2014)
8. Nangia, U., Katz, D.S., et al.: Track 1 paper: surveying the us national postdoctoral association regarding software use and training in research. In: Workshop on Sustainable Software for Science: Practice and Experiences (WSSSPE 5.1) (2017)

9. Heaton, D., Carver, J.C.: Claims about the use of software engineering practices in science: a systematic literature review. Inf. Softw. Technol. **67**, 207–219 (2015)

10. Arvanitou, E.M., Ampatzoglou, A., Chatzigeorgiou, A., Carver, J.C.: Software engineering practices for scientific software development: a systematic mapping study. J. Syst. Softw. **172**, 110848 (2021)

11. Carver, J.C., Weber, N., Ram, K., Gesing, S., Katz, D.S.: A survey of the state of the practice for research software in the united states. PeerJ Comput. Sci. **8**, e963 (2022)

12. Geethalakshmi, S., Shanmugam, A.: Success and failure of software development: practitioners' perspective. In: Proceedings of the International MultiConference of Engineers & Computer Scientists, pp. 915–921 (2008)

13. de Souza, M.R., Haines, R., Vigo, M., Jay, C.: What makes research software sustainable? An interview study with research software engineers. In: IEEE/ACM 12th International Workshop on Cooperative and Human Aspects of Software Engineering (CHASE), pp. 135–138. IEEE 2019 (2019)

14. Brous, P., Janssen, M., Krans, R.: Data governance as success factor for data science. In: Hattingh, M., Matthee, M., Smuts, H., Pappas, I., Dwivedi, Y.K., Mäntymäki, M. (eds.) I3E 2020. LNCS, vol. 12066, pp. 431–442. Springer, Cham (2020). https://doi.org/10.1007/978-3-030-44999-5_36

15. Reel, J.S.: Critical success factors in software projects. IEEE Softw. **16**(3), 18–23 (1999)

16. Nasir, M.H.N., Sahibuddin, S.: Critical success factors for software projects: a comparative study. Sci. Res. Essays **6**(10), 2174–2186 (2011)

17. Chow, T., Cao, D.B.: A survey study of critical success factors in agile software projects. J. Syst. Softw. **81**(6), 961–971 (2008)

18. Misra, S.C., Kumar, V., Kumar, U.: Identifying some important success factors in adopting agile software development practices. J. Syst. Softw. **82**(11), 1869–1890 (2009)

19. Misra, S.C., Kumar, V., Kumar, U.: Success factors of agile software development. Softw. Eng. Res. Pract. **1**, 233–239 (2006)

20. Aldahmash, A., Gravell, A.M., Howard, Y.: A review on the critical success factors of agile software development. In: Stolfa, J., Stolfa, S., O'Connor, R.V., Messnarz, R. (eds.) EuroSPI 2017. CCIS, vol. 748, pp. 504–512. Springer, Cham (2017). https://doi.org/10.1007/978-3-319-64218-5_41

21. Lindsjørn, Y., Sjøberg, D.I., Dingsøyr, T., Bergersen, G.R., Dybå, T.: Teamwork quality and project success in software development: a survey of agile development teams. J. Syst. Softw. **122**, 274–286 (2016)

22. Wohlin, C., Runeson, P., Höst, M., Ohlsson, M.C., Regnell, B., Wesslén, A.: Experimentation in Software Engineering. Springer Science & Business Media, Berlin, Heidelberg (2012). https://doi.org/10.1007/978-3-642-29044-2

23. Hannay, J.E., MacLeod, C., Singer, J., Langtangen, H.P., Pfahl, D., Wilson, G.: How do scientists develop and use scientific software? In: ICSE Workshop on Software Engineering for Computational Science and Engineering, pp. 1–8. IEEE 2009 (2009)

24. Abran, A., Moore, J.W., Bourque, P., Dupuis, R., Tripp, L.: Software engineering body of knowledge. IEEE Computer Society, Angela Burgess, p. 25 (2004)

25. Petersen, K., Vakkalanka, S., Kuzniarz, L.: Guidelines for conducting systematic mapping studies in software engineering: an update. Inf. Softw. Technol. **64**, 1–18 (2015)

26. Mourão, E., Pimentel, J.F., Murta, L., Kalinowski, M., Mendes, E., Wohlin, C.: On the performance of hybrid search strategies for systematic literature reviews in software engineering. Inf. Softw. Technol. **123**, 106294 (2020)
27. Kitchenham, B.A., Pfleeger, S.L.: Personal opinion surveys. In: Shull, F., Singer, J., Sjøberg, D.I.K. (eds.) Guide to Advanced Empirical Software Engineering, pp. 63–92. Springer, London (2008). https://doi.org/10.1007/978-1-84800-044-5_3
28. Basili, V.R., Caldiera, G., Rombach, H.D.: Goal, question metric paradigm. encyclopedia of software engineering, vol. 1 (1994)
29. Sjøberg, D.I., et al.: A survey of controlled experiments in software engineering. IEEE Trans. Softw. Eng. **31**(9), 733–753 (2005)
30. Nguyen, D.S.: Success factors that influence agile software development project success. Am Sci. Res. J. Eng. Technol. Sci. (ASRJETS) **17**(1) 171–222 (2016)

Influence of Personal Cultural Orientations in Artificial Intelligence Adoption in Small and Medium-Sized Enterprises

Diego Fernando Plata Lerma(✉) ⓘ, Michael Adu Kwarteng ⓘ, and Michal Pílik ⓘ

Tomas Bata University, Zlin 76001, Czech Republic
`podatelna@utb.cz`

Abstract. This study aims to propose a theoretical model that examines the significance of personal cultural orientations, specifically focusing on innovativeness, independence, and ambiguity intolerance, in the adoption of artificial intelligence (AI) within small and medium-sized enterprises (SMEs). Additionally, the study establishes a relationship between personal cultural orientations and the Unified Theory of Acceptance and Use of Technology (UTAUT), particularly considering performance expectancy and facilitating conditions. SMEs face unique challenges and barriers in their pursuit of competitiveness, which necessitate alternative approaches and methodologies to foster the acceptance of new innovations like AI, beyond traditional technology adoption models. Employing a qualitative methodology, emphasizing documentary research, and utilizing inferential and deductive reasoning, a theoretical model is proposed. This model aims to demonstrate how analysing personal cultural orientations can facilitate the design of effective strategies and policies to support SMEs' AI adoption, promoting their growth and sustainability in a technology-driven and highly volatile environment.

Keywords: Artificial intelligence · personal cultural orientations · SMEs · UTAUT

1 Introduction

Artificial intelligence (AI) has garnered momentum in the past decade after experiencing periods of scepticism and pessimism about its potential. It has radically transformed traditional work methods making it applicable in diverse fields, including healthcare, finance, e commerce, cybersecurity, transportation customer service and predictive analytics (Yang et al., 2021; Skilton & Hovsepian, 2017). The adoption of AI technology is no longer exclusively associated with large companies from developed countries (OECD, 2021a, 2021b). SMEs are also increasingly investing in them due to cost efficient advancements that enable small businesses to leverage the tools benefits without significant capital investment (Ikumoro & Jawad, 2019). The distinct shift towards AI adoption emphasizes scientific and academic principles such as data driven decision making critical for extracting valuable insights from vast datasets (Garzoni et al., 2020).

© IFIP International Federation for Information Processing 2023
Published by Springer Nature Switzerland AG 2023
M. Janssen et al. (Eds.): I3E 2023, LNCS 14316, pp. 27–40, 2023.
https://doi.org/10.1007/978-3-031-50040-4_3

In the face of increasing market competition, SMEs are exploring novel strategies to maintain their relevance and attain a competitive advantage. AI presents a potentially fruitful avenue for realizing these objectives, as posited by Baabdullah et al. (2021). The utility of AI systems in promoting the growth and efficiency of small and medium-sized enterprises (SMEs) while reducing expenses has been demonstrated by their scalability and flexibility (Drydakis, 2022). Notwithstanding the potential advantages that the integration of AI can offer various economic domains, SMEs encounter notable obstacles and difficulties, as reported by the OECD (2021b). The capacity of organizations to invest in AI is frequently restricted by financial limitations, which stem from the considerable expenses involved in implementing, establishing infrastructure, and acquiring expertise (Wang et al., 2022). The authors Rozmi et al. (2019) have identified a notable challenge for SMEs owners and decision- makers, which is the limited understanding and awareness of the potential benefits and applications of AI. This knowledge gap has been identified as a significant obstacle for many SMEs.

The impact of cultural factors on the adoption of emerging technologies, such as AI, has been acknowledged in academic literature (Behl et al., 2022; Robinson, 2020; Tam & Oliveira, 2019). The influence of culture on individuals' attitudes and behaviors is significant, as it affects their adoption and implementation of technological advancements. This has been noted by Semrau et al. (2016) and Sharma (2010). Comprehending the challenges and opportunities associated with technology adoption necessitates an understanding of the cultural underpinnings. This understanding is crucial in developing culturally sensitive strategies that can facilitate successful implementation, as posited by Vos and Boonstra (2022).

Earlier investigations have investigated the impact of cultural variables on the adoption of AI. However, there exists a knowledge gap regarding this phenomenon in the Latin American area. Muñoz et al. (2021) assert that Latin American nations possess distinctive societal norms, values, and historical backgrounds, which contribute to a distinct landscape for SMEs seeking to incorporate AI technologies. The objective of this research is to analyse the relationship between cultural values and the adoption of artificial intelligence in the Latin American region. The study will investigate the various factors that may influence the intentions of SMEs managers/owners to adopt AI technology.

Previous research efforts have provided insights into the impact of cultural elements on the adoption of AI (Zhang et al., 2011); yet, further investigation is necessary to examine this occurrence in the Latin American area. McCoy et al. (2005) conducted an empirical study on the Technology Acceptance Model (TAM) in Uruguay and determined that further research is necessary in the region to overcome the challenges posed by cultural measurements. Muñoz et al. (2021) assert that the Latin American region is distinguished by its distinctive societal norms, values, and historical backgrounds, which create a unique environment for small and medium-sized enterprises (SMEs) that aim to incorporate AI technologies. The objective of this study is to investigate the potential impact of cultural values on the adoption of AI by SMEs. Specifically, this research aims to identify the factors or issues that may influence the adoption intentions of SME managers/owners.

Drawing upon Sharma's (2010) cultural orientations (CO) framework and Venkatesh's (2003) unified theory of acceptance and use of technology (UTAUT), this article investigates the connections between innovativeness, independence, and risk aversion (CO) on one hand, and performance expectancy and facilitating conditions (UTAUT) on the other. The inclusion of control variables such as age and firm size ensures a comprehensive analysis of the relationships between these constructs. By merging an expanded technology model with cultural values, this study contributes to a deeper understanding of the challenges managers may face when adopting new digital technologies. Furthermore, by focusing on AI within a non-developed country, we contribute to the limited body of research in this area. Our findings will provide valuable insights for policymakers, researchers, and industry practitioners, enabling them to devise customized strategies that account for the cultural sensitivities of SMEs in emerging countries. Ultimately, this will foster successful AI implementation and drive economic growth in these regions.

2 Literature Review

2.1 Personal Cultural Orientations

The task of conceptualizing culture is a complex undertaking due to its intrinsically dynamic and continuously evolving character. Edward Burnett Tylor, an anthropologist, made one of the initial efforts to articulate the definition of the notion of culture. Tylor's definition of culture, as stated in his work, encompasses a comprehensive range of elements, including but not limited to knowledge, beliefs, art, morality, laws, customs, and various other capabilities and habits that are acquired by individuals as members of a society (Taylor, 1871). As per Trompenaars and Hampden-Turner's (1996) definition, culture pertains to the communal approach adopted by individuals to confront obstacles and reconcile differences. According to Hofstede's (1984) perspective, culture is a shared cognitive framework that shapes the way individuals perceive and interact with the world.

The investigation of disparities in technology adoption across cultures frequently employs Hofstede's cultural dimensions, including individualism, power distance, uncertainty avoidance, masculinity, and long-term orientation, as national metrics (McCoy et al., 2005). Notwithstanding, certain academics contend that there exists a differentiation between Hofstede's cultural dimensions at the national level and the scrutiny of cultural values at the individual level (Coon & Kemmelmeinier, 2002; Mehta, 2018). The acknowledgement of heterogeneity within a nation underscores the necessity of a holistic strategy that accommodates distinct viewpoints and ethnic disparities (Schaffer & Jordan, 2003).

The proposed theory by Sharma (2010) presents a perspective on personal cultural orientations that surpasses the scope of macro-level frameworks. It recognizes the active participation of individuals in shaping and interpreting cultural values. This study incorporates Sharma's theory and extends it to the Latin American context in order to facilitate a more rigorous multi-dimensional analysis. Sharma's (2010) concept proposes a reformulation of Hofstede's dimensions, incorporating three fundamental dimensions, namely risk aversion (RSK), ambiguity intolerance (AMB), and innovativeness (INN).

2.1.1 Risk Aversion

Risk aversion refers to the degree to which individuals exhibit a reluctance to engage in risky decision-making or take risks. SMEs are frequently confronted with elevated risk in relation to investment in innovative systems within the technology adoption framework. This is primarily due to their restricted resources and the volatile nature of the market. According to Vekatesh (2003), managers who exhibit risk-averse tendencies may opt to uphold the current state of affairs and allocate resources towards established systems, especially when contemplating the considerable unpredictability linked with investments in AI. The dimension RSK is indicative of risk aversion, which pertains to the degree of hesitation among managers in making decisions that involve risk (Robinson, 2020).

2.1.2 Ambiguity Intolerance

Ambiguity intolerance pertains to an individual's capacity to endure ambiguity, specifically in novel circumstances that involve new technologies. This pertains to the degree to which individuals experience a sense of apprehension in response to uncertain or unfamiliar circumstances, as posited by Hofstede (2001). The relevance of predictability, explicit rules, structured situations, and previous positive experiences is evident in the context of SMEs' adoption intentions. Individuals who possess a low tolerance for ambiguity may encounter unease when faced with uncertain situations and may demonstrate a proclivity towards seeking security, predictability, and conformity (Papacharissi & Rubin, 2000; Dougas et al., 2005; Sharma, 2010).

2.1.3 Innovativeness

The term "innovativeness" pertains to an individual's self-perception of their capability to execute a task utilizing a technological framework. The adoption of information technology is heavily influenced by a crucial factor, which is the level of ease with which individuals acquire digital skills. According to Dholakia and Kshetri (2004), the absence of creativity and originality among individuals responsible for making decisions can impede the assimilation of novel technologies in SMEs. The assessment of a new technology's usefulness, ease of use, and facilitating conditions necessitates a sense of assurance in one's knowledge and IT competencies (Grandón & Ramírez-Correa, 2018).

2.2 Unified Theory of Adoption and Use of Technology

The Unified Theory of Adoption and Use of Technology (UTAUT) offers a comprehensive framework for examining the adoption of digital technology in diverse economic contexts, as evidenced by the works of Alhaimer (2019) and Alkhowaiter (2020). The UTAUT framework is an integration of eight established theories and models in the field of information systems. These include the theory of reasoned action (TRA), social cognitive theory (SCT), technology acceptance model (TAM), theory of planned behavior (TPB), model of PC utilization (MPCU), motivational model (MM), decomposed theory of planned behavior (DTPB), and innovation diffusion theory (IDT) (Venkatesh et al., 2003).

UTAUT posits that the determinants of an individual's intention to adopt a technology include performance expectancy (PE), effort expectancy (EE), social influence (SI), and facilitating conditions (FC). The concept of PE pertains to the anticipation of favourable outcomes resulting from the adoption of a particular conduct, and it has been established as a robust determinant of the inclination to utilize a technological innovation (Venkatesh, 2003).

2.2.1 Performance Expectancy

According to the Unified Theory of Acceptance and Use of Technology (UTAUT), individuals are more inclined to participate in a particular behavior when they anticipate receiving favorable outcomes as a result of their actions. According to Compeau and Higgins (1995), the potential for rewards creates a strong inclination for individuals to form favorable attitudes and preferences towards a particular behavior. Several scholars have posited that perceived ease of use (PE) is the most robust determinant of an individual's inclination to employ a specific system or technology (Compeau & Higgins, 1995). Furthermore, PE may serve as a crucial element in facilitating or impeding the adoption of technology by SMEs.

2.2.2 Facilitating Conditions

Facilitating conditions pertain to the managerial viewpoint regarding the resources and assistance that are accessible to execute a behaviour through a digital system (Brown & Venkatesh, 2005). The construct of facilitating conditions pertains to the SME's perception of the adequacy of technical infrastructure for the effective utilization of a particular technology as and when needed (Im et al., 2011). The reliance SMEs on the existence of a particular organizational or technical entity in the event of any unforeseen circumstances has a significant impact on their inclination towards technology adoption (Rozmi, 2019). This inclination is influenced by factors such as formal training, guidance, infrastructure, and system compatibility, as suggested by various studies. FC constitutes a crucial determinant in the adoption of IT innovation, serving as a potent motivator that engenders a favourable influence on the utilization of technology for procuring goods or services.

3 Rationale of the Study

The rationale for this study stems from the recognition that the adoption of AI technologies within organizations is a complex process influenced by various factors, including personal cultural orientations. Understanding the dynamics of AI adoption and its relationship with cultural values is crucial for organizations aiming to leverage AI effectively and gain a competitive advantage. The conceptualization of culture as a dynamic and ever-evolving phenomenon highlights the need to move beyond macro-level cultural frameworks and consider individual perspectives. By incorporating personal cultural orientations, such as risk aversion, ambiguity intolerance, and innovativeness, this study aims to provide a more comprehensive and robust analysis of the factors influencing AI adoption in the Latin American context.

Moreover, existing theoretical frameworks, such as the Unified Theory of Adoption and Use of Technology (UTAUT), have demonstrated their effectiveness in explaining technology adoption behaviors. By focusing on the constructs of performance expectancy and facilitating conditions from the UTAUT model, this study aims to provide a theoretical foundation for understanding the drivers and facilitators of AI adoption. The integration of personal cultural orientations and the UTAUT model in this study offers a unique perspective on AI adoption, considering both the individual's cultural values and the key determinants of technology adoption. By exploring how personal cultural orientations interact with performance expectancy and facilitating conditions, this research seeks to shed light on the complex interplay between cultural factors and technology adoption behaviours.

4   Methodology

4.1   Aim

The main aim of this study is to investigate the interplay between personal cultural orientations and the adoption of artificial intelligence within the context of the Latin American region. Specifically, the study aims to examine the influence of risk aversion, ambiguity intolerance, and innovativeness on SME managers/owners' adoption intentions regarding AI technologies. By incorporating personal cultural orientations and drawing upon the UTAUT framework, this research seeks to provide a comprehensive understanding of the factors that affect AI adoption in SMEs. The findings will contribute to the existing body of knowledge by shedding light on the complex relationship between cultural values and technology adoption behaviours, with the ultimate goal of facilitating successful AI implementation and driving economic growth in the Latin American region.

4.2   Design and Setting of the Study

The study methodology utilized is qualitative in nature, with a particular emphasis on conducting documentary research. This implies that the study primarily relies on information obtained from diverse sources such as books, articles, videos, journals, periodicals, and other relevant materials that the researchers deemed pertinent to their research objectives. These sources were carefully chosen based on their connection and relevance to the research topic. Moreover, within the qualitative framework and the emphasis on documentary research, the researchers have employed inferential and deductive reasoning techniques to derive insights and make logical deductions.

Documentary research serves as a valuable qualitative approach to explore the concepts, statements, and perspectives related to personal cultural orientations and AI adoption within the UTAUT framework. This methodology allows researchers to delve into documented sources that offer insights into the interplay between personal cultural orientations and the acceptance of AI technologies.

Similarly, employing deductive thinking enables the linkage of expressions associated with culture (innovativeness, independence, risk aversion) to technology adoption constructs. This approach highlights commonalities between them and emphasizes the importance of their interrelation, thus shedding light on the elements that constitute the relationship between culture and technology adoption.

Moreover, inferential reasoning facilitates the exploration of how specific elements of personal cultural orientations relate to different dimensions of AI adoption as delineated by the UTAUT framework. The combination of qualitative methods, particularly documentary research, with deductive and inferential reasoning within the UTAUT framework, offers a comprehensive and nuanced understanding of the relationship between personal cultural orientations and AI adoption. This scholarly approach illuminates the underlying mechanisms and factors that shape individuals' attitudes and behaviours towards the adoption of AI technologies in diverse cultural contexts.

Nonetheless, it is crucial to emphasize that both inferential reasoning and deductive reasoning play integral roles in the logical process employed to develop the proposed disruptive triad model in this study.

5   Description of All Processes and Methodologies Employed

The current research adopts a post positivist orientation to the extent that it argues that background theories can influence what is observed objectivity in understanding and verifying the realities of this world. Therefore, the literature review related to AI adoption was carried out with articles published in journals indexed mainly in Scopus and Web of Science databases. The information collected and analysed is assessed with the aim of proposing a conceptual model (Fig. 1) merging the UTAUT model and personal values orientations (Sharma, 2010). Consequently, the construction of the theoretical model involved a rigorous methodology that encompassed the following processes:

1. Conceptual and Theoretical Investigation: Extensive research was conducted to delve into the conceptual and theoretical aspects of personal cultural orientations and AI adoption. Multiple scholarly sources were consulted to gain insights from various authors and researchers who have explored these topics.
2. Examination of Previous Research: Existing studies and literature on personal cultural orientations and AI adoption were examined to identify any existing frameworks or models that directly addressed the relationship between these two variables. Although no direct coincidences with the proposed model were found, this examination served as a foundation for understanding the existing knowledge landscape.
3. Analysis of Individual Element Impact: Each component was individually examined to assess its impact on various aspects, such as attitudes, behaviours, and decision-making processes. Through deductive and inferential reasoning, the study sought to explore the potential synergistic effects of combining these elements within the context of AI adoption.
4. Integration of personal cultural orientations expressions: The expressions of personal cultural orientations and their influence on AI adoption were synthesized into a unified theoretical model. This integration involved considering the theoretical elements supported by relevant studies and empirical evidence. By establishing connections between personal cultural orientations and AI adoption, the model aimed to provide insights into the interplay between these variables and their implications for organizations.

By following this methodological approach, the theoretical model for the AI adoption within the domain of personal cultural orientations was developed. This systematic process ensured a comprehensive exploration of the interrelationships and potential synergies between these elements. The resulting model contributes to the understanding of how personal cultural orientations influence the adoption and utilization of AI technologies, offering valuable insights for researchers, practitioners, and policymakers in this field.

6 Limitations

The utilization of qualitative methodology and dependence on documentary research may introduce the possibility of subjectivity and bias in the interpretation of data. The analysis and conclusions drawn from the collected information may be influenced by the researchers' own perspectives and biases. The present study aims to investigate the interrelationships among personal cultural orientations, performance expectancy, and facilitating conditions. The cross-sectional nature of the research design precludes the determination of causality, despite the identification of correlations and associations in the study. To establish causal relationships with greater certainty, it would be necessary to employ longitudinal studies or experimental designs.

7 Results and Discussion

7.1 Results

Once the cultural concepts associated with AI adoption intentions among SMEs have been explained, such as independence, risk aversion and ambiguity intolerance, as well as their relationship with the technology constructs, performance expectancy and facilitating conditions, it is possible, then, to consider that the result of this study is graphically represented in the theoretical model proposed in Fig. 1.

The diagram depicted in Fig. 1 showcases the correlation between individual cultural values such as innovativeness, independence, and ambiguity intolerance, and the fundamental factors of performance expectancy and facilitating conditions, which serve as the basis for the adoption intentions of AI in SMEs. The incorporation of control variables, namely company age and size, was undertaken to account for the potential influence of established networks, customer relationships, and industry knowledge possessed by older companies on their decision-making and adoption of novel technologies, such as AI. Through the implementation of age control measures, it becomes feasible to evaluate whether the impact of a company's age on its intentions to adopt AI is distinguishable from the influence of cultural orientations and other pertinent factors. In addition, firms possessing greater longevity in the industry may encounter obstacles associated with organizational inertia and a reluctance to embrace change. The entrenched practices and procedures of an organization may impede the assimilation of novel technologies.

Moreover, there exists a positive correlation between the magnitude of a corporation and its accessible resources, encompassing monetary capital, personnel, and technological framework. Organizations of greater magnitude may possess a greater abundance of resources to allocate towards the integration of AI and may encounter distinct hurdles in the process, as opposed to their smaller counterparts. Furthermore, the magnitude of a company can serve as an indicator of its organizational framework, intricacy, and methods of decision-making. Organizations of greater magnitude may exhibit intricacies in their hierarchical structures, departmental arrangements, and mechanisms for decision-making.

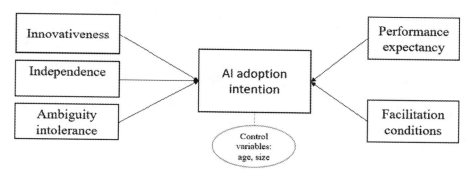

Fig. 1. Proposed research framework. Source: own.

8 Discussion

Scholars have conducted thorough investigations on cultural orientations and the adoption of technology, providing insight into the intricate correlation between culture and the acceptance of technology (Zhang et al., 2011; Syed and Malik, 2014; Tam & Oliveira, 2019). Although the current body of literature has provided valuable insights, additional research is necessary, particularly with regards to the individual perspective and within the context of Latin America (McCoy et al, 2005). Through a thorough exploration of an individual's cultural orientations and their impact on the adoption of technology, scholars can reveal intricate elements that mold the behavioural intentions of managers/owners of SMEs.

Drawing logical connections between variables, this research aims to establish coherent connections among various variables and explore the potential outcomes and importance of the proposed framework. The cultural value of independence, which prioritizes self-reliance and autonomy, is a crucial determinant of individuals' attitudes and behaviors towards technology adoption (Drykakis, 2022). Within the domain of AI adoption, those who prioritize independence may view AI technologies as a mechanism to augment their individual autonomy and capacity for making decisions. According to Mehta's (2018) findings, prior studies have suggested that individuals who possess a robust sense of autonomy are more predisposed to adopting technological innovations that offer them increased agency and adaptability. The reluctance to participate in specific activities can be ascribed to apprehensions regarding breaches of privacy and the potential repercussions on interpersonal connections. Conversely, those who place a premium on individualism within their cultural framework may perceive AI as a mechanism for enhancing personal efficiency and output, thereby resulting in a greater degree of receptivity and assimilation (Mueller, 2001).

Ambiguity intolerance refers to the uncomfortable or discomfort that people experience when confronted with ambiguity and a lack of clarity (Sharma, 2018). According to Dougas et al., (2005), individuals with a high ambiguity intolerance regard ambiguous circumstances as dangerous. Similarly, individuals with a high level of ambiguity intolerance may be skeptical of AI technology due to their apparent complexity and unknown outcomes and see ambiguous situations as potential sources of threats (Papacharissi & Rubin, 2000). Consequently, individuals with a low tolerance for ambiguity may be concerned about adopting AI due to the perceived lack of transparency in AI's decision-making processes and its inability to provide assurance in uncertain scenarios Furthermore, managers with lesser tolerance for unclear situations, may have lower performance expectations because they doubt the predictability and reliability of AI systems. Developing trust in AI may be especially difficult for those who have a high ambiguity intolerance, because AI recommendations may be interpreted as dangerous threats rather than helpful suggestions.

While digitalization processes entail many potential benefits for SMEs, they are also associated with high risks, especially for new technologies like AI. Risk aversion reflects individuals' preferences for avoiding risks and uncertainties (Sharma, 2018). Individuals that are particularly risk-averse are more likely to be cautious about AI adoption due to their concerns about the potential risks linked with AI technologies. Their proclivity to avoid risks may influence their assessment of AI's predicted performance, as they weigh the potential benefits against the perceived hazards and uncertainties (Robinson, 2020). Certainly, integrating AI technology in SMEs can represent considerable dangers, which are heightened in family-owned businesses. However, it is critical to remember that the dangers of not implementing these new technologies can be even bigger in terms of potential loss of competitiveness and effectiveness (OECD, 2021a, 2021b). SMEs may miss out on prospects for better operational efficiency, enhanced decision-making capabilities, and market competitive advantage if they do not embrace AI. While there are inherent hazards, the risks of not adopting AI should also be carefully addressed in order to make informed judgments about technology integration.

On the other hand, the UTAUT model provides a framework to understand individuals' technology adoption behaviors based on four key factors: performance expectancy, effort expectancy, social influence, and facilitating conditions (Venkatesh et al., 2003). In this analysis, we focused on the variables of performance expectancy and facilitating conditions. According to Venkatesh (2003), performance expectancy refers to an individual's belief that utilizing a system or technology will help them perform better at work. Sheeshka et al. (1993) contend that anticipated outcomes influence performance expectations, and other studies have interpreted this idea as outcome expectancy (Bandura, 1997b). PE has been established as the most powerful predictor of intention to use a specific system or technology even in emerging countries contexts (Khayer et al, 2020). Therefore, this construct is imperative to be considered in the SMEs behaviours intentions analysis and it is expected to positively affect the managers' decisions of AI adoption.

Furthermore, facilitating conditions encompass technical features within an organizational context that aid in the removal of barriers to technology utilization (Venkatesh, 2003). Individuals' behavioral intentions can be influenced by the provision of appropriate organizational or technological resources, such as training opportunities or system compatibility, according to Ikumoro et al., (2019). These resources are critical in molding people's propensity to adopt and use technology effectively. Facilitating conditions contribute to the creation of an environment suitable to digitalization uptake and usage within SMEs by providing the required assistance and resources (Rozmi, 2019). Researchers and practitioners can assess an organization's preparedness to adopt digitalization and identify potential impediments to its implementation by using FC as a variable. Understanding the availability and effectiveness of favourable conditions enables the formulation of plans to overcome any gaps or constraints, hence increasing the likelihood of successful AI adoption.

9   Conclusion

Latin American cultures, with their various socioeconomic gaps and varying levels of technological penetration, provide a fertile ground for studying technology adoption patterns. This research methodology lays the groundwork for future studies that will duplicate and investigate AI adoption in diverse Latin American contexts, providing a more in-depth understanding of the cultural, social, and economic elements that influence technological acceptance.

The significance of cultural orientations and the UTAUT model in understanding the adoption of artificial AI technology in Latin American contexts has been highlighted in this study. We investigated the potential influence of cultural orientations such as independence, ambiguity intolerance, and risk aversion on individuals' views and behaviors toward AI adoption. This study acknowledges that cultural values, norms, and beliefs influence individuals' attitudes and behaviors toward technology adoption. The comprehensive framework created as a result of this integration allows for a more nuanced understanding of how socio-cultural issues influence technology acceptance.

Overall, this proposed research model offers a systematic and replicable approach for investigating AI adoption in Latin America, emphasizing the influence of cultural orientations and integrating key variables from the UTAUT model. By leveraging existing knowledge and incorporating cultural dimensions specific to Latin American contexts, this study has the potential to enhance our understanding of technology acceptance and adoption, contribute to theoretical advancements, and offer practical implications for promoting AI adoption in the region.

10   Theoretical and Managerial Implications

The findings of this study have theoretical and practical implications. Theoretically, this research contributes to the existing literature by highlighting the importance of considering cultural orientations when investigating technology adoption. By integrating cultural orientations and the UTAUT model, we have developed a comprehensive framework that captures the interplay between socio-cultural factors and individuals' acceptance of AI technologies.

Practically, the insights gained from this study can inform the design of targeted interventions and strategies for promoting AI adoption in Latin American contexts. Recognizing and accommodating cultural variations, such as independence, ambiguity intolerance, and risk aversion, can facilitate the successful implementation of AI technologies and address potential barriers to adoption.

While this study has provided a solid theoretical foundation, there is still ample room for further research. Future studies could delve deeper into the specific mechanisms through which cultural orientations interact with performance expectancy and facilitating conditions, exploring additional cultural variables and their impact on AI adoption. Moreover, replication of this study in diverse Latin American contexts can offer valuable insights into regional nuances and contribute to the generalizability of the proposed model.

Ultimately, this research sets the stage for a comprehensive understanding of AI adoption in Latin America, providing a theoretical framework that can guide future investigations and empirical studies. By recognizing and addressing the influence of cultural orientations and the UTAUT variables, we can facilitate the successful integration of AI technologies across a wide range of sectors, contributing to technological advancements and societal progress in the region.

References

Baabdullah, A.M., Alalwan, A.A., Slade, E.L., Raman, R., Khatatneh, K.F.: SMEs and artificial intelligence (AI): antecedents and consequences of AI-based B2B practices. Ind. Market. Manag. **98**(January), 255–270 (2021). https://doi.org/10.1016/j.indmarman.2021.09.003

Behl, A., Chavan, M., Jain, K., Sharma, I., Pereira, V.E., Zhang, J.Z.: The role of organizational culture and voluntariness in the adoption of artificial intelligence for disaster relief operations. Int. J. Manpower **43**(2), 569–586 (2022). https://doi.org/10.1108/IJM-03-2021-0178

Compeau, D.R., Higgins, C.A.: Computer self-efficacy: development of a measure and initial test. MIS Q. **19**, 189–211 (1995)

Derouin, R.E., Fritzsche, B.A., Salas, E.: E-learning in organizations. J. Manag. **31**(6), 920–940 (2005)

Dugas, M.J., Hedayati, M., Karavidas, A., Buhr, K., Francis, K., Phillips, N.A.: Intolerance of uncertainty and information processing: evidence of biased recall and interpretations. Cogn Ther Res 1(29), 57–70 (2005). https://doi.org/10.1007/s10608-005-1648-9

Dholakia, R.R., Kshetri, N.: Factors impacting the adoption of the Internet among SMEs. Small Bus. Econ. **23**(4), 311–322 (2004). https://doi.org/10.1023/B:SBEJ.0000032036.90353.1F

Drydakis, N.: Artificial intelligence and reduced SMEs' business risks. a dynamic capabilities analysis during the COVID-19 pandemic. Inform. Syst. Front. **24**(4), 1223–1247 (2022). https://doi.org/10.1007/s10796-022-10249-6

Garzoni, A., De Turi, I., Secundo, G., Del Vecchio, P.: Fostering digital transformation of SMEs: a four levels approach. Manag. Decis. **58**(8), 1543–1562 (2020). https://doi.org/10.1108/MD-07-2019-0939

Grandón, E.E., Ramírez-Correa, P.: Managers/owners' innovativeness and electronic commerce acceptance in Chilean SMES: a multi-group analysis based on a structural equation model. J. Theor. Appl. Electron. Commer. Res. **13**(3), 1–16 (2018). https://doi.org/10.4067/S0718-187 62018000300102

Hansen, E.B., Bøgh, S.: Artificial intelligence and internet of things in small and medium-sized enterprises: a survey. J. Manuf. Syst. **58**(August 2020), 362–372 (2021). https://doi.org/10.1016/j.jmsy.2020.08.009

Ikumoro, A.O., Jawad, M.S.: Intention to use intelligent conversational agents in e-commerce among malaysian SMEs: an integrated conceptual framework based on tri-theories including unified theory of acceptance, use of technology (UTAUT), and T-O-E. Int. J. Acad. Res. Bus. Soc. Sci. **9**(11), 205–235 (2019). https://doi.org/10.6007/IJARBSS/v9-i11/6544

Im, I., Hong, S., Kang, M.S.: An international comparison of technology adoption: testing the UTAUT model. Inform. Manag. **48**(1), 1–8 (2011). https://doi.org/10.1016/j.im.2010.09.001

Khayer, A., Jahan, N., Hossain, M.N., Hossain, M.Y.: The Adoption of cloud computing in small and medium enterprises: a developing country perspective. VJIKMS **1**(51), 64–91 (2020). https://doi.org/10.1108/vjikms-05-2019-0064

McSweeney, B.: Hofstede's model of national cultural differences and their consequences: a triumph of faith – a failure of analysis. Hum. Relat. **55**(1), 89–118 (2002). https://doi.org/10.1177/0018726702551004

McCoy, S., Everard, A., Jones, B.M.: An examination of the technology acceptance model in Uruguay and the us: a focus on culture. J. Global Inform. Technol. Manag. **8**(2), 27–45 (2005). https://doi.org/10.1080/1097198X.2005.10856395

Mehta, A.: The Influence of Values on the Adoption of Educational Technology. The University of Leeds, August, 75383 (2018)

Muñoz, V., Tamayo, E., Guio, A.: The Colombian case : adopting collaborative governance as a path for implementing ethical artificial intelligence Víctor Muñoz. http://repositorio.udesa.edu.ar/jspui/handle/10908/18743   https://repositorio.udesa.edu.ar/jspui/bitstream/10908/18743/1/The%20Colombian%20case%20adopting%20collaborative%20governance%20as%20a%20path%20for%20implementing%20ethical%20artificial%20intelligence.pdf (2021)

OECD: Digital Transformation in the Era of Covid-19. Digital Economy Outlook 2020 Supplement (2021a). https://doi.org/10.1007/978-3-030-80840-2_10

OECD: The Digital Transformation of SMEs. In OECD Publishing. https://www.oecd-ilibrary.org/industry-and-services/the-digital-transformation-of-smes_bdb9256a-en (2021b)

Oyserman, D., Kemmelmeier, M., Coon, H.: Cultural psychology, a new look: Reply to Bond (2002), Fiske (2002), Kitayama (2002), and Miller. Psychol. Bull. **128**(1), 110–117 (2002)

Papacharissi, Z., Rubin, A.M.: Predictors of Internet use. J. Broadcast. Electron. Media **44**(2), 175–196 (2000). https://doi.org/10.1207/s15506878jobem4402_2

Robinson, S.C.: Trust, transparency, and openness: how inclusion of cultural values shapes Nordic national public policy strategies for artificial intelligence (AI). Technol. Soc. **63**, 101421 (2020). https://doi.org/10.1016/j.techsoc.2020.101421

Rozmi, A.N.A., Bakar, M.I.A., Abdul Hadi, A.R., Imran Nordin, A.: Investigating the intentions to adopt ICT in Malaysian SMEs using the UTAUT model. In: Zaman, H.B., Smeaton, A.F., Shih, T.K., Velastin, S., Terutoshi, T., Ali, N.M., Ahmad, M.N. (eds.) Advances in Visual Informatics: 6th International Visual Informatics Conference, IVIC 2019, Bangi, Malaysia, November 19–21, 2019, Proceedings, pp. 477–487. Springer International Publishing, Cham (2019). https://doi.org/10.1007/978-3-030-34032-2_42

Schaffer, B.S., Riordan, C.M.: A review of cross-cultural methodologies for organizational research: a best-practices approach. Organ. Res. Methods **6**(2), 169–215 (2016). https://doi.org/10.1177/1094428103251542

Semrau, T., Ambos, T., Kraus, S.: Entrepreneurial orientation and SME performance across societal cultures: an international study. J. Bus. Res. **69**(5), 1928–1932 (2016). https://doi.org/10.1016/J.JBUSRES.2015.10.082

Sharma, P.: Measuring personal cultural orientations: scale development and validation. J. Acad. Market. Sci. **38**(6), 787–806 (2010). https://doi.org/10.1007/s11747-009-0184-7

Skilton, M., Hovsepian, F.: The 4th industrial revolution: responding to the impact of artificial intelligence on business. In: The 4th Industrial Revolution: Responding to the Impact of Artificial Intelligence on Business, pp. 1–315 (2017). https://doi.org/10.1007/978-3-319-62479-2

Syed, H., Malik, A.: Comparative study of effect of culture on technology adoption in Pakistan and USA. Bus. Manag. Rev. 5(1), 42–51 (2014)

Tam, C., Oliveira, T.: Does culture influence m-banking use and individual performance? Inform. Manag. 56(3), 356–363 (2019). https://doi.org/10.1016/j.im.2018.07.009

Taylor, E.B.: Primitive Culture, Researches into the Development of Mythology, Philosophy, Religion Language, Art and Custom (1871)

Trompenaars, F., Hampden-Turner, C.: Riding the Waves of Culture Reducing Lines, Expanding Circles. January 1998 (1996)

Vos, J.F.J., Boonstra, A.: The influence of cultural values on enterprise system adoption, towards a culture – enterprise system alignment theory. Int. J. Inform. Manag. (2022). https://doi.org/10.1016/J.IJINFOMGT.2021.102453

Wang, J., Lu, Y., Fan, S., Hu, P., Wang, B.: How to survive in the age of artificial intelligence? Exploring the intelligent transformations of SMEs in central China. Int. J. Emerg. Markets 17(4), 1143–1162 (2022). https://doi.org/10.1108/IJOEM-06-2021-0985

Yang, Z., Chang, J., Huang, L., Mardani, A.: Digital transformation solutions of entrepreneurial SMEs based on an information error-driven T-spherical fuzzy cloud algorithm. Int. J. Inform. Manag. 69, 102384 (2023). https://doi.org/10.1016/j.ijinfomgt.2021.102384

Zhang, A., Yue, X., Kong, Y.: Exploring culture factors affecting the adoption of mobile payment. In: Proceedings – 2011 10th International Conference on Mobile Business, ICMB 2011, pp. 263–267 (2011). https://doi.org/10.1109/ICMB.2011.32

Human-AI Collaboration in Public Services: The Case of Sick Leave Case Handling

Christer Eriksson[1], Kristian Olsen[1], Stefan Schmager[1(✉)] ⓘ, Ilias O. Pappas[1,2] ⓘ, and Polyxeni Vassilakopoulou[1] ⓘ

[1] University of Agder, 4630 Kristiansand, Norway
`stefan.schmager@uia.no`
[2] Norwegian Univrsity of Science and Technology, 7491 Trondheim, Norway

Abstract. This research paper explores Human-AI Collaboration in public services, focusing on the needs and understanding of AI among caseworkers in a public welfare organisation dealing with sick leave cases. Conducting a foresight study with 19 caseworkers we identify roles that AI systems can take contributing to improved services for citizens, more fulfilling everyday work for caseworkers and more efficient use of public resources. Our research delves into the entirety of tasks involved in sick leave case handling expanding beyond the digital touchpoints between humans and AI. It goes beyond human-AI interaction to encompass the broader scope of collaboration between humans and machines as joint cognitive systems and suggests thinking of AI as a collaborator that undertakes specific roles.

Keywords: Human-AI collaboration · Public Services · Joint Cognitive System

1 Introduction

The field of Artificial Intelligence (AI), which originated in the 1950s [1], has witnessed a surge in interest from both academia and industry over the past decade [2]. AI has the capability to handle tasks that were traditionally reserved for humans, either partially or entirely [3], thereby enhancing efficiency across various sectors, including public services. AI applications are currently the most important information system innovations for the public sector [4]. AI can reduce administrative burdens and encourage resource reallocation [5]. For instance, the use of AI-based chatbots is now widespread in public services [6].

While AI offers many potential benefits, it also presents challenges in terms of organizational changes and social impacts [7, 8]. Information Systems researchers, with their sociotechnical understanding, are well-equipped to investigate these issues [9, 10]. A growing volume of research has been investigating how AI can be introduced in organisational settings by focusing on Human-AI interaction [2, 11]. However, interaction is not synonymous with collaboration. Most human activities today involve collaboration; therefore, to adequately integrate AI into workflows, it is critical to research and plan for a Human-AI collaboration future of work [11]. Rather than just examining how humans

© IFIP International Federation for Information Processing 2023
Published by Springer Nature Switzerland AG 2023
M. Janssen et al. (Eds.): I3E 2023, LNCS 14316, pp. 41–53, 2023.
https://doi.org/10.1007/978-3-031-50040-4_4

and AI interact, we must investigate how they can collaborate effectively as partners. As AI becomes more advanced, the most relevant question is not whether AI will replace humans but how humans and AI can joint efforts through collaboration.

Considering human-AI collaboration as opposed to just interaction helps framing AI implementation in a way that leverages the respective strengths of humans and technology. Organizations that design and plan for collaboration between humans and machines have the potential to achieve substantial benefits [12]. This way, they can evolve their practices involving humans and AI in work rather than just implementing new technologies [13]. A thorough understanding of human-AI collaboration dynamics could guide the design of AI systems that augment – rather than compete with – human capabilities and roles. The shift from a focus on interaction to collaboration is crucial for maximizing the benefits of AI while mitigating potential drawbacks for individuals, organizations and society.

The aim of this research is to examine the collaboration potential between humans and AI in the context of public services with a specific focus on understanding the requirements and perspectives of caseworkers at the Norwegian Labour and Welfare Administration (NAV). A core responsibility of NAV caseworkers is to assist citizens on sick leave in returning to work. Our research focuses on the caseworkers' views as there is limited previous research from their perspective. While prior research has examined citizens' perspectives, more work is needed to investigate the stances of public servants for AI-supported public services [14]. To help shed more light on this, we formulated the following research question: *What are caseworkers' needs for Human-AI collaboration in public services?* To answer this research question, we analyzed data collected via interviews with NAV caseworkers. The findings provide insights into how AI can be designed and implemented by taking into account the needs and values of public servants delivering government services on the frontlines. Ultimately, the research can inform policy and practice around human-AI collaboration in welfare administration and other domains of the public sector.

The remainder of this paper is structured as follows. We begin by presenting the theoretical background. Subsequently, the research method for data collection and analysis is described. The key findings, categorized into themes, are then presented and discussed before concluding.

2   Theoretical Background: Joint Cognitive Systems

For this study, we draw theoretically from the early work on Human-AI collaboration by Woods and the concept of "joint cognitive systems" [15]. Taking a joint cognitive system perspective allows to bring in focus the cognitive functions that human operators and technologies accomplish in collaboration. Woods developed the concept by hypothesizing a setting where an artificial agent (the machine expert) can offer some sort of problem-solving, while a human supports data gathering and accepts or overrides the machine's solution (Fig. 1). This is the decision support paradigm which Woods suggests that has to be replaced by a new joint cognitive system paradigm. The joint cognitive system paradigm defines the artificial agent as a resource or source of information for a human problem solver. The human problem solver is in charge; the artificial agent functions more as a staff member. Woods [15] argues that a problem-driven approach, rather than a technology-driven approach, is important. Cognitive work is accomplished by a collection of people and technologies coordinating with each other to solve problems in specific work contexts. Rather than simply offering solutions, artificial agents can be built to support problem formulation and solution evaluation providing informative counsel.

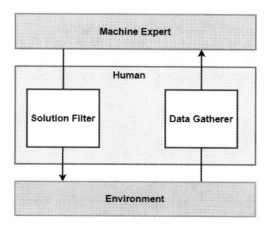

Fig. 1. A joint cognitive system implicit in human-machine interaction (adapted from [15]).

The Joint Cognitive Systems concept was proposed more than three decades ago; however, it is nowadays more relevant than ever gaining interest in recent research. For instance, Balakrishnan and Dwivedi [16] use the concept to research the role of cognitive absorption in building user trust and experience for chatbot use. IJtsma et al. [17] use the concept in their research on making informed design decisions when determining the allocation of work and interaction modes for human-robot teams [17]. Stowers et al. [18] build on the joint cognitive systems concept in their research on the impact of agent transparency on operator performance, response time, perceived workload, perceived usability, and operator trust in the context of human-machine collaboration. Marathe et al. [19] use it in their research on bidirectional communication for effective human-agent teaming, which is an approach that fosters communication between human and intelligent agents to improve mutual understanding and enable effective task coordination. More recently, Xu and Gao [20] proposed a conceptual framework of human-AI joint cognitive systems for developing effective human-AI teaming. They suggest that such a framework can facilitate teaming while enabling human-centred AI [21] augmenting human capabilities and raising joint performance.

In line with Woods' conceptualization, we view human caseworkers and AI systems as complementary components of a combined sociotechnical system aimed at delivering effective public services through nuanced decision-making and personalized case handling. In this joint cognitive system, AI can support problem solving while humans can remain ultimately responsible for the complex judgments and personal interactions required.

3   Case Background and Method

The Norwegian Labour and Welfare Administration (NAV) administers approximately a third of the Norwegian national budget through schemes such as work assessment allowance, sickness benefits, and unemployment benefits. NAV´s main goal is to get more people active and in work, having fewer people relying on benefits [22]. Handling sick leave cases revolves around promoting citizens' transition back to work, as well as helping with other activity needs in times of sickness. NAV created an AI lab in 2017. There are many relevant application areas for AI in NAV, one of which is the area of sick leave handling [23]. Reducing workplace absenteeism due to illness is a government priority in Norway [24] hence, the use of AI to improve the follow-up of people on sick holds great appeal. NAV is responsible for following up of sick leave on the basis of legal requirements in the Working Environment Act and the National Insurance Act. As a major public player, NAV is aware of its special responsibility, and wants to use AI in a responsible manner, an AI tool for sick-leave has been developed but is not deployed yet as the legal provisions, the perspectives of citizens and the needs of case workers are being explored.

For our investigation around caseworkers' needs for Human-AI collaboration in public services we focused on the use of AI for handling sick-leaves as this is a priority area. for the government. To ensure the participation and collaboration of employees, we employed foresight methods [25, 26]. Foresight thinking allows people to think ahead and to consider, model, and respond to future eventualities. It provides interesting opportunities and insights into imagining and shaping a social, fair, and just future [27]. It's a process to make sense of an uncertain and complex future environment, using as wide a frame as possible.

3.1   Data Collection

We conducted a foresight study exploring how caseworkers at NAV both understand and envision AI in their work. We performed semi-structured interviews [28] allowing for additional questions and inquiries depending on the flow of the conversation. We developed an interview guide which includes three parts: 1) demographic, occupational and technology literacy information; 2) questions about the caseworker's current processes; 3) probes into different potential future scenarios.

The first part contained general questions about the participants, such as their age, official job title, and how long they have been in their roles. We also asked about their knowledge about AI. These questions were asked to give us a better context when analyzing the data later and to engage the participants in the interview process. The second part contained questions about their current processes as caseworkers in NAV. We asked participants to tell us what their individual daily work tasks entail, e.g., decisions they make, dialogue meetings, types of support. We also asked a follow-up question about how they thought AI could be used for their tasks. These questions were asked to better understand what the caseworkers do in their work and how AI could help them. In the third part, we applied a foresight method by providing the participants with a hypothetical scenario and asking questions about potential future developments. As the foresight method aimed to explore possible futures in relation to AI in the workplace, the scenario was based on an AI decision support system that could predict the duration of a citizen's sick leave. Based on the scenario the participants were asked to think about how different futures might look like. The different futures were split into four directions: best-case/worst-case, probable, preferred, and possible futures. As non-experts in the field of AI, the fictive scenario made it easier for them to think and describe how AI could help or make things worse in the future. This gave us more insight into what caseworkers want from an AI system in the future, and what they are worried could go wrong utilizing AI in their work.

We interviewed a total of 19 caseworkers that work at three different NAV offices. Each interview was recorded and then transcribed. The first interviews took place in digital form in November 2022, we continued with in person interviews in the period December 2022 to March 2023. For practical reasons, the interviews in December were group interviews where two caseworkers participated together. The interviews in January and March were one-on-one interviews. An overview of all interviews performed is provided in Table 1. The research was approved by the Norwegian center for research data (NSD). All interviewees participated voluntarily and were given a consent form with information on the study purpose and the data use.

Table 1. Overview of interviews.

Date	Code	Mode	Duration
14.11.2022	P1	Digital interview	30 min
18.11.2022	P2	Digital interview	30 min
23.11.2022	P3	Digital interview	30 min
07.12.2022	S1	2-People group interview	45 min
07.12.2022	S2	2-People group interview	45 min
07.12.2022	S3	2-People group interview	45 min
07.12.2022	S4	2-People group interview	45 min
07.12.2022	S5	2-People group interview	45 min
07.12.2022	S6	2-People group interview	45 min
07.12.2022	S7	2-People group interview	45 min
07.12.2022	S8	2-People group interview	45 min
26.01.2023	S9	Face-to-face interview	45 min
26.01.2023	S10	Face-to-face interview	45 min
26.01.2023	S11	Face-to-face interview	45 min
26.01.2023	S12	Face-to-face interview	45 min
23.03.2023	S13	Face-to-face interview	45 min
23.03.2023	S14	Face-to-face interview	45 min
23.03.2023	S15	Face-to-face interview	45 min
23.03.2023	S16	Face-to-face interview	45 min

3.2 Data Analysis

We used thematic analysis to get insights from the data collected. Thematic analysis is a method for identifying, analyzing and reporting themes that allows flexibility and interpretation [29] yielding rich, detailed, yet complex accounts of data. The data from the transcriptions were coded and grouped into themes [30]. The thematic analysis allowed us to explore and organize ideas identifying patterns [31, 32]. The key steps followed include: a) data familiarization: we went through all interview transcripts to become familiar and begin recording initial ideas; b) code generation: we systematically assigned codes to condense the interview content; c) themes identification and review: we sorted the different codes into themes collating coded data extracts, we refined and redefined themes moving back and forth between the entire data set, the coded extracts of data, and the identified themes. The flexibility inherent in thematic analysis enabled us to organize broad patterns in a way that told a "story" relevant to the research aims. The section that follows provides an overview of the findings.

4   Findings

Overall, we found that caseworkers see AI as an opportunity to overhaul outdated systems and "old-fashioned" approaches to serving citizens. Several interviewees made bold statements:

> "The way we work today has to change. We are behind, we work on old systems, and we work in the old-fashioned way towards the users and the people on sick leave. (...) I think that machines can do something to make things easier every day" (S11).

> "It is possible to reorganize the whole way of working, I think there is a huge potential for AI" (S13).

The caseworkers expressed optimistic yet circumspect perspectives about the introduction of AI. They pointed to potential benefits of AI-enabled profiling for prioritizing and better targeting the cases they handle. They also mentioned the potential to use AI for fetching and processing data, preparing reports, and performing simple standardized tasks. However, the caseworkers acknowledged that AI could not fully replace human workers due to the complexities and uncertainties surrounding sick-leave handling and the need to consider soft data. They also noted that AI could be one of multiple avenues for the organization to improve services, rather than a silver- bullet solution for everything. In the subsections below we elaborate on these caseworker perspectives.

4.1 Using AI for Sorting Out Cases, Prioritising and Targeting

The caseworkers indicated that they could benefit from AI assistance for prioritizing which citizens need the most support or personal interaction.

> "How do you sort out those who need the most attention, and the ones who need the most follow-up? (…) It needs to be focused on finding the people who needs us the most. That is something that artificial intelligence could help with" (S14).

"We could use our time on the most important cases, those who really need it. Those with low resources who can not take care of themselves" (S4).

The study participants explained that improved case prioritization could help reduce unnecessary meetings enabling them to devote more time and attention to people that really need these meetings.

"Maybe we could be more ON in the cases we have, have fewer and better cases, and be more often in them. As long as a meeting is not requested, and we have the information we need, and their workplace does not request a meeting, and they are working like 50%, they are rolling in the system, then maybe we could be more on them to push them a bit faster back to work. Or what we could do to make that happen, and what they can do for themselves. We could use our time on those who needs us the most" (S3).

"Previously there have been many dialogue meetings that have been unnecessary. There has been a policy that all dialogue meetings should be held, and then there were some meetings that were unnecessary for both doctors and employers" (S14).

When we asked a follow-up question about how caseworkers would utilize their time if they did not have meetings they deemed as unnecessary, they mentioned that they would focus more on the people that need extra support:

"If I did not have to have a dialogue meeting, I could have spent more time with those who need it" (S15).

The caseworkers see potential value in AI-assisted case prioritization for better targeting their limited time and resources towards citizens who need the most support. While welcoming technologies that can optimize their processes, the caseworkers underscored that empowering personnel to provide personalized service remains essential for achieving NAV's core mission.

4.2   Using AI for Automating Data Retrieval and Processing, Reporting and Simple Tasks

The caseworkers hope that AI can simplify their daily work by making information readily available.

"It could retrieve information from the doctor's report. If an AI could enter all the parameters we consider, it would have helped a lot. Then we could avoid having to write everything... and it would save us time." (P3).

"I would hope that AI simplifies my daily work. (…) That I can see clearer in a situation because I get information. I free up more working hours to do the tasks which are important" (S14).

"We work so cumbersome, as we work in five different systems. So, if you have to check a case, you at least go through four of these systems (…) I think I would have liked logging into one system and collected all the information there, rather

than have to work on a case and having to open many different systems and go back and forth all the time" (S12).

Participants also expect that AI can help in preparing reports and automating simple tasks. For instance, interviewees stated:

"Reports could have been much more automated. That would save us a lot of time, and certainly cooperation partners too" (S16).

"I would very much like to have a robot that automatically does simple things, for example, paying out sick pay... The robot should be put-in as much as possible" (S9).

"I wish for a system that could call-in and find a time for the citizen, the supervisor and the doctor, when it comes to dialogue meetings. With this, we would not have to spend half an hour to sit on the phone to find when the doctors are available" (S15).

During the interviews, it was brought one of the participants brought-up an in-house initiative to support writing with the use of pre-existing sections of standardized text. This indicates the potential of AI to support writing tasks.

"You know Wiki in Teams? It is a function in Teams where you can put standard text that we use again and again (...) you just give it a number, so it is very easy to find it back (...) I developed that here, in-house, it saves a lot of time" (S13).

The caseworkers hope that AI can simplify their work by making information readily accessible, automating routine tasks, and assisting with writing. They anticipate that AI could alleviate some administrative burden and make their work more efficient.

4.3   Using AI as a Helper Rather than a Substitute

When asked about what they would expect to happen with AI in the future, many caseworkers stated that there will always be a need for a human to take final decisions even if AI systems will be introduced to give recommendations.

"AI can help us in cases of doubt by giving a recommendation, so we do not have to think about it so much more it if comes with a certain outcome. Then it will be easier for us to make a decision" (P3).

"I think there must be a human advisor. It is fine with simple functions like moving tasks and such, but if you have more complex situations, there is a lot of discretion here. In my head a machine cannot assess discretion. So, I think there must be a human being in the final process the final piece of quality assurance is where a human is needed" (S14).

"I would like a good combination of talking to people and having support in the form of an artificial intelligence. Where you can have an assembly line, it is very sensible. You must never forget that you must talk to people" (S9).

When asked about how they would feel if a machine acted as a co-worker, several participants said that it sounds exciting as long as they have the control, and that humans direct the AI. This was expressed in multiple different ways:

"I think that it would be a little more exciting, if it was still me who had the control. You can get new ideas or encyclopedias and use them as help, so to speak" (S9).

"It can be a certain help, but NAV must be person-based I think, because of what we do"(S7).

"It must be controlled so that we see that things work, that it is directed" (S14).

Several interviewees also pointed to the importance of having face to face, on-site meetings to assess the specific circumstances.

"We can of course just have video meetings, but what happens when they come into our office, and you sit down and talk with them, and you see, do you get eye-contact? Do they smell alcohol? Can they read? There are a lot of things like that about people that a machine would never be able to catch" (S13)

"We have a lot of digital meetings every day, but when we sit around a table, we often have better meetings. I do not know why, but we have better contact and body language. Maybe the user is sitting alone at home, sometimes it could be difficult, they cry and are very alone, and I do not like that ...we are going to be a more digitized society, which is fine, but I do not think we should stop having that human connection.

... I notice that often if I have met a person once in a meeting, they also feel safer chatting digitally later as they know who they are talking to on the other end. So, I believe we should keep talking to people" (S5).

" I like to speak with people. I do not think everything can be done by technology, because I have to speak with them" (S5).

One of the interviewees explained that there are legal limitations related to what can be automated. The interviewee stated that NAV tried to automate some decision- making processes in the past, but this stopped due to legal restrictions.

"They (NAV management) tried to achieve automation for the 14A decision which was stopped. They did not get far as to be allowed to send a decision without a human being involved... we depend on good questions being asked to the user, and that the user has good self-awareness. So, if we fail at one of the two things there, it doesn't help us much" (P1).

The caseworkers consistently emphasized that humans will remain necessary for complex decision-making due to the nuances involved in individual cases. Personal interactions, meetings, and "human connections" were seen as crucial for assessing cases, building trust, and providing emotional support. The caseworkers expressed a desire to maintain control over AI and envisioned AI acting as an assistant rather than a replacement. Ultimately, caseworkers view AI as a potential helper that would still require human oversight, judgment and empathy to achieve NAV's core mission of serving citizens facing difficulties.

5 Discussion

Prior studies have indicated that organizations can be more efficient if humans collaborate with AI, rather than if AI replaces humans [11, 12]. The caseworkers interviewed in this study share a similar view, indicating that AI's role should be to augment – not supplant – their efforts to effectively support citizens. They felt AI could aid certain tasks and processes but emphasized that human judgment, empathy and personalized attention would remain crucial for fulfilling NAV's mandate. Humans are complex, and human discretion is hard for a machine to comprehend [33]. Rather than replacing caseworkers, AI can become a complementary helper, in a human-AI collaborative endeavour to enhance decision-making capabilities and efficiency.

The positive stances of caseworkers create opportunities for cultivating novelty and stimulating innovation from within. Prior research has indicated that public sector organizations would benefit from a process that rewards disruption from within as they have a moderate track record of IS innovation results [6]. Velsberg and colleagues [13] suggest that the realization of smartness in the public sector requires a willingness to explore and adopt new work practices instead of simply implementing emerging technologies. The findings from this study imply that there is significant room for digital intrapreneurship [34, 35] in NAV. AI-related innovations can sprout from workers´ resourcefulness leveraging the in-house skills and capabilities of the AI lab.

Building on the Joint Cognitive Systems conceptualization [15], Human-AI collaboration could be established in NAV bringing together both human and artificial agents´ qualities. An example could be when a meeting is initiated between a caseworker and a citizen. An AI system can collate data related to the citizen (sick leave data and other related data), and the case worker can add additional data from dialogue meetings and verify data. The AI system can analyze the data using powerful algorithms and give results in the form of suggestions to aid the caseworker in reaching good decisions. The results should be understandable for humans through explainable AI methods, so the caseworker can understand what the results mean and how the AI developed the resulting suggestions. The caseworker can use the AI help to reach a decision and give the citizen the appropriate service based on their discretion. The caseworker should also be able to relay the resulting information to the citizen in a clear and comprehensible way to maintain trust and accountability. The insights from this study cover the entirety of tasks involved in sick leave case handling expanding beyond the digital touchpoints between humans and AI. The findings go beyond human-AI interaction to encompass the broader scope of collaboration between humans and machines as joint cognitive systems and suggests thinking of AI as a collaborator that undertakes specific roles.

The findings highlight the importance of balancing between efficient public service (which can be facilitated through automation), and AI accountability (which requires control mechanisms and strong roles for humans). This balance has long been a challenge in public services [36], and with the advancements in AI, it has become even more crucial. Further research is required to delve deeper into this topic. Public organizations need to take a comprehensive view on AI accountability being able to answer for and justify actions related to AI, ensuring the ability of stakeholders to interrogate about AI and sanctioning when AI systems work in unacceptable ways [37]. Further research is needed on how this can be achieved in practice. Overall, the responsible development and deployment of AI is an area of research that requires significant further development, and Information Systems researchers, with their sociotechnical understanding, are well-suited to contribute to this crucial endeavour [9, 10]. Further research could extend across countries as cultural identity and overall digital literacy may influence stances on AI [14]. This is an exciting research opportunity to see how human-AI collaboration differs cross-culturally.

Implementing human-AI collaboration into public services could help the Norwegian government in reaching United Nations' sustainable development goals (SDGs) such as reduced inequalities by ensuring access to high quality public services for all; decent work and economic growth by helping more people get back to work faster; and good health and well-being by helping more citizens and guiding them getting the help they need [38].

6 Conclusion

This study provides valuable insights into caseworkers' needs for human-AI collaboration in public services. The findings highlight both opportunities and challenges for introducing AI in welfare administration. The caseworkers expressed optimistic yet circumspect perspectives about the introduction of AI. On the one hand, caseworkers see potential for AI to improve prioritization, data retrieval, reporting and simple tasks – thereby simplifying and making their work more efficient. On the other hand, they emphasize that AI cannot fully replace humans due to the complexity of sick leave cases and the need for empathy, discretion and personal connections. Caseworkers envision AI playing an assisting rather than substitutive role, where artificial agents aid – rather than compete with humans. Realizing such human-AI synergies in practice requires thoughtful design of socio-technical systems that account for the contextual specificities and values of public service provision [14, 39].

Our research is not without limitations. We focused solely on one public organization and on one specific service to citizens (sick-leaves). Therefore, caution should be exercised in generalizing the findings to other contexts. Future investigations could explore the perspectives of public servants on AI across different contexts, aiming to identify both commonalities and variations across settings. Furthermore, this is a foresight study. The participants have not experienced the use of AI yet in their everyday tasks, they have been stimulated to think of future scenarios. The strength of the study is that the participants have not been limited in their thinking by systems that already provide specific action possibilities and action constraints. Further studies in workplaces where AI has already been introduced can bring additional insights into the dynamic relationships between humans and AI within organizational contexts. A stream of in-depth, contextualized research investigations can generate much needed knowledge for cultivating productive human-AI collaborations.

References

1. McCarthy, J.J., Minsky, M., Rochester, N., Shannon, C.E.: A Proposal for the Dartmouth summer research project on artificial intelligence, August 31, 1955. AI Mag. **27**(4), 12 (2006)
2. Meske, C., Bunde, E., Schneider, J., Gersch, M.: Explainable artificial intelligence: objectives, stakeholders, and future research opportunities. Inf. Syst. Manag. **39**(1), 53–63 (2022)
3. Park, S.Y., et al.: Identifying challenges and opportunities in human-AI collaboration in healthcare. In: Conference Companion Publication of the 2019 on Computer Supported Cooperative Work and Social Computing, Association for Computing Machinery, pp. 506–510 (2019)
4. Benbunan-Fich, R., Desouza, K.C., Andersen, K.V.: IT-enabled innovation in the public sector: introduction to the special issue. Eur. J. Inf. Syst. **29**(4), 323–328 (2020)
5. Eggers, W., Fishman, T., Kishnani, P.: AI-Augmented Human Services: Using Cognitive Technologies to Transform Program Delivery (2017)
6. Vassilakopoulou, P., Haug, A., Salvesen, L.M., Pappas, I.O.: Developing human/AI interactions for chat-based customer services: lessons learned from the Norwegian government. Eur. J. Inf. Syst. **32**(1), 10–22 (2023)
7. Dennehy, D., Griva, A., Pouloudi, N., Mäntymäki, M., Pappas, I.: Artificial Intelligence for Decision-Making and the Future of Work (2023)
8. Dennehy, D., Griva, A., Pouloudi, N., Dwivedi, Y.K., Mäntymäki, M., Pappas, I.O.: Artificial intelligence (AI) and information systems: perspectives to responsible AI. Inf. Syst. Front. **25**(1), 1–7 (2023)
9. Vassilakopoulou, P., Parmiggiani, E., Shollo, A., Grisot, M.: Responsible AI: Concepts, critical perspectives and an Information Systems research agenda. Scand. J. Inf. Syst. **34**(2), 3 (2022)
10. Akbari, P., Pappas, I., Vassilakopoulou, P.: Justice as Fairness: a hierarchical framework of responsible AI principles. In: ECIS 2023 (2023)
11. Wang, D., et al.: From Human-Human Collaboration to Human-AI Collaboration (2020)
12. McKinsey: Forging the Human–Machine Alliance (2022)
13. Velsberg, O., Westergren, U.H., Jonsson, K.: Exploring smartness in public sector innovation – creating smart public services with the Internet of Things. Eur. J. Inf. Syst. **29**(4), 350–368 (2020)
14. Schmager, S., Vassilakopoulou, P., Grøder, C., Parmiggiani, E., Pappas, I.: What do citizens think of AI adoption in public services? Exploratory research on citizen attitudes through a social contract lens. In: Proceedings of the 56th Annual Hawaii International Conference on System Sciences. HICSS Conference Office, vol. 436, pp. 4472–4481 (2023). ISBN 978-0-9981331-6-4
15. Woods, D.D.: Cognitive technologies: the design of joint human-machine cognitive systems. AI Mag. **6**(4), 86–92 (1986)
16. Balakrishnan, J., Dwivedi, Y.K.: Role of cognitive absorption in building user trust and experience. Psychol. Mark. **38**(4), 643–668 (2021)
17. Ijtsma, M., Ma, L.M., Pritchett, A.R., Feigh, K.M.: Computational methodology for the allocation of work and interaction in human-robot teams. J. Cogn. Eng. Decis. Making **13**(4), 221–241 (2019)
18. Stowers, K., Kasdaglis, N., Rupp, M., Chen, J., Barber, D., Barnes, M.: Insights into human-agent teaming: intelligent agent transparency and uncertainty, in advances in human factors in robots and unmanned systems. In: Savage-Knepshield, P., Chen, J. (eds.) Springer International Publishing, pp. 149–160 (2017)
19. Marathe, A.R., Schaefer, K.E., Evans, A.W., Metcalfe, J.S.: Bidirectional communication for effective human-agent teaming, in virtual, augmented and mixed reality: interaction, navigation, visualization, embodiment, and simulation. In: Chen, J.Y.C., Fragomeni, G. (eds.) Springer International Publishing, pp. 338–350 (2018)

20. Xu, W., Gao, Z.: Applying human-centered AI in developing effective human-AI teaming: A perspective of human-AI joint cognitive systems. arXiv preprint arXiv:2307.03913 (2023)
21. Schmager, S., Pappas, I., Vassilakopoulou, P.: Defining Human-centered AI: a comprehensive review of HCAI literature. In: Proceedings of the Mediterranean Conference on Information Systems 2023 (2023)
22. Nav, Hva er NAV? – nav.no. (2023)
23. Jensen, M.V., Lyngstad, C.P.: Innspill til strategi for kunstig intelligens (2019)
24. Fineide, M.J., Hansen, G.V., Haug, E.: How does a new working method in the Norwegian Labour and Welfare Organization (NAV) succeed in reducing sick leave rates? Int. J. Integr. Care 19(4), 169 (2019)
25. Neuhoff, R., Simeone, L., Laursen, L.H.: Exploring how design-driven foresight can support strategic thinking in relation to sustainability and circular policy making. In: European Academy of Design Conference: Safe Harbours. The European Academy of Design (2021)
26. Ramos, J., Sweeney, J.A., Peach, K., Smith, L.: Our futures: by the people, for the people. NESTA, London (2019)
27. Inayatullah, S.: Methods and Epistemologies in Futures Studies, Knowledge Base of Futures Studies, 1st edn. Foresight International, Brisbane (2000)
28. Oates, B.J., Griffiths, M., McLean, R.: Researching Information Systems and Computing. Sage Publications Limited (2022)
29. Braun, V., Clarke, V.: Using thematic analysis in psychology. Qual. Res. Psychol. 3(2), 77–101 (2006)
30. Castleberry, A., Nolen, A.: Thematic analysis of qualitative research data: is it as easy as it sounds? Curr. Pharm. Teach. Learn. 10(6), 807–815 (2018)
31. Guest, G., Mclellan, E.: Distinguishing the trees from the forest: applying cluster analysis to thematic qualitative data. Field Methods 15(2), 186–201 (2003)
32. Richards, T., et al.: Using hierarchical categories in qualitative data analysis. In: Computer-Aided Qualitative Data Analysis: Theory, Methods, and Practice, pp. 80–95 (1995)
33. Young, M.R., Bullock, J.B., Lecy, J.D.: Artificial discretion as a tool of governance: a framework for understanding the impact of artificial intelligence on public administration. Perspect. Public Manag. Governance 2, 301–313 (2019)
34. Vassilakopoulou, P., Grisot, M.: Effectual tactics in digital intrapreneurship: a process model. J. Strateg. Inf. Syst. 29(3), 101617 (2020)
35. Opland, L.E., Pappas, I.O., Engesmo, J., Jaccheri, L.: Employee-driven digital innovation: a systematic review and a research agenda. J. Bus. Res. 143, 255–271 (2022)
36. Gayialis, S.P., Papadopoulos, G.A., Ponis, S.T., Vassilakopoulou, P., Tatsiopoulos, I.P.: Integrating process modeling and simulation with benchmarking using a business process management system for local government. Int. J. Comput. Theory Eng. 8(6), 482 (2016)
37. Kempton, A.M., Parmiggiani, E., Vassilakopoulou, P.: Accountability in Managing Artificial Intelligence: State of the Art and a way forward for Information Systems Research (2023)
38. United Nations: Take Action for the Sustainable Development Goals – United Nations Sustainable Development. (2020)
39. Schmager, S.: From commercial agreements to the social contract: human-centered AI guidelines for public services. In: Proceedings of the Mediterranean Conference on Information Systems 2022 (2022)

Creating Demand for AI-Based Subscription of Physical Goods: A Consumer Perspective in the Food Industry

Dinara Davlembayeva[1]([✉]) [iD], Davit Marikyan[2] [iD], Eleonora Pantano[2] [iD],
Francesca Serravalle[3] [iD], and David Babayan[4]

[1] Cardiff Business School, Cardiff University, Cardiff CF10 3EU, UK
davlembayevad@cardiff.ac.uk
[2] University of Bristol Business School, Bristol BS8 1SD, UK
[3] Department of Management "Valter Cantino", University of Turin, 10134 Turin, Italy
[4] Lomonosov Moscow State University, Moscow 119234, Russia

Abstract. Subscription platforms based on artificial intelligence (AI) that offer the delivery of physical goods represent a new frontier in retailing. Therefore, empirical investigation into consumers' views on the factors driving their motivation to use such platforms is necessary. Considering the lack of research on this front, this study aims to examine consumers' insights into the enabling and constraining technological affordances of platforms that inhibit or facilitate subscription motivation. Drawing on Regulatory Focus Theory, this study tests the effects of situational prevention-focused and promotion-focused factors on subscription intention. Based on data from 290 respondents, we found that intention is positively influenced by perceived functional congruity, which is determined by perceived service personalization and ease of use. In contrast, the effect of psychological reactance associated with perceived lack of control over service delivery is negative. These findings advance our understanding of the features of platforms offering physical goods subscription services that drive the predisposition to use such platforms, thus informing retailers on how AI can support platform expansion.

Keywords: Artificial Intelligence · Subscription Platforms · Platformisation · Food Industry · Physical Goods

1 Introduction

The recent progress in technology has led to a new form of retail channels based on subscriptions, which transcend traditional distribution networks [1]. For instance, subscriptions to online platform-based services like streaming TV and online sports (e.g., Netflix, Disney+, BT Sport, Amazon Prime, etc.) have experienced a global surge. Although subscription services predominantly revolve around digital goods, retailers of physical products have begun offering subscription plans, thus presaging a promising

© IFIP International Federation for Information Processing 2023
Published by Springer Nature Switzerland AG 2023
M. Janssen et al. (Eds.): I3E 2023, LNCS 14316, pp. 54–68, 2023.
https://doi.org/10.1007/978-3-031-50040-4_5

future for the development of subscription-based retail platforms. The role of AI in the functioning of such platforms will be crucial. Taking the analogy of streaming services, such as Netflix, AI can facilitate the delivery of new products based on past purchases and interactions on the platform. This will be possible due to AI's capabilities to automatically detect the characteristics of accessed products and match them with similar ones. Consequently, platform- and subscription-based expansion strategies, based on the employment of AI, represent a new frontier in the retailing of physical goods.

While the advancement of retail subscription services using AI promises to enhance the customer experience, it does have unequivocal implications for customers and companies. Subscription plans can lead to attachment to the retail brand offering the subscription [2]. Their purchase can also involve a certain level of risk and a loss of perceived control over the plan, which can be mitigated by reducing the length of the subscription (e.g., from one year to a monthly basis) [3]. Moreover, recent studies have highlighted that subscriptions might have a negative impact on retailers' incremental profit since they may cannibalize sales from the offline channel while incurring delivery costs [4].

The potential development of subscription services enabled by AI and their ambiguous implications necessitate empirical investigation into consumers' views on retail subscription platforms. However, evidence in the retail and distribution management literature on this topic is limited. Existing research on subscription services for physical goods has primarily focused on the rental of luxury products [5], and studied the delivery of fashion items, highlighting specific benefits for consumers in terms of convenience, excitement, surprise, and self-gratification [6–9]. Other studies have explored the role of customer heterogeneity and subscription length in the demand for services from market and design perspectives [10, 11]. Nevertheless, recent research largely stressed the challenges and threats when consumers interact with AI in retail settings [12–14]. As such, the consumers' insights into the enabling and constraining technological affordances of platforms have not been explored, despite the importance of such evidence in understanding how AI can support platform expansion (platformisation) for retailers of physical goods.

To address the above gap, we empirically examine the motivation to use subscription retail platforms for physical goods enabled by AI, and the impact of contrasting beliefs about technological affordances that facilitate or inhibit motivation to use them. To this end, this study adopts the Regulatory Focus theory [15] and builds on relevant literature [16–23] to identify the factors that promote or prevent motivation to use subscription platforms. The remainder of the paper will discuss the theoretical background underpinning this study and the hypotheses. Next, we will explain the methodological approaches adopted for this study, followed by the results and discussion of findings. The paper will conclude with a summary of the results and key contributions.

2 Theoretical Foundation and Hypotheses

2.1 Regulatory Focus Theory

This study adopts the Regulatory Focus Theory (RFT) developed by Higgins [24] to explain the underpinnings of motivation to use AI-powered subscription platforms in the context of retailing. RFT describes the self-regulation mechanisms – both inherent to people and situationally induced – that can explain individuals' predisposition vs. aversive reaction to the same event or stimuli [15]. The predisposition and aversive responses represent promotion-focused and prevention-focused regulatory processes. Promotion-focused self-regulation hinges on the salience of needs for growth/development and aspirations. Simply put, the motivation to engage in behaviour is stimulated by the belief in the ability to attain positive outcomes. In contrast, prevention-focused self-regulation manifests itself when an individual is guided by the need to avoid adverse outcomes. When such a regulatory process takes place, individuals experience the salience of the need for safety and risk aversion [25].

RFT is deemed instrumental for the context of this research, given the polarisation of beliefs that could be potentially raised by the embeddedness of AI algorithms in subscription platforms. On the one hand, complete automation of services and proactive service personalisation enabled by AI can help improve service value and tailor services to the needs of customers [18, 26]. Thus, AI-based subscription platforms can be instrumental for customers due to their functional congruity. *Functional congruity* is conceptualised as the match between consumers' perception of the utilitarian attributes of the system and consumers' ideal expectations of those attributes [27]. On the other hand, the autonomy of system decision-making can indicate limited consumers' power and control over experience, thus undermining the psychological acceptance of the system and triggering psychological reactance [18]. Psychological reactance is a state instigated by the perception of a threat to one's freedom [28]. As such, the use of RFT enables us to accommodate the objective of the study aimed to explore both enabling and constraining affordances of platforms contributing to the perception of functional congruity and psychological reactance. The next section discusses perceived functional congruity and psychological reactance and their predictors as the reflection of promotion and prevention motivational orientation when it comes to the use of AI-based subscription retail platforms (Fig. 1).

2.2 Hypothesis Development

Situational Promotion-Focused Predictors

The perception of functional congruity is argued to be shaped by utilitarian beliefs [29]. Based on the literature on AI-based technologies and recommender platforms, one of the most critical utilitarian factors regarding the use and adoption of technology is perceived personalization and ease of use [16–19]. Personalisation refers to the degree to which an AI platform can be tailored to satisfy individual needs. Previous research extensively discussed the role of personalization in users' experiences when interacting with AI-based devices such as chatbots, voice-based digital assistants, and smart home technologies (e.g., Google Home, Amazon Alexa) [20, 21, 30, 31]. Personalization of services and goods plays a significant role in adoption and decision-making processes [16, 17]. Many organizations and developers strive to acquire and share data for marketing/retail purposes to offer better and more personalized offers to their customers [16, 32, 33]. Given that the ultimate goal of offering personalized services/offers is to better cater to consumers' needs, it can be concluded that personalization would be well-received by consumers [16, 33]. Perceived ease of use can be defined as "*the degree to which an individual believes that using a particular system would be free of effort*" [34]. In this context, perceived ease of use refers to individuals' beliefs regarding the effort they need to invest to use or set up a plan employing an AI-based subscription platform. Perceived ease of use has been established to have a strong and significant impact on individuals' attitudes, intentions, and usage behaviour [20, 34–37]. The literature provides evidence that the lower the effort individuals need to invest to use the system, the higher their intention to use it [20, 35]. For instance, it was found that when individuals believe that new innovative technologies, such as AI-based technologies, will be easier to use for work purposes, they tend to adopt and use them in their daily routines [20]. Given the above evidence and the argument that functional congruity is affected by external utilitarian cues of an object, we hypothesize the following:

> **H1:** *(a) Perceived personalisation and (b) ease of use are positively related to the perception of functional congruity.*

Situational Prevention-Focused Predictors

System decision autonomy captures individuals' views about technology (e.g., AI-based recommender platform) that has full autonomy or freedom to select products/services for them. Semi-autonomous and autonomous systems are used in various applications, such as automotive, smart technologies, tourism, and robotics, among others [20–23, 38]. The advancement of technology and widespread adoption of different smart technologies have motivated individuals to rely more on the autonomous features of technology, particularly in the work environment [30, 39]. However, there is a viewpoint that despite the capabilities of technology to be fully autonomous, people still prefer to supervise it and have control over it [23]. Control is defined as *"perceived ease or difficulty of performing the behaviour"* [40], in IS context it is *"a perception of internal and external constraints on behaviour"* [41]. The perception of control is important for individuals as they feel that they have the opportunity to influence or change aspects of the environment, which can impact events related to them. This becomes particularly important when it comes to the use of new or innovative technologies/systems [42]. A lack of control or awareness of how to manage systems can result in negative consequences [43]. Thus, individuals tend to prefer having control over technologies to avoid any negative results.

Given the evidence above and the principles of reactance theory, which assumes that individuals expect to have freedom in different aspects of their lives (especially when it comes to the opportunity to select alternative products or services when it comes to consumption scenarios) [44], we hypothesise that:

> **H2:** *(a) Perceived autonomy of a platform in decision-making and (b) lack of control are positively related to psychological reactance.*

Predictors of Use Intention

In this study, we hypothesise that perceived functional congruity and psychological reactance have opposite effects on intention. Many studies found that functional congruity directly predicts an individual's behaviour [29, 45–47]. It impacts individuals' attitudes [48], purchase intention [49] and satisfaction [50]. On the contrary, psychological reactance was found to be an inhibitor of behaviour [51]. The theory of psychological reactance can explain the negative relationship. The theory postulates that individuals perceive themselves to be entitled to have some degree of freedom to engage in certain behaviours [28, 52]. When individuals feel that their freedom to engage in certain behaviours is threatened or diminished, they become motivated to restore it and eliminate the threat reducing their freedom [28, 52, 53]. In the decision-making and consumption scenarios, individuals anticipate having the freedom to choose and the opportunity to select alternative products or services [44, 53]. For example, during COVID-19 many governments limited individuals' freedom to go out shopping, which resulted in psychological reactance and motivated individuals to get engaged in revenge buying to counteract the imposed restrictions [51]. Some aspects of AI-based recommender platforms, such as system decision autonomy and lack of control may limit the individuals' freedom to select products can lead to psychological reactance. Following the principles of the theory of psychological reactance [44, 52, 53], it is more likely that when such a psychological state is aroused, individuals will attempt to avoid using technology which limits their freedom. Given the evidence above we hypothesise that:

H3: The perception of functional congruity is positively related to the intention to use platforms.

H4: Psychological reactance is negatively related to the intention to use platforms.

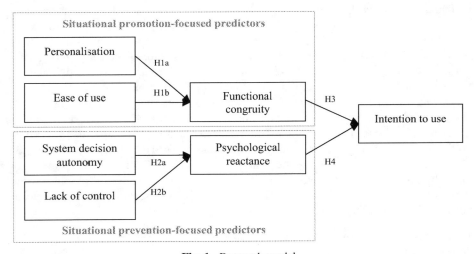

Fig. 1. Research model

3   Methodology

We conducted a cross-sectional survey distributed via Prolific, a research platform assisting in the collection of data from a target sample. A sample for data collection was purposive. Considering the objectives of the research to explore the intentions of potential users of subscription platforms, the survey was open to individuals of any occupation, gender, age, skill or experience. However, to ensure the comprehension of the questions in English and the accuracy of responses, the survey was restricted to respondents from the United Kingdom and the USA. Prior to data collection, we conducted a pilot study based on 10 respondents to eliminate the possibility of ambiguous questions and technical errors. The final questionnaire contained four blocks: 1) the introduction detailing the purpose of the study and consent form; 2) the vignette; 3) the questions measuring respondents' perceptions, the motivations for using subscription platforms for the delivery of physical goods, and the perceived behavioural consequences of usage; 4) the questions for a socio-demographic profile of the sample. The vignette described a hypothetical scenario about the services of an AI-based subscription platform in the context of food retailing. First, the respondents were asked to imagine the scenario of using a subscription-based grocery platform giving access to a range of products and enabling users to manually select orders for home delivery. Then, the respondents were given an alternative option of a service, based on artificial intelligence algorithms. Compared to an existing subscription service, the platform customises and automatically preselects products for customers. The respondents have explained the functionality and services of the AI-based subscription platform. The final data set consisted of 290 responses (Table 1).

Table 1. Demographic profile of respondents

	Demographic data	Number of respondents	Percentage of respondents
Gender	Male	107	36.9
	Female	175	60.3
	Non-binary	6	2.1
	Prefer not to say	2	0.7
Age	18–19	4	1.4
	20 – 29	84	29.0
	30 – 39	90	31.0
	40 – 49	55	19.0
	50 – 59	41	14.1
	60 and over	16	5.5
Education	Some high school or less	6	2.1
	High school graduate or equivalent	44	15.2
	Vocational/technical school (two-year program)	15	5.2

(continued)

Table 1. (*continued*)

	Demographic data	Number of respondents	Percentage of respondents
	Some college, but no degree	46	15.9
	College graduate (four-year program)	83	28.6
	Some graduate school, but not degree	5	1.7
	Graduate degree (MSc, MBA, PhD, etc.)	80	27.6
	Professional degree (M.D., J.D., etc.)	11	3.8
Annual income	$0 – $24,999	97	33.4
	$25,000 – $49,999	122	42.1
	$50,000 – $74,999	51	17.6
	$75,000 – $99,999	9	3.1
	More than $100,000	11	3.8
	Prefer not to say	0	0

Measurement items of the tested variables were adopted from and validated by prior studies (Table 2). A 7-point Likert scale was used for all items, whereby the score of "1" denoted strong disagreement, "7" meant strong agreement and "4" was a midpoint for an undetermined stance regarding a question.

The research model was tested using covariance-based structural equation modelling (CB-SEM) with SPSS Amos software. First, confirmatory factor analysis (CFA) was performed to test the reliability and validity of the measurement model. Model fit indices ($\chi^2(384) = 934.105$, P = .00, CMIN/DF = 2.433, CFI = 0.923, RMSEA = 0.070) were satisfactory. The reliability and the convergent and discriminant validity of scales were confirmed by Cronbach's alpha values above 0.7, composite reliability values (C.R.) above 0.7, average variance extracted (AVE) higher than 0.5 and the square root of AVE higher than the between-constructs correlation (Table 3) [60]. Also, since the data was collected from a single source, common method bias (CMB) was checked using Harman's single-factors method [61]. A single factor accounted for 37% of the total variance, which is below the threshold of 50%, thus suggesting that the variance is not attributable to the measurement method [61].

The second step prior to path analysis was the evaluation of the structural model, which showed satisfactory model fit: $\chi2(393) = 966.893$, P = .00, CMIN/DF = 2.460, CFI = 0.920, RMSEA = 0.071.

Table 2. Measurement items

Items	Factor Loading
Personalisation [54]	
I think that the use of the AI-powered subscription platform... will help address my dietary needs	0.779
would be personalised to my dietary needs	0.862
would be customised exactly to my dietary requirements	0.816
would result in the delivery of products that I need	0.739
Ease of use [55]	
would be clear and understandable	0.628
would not require a lot of my mental effort	0.668
would be easy	0.799
It would be easy to get the subscription platform to do what I want it to do	0.755
Functional congruity [56]	
I think that the AI-powered subscription platform... would provide the services I desire	0.611
would perform better on the functional attributes I value most, such as product selection and delivery	0.576
would meet all the needs when it comes to product selection and delivery	0.576
would provide value that is consistent with what I expect from a subscription-based platform	0.653
Decision autonomy [57]	
In think that when it comes to the selection and delivery of products, the AI-powered subscription platform... would have the freedom to make decisions for me	0.681
would make decisions independent of me	0.645
would have a great deal of freedom to assemble orders for me	0.705
would be empowered to make decisions for me	0.662
would be independent when making decisions	0.656
would assemble orders the way it sees fit	0.561
Lack of control [57]	
I think that when using the AI-powered subscription platform... the decisions regarding product selection and delivery would be out of my hands	0.761
I would have no control over the decisions regarding product selection and delivery	0.808
I would not be in charge of my own experience of using the services	0.815

(*continued*)

Table 2. (*continued*)

Items	Factor Loading
I would feel lack of control	0.779
I think that things would be out of my control	0.813
I would have no influence over the selection and delivery of products for my orders	0.738
Psychological reactance [58]	
The use of AI algorithms in the subscription service for product selection and delivery… would restrict my choices	0.925
would make me limited in my choices	0.904
would impact my freedom of choice	0.834
Intention [59]	
If I am offered to use the AI-powered subscription platform for product selection and delivery… I intend to use it	0.850
I would always try to use it	0.844
I would plan to use it	0.868

Table 3. Reliability, convergent and discriminant validity test

	CR	AVE	α	1	2	3	4	5	6	7
LC	0.941	0.726	0.940	**0.852**						
DA	0.885	0.562	0.883	0.246	**0.750**					
PE	0.916	0.732	0.911	−0.282	0.312	**0.856**				
EoU	0.848	0.584	0.847	−0.427	0.265	0.626	**0.764**			
FC	0.875	0.638	0.875	−0.493	0.217	0.644	0.754	**0.798**		
IN	0.956	0.878	0.955	−0.440	0.049	0.371	0.477	0.648	**0.937**	
PS	0.941	0.843	0.938	0.648	0.092	−0.261	−0.406	−0.488	−0.481	**0.918**

Notes: Diagonal figures represent the square root of the average variance extracted (AVE) and the figures below represent the between-constructs correlations
PS – Psychological Reactance, DA – decision autonomy, PE – personalisation, EoU – ease of use, LC – lack of control, FC – functional congruity, IN – intention

4   Results and Discussion

The analysis of the structural model showed that the hypotheses were supported (Table 4). The model explained 63% of the variance for perceived functional congruity, 43% for psychological reactance and 42% for intention.

Table 4. Path analysis results

Hypotheses	Path	Coef.	t-test
H1a	Personalisation -> Functional congruity	0.256	3.905 ***
H1b	Ease of use -> Functional congruity	0.61	8.358 ***
H2a	System decision autonomy -> Psychological reactance	−0.081	−1.547 ns
H2b	Lack of control -> Psychological reactance	0.673	11.282 ***
H3	Functional congruity -> Intention	0.534	9.335 ***
H4	Psychological reactance -> Intention	−0.257	−4.998 ***

Significant at p: ns ≥ 0.05; *<0.05; **<0.01; ***<0.001.

Our results show the situational promotion-focused predictors and situational prevention-focused predictors of the adoption of subscription services for physical goods, specifically in the case of food. We identify the drivers of adopting subscription services for physical goods in terms of perceived personalization, ease of use, and functional congruity. We also examine discouraging factors in terms of the perceived autonomy of the system and psychological reactance. Specifically, our findings show that perceived personalization and the ease of platforms' use positively impact functional congruity (H1a coeff. = 0.256, t-test = 3.905; H1b coeff. = 0.61, t-test = 8.358, respectively). In other words, if the platform supports personalisation (for instance, by allowing consumers to have customised boxes based on product preferences, typology and usage, frequency of delivery, novelty/exclusivity of the product, etc.) and offers easy-to-use interfaces (for instance, consumers can easily select their needs and expectations for the delivered products), consumers' perception of the platform's utilitarian attributes and their ideal expectations of those attributes are aligned (functional attributes).

Our results also demonstrate that the perceived autonomy of the platform in making decisions about the products has a minimal influence on consumers' psychological reactance (H2a coeff. = −0.081, t-test = −1.547). This means that the level of autonomy of the platform has only a marginal impact on consumers' feelings of freedom in choosing the products to be delivered. On the contrary, the lack of control positively affects psychological reactance (H2b coeff. = 0.673, t-test = 11.282). Moreover, the perception of functional congruity positively impacts the intention to use the subscription platform (H3 coeff. = 0.534, t-test = 9.335). Therefore, when consumers' perceptions of the platform's utilitarian attributes and their ideal expectations align, they intend to subscribe to the delivery of physical goods.

Finally, psychological reactance negatively impacts the intention to use these platforms (H4 coeff. = −0.257, t-test = −4.998). That means that the higher consumers' need to feel independent in their choices (including the choice to purchase certain physical products), the lower their intention to adopt subscription services for physical goods, as they would perceive them as limiting their freedom.

5 Conclusion and Contributions

This study addressed the gap in current research, lacking insights into consumers' perspectives on the enabling and constraining technological affordances that inhibit or facilitate the use of AI-enabled subscription services for physical goods. Drawing on RFT and relevant literature [15–23], we identified situational prevention-focused and promotion-focused predictors of intention to use subscription retail services. We found that the perception of functional congruity, associated with perceived service personalization and ease of use, increases intention to use. Conversely, psychological reactance resulting from the perception of a lack of personal control over service delivery decreases motivation to use. These findings advance our understanding of the features of platforms offering physical goods subscription services that drive the predisposition to use such platforms. This evidence is novel considering that previous research on subscription-based delivery of physical products has only focused on certain benefits of fashion item delivery services [6–9], as well as market and design perspectives on exploring consumers' use of such services [10, 11]. In our research, we examine the extent to which "platformisation" of retailing with the help of AI can potentially be more efficient in capitalizing consumer demand than traditional business models, by aiding the transition from subscription services offering rented products, such as luxury goods [5], to the subscription for ownership-based products, such as food. By doing so, our research emphasizes how AI might support and even replace consumer decision-making, by making autonomous purchase decisions regarding physical goods, thus contributing to the debate on consumers' interaction with AI [12–14]. The focus on a specific form of interaction (i.e. subscription for physical goods), whereby the interaction occurs to support AI in selecting and buying products on behalf of the consumer, extends the knowledge in past studies on human-AI interactions [12, 38].

From a practical standpoint, this study's findings provide valuable insights for brands regarding the effectiveness of specific platform features and functions in driving demand for physical goods offered through AI-based subscription plans. Our results demonstrate a strong consumer willingness to embrace subscription plans, prompting retailers to seriously consider this option for both customer retention and acquisition. More specifically, our findings recommend that retailers should incorporate options for personalization within their service offerings. This includes not only tailoring subscription frequencies and allowing temporary suspensions but also enabling the creation of highly customized shopping carts for in-person grocery visits.

6 Future Research Directions

Our research offers an initial exploration of subscription services for physical goods, with a broader focus beyond just the fashion industry. Nevertheless, it's important to note that our sample was drawn from two countries, the UK and US, where subscription plans for physical goods, even those with minimal personalization, are already widely adopted. Consequently, the familiarity of our sample with these plans, as well as their general technological awareness, may have influenced their responses. To enhance the generalizability of our findings, future studies should consider diversifying their samples by including participants from countries with varying levels of technological development and differing access to subscription plans, such as Italy, India, and others. Moreover, we strongly encourage future research to employ larger sample sizes to further strengthen the validity of our results. Also, more studies are required to identify any difference in consumers' adoptions according to product categories and subcategories (e.g., electronics versus grocery, fast fashion versus luxury products, etc.), lifestyle/working conditions or generational cohorts (e.g., will younger VS older segments be more willing to adopt subscription plans?).

References

1. Pasirayi, S., Fennell, P.B.: The effect of subscription-based direct-to-consumer channel additions on firm value. J. Bus. Res. **123**, 355–366 (2021)
2. Kerschbaumer, R.H., et al.: Subscription commerce: an attachment theory perspective. Int. Rev. Retail, Distrib. Consum. Res. **33**(1), 92–115 (2023)
3. Roy, A., Ortiz, M.: Is it risky to subscribe? Perceived control and subscription choice. Psychol. Market. **40**(2), 365–372 (2023)
4. Wagner, L., Pinto, C., Amorim, P.: On the value of subscription models for online grocery retail. Eur. J. Oper. Res. **294**(3), 874–894 (2021)
5. Pantano, E., Stylos, N.: The Cinderella moment: exploring consumers' motivations to engage with renting as collaborative luxury consumption mode. Psychol. Market. **37**(5), 740–753 (2020)
6. Bhatt, D., Kim, H.-S., Bhatt, S.: Shopping motivations of fashion subscription service consumers. Int. Rev. Retail, Distrib. Consum. Res. **31**(5), 549–565 (2021)
7. Tao, Q., Xu, Y.: Fashion subscription retailing: an exploratory study of consumer perceptions. J. Fashion Market. Manag.: An Int. J. **22**(4) (2018)
8. Bray, J., et al.: Thinking inside the box: an empirical exploration of subscription retailing. J. Retailing Consum. Serv. **58**, 102333 (2021)
9. Bischof, S.F., Boettger, T.M., Rudolph, T.: Curated subscription commerce: a theoretical conceptualization. J. Retail. Consum. Serv. **54**, 101822 (2020)
10. Niculescu, M.F., Shin, H., Whang, S.: Underlying consumer heterogeneity in markets for subscription-based IT services with network effects. Inform. Syst. Res. **23**(4), 1322–1341 (2012)
11. Feng, N., et al.: Designing subscription menu for software products: whether to release a long-length option. Inform. Manag. **59**(6), 103665 (2022)
12. Pantano, E., Scarpi, D.: I, robot, you, consumer: measuring artificial intelligence types and their effect on consumers emotions in service. J. Serv. Res. **25**(4), 583–600 (2022)
13. Wirtz, J., et al.: Corporate digital responsibility in service firms and their ecosystems. J. Serv. Res. **26**(2), 173–190 (2023)

14. Kopalle, P.K., et al.: Examining artificial intelligence (AI) technologies in marketing via a global lens: current trends and future research opportunities. Int. J. Res. Market. **39**(2), 522–540 (2022)
15. Higgins, E.T.: Regulatory focus theory. In: Van Lange, P., Kruglanski, A., Higgins, E. (eds.) Handbook of Theories of Social Psychology: Vol. 1, pp. 483–504. SAGE Publications Ltd, 1 Oliver's Yard, 55 City Road, London EC1Y 1SP United Kingdom (2012). https://doi.org/10.4135/9781446249215.n24
16. Kronemann, B., et al.: How AI encourages consumers to share their secrets? The role of anthropomorphism, personalisation, and privacy concerns and avenues for future research. Spanish J. Market.-ESIC **27**(1), 2–19 (2023)
17. Nawaz, I.Y.: Characteristics of millennials and technology adoption in the digital age. In: Dadwal, S.S. (ed.) Handbook of Research on Innovations in Technology and Marketing for the Connected Consumer, pp. 241–262. IGI Global (2020). https://doi.org/10.4018/978-1-7998-0131-3.ch012
18. Zhang, B., Sundar, S.S.: Proactive vs. reactive personalization: can customization of privacy enhance user experience? Int. J. Human-Comput. Stud. **128**, 86–99 (2019)
19. Childers, T.L., et al.: Hedonic and utilitarian motivations for online retail shopping behavior. J. Retail. **77**(4), 511–535 (2001)
20. Marikyan, D., et al.: Working in a smart home environment: examining the impact on productivity, well-being and future use intention. Internet Res. (2023)
21. Marikyan, D., Papagiannidis, S., Alamanos, E.: A systematic review of the smart home literature: a user perspective. Technol. Forecast. Soc. Change **138**, 139–154 (2019)
22. Li, L., Ota, K., Dong, M.: Humanlike driving: empirical decision-making system for autonomous vehicles. IEEE Trans. Veh. Technol. **67**(8), 6814–6823 (2018)
23. Endsley, M.R.: From here to autonomy: lessons learned from human–automation research. Hum. Factors **59**(1), 5–27 (2017)
24. Higgins, E.T.: Beyond pleasure and pain. Am. Psychol. **52**(12), 1280 (1997)
25. Brockner, J., Higgins, E.T.: Regulatory focus theory: implications for the study of emotions at work. Organ. Behav. Hum. Decis. Processes **86**(1), 35–66 (2001)
26. Zimmermann, R., et al.: Enhancing brick-and-mortar store shopping experience with an augmented reality shopping assistant application using personalized recommendations and explainable artificial intelligence. J. Res. Interact. Mark. **17**(2), 273–298 (2023)
27. Sirgy, M.J., Johar, J.: Toward an integrated model of self-congruity and functional congruity. ACR Eur. Adv. **4**, 252–256 (1999)
28. Brehm, S.S., Brehm, J.W.: Psychological Reactance: A Theory of Freedom and Control. Academic Press (2013)
29. Sirgy, M.J., et al.: Self-congruity versus functional congruity: predictors of consumer behavior. J. Acad. Market. Sci. **19**, 363–375 (1991)
30. Marikyan, D., et al.: "Alexa, let's talk about my productivity": the impact of digital assistants on work productivity. J. Bus. Res. **142**, 572–584 (2022)
31. Balakrishnan, J., Dwivedi, Y.K.: Conversational commerce: entering the next stage of AI-powered digital assistants. Ann. Operat. Res. 1–35 (2021). https://doi.org/10.1007/s10479-021-04049-5
32. Pansari, A., Kumar, V.: Customer engagement: the construct, antecedents, and consequences. J. Acad. Market. Sci. **45**, 294–311 (2017)
33. Barth, S., De Jong, M.D.: The privacy paradox–Investigating discrepancies between expressed privacy concerns and actual online behavior–A systematic literature review. Telematics Inform. **34**(7), 1038–1058 (2017)
34. Davis, F.D.: Perceived usefulness, perceived ease of use, and user acceptance of information technology. MIS Q. **13**(3), 319–340 (1989). https://doi.org/10.2307/249008

35. King, W.R., He, J.: A meta-analysis of the technology acceptance model. Inform. Manag. **43**(6), 740–755 (2006)
36. Davis, F.D.: User acceptance of information technology: system characteristics, user perceptions and behavioral impacts. Int. J. Man-Mach. Stud. **38**(3), 475–487 (1993)
37. Papagiannidis, S., Davlembayeva, D.: Bringing smart home technology to peer-to-peer accommodation: exploring the drivers of intention to stay in smart accommodation. Inform. Syst. Front. **24**(4), 1189–1208 (2022)
38. Kim, H., So, K.K.F., Wirtz, J.: Service robots: Applying social exchange theory to better understand human–robot interactions. Tourism Manag. **92**, 104537 (2022)
39. Papagiannidis, S., Marikyan, D.: Smart offices: a productivity and well-being perspective. Int. J. Inform. Manag. **51**, 102027 (2020)
40. Ajzen, I.: The theory of planned behavior. Organ. Behav. Hum. Dec. Proc. **50**(2), 179–211 (1991)
41. Taylor, S., Todd, P.A.: Understanding information technology usage: a test of competing models. Inform. Syst. Res. **6**(2), 144–176 (1995)
42. Wnuk, A., Oleksy, T., Maison, D.: The acceptance of Covid-19 tracking technologies: the role of perceived threat, lack of control, and ideological beliefs. PloS one **15**(9), e0238973 (2020)
43. Straub, D.W., Welke, R.J.: Coping with systems risk: Security planning models for management decision making. MIS Q. **22**(4), 441 (1998). https://doi.org/10.2307/249551
44. Clee, M.A., Wicklund, R.A.: Consumer behavior and psychological reactance. J. Consum. Res. **6**(4), 389–405 (1980)
45. Sirgy, M.J., Samli, A.C.: A path analytic model of store loyalty involving self-concept, store image, geographic loyalty, and socioeconomic status. J. Acad. Market. Sci. **13**, 265–291 (1985)
46. Suh, K.-S., Kim, H., Suh, E.K.: What if your avatar looks like you? Dual-congruity perspectives for avatar use. MIS Q. **35**, 711–729 (2011)
47. Wu, S., et al.: Self-image congruence, functional congruence, and mobile app intention to use. Mobile Inform. Syst. **2020**, 1–17 (2020)
48. Su, N., Reynolds, D.: Effects of brand personality dimensions on consumers' perceived self-image congruity and functional congruity with hotel brands. Int. J. Hospitality Manag. **66**, 1–12 (2017)
49. Jing, R.: A brief analysis of the influencing mechanism of Internet financial behavior: based on congruity perspective. In: 2018 International Conference on Economics, Business, Management and Corporate Social Responsibility (EBMCSR 2018). Atlantis Press (2018)
50. Kumar, V., Nayak, J.K.: The role of self-congruity and functional congruity in influencing tourists' post visit behaviour. Adv. Hospitality Tourism Res. (AHTR) **2**(2), 24–44 (2014)
51. Gupta, A.S., Mukherjee, J.: Decoding revenge buying in retail: role of psychological reactance and perceived stress. Int. J. Retail Distrib. Manag. **50**(11), 1378–1394 (2022). https://doi.org/10.1108/IJRDM-01-2022-0022
52. Brehm, J.W.: A Theory of Psychological Reactance. Academic Press (1966)
53. Rosenberg, B.D., Siegel, J.T.: A 50-year review of psychological reactance theory: do not read this article. Motiv. Sci. **4**(4), 281 (2018)
54. Veloutsou, C., McAlonan, A.: Loyalty and or disloyalty to a search engine: the case of young Millennials. J. Consum. Market. **29**(2), 125–135 (2012)
55. Venkatesh, V., Bala, H.: Technology acceptance model 3 and a research agenda on interventions. Dec. Sci. **39**(2), 273–315 (2008)
56. Sop, S.A., Kozak, N.: Effects of brand personality, self-congruity and functional congruity on hotel brand loyalty. J. Hospitality Market. Manag. **28**(8), 926–956 (2019)
57. Zhang, P., Meng, F., So, K.K.F.: Cocreation experience in peer-to-peer accommodations: conceptualization and scale development. J. Travel Res. **60**(6), 1333–1351 (2021)

58. Lee, G., Lee, J., Sanford, C.: The roles of self-concept clarity and psychological reactance in compliance with product and service recommendations. Comput. Hum. Behav. **26**(6), 1481–1487 (2010)
59. Venkatesh, V., Thong, J.Y., Xu, X.: Consumer acceptance and use of information technology: extending the unified theory of acceptance and use of technology. MIS Q. **36**, 157–178 (2012)
60. Hair, J.F., et al.: Multivariate Data Analysis: Pearson New, International Pearson Education Limited, Essex (2014)
61. Podsakoff, P.M., et al.: Common method biases in behavioral research: a critical review of the literature and recommended remedies. J. Appl. Psychol. **88**(5), 879 (2003)

Exploring the Transformative Impact of Generative AI on Higher Education

Tegwen Malik[1,2(✉)] 🅳, Laurie Hughes[3] 🅳, Yogesh K. Dwivedi[1,2,4] 🅳,
and Sandra Dettmer[1] 🅳

[1] School of Management, Swansea University – Bay Campus, Swansea SA1 8EN, Wales, UK
{f.t.malik,y.k.dwivedi}@swansea.ac.uk
[2] Digital Futures for Sustainable Business and Society Research Group, School of Management,
Swansea University – Bay Campus, Swansea, UK
[3] Edith Cowan University, School of Business and Law, 270 Joondalup Drive, Joondalup,
WA 6027, Australia
david.hughes@ecu.edu.au
[4] Symbiosis Institute of Business Management, Pune and Symbiosis International (Deemed
University), Pune, Maharashtra, India

Abstract. The launch and subsequent rapid adoption of ChatGPT has initiated significant debate within the academic and practice-based community generating both fear and anxiety that is also contrasted with a sense of opportunity and excitement within the sector. The use of Generative AI (GenAI) within Higher Education (HE) has significant implications from both student and staff perspectives directly impacting existing pedagogic and assessment practice as well as policy across the education system. We seek to explore these areas to better understand the impact on HE from the widespread use of generative AI. Through a qualitative lens, this study has explored the thoughts and feeling of staff and students on the adoption of generative AI giving the sector valuable insights. Our findings highlight the complexities in decision and policy making where staff and students exhibit a wide spectrum of views and feelings on the use of generative AI with their fears and uncertainty being exacerbated with absence of formative and clear guidance. This research paper also highlights some of the innovative uses of generative AI and discusses how students use the technology to pragmatically support their learning but also engage in unethical practice, offering valuable and timely insight to ChatGPT use within a HE context.

Keywords: Generative AI · ChatGPT · Education

1 Introduction

The emergence of Artificial Intelligence (AI) has sparked extensive discussions within academia and the public discourse since the launch of ChatGPT in November 2022 and subsequent releases of Large Language Model (LLM) based Generative AI (GenAI) products by major tech companies like Google and Microsoft. OpenAI's ChatGPT

© IFIP International Federation for Information Processing 2023
Published by Springer Nature Switzerland AG 2023
M. Janssen et al. (Eds.): I3E 2023, LNCS 14316, pp. 69–77, 2023.
https://doi.org/10.1007/978-3-031-50040-4_6

(which is the most widely adopted LLM) utilizes a pre-trained transformer model trained on a diverse dataset comprising internet pages, academic articles, books, and social media content. It has the capability to generate text responses and interactions that exhibit human-like levels of creativity and proficiency, enabling a wide range of applications [1].

The disruptive impact of ChatGPT is evident from its rapid global adoption having gained one million users in just five days after launching in November 2022 [2]. According to a report from Reuters [3], within just over three months ChatGPT amassed approximately 123 million active monthly users, with an average of 13 million daily visitors making it the fastest growing internet application in history. Furthermore, Google's recent announcement in May 2023 regarding their AI language model, PaLM2, and its integration into more than 25 products, including Google Maps and Gmail, highlights how Google envisions a future where LLM-based tools, like PaLM2, become an ordinary part of everyday life. Additionally, Google's own LLM – Bard will soon allow users to utilise image-based prompts in addition to text, highlighting the rapid advancements in GenAI technology [4]. These developments highlight the significant impact and rapid transformative progress in GenAI applications, starkly illustrating the breakneck speed of innovation.

The academic and practice-based literature has discussed the potential impact from GenAI, highlighting the range of industries that are likely to be disrupted by this technology, including: content creation and media, education, customer service and support, healthcare and medicine, music production, artistry, illustration and design, finance and insurance, manufacturing and supply chain, gaming and entertainment, legal services, and compliance [1]. Furthermore, researchers have raised a number of concerns about the potential risks, ethical implications and social as well as economic impact of GenAI. These concerns are related to a number of areas, mainly the role of humans in the creative process, the potential for bias and discrimination, high levels of job loss through automation of traditional cognitive and creative tasks, forcing people to retrain and potentially move up in the value chain to conduct as yet undefined roles that utilise this new technology [1]. However, to-date, emerging research on this topic has generally followed an opinion-based narrative, where studies have either developed an informative discourse on the disruption from GenAI at a societal level, or focussed on specific sectors such as higher education, with greater access to empirical data sources and perspectives. What is clear is that the existing literature has yet to fully explore the full range of perspectives on how this new and rapidly evolving technology can fully impact the HE sector and develop the detailed implications for organisations and decision makers to capitalise on the potential of GenAI [5–7].

Our research seeks to better understand how the use of GenAI could impact current academic policy and assessment practice within Higher Education. Therefore, we pose the following research questions (RQ):

RQ1: What are the HE student and staff perspectives on the pedagogic and assessment impact from ChatGPT and any other forms of generative AI?

RQ2: What are the HE student and staff perspectives on the policy implications from widespread adoption of ChatGPT and any other forms of generative AI?

By analysing the disruption through the lens of both academics and students, we empirically investigate the impact from GenAI, identifying a range of perspectives, numerous challenges and opportunities for the enhancement of the learning experience through the adoption of GenAI within HE settings.

The remainder of this paper is as follows: Sect. 2 explores the current literature on GenAI and its impact on HE, Sect. 3 outlines the methodology used to conduct this research, Sect. 4 highlights the key findings and develops a discussion of the core aspects. The paper is concluded in the final section where key areas are highlighted.

2 Generative AI and Higher Education

The impact of AI on education is an increasingly discussed topic and emerging research area, as technology continues to play a significant role in pedagogical approaches and student learning, particularly within HE [8]. The launch of OpenAI's ChatGPT in November 2022 followed by other LLMs based GenAI platforms from Google and Microsoft, has the potential to radically disrupt traditional approaches to HE in the context of pedagogy and student assessment. The recent guidance published by the Quality Assurance Agency for Higher Education in their report titled: '*Maintaining quality and standards in the ChatGPT era: QAA advice on the opportunities and challenges posed by Generative Artificial Intelligence*', highlights the policy and assessment implications from GenAI use in HE, advocating the development of "sophisticated policies that are appropriate to their teaching and learning strategy" [9]. The HE sector, having encountered huge disruption due to Covid-19 is now facing significant challenges around how to react to the rapid pace and widespread adoption of GenAI, whilst attempting to formulate policy within a rapidly changing environment [1, 10].

Since the launch of ChatGPT in November 2022, an emerging GenAI focussed theme has developed within the extant literature, where studies have explored some of the key implications of widespread adoption of GenAI [1]. A number of studies have discussed the implications for the HE sector, where researchers have highlighted many of the pedagogic and assessment areas that could be affected and the subsequent impact on policy. Researchers have developed various narratives from both positive and negative perspectives, where studies have attempted to assess the change to existing practice. Generally, the literature seems to have followed an opinion-based narrative, somewhat lacking an empirical focus to develop greater rigor and structure to this important research area [11, 12]. A number of studies have explored the potential restriction of ChatGPT and other GenAI tools, following the Oxford and Cambridge universities announcement, advocating the banning of the technology over plagiarism fears [13, 14]. The GenAI focussed literature has also discussed the impact on pedagogy and assessment within HE settings. Studies have highlighted the widespread student use of the technology and the impact on academic integrity as GenAI output is used verbatim for assessment [15]. There exists both a positive and negative narrative within the literature on the impact of widespread adoption of GenAI within HE. What is clear is that further research is needed to empirically understand the thoughts and feelings of decision makers and to fully understand the implications of extensive use by both staff and students [1].

3 Methodology

To develop the required insight around the impact of GenAI within HE, we adopted a qualitative approach to fully understand the thoughts and feelings of this study's participants on their perspectives related to the use of GenAI. By utilising a qualitative approach, we were better able to develop the necessary flexibility and adaptability to follow the various threads of participant perspectives to understand the pedagogic and assessment impact.

The chosen research methodology approach is depicted in Fig. 1. In alignment with Cassell [16], the research design followed a semi-structured format to allow the necessary flexibility and adaptability within each of the interviews to allow the interviewer to pursue specific points and clarify perspectives as required depending on the direction and feedback within the interviews. Participants were selected at random and included both university staff and students.

This research adopted a theoretical saturation approach from grounded theory [17]. The number of participants was not fixed or constrained at the onset but governed by the acquisition of new insight and knowledge [18]. At the point when the research team could see that no new information was being acquired from study participants, it was judged that no further interviews were needed and that the required threshold of data had been achieved as the interview phase had reached the required saturation level from participants.

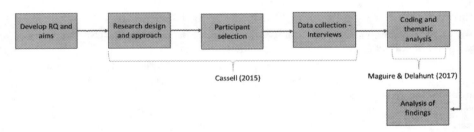

Fig. 1. Methodological Approach

In alignment with previous qualitative studies [19], interviews were conducted by the research team with 29 participants (15 staff and 14 students) throughout April and May 2023 and recorded via Zoom. Although the interview questions were transcribed in advance of the interviews, the format allowed the interviewer to follow up with further questions and clarifications as needed. The research team interviewed students at all the different levels of study within a university setting from first year undergraduates (UGs) to final year UGs through to postgraduate (PG) taught students up to PG research students. Likewise, the staff that were interviewed had a range of backgrounds, namely lecturers, senior lectures, associate professors, professors, programme directors and leads of learning and teaching. Staff also came from a range of subject specific backgrounds. Interviews were transcribed and coded in alignment with the approach advocated by Maguire & Delahunt [20] where key passages where coded and subsequently aligned with the emerging themes. The final coded and thematic interview data was further processed to collate the key research outcomes and final analysis.

4 Findings and Discussions

Having conducted and coded the staff and student interviews in alignment with the strategy utilised by Maguire and Delahunt [20], this section utilises quotes from staff and students to develop a narrative that tells a story through the lens of this paper's research questions. This is an approach that has been utilised within the literature [21]. Findings are discussed in this section under the relevant themes identified which have been highlighted in bold in the following narrative. As prescribed in Maguire and Delahunt [20] the themes emerged from conducting a reflective thematic analysis of the transcribed interview data.

Initially the research questions focused on participants' **Feelings about GenAI (specifically ChatGPT)**. Staff were found to have a range of feelings from "*very excited*", "*poses problems, but is useful*", "*I would like to know a lot more about it but it's difficult to know where to start*", "*I haven't really had the time to explore it*" through to those members of staff who said that they are "*quite tech adverse*" which they felt causes them to feel "*anxiety and resistance*" to this GenAI technology and those members of staff who said that they "*can't completely understand the whole process*" and as such they said "*I seem to be quite resistant to learning it*". Likewise, students also expressed a variety of different feelings about ChatGPT, they shared that they "*think it's quite cool*" and that "*you're able to ask it anything and it will give you an answer*" and they also said that they "*recognise the value of it as a learning tool*". Simultaneously, students voiced concerns and uncertainties as evident in the quotes "*I don't trust it*" and "*that is frightening*". It was from this that the theme **GenAI as Support** was identified from these interviews where students with learning difficulties shared that they are utilising ChatGPT to support them to "*alleviate a lot of my worries and kind of thoughts*" and to "*use it for a kind of mental reassurance*" and another shared that "*particularly for me with autism and how I am, how I operate mentally. It's definitely a help to kind of someone who kind of overthinks and stuff. It's very helpful and kind of having that clarification that a certain idea that you have is actually okay*".

Use and Impact of GenAI (ChatGPT) for Assessment was the next theme explored with participants. From a staff perspective they could recognise the limitations of Chat-GPT for assessment with one member of staff saying that you "*could only get about 30 or 40% of what you need for you answers*" using ChatGPT with most staff recognising that GenAI leads to "*academic misconduct issues*" but they shared that at the end of the day "*I can only be suspicious that some wrong-doing has happened. I can't prove it*". In terms of assessment some staff thought that a number of these issues could be overcome by focusing assessment strategies more on "*critical thinking and the reflectivity*" type of narrative from students instead. When the **Use and Impact of GenAI (ChatGPT) for Assessment** was explored with students, they shared that ChatGPT is "*being used and abused at the minute across the student base*" and students are looking at "*how far can I push the boundaries*" of this GenAI within a university setting. Students also shared that "*sometimes there's a lot of value in what it provides to you, especially if you've got* *a very relatively technical assignment question*" but, as one student said, "*I work hard for the kind of things that I put in. But then, realizing that students are cheating with ChatGPT – they can do half the effort in half the time to get them through*" so the fairness in terms of equitable use of ChatGPT was questioned here whilst at the same time they felt that "*We need to kind of recognize the value of it as a learning tool*". In general, students were clearly much more trusting and enthusiastic about ChatGPT than staff, but both expressed a degree of uncertainty and caution in its use assessment purposes, particularly final year undergraduate students and PhD students.

Finally, this study explored participants' **Thoughts on Student Use of GenAI** (specifically ChatGPT). Staff commented that within academia, we "*need students to demonstrate critical thinking and analysis of content to show their understanding and reflective learning*" but that unlike academic staff, "*students don't necessarily have the evaluation criteria or ability as part of their training yet to validate ChatGPT output*". Ultimately, as "*academics generally, we have better evaluation skills, so we're more likely to understand that you can't just take it as it is, whereas if it's a student using the content they're going to be trying to copy and paste*". ChatGPT is being discussed widely within the academic community and it is interesting to note that students think that "*it's gonna have a very profound impact on academia and I feel like it's definitely something that you can't ignore*"; in fact students felt that "*Universities are gonna have to kind of embrace it*" and they are also questioning that if universities do not come up with an effective AI policy and assessment strategy that takes account of GenAI and the likes of ChatGPT then "*is there an actual value to a degree now?*". This last student quote is a wakeup call in some ways to the HE sector that if GenAI is not mindfully integrated within academia the value of a degree could be devalued in a short space of time.

Moving forward, from a student and staff perspective, the final theme explored was that of a **ChatGPT Policy**. Staff voiced that "*it has to be adaptive*" and that any policy should reflect that "*if you're found to be using it [ChatGPT] to actually generate content rather than search for how to find content or how to find a reference. Then obviously, you should suffer the same penalties as anybody else committing AI academic misconduct*". Students shared that from their perspective "*a lot of us are now aware that the university systems are kind of trying to clamp down on it*" but they also stated that "*by the time you try and clamp down on it becomes even more intelligent*" and so they rightly highlighted this catch 22 that academia needs to consider when developing a usage policy and when ensuring staff are AI literate, something that the Russell Group [22] recently discussed in their published statement.

To pull this participant narrative together under the two RQs:

RQ1: Both students and staff acknowledged both the threat and opportunity posed by GenAI, specifically ChatGPT within the HE sector. Whereas some students acknowledged using GenAI to support their learning, others especially post-graduate students emphasized that they do not engage with it as part of their individual studies and conveyed a more critical perspective with respect to skill acquisition and uncertainties around the impact on assessment and fairness. However, students voiced overwhelming support for using it as a learning tool within the classroom. Staff perspectives on the use of Chat-GPT and GenAI for assessment demonstrated some angst and vulnerability. This was especially true for staff being left to their own devices and being solely responsible for creating GenAI proof forms of assessment without adequate training and support.

RQ2: Students felt they were in an information vacuum with only a limited GenAI policy and unclear guidance on how they could utilise GenAI tools effectively within an HE environment. Staff were also unclear on how to implement any AI policy (especially those with limited technical expertise in this area) and how best to apply academic judgement effectively within an assessment context.

The rapid adoption and evolution of GenAI has meant that decision makers have needed to review existing policies and guidelines as well as consider support mechanisms for staff and students. The key issue here is the significant pace of change where academics are forced to reconsider and adapt existing teaching practice and traditional methods of assessment.

5 Conclusions

This research offers valuable contribution to the pedagogical discourse where we articulate both the student and staff perspectives, identifying the significant challenges (and opportunities) for educators and policy decision makers. This study's findings can be used to inform academics on the impact of generative AI from the lens of both students and staff and how decision and policy makers can best utilise this disruptive technology within HE settings.

Overall, the analysis of staff and student quotes demonstrates a mixed response with respect to their feelings towards GenAI. This paper also highlights the fact that current assessment approaches do not factor in the use of GenAI with staff and students expressing the need for clear guidance and AI policy for assessment purposes that either explicitly incorporates GenAI usage or negates its use. It was also clear that a greater level of education is needed for staff around GenAI and its impact on both pedagogy and assessment with academic integrity guidelines needing to be much more explicit to guide students on the acceptable GenAI use. Currently students expressed uncertainty and confusion on current policy and this study suggest that any university AI policy needs to be very prescriptive to better guide and inform students moving forward. Ultimately, GenAI and the likes of ChatGPT are here to stay and this technology is only going to get better and more efficient and more capable very quickly, as such, this is not an issue that can be addressed by individual institutions, the sector will need to work together collaboratively to ensure that the integrity and value of degrees remain valued by employees and students alike.

References

1. Dwivedi, Y.K., et al.: "So what if ChatGPT wrote it?" Multidisciplinary perspectives on opportunities, challenges and implications of generative conversational AI for research, practice and policy. Int. J. Inf. Manage. **71**, 102642 (2023)

2. Statista: One Million Users (2023). https://www.statista.com/chart/29174/time-to-one-million-users/. Accessed on 14 July 2023
3. Reuters: ChatGPT sets record for fastest-growing user base – analyst note (2023). https://www.reuters.com/technology/chatgpt-sets-record-fastest-growing-user-base-analyst-note-2023-02-01/. Accessed on 14th July 2023
4. Heikkila, M.: MIT Technology Review: Google is throwing generative AI at everything (2023). https://www.technologyreview.com/2023/05/10/1072880/google-is-throwing-generative-ai-at-everything/. Accessed on 11 May 2023
5. Ausat, A.M.A., Azzaakiyyah, H.K., Permana, R.M., Riady, Y., Suherlan, S.: The role of ChatGPT in enabling MSMEs to compete in the digital age. Innovative: J. Soc. Sci. Res. **3**(2), 622–631 (2023)
6. Beerbaum, D.O.: Generative artificial intelligence (GAI) ethics taxonomy-applying chat GPT for robotic process automation (GAI-RPA) as business case. SSRN Electron. J. (2023). Available at SSRN 4385025
7. George, A.S., George, A.H.: A review of ChatGPT AI's impact on several business sectors. Partners Univers. Int. Innov. J. **1**(1), 9–23 (2023)
8. Dwivedi, Y.K., et al.: Artificial intelligence (AI): multidisciplinary perspectives on emerging challenges, opportunities, and agenda for research, practice and policy. Int. J. Inf. Manag. **57**, 101994 (2021)
9. QAA: Maintaining quality and standards in the ChatGPT era: QAA advice on the opportunities and challenges posed by Generative Artificial Intelligence, p. 2. https://www.qaa.ac.uk/docs/qaa/members/maintaining-quality-and-standards-in-the-chatgpt-era.pdf (2023)
10. Farrokhnia, M., Banihashem, S.K., Noroozi, O., Wals, A.: A SWOT analysis of ChatGPT: implications for educational practice and research. Innov. Educ. Teach. Int. (2023). https://doi.org/10.1080/14703297.2023.2195846
11. Biswas, S.: Role of Chat GPT in Education (2023). Available at SSRN 4369981
12. Shidiq, M.: The use of artificial intelligence-based chat-gpt and its challenges for the world of education; from the viewpoint of the development of creative writing skills. In: Proceeding of International Conference on Education, Society and Humanity, vol. 1, no. 1, pp. 353–357 (2023)
13. UWN: Oxford and Cambridge ban ChatGPT over plagiarism fears. https://www.universityworldnews.com/post.php?story=20230304105854982 (2023). Accessed on 14 July 2023
14. Yu, H.: Reflection on whether Chat GPT should be banned by academia from the perspective of education and teaching. Front. Psychol. **14**, 1181712 (2023)
15. Tajik, E., Tajik, F.: A comprehensive Examination of the potential application of Chat GPT in Higher Education Institutions. TechRxiv. Preprint, pp. 1–10 (2023)
16. Cassell, C.: Conducting Research Interviews for Business and Management Students. SAGE Publications Ltd, 1 Oliver's Yard, 55 City Road London EC1Y 1SP (2015). https://doi.org/10.4135/9781529716726
17. Douglas, D.: Grounded theories of management: a methodological review. Manag. Res. News **26**(5), 44–52 (2003)
18. Sandelowski, M.: Qualitative analysis: what it is and how to begin. Res. Nurs. Health **18**(4), 371–375 (1995)
19. Hennink, M., Kaiser, B.N.: Sample sizes for saturation in qualitative research: a systematic review of empirical tests. Soc. Sci. Med. **292**, 114523 (2022)
20. Maguire, M., Delahunt, B.: Doing a thematic analysis: a practical, step-by-step guide for learning and teaching scholars. All Ireland J. High. Educ. **9**(3), 3351–33514 (2017)

21. Gioia, D.A., Corley, K.G., Hamilton, A.L.: Seeking qualitative rigor in inductive research: notes on the Gioia methodology. Organ. Res. Methods **16**(1), 15–31 (2013)
22. Russell Group: New principles on use of AI in education (Russell Group principles on the use of generative AI tools in education). https://russellgroup.ac.uk/news/new-principles-on-use-of-ai-in-education/ (2023)

Understanding DevOps Critical Success Factors: Insights from Professionals

Nasreen Azad[1]([envelope]) [ID], Sami Hyrynsalmi[1] [ID], and Matti Mäntymäki[2] [ID]

[1] LUT University, Lappeenranta, Lahti, Finland
nasren.azad@lut.fi
[2] Turku School of Economics, University of Turku, Turku, Finland

Abstract. This paper explores the factors that contribute to the success of software development undertaken with DevOps practices. DevOps is a set of practices that aims to increase software development process efficiency by reducing barriers between operation and development teams. Despite the wealth of information available on DevOps practices, adoption, and the respective challenges, there is a dearth of research focusing specifically on the DevOps critical success factors. This paper seeks to fill this gap by analyzing and discussing the key factors that are essential for success in software development with DevOps. To this end, we have conducted an open-ended survey among 72 DevOps professionals. By employing the Gioia method, we elaborate on the professionals' perspectives on the DevOps success factors identified and connect them to the prior literature. These success factors encompass intra-organizational collaboration, organizational hierarchy, strategic planning, team dynamics, cultural shift, performance engineering, integration, build and test automation, infrastructure, and DevOps as a service. We propose five DevOps implementation advice that could benefit companies while implementing DevOps practices. Those include management support, investment in DevOps tools, sharing knowledge within teams, sharing responsibility in teams, being willing to explore and experiment with the practices, and being agile are crucial for DevOps performance and organizational success.

Keywords: DevOps · Critical success factors · Continuous delivery · Continuous development · DevOps survey · Software development · Success factors validation · Gioia method · Qualitative research

1 Introduction

The software development process has undergone considerable changes in the past years [6, 22, 33]. Today developers can initiate the software development process quicker than before and the results can be accessed faster [33]. Compared to the waterfall model of software development, DevOps has lifecycle increased the efficiency of the post-deployment phase of the software development lifecycle [1, 33].

M. Janssen et al. (Eds.): I3E 2023, LNCS 14316, pp. 78–90, 2023.
https://doi.org/10.1007/978-3-031-50040-4_7

DevOps is a set of organizational practices aimed at enhancing collaboration between development (Dev) and operations (Ops) team members [2,5,19]. DevOps practices in the organization aim to provide (1) better user feedback and experience, (2) reduced time for the development process, (3) speed up deployment rates, (4) time optimization to recover deployment and implementation cost [15,21]. DevOps combines IT culture, practices, and tools that increase an organization's ability to deliver applications and services at high velocity [8,31]. Despite the considerable scholarly interest in DevOps, research focusing specifically on the success factors of DevOps has remained scant [4,6,8]. To address this gap, we have the following research questions in order to understand the facts for critical success factors and respective organizational practices:

RQ1: What are the critical success factors of DevOps as reported by the professionals?

RQ2: How do these factors impact DevOps practices?

To this end, we adopt the DevOps critical success factor model proposed by Azad and Hyrynsalmi (2021) [4,5]. We have undertaken an open-ended online survey among 72 DevOps professionals from different organizations. We use the Gioa method to analyze the data [17,18,22,23].

This research contributes to the DevOps literature by identifying a set of DevOps success factors and thus providing guidance to practitioners on how to successfully utilize DevOps and giving guidelines to the practitioners on key success factors [3,5,8]. We believe that the findings will be helpful for the professionals, consultants, and researchers' further exploration. In doing so, we contribute to the growing literature of DevOps by empirically supporting the DevOps critical success factor model [3–5].

2 Background

2.1 DevOps Concept and Process

DevOps increases the performance of software products and services and ensures the collaboration, integration, and communication process [6]. There are many concepts surrounding DevOps but there is no specific DevOps definition to follow [20]. The purpose of DevOps is to eliminate the gap among teams so that software development can be done efficiently [32]. The development teams deliver the software features more frequently. Then the operations teams work on the features. Thus, the main advantage DevOps serves here is delivering faster features to customers. DevOps merges the development teams and operation teams to work together to achieve a faster software development process [32]. Jabbari et al. [20] have conducted a comprehensive content analysis and found eight components of DevOps and defined DevOps as a development methodology that eliminates the gap between Dev and ops teams. They also suggested that communication and collaboration, continuous integration, delivery with automated deployment, and ensuring quality assurance can be achieved by DevOps [20].

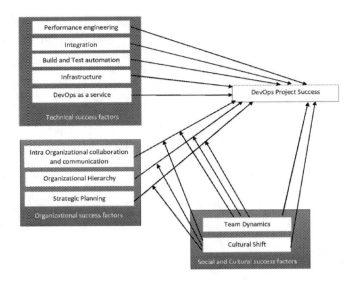

Fig. 1. The DevOps Critical Success Factor model (adapted from [4]).

2.2 DevOps Critical Success Factors

The management literature discussed the critical success factors at the beginning of the 1960s [4,14]. There has been much literature on critical success factors related to their impacts and roles in the organization. Critical success factors can be explained as *"key areas of processes where acceptable results are required for specific managers to achieve the goal"* [9]. Shahin et al. [27] discussed that when practitioners are aware of the critical success factors beforehand, it will help the organization to handle continuous practices and smooth integration of DevOps process [3,5].

Prior literature suggests how performance engineering complexity can be addressed for a DevOps project's success [4,8]. According to Bezemer et al., performance engineering approaches should be lightweight to address DevOps performance in the organization [8]. Performance measurement [30], Software release [10], and [10] Seamless upgrades [13] are also the important factors. According to Chen et al. [12] performance regression needs to be identified at the beginning of the source code level so that DevOps operations can run smoothly. According to Claps et al. [13] continuous integration process has an impact on DevOps success. Furthermore, automatic testing technique improvement [25], test automation [25], verification of soundness [7], automation tools [7] may affect the success of DevOps.

Azad and Hyrynsalmi [4,5] proposed a synthesized framework for the critical success factors of DevOps projects. According to them, there are ten major factors which are categorized as technical, organizational, social and cultural factor groups. The framework is shown in Fig. 1. However, their model is based on synthesizing extant scientific literature on DevOps and it has not been thus far empirically evaluated. In this paper, we adopt and aim to provide the first empirical verification for this model.

3 Research Approach

3.1 Survey Design and Data Collection

An open-ended survey was designed to understand DevOps practices, DevOps implementation, and adoption in organizations. We have used an open-ended survey questionnaire as the method is suitable for a large number of respondents [26]. For the questionnaire, we have developed 25 questions. The questionnaire had themes related to DevOps operational practices, development practices, team culture, collaboration between teams, and the impact of success factors throughout the whole process of the DevOps lifecycle.We shared the survey link through social media platforms; Facebook, LinkedIn, and Twitter were specifically used in the first stage of data collection.

In the second stage of data collection, we conducted our survey with the help of a prolific data collection tool. We conducted the survey with prolific because we could not get sufficient data from social networking sites. We got 91 responses by combining two stages of data collection. Finally, we could use 72 responses for data analysis.

3.2 Data Analysis

For the data analysis, we have employed the Gioia method proposed by Gioia et al. (2013) [17]. Our analysis followed an iterative process that involved the repetition of steps for data analysis. A total of 75 pages were generated from the data collection. Based on our understanding we have iteratively conducted the data analysis process [28].

For the analysis, open coding has been used [28]. While doing the analysis we went through the survey transcript and assigned codes to describe the survey content [24]. As a guideline, we have followed research questions for forming the coding of the first round. From the empirical data, we looked for code similarities and dissimilarities based on various segments of the data [24]. This way of coding is similar to Grounded theory research because constant comparison is one of the key aspects of grounded theory and we have followed constant comparison for the data analysis [28]. We have listed an example of coding activities in Table 1. While doing coding we got 21 codes after our analysis of the survey data. In Table 1 we have shown a list of codes, code descriptions, and quotes from the professionals as an example table.

Then we moved to the second phase of the coding process. According to Charmaz (1990) to create second-order codes for concepts it is necessary to categorize the first-phase codes [11]. Thus, the second phase codes are combined with the first phase codes [16]. We have also used memoing techniques during the data analysis process. It helped us to understand more insights and perspectives of professionals regarding critical success factors.

Table 1. Coding used for survey data

List of codes	Description of codes	Quotes from Professionals
Collaboration between DevOps teams	Good collaboration in teams helps team members perform better	"In our organization, DevOps (Development and Operations) is a discipline that increases communication, collaboration, integration and even fusion between application development and operations with the goal of promoting fast, consistent, high-quality, scalable application releases. It is a method of bringing developers, IT operations and Quality Assurance (QA) team together"
Effective communications techniques	Techniques that help team members to communicate	"...The product owner and team lead discusses with teams before taking decisions on existing issues and need. "
Superiors' guidance	Superiors' guidance speeds up the working process in teams	"..The product management team is responsible for the functional (business) requirement and the technology team (Technology Architects) is responsible for taking non-functional (technical) requirements based on the business requirements and available resources. It is important to have some guidance from manager or superiors so that the team has a clear idea about the tasks they should be doing."
Instructions are good for progress	"Superiors' instructions from fellow team members gives a better working environment	"Usually, the team consists of DevOps Lead/Architect, a few Junior-Mid-Senior Developers with similar kind of skill set. Lead developer usually distributes the work among the other team members and provides the guidelines for expected outcomes""
IT and Business have common goals	The goal for a company should align together for IT and business objectives	"DevOps helps in faster and cheaper delivery of software products, increasing velocity of change and time to market, empowering people in their work, autonomous teams, and less downtime due to more controlled changes are positive impacts to name a few"

In the third phase of analysis, we have aggregated the themes into three main aggregate categories including Organizational success factors, Cultural and Social success factors, and Technical success factors. In Fig. 2 we have shown the data analysis process with themes.

4   Results

4.1   Organizational Success Factors

Intra-Organizational Collaboration or Communication. Intra-organizational collaboration or communication is the second-order theme for organizational success factors. From the analysis, we have observed that collaboration between the Dev and Ops team and effective communication techniques are crucial for DevOps success [3]. According to Luz et al. (2018), collaboration culture is one of the core themes for success in a DevOps environment. One of the respondents quoted:

> "In our organization, Development, and test teams work together and share the responsibility together. Product management takes care of configuration and release management. A separate management team takes care of the bugs and issues in software life cycles. Thus teams work under better collaboration and communication"

Organizational Hierarchy. Organizational hierarchy is a second-order theme for organizational success factors. According to our analysis, a superior's guidance and instructions while working are beneficial for teams. DevOps professionals are willing to get instructions from superiors. Guidance from a lead person who can provide instructions impacts the team in a positive way. Without a lead person, there could be some difficulties in teamwork [3,5]. An example quote is given below.

> "The teams have meetings periodically to prioritize the task. Based on the business requirements product management assign the level of priority. Business requirements are set based on market demand and future prospects. Production and development should run smoothly. Every project has a leader who is responsible for the decision-making and prioritizing tasks for the team."

Strategic Planning. From a strategic point of view, the product management team is responsible for maintaining the business requirements discussed by [3,4]. The responsibility of the technology team is to handle the technical requirements based on resource availability. Our research findings suggest that project planning is related to initiatives, resources, and budget. While planning for a project, IT and the business should have similar goals and objectives.

For example, one respondent's answers:

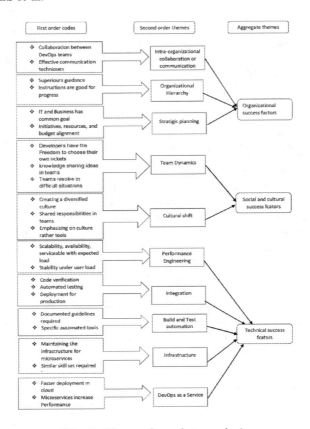

Fig. 2. Themes from data analysis

"..The product management team handles the functional requirements and the technology team is responsible for nonfunctional requirements. All these requirements could be addressed through the availability of resources and business needs..."

4.2   Social and Cultural Factors

Team Dynamics. Team Dynamics is essential for DevOps success. Sharing knowledge and spreading ideas While working in a team is a good practice. This in turn helps the team members to improve their work efficiency. When Team dynamics exist in a team that benefits the DevOps team in many ways. Among those include collaboration, trust building, better workflow, and common ways of working in the team.

For example, respondents reported on the following issues:

"Lead developer usually distributes the work among the other team members and provides the guidelines for expected outcomes. Faster delivery times, increased quality, early defect detection, improved security, and happier developers are our team dynamics ".

Cultural Shift. The cultural shift has a huge impact on DevOps success in organizations. In an organization, there are barriers related to technical issues however, the barriers related to cultural issues are even more important when adopting DevOps. From the respondents' answers, we have found that organizational culture plays a vital role in achieving the project's objective. Sharing the experience and creating a diversified culture helps the team to progress better. An example quote is given below.

"Team collaboration helps us to build awesome products for clients. The company culture we have is collaborative, flexible, supportive, focused, goal-oriented, can do attitude. Our company has Very well adopted DevOps culture in every stage of the development life cycles".

4.3 Technical Factors

Performance Engineering. For any software, performance engineering is a complex activity. It requires adequate knowledge to understand the software life cycle. In DevOps there is a low adoption of performance engineering. The reason behind low adoption is that the performance engineering approaches are not designed for DevOps context. There are many existing tools that are used for DevOps settings in organizations, for example Docker and Puppet but they do not align smoothly with the performance engineering process [8]. One respondent quoted:

"CI/CD pipeline execution time which is related to the developer's work to mark a ticket ready, tasks prevent the pipeline to be executed properly, customer support needs, e.g. a temporary review site to showcase the provided solution, version discrepancy that halts new feature to be released.".

Integration. Continuous integration tools do several automated actions that help the system to work together for the pipeline. Some of the pipeline stages include package generation, automated test execution, code verification, and deployment for the production and development environments. The developers are the responsible actors for defining pipeline structures. On the other hand, operators are responsible for defining collaboration for deployment phases. They are also responsible for the continuous integration. One of the respondents quoted:

"Continuous integration is an essential step where developers merge the codes so that they can run the automated builds and tests".

Build and Test Automation. Build and test automation is another subcategory of the technical success factors. Based on our data analysis, we have found that test automation, automatic testing, and improvement of techniques might impact the success of DevOps. In teams, different automation techniques are used. Some of the automation includes verification of soundness, automation-specific tools, build and process automation etc.

For example, one respondent quoted that:

> "For the integration process our company uses various tools. Some of the tools includes Version control (Git), dependency management tools for programming languages, testing frameworks, container technologies, Continuous Integration and Delivery tools (CI/CD), cloud platforms, configuration management tools, infrastructure as code tools".

Infrastructure. For software process integration the infrastructure play a crucial role. Infrastructure helps the DevOps teams to handle the software and hardware issues and make sure the software to be deployed when required. For a better execution of DevOps practices in the organization, it is necessary to have infrastructure provisioning and infrastructure development. One respondent quoted:

> "Depending on the project, there could be a central "DevOps" team which provides services, tooling, and support for software development teams. Or, the software development team(s) can manage everything by themselves".

DevOps as a Service. Micro-services are part of the cloud infrastructure. It is essential for future DevOps development.Because microservices can enable faster deployments in the cloud without hampering the performance of the software process. DevOps adoption ideology suggests that separate software teams are responsible for the different stages of software applications and allow the team to develop, test, handle failures and act independently [29]. One responded quoted that:

> "Microservices increase productivity by embracing a common toolset that can be used by both teams. The common toolset creates a common terminology by understanding the requirements, problems, and dependencies of the system. ".

We have presented the three analysis stages of themes in Fig. 2 and the respective data-structure processes are summarized in the figure.

5   Discussion

5.1   Key Findings

While more support was found for organizational, social, and cultural factors, technical factors were present in the data [29]. However, the technical problems and solutions are quite specific and not that often reported. Yet, there are exceptions as, for example, there are several issues belonging to Build and Test automation technical factors. Furthermore, it is worth noting that in all organizations whether producing software or not organizational, cultural, and social aspects are present when new practices and processes are taken into use. Therefore, their presence in the list of the critical success factors of DevOps usage is not a surprise [4].

Overall, this study offers empirical support for the DevOps critical success factors model synthesized from the literature by [4]. Issues belonging to each factor were found in the analysis.

The roles of DevOps for all organizations are not similar. According to our survey, we have got different answers regarding the meaning of DevOps for various companies. Professionals stated that company culture, practices, maintaining coding standards, testing, set of processes for production release, technical tools, business culture, and framework, breezing the gaps between Dev and Ops teams, infrastructure Update, software updates, automation, less repetition in the working process, frequent delivery of updates and features are all important to consider for the DevOps practices in organizations.

5.2 Implications

Based on the responses we have received, we propose five DevOps implementation advice that could benefit companies while implementing DevOps practices. These include management support, investing in DevOps tools, sharing knowledge and responsibility, being willing to experiment and evolve, and building a strong developer-lead culture.

Management Support. Better management support is adequate for the teams. One of the reasons for not having better management support could be, that there is not yet enough skill to handle different management issues for DevOps. The management needs to support and understand the software development process otherwise the teams might suffer.

Invest in DevOps Tools. Investing in DevOps tools is needed. The support from the proper tools can create an environment where the professionals can execute the process and release faster without any hassle. There should be training for the DevOps engineers so that new tools will be easy to handle.

Share Knowledge and Responsibility. Sharing knowledge and responsibility is one of the most crucial aspects of using DevOps. In previous times working in the software industry did not have a shared responsibility concept. DevOps introduced that professionals will work together to fulfill a common goal of a project.

Willing to Experiment and Evolve. A willing team is a team that can handle any new challenges while working on a project. DevOps teams should be willing to experiment and evolve when needed and build a strong DevOps lead culture.

Build a Strong Developer Lead Culture. Building a strong developer team is a requirement for DevOps use in companies. Focusing only on the tools and automation is not always the best way to handle various DevOps issues. At the same time, culture and ways of working are usually more important facts for organizations using DevOps practices.

5.3   Limitations and Future Research

First, due to the nature of the data collection, the results are evidently limited to the data available and cannot be directly generalized. Hence, a natural future research direction would be to obtain a more extensive set of empirical data. Second, in this study we focused on DevOps in a general sense. However, there are specific adaptations of DevOps such as MLOps. Thus, future research could focus specifically on the success factors of MLOps.

6   Conclusion

The purpose of the paper was to explore DevOps key success factors and organizational practices for software development. The DevOps success factors identified include intra-organizational collaboration or communication, organizational hierarchy, strategic planning, team dynamics, cultural shift, performance engineering, integration, build and test automation, infrastructure, and DevOps as a service. We have further discussed that management support, investing in DevOps tools, sharing knowledge in teams, sharing responsibility, exploring and experimenting with the practices, and being agile play a vital role in DevOps performance and contribute to DevOps success.

References

1. Abdelkebir, S., Maleh, Y., Belaissaoui, M.: An agile framework for its management in organizations: a case study based on devops. In: Proceedings of the 2nd International Conference on Computing and Wireless Communication Systems, pp. 1–8 (2017)
2. Amaro, R., Pereira, R., da Silva, M.M.: Capabilities and practices in DevOps: a multivocal literature review. IEEE Trans. Software Eng. **49**(2), 883–901 (2022)
3. Azad, N.: Understanding DevOps critical success factors and organizational practices. In: 2022 IEEE/ACM International Workshop on Software-Intensive Business (IWSiB), pp. 83–90. IEEE (2022)

4. Azad, N., Hyrynsalmi, S.: What are critical success factors of DevOps projects? a systematic literature review. In: Wang, X., Martini, A., Nguyen-Duc, A., Stray, V. (eds.) ICSOB 2021. LNBIP, vol. 434, pp. 221–237. Springer, Cham (2021). https:// doi.org/10.1007/978-3-030-91983-2_17

5. Azad, N., Hyrynsalmi, S.: DevOps critical succes factors-a systematic literature review. Inf.Softw. Technol. 107150 (2023)

6. Bass, L., Weber, I., Zhu, L.: DevOps: A software Architect's Perspective. Addison-Wesley Professional, Boston (2015)

7. Ben Mesmia, W., Escheikh, M., Barkaoui, K.: DevOps workflow verification and duration prediction using non-Markovian stochastic petri nets. J. Softw. Evol. Process 33(3), e2329 (2021)

8. Bezemer, C.P., et al.: How is performance addressed in DevOps? In: Proceedings of the 2019 ACM/SPEC International Conference on Performance Engineering, pp. 45–50 (2019)

9. Bullen, C.V., Rockart, J.F.: A primer on critical success factors. Working papers 1220–81. Report (Alfred P. Sloan School of Management. Center for Information Systems Research); no. 69, Massachusetts Institute of Technology (MIT), Sloan School of Management (1981). https://EconPapers.repec.org/RePEc:mit:sloanp: 1988

10. Callanan, M., Spillane, A.: DevOps: making it easy to do the right thing. IEEE Softw. 33(3), 53–59 (2016)

11. Charmaz, K.: 'discovering' chronic illness: using grounded theory. Soc. Sci. Med. 30(11), 1161–1172 (1990)

12. Chen, J.: Performance regression detection in DevOps. In: 2020 IEEE/ACM 42nd International Conference on Software Engineering: Companion Proceedings (ICSE-Companion), pp. 206–209. IEEE (2020)

13. Claps, G.G., Svensson, R.B., Aurum, A.: On the journey to continuous deployment: technical and social challenges along the way. Inf. Softw. Technol. 57, 21–31 (2015)

14. Dickinson, R.A., Ferguson, C.R., Sircar, S.: Critical success factors and small business. Am. J. Small Bus. 8(3), 49–57 (1984)

15. Forsgren, N., Smith, D., Humble, J., Frazelle, J.: 2019 accelerate state of DevOps report (2019)

16. Gartner, I.: Gartner it glossary DevOps. Gartner IT Glossary (2017)

17. Gioia, D.A., Corley, K.G., Hamilton, A.L.: Seeking qualitative rigor in inductive research: notes on the Gioia methodology. Organ. Res. Methods 16(1), 15–31 (2013)

18. Gioia, D.A., Patvardhan, S.D., Hamilton, A.L., Corley, K.G.: Organizational identity formation and change. Acad. Manag. Ann. 7(1), 123–193 (2013)

19. Humble, J., Molesky, J.: Why enterprises must adopt DevOps to enable continuous delivery. Cutter IT J. 24(8), 6 (2011)

20. Jabbari, R., bin Ali, N., Petersen, K., Tanveer, B.: What is DevOps? A systematic mapping study on definitions and practices. In: Proceedings of the Scientific Workshop Proceedings of XP2016, pp. 1–11 (2016)

21. Kurkela, M.: Devops capability assessment in a software development team (2020)

22. Laato, S., Mäntymäki, M., Islam, A.N., Hyrynsalmi, S., Birkstedt, T.: Trends and trajectories in the software industry: implications for the future of work. Inf. Syst. Front. 25(2), 929–944 (2023)

23. Mäntymäki, M., Hyrynsalmi, S., Koskenvoima, A.: How do small and medium-sized game companies use analytics? an attention-based view of game analytics. Inf. Syst. Front. 22, 1163–1178 (2020)

24. Miles, M.B., Huberman, A.M.: Qualitative Data Analysis: An Expanded Source-book. Sage, Thousand Oaks (1994)
25. Riungu-Kalliosaari, L., Mäkinen, S., Lwakatare, L.E., Tiihonen, J., Männistö, T.: DevOps adoption benefits and challenges in practice: a case study. In: Abrahams-son, P., Jedlitschka, A., Nguyen Duc, A., Felderer, M., Amasaki, S., Mikkonen, T. (eds.) PROFES 2016. LNCS, vol. 10027, pp. 590–597. Springer, Cham (2016). https://doi.org/10.1007/978-3-319-49094-6_44
26. Schluter, J., Seaton, P., Chaboyer, W.: Critical incident technique: a user's guide for nurse researchers. J. Adv. Nurs. 61(1), 107–114 (2008)
27. Shahin, M., Babar, M.A., Zahedi, M., Zhu, L.: Beyond continuous delivery: an empirical investigation of continuous deployment challenges. In: 2017 ACM/IEEE International Symposium on Empirical Software Engineering and Measurement (ESEM), pp. 111–120. IEEE (2017)
28. Strauss, A., Corbin, J.: Basics of qualitative research techniques (1998)
29. Trihinas, D., Tryfonos, A., Dikaiakos, M.D., Pallis, G.: DevOps as a service: pushing the boundaries of microservice adoption. IEEE Internet Comput. 22(3), 65–71 (2018)
30. Tsanos, C.S., Zografos, K.G., Harrison, A.: Developing a conceptual model for examining the supply chain relationships between behavioural antecedents of collaboration, integration and performance. Int. J. Logistics Manag. 25, 418–462 (2014)
31. Van Belzen, M., DeKruiff, D., Trienekens, J.J.: Success factors of collaboration in the context of devops. In: Proceedings of the 12th IADIS International Conference Information Systems 2019, IS 2019, pp. 26–34 (2019)
32. Zarour, M., Alhammad, N., Alenezi, M., Alsarayrah, K.: A research on DevOps maturity models. Int. J. Recent Technol. Eng. 8(3), 4854–4862 (2019)
33. Zhu, L., Bass, L., Champlin-Scharff, G.: DevOps and its practices. IEEE Softw. 33(3), 32–34 (2016)

Integrating Machine Learning for Predicting Future Automobile Prices: A Practical Solution for Enhanced Decision-Making in the Automotive Industry

Marcelo Carneiro Gonçalves(✉) 🆔, Thiago Roger Machado,
Elpidio Oscar Benitez Nara🆔, Izamara Cristina Palheta Dias🆔, and Lucas Vianna Vaz

Pontifical Catholic University of Paraná, Curitiba, PR 80215-901, Brazil
{Carneiro.marcelo,elpidio.nara}@pucpr.br, {thiago.roger,
izamara.dias,lucas.vaz}@pucpr.edu.br

Abstract. This article presents a study conducted in a vehicle dealership company located in Southern Brazil. The company has been operating in the market since 2018 and faces challenges related to the lack of an automated and quantitatively based flow for negotiation, vehicle valuation, and inventory management. The absence of an automated Production Planning and Control (PPC) system and advanced techniques such as Machine Learning makes it difficult for the company to establish efficient pricing strategies, manage inventory, and make accurate decisions, which can negatively impact overall business performance. This study aims to implement a model that utilizes PPC and Machine Learning techniques to predict the selling price of vehicles.

To achieve this goal, the research followed these steps: conducting a literature review on Machine Learning and PPC focused on Sales and Operations Planning (S&OP), analyzing the company's current procedure through a BPMN diagram, collecting data from the top 5 vehicles with the highest turnover in the company.

The study resulted in the implementation of an automated PPC and Machine Learning flow, enhancing the company's sales management.

Keywords: Vehicle Sales · Machine Learning Techniques · Production Planning and Control

1 Introduction

In a competitive market scenario, companies seek to avoid wastage, increase profits, and improve their work methodologies, thus searching for tools and strategies for informed decision-making [1, 2]. Well-defined and executed planning can be the key to enhancing a company's performance, and efficient resource management has become a significant differentiator in the market [3]. However, companies can reduce their logistical costs and avoid unnecessary expenses, thereby maximizing profits and improving operational

Published by Springer Nature Switzerland AG 2023
M. Janssen et al. (Eds.): I3E 2023, LNCS 14316, pp. 91–103, 2023.
https://doi.org/10.1007/978-3-031-50040-4_8

performance. To achieve this, it is necessary to utilize historical data already collected by the organization and quantitatively perform forecasting models, leading to optimized and efficient inventory management to meet demand and increase organizational profits [4]. Production Planning and Control (PPC) were employed for demand forecasting, providing more precise insights that enable better resource utilization [5]. The major problems in planning and control are among the main causes of low sector productivity, high losses, and poor product quality. Therefore, successful PPC implementation requires leveraging the company's historical data and thorough evaluation. Planning is a decision-making process that facilitates understanding of business objectives and produces essential reference information to monitor and control project execution [6]. Within PPC, Sales and Operations Planning (S&OP) plays a crucial role, aiming to strategize and implement business plans, bringing greater value to the enterprise [7]. It anticipates company needs and constraints, aligning internal departments. S&OP has proven to be highly effective in resolving various production, finance, and sales challenges. As a result, the expected outcomes include increased inventory turnover, reduced unnecessary purchases, expenditures, and improved management aided by artificial intelligence tools [8]. Artificial Intelligence (AI) has been transforming the world, automating, enhancing, or optimizing tasks previously performed solely by humans. Consequently, companies have adapted to this new landscape to remain competitive and achieve high performance, utilizing AI as a significant resource [9].

Within the AI field, Machine Learning allows machines to learn and adapt from an initial program and finite pre-determined dataset without the need for further programming. This ability to receive and learn from data makes Machine Learning a powerful tool for system development, data analysis, and decision-making assistance [9].

The objective of this study is to implement a decision-making flow in vehicle sales management, considering Machine Learning concepts. The steps to achieve this objective are as follows: a) Collect data for forecasting; b) Analyze and treat the data; c) Apply Machine Learning forecasting methods; d) Choose the best method based on the lowest error; e) Implement a flow for decision-making on vehicle lot permanence; f) Validate with stakeholders. The subject company under study has a branch located in Curitiba, solely engaged in vehicle sales, with a wide variety of models in stock. The organization lacks a scientific method to make informed decisions regarding vehicle inventory management and lot permanence. Currently, this is done through the owner's know-how.

2   Methodology

This study followed a set of detailed methodological procedures, as described below. The research began with a literature review using the Scopus and Science Direct databases. Relevant scientific papers on Production Planning and Control (PPC) and machine learning techniques were sought. A thorough analysis of the current company process was conducted using BPMN (Business Process Model and Notation) tool. This mapping helped identify key points for the application of machine learning techniques.

Data collection was carried out in collaboration with the company, which selected the 5 most frequently rotated vehicles for analysis. The predictor variables used were the year, month, and model of the vehicles. For the collection of the dependent variable, historical data from the FIPE table on the selling prices of the selected vehicles were used. Google Colab, a cloud-based platform that allows the execution of Python language codes, was employed for data analysis. Prediction algorithms such as K-Nearest Neighbor, Random Forest, Support Vector Machines, Gradient Boosting Machine, and Linear Regression were incorporated. The codes were pre-modeled and subsequently modified to address the specific problem of this study. The selection of machine learning techniques was based on their prominence in the literature, as indicated in the review conducted by [10]. To evaluate the constructed models, various error-based metrics were used, including Mean Absolute Error (MAE), Mean Absolute Percentage Error (MAPE), Mean Squared Error (MSE), and Root Mean Squared Error (RMSE). These metrics were chosen due to their widespread use in the literature for regression cases, as noted by [10]. This study was conducted in accordance with ethical guidelines. The company provided access to the data, and all procedures followed established ethical standards, including approval by the ethics committee and ensuring participant anonymity. The obtained results were presented to the company's managers to assess their alignment with actual pricing practices for different types of projects and clients. The detailed description of the methodological procedures provides a solid foundation for understanding and replicating this study. The carefully planned steps ensured the validity and reliability of the obtained results, offering an innovative contribution in the context of vehicle sales management using Machine Learning concepts.

3   Theoretical Background

3.1   Production Planning and Control (PPC) in Sales Management

Production Planning and Control (PPC) is an essential component of Sales Management, as it establishes a framework for efficiently managing the production and distribution of vehicles in response to market demand. By implementing effective PPC strategies, the vehicle dealership company can optimize its production schedules, ensuring that the right mix of vehicle models is readily available to meet customer preferences. Additionally, PPC aids in balancing inventory levels, minimizing excess stock while avoiding shortages, which can lead to lost sales opportunities. [11] emphasize that an integrated PPC approach contributes to better supply chain visibility, enabling the company to synchronize its production plans with sales forecasts and thereby enhance overall operational efficiency. Through the integration of sales data into PPC, the company can more accurately predict fluctuations in demand, anticipate seasonal trends, and proactively address potential imbalances in vehicle inventory. Furthermore, the adoption of advanced optimization techniques in PPC can substantially benefit sales performance. Researchers such [12] highlight the advantages of applying mathematical optimization models, which can determine the optimal production plan that minimizes costs while meeting sales targets. These models consider various constraints, such as production capacities, storage limitations, and customer demand, to devise an efficient production schedule that maximizes revenue and profit margins. By leveraging such techniques, the vehicle dealership company can streamline its production processes, reduce lead times, and offer more competitive pricing to customers. Moreover, implementing responsive

PPC systems can lead to increased customer satisfaction, as it ensures the availability of preferred vehicle models when and where customers need them, enhancing the company's reputation and market competitiveness.

3.2 Integration of Sales and Operations Planning (S&OP)

Incorporating Sales and Operations Planning (S&OP) practices into the vehicle dealership company's operations fosters seamless coordination between sales, marketing, and production teams, aligning their efforts to achieve common business goals. As outlined by [13], successful S&OP implementation relies on effective cross-functional communication, fostering a collaborative environment that allows all stakeholders to share insights and make informed decisions. By holding regular S&OP meetings, the company can ensure that sales forecasts, marketing strategies, and production plans are consistently aligned with the dynamic market conditions and customer demands. This alignment reduces the risk of potential bottlenecks and uncertainties, enhancing the company's ability to swiftly adapt to changing market trends and outperform competitors.

Moreover, S&OP empowers the vehicle dealership company to proactively respond to potential supply chain disruptions and fluctuations in vehicle demand. Researchers like [14] emphasize that proactive risk management, integrated within S&OP, helps identify potential challenges and devise contingency plans to mitigate their impact. By considering potential disruptions, such as supply shortages or delays, in the decision-making process, the company can enhance its resilience and maintain a steady supply of vehicles to meet customer needs consistently. Through S&OP's integration, the vehicle dealership company can optimize its sales forecasting accuracy, leading to improved inventory planning and enhanced customer service levels. This integration of Sales and Operations Planning strengthens the company's ability to navigate complex market conditions, contributing to sustainable growth and profitability [15, 16].

3.3 Machine Learning and its Techniques in Service-Based Scenarios

Machine Learning (ML) has emerged as a powerful tool in various industries, including service-oriented businesses. ML techniques enable data-driven decision-making, predictive analysis, and process optimization, contributing to improved service quality, customer satisfaction, and operational efficiency. In the context of the vehicle dealership company, ML offers valuable insights for sales management, demand forecasting, and pricing optimization. Here, we explore five ML techniques: K-Nearest Neighbor, Random Forest, Support Vector Machines, Gradient Boosting Machine, and Linear Regression, along with examples of authors who have successfully applied these methods in service-related scenarios [17]. K-Nearest Neighbor is a simple yet effective ML algorithm used for classification and regression tasks. In service applications, KNN has proven useful for customer segmentation and personalized service delivery. In the vehicle dealership context, KNN could be leveraged to group customers with similar preferences or buying behaviors, helping the company to develop targeted marketing strategies and optimize sales efforts [18]. Random Forest is an ensemble learning method that combines multiple decision trees to improve prediction accuracy and reduce overfitting. This technique has demonstrated its value in customer churn prediction and recommendation systems in service industries. In the vehicle dealership setting, Random Forest can be applied to forecast customer preferences and anticipate potential shifts in demand, guiding the company in optimizing inventory management and pricing decisions [19]. Support Vector Machines are powerful classifiers widely used in various service domains, such as sentiment analysis and customer sentiment prediction. In the vehicle dealership domain, SVM can be employed for sentiment analysis of customer feedback and reviews, enabling the company to gauge customer satisfaction and identify areas for improvement in their sales and after-sales services [20]. Gradient Boosting Machine is an ensemble technique that sequentially builds weak learners into a strong predictive model. GBM has been successfully applied in various service sectors for demand forecasting and resource optimization. In the vehicle dealership industry, GBM could be employed to forecast demand for different vehicle models and optimize inventory levels, contributing to more accurate production planning and effective sales strategies [21]. Linear Regression is a fundamental ML technique used for predicting numerical values based on linear relationships between variables. In service-oriented applications, Linear Regression is often employed for price optimization and demand forecasting. For the vehicle dealership company, Linear Regression can be applied to predict vehicle prices based on historical data, facilitating more precise pricing decisions and ensuring competitiveness in the market [22–25]. These ML techniques, together with data from the vehicle dealership company, hold significant potential for enhancing sales management, demand forecasting, and pricing strategies. By drawing insights from these examples, the company can leverage Machine Learning to gain a competitive advantage, improve customer satisfaction, and optimize its overall sales performance.

4 Demand Forecasting and Decision-Making Analysis

4.1 Process Mapping

The present study was conducted at a vehicle dealership company, referred to as Company M for anonymity purposes. Company M has been operational since 2018, employing a team of 5 direct employees and averaging approximately 20 monthly vehicle sales. Committed to delivering an exceptional customer experience, the company offers comprehensive information and support from the beginning of negotiations to post-sales service. However, despite the owner's expertise and the provided structure, continuous improvement is essential to remain competitive in the market and sustain growth by adapting to customer needs. The project was initiated with the aim of aiding in the development and management of Company M. Through insightful discussions with the team, it was identified that the company faced challenges in maintaining optimal control over its vehicle inventory. Additionally, there was a lack of documented or scientifically supported procedures to effectively manage the decision-making process regarding the retention or release of vehicles in stock, as well as determining the ideal pricing strategies. To address these challenges, the current company process was meticulously mapped using Business Process Model and Notation (BPMN), a widely recognized tool for visualizing and analyzing business processes. BPMN is of utmost importance in this research as it provides a standardized and clear representation of Company M's business processes. By utilizing BPMN, the research team was able to map out the various steps involved in the sales and inventory management processes, enabling a comprehensive understanding of the workflow and identifying potential areas for improvement. This visualization fosters effective communication among team members, highlighting any bottlenecks, redundancies, or inefficiencies that may impact the company's overall performance. As a result, BPMN serves as a critical foundation for the subsequent analysis and application of Machine Learning techniques, enabling Company M to make informed decisions based on a well-documented and optimized process flow.

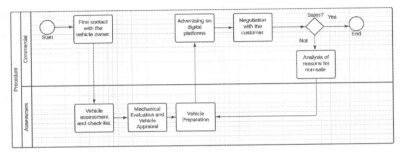

Fig. 1. Company current process.

As observed in Fig. 1, the commercial team is responsible for making the first contact with the customer to gather specific information about the vehicle, such as its history, value, and optional features it possesses. Subsequently, the vehicle goes through a Check List performed by the evaluation department to assess its actual conditions and determine necessary adjustments. After the initial check, a mechanical inspection and expertise are conducted to ascertain whether the vehicle has been previously involved in accidents or has a history of being auctioned. Following this, the next step involves preparing the car by addressing the previously identified checklist items. Afterwards, the vehicle is washed and sanitized to facilitate its commercialization. Once the preparation is completed, the vehicle is taken to the yard for photographs, which will be used for advertising on digital platforms. The dissemination of information is of paramount importance in this process since it allows the product to reach potential customers. Upon reaching these potential customers, the team receives messages and visits to the store, enabling direct interactions between the customers and the sales team. If these negotiations result in a sale, the process concludes. However, if the vehicle remains unsold after a period of 60 days, the commercial team explores potential reasons, with common factors being the market price, Fipe table values, the vehicle's current condition, missing information, or issues related to customer service. After this analysis, the vehicle is returned for preparation and re-announced on digital channels.

4.2 Data Collection and Comparative Analysis of Machine Learning Techniques

The collected data refers to five selected vehicle models that have been previously sold by the company and have shown good turnover. These vehicles belong to different categories, have varying years of manufacture, colors, brands, and versions. The models are as follows: (i) Golf Highline 1.4 TSI 2015, (ii) Cruze 1.4 LTZ Sedan 2017, (iii) Palio 1.0 Economy Fire Flex 4p 2014, (iv) Argo HGT 1.8 Aut 2018, and (v) Evoque 2.0 Dynamic 2013. The independent variables were the month and year of each vehicle model, while the dependent variable was the vehicle's price, obtained from the Fipe table website [26]. The analyzed interval spans from each model's launch year to the current year. It is worth noting that vehicles start being manufactured and sold one year earlier; for example, a 2016 model's Fipe valuation begins in 2015. Below are the individual models and the respective data collection intervals: Argo (July 2017–April 2023); Cruze (July 2016–April 2023); Evoque (January 2013–April 2023); Palio (May 2013–April 2023) and Golf (September 2014–April 2023). To perform the model, forecasting methods previously described were employed, namely GBM, SVM, RF, KNN, and LR. Thus, 90% of the data was used for model training, and the remaining 10% for testing. This choice was motivated by the limited availability of training data. The hyperparameters for the K-Nearest Neighbors (KNN) algorithm are: n_neighbors = 20, weights = 'uniform', algorithm = 'auto', p = 2, and metric = 'minkowski'. For the Random Forest algorithm, the main hyperparameters include criterion = squared_error', max_depth = None, min_samples_split = 2, min_samples_leaf = 1, and max_features = None. In the case of Support Vector Regression (SVR), the key hyperparameters are kernel = 'rbf', gamma = 'scale', C = 1.0, and epsilon = 0.1. Lastly, the Gradient Boosting Regressor (GBR) utilizes loss = 'squared_error', learning_rate = 0.1, n_estimators = 100, and max_depth = 3 as important hyperparameters. For Linear Regression (RL), the relevant hyperparameters are fit_intercept = bool and copy_X = bool. These hyperparameters play a critical role in configuring the respective models and can significantly influence their performance on specific datasets and regression tasks. Table 1 allows us to analyze the application of the 5 demand forecasting techniques (GB, KNN, SVM, RF, and LR) measured by the 4 error metrics (MAE, MAPE, MSE, and RMSE) on the Argo model's database.

Table 1. Argo Results.

	MAE	MAPE	MSE	RMSE
Gradient Boosting	1443.46209	0.02232	3,5236E+12	1877.12585
KNN	2986.13125	0.04637	8,96799E+12	2994.66033
SVM	1828.50004	0.02834	3,62371E+12	1903.60530
Random Forest	1401.25000	0.02767	3.667120*06	1901.76556
Linear Regression	7226.94076	0.11223	5,24102E+13	7239.48658

In Table 1, it was observed that for the Argo model, the technique with the lowest error (MAPE) was Random Forest with a value of 2.167%. The algorithm considered up to 5 decimal places. Table 2 allows us to analyze the application of the 5 demand forecasting techniques (GB, KNN, SVM, RF, and LR) measured by the 4 error metrics (MAE, MAPE, MSE, and RMSE) on the Cruze model's database.

Table 2. Cruze Results.

	MAE	MAPE	MSE	RMSE
Gradient Boosting	2165.55708	0.02472	8,73687E+12	2955.81951
KNN	3335.48889	0.03727	1,16069E+13	3406.89194
SVM	2132.38887	0.02374	5,01421E+12	2239.24333
Random Forest	2673.44444	0.03034	1,00669E+13	3172.82935
Linear Regression	1672.79412	0.01896	3,82141E+12	1954.84283

In Table 2, it was observed that for the Cruze model, the technique with the lowest error (MAPE) was Linear Regression with a value of 1.896%. Table 3 allows us to analyze the application of the 5 demand forecasting techniques (GB, KNN, SVM, RF, and LR) measured by the 4 error metrics (MAE, MAPE, MSE, and RMSE) on the Evoque model's database.

Table 3. Evoque Results.

	MAE	MAPE	MSE	RMSE
Gradient Boosting	1928.61199	0.01015	9,093E+12	3015.46008
KNN	21724.34615	0.11443	5,09503E+14	22572.16682
SVM	63690.38267	0.33596	4,05837E+15	63705.31143
Random Forest	1897.30769	0.00998	7,73123E+12	2780.50962
Linear Regression	11013.15086	0.05807	1,30777E+14	11435.79618

In Table 3, it was observed that for the Evoque model, the technique with the lowest error (MAPE) was Random Forest with a value of 0.998%. Table 4 allows us to analyze the application of the 5 demand forecasting techniques (GB, KNN, SVM, RF, and LR) measured by the 4 error metrics (MAE, MAPE, MSE, and RMSE) on the Palio model's database.

Table 4. Palio Results.

	MAE	MAPE	MSE	RMSE
Gradient Boosting	303.47758	0.01256	1.47397E+05	338.73246
KNN	200.41538	0.00832	4.842467E+04	220.05606
SVM	206.19228	0.00856	5.235609E+04	228.81452
Random Forest	293.46154	0.01221	1,05979E+11	325.54463
Linear Regression	2056.64697	0.08526	4,32755E+12	2080.27676

In Table 4, it was observed that for the Palio model, the technique with the lowest error (MAPE) was KNN with a value of 0.832%. Table 5 allows us to analyze the application of the 5 demand forecasting techniques (GB, KNN, SVM, RF, and LR) measured by the 4 error metrics (MAE, MAPE, MSE, and RMSE) on the Golf model's database.

Table 5. Golf Results.

	MAE	MAPE	MSE	RMSE
Gradient Boosting	2569.34740	0.03112	9,02588E+12	3004.30943
KNN	9533.80727	0.11350	9,54868E+13	9771.73677
SVM	8183.45442	0.09730	7,18444E+13	8476.10803
Random Forest	2477.81818	0.03002	8,43925E+12	2905.03938
Linear Regression	7372.17104	0.08755	5,97038E+13	7726.82049

In Table 5, it was observed that for the Golf model, the technique with the lowest error (MAPE) was Random Forest with a value of 3.002%.

Machine Learning techniques were employed to develop tables for each analyzed vehicle, aiming to find the best model with the lowest error using MAE, MAPE, MSE, and RMSE metrics. Each vehicle exhibits unique characteristics, leading to variations in error values when comparing them. As a result, some errors may be larger or smaller depending on the analyzed tables.

4.3   Demand Forecasting-Driven Decision-Making Process and Validation

Making decisions on whether a vehicle can remain in the yard is of paramount importance for the organization's development, as it ensures inventory renewal and facilitates sales. To achieve this, Machine Learning was utilized to forecast the trend of the Fipe table values for the 5 analyzed vehicle models, which can be increasing, decreasing, or constant. As the value ranges were input until April, the forecast extends to the following 3 consecutive months (Table 6).

Table 6. Prediction.

	May	June	July
Golf	84.475,00	83.645,00	84.097,00
Pálio	27.472,75	27.539,65	27.279,00
Evoque	124.950,00	124.950,00	124.950,00
Cruze	83.789,96	83.645,02	83.500,08
Argo	69.532,00	69.532,00	69.532,00

Based on this forecast information, it is possible to make more informed and decisive decisions by observing increasing, decreasing, or constant trends. Consequently, the following analysis can be conducted during a meeting with stakeholders for vehicles exhibiting: (i) an increasing trend: the car's value will be updated with the rise and can remain in the yard until its sale is finalized. (ii) For decreasing trends: prices will be reassessed and adjusted to the forecasted value to facilitate quicker sales, with updates reflecting a reduction in accordance with the forecast. (iii) For constant trends: vehicle prices will be maintained, and the cars will be kept in the yard. In Fig. 2, we present a BPMN diagram outlining the new decision-making process for the company, which now includes the demand forecasting procedure.

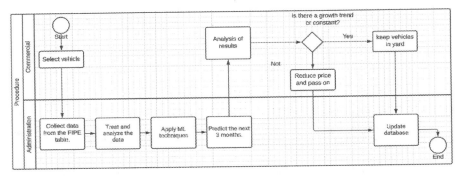

Fig. 2. Making-decision process.

The process begins by selecting the vehicle, model, and year. Next, historical values are fetched from the Fipe table, covering the period from the vehicle's launch year to the closest previous month. These data undergo treatment, analysis, and are organized into a labeled table. Subsequently, the data is uploaded to GitHub, a cloud-based repository, to leverage forecasting techniques. Google Colab, a cloud-based tool utilizing Python, is then employed to identify the optimal forecasting technique for the model, resulting in a future prediction spanning a predetermined three-month period, as defined by stakeholders. This forecast enables the identification of potential trends. The team convenes to discuss the evaluated vehicle, considering unique characteristics not accounted for in the Fipe table [26]. Using the trend information, vehicles experiencing upward or constant trends are retained in the yard for sale. However, if a downward trend is detected, prices are reduced to facilitate quicker sales or the vehicle is made available to other companies. This newly integrated BPMN process streamlines decision-making by incorporating data-driven demand forecasting, enabling the company to make more informed and proactive choices, ultimately leading to improved business outcomes.

The present study proposal was presented to the company's director and their team, showcasing the developed points and how they could be applied to the business with the aim of increasing revenue and improving vehicle pricing. This, in turn, would lead to more informed decisions regarding the vehicles in the yard. However, the proposal was presented as an auxiliary method for decision-making within the company.

As feedback, stakeholders expressed satisfaction with the achieved results. Additionally, as suggestions for improvement, they proposed expanding the application of this work beyond existing yard vehicles, utilizing the technique for vehicle pricing at the time of purchase. The team also recommended incorporating more external criteria into the model to ensure comprehensive decision-making. The validation session allowed for fruitful discussions, and the positive feedback and insightful suggestions from the stakeholders will contribute to further refining and optimizing the proposed methods. The company can now consider implementing these strategies to drive better outcomes, bolstering revenue growth, and facilitating well-informed decisions both for existing inventory and new vehicle acquisitions. By embracing these improvements, the organization can fortify its position in the market and maintain a competitive edge.

5   Final Considerations

Throughout this work, a solution for predicting future automobile prices was devel-oped using concepts of Machine Learning and PPC techniques. To achieve this goal, various steps were undertaken, including a literature review, mapping of the current company procedure, and the creation of a BPMN diagram to demonstrate the employed methodology. This solution presents itself as an alternative to be in-corporated into the company's current decision-making procedures, not to be considered an exclusive approach but rather a supportive tool. With the use of Machine Learning, it be-comes evident that the company can achieve enhanced performance and maintain competitiveness in the market. The use of the FIPE dataset for the 5 most frequently traded vehicles adds originality to this research, as there have been few studies exploring this specific dataset for predicting future vehicle prices. The FIPE serves as a reliable and comprehensive source of vehicle price information, and selecting the top 5 vehicles in terms of turnover adds practical relevance to the obtained results. This approach paves the way for further studies and research that can explore the full potential of this specific dataset in other automotive market analysis applications.

The limitations of the work were related to the number of vehicles used in the research. As for future work, the use of new predictor variables in the process is suggested.

In conclusion, this work represents an important step towards integrating artificial intelligence concepts and predictive analysis in the automotive market context. The use of an innovative dataset based on the FIPE table and the development of a practical and applicable solution for decision-making contribute not only to academia, providing valuable references and insights for future research, but also to external practices, allowing companies in the automotive sector to benefit from the application of these techniques and stand out in an increasingly competitive market.

Acknowledgments. The authors would like to thank the Pontifical Catholic University of Paraná (PUCPR) and PPGEPS-PUCPR.

References

1. Serra, F., Nara, E., Gonçalves, M., Costa, S., Bortoluzzi, S.: Preliminary construct for decision making in organizations: a systemic approach. In: Deschamps, F., de Lima, E.P., da Costa, S.E.G., Trentin, M.G. (eds.) Proceedings of the 11th International Conference on Production Research – Americas: ICPR Americas 2022, pp. 639–646. Springer Nature Switzerland, Cham (2023). https://doi.org/10.1007/978-3-031-36121-0_81

2. Baierle, I.C., Schaefer, J.L., Sellitto, M.A., Furtado, J.C., Nara, E.O.B.: Moona software for survey classification and evaluation of criteria to support decision-making for properties portfolio. Int. J. Strateg. Property Manag. **24**(2), 226–236 (2020)

3. Nora, L.D.D., Siluk, J.C.M., Júnior, A.L.N., Nara, E.O.B., Furtado, J.C.: The performance measurement of innovation and competitiveness in the telecommunications services sector. Int. J. Bus. Excell. **9**(2), 210–224 (2016)

4. Schaefer, J.L., Baierle, I.C., Sellitto, M.A., Furtado, J.C., Nara, E.O.B.: Competitiveness scale as a basis for Brazilian small and medium-sized enterprises. EMJ – Eng. Manag. J. **33**(4), 255–271 (2021)

5. Hamasaki, K., Gonçalves, M.C., Junior, O.C., Nara, E.O.B., Wollmann, R.R.G.: Robust linear programming application for the production planning problem. In: Deschamps, F., de Lima, E.P., da Costa, S.E.G., Trentin, M.G. (eds.) Proceedings of the 11th International Conference on Production Research – Americas: ICPR Americas 2022, pp. 647–654. Springer Nature Switzerland, Cham (2023). https://doi.org/10.1007/978-3-031-36121-0_82

6. Dias, I., Sampaio, R., Wollmann, R., Goncalves, M., Nara, E.: A decomposition scheme in production planning based on linear programming that incorporates the concept of a dynamic planning environment. In: International Joint Conference on Industrial Engineering and Operations Management, IJCIEOM 2022. Springer Proceedings in Mathematics and Statistics (2023)

7. Agostini, L., Filippini, R.: Organizational and managerial challenges in the path toward Industry 4.0. Eur. J. Innov. Manag. **22**(3), 406–421 (2019). https://doi.org/10.1108/EJIM-02-2018-0030

8. Gonçalves, M.C., Nara, E.O.B., dos Santos, I.M., Mateus, I.B., do Amaral, L.M.B.: Comparative analysis of machine learning techniques via data mining in a railroad company. In: Deschamps, F., de Lima, E.P., da Costa, S.E.G., Trentin, M.G. (eds.) Proceedings of the 11th International Conference on Production Research – Americas: ICPR Americas 2022, pp. 655–664. Springer Nature Switzerland, Cham (2023). https://doi.org/10.1007/978-3-031-36121-0_83

9. Usuga Cadavid, J.P., Lamouri, S., Grabot, B., Fortin, A.: Machine learning in production planning and control: a review of empirical literature. IFAC-PapersOnLine **52**(13), 385–390 (2019). https://doi.org/10.1016/j.ifacol.2019.11.155

10. Goncalves, M., Pereira, A., Ferraz, T., Nara, E., Dias, I.: Predicting project sales prices using machine learning techniques: a case study in a project consultancy. In: International Joint Conference on Industrial Engineering and Operations Management, IJCIEOM 2022. Springer Proceedings in Mathematics and Statistics (2023)

11. Alvarez, P.P., Espinoza, A., Maturana, S., Vera, J.: Improving consistency in hierarchical tactical and operational planning using Robust Optimization. Comput. Ind. Eng. **139**, 106112 (2020). https://doi.org/10.1016/j.cie.2019.106112

12. Zanjani, M.K., Nourelfath, M., Ait-Kadi, D.: A multi-stage stochastic programming approach for production planning with uncertainty in the quality of raw materials and demand. Int. J. Product. Res. **48**(16), 4701–4723 (2010). https://doi.org/10.1080/00207540903055727

13. Chen, I.J.: Planning for ERP systems: analysis and future trend. Bus. Process Manag. J. **7**(5), 374–386 (2001). https://doi.org/10.1108/14637150110406768

14. Gonçalves, M.C., Wollmann, R.R.G., Sampaio, R.J.B.: Proposal of a numerical approximation theory to solve the robust convex problem of production planning. Int. J. Operat. Res. **1**(1), 1 (2022). https://doi.org/10.1504/IJOR.2022.10049618

15. Goncalves, M., Sampaio, R., Wollmann, R., Nara, E., Dias, I.: Using robust approach concept to solve the production planning problem in manufacturing systems. In: International Joint Conference on Industrial Engineering and Operations Management, IJCIEOM 2022. Springer Proceedings in Mathematics and Statistics (2023)

16. Lourenço, F., Nara, E., Gonçalves, M., Canciglieri, O.: Preliminary construct of sustainable product development with a focus on the brazilian reality: a review and bibliometric analysis. In: Filho, W.L., Frankenberger, F., Tortato, U. (eds.) Sustainability in Practice: Addressing Challenges and Creating Opportunities in Latin America, pp. 197–220. Springer Nature Switzerland, Cham (2023). https://doi.org/10.1007/978-3-031-34436-7_12

17. Morin, M., Gaudreault, J., Brotherton, E., Paradis, F., Rolland, A., Wery, J., Laviolette, F.: Machine learning-based models of sawmills for better wood allocation planning. Int. J. Product. Econ. **222**, 107508 (2020). https://doi.org/10.1016/j.ijpe.2019.09.029

18. Chabanet, S., Thomas, P., El-Haouzi, H.B., Morin, M., Gaudreault, J.: A kNN approach based on ICP metrics for 3D scans matching: an application to the sawing process. IFAC-PapersOnLine **54**(1), 396–401 (2021). https://doi.org/10.1016/j.ifacol.2021.08.045

19. Bertolini, M., Mezzogori, D., Neroni, M., Zammori, F.: Machine Learning for industrial applications: a comprehensive literature review. Expert Syst. Appl. **175**, 114820 (2021). https://doi.org/10.1016/j.eswa.2021.114820

20. Baumung, W., Fomin, V.V.: Predicting production times through machine learning for scheduling additive manufacturing orders in a PPC system. In: Proceedings of 2019 IEEE International Conference of Intelligent Applied Systems on Engineering, ICIASE 2019, art. no. 9074152, pp. 47–50 (2019). https://doi.org/10.1109/ICIASE45644.2019.9074152

21. Ritto, T.G., Rochinha, F.A.: Digital twin, physics-based model, and machine learning applied to damage detection in structures. Mech. Syst. Signal Process. **155**, 107614 (2021). https://doi.org/10.1016/j.ymssp.2021.107614

22. Morin, M., Paradis, F., Rolland, A., Wery, J., Gaudreault, J., Laviolette, F.: Machine learning-based metamodels for sawing simulation. In: Proceedings – Winter Simulation Conference, 2016-February, art. no. 7408329, pp. 2160–2171 (2015). https://doi.org/10.1109/WSC.2015.7408329

23. Gonçalves, M.C., Canciglieri, A.B., Strobel, K.M., Antunes, M.F., Zanellato, R.R.: Application of operational research in process optimization in the cement industry. J. Eng. Technol. Ind. Appl. **6**(24), 36–40 (2020). https://doi.org/10.5935/jetia.v6i24.677

24. De Faria, G.L., Gonçalves, M.C.: Proposition of a lean flow of processes based on the concept of process mapping for a Bubalinocultura based dairy. J. Eng. Technol. Ind. Appl. **5**(18), 23–28 (2019). https://doi.org/10.5935/2447-0228.20190022

25. Junior, O.J.T., Gonçalves, M.C.: Application of quality and productivity improvement tools in a Potato Chips Production Line. J. Eng. Technol. Ind. Appl. **5**(18), 65–72 (2019). https://doi.org/10.5935/2447-0228.20190029

26. FIPE: https://veiculos.fipe.org.br/. Last accessed 18 Jul 2023

Digital Transformation and New Technologies

How Supervisory Board Members Influence Digital Strategy: Towards a Framework for Digital Strategy Governance

Simone L. van Golden[1]([envelope]) [iD], Marijn Janssen[2] [iD], and Henk Kievit[1] [iD]

[1] Center for Entrepreneurship, Governance and Stewardship, Nyenrode Business University, Breukelen, The Netherlands
S.vangolden@my.nyenrode.nl, H.Kievit@nyenrode.nl
[2] TU Delft, Department of Technology, Policy and Management, Delft, The Netherlands
M.f.w.h.a.janssen@tudelft.nl

Abstract. Since digital opportunities will continue altering business models, organizations need to formulate and execute digital strategies to sustain long-term value. A digital strategy is governed by the organization's board. A board consists of executive and non-executive members, whereas in a two-tier system, the non-executive members form a supervisory board that is decoupled from the executive board. We present a framework illustrating how the actions of supervisory board members might influence digital strategy. We developed this framework based on a structured literature review with insights from corporate governance, strategic management, and board-level IT governance. We found that supervisory board members execute a variety of actions to take and shape strategic decisions and shape the strategic content, context, and conduct within their organization. We integrated our findings into sixteen potential actions that supervisory board members can take to influence digital strategy formulation, execution, and context. Further research should evaluate the framework and investigate the impact of their actions on digital strategies.

Keywords: digital strategy · digital strategy governance · supervisory board member · board-level IT governance · board member actions

1 Introduction

Organizations can formulate and execute a digital strategy to create and sustain organizational distinctiveness with digital capabilities. In line with this strategy, organizations explore digital opportunities and integrate these into their business. Since digital solutions can add business value but may also entail organizational risks [1], boards should be involved in digital strategy. Boards that are actively involved in formulating strategy add organizational value. Their involvement improves financial performance, competitive power, and innovation [2]. This implies that active involvement in digital strategy governance might also add organizational value. Unfortunately, there seems to be a lack of

© IFIP International Federation for Information Processing 2023
Published by Springer Nature Switzerland AG 2023
M. Janssen et al. (Eds.): I3E 2023, LNCS 14316, pp. 107–126, 2023.
https://doi.org/10.1007/978-3-031-50040-4_9

involvement of boards in digital strategy: "Boards of directors do not participate nearly enough in major technology decisions, are surprisingly out of the technology loop on technology issues and are therefore missing opportunities to optimize operational and strategic technology investments" [3, p. 373].

Boards consist of executive and non-executive members. In a two-tier structure, the non-executive board members form a supervisory board. As part of their governance, these supervisory board members control and advise the executive board members, who are responsible for effectively implementing strategic activities to compete with rivals and create long-term value.

How supervisory board members influence digital strategy has not been researched. However, there is related research in adjacent domains such as corporate governance, strategic management, and board-level IT governance from which can be learned.

In the domain of corporate governance and strategic management, researchers investigated different levels of involvement in strategy by non-executive board members [4, 5]. These board members influence strategy by taking strategic decisions, shaping strategic decisions, and shaping content, context, and conduct by which strategy evolves [4–7]. We expect these levels of board involvement also to be applicable to the involvement of the supervisory board members in digital strategy.

In the domain of board-level IT governance, researchers investigated structures, processes, and relational mechanisms [8, 9] that aim to ensure that IT is used effectively such that: "(1) IT is aligned with the enterprise, (2) IT allows the organization to exploit opportunities, (3) IT resources are used responsibly, and (4) IT risks are managed appropriately" [10, p. 224]. Effective use of IT by good board-level IT governance ultimately leads to better organizational performance [8, 10–12].

Different researchers of board-level IT governance investigated how these structures, processes, and mechanisms are used at the board level to govern IT [10, 13–15]. Other board-level IT governance researchers investigated the different roles that boards can fulfill while governing IT [1, 8, 16]. Also, some researchers specifically list questions that boards should ask about digital initiatives, projects, and organizational processes [11, 17–19]. Despite previous researchers of board-level IT governance plea for more research into how boards currently engage in board-level IT governance and actually take their responsibilities [15, 17], we were unable to find scientific insights into how independent non-executive supervisory board members, in a two-tier system, act to influence digital strategy. Empirical research inside boardrooms is needed to understand the complex processes and interactions concerning strategy [20] and the way boards address emerging technological threats and opportunities in their governance [21].

There is a void in research in understanding how the actions of supervisory board members influence digital strategy. In this paper, we develop a framework for digital strategy governance that presents how the actions of supervisory board members might influence the formulation and execution of a digital strategy as well as the context in which supervisory board members act. We focus on a two-tier governance system. We introduce our key concepts in Sect. 2. Next, we structurally review and integrate literature from adjacent domains in Sects. 3 and 4, which leads to our framework in Sect. 5. In Sect. 6 we summarize our findings, discuss the limitations of our research and give suggestions for further research.

2 Literature Background

Since we aim to develop a framework for digital strategy governance that shows how supervisory board members influence digital strategy, we will discuss two relevant key concepts in this chapter: (1) digital strategy and (2) digital strategy governance by the board.

2.1 Digital Strategy

Research shows that a digital 'mature' organization distinguishes itself from the rest by explicitly having a digital strategy that builds on the potential of digital technologies [22]. Traditionally researchers investigated the exploitation of IT in support of business strategies, but recent research investigates the exploration of new valuable uses of IT instead [23]. In this scenario, IT strategy is no longer a strategy in functional areas such as operations, purchasing, supply chain, and marketing, but has become an integrated part of a business strategy [24–28]. This means that in this digital era digital strategy should no longer be positioned below business strategy but should be treated as a business strategy itself.

A digital strategy uses digital resources to drive competitive advantage and create differential value [25]. The integration of existing business capabilities with new digital capabilities of powerful, readily accessible technologies can offer a company real distinctiveness which should not be easy to imitate by competitors [29]. Based on Ross et al. [29] and Bharadwaj et al. [25] in this research we define digital strategy as *an organizational strategy formulated and executed by using the capabilities of powerful, accessible technologies to create differential value in constantly changing market conditions.*

An organization should formulate and execute its digital strategy to become digitally mature. This strategy can entail (1) digitization, changing from analog to digital data, (2) digitalization, supporting processes with digital technology, or (3) digital transformation. With digital transformation organizations alter their value creation processes and change their business model. During this change, they need to manage necessary structural changes and organizational barriers which could affect the required transformation in a positive or negative way [30].

A digital strategy can create strategic business value for organizations through (1) improvement of decision-making processes, (2) use of resources in a more efficient way, (3) serving customers in a more effective manner, (4) successfully becoming part of a digital ecosystem or (5) innovating their business model. As such, a digital strategy is a relevant response to market disruptions and necessary to generate long-term value.

A digital strategy consists of different phases and activities. We divide digital strategy into two iterative phases, in line with Peppard & Ward [28] and Azlan Annuar [7]. We call these two phases digital strategy formulation and digital strategy execution. During digital strategy formulation it is necessary to (1) get insight and understand digital opportunities, threats, and their impact, (2) envision business model change alternatives driven by technological possibilities, (3) critically evaluate these alternatives and (4) include relevant stakeholders when defining and communicating the vision [31]. During digital strategy execution, it is relevant to monitor progress but also to constantly sense the environment and decide whether adjustment of the digital course is necessary. Therefore, a constant iterative process between formulation and execution occurs, which we call digital strategizing.

2.2 Digital Strategy Governance by the Board

Boards can consist of one or two tiers. A two-tier board structure strictly separates responsibilities between executive management and non-executive independent supervisors. Executives run a company, set the strategic direction, and are primarily responsible for its continuity, whereas the non-executive supervisory board needs to ensure the organization's long-term performance by controlling and advising the executives [32–34]. As such, non-executive board members fulfill controlling and advisory roles [20, 35–37] and can be involved in strategy at different levels: by taking and shaping strategic decisions, shaping strategic content, and shaping strategic context and conduct [4, 5, 7].

Boards control managerial IT-related decisions and actions and offer IT-related advice and direction [16] that might influence digital strategy. Board members should "encourage, push for change and progress, see the big picture, and review and question" [38, p. 45] the digital strategy set by executive management. Additionally, board members are supposed to sense the environment and shape the context to execute the digital strategy successfully.

The involvement of boards in strategy varies: All boards take controlling strategic decisions "where influence is exerted inside the boardroom and the board takes decisions to either accept, reject or refer proposals" [5, p. 65]. About half of all boards also shape strategic decisions by giving advice. Only fifteen percent of the boards are deeply involved and shape strategic context, conduct, and content [5], such as IT governance structures and processes and the specific content of the digital strategy. "Some boards may also get too much involved with strategy development and heavily constrain and/or discount executives' strategic discretion" [32, p. 57].

Although supervisory board members do not set the strategy directly, they can significantly impact it [39]. Given the relevance of digital strategy and the impact supervisory board members might have on it, we investigated how board members of the supervisory board might influence the digital strategy with their actions. Our research starts with a literature review in Sects. 3 and 4 leading to our framework in Sect. 5.

3   Research Method: Systematic Literature Review

We reviewed the existing scientific literature to answer the following research question: *Which specific actions might supervisory board members take that could influence digital strategy?*

During our literature review, we searched the Scopus database several times. We specifically searched for English-written, peer-reviewed journal papers and conference proceedings with specific terms related to our research question in their title, abstract, or keywords. Our search took place in April 2023.

At first, we searched for papers containing Supervisory Board AND Influence AND Digital Strategy, or similar terms as shown in the search string details in Table 1.

Table 1. Search string of supervisory board influence on digital strategy

Search string	Search string details
Supervisory Board	(non-executive* OR "supervisory board")
AND	AND
Influence	(strategize OR act* OR influenc* OR govern* OR role OR contribut* OR involv* OR monitor* OR supervis* OR advis*)
AND	AND
Digital Strategy	(digital* strateg* OR "digital* business strateg*" OR "digital* transformation" OR "information technology strateg*" OR "information system* strateg*" OR "IT strateg*" OR "IS strateg*")

This first search string did not give any results, which confirms a gap in the scientific literature about how supervisory board members influence digital strategy. Therefore, we structurally broadened our search in three different ways, as illustrated in Fig. 1.

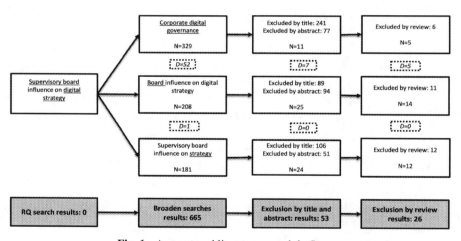

Fig. 1. A structured literature search in Scopus

First, we expanded our search to the research area of 'corporate digital governance'. Since we define digital strategy as part of the corporate strategy, supervision of this digital strategy could be part of corporate governance. We used a combination of three search strings and searched for: ((Corporate Governance AND Digital Strategy) OR (Corporate Governance AND Information Technology) OR (Corporate Digital Governance)). The details of these search strings are shown in Table 2. This search resulted in 329 papers as shown in Fig. 1.

Table 2. Search strings of corporate digital governance

Search string 1	Search string details
Corporate Governance	("Corporate Govern*" OR "Corporate strategy governan*")
AND	AND
Digital Strategy	(digital* strateg* OR "digital* business strateg*" OR "digital* transformation" OR "information technology strateg*" OR "information system* strateg*" OR "IT strateg*" OR "IS strateg*")
Search string 2	Search string details
Corporate Governance	("Corporate Govern*" OR "Corporate strategy governan*")
AND	AND
Information Technology	"Information Technology"
Search string 3	Search string details
Corporate Digital Governance	("Corporate Digital* Govern*" OR "Digital* Corporate Govern*" OR "Corporate Technology Governan*" OR "Corporate Information Technology Govern*" OR "Corporate IT Govern*" OR "Enterprise Business Technology Govern*")

Secondly, we broadened our search from the supervisory board level to the board level because we suspect that prior research on one-tier boards might contain board member actions that could also occur in a two-tier structure at the supervisory board level. As shown in Table 3, we combined three strings: (Board AND Digital Strategy), (Board AND IT Governance) and (Board AND Influence AND Information Technology). The combination of these strings resulted in 208 papers (see Fig. 1).

Table 3. Search strings of board influence on digital strategy

Search string 1	Search string details
Board	(Boardroom OR board-level OR "board level" OR board-member OR "board member" OR "board of directors" OR "boards of directors" OR "corporate board*" OR non-executive* OR "supervisory board*")
AND	AND
Digital Strategy	(digital* strateg* OR "digital* business strateg*" OR "digital* transformation" OR "information technology strateg*" OR "information system* strateg*" OR "IT strateg*" OR "IS strateg*")
Search string 2	Search string details
Board	(Boardroom OR board-level OR "board level" OR board-member OR "board member" OR "board of directors" OR "boards of directors" OR "corporate board*" OR non-executive* OR "supervisory board*")

(*continued*)

Table 3. (*continued*)

AND	AND
IT Governance	"IT govern*"
Search string 3	*Search string details*
Board	(boardroom OR board-level OR "board level" OR board-member OR "board member" OR "board of directors" OR "boards of directors" OR "corporate board*" OR non-executive* OR "supervisory board*")
AND	AND
Influence	(strategize OR act* OR influenc* OR govern* OR role OR contribut* OR involv* OR monitor* OR supervis* OR advis*)
AND	AND
Information Technology	Information Technology

Thirdly, we searched the Scopus database for literature about the influence of supervisory (and non-executive) board members on strategy in general. We believe that the actions these board members take to influence corporate strategy could also be taken to influence the digital strategy. In this third search, we included the elements Supervisory Board AND Influence AND Strategy, see Table 4, resulting in 181 papers as shown in Fig. 1.

Table 4. Search string of supervisory board member influence on strategy

Search string	*Search string details*
Supervisory Board	(non-executive* OR "supervisory board")
AND	AND
Influence	(strategize OR act* OR influenc* OR govern* OR role OR contribut* OR involv* OR monitor* OR supervis* OR advis*)
AND	AND
Strategy	strateg*

As shown in Fig. 1, our search results contained duplicates (D); 52 papers were found in both our 'corporate digital governance' search as well as in our 'board influence on digital strategy' search. In addition, one paper was found in both our 'board influence on digital strategy' search as well as in our 'supervisory board influence on strategy' search. There were no duplicates in the 'corporate digital governance' and 'supervisory board influence on strategy' searches. We eliminated these 53 duplicates, leading to a total of 665 papers that could contain specific actions that supervisory board members might take to influence digital strategy (see Fig. 1).

The 665 papers we found were scanned by title. Based on their title, we excluded the papers that we were sure of that would not provide insight into board-level actions that might influence strategy. As shown in Fig. 1, we excluded 241 of the 'corporate digital governance' papers, 89 of the 'board-level' papers, and 106 of the 'strategy' papers. Next, we scanned the abstracts of the remaining papers and excluded those that did not contain potential influential actions, or were not focused on board-level or board members. Since we were searching for actions that influence the digital strategy, we also excluded papers where 'digital' seemed to be the cause or tool and not the outcome, for example, (1) papers investigating the role of technology on governance or strategy and (2) papers investigating the use of digital techniques during board level decision-making. After this, we ended up with 11 papers about 'corporate digital governance', 25 papers about 'board influence on digital strategy', and 24 papers about 'the supervisory board's influence on strategy'. After we excluded the seven duplicate papers, 53 unique papers remained, see Fig. 1.

We reviewed these 53 papers in detail to determine whether they could answer our research question. We excluded papers about the implementation of governance frameworks and structures as well as papers specifically about antecedents of IT governance, IT investments, or strategic board involvement. Finally, we ended up with 26 relevant papers. Of these 26 papers, all 5 results in our 'corporate digital governance' search were duplicates of results from our 'board influence on digital strategy' search (see Fig. 1), which means the literature search on 'corporate digital strategy' did not contribute to our results. Therefore, in the rest of this paper, we will only refer to two categories: (1) board influence on digital strategy, and (2) supervisory board influence on strategy. The resulting 26 papers of our review are presented, split by research category, and sorted by year of publication, in Tables 7 and 8 in the Appendix.

4   Data Analysis

We analyzed the selected papers to develop a framework that indicates how supervisory board members influence digital strategy: a framework for digital strategy governance. In this chapter, we first present some research characteristics, such as publications over time, research methods, and research theories. Thereafter, we answer our research question and give insight into the different types of actions that supervisory board members could take to influence digital strategy. At last, we also describe factors that might influence these actions. Based on our data analysis, we present our framework in Sect. 5.

4.1   Previous Research Characteristics.

As shown in Tables 7 and 8 in the Appendix and in Fig. 2, scientific research into the board's influence on digital strategy as well as the supervisory[1] board's influence on strategy started at the end of the '90s and still continues. Despite the increase in the strategic relevance of IT, scientific research in the fields related to supervising digital strategy does not appear to be expanding.

---

[1] Most researchers of the papers we selected as part of our 'supervisory board influence on strategy' search, investigated one-tier boards with a specific focus on the role of the non-executive board members.

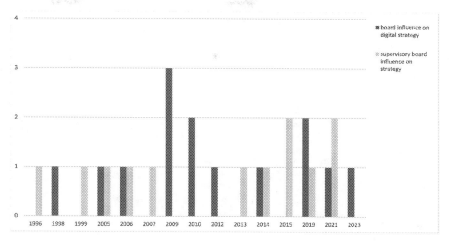

Fig. 2. Year of publication of selected papers

In the rest of this section, we present the different research methods and scientific theories that were applied in the papers we included in our review.

Research Methods
Scientific research into the board's involvement in IT as well as the supervisory board's involvement in strategy is conducted using different research methods as shown in Fig. 3. Researchers in these areas used literature reviews [1, 15, 40], case studies [19, 45], interview techniques [4, 5, 7, 33, 34, 42–44] and surveys [8, 17, 18, 47–50]. One researcher observed board meetings [46] and some researchers supplemented their surveys with interviews [3, 18] or in-depth analysis [10] to conduct mixed-method research. One relevant paper is mainly based on the practical experience of the authors [11]. One paper did not mention a specific research method [41].

The research methods used to investigate this phenomenon, differ per research area as presented in Fig. 3. In the research area of supervisory board influence on strategy only qualitative and quantitative research is conducted. In the research area of board influence on digital strategy, researchers also conducted literature reviews and mixed-method research. The qualitative research method used also varies per research area.

Research Theories
We analyzed the scientific theories mentioned in our paper selection. Our analysis supports the findings of Madhani [51], who states that different scientific theories are applicable at the board level. These different theories support the different roles and responsibilities of board members.

Agency theory supports the controlling and monitoring role of the board as mentioned by most of the researchers [1, 4, 5, 15, 16, 34, 43, 44, 48, 50]. In addition to agency theory, many researchers mention resource dependency theory [1, 4, 15, 16, 32, 33, 48, 50] or the resource-based perspective [10, 15, 16]. In line with the advisory role of the board, researchers often mention stewardship theory [1, 15, 16, 44, 48]. In addition to

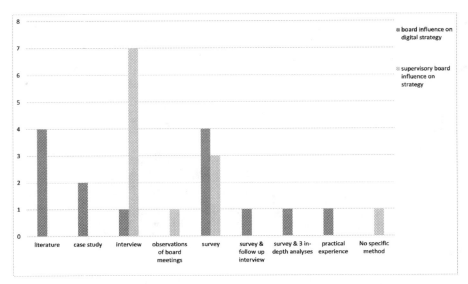

Fig. 3. Research method of selected papers

the aforementioned theories, involvement of boards in strategy can also be supported by stakeholder theory [15, 16] upper echelons theory [32, 40], strategic choice theory [8, 15, 16, 40], signaling theory [16], institutional theory [8, 40], a class hegemony perspective [4, 32, 48], a legalistic perspective [32] and a contingency view [10, 15, 17].

We think that the diversity of theoretical views to explain the involvement of boards aligns with the broad and overarching responsibility that board members bear. Following the lead of other researchers [16, 32, 40, 51] we think that different theoretical perspectives can coexist and offer complementary views to explain board phenomena.

4.2 Actions that Might Influence Digital Strategy

Based on our 26 papers, we identified and listed over 200 potential actions that supervisory boards or their members can take to influence digital strategy. Since some papers are written by the same authors and refer to identical research data, our list of actions contained duplicates. Also, various papers label actions differently but in our interpretation these actions are quite the same and can be merged into the same category.

We interpreted and classified our identified actions in a list of 16 categories that might influence (1) the formulation of digital strategy, (2) both formulating and executing digital strategy, (3) the execution of digital strategy or (4) the board-level context of digital strategy, see Table 5. Supervisory board members might take any of these actions to influence digital strategy as part of their controlling and advising role.

Table 5. Supervisory board member actions that might influence digital strategy

Actions	Influence on digital strategy formulation	Influence on digital strategy execution	Actions that influence board-level context	Found in references
Review and criticize plans	X			[7, 11, 16, 18, 33, 40–42, 44]
Approve plans and budget	X			[5, 7, 18, 19, 33, 42, 49]
Determine KPIs	X			[1, 10, 11, 16, 18, 43, 49, 50]
Ask questions	X	X		[7, 11, 15, 17, 33, 41, 46, 47]
Direct executive attention	X	X		[16, 18, 40]
Approve executive decisions	X	X		[1, 4, 5, 7, 10, 11, 15] [16, 18, 40, 42, 49, 50]
Monitor (and evaluate) executive actions	X	X		[8, 11, 16, 40–44]
Executive coaching and mentoring	X	X		[1, 4, 5, 11, 16, 33, 48]
Provide substantive advice	X	X		[1, 7, 10, 11, 16, 18] [41–43, 48–50]
Sense environment for opportunities and threats	X	X		[7, 11, 16, 18, 40, 48]
Stakeholder management (communication and interaction)	X	X		[10, 16, 41–43]
Monitor (and evaluate) execution of plans		X		[1, 3, 5, 7, 10, 11, 15, 16] [18, 34, 40–45, 48–50]
Use relational capital (network)		X		[1, 3, 11, 15, 16, 18, 41, 48]
Implement or change governance structure or processes			X	[1, 3, 7, 8, 10, 11, 16] [18, 40–42, 44, 45, 50]
Shape values and culture			X	[16, 18, 41, 42, 44]
Appoint and dismiss executives, determine compensation, and steer executive development			X	[11, 18, 42–44]

4.3 Factors that Influence Actions Board Members Take

Most of the papers we reviewed did not only mention actions but also mentioned factors that affect which actions a (supervisory) board member might take. These factors were mentioned related to other outcomes than digital strategy, such as IT governance, workings of the board, board involvement, board effectiveness, firm performance, and non-executive director roles. Although these influential factors were not explicitly investigated in our research context, we expect these to also be applicable to the influence of supervisory board members on digital strategy. We divided these influential factors into three different context levels: (1) organizational context, (2) board-level context, and (3) board member characteristics, as presented in Table 6.

Table 6. Contextual elements that might affect how supervisory board members act

Factors that might influence how board members act	Organizational context	Booard-level context	Booard member characteristics	Found in references
Ownership structure, power between internal and external stakeholders	X			[43, 44]
Company lifecycle or age	X			[4, 8, 15, 43]
Role of IT in organization (IT usage mode)	X			[8, 10, 11, 15, 17, 40]
Country, Legal environment, IT intensity of industry	X			[15, 18, 49]
Turbulence of the environment (f.e. potential crisis)	X			[18, 34]
Governance structures and processes		X		[3, 4, 15, 16, 18, 40, 43, 44]
Board size		X		[8, 15, 16, 50]
Insider or founder representation on the board		X		[8, 15, 16, 44]
Board independence		X		[50]
Cognitive diversity of non-executive directors		X		[16, 48]
Board IT competency		X		[8, 15, 16, 18, 40]
Board culture and teamwork		X		[4, 5, 44]
Governing style		X		[15, 18, 42]
Director age			X	[15, 40]
Human capital and relational capital			X	[16, 48]
Attitude and beliefs, perceived self-efficacy and motivational factors			X	[15, 48]
IT background, education, experience, (IT) expertise and skills			X	[1, 11, 16, 33, 40, 44, 48]
Skills, the ability to work as a group, sensitivity to board dynamics and personal power and Influential style			X	[5, 33, 42, 43]

5   Towards a Framework for Digital Strategy Governance

Despite we found no scientific literature on the influence of supervisory board members on digital strategy, we developed a framework for digital strategy governance. Our framework presents actions we abstracted from research in corporate governance, strategic management, and board-level IT governance, where we suppose these actions also to apply to digital strategy. Our framework for digital strategy governance is presented in Fig. 4. Central in our framework are the actions of supervisory board members, which influence digital strategy.

A digital strategy consists of two iterative phases [7, 28]. We call these (1) digital strategy formulation and (2) digital strategy execution. By evaluating the performance of past strategies, and considering current strategic performance, the strategic plan might be adjusted [50].

Supervisory board members might take different actions to influence (1) the formulation of digital strategy, (2) both formulating and executing digital strategy, (3) the execution of digital strategy, and (4) the board-level context within which actions take place (see Table 5).

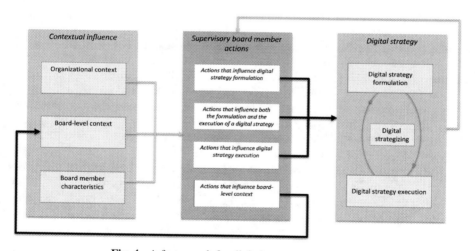

Fig. 4. A framework for digital strategy governance

To influence the formulation of a digital strategy, supervisory board members control executives by reviewing, criticizing, and approving strategic plans [7, 11, 16, 18, 33, 40–42, 44] as well as determining KPIs [1, 10, 11, 16, 18, 43, 49, 50] to be able to control the execution.

During digital strategy execution, determined KPIs can give insight into IT-related risks, such as IT competence risk, infrastructure risk, project risk, business continuity risk, and information risk [11, 16, 43, 45]. To monitor progress, special board meetings might occur [7] where the CIO presents the progress to the full board so that IT-related risks, assets, and projects can be discussed [40].

Furthermore, to influence the digital strategy execution, supervisory board members can interact with external as well as internal stakeholders or use their relational capital to get access to relevant resources such as IT providers [3, 16], capital [16] and expertise [11, 18]. They can also use their network to share problems [41] or to visit other organizations and observe their technology approaches and digital strategies [11].

During both the formulation and execution of a digital strategy, supervisory board members need to assure that decision-making in the board is driven by its strategy [41]. Therefore, they can ask questions [7, 11, 15, 17, 33, 41, 46, 47] and they need to approve strategic decisions with fundamental operational or financial impact [1, 7, 15, 16, 18, 49]. Also, they need to approve major decisions about the use of resources, investments, or divestments [42]. Next to the approval of decisions, supervisory board members need to evaluate if the executives have applied the correct decision-making processes [44] and "evaluate whether the executives have established the correct procedures to adequately manage IT" [16, p. 6049].

Also, during the formulation and execution of a digital strategy, supervisory board members can provide substantive advice [1, 7, 10, 11, 16, 18, 41–43, 48–50] and direct executive attention [16, 18, 40] To be able to give substantive advice, supervisory board members need to scan their environment [7, 16, 48] and identify threats and opportunities. They can use IT risk management insights from other organizations [18] and need to keep abreast of technological trends [11, 40]. Based on their knowledge and experience they can also coach and advise executives during individual consultations [4, 8, 11, 16, 48] or during strategy-making sessions [48, 49]. Furthermore, they might explicitly direct the executive's attention [16] to (1) IT issues and risks [10, 18], (2) IT innovation and trends [18], or (3) to put IT on the agenda of the board meetings and strategy discussions [40, 41]. As such, the advice given by the supervisory board members can be risk-related [10, 43], but can also be opportunity-driven [18].

At last, supervisory board members can change the board-level context. "They can create an atmosphere of joint accountability and support regarding IT" [16, 18, p. 62] and facilitate a culture that shares appropriate information and encourages risk awareness [44]. Also, they might change the board-level IT governance structure by initializing a specific IT risk committee [1], a strategic IT committee [3, 8, 10, 11, 40], assigning IT responsibilities to existing committees or assign a board IT representative [11, 45]. The board-level context can also be changed because the supervisory board acts as the employer of all board members. As such, they can even be involved in steering the executive development plans [44]. This implies that supervisory board members influence the expertise on board.

Our framework also indicates which contextual elements might affect supervisory board members' actions. Contextual elements occur at different levels. At the organizational level, elements such as ownership structure [43, 44], company age [4, 8, 15, 43], the role of IT in the organization [8, 10, 11, 15, 17, 40], legislation and regulations [15, 49], and turbulence of the environment [18, 34], influence the actions of supervisory board members. At the board level, the IT governance structures, processes, and relational mechanisms [3, 4, 15, 16, 18, 40, 43, 44], as well as board size [8, 15, 16, 50], board IT competency [8, 15, 16, 18, 40], and governing style [15, 18, 42], impact the

actions of supervisory board members. At the board member level, different characteristics impact their actions such as beliefs, age, experience, expertise, and skills [1, 11, 16, 33, 40, 44, 48].

Based on our framework we expect that supervisory board members influence digital strategy formulation, execution, and context with more than just asking questions. Their different actions are not only driven by their personal characteristics but are also affected by the organizational and board-level context.

6 Conclusions and Further Research

In this paper, we presented a framework based on different research streams, giving insight into the actions supervisory board members can take to influence digital strategy. As far as we know, we were the first to scientifically review, analyze and integrate literature to develop a framework for digital strategy governance. Supervisory board members can use this framework to become more aware of different alternative actions and the influence of their actions on digital strategy.

Our findings indicate that supervisory board members can ask questions but can also take a variety of other actions to influence the digital strategy. With this repertoire of actions, they can directly influence the formulation and execution of a digital strategy, but they can also influence the board-level context, which in turn appears to affect their own actions. Apart from the board-level context as an influential factor, we also expect the organizational context and the board member characteristics to influence how supervisory board members act.

As with any research, our research has some limitations. First, since we could not find specific scientific literature to answer our research question, we interpreted and integrated literature from adjacent domains. This literature is mostly based on research in one-tier boards. Further empirical and practical research is needed to investigate how supervisory board members in two-tier boards, influence digital strategy. Additionally, since different theoretical perspectives can coexist to explain board phenomena, more research is necessary to investigate how these theories support our framework.

Another limitation concerns our influential factors because we only aggregated contextual factors from papers that contained potential actions of supervisory board mem-
bers. Papers that did not contain actions were excluded, even though some of these papers specifically investigated antecedents of board-level IT governance or the involvement of boards in strategy. Further research in practice to investigate how any of these factors affect supervisory board members' actions to influence digital strategy is recommended.

In conclusion, our emerging framework for digital strategy governance can be further researched, refined, and evaluated by investigating how our described actions occur in supervisory boards and how they vary in different contexts.

Appendix

Table 7. In-dept reviewed papers of board influence on digital strategy

Authors	Title	Journal
Damodaran L. [19]	Development of a user-centred IT strategy: A case study	(1998) Behaviour and Information Technology, 17 (3), pp. 127–134
Nolan R., McFarlan F.W. [11]	Information technology and the board of directors	(2005) Harvard Business Review, 83 (10), pp. 96–106 + 157
Mähring M. [40]	The role of the board of directors in IT governance: A review and agenda for research	(2006) Association for Information Systems 12th Americas Conference On Information Systems, AMCIS
Parent M., Reich B.H. [45]	Governing information technology risk	(2009) California Management Review, 51 (3), pp. 134–152 + 5
Andriole S.J. [3]	Boards of directors and technology governance: The surprising state of the practice	(2009) Communications of the Association for Information Systems, 24 (1), pp. 373–394
Bart C., Turel O. [47]	The role of the board in IT governance: Current and desired oversight practices	(2009) International Journal of Business Governance and Ethics, 4 (4), pp. 316–329
Bart C., Turel O. [17]	IT and the board of directors: An empirical investigation into the "Governance questions" Canadian board members ask about IT	(2010) Journal of Information Systems, 24 (2), pp. 147–172
O'Shannassy T. [33]	Board and CEO practice in modern strategy-making: How is strategy developed, who is the boss and in what circumstances?	(2010) Journal of Management and Organization, 16 (2), pp. 280–298
Jewer J., McKay K.N. [8]	Antecedents and consequences of board IT governance: Institutional and strategic choice perspectives	(2012) Journal of the Association for Information Systems, 13 (7), pp. 581–617
Turel O., Bart C. [10]	Board-level IT governance and organizational performance	(2014) European Journal of Information Systems, 23 (2), pp. 223–239
Caluwe L., De Haes S. [15]	Board Level IT Governance: A Scoping Review to Set the Research Agenda	(2019) Information Systems Management, 36 (3), pp. 262–283
Turel O., Liu P., Bart C. [18]	Board-Level IT Governance	(2019) IT Professional, 21 (2), art. no. 8676129, pp. 58–65
Caluwe L., de Haes S., Wilkin C., Huygh T. [16]	How boards of directors can contribute to governing IT	(2021) Proceedings of the Annual Hawaii International Conference on System Sciences, 2020-January, pp. 6047–6056
Matta M., Cavusoglu H., Benbasat I. [1]	Understanding the Board's Involvement in Information Technology Governance	(2022) Information Systems Management

Table 8. In-dept reviewed papers of supervisory board influence on strategy

Authors	Title	Journal
McNulty T., Pettigrew A. [42]	The Contribution, Power and Influence of Part-time Board Members	(1996) Corporate Governance: An International Review, 4 (3), pp. 160–179
McNulty T., Pettigrew A. [4]	Strategists on the board	(1999) Organization Studies, 20 (1), pp. 47–74
Long T., Dulewicz V., Gay K. [43]	The role of the non-executive director: Findings of an empirical investigation into the differences between listed and unlisted UK boards	(2005) Corporate Governance: An International Review, 13 (5), pp. 667–679
Kemp S. [5]	In the driver's seat or rubber stamp?: The role of the board in providing strategic guidance in Australian boardrooms	(2006) Management Decision, 44 (1), pp. 56–73
Long T. [44]	The evolution of FTSE 250 boards of directors: Key factors influencing board performance and effectiveness	(2007) Journal of General Management, 32 (3), pp. 45–60
Eulerich M., Stiglbauer M. [34]	The supervision of strategy and risk in German two-tier boards: Lessons learned from the crisis	(2013) International Journal of Management Practice, 6 (3), pp. 220–234
Azlan Annuar H. [7]	Independent non-executive directors strategic role – some evidence from Malaysia	(2014) Corporate Governance (Bingley), 14 (3), pp. 339–351
Sheaff R., Endacott R., Jones R., Woodward V. [46]	Interaction between non-executive and executive directors in English National Health Service trust boards: An observational study	(2015) BMC Health Services Research, 15 (1), art. no. 470
Deffenbaugh J. [41]	Houston, we've had a problem here: Tackling board governance	(2015) British Journal of Health Care Management, 21 (7), pp. 304–309
Hom C.L., Samson D., Cebon P.B., Cregan C. [48]	Inside the black box: an investigation of non-executive director activity through the lens of dynamic capability	(2021) Asia Pacific Journal of Management, 38 (3), pp. 857–895
De Haas R., Ferreira D., Kirchmaier T.[49]	The inner workings of the board: Evidence from emerging markets	(2021) Emerging Markets Review, 48, art. no. 100777
Cindrić L. [50]	Supervisory Board's Contribution to Corporate Strategy: Evidence from Croatian Companies	(2021) Studies in Business and Economics, 16 (1), pp. 42–50

References

1. Matta, M., Cavusoglu, H., Benbasat, I.: Understanding the board's involvement in information technology governance. Inf. Syst. Manag. (2022). https://doi.org/10.1080/10580530.2022.2074580
2. Zhu, H., Wang, P., Bart, C.: Board processes, board strategic involvement, and organizational performance in for-profit and non-profit organizations. J. Bus. Ethics **136**(2), 311–328 (2016). https://doi.org/10.1007/s10551-014-2512-1
3. Andriole, S.J.: Boards of directors and technology governance: the surprising state of the practice. Commun. Assoc. Inf. Syst. **24**(1), 373–394 (2009). https://doi.org/10.17705/1cais.02422
4. McNulty, T., Pettigrew, A.: Strategists on the board. Organ. Stud. **20**(1), 47–74 (1999). https://doi.org/10.1177/0170840699201003
5. Kemp, S.: In the driver's seat or rubber stamp?: the role of the board in providing strategic guidance in Australian boardrooms. Manag. Decis. **44**(1), 56–73 (2006). https://doi.org/10.1108/00251740610641463
6. Åberg, C., Kazemargi, N., Bankewitz, M.: Strategists on the board in a digital era. Bus. Manag. Res. **6**(2), 40 (2017). https://doi.org/10.5430/bmr.v6n2p40
7. Azlan Annuar, H.: Independent non-executive directors strategic role – some evidence from Malaysia. Corp. Gov. (Bingley) **14**(3), 339–351 (2014). https://doi.org/10.1108/CG-10-2011-0075
8. Jewer, J., Mckay, K.N.: Antecedents and consequences of board IT governance: institutional and strategic choice perspectives. J. Assoc. Inf. Syst. **13**(7), 581–617 (2012)
9. de Haes, S., van Grembergen, W.: IT Governance and Its Mechanisms. www.isaca.org (2004)
10. Turel, O., Bart, C.: Board-level IT governance and organizational performance. Eur. J. Inf. Syst. **23**(2), 223–239 (2014). https://doi.org/10.1057/ejis.2012.61
11. Nolan, R., McFarlan, F.W.: Information technology and the board of directors. Harv. Bus. Rev. (2005). www.hbr.org
12. Turel, O., Liu, P., Bart, C.: Board-level information technology governance effects on organizational performance: the roles of strategic alignment and authoritarian governance style. Inf. Syst. Manag. **34**(2), 117–136 (2017). https://doi.org/10.1080/10580530.2017.1288523
13. de Haes, S., van Grembergen, W.: Analysing the relationship between IT governance and business/IT alignment maturity. In: Proceedings of the 41st Hawaii International Conference on System Sciences (2008)
14. Turel, O., Liu, P., Bart, C.: Is board IT governance a silver bullet? A capability complementarity and shaping view. Int. J. Account. Inf. Syst. **33**, 32–46 (2019). https://doi.org/10.1016/j.accinf.2019.03.002
15. Caluwe, L., De Haes, S.: Board level IT governance: a scoping review to set the research agenda. Inf. Syst. Manag. **36**(3), 262–283 (2019). https://doi.org/10.1080/10580530.2019.1620505
16. Caluwe, L., Wilkin, C., De Haes, S., Huygh, T.: How boards of directors can contribute to governing IT. In: Proceedings of the 54th Hawaii International Conference on System Sciences (2021). https://hdl.handle.net/10125/71351
17. Bart, C., Turel, O.: IT and the board of directors: an empirical investigation into the 'Governance questions' Canadian board members ask about IT. J. Inf. Syst. **24**(2), 147–172 (2010). https://doi.org/10.2308/jis.2010.24.2.147
18. Turel, O., Liu, P., Bart, C.: Board-level IT governance. IT Prof **21**(2), 58–65 (2019). https://doi.org/10.1109/MITP.2019.2892937
19. Damodaran, L.: Development of a user-centred IT strategy: a case study. Behav. Inform. Technol. **17**(3), 127–134 (1998). https://doi.org/10.1080/014492998119472

20. Watson, C., Ireland, A.: Boards in action: processes and practices of 'strategising' in the Boardroom. J. Manage. Governance **25**(3), 933–966 (2021). https://doi.org/10.1007/s10997-020-09545-7
21. Klarner, P., Yoshikawa, T., Hitt, M.A.: A capability-based view of boards: a new conceptual framework for board governance. Acad. Manag. Perspect. **35**(1), 123–141 (2021). https://doi.org/10.5465/AMP.2017.0030
22. Kane, G.C., Palmer, D., Phillips, A.N., Kiron, D., Buckley, N.: Strategy, not technology, drives digital transformation. MIT Sloan Manage. Rev. (2015). http://sloanreview.mit.edu/projects/strategy-not-technology-drives-digital-transformation
23. Teubner, R.A., Stockhinger, J.: Literature review: understanding information systems strategy in the digital age. J. Strateg. Inform. Syst. **29**(4), 101642 (2020). https://doi.org/10.1016/j.jsis.2020.101642
24. El-Masri, M., Orozco, J., Tarhini, A., Tarhini, T.: The impact of is-business alignment practices on organizational choice of IS-business alignment strategies. In: PACIS 2015 Proceedings (2015)
25. Bharadwaj, A., El Sawy, O.A., Pavlou, P.A., Venkatraman, N.: Digital business strategy: toward a next generation of insights. MIS Q. **37**(2), 471–482 (2013)
26. Lipsmeier, A., Kühn, A., Joppen, R., Dumitrescu, R.: Process for the development of a digital strategy. Procedia CIRP **88**, 173–178 (2020). https://doi.org/10.1016/j.procir.2020.05.031
27. Drnevich, P.L., Croson, D.C.: Information technology and business-level strategy: toward an integrated theoretical perspective. MIS Q. **37**(2), 483–509 (2013)
28. Peppard, J., Ward, J.: The Strategic Management of Information Systems. Building a Digital Strategy, 4th edn. (2016)
29. Ross, J.W., Sebastian, I.M., Beath, C., Moloney, K.G., Mocker, M., Fonstad, N.O.: Designing and executing digital strategies. In: Thirty Seventh International Conference on Information Systems, Dublin (2016)
30. Vial, G.: Understanding digital transformation: a review and a research agenda. J. Strateg. Inform. Syst. **28**(2), 118–144 (2019). https://doi.org/10.1016/j.jsis.2019.01.003
31. Ziyadin, S., Suieubayeva, S., Utegenova, A.: Digital transformation in business. In: Ashmarina, S.I., Vochozka, M., Mantulenko, V.V. (eds.) Digital Age: Chances, Challenges and Future, pp. 408–415. Springer International Publishing, Cham (2020). https://doi.org/10.1007/978-3-030-27015-5_49
32. Talaulicar, W.Q., Judge, T.: Board involvement in the strategic decision making process: a comprehensive review. Ann. Corp. Governance **2**(2), 51–169 (2017). https://doi.org/10.1561/109.00000005
33. O'Shannassy, T.: Board and CEO practice in modern strategy-making: how is strategy developed, who is the boss and in what circumstances? J. Manag. Organ. **16**(2), 280–298 (2010). https://doi.org/10.5172/jmo.16.2.280
34. Eulerich, M., Stiglbauer, M.: The supervision of strategy and risk in German two-tier boards: lessons learned from the crisis. Int. J. Manag. Pract. **6**(3), 220 (2013). https://doi.org/10.1504/IJMP.2013.055832
35. Zahra, S.A., Pearce, J.A.: Boards of directors and corporate financial performance: a review and integrative model. J. Manage. **15**(2), 291–334 (1989). https://doi.org/10.1177/014920638901500208
36. Klarner, P., Probst, G., Useem, M.: Opening the black box: unpacking board involvement in innovation. Strateg. Organ. **18**(4), 487–519 (2020). https://doi.org/10.1177/1476127019839321
37. Brauer, M., Schmidt, S.L.: Defining the strategic role of boards and measuring boards' effectiveness in strategy implementation. Corp. Gov. **8**(5), 649–660 (2008). https://doi.org/10.1108/14720700810913304

38. Weill, P., Apel, T., Woerner, S., Banner, J.: It pays to have a digitally savvy board. MIT Sloan Manag. Rev., 41–45 (2019)
39. Jasiński, B.: The role of the supervisory board in the process of shaping the company's innovativeness (2022). https://www.wir.ue.wroc.pl
40. Mähring, M. : The Role of the Board of Directors in IT Governance: A Review and Agenda for Research (2006). http://aisel.aisnet.org/amcis2006/377
41. Deffenbaugh, J.: Houston, we've had a problem here: Tackling board governance. Br. J. Healthc. Manag. 21(7), 304–309 (2015). https://doi.org/10.12968/bjhc.2015.21.7.304
42. Mcnulty, T., Pettigrew, A.: The contribution, power and influence of part-time board members. Corp. Governance: An Int. Rev. 4(3), 160–179 (1996). https://doi.org/10.1111/j.1467-8683. 1996.tb00145.x
43. Long, T., Dulewicz, V., Gay, K.: The Role of the Non-executive Director: findings of an empirical investigation into the differences between listed and unlisted UK boards. Corp. Governance: An Int. Rev. 13(5), 667–679 (2005). https://doi.org/10.1111/j.1467-8683.2005. 00458.x
44. Long, T.: The evolution of FTSE 250 boards of directors: key factors influencing board performance and effectiveness. J. Gen. Manag. 32(3), 45–60 (2007)
45. Parent, M., Reich, B.H.: Governing information technology risk. California Manag. Rev. 51(3), 134–152 (2009). https://doi.org/10.2307/41166497
46. Sheaff, R., Endacott, R., Jones, R., Woodward, V.: Interaction between non-executive and executive directors in English National Health Service trust boards: an observational study. BMC Health Serv. Res. (2015). https://doi.org/10.1186/s12913-015-1127-2
47. Bart, C., Turel, O.: The role of the board in IT governance: current and desired oversight practices. Int. J. Bus. Governance Ethics 4(4), 316 (2009). http://www.corporatemissionsinc. com
48. Hom, C.L., Samson, D., Cebon, P.B., Cregan, C.: Inside the black box: an investigation of non-executive director activity through the lens of dynamic capability. Asia Pac. J. Manag. 38(3), 857–895 (2021). https://doi.org/10.1007/s10490-019-09693-x
49. De Haas, R., Ferreira, D., Kirchmaier, T.: The inner workings of the board: evidence from emerging markets. Emerg. Markets Rev. 48, 100777 (2021). https://doi.org/10.1016/j.eme mar.2020.100777
50. Cindrić, L.: Supervisory board's contribution to corporate strategy: evidence from croatian companies. Stud. Bus. Econ. 16(1), 42–50 (2021). https://doi.org/10.2478/sbe-2021-0004
51. Madhani, P.M.: Diverse roles of corporate board: review of various corporate governance theories. The IUP J. Corp. Gov. 16(2), 7–28 (2017). https://ssrn.com/abstract=2981605

Benchmarking Open Government Data (OGD) Curriculum in Universities

Georgios Papageorgiou[1], Ricardo Matheus[2], Charalampos Alexopoulos[1],
Guilherme Wiedenhöft[3], Euripides Loukis[1], Nina Rizun[4], Yannis Charalabidis[1],
and Stuti Saxena[5(✉)]

[1] University of the Aegean, Mitilini, Greece
[2] TU Delft, Delft, The Netherlands
[3] Federal University of RioGrande, RioGrande, Brazil
[4] Gdansk University of Technology, Gdańsk, Poland
[5] Nainital, India

stutisaxenaogd.vishnu@gmail.com

Abstract. Whilst there is a need for furthering the engagement of the universities in imbibing the Open Government Data (OGD) curriculum in their graduate and postgraduate courses, there has been no systematic research focused on the identification of the qualitative benchmarking regarding the curriculum of OGD-focused academic programmes. Benchmarking the OGD curriculum with the adoption of best practices among the universities is pertinent given the significant role of the students and other faculty members in the value derivation and innovation pursuits in their current and futuristic capacities. Drawing inferences from the QS World University rankings, 2023, via the BEKA (benchmarking, evidencing, knowing, applying) analysis, this paper identifies the best practices in qualitative terms for furthering dialogue and discourse among the university stakeholders and others in the OGD ecosystem. Specifically, a detailed course structure is provided for OGD courses which may serve as benchmarks for further foundation-laying of OGD curriculum in different varsities. As a first contribution towards identification of the best practices in the OGD-focused curriculum designing, the study contributes towards OGD literature, in general, and the benchmarking practices in OGD-focused discourse, in specific.

Keywords: Open government data · OGD · curriculum · benchmarking · qualitative analysis

1 Introduction

Despite the cruciality of Open Government Data (OGD) initiatives in terms of their applications in furthering value derivation and innovation [1] by the myriad stakeholders [2] thereby contributing to the economic growth of the country [3], the infusion and integration of OGD-based curriculum in the universities is yet to attain its credible standard. This is surprising given the upsurge in OGD-hinged research and conferences

M. Janssen et al. (Eds.): I3E 2023, LNCS 14316, pp. 127–138, 2023.
https://doi.org/10.1007/978-3-031-50040-4_10

and other forums for deliberation and discussion on OGD's status and progress so far [4–6]. OGD curriculum should taken into consideration the technical, operational and application dimensions with the invocation of contemporary case studies and relevant examples underlining the drivers, barriers and possibilities of OGD for the OGD suppliers and OGD users/prosumers hailing from a cross-section of society including the citizens, software app developers, professionals, and the like. The present study seeks to present a benchmarking framework to identify the best practices in designing OGD curriculum in universities by deploying the BEKA (benchmarking, evidencing, knowing, applying) evaluation framework [7–9]. BEKA evaluation framework rests on the premise that curriculum designing should incorporate dimensions of currency, relevance, strategic execution, scrutiny, feedback and control mechanisms. Specifically, the BEKA evaluation framework shall be applied across the key parameters of OGD curriculum sourced from the top-notch universities identified in the QS World University Rankings, 2023 [10][1].

The overarching research question for the study is: *"What is the basic OGD curriculum framework which may be followed as a benchmark for the other universities to further the expanse of OGD in academic arena?"* Furthermore, the study's originality rests on the fact that this is the first attempt at providing a benchmark for OGD-focused curriculum in the universities. Thus, apart from contributing towards the extant OGD literature thereby providing leads for further exploration, the study has significant insights for the academic practitioners as well as policy-makers too. The remainder of the paper is sequenced as follows: Sect. 2 provides a brief about OGD, Sect. 3 provides the research methodology and Sect. 4 elaborates upon the application of BEKA evaluation framework for deducing benchmarks for designing OGD curriculum alongside the Discussion of the findings while Sect. 5 concludes the study along with academic and practical implications.

2   Related Research

OGD
OGD refers to the strucrural and functional datasets pertaining to the administrative entites wherein these datasets are published on dedicated web portlas [11]. The objectives of OGD initiatives are furthering transparency, citizen collaboration and trust [12]. As far as providing the necessary impetus to citizen collaboration and participation is concerned, it is anticipated that stakeholders hailing from diverse societal segments, including the citizens, professionals, software app developers and the like, would re-use the datasets for value creation and innovation by interlinking them [13, 14]. OGD are accessible in machine-readable formats and are license-free [15]. With the possibilities of value derivation and innovation, it is liable that ecomic growth of the country would result from such pursuits [3, 16].

OGD Adoption Among the Government Agencies
As such, extant research has underlined the drivers, barriers and possibilities for OGD

---

[1] Universities filtered for the analysis are available at the github repository.

re-use by the different stakeholders. For instance, organizational entities adopt OGD contingent upon the perceived benefits, organizational reasiness and contextual factors-case in point being Taiwanese government entities [17]. Similarly, in the Malaysian context, it was found that public sector entities considered organizational context (top management support, organizational culture) and technological context (complexity, relative advantage) as pertinent for being adopted [18]. In the context of Madrid, the adoption of OGD was considered important from the perspective of the policy entrepreneurs who championed the case of OGD Initiatives for frthering transparency and citizen participation in the administrative system including the OGD policies [19]. Across the four European countries of France, Italy, Spain and the United Kingdom, it was shown that factors such as the need for furthering innovation and transparency apart from providing the necessary impetus to public-private collaboration are responsible for OGD adoption by the governments [20]. Government agencies in Pakistan are liable to adopt OGD given the judicious availability of technical and technological capacities [21]. For US, an innovative and flexible organizational culture was considered pertinent for government agencies to adopt OGD [22]. In the context of Australian government entities, it was found that political and bureaucratic leadership, institutional pressure, digital technologies, perceived interoperability, organizational readiness and management commitment are significant determinants of OGD adoption [23, 24]. It has been attested that incentives should be provided to the OGD implementors and strategists in the government bodies for furthering OGD adoption [25] given the tendency to resist adoption of OGD given the increase in workload and general unwillingness, etc. [26]-case in point being the Chinese government bodies. Finally, in the case of Tanzania, it was clinched that there are organizational, social, lega and technical barriers towards OGD initiative's institutionalization [27].

OGD Adoption Among the Users

Among the first significant studies on OGD adoption among the users may be counted the work of Zuiderwijk and her colleagues [28] wherein it was attested that users' (i.e. the conference participants, citizens, researchers, citizens and civil servants) engagement with OGD is furthered by the determinants like performance expectancy, effort expectancy, social influence and voluntariness of use-the constituent constructs of the Unified Theory of Acceptance and Use of Technology (UTAUT). Among the users belonging to different backgrounds, performance expectancy, effort expectancy, social influence and facilitating conditions were found to have direct impact on users' satisfaction with OGD usage [29]. In the UK, citizens' adoption of OGD was found to be a factor of relative advantage, compatibility and observability [30]. Likewise, OGD adoption and usage among the university students was determined by a host of factors including the anticipated role of OGD for academic performance and credibility of OGD and its sources [31]. Among the German citizens, it was attested that ease of use, usefulness, intrinsic motivation and internet competence determined the propensity of OGD adoption and usage [32]. Based on a heterogenous set of Taiwanese user innovators hailing from diverse backgrounds like academics, administration, managers, information technology specialists and managers, etc., it was attested that computer self-efficacy and social influence were significant determinants of OGD adoption [33]. In another study involving a heterogenous cohort of users based in India, it was found that apart from the significant influence of performance expectancy, effort expectancy, facilitating conditions and social influence, the purposes of using OGD among the males and females differed with the former preferring OGD usage for professional purposes and latter tapping OGD for non-professional and personal use as well [34]. In another developing country's context, it was found that citizens' requirement in terms of urgency, skills and usage of social media determined OGD adoption [35]. An empirical study contextualized in Brazil showed that apart from the influence of perceived ease of use, usefulness, intrinsic motivation, political satisfaction, government trust and internet use, demographic variables like education, income and region also determined the OGD adoption propensities in direct and indirect ways [36]. Even in the case of Bangladesh, it was found that OGD adoption among the citizens was a function of performance expectancy, effort expectancy, social influence, system quality and information quality [37]. In Saudi Arabian context, it was inferred that the OGD adoption and usage was pronounced among the researchers and scholars on account of the possibilities of facilitating research [38]. Finally, it has been shown in a longitudinal study covering 90 countries across 2013-2016 that OGD publishing has been found to have direct impact on furthering entrepreneurship [39].

Research Rationale

Given the impetus upon value derivation and innovation by the stakeholders, it is essential to understand how OGD curriculum may be better integrated in the higher education system for benefitting the academic community, and, the community, in turn. Keeping this dimension into consideration, the present research seeks to present a benchmarking framework regarding the OGD curriculum designing in the universities. Furthermore, a basic OGD courseware is provided to serve as a benchmark for universities to adopt in order to broadbase the expanse of OGD.

3 Research Methodology

BEKA analysis was used for the study. The first stage is benchmarking for which the curriculum of the top-notch universities [10] having integrated OGD syllabus in their certificate/undergraduate/postgraduate programmes were studied and compared. In the second stage of evidencing, the aims of the OGD-focused curriculum across the universities were compared and contrasted alongside the conducting of interviews with the researchers and course instructors of OGD to arrive at the key concentration areas of OGD curriculum [40–42]. Since the present study sought to address a novel RQ for which OGD literature is yet to identify the rubrics, semi-structured interviews were conducted with academic professionals [43–45]. The third stage pertains to knowing and applying which includes interviewing the key experts vis-a-vis the 3 key concentration areas of OGD curriculum, viz., data analytics and programming languages; application of OGD via value derivation and innovation for user groups; and, research-focused or other domains. At the end of this analysis, the 'stated' and 'unstated' facets of OGD curriculum were identified [7, 9] (Table 1).

Table 1. Curriculum features derived from BEKA analysis

Stated facets of OGD curriculum	Unstated facets of OGD curriculum
Data analytics and programming should be a part of the curriculum	Such courses may be best positioned alongside applicative dimensions such as OGD linkages and interoperability, Big Data analytics, etc
Value derivation and innovation applications ought to be integrated in the curriculum	Utility, facilitators, barriers and potential of OGD needs to factor into account the state-of-the-art technologies including the Artificial Intelligence, Internet of Things, Blockchain, etc. Wherein stakeholders across myriad professional and non-professional streams might derive value and innovate upon their products/services, etc
Research/other usage	Inter-disciplinarity is essential for driving home the nuances of OGD re-use across a range of socio-economic sectors

4 Findings and Discussion

Benchmarking implies that a criterion is set against which the quality of an object or entity is estimated and assessed [46]. For the present study, the benchmarking of OGD curricula was attempted with the OGD-hinged curriculum being followed in the top-notch universities in the form of certificate/undergraduate/postgraduate programmes-this is in line with the previous research protocols [47]. Therefore, a two-pronged approach was adopted wherein evidentiary support lent by the OGD-hinged curriculum across the universities and the interviews of key stakeholders were scanned [48]. The curriculum was studied across horizontal (i.e. inter-university) and vertical (i.e. certificate, undergraduate versus postgraduate programmes) lines.

In the second stage of Evidencing, the universities' OGD curriculum was assessed based on the three-fold criteria: data analytics and programming, value derivation and innovation, and, research/other. For this, the OGD curriculum being offered by the university programme/course was studied in terms of its aims, syllabus, credits offered, fee structure, duration of the course, delivery mechanisms, assessment methods and the resources provisioned for the said course/programme. This step was important to ensure that the comparison may be done against the established benchmarks. Also, the curriculum 'stated' and 'unstated' aims and focus were studied across horizontal and vertical dimensions. Furthermore, content description, relevance and currency of the programme was studied alongside the objectives and aims and other metrics. A downside to the analysis relates to the fact that the figures for actual student enrollment or retention were not available to the researchers at the point of writing.

In the third stage of Knowing, the attempt is made to include the knowledge and the deeper comprehension of the relevant OGD professionals and experts regarding the curriculum. Therefore, interviews were undertaken with the experts who are researchers and/or teaching OGD-specific themes (Table 2). Such expert opinion is conducive towards identifying the lacunae and strengths of a curricula besides assessing the requirements and constraints associated with floating an 'ideal' OGD curriculum to facilitate teaching-learning process. Therefore, the experts' views were synthesized by the authors themselves to arrive at the inferences.

Table 2. Experts' background

Expert's academic background/*country*/research interests →
- Technology, Policy and Management, *The Netherlands*, Digital transformation, Business intelligence, Data protection
- Business Analytics, *Poland*, Big Data, Computational and Linguistic Analytics, Smart Sustainable Cities
- Business-Society Management, *The Netherlands*, Policy and governance, Planning and decision-making in China, Transport infrastructures, Sustainable urban development
- Information and Communications Systems Engineering, *Greece*, Data mining, Computer security and reliability, Artificial Intelligence
- Information and Communications Systems Engineering, *Greece*, Cybersecurity, Data privacy, Digital forensics, Gamification strategies, Open and linked data ecosystems

---

The model curriculum is designed as per Table 3.

Table 3. Model OGD Curriculum

Open Government Data (OGD) Curriculum
Programme & Course Structure
Vision: As the dawn of globalized higher education policies unravel their shimmer across the higher education landscape, it behooves upon the stakeholders to conceive a roadmap for refurbishing the ecosystem from the perspective of the undergraduate and postgraduate degree courses. In this vein, the state-of-the-art technological interfaces[a] upon the socio-economic fabric are seemingly perceptible wherein the administrative datasets published via the dedicated web portals, so-called the Open Government Data (OGD), are making giant strides not only in terms of refurbishing the image of the government in terms of increased transparency but also in terms of unfolding the possibilities of value derivation and innovation by a range of stakeholders, including the citizens, professionals, businesses, and the like. Thus, the globally-acclaimed (*Name of the University*) is poised to launch a full-fledged ***Open Government Data (OGD)*** Course wherein the infusion of specialized programming, advanced analytics, Artificial Intelligence (AI) and Machine Learning (ML) in the multi-pronged heterogeneous OGD shall culminate in an integrated degree programme
Purpose: As a step forward towards (*University vision*), the purport of the ***Open Government Data (OGD)*** integrated programme is to churn out technologically-grounded youth with a social visage such that their vaulting spree in their preferred career gets the best niche and recognition
Structure: The 5-year integrated ***Open Government Data (OGD)*** programme is a platform for furthering the already-established (University's) transformational learning teaching-learning process. The five-year integrated programme runs across 10 semesters interspersed with internships, hackathons and attache opporunities. The flagship programme shall progress from preliminaries (Pre) edifice (First and Second Semester) prior to scaling (Sc) itself from Third until Sixth Semester and attaining its avowed tour de force (TdF) state from Seventh until Tenth Semester

---

Open Government Data (OGD) First Semester

OGD Pre-I (7C)	Foundations of Statistics-I	Fundamentals of Computing & Data Science	R programming[b]	GitHub notebook[c]
	Introduction to Open Government Data (OGD)	Core Course-1 (Facilitating and Dampening forces for OGD initiatives)	Core Course-2 (OGD Ecosystem)	Microsoft Office-Word[d] & Microsoft Power Point[e]

(*continued*)

Table 3. (*continued*)

Open Government Data (OGD) Second Semester			
OGD Pre-II (7C)	Foundations of Statistics-II	R programming[f]	GitHub notebook[g]	Microsoft Office-Excel[h]
	Core Course-3 (Case studies of OGD Initiatives by governments-I)	Core Course-4 (Re-using OGD by stakeholders-I)	Core Course-5 (OGD Quality Metrics and Benchmarking-I)	Core Course-6 (Institutional dimensions of OGD-I)
Open Government Data (OGD) Third Semester				
OGDSc-I (7C)	Foundations of Statistics-III	Python language[i]	Apache Hadoop[j]	D3.js[k]
	Core Course-7 (Case studies of OGD Initiatives by governments-II)	Core Course-8 (Re-using OGD by stakeholders-II)	Core Course-9 (OGD Quality Metrics and Benchmarking-II)	Elective-½ (Institutional dimensions of OGD-II)
Open Government Data (OGD) Fourth Semester				
OGD Sc-II (7C)	Foundations of Statistics-IV	Python language[l]	Apache Hadoop[m]	D3.js[n]
	Core Course-10 (Case studies of OGD Initiatives by governments-III)	Core Course-11 (Re-using OGD by stakeholders-II)	Elective ¾ (OGD Quality Metrics and Benchmarking-III)	Elective-$^5/_6$ (Institutional dimensions of OGD-III)
	Summer Internship (preferably with a government organization with value derivation/innovation applications			
Open Government Data (OGD) Fifth Semester				
OGD Sc-III (9C)	Statistics for society-I	PyTorch[o]	Apache MXNet[p]	Apache CouchDB[q]
	Core Course-12 (Case studies of OGD Initiatives by governments-IV)	Core Course-13 (Re-using OGD by stakeholders-IV)	Elective $^7/_8$ (OGD Quality Metrics and Benchmarking-IV)	Elective 9/10 (Institutional dimensions of OGD-IV)
Open Government Data (OGD) Sixth Semester				
OGD Sc-IV (7C)	Statistics for so ciety-II	PyTorch[r]	Apache MXNet[s]	Apache CouchDB[t]
	Core Course-14 (Case studies of OGD Initiatives by governments-V)	Core Course-15 (Re-using OGD by stakeholders-V)	Elective 10/11 (OGD Quality Metrics and Benchmarking-V)	Elective 12/13 (Institutional dimensions of OGD-V)
Open Government Data (OGD) Seventh Semester				
OGD TdF-I (7C)	Cloud computing-I	IBM Cognos[u]	RawGraphs[v]	SPSS[w]
	Core Course-16 (OGD & Law-I)	Elective Course-14/15 (OGD & Artificial Intelligence (AI))	Hackathon-I	
Open Government Data (OGD) Eighth Semester				
OGD TdF-II (7C)	Cloud computing-II	IBM Cognos[x]	RawGraphs[y]	SPSS[z]
	Core Course-17 (OGD & Law-II)	Elective Course-16/17 (OGD Prosumers-II)	Hackathon-II	
Open Government Data (OGD) Ninth Semester				
OGD TdF-III (7C)	IBM Cloud Paks[aa]	Watson Studio[ab]	Attache-I programme (Innovative solutions' application in an organization under the aegis of an official/personnel)	
	Core Course-18 (OGD Psychology and Marketing-I)	Elective Course-18/19 (OGD Prosumers-III)	Attache-II programme (Innovative solutions' application in an organization under the aegis of an official/personnel)	
Open Government Data (OGD) Tenth Semester				
OGD TdF-IV (7C)	IBM Cloud Paks[ac]	Watson Studio[ad]	Reflection & The Grand Finale (Channelizing national and international dialogue, discussion and analysis of the learning so far and projecting its applications for Society 6.0 & Industry 5.0)	

(*continued*)

Table 3. (*continued*)

	Core Course-19 (OGD Psychology and Marketing-II)	Elective Course-20/21 (OGD Prosumers-IV)		
	Snapshot of the 5-year Open Government Data (OGD) (C: Credits) *Pre-requisites:* A penchant for learning is all that is required so that whilst you're standing on the shoulders of giants, your job market pitch is well above the threshold decibels! Easy, huh! So, plunge in			

[a] BM (2022). What is data science? Available at https://www.ibm.com/topics/data-science accessed on 2nd February, 2023

[b] R programming (2023). R 4.2.2. https://www.r-project.org/.

[c] GutHub (2023). GitHub. https://github.com/.

[d] MS Word (2023). https://www.microsoft.com/en-ww/microsoft-365/word?activetab=tabs%3af aqheaderregion3.

[e] MS Power Point (2023). MS Power Point. https://www.microsoft.com/en-in/microsoft-365/pow erpoint.

[f] R programming (2023). R 4.2.2. https://www.r-project.org/.

[g] GutHub (2023). GitHub. https://github.com/.

[h] MS Excel (2023). MS Excel. https://www.microsoft.com/en-ww/microsoft-365/excel.

[i] Python (2023). Python 3.11.1. https://www.python.org/.

[j] Apache Hadoop (2023). Apache Hadoop 3.3.4. https://hadoop.apache.org/.

[k] D3.js (2023).d3-7.8.2.tgz. https://d3js.org/.

[l] Python (2023). Python 3.11.1. https://www.python.org/.

[m] Apache Hadoop (2023). Apache Hadoop 3.3.4. https://hadoop.apache.org/.

[n] D3.js (2023).d3–7.8.2.tgz. https://d3js.org/.

[o] PyTorch (2023). PyTorch 1.13.1. https://pytorch.org/.

[p] Apache MXNet (2023). Apache MXNet 1.9.1. https://mxnet.apache.org/versions/1.9.1/.

[q] Apache CouchDB (2023). Apache CouchDB 3.3.1. https://couchdb.apache.org/.

[r] PyTorch (2023). PyTorch 1.13.1. https://pytorch.org/.

[s] Apache MXNet (2023). Apache MXNet 1.9.1. https://mxnet.apache.org/versions/1.9.1/.

[t] Apache CouchDB (2023). Apache CouchDB 3.3.1. https://couchdb.apache.org/.

[u] Cognos Analytics (2023). Watson 11.2.2. https://www.ibm.com/in-en/products/cognos-ana lytics.

[v] RawGraphs (2023). RawGraphs 2.0. https://www.rawgraphs.io/.

[w] SPSS (2023). IBM SPSS 29.0 software. https://www.ibm.com/products/spss-statistics-gra dpack#3066862.

[x] Cognos Analytics (2023). Watson 11.2.2. https://www.ibm.com/in-en/products/cognos-ana lytics.

[y] RawGraphs (2023). RawGraphs 2.0. https://www.rawgraphs.io/.

[z] SPSS (2023). IBM SPSS 29.0 software. https://www.ibm.com/products/spss-statistics-gra dpack#3066862.

[aa] IBM Cloud Paks (2023). IBM Cloud Paks. https://www.ibm.com/cloud-paks.

[ab] IBM Watson Studio. https://www.ibm.com/cloud/watson-studio/autoai.

[ac] IBM Cloud Paks (2023). IBM Cloud Paks. https://www.ibm.com/cloud-paks.

[ad] IBM Watson Studio. https://www.ibm.com/cloud/watson-studio/autoai.

5 Conclusion

In order to arrive at a somewhat 'ideal' OGD curriculum against which the universities could benchmark their OGD curriculum, the present study sought to present a BEKA analysis of the OGD curriculum across certificate/undergraduate/postgraduate programmes across universities as per the QS World University Rankings, 2023. Whilst the first three components of BEKA could be done in this study backed by expert opinion, the fourth stage of empirically validating the OGD curriculum shall be attempted in the successive research. However, as a primer towards furthering a benchmarking analysis in the realm of OGD curriculum, the study adds to the OGD literature as also pushing forth a sense of urgency as far as refurbishing and institutionalizing state-of-the-art OGD curriculum is concerned which caters to the needs of the different stakeholders.

The study leaves academic implications in that further research is warranted to undertake the fourth stage of BEKA across developed and developing countries to draw inferences regarding the benchmarked OGD curriculum as per the students' needs and expectations alongside the resources available in the different contexts and programme formats. The study holds practitioner implications as well in terms of the policy-makers' involvement in refurbishing the OGD initiatives per se for furthering value derivation and innovation pursuits by the stakeholders which would sped up dialogue and deliberation upon the restructuring and rejigging OGD curriclum formats in the universities.

References

1. Jetzek, T., Avital, M., Bjorn-Andersem, N.: Data-driven innovation through open government data. J. Theor. Appl. Electron. Commer. Res. **9**(2), 100–120 (2012). https://doi.org/10.4067/S0718-18762014000200008
2. Ubaldi, B.: Open government data: towards empirical analysis of open government data initiatives. In: OECD Working Papers on Public Governance, vol. 22. OECD Publishing Press (2013). https://doi.org/10.1787/5k46bj4f03s7-en
3. Zeleti, F.A., Ojo, A., Curry, E.: Exploring the economic value of open government data. Gov. Inf. Q. **33**(3), 535–551 (2016). https://doi.org/10.1016/j.giq.2016.01.008
4. Charalabidis, Y., Alexopoulos, C., Loukis, E.: A taxonomy of open government data research areas and topics. J. Organ. Comput. Electron. Comm. **26**(1–2), 41–63 (2016). https://doi.org/10.1080/10919392.2015.1124720
5. Wirtz, B.W., Becker, M., Weyerer, J.C.: Open government: development, concept, and future research directions. Int. J. Public Admin. **46**(12), 797–812 (2023). https://doi.org/10.1080/01900692.2021.2019273
6. Mohamad, A.N., Sylvester, A., Campbell-Meier, J.: Towards a taxonomy of research areas in open government data. Online Inform. Rev. (2023). https://doi.org/10.1108/OIR-02-2022-0117
7. Glatthorn, A.A.: Curriculum Leadership. Scott, Foresman and Company, Glenview, Illinois (1987)
8. Glatthorn, A.A.: Curriculum alignment revisted. J. Curriculum Supervision **15**(1), 26–34. (1999). https://www.proquest.com/docview/196371805
9. Print, M.: Curriculum Development and Design. Allen and Unwin, St Leonards, NSW (1993)
10. QS World University Rankings. https://www.topuniversities.com/qs-world-university-rankings/methodology (2023)

11. Gao, Y., Janssen, M., Zhang, C.: Understanding the evolution of open government data research: towards open data sustainability and smartness. Int. Rev. Adm. Sci. **89**(1), 59–75 (2023). https://doi.org/10.1177/00208523211009955

12. Coglianese, C.: The transparency president? the Obama administration and open government. Governance-An Int. J. Policy, Adm., Institutions **22**(4), 529–544 (2009). https://doi.org/10.1111/j.1468-0491.2009.01451.x

13. Evans, A.M., Campos, A.: Open government initiatives: Challenges of citizen participation. J. Policy Anal. Manage. **32**(1), 172–185 (2013). https://doi.org/10.1002/pam.21651

14. Gonzalez-Zapata, F., Heeks, R.: The multiple meanings of open government data: understanding different stakeholders and their perspectives. Gov. Inform. Q. **32**(4), 441–452 (2015). https://doi.org/10.1016/j.giq.2015.09.001

15. Kalampokis, E., Tambouris, E., Tarabanis, K.: Open government data: a stage model. In: Janssen, M., Scholl, H.J., Wimmer, M.A., Tan, Y.H. (eds.) Electronic Government, pp. 235–246. Springer Berlin Heidelberg, Berlin, Heidelberg (2011). https://doi.org/10.1007/978-3-642-22878-0_20

16. Saxena, S.: Prospects of open government data (OGD) in facilitating the economic diversification of GCC region. Inform. Learn. Sci. **118**(5/6), 214–234 (2017). https://doi.org/10.1108/ILS-04-2017-0023

17. Wang, H.J., Jin, L.: Adoption of open government data among government agencies. Gov. Inf. Q. **33**(1), 80–88 (2016). https://doi.org/10.1016/j.giq.2015.11.004

18. Mustapa, M.N., Hamid, S., Md Nasaruddin, F.H.: Factors influencing open government data post-adoption in the public sector: the perspective of data providers. PLOS ONE **17**(11), e0276860 (2022). https://doi.org/10.1371/journal.pone.0276860

19. Ruvalcaba-Gomez, E.A., Criado, J.I., Gil-Garcia, J.R.: Analyzing open government policy adoption through the multiple streams framework: the roles of policy entrepreneurs in the case of Madrid. Public Policy Admin. **38**(2), 233–264 (2023). https://doi.org/10.1177/0952076720936349

20. De Blasio, E., Selva, D.: Why choose open government? Motivations for the adoption of open government policies in four European countries. Policy Internet **8**(3), 225–247 (2016). https://doi.org/10.1002/poi3.118

21. Khurshid, M.M., Zakaria, N.H., Arfeen, M.I., Rashid, A., Shehzad, H.M.F., Ahmad, M.N.: An intention-adoption behavioral model for open government data in pakistan's public sector organizations–an exploratory study. In: Sharma, S.K., Dwivedi, Y.K., Metri, B., Rana, N.P. (eds.) Re-imagining Diffusion and Adoption of Information Technology and Systems: A Continuing Conversation: IFIP WG 8.6 International Conference on Transfer and Diffusion of IT, TDIT 2020, Tiruchirappalli, India, December 18–19, 2020, Proceedings, Part I, pp. 377–388. Springer International Publishing, Cham (2020). https://doi.org/10.1007/978-3-030-64849-7_34

22. Grimmelikhuijsen, S.G., Feeney, M.K.: Developing and testing an integrative framework for open government adoption in local governments. Public Admin. Rev. **77**(4), 579–590 (2017). https://doi.org/10.1111/puar.12689

23. Chatfield, A.T., Reddick, C.G.: The role of policy entrepreneurs in open government data policy innovation diffusion: an analysis of Australian Federal and State governments. Gov. Inf. Q. **35**(1), 123–134 (2018). https://doi.org/10.1016/j.giq.2017.10.004

24. Hossain, M.A., Chan, C.: Open data adoption in Australian government agencies: an exploratory study. In: Australian Conference on Information Systems, Adelaide. (2015). https://doi.org/10.48550/arXiv.1606.02500

25. Zhang, H., Bi, Y., Kang, F., Wang, Z.: Incentive mechanisms for government officials' implementing open government data in China. Online Inform. Rev. **46**(2), 224–243 (2022). https://doi.org/10.1108/OIR-05-2020-0154

26. Li, S., Chen, Y.: Explaining the resistance of data providers to open government data. Aslib J. Inf. Manag. **73**(4), 560–577 (2021). https://doi.org/10.1108/AJIM-09-2020-0270

27. Shao, D.D., Saxena, S.: Barriers to open government data (OGD) initiative in Tanzania: stakeholders' perspectives. Growth Chang. **50**(1), 470–485 (2019). https://doi.org/10.1111/grow.12282

28. Zuiderwijk, A., Janssen, M., Dwivedi, Y.K.: Acceptance and use predictors of open data technologies: drawing upon the unified theory of acceptance and use of technology. Gov. Inf. Q. **32**(4), 429–440 (2015). https://doi.org/10.1016/j.giq.2015.09.005

29. Islam, M.T., Talukder, M.S., Khayer, A., Islam, A.K.M.N.: Exploring continuance intention toward open government data technologies: an integrated approach. VINE J. Inform. Knowl. Manag. Syst. **53**(4), 785–807 (2023). https://doi.org/10.1108/VJIKMS-10-2020-0195

30. Weerakkody, V., Irani, Z., Kapoor, K., Sivarajah, U., Dwivedi, Y.K.: Open data and its usability: an empirical view from the citizen's perspective. Inf. Syst. Front. **19**, 285–300 (2017). https://doi.org/10.1007/s10796-016-9679-1

31. Lnenicka, M., Nikiforova, A., Saxena, S., Singh, P.: Investigation into the adoption of open government data among students: the behavioral intention-based comparison of three countries. Aslib J. Inf. Manag. **74**(3), 549–567 (2022). https://doi.org/10.1108/AJIM-08-2021-0249

32. Wirtz, B.W., Weyerer, J.C., Rosch, M.: Citizen and open government: an empirical analysis of antecedents of open government data. Int. J. Public Admin. **41**(4), 308–320 (2018). https://doi.org/10.1080/01900692.2016.1263659

33. Wang, H.J.: Adoption of open government data: perspectives of user innovators. Inform. Res. **25**(1). (2020). https://informationr.net/ir/25-1/paper849.html

34. Saxena, S., Janssen, M.: Examining open government data (OGD) usage in India through UTAUT framework. Foresight **19**(4), 421–436 (2017). https://doi.org/10.1108/FS-02-2017-0003

35. Purwanto, A., Zuiderwijk, A., Janssen, M.: Citizen engagement with open government data: lessons learned from Indonesia's presidential election. Transfor. Govern.: People, Process Policy **14**(1), 1–30 (2020). https://doi.org/10.1108/TG-06-2019-0051

36. De Souza, A.A.C., d'Angelo, M.J., Filho, R.N.L.: Effects of predictors of citizens' attitudes and intention to use open government data and government 2.0. Govern. Inform. Q. **39**(2), 101663 (2022). https://doi.org/10.1016/j.giq.2021.101663

37. Talukder, M.S., Shen, L., Talukder, M.F.H., Bao, Y.: Determinants of user acceptance and use of open government data (OGD): an empirical investigation in Bangladesh. Technol. Soc. **56**, 147–156 (2019). https://doi.org/10.1016/j.techsoc.2018.09.013

38. Shehata, A., Elgllab, M.: Saudi scholars' perceptions and use of open government data portals at Sharqa University, Saudi Arabia. IFLA J. **47**(4), 493–504 (2021). https://doi.org/10.1177/03400352211023834

39. Huber, F., Ponce, A., Rentocchini, F., Walnwright, T.: The wealth of (open data) nations? Open government data, country-level institutions and entrepreneurial activity. Ind. Innov. **29**(8), 992–1023 (2022). https://doi.org/10.1080/13662716.2022.2109455

40. Krathwohl, D.R.: Educational and social science research. In: Cranton, P. (ed.) Planning Instruction for Adult Learners, 2nd edn. Wall and Emerson Inc, Toronto (1998)

41. Cranton, P.: Planning Instruction for Adult Learners. Wall and Emerson Inc., Toronto (2000)

42. Watchtler, C., Troein, M.: A hidden curriculum: mapping cultural competency in a medical programme. Med. Educ. **37**(10), 861–868 (2003). https://doi.org/10.1046/j.1365-2923.2003.01624.x

43. Doringer, S.: 'The problem-centered expert interview' Combining qualitative interviewing approaches for investigating implicit expert knowledge. Int. J. Soc. Res. Methodol. **24**(3), 265–278 (2021). https://doi.org/10.1080/13645579.2020.1766777

44. Maylor, H., Blackmon, K. Huemann, M.: Researching Business and Management, 2nd edn. Palgrave, McMillan Education, UK (2017)
45. Saunders, M., Lewis, P., Thornhill, A.: Research Methods for Business Students. Prentice Hall, Harlow, England (2007)
46. Vlasceanu, L., Grunberg, L., Parlea, D.: Quality Assurance and Accreditation: A Glossary of Basic Terms and Definitions. UNESCO, Bucharest (2007)
47. Robley, W., Whittle, S., Murdoch-Eaton, D.: Mapping generic skills curricula: outcomes and discussion. J. Furth. High. Educ. 29(4), 321–330 (2005). https://doi.org/10.1080/030987705 00353342
48. Keough, J.J., Fourie, W.J., Watson, S., Gay, H.: Involving the stakeholders in the curriculum process: a recipe for success? Nurse Educ. Today 30, 37–43 (2010). https://doi.org/10.1016/j.nedt.2009.05.017
49. Dean, J., Kenworthy, N. The principles of learning. In: Nicklin, P., Kenworthy, N. (eds.) Teaching & Assessing in Nursing Practice-An Experiential Approach. Bailliere Tindall: Edinburgh (2000)

Transforming the Internal Audit Function (IAF): An Integrated MICMAC-ISM Approach for Unravelling the Relationship Among Challenges

Mochammad Gilang Ramadhan(✉) ⓘ, Marijn Janssen ⓘ, and Haiko van der Voort ⓘ

Delft University of Technology, Delft, The Netherlands
m.g.ramadhan@tudelft.nl

Abstract. The transformation toward the use of data analytics requires overcoming many challenges. Nevertheless, the interconnections between the challenges are unclear. Gaining knowledge about these interconnections is important to prioritize strategies that aim to stimulate the transformation. This paper unravels the relationship among Audit Analytics (AA) implementation challenges to transform the Internal Audit Function (IAF) using *Matrice d'Impacts Croisés Multiplication Appliqués à un Classement* (MICMAC) – Interpretative Structural Modelling (ISM) (or MICMAC-ISM) to develop a hierarchical model and determine the relationships among the challenges and the degree of power of each challenge. We collect data from internal auditors experienced in using audit analytics. They suggest that cultural challenges, along with technical challenges, are critical for enabling transformation. Moreover, combinations of approaches are required to address the complex interrelationships among challenges to initiate transformation. The analysis suggests that AA implementation requires a top-down approach to address cultural challenges blended with a bottom-up strategy to overcome technical challenges.

Keywords: Audit Analytics · Internal Audit Function · MICMAC-ISM · Transformation

1 Introduction

Audit Analytics (AA) can potentially transform auditing, including Internal Audit Function (IAF). AA can be defined as "*the process of identifying, gathering, validating, analyzing, and interpreting digital data using information technology to further the purpose and mission of internal auditing*" [1]. The use of AA by IAF is more than a mere change of approach. AA reshapes all facets of the organization, including the required auditor's skill, the data collection and analysis, and how to deliver the results [2]. AA also influences the relationships and interactions between IAF and its stakeholders, such as data access and analytics process [3, 4]. The fundamental adjustments imply the need to adapt the current practices, actors, structures, and values [5] for AA implementation, which resembles a transformational effort by IAF.

© IFIP International Federation for Information Processing 2023
Published by Springer Nature Switzerland AG 2023
M. Janssen et al. (Eds.): I3E 2023, LNCS 14316, pp. 139–155, 2023.
https://doi.org/10.1007/978-3-031-50040-4_11

AA encompasses various types of techniques, from simple ones like computer-assisted audit techniques (CAAT), to more sophisticated ones like continuous auditing (CA), and advanced use of machine learning for fraud detection [6–9]. This approach enables IAF to improve its services' effectiveness and efficiency through real-time (or near real-time) testing and reporting, expansion of services and testing coverage, and providing insight and foresight for the organization to anticipate future risks and opportunities [9–12]. AA also allows for engagement to be performed remotely [13], which provides a significant benefit in the post-pandemic era.

While the potential benefit of AA is widely recognized, the use of this practice is surprisingly low [12, 14–16]. In this regard, IAF faces many challenges in implementing AA, ranging from organizational (e.g., funding, (internal) audit process, auditor's skills) to technological (e.g., IT infrastructure, data) and even (organization's) cultural aspects [17–21]. However, although challenges of AA implementation are mentioned, the extant literature lacks an understanding of their relationships and significance. Gaining knowledge about these interconnections is important to prioritize strategies that aim to stimulate the transformation. This understanding is needed to lay the ground for developing a transformation framework that can overcome the challenges and assist practitioners in addressing those challenges based on their interrelationships.

Therefore, this paper aims to fill the void in the extant literature by unraveling the relationships among challenges for AA implementation by IAF. For this purpose, this paper is structured as follows. The next section describes the research approach, followed by an explanation of data collection and analysis using the MICMAC-ISM approach to lay out the interrelation of challenges as this research's finding. The subsequent section discusses the resulting model's interpretation along with the scientific and practical implications. The final section concludes the paper and suggests fruitful endeavours for future research.

2 Research Approach

2.1 Literature Research

This research refers to the previous literature review by Ramadhan et al. [1], which covers the extant literature discusses various aspects of AA from different perspectives and overview of challenges. The literature review obtained insight into the challenges related to AA implementation in IAF. It searched the literature using the keywords "audit analytics", "continuous audit", and "audit data analytics", combined with "implementation", "challenges", "factors", and "barriers", which resulted in 15 search strings. This approach aligns with the suggestion from vom Brocke et al. [22] to help ensure the relevance of the search results. The review focused on articles discussing AA in IAF settings. Nevertheless, some general and external audit literature relevant to IAF were found and included. The resulting articles were filtered based on their format and relevance, i.e., scientific publications (journal and conference paper and book section with an explicit method) and primary study of AA in the internal audit field or general audit with relevance to internal audit activity.

2.2 Analysis of the Challenges

This research adopted the *Matrice d'Impacts Croisés Multiplication Appliqués à un Classement* (MICMAC) – Interpretative Structural Modelling (ISM) (or MICMAC-ISM for short) method. MICMAC-ISM has been successfully utilized in studies on the barriers to innovation or technology implementation e.g., [23–26], which characterizes AA implementation. MICMAC-ISM assists in analyzing the complex and multifaceted system using a systematic approach to acquire practitioners' views on the matter being analyzed [23, 27] (see Fig. 1). This approach is arguably more robust and comprehensive than other multi-criteria decision-making approach like analytic network process (ANP) and analytical hierarchy process (AHP) [24, 26]. Further, practitioners' opinions incorporate their experience and the dynamics in the field over time, which improves the reliability of the analysis result.

For this research, the respondents were practitioners from IAF in a government institution with experience using AA in their internal audit activities. The setting and respondents were chosen since it has the revelatory characteristic of an emergent phenomenon being studied.

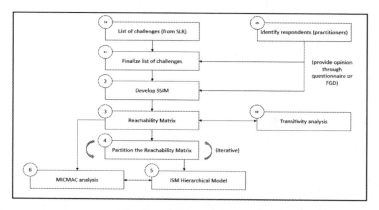

Fig. 1. MICMAC-ISM Steps

The first step was to finalize the challenges based on the practitioners' opinions. The respondent(s) are auditors with more than five years of experience, which included:

a) Auditors from IAF using AA in their (internal) audit projects, and
b) Employees of IAF who are involved in the development of AA in their institution.

This research asked respondents' views on the identified factors, i.e., their significance and additional factor(s), if any, using a questionnaire listing the factors (and a follow-up structured interview). The first step resulted in the final list of challenges.

The second step was to test the contextual relationship among the final list of challenges to develop the Structural Self-Interaction Matrix (SSIM). For this purpose, using the focused group discussion (FGD), participants were asked to determine the relationship between a pair of challenges. The SSIM was determined based on consensus among participants.

The SSIM transformed into a reachability matrix in the third step, i.e., a matrix showing relationships among challenges using binary notation (1 and 0, with 1 influencing another challenge and 0 influenced by another challenge). Transitivity analysis was performed to develop the final reachability matrix (FRM). In the fourth step, the FRM was partitioned iteratively to develop the hierarchy of challenges as the fifth step. Finally, MICMAC analysis used the final reachability matrix (FRM) to identify each factor's driving power and dependency. The MICMAC analysis then determines the position of each challenge as:

1) Autonomous, scored low in both driving power and dependence;
2) Independent, which has a high driving power;
3) Linkage, which is relatively high in both driving power and dependence; or
4) Dependent, scored high in dependence and low in driving power which informs that other challenges mostly influence the (said) challenge.

3 Data Analysis and Findings

3.1 Challenges of AA Implementation by IAF

A broad set of challenges emerged from the literature review. Some were organizational, whereas others were technical. Some challenges are related to the organization's operation or within the scope of authority of the organization, such as 'auditors' competence', 'cultural readiness', and 'organization and business complexity' [3, 18, 28, 29]. Other challenges refer to factors that are forced by authoritative entities like 'inadequate audit standard/guidelines' or 'independence impairment' [3, 4]. Moreover, as a technology-based innovation, some AA challenges pertinent to technology, such as 'data security concerns' or 'infrastructure capabilities' [30, 31]. Furthermore, some challenges reflect the problem related to audit activities, such as 'limited AA use-case', 'dynamics in audit process', or 'counter analytics' [3, 17, 32].

We follow up on the initial results with a group of practitioners. The respondents provided their views on the list of challenges using questionnaires and follow-up interviews[1]. Eleven practitioners participated in finalizing the list of challenges through questionnaires and follow-up interviews. All of the respondents have more than six years of experience in the internal audit, are involved in three or more AA projects, and hold relevant professional credentials in the technology-related audit fields, like certified Indonesian government auditor (JFA) or Certified Information System Auditor (CISA).

---

[1] The data collected from the respondents (presented throughout this paper) were in Indonesian, which was translated into English.

The questionnaire and interview used a 5-points Lickert scale (from 1-very insignif-icant, 3-neutral, to 5-very significant) and a narrative description to capture the respon-dents' opinions on the significance of each challenge. The significance of each challenge is assessed based on the view of participants from different organization units, i.e., the audit unit and research and development unit (or "Innovation Unit", in Krieger et al.'s [4] term). We considered the overall average score and the score from each business units to obtain more-balanced views of the challenges' significance to be included in the next analysis.

Further, we obtained follow-up interviews with some of the respondents to capture the importance (or lack of it) of the challenges. The follow up interviews provided additional insight. For instance, respondents #2 and #8 stated that some cultural characteristics like "reluctant to change", "expect instant result", and "fear of missing out", which are common in technology-based innovation in an organization, can significantly hinder AA implementation in IAF (see Table 1).

Table 1. List of Challenges (adapted from Ramadhan et al. [1])

#	Challenge	Description	References	Average Score (Audit)	Average Score (R&D)	**Average Score (overall)**
1	Inaccessible Data (for AA purposes)	Unavailability of digital data for the auditor to collect, evaluate, and analyze in the context of AA (including authorization, approval, and provision)	[18, 33]	4.43	5.00	4.64
2	Data Security Concerns	Concern regarding data confidentiality[1], i.e., the need to ensure data is accessible only to those with proper authorization, might affect data exchange among business/data owners and including IAF	[30]	3.43	4.25	3.73

(continued)

Table 1. (*continued*)

#	Challenge	Description	References	Average Score (Audit)	Average Score (R&D)	**Average Score (overall)**
3	Missing Data	Unavailability of data in the digital form required for AA within an organization's data ecosystem (including database or data warehouse)	[3, 18]	4.00	4.25	4.09
4	Lack of Cultural Readiness	Limited organizations' and IAF's awareness of the importance and benefit of AA and commitment to do the necessary process to implement AA	[3, 19, 21, 31]	4.86	4.25	4.64
5	Different Stakeholder's Interests	Problems due to varieties of perceptions, preferences, support, and interests among the related actors on the use of AA by IAF	[28, 34]	4.14	4.75	4.37
6	Auditor's AA-related Skills	The limitation of the Internal auditor's ability to perform the necessary task (e.g., obtain business understanding in IT-based environment, scripting, statistical knowledge) to use AA	[20, 29]	4.14	4.25	4.18

(*continued*)

Table 1. (*continued*)

#	Challenge	Description	References	Average Score (Audit)	Average Score (R&D)	**Average Score (overall)**
7	Dynamics in Audit Process	Unclear interaction mechanisms and dynamics between the auditor, client, and other stakeholders in internal audit tasks (or other related activities), including the use of AA in internal audit tasks	[17, 19, 35]	3.71	4.50	4.00
8	Organization and Business Complexity	Complex organizational structure and business processes, e.g. involving multiple systems and actors with different rules and regulations, including IT system complexity and variations, influence the effort required to implement AA	[18, 31]	3.71	3.75	3.73
9	Limited Use-Case availability	Limited audit analytics use cases appropriate for an assurance engagement by IAF. Audit analytics use-case includes the engagement objectives, analysis techniques, and data requirements for internal audit tasks	[4, 32, 36]	3.86	3.50	3.73

(*continued*)

Table 1. (*continued*)

#	Challenge	Description	References	Average Score (Audit)	Average Score (R&D)	**Average Score (overall)**
10	Inadequate (Internal) Audit Standard/ Guideline	Lack of (Internal) audit standard and its derivation, including guidelines or procedures; which inform how (internal) audit perform/conduct the use of AA in internal audit tasks, including the impairment in independence and objectivity and how to mitigate it	[3, 4, 19]	3.57	3.75	3.64

[1] In most references, data security often refers to confidentiality, integrity, and availability (known as CIA triad). However, in this paper, security particularly refers to confidentiality.

3.2 Structural Self-Interaction (SSIM) and Reachability Matrix

The SSIM was developed based on the consensus among FGD participants. For this purpose, we conducted FGD to an audit team experienced in using AA in internal audit tasks, from *simple* CAAT to developing a web-based application for CA (with testing automation). The team consists of one audit manager, one audit team leader, and three audit team members (with one skilled as a programmer and two skilled as a data engineer and database administrator). The FGD aims to map the relationship between a pair of challenges to develop the SSIM for MICMAC-ISM analysis. Each relationship is denoted as follows:

1) V, if the challenge on the left side of the table (L) affects the challenge on the top side of the table (T);
2) A, if challenge L is affected by challenge T;
3) X, if both challenges (L and T) affect each other; and
4) O, if both challenges (L and T) do not affect each other.

The resulted SSIM transformed into a reachability matrix using binary notation, i.e., 1 and 0. The reachability matrix was presented as follows:

1) 'V' results in 1 for challenge L and 0 for challenge T;
2) 'A' results in 0 for challenge L and 1 for challenge T;
3) 'X' results in 1 for both challenges L and T; and
4) 'O' results in 0 for both challenges L and T.

Further elaboration used transitivity analysis to develop the final reachability matrix. Transitivity analysis added notation 1 for a pair of unrelated challenges but related through another challenge (see Table 2).

Table 2. Final Reachability Matrix

Challenge	10	9	8	7	6	5	4	3	2	1	Driving Power
1	0	1	1*	1*	1	0	0	0	0	1	5
2	0	1*	0	1	1*	1	0	0	1	1	6
3	1	1	0	1	1*	0	0	1	0	1	6
4	1	1	1	1*	1	1	1	1	1	1	10
5	0	0	0	1	0	1	0	0	0	1*	3
6	0	1	1	1	1	0	0	0	0	1	5
7	0	1*	0	1	1*	0	0	0	0	1	4
8	0	1*	1	1	1	0	0	0	0	1*	5
9	0	1	0	1	1*	0	0	0	0	1	4
10	1	1	1*	1	1	0	0	0	0	1	6
Dependence	3	9	5	10	9	3	1	2	2	10	

*) adding transitivity

3.3 MICMAC (Cross-Impact Matrix-Multiplication Applied to Classification) and ISM Analysis

MICMAC analysis uses the final reachability matrix (FRM) to identify each factor's driving power and dependency. Driving power reflects the measured factor's influence on other factors, which is calculated as the sum of the associate row in the FRM; whereas dependence reflects other factors' influence on the measured factor, which is calculated as the sum of the associate column in the FRM [24, 37]. The result of MICMAC analysis is presented in the Fig. 2 below.

The team's consensus suggested that the lack of cultural readiness (C4) is the most independent challenge with strong driving powers, thus influential to other challenges. This notion suggests that addressing this challenge may benefit in solving problems derived from other challenges and eventually help the AA implementation. In contrast, inaccessible data (C1), limited AA-related skills (C6), dynamics in the audit process (C7), and limited use-case (C9) have a high dependence on other challenges, which implies that other challenges influence them. This notion indicates that they need the other challenges to be solved to reduce or eliminate their effect on AA implementation. Therefore, practitioners can focus on addressing other challenges, which will indirectly address these challenges with high dependence.

The final step was to define the levels of the challenges based on the reachability and antecedent set of each factor. The reachability set (R(Ci)) consists of the (analyzed) challenge and other challenges influenced by the said challenge. Meanwhile, the antecedent set (A(Ci)) consists of (the analyzed) challenge and other challenges that affect the said

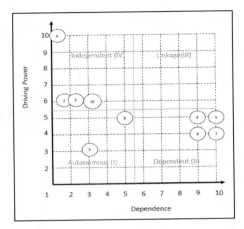

Fig. 2. MICMAC Analysis for AA Implementation Challenges

challenge. The challenges in which the reachability set equals the intersection set are put at the first (highest) level and removed from the list. The process performs iteratively for the remainder of the challenges until all the challenges' levels are defined (until the bottom level). The ISM analysis result is presented in the Fig. 3 below.

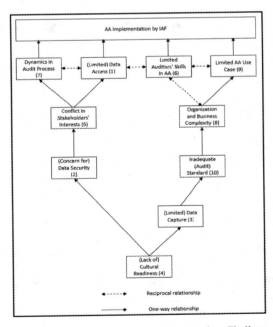

Fig. 3. ISM Analysis for AA Implementation Challenges

The hierarchical model visualizes the interrelations among challenges. The independent challenges with strong driving powers tend to be the foundational challenge (low-level). The team seemed to agree on the importance of the lack of culture (C4) as the foundational level challenge and that the inaccessible data (C1), AA-related audit skills (C6), dynamics in the audit process (C7), and limited use-case (C9) have the most direct impact on AA implementation (high-level challenges). This result reinstates the MICMAC analysis.

4   Discussion

4.1   Model Interpretation and its Scientific Value

AA implementation as a transformational change urges IAF to adjust its culture, process, and resources simultaneously. In this regard, MICMAC-ISM's resulting models help to conceptualize the layers and interrelationships among those challenges. This section elaborates on the meaning of the result of the MICMAC-ISM analysis.

Participants are concerned with the lack of cultural readiness (C4) as one of the critical challenges, which affects the data-related challenges, i.e., security (C2) and capture (C3). In this regard, the lack of cultural readiness renders the organization focused on confidentiality while undermining the value of data sharing and interconnection. And implies limited initiative to digitalize business processe. Therefore, addressing the cultural issue is one of the critical tasks in initiating AA implementation by IAF.

Interestingly, the extant literature focused on the cultural issue from the auditors' side. This research, however, suggests that it extends beyond the scope of auditors (or IAF as an entity) and reaches its stakeholders. Therefore, addressing cultural readiness should be directed towards the auditors (e.g., to overcome the auditors' resistance) and the stakeholders, such as audit clients or data owners.

The subsequent layers of challenges focused on data-related issues, which influence organizational and regulation-related issues. The participants agreed with those challenges' influence on other challenges. "[…] if the client is overly concerned with their data confidentiality, this (concern) will be reflected in their interests towards AA implementation by IAF […]", said one of the participants. This notion reaffirms the previous discussion to include external stakeholders of IAF (e.g., the client) in the AA implementation effort.

The higher-level challenges consist of technical challenges which are directly influence the use of AA in audit activities. Many other challenges influence those challenges, although they also influence each other. For instance, one participant suggested that "[…] dynamics during audit assignment affect communication between auditors and the client, which may eventually lead to the challenge of data access […]", to which another participant replied, "[…] while I agree with that statement, I can also see that the difficulty in accessing data may lead to more 'dynamics' during the audit assignment […]".

This research contributes to the advancement of this field by theorizing the contextual relationships and interrelation among those challenges to better understand the challenges around AA implementation and how those challenges simultaneously affect AA implementation. This result sheds light on why AA implementation is low despite its promised benefits. This research also addresses the need to examine the relationships between AA implementation and contextual factors, as [4] suggested. Hence, this result suggests that interdisciplinary research is promising for advancing this field.

This study also contributes to the advancement of the method. To the best of our knowledge, this research is the first to use the MICMAC-ISM approach to unravel the contextual relationships among key challenges of AA implementation. Furthermore, unlike other MICMAC-ISM research, which mainly relies on survey data, we opt to obtain an in-depth view of the contextual relationships among the selected challenges through FGD sessions in the next phase. Therefore, it enables us to obtain the 'quantized' data about the relationships among challenges (i.e., influencing or influenced; presented in binary 1 or 0) and unravel the reasoning behind their view to enrich the analysis. This approach strengthens the use of MICMAC-ISM by decomposing its complex socio-technical challenges and incorporates the contextual factor in analyzing the phenomena; thus, improves the scientific and practical relevance of the findings from this method.

4.2 Practical Implications

This section discusses the implication of the developed model and the possible strategies to overcome the challenges.

AA implementation requires the IAF and the organization it belongs to adjust its current values and practices, which is indicated by the significance of the cultural challenge (C4). The model also acknowledges that technical challenges have an immediate influence on the use of AA in an engagement.

Transformational change requires the organization to develop a sense of urgency, form a coalition, and develop and communicate the vision for change within the organization that wants to transform [38]. This approach will assist in addressing the cultural issue in AA implementation, which may also help address other challenges. For instance, cultural readiness may develop the clients' understanding of the benefit of AA and, further, pave common perception on addressing data security concerns and access provision. These efforts typically require a top-down approach.

However, addressing cultural issues is a long-term effort with no guarantee of an immediate result. Also, there are caveats in the transformation effort's initial steps, such as the lack of patience or overconfidence in the organization's ability to change [38]. Therefore, another strategy is to address challenges with a more direct impact on AA implementation and more manageable processes and results. For instance, the IAF may initiate relevant training related to AA use for the auditors [3, 29]. This approach may help the transformation through visible results such as improved auditors' AA-related skills or concrete ideas for an AA project and address C6 and C9.

The implication of AA implementation as a transformational change may also require adjustment in regulatory settings, e.g., internal audit standards at the industry level or internal audit charter containing internal audit result communication and follow-up protocol at the organization level [12, 39]. Moreover, this regulation should encompass the responsibilities of all related parties, i.e., the responsibility of the governing body and audit clients, such as providing (data) access for internal audit purposes [40], and the IAF to mitigate the risks associated with the transfer and use of (internal audit) client's data, such as security and contextual integrity risks [41–43]. Furthermore, the emergence and growth of predictive and prescriptive analytics may obscure the barrier between assurance and consulting activities [3]. Therefore, a regulatory update might be required to safeguard IAF's conformity with independence and objectivity standard. In addition, the required skills to implement AA may also transcend beyond the internal hiring and training strategy by IAF. Hence, there is a need to adjust and improve academic and professional curricula to incorporate AA-related skills for auditors [44, 45]. These types of efforts combine top-down and bottom-up approaches, incorporating mid- and long-term strategies aimed at a more fundamental change in organizational aspects and short-term effort with expected immediate technical results.

In practice, this combination of approaches can be translated into an AA implementation roadmap involving various stakeholders in its development and incorporating different elements. For instance, a long-term roadmap can contain a communication plan to persuade all actors to embrace AA. It also comprises competency requirements and a training plan for auditors and pilot projects as a quick-win strategy to acclimatize the organization and IAF with AA's actual practice and benefits. Furthermore, this roadmap may include efforts to update the professional standards and curricula. The formalized and enacted roadmap represents the top-down or strategic approach, while the pilot project (combined with the training plan) supports the roadmap from the operational or bottom-up perspective.

4.3   Limitations and Future Research

We identify several limitations of this study. First, the specific context of the research may suffer from the findings' limited generalizability and external validity. In addition, the identified key challenges in this study derived from the respondents within this study context, which may be different in another setting. Moreover, this research's approach also suggests that the result of MICMAC-ISM considerably depends on the respondents' knowledge and experience of the analyzed matter and may limit its applicability in a particular context. In addition, although mitigated by the use of multiple respondents and consensus among respondents, this method also acknowledges the nature of possible subjectivity of the respondents.

Therefore, working on the limitations above, future research may enhance this field by examining the challenges of AA implementation in a different setting, which includes the identification of challenges and the analysis of contextual relationships among the challenges. An in-depth case study to reflect on this research's result will also be beneficial for the advancement of this field and may reaffirm or extend this research's findings. In addition, to address the possible limited expertise of practitioners, future works may opt to use experts who meet the criteria suggested by [46]. Finally, developing a framework for AA implementation based on the hierarchical model of the challenges will be fruitful in advancing this research field.

5   Conclusion

This paper views AA implementation as a transformational change for IAF. The developed MICMAC-ISM model assists AA implementation by unraveling how the challenges are interrelated and influence AA implementation.

This research analyzes the relationship between the ten challenges of AA implementation. This way, different layers of challenges to AA implementation were identified, from the foundation level with the strongest driving power to the top level directly impacting AA use. We found that the cultural readiness issue (C4) is a critical challenge to address in an AA implementation. The next layer is data-related and organizational issues, which are influenced by cultural issues but indirectly influence technical challenges. The final layer is technical challenges with a more direct impact on AA implementation, such as data access (C1), AA-related skills (C6), or limited AA use-case (C9). The interrelation and hierarchy of challenges help practitioners and academics to understand the contextual factors around AA implementation better. The resulting MICMAC-ISM model also emphasizes the nature of AA implementation as a digital transformation effort for IAF.

Therefore, this research suggests combining a top-down and bottom-up approach and long and short-term efforts to address challenges and implement AA as a transformational effort. Finally, this research finds that AA implementation requires action beyond IAF as an organization and the organization to which the IAF belongs and suggests that AA implementation needs to reach policymakers and professional bodies, such as to develop a sound internal audit standard to mitigate risks associated with AA and improve academic and professional curricula for the internal auditor.

Acknowledgement. We thank the reviewers for valuable comments to improve this paper. This paper is supported by the Indonesia Endowment Fund for Education (LPDP) through a doctoral scholarship for M. G. Ramadhan. LPDP had no involvement in the design and execution of this paper.

References

1. Ramadhan, M.G., Janssen, M., van der Voort, H.: Driving and inhibiting factors for implementing audit analytics in an internal audit function. J. Emerg. Technol. Account. **20**, 1–29 (2023). https://doi.org/10.2308/JETA-2022-035
2. Vasarhelyi, M.A., Alles, M., Kuenkaikaew, S., Littley, J.: The acceptance and adoption of continuous auditing by internal auditors: a micro analysis. Int. J. Account. Inf. Syst. **13**(3), 267–281 (2012). https://doi.org/10.1016/j.accinf.2012.06.011
3. Austin, A.A., Carpenter, T., Christ, M.H., Nielson, C.: The Data Analytics Transformation: Evidence From Auditors, CFOs, and Standard-Setters (2018) [Online]. Available: https://pdfs.semanticscholar.org/e308/2c715f168c2c2569ebe93ad449117858234e.pdf
4. Krieger, F., Drews, P., Velte, P.: Explaining the (non-) adoption of advanced data analytics in auditing: a process theory. Int. J. Account. Inf. Syst. **41**, 100511 (2021). https://doi.org/10.1016/j.accinf.2021.100511
5. Hinings, B., Gegenhuber, T., Greenwood, R.: Digital innovation and transformation: an institutional perspective. Inf. Organ. **28**(1), 52–61 (2018). https://doi.org/10.1016/j.infoandorg.2018.02.004
6. Bumgarner, N., Vasarhelyi, M.A.: Continuous Auditing—A New View. In: Chan, D.Y., Chiu, V., Vasarhelyi, M.A. (eds.) Audit Analytics and Continuous Audit: Theory and Application (Rutgers Study in Accounting Analytics), 1st edn., pp. 7–52. Emerald Publishing Limited, Bingley, UK (2018)

7. Craja, P., Kim, A., Lessmann, S.: Deep learning for detecting financial statement fraud. Decis. Support Syst. **139**(May), 113421 (2020). https://doi.org/10.1016/j.dss.2020.113421

8. No, W.G., Lee, K., Huang, F., Li, Q.: Multidimensional audit data selection (MADS): a framework for using data analytics in the audit data selection process. Account. Horizons **33**(3), 127–140 (2019). https://doi.org/10.2308/acch-52453

9. Stippich, W.W., Preber, B.J.: Data Analytics: Elevating Internal Audit Value. IIARF, Altamonte Springs, Florida, USA (2016)

10. Ames, B.C., et al.: Global Technology Audit Guide 3 - Continous Auditing: Coordinating Continous Auditing and Monitoring to Provide Continous Assurance. The Institute of Internal Auditor, Altamonte Springs, Florida, USA (2015)

11. Barr- Pulliam, D., Brown-Liburd, H.L., Sanderson, K.: The effects of the internal control opinion and use of audit data analytics on perceptions of audit quality, assurance, and auditor negligence. Audit. A J. Pract. **41**(1), 24–48 (2022) [Online]. Available: https://papers.ssrn.com/sol3/papers.cfm?abstract_id=3021493

12. Li, H., Dai, J., Gershberg, T., Vasarhelyi, M.A.: Understanding usage and value of audit analytics for internal auditors: an organizational approach. Int. J. Account. Inf. Syst. **28**(November), 59–76 (2018). https://doi.org/10.1016/j.accinf.2017.12.005

13. Byrnes, E.P.C., et al.: Evolution of auditing : from the traditional approach to the future audit. In: Audit Analytics and Continuous Audit: Looking Toward the Future, pp. 285–297 (2018)

14. Cardoni, A., Kiseleva, E., De Luca, F.: Continuous auditing and data mining for strategic risk control and anticorruption: creating 'fair' value in the digital age. Bus. Strateg. Environ. **29**(8), 3072–3085 (2020). https://doi.org/10.1002/bse.2558

15. Gonzalez, G.C., Sharma, P.N., Galletta, D.F.: The antecedents of the use of continuous auditing in the internal auditing context. Int. J. Account. Inf. Syst. **13**(3), 248–262 (2012). https://doi.org/10.1016/j.accinf.2012.06.009

16. Wang, T., Cuthbertson, R.: Eight issues on audit data analytics we would like researched. J. Inf. Syst. **29**(1), 155–162 (2015). https://doi.org/10.2308/isys-50955

17. Eilifsen, A., Kinserdal, F., Messier, W.F., McKee, T.E.: An exploratory study into the use of audit data analytics on audit engagements. Account. Horizons **34**(4), 75–103 (2020). https://doi.org/10.2308/HORIZONS-19-121

18. de Freitas, M.M., Codesso, M., Augusto, A.L.R.: Implementation of continuous audit on the Brazilian navy payroll. J. Emerg. Technol. Account. **17**(2), 157–171 (2020). https://doi.org/10.2308/JETA-2020-047

19. Chaqiqi, A., Nugroho, A.: Readiness analysis of data analytics audit implementation in inspectorate general of the ministry of finance: an indonesian case. Indones. J. Account. Res. **24**(02), 147–162 (2021). https://doi.org/10.33312/ijar.513

20. Soedarsono, S., Mulyani, S., Tugiman, H., Suhardi, D.: Information quality and management support as key factors in the applications of continuous auditing and continuous monitoring: an empirical study in the government sector of Indonesia. Contemp. Econ. **13**(3), 335–350 (2019) [Online]. Available: https://www.ceeol.com/search/article-detail?id=974395

21. Vasarhelyi, M.A., Halper, F.B.: The Continuous Audit of Online Systems. In: Chan, D.Y., Chiu, V., Vasarhelyi, M.A. (eds.) Audit Analytics and Continuous Audit: Theory and Application (Rutgers Study in Accounting Analytics), 1st edn., pp. 87–104. Emerald Publishing Limited, Bingley, UK (2018)

22. vom Brocke, J., Simons, A., Riemer, K., Niehaves, B., Plattfaut, R., Cleven, A.: Standing on the shoulders of giants: challenges and recommendations of literature search in information systems research. Commun. Assoc. Inf. Syst. **37**, 205–224 (2015). https://doi.org/10.17705/1cais.03709

23. Dube, A.S., Gawande, R.S.: Analysis of green supply chain barriers using integrated ISM-fuzzy MICMAC approach. Benchmarking An Int. J. **23**(6), 1558–1578 (2016). https://doi.org/10.1108/BIJ-06-2015-0057

24. Janssen, M., Luthra, S., Mangla, S., Rana, N.P., Dwivedi, Y.K.: Challenges for adopting and implementing IoT in smart cities. Internet Res. **29**(6), 1589–1616 (2019). https://doi.org/10.1108/INTR-06-2018-0252

25. Katiyar, R., Barua, M.K., Meena, P.L.: Analysing the interactions among the barriers of supply chain performance measurement: an ISM with fuzzy MICMAC approach. Glob. Bus. Rev. **19**(1), 48–68 (2018). https://doi.org/10.1177/0972150917713283

26. Sharma, S.K., Metri, B., Dwivedi, Y.K., Rana, N.P.: Challenges common service centers (CSCs) face in delivering e-government services in rural India. Gov. Inf. Q. **38**(2), 101573 (2021). https://doi.org/10.1016/j.giq.2021.101573

27. Sindhwani, R., Mittal, V.K., Singh, P.L., Kalsariya, V., Salroo, F.: Modelling and analysis of energy efficiency drivers by fuzzy ISM and fuzzy MICMAC approach. Int. J. Product. Qual. Manag. **25**(2), 225 (2018). https://doi.org/10.1504/IJPQM.2018.094768

28. Tang, F., Norman, C.S., Vendrzyk, V.P.: Exploring perceptions of data analytics in the internal audit function. Behav. Inf. Technol. **36**(11), 1125–1136 (2017). https://doi.org/10.1080/0144929X.2017.1355014

29. Hampton, C., Stratopoulos, T.C.: Audit data analytics use: an exploratory analysis. SSRN Electron. J. (2016). https://doi.org/10.2139/ssrn.2877358

30. Haynes, R., Li, C.: Continuous audit and enterprise resource planning systems: a case study of ERP rollouts in the houston, TX oil and gas industries. J. Emerg. Technol. Account. **13**(1), 171–179 (2016). https://doi.org/10.2308/jeta-51446

31. Brennan, G., Teeter, R.A.: Aiding the audit: using the IT audit as a springboard for continuous controls monitoring. SSRN Electron. J. **3**, 129–136 (2010). https://doi.org/10.2139/ssrn.1668743

32. Codesso, M., de Freitas, M.M., Wang, X., de Carvalho, A., da Silva Filho, A.A.: Continuous audit implementation at Cia. Hering in Brazil. J. Emerg. Technol. Account. **17**(2), 103–118 (2020)

33. Rakipi, R., De Santis, F., D'Onza, G.: Correlates of the internal audit function's use of data analytics in the big data era: global evidence. J. Int. Accounting, Audit. Tax **42**, 100357 (2021). https://doi.org/10.1016/j.intaccaudtax.2020.100357

34. Earley, C.E.: Data analytics in auditing: opportunities and challenges. Bus. Horiz. **58**(5), 493–500 (2015). https://doi.org/10.1016/j.bushor.2015.05.002

35. Debreceny, R., Gray, G.L., Tham, W., Goh, K., Tang, P.: The development of embedded audit modules to support continuous monitoring in the electronic commerce environment. Int. J. Audit. **7**(2), 169–185 (2003). https://doi.org/10.1111/1099-1123.00067

36. Malaescu, I., Sutton, S.G.: The reliance of external auditors on internal audit's use of continuous audit. J. Inf. Syst. **29**(1), 95–114 (2015). https://doi.org/10.2308/isys-50899

37. Luthra, S., Luthra, S., Haleem, A.: Hurdles in Implementing sustainable supply chain management: an analysis of indian automobile sector. Procedia – Soc. Behav. Sci. **189**, 175–183 (2015). https://doi.org/10.1016/j.sbspro.2015.03.212

38. Kotter, J. P.: Leading Change: Why transformation efforts fail? Harv. Bus. Rev. (March-April), 59–67 (1995)

39. Kearns, G., Barker, K., Danese, S.: Developing a forensic continuous audit model. J. Digit. Forensics, Secur. Law **6**(2), 25–48 (2011). https://doi.org/10.15394/jdfsl.2011.1094

40. Woodroof, J., Searcy, D.: Continuous audit model development and implementation within a debt covenant compliance domain. Int. J. Account. Inf. Syst. **2**(3), 169–191 (2001). https://doi.org/10.1016/S1467-0895(01)00019-7

41. Koskivaara, E.: Integrating analytical procedures into the continuous audit environment. JISTEM J. Inf. Syst. Technol. Manag. **3**(3), 331–346 (2006). https://doi.org/10.4301/S1807-17752006000300005

42. Burns, M.B., Igou, A.: 'Alexa, write an audit opinion': adopting intelligent virtual assistants in accounting workplaces. J. Emerg. Technol. Account. **16**(1), 81–92 (2019). https://doi.org/10.2308/jeta-52424

43. Winter, J.S., Davidson, E.: Big data governance of personal health information and challenges to contextual integrity. Inf. Soc. **35**(1), 36–51 (2019). https://doi.org/10.1080/01972243.2018.1542648

44. Joshi, P., Marthandan, G.: Continuous internal auditing: can big data analytics help. Int. J. Accounting, Audit. Perform. Eval. **16**(1), 25 (2020). https://doi.org/10.1504/IJAAPE.2020.106766

45. Gambetta, N., García-Benau, M.A., Zorio-Grima, A.: Data analytics in banks' audit: the case of loan loss provisions in Uruguay. J. Bus. Res. **69**(11), 4793–4797 (2016). https://doi.org/10.1016/j.jbusres.2016.04.032

46. Shanteau, J., Weiss, D.J., Thomas, R.P., Pounds, J.C.: Performance based assessment of expertise: how to decide if someone is an expert or not. Eur. J. Oper. Res. **136**, 253–263 (2002)

E-channel Selection Intention: Role of Users' IT Characteristics and IT Usage

Sakshi Srivastava[1] and Gaurav Dixit[1,2(✉)]

[1] Department of Management Studies, Indian Institute of Technology Roorkee, Roorkee, India
gaurav.dixit@ms.iitr.ac.in
[2] Mehta Family School of Data Science and Artificial Intelligence, Indian Institute of Technology Roorkee, Roorkee, India

Abstract. The last decade's technological advances have enabled firms to offer their services to users through multiple digital channels like PC, mobile, and wearable computing devices. Consequently, users tend to cultivate their preferences towards the PC channels (desktop website or app) or mobile channels (app or website) for various online activities like informative content, entertainment, transactions, and location-based services. In this research, we study how users' IT characteristics, such as computer self-efficacy, privacy concerns, perceived Internet security, and personal innovativeness in IT, affect their IT usage for online activities, thereby influencing their e-channel selection intention. We plan to collect data from online users and apply structural equation modelling to test these relationships. The findings of our study are likely to develop a better understanding of users' cognitive processes around e-channel selection for online activities. Our study is expected to provide strong implications for Internet and e-commerce firms to optimise user engagement and experience across various e-channels.

Keywords: e-channel · Selection intention · Online activities

1 Introduction

The rapid development of ICTs and widespread Internet penetration in the last decade has changed how users communicate with each other, search for information, and fulfil their utilitarian and hedonic needs [1]. Moreover, with the addition of the mobile Internet as a new channel, users' accessibility to the Internet has widened to multiple devices like smartphones, tablets, smart TVs, and wearable devices [2]. According to a recent report, users across the globe own 3.6 devices and connections on average [3]. At the same time, it allows them to explore and use multiple e-channels, like desktop websites and apps in the PC computing environment and mobile websites and apps in the mobile computing environment. The presence of multiple e-channels might necessitate users to decide the most appropriate e-channel for specific online activities [4]. For instance, Singh and Swait [2] found that users typically used mobile channels to search for information during their commute or waiting time. Alternatively, they preferred PCs

M. Janssen et al. (Eds.): I3E 2023, LNCS 14316, pp. 156–165, 2023.
https://doi.org/10.1007/978-3-031-50040-4_12

to navigate several websites and conduct price comparisons. These findings imply that users' cognitive processes for selecting e-channels are often complex and shaped by their perceptions of e-channels [5]. As such, variances in e-channel attributes make it increasingly crucial for industry practitioners to understand users' cognitive processes around e-channel selection. Understanding how users cultivate preferences towards e-channels could help practitioners roll offerings that better cater to their requirements. For example, gaining insights into users' channel selection behaviour enabled entertainment services firms to rework their pricing strategies and offer different subscription plans across channels to capture a broader audience [6]. As people's lives continue to integrate with the Internet, it becomes essential to understand factors affecting users' e-channel selection behaviour. Therefore, this study examines "how users' intentions for e-channel selection are formed".

The existing research has identified several antecedents of channel selection behaviour, like channel characteristics [7], shopping orientations [8], and user motivation [9]. However, these studies primarily focus on the offline-online scenarios related to channel selection intentions. They do not consider the different categories of e-channels and the factors that shape users' preferences for selecting them. Furthermore, with the growing multiplicity of e-channels and their potential to fulfil users' utilitarian and hedonic needs, it seems surprising that few studies recognise diverse online channels and their touchpoints [10]. Amongst such studies, Chen et al. [11] explored how specificity about goal and product knowledge affected users' choice of online channels. Wagner et al. [10] emphasised the significance of technological and contextual factors in predicting users' intentions to utilise e-channels. De Haan et al. [12] examined how switching between mobile and fixed devices affected users' purchase behaviours. However, all three studies predominantly focused on users' online channel selection behaviours in retail. Moreover, these studies mainly emphasised e-channel selection in the pre-adoption and usage context. On the other hand, the existing literature is somewhat silent in understanding the impact of users' behavioural factors on the continued use of online technologies [13]. Therefore, this research examines how regularly performing online activities shapes users' preferences for e-channels in the post-adoption context. Additionally, while the extant IS studies advance our understanding of users' cognitive processes for making decisions on separate channels, they seldom discuss the impact of users' IT characteristics on e-channel selection intentions.

We, specifically, address this gap by developing a conceptual model to investigate how users' IT characteristics affect IT usage for online activities, which in turn influences their e-channel selection intention. Previous studies have extensively explored the role of users' IT characteristics like personal innovativeness, computer self-efficacy, perceived Internet security, and privacy concerns in IS literature. For example, Palash et al. [14] found that personal innovativeness in IT (PIIT) demonstrated a significant moderating effect on the association between perceived risk and users' inclination towards using facial recognition for digital payments. Gupta et al. [15] found that users' self-efficacy and perceived security positively influenced the continued use of m-wallets. Furthermore, Wottrich et al. [16] found that privacy concerns negatively affected users' intentions to accept online app requests. In this context, the current research proposes that users' IT characteristics affect usage for various online activities, influencing their e-channel selection. We further assume that when users regularly perform online activities through e-channels, a relatively stable pattern of their e-channel selection intention emerges. Hence, in this research, we describe the term 'e-channel selection intention' to include the adoption and continued use of e-channels. As indicated by Goeke et al. [17], the initial adoption of an IS artefact does not lead to its increased levels of usage. Instead, it typically indicates its initial trial and workability to the users [18]. The long-term success of any IS artefact depends on its regular and frequent usage [19]. Hence, firms can only attain continued success for their e-channel offerings by optimising users' experience across different channels. It further raises the need to understand the role of user IT characteristics in influencing IT usage for online activities and the continued intentions towards e-channel selection. Given the context, this study develops a conceptual model to address the following objectives: (1) exploring the role of users' IT characteristics on IT usage for online activities and (2) investigating the influence of users' IT usage on their e-channel selection intentions.

2   Theoretical Background

2.1   E-channel Selection Intention

In a multichannel setting, firms are often concerned about the channels users plan to leverage for their online activities [4]. Prior studies have identified several antecedents affecting users' intention for channel selection. Gené Albesa [20] revealed the significance of social relationships, channel convenience, channel knowledge, and privacy in influencing users' channel behaviour in banking services. Likewise, Konuş et al. [21] examined the role of loyalty, enjoyment, and innovativeness to classify customers into three segments: uninvolved shoppers, store-focused customers, and multichannel enthusiasts.

While channel selection is not new, advancements in ICT and the availability of multiple devices (like smartphones and tablets) have further spurred the interest of academicians and practitioners in this field. For instance, Acquila-Natale and Iglesias-Pradas [22] employed elements like perceived quality, brand knowledge, non-monetary costs, monetary costs, hedonic aspects, user demographics, and lock-in variables to predict users' single or multichannel behaviours. Richard and Purnell [23] explored the role of channel attributes like structural assurance, channel experience, and channel convenience in affecting users' satisfaction and preferences for a channel. Xu and Jackson [4] focused on understanding the effect of channel transparency, convenience, and uniformity on channel selection intention by influencing user perception. Similarly, Maity and Dass [7] found that users preferred channels with medium-to-high media richness (like e-commerce and offline stores) for complex tasks and low-media richness channels (e.g., mobile commerce) for straightforward tasks.

Such spillover effects typically observed in online-offline channels could also be experienced across devices. For example, De Haan et al. [12] observed how switching from a more portable device (e.g., smartphone) to a fixed device (e.g., PC) often resulted in greater sales conversion probability. In a randomised experimental study, Naegelein et al. [24] explored how different visual product presentation techniques (e.g., zoom technology) on mobile and PC-based channels affect online sales performance. The growing diversity in Internet-enabled devices has made users' experiences versatile and complex [10]. Thus, differences in technological features and interactive functionalities across mobile and PC channels further introduce opportunities and constraints for users. Consequently, users with varying IT expertise and experience would utilise mobile and PC-based devices differently [25].

Given this context, we expect users' IT characteristics, such as PIIT, computer self-efficacy, perceived Internet security, and privacy concerns, to be crucial in shaping their intentions towards e-channel selection. The more users are familiar with e-channels, the more they are motivated to continue using them for future online activities [25]. Furthermore, we argue that with increased utilisation of e-channels, relatively stable patterns of users' intentions for e-channel selection begin to emerge. It is important to note that an IS artefact's commercial success depends on its continued use instead of its mere adoption [19]. If users no longer feel safe, enthusiastic, and efficacious in utilising an e-channel, this might eventually result in its disuse [26]. While there has been much discussion on the antecedents for adopting e-channels, the extant IS literature is relatively silent on how users' IT characteristics and IT usage for various online activities determine their intentions for e-channel selection in the post-adoption context. Therefore, in this research, we examine the role of users' IT characteristics in utilising e-channels for performing various online activities. We further investigate the effect of users' IT usage on their intentions towards selecting and continually using e-channels in the post-adoption context.

3   Hypothesis Development

We now discuss our proposed research model and its related hypotheses, as shown in Fig. 1. Agarwal and Prasad [27] conceptualised PIIT to explain users' willingness to accept and utilise new IT artefacts. It reflects a user's curiosity in influencing their decision to adopt and use IT artefacts [14]. In contrast to late adopters, users with high innovativeness generally have a greater tendency to identify the potential benefits of a new IT artefact in its early stage of diffusion [28]. They often develop positive perceptions towards trying new channels and technologies [21]. Prior studies have highlighted PIIT as a critical factor in understanding the adoption and behavioral usage intention for different e-channels [28, 29]. Thakur and Srivastava [30] noted that the impact of personal innovativeness on behavioral intentions to use mobile payments is significantly different among users and non-users, further emphasizing its importance in influencing the usage of e-channels. Hence, users with higher PIIT will be more inclined to experiment with newer functions and features of e-channels, thereby leading to increased IT usage. We, therefore, posit:

H1: Personal innovativeness positively affects users' IT usage for online activities.

Compeau and Higgins [31] extended the concept of self-efficacy to the IT domain and described it as individuals' belief in their ability to use computing systems competently. Prior studies have explained how users' higher self-efficacy is linked to increased IT usage [32]. Lu and Su [33] claimed that users would be more likely to perform complex smartphone functions when they are more confident with their mobile-related skills. Chang et al. [34] highlighted that higher self-efficacy regarding mobile channels motivated users to switch from physical store shopping to an online environment. Moreover, when users feel confident in utilising e-channels after the initial use, they will more likely be inclined towards leveraging these e-channels for their future online activities, resulting in increased IT usage [26]:

H2: Computer self-efficacy positively affects users' IT usage for online activities.

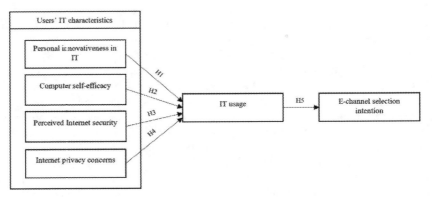

Fig. 1. Proposed research model

Perceived Internet security reflects users' belief that unauthorised parties will not view, store, or manipulate their personal and monetary information when performing online transactions [35]. Because of their varying experiences, users tend to develop different attitudes towards e-channels for executing online activities [36]. For instance, users who view the Internet as less secure will be less likely to utilise it frequently [37]. Alternatively, a higher perception of the in-built security features of e-channels gives users the confidence to conduct online transactions, eventually leading to increased IT usage [15]. Therefore, we posit:

H3: Perceived Internet security positively affects users' IT usage for online activities.

Advancements in digitisation make it easy for businesses to capture users' personal information, browsing patterns, and other digital footprints, thus raising their concern over information divulging and misuse [38]. Prior studies have demonstrated that users' growing privacy concerns may negatively affect their technology acceptance [39]. However, a user's decision to adopt an e-channel is typically based on the cost-benefit trade-off [40]. Although users are generally anxious about their online privacy, they seem willing to share their personal information for perceived benefits [41]. Thus, it can be argued that users might differ in their experiences and coping mechanisms towards privacy concerns [16]. Users who are highly concerned for their privacy may respond more negatively towards IT usage than those with low privacy concerns. Therefore, we hypothesise:

H4: High Internet privacy concerns negatively affect users' IT usage for online activities.

Self-determination theory (SDT) says that fulfilling users' basic innate needs, such as autonomy, relatedness, and competence, could be a strong intrinsic force in shaping their attitudes and behaviour [42]. The extent to which these innate psychological needs are fulfilled enables users to engage in a specific situation, whereas, when unfulfilled, it diminishes their motivation and psychological well-being [43]. Previous studies have indicated that satisfying users' innate psychological needs intrinsically motivates their positive attitudes and behaviour towards IT artefacts [44, 45]. In e-channel selection, we expect users to exercise autonomy in selecting and using channels that activate their sense of motivation, satisfaction, and emotional well-being. For instance, based on their perceptions towards innovativeness, competence, privacy and security concerns, they can select an appropriate e-channel from the multiple alternatives. For instance, while users may find it convenient to use mobile devices for making payments at retailers' stores, they may prefer PC-based channels for more significant transactions. Similarly, users may utilise mobile devices to watch TikTok videos and prefer Smart TV or PC channels to watch movies with family and friends. Moreover, as they repeatedly engage with their preferred e-channel choices, their long-term preferences for e-channel selection will begin to emerge and stabilise. Given the context, we posit:

H5: Users' IT usage for online activities positively affects their intention for e-channel selection.

4 Proposed Research Methodology

In this research study, we plan to measure users' IT characteristics by adapting scales from the existing literature. We will utilise the 4-item scale Agarwal and Prasad [27] developed to measure PIIT. The measurement scale for computer self-efficacy (4-item) and perceived Internet security (3-item) will be along the lines of O'Cass and Fenech [37]. We will use the 3-item scale from Cheung and Lee [46] to measure Internet privacy concerns. Furthermore, we plan to use single-item observed variables for the four IT use activities based on the work of Mahatanankoon et al. [47] and Agarwal and Dixit [48]. These observed variables will reflect users' frequency of online and digital activities associated with entertainment, transaction-based, content delivery, and location-based services. Finally, to study the construct of e-channel choice intentions, we plan to use the 8-item measurement scale by Xu and Jackson [4]. Based on these scales, we will prepare a structured questionnaire and collect responses from individuals who use e-channels to perform various online activities. Upon collecting the data, we will use structural equation modelling (SEM) to analyse the proposed research model for confirmatory factor analysis. Furthermore, another crucial aspect is determining the sample size. Several researchers assert utilising participant-to-item ratio, typically in the range of 10–20:1, for sample size determination [49–51]. According to Kass and Tinsley [52], a sample size greater than 300 is adequate, while other scholars suggested a minimum sample size of 200 [53]. Based on this discussion, we plan to gather data from around 450 respondents for the current study.

5 Potential Contribution

We expect this research to make the following contributions to the IS literature. First, by focusing on user-oriented variables, this study is likely to provide a better comprehension of the cognitive processes towards e-channel selection intentions for online activities. The literature examining the relationship between users' behavioural factors and the continuance intentions for IS artefacts is relatively scarce [13]. This study makes an early attempt to explore how users' IT characteristics and IT usage determine their intentions to select and continue using e-channels. Second, this study delineates the term 'e-channel selection intention' to include the adoption and continued use of e-channels. In doing so, we contribute to IS literature by emphasising the post-adoption context of the e-channel selection intention. Third, we extend the extant IS literature by exploring users' channel selection behaviour in the context of online channels. Within the multichannel environment, previous research has primarily focused on 'online-offline' channels [4]. In contrast, we emphasise how expanding the number of e-channels might necessitate users to select the most appropriate channel for specific online activities and, over time, result in the stabilisation of their preferences. Fourth, past studies have investigated users' likelihood of adopting and using e-channels [11, 26]. However, often, these studies do not specify the online activities users usually undertake. In this study, we specifically explore the association of how users' engagement in various online activities leads to the emergence of a relatively stable pattern for their e-channel selection. Moreover, this study further contributes to the extant IS research by focusing on how users' IT characteristics affect the four types of IT usage activities.

We also offer some exciting implications for business managers. First, this study highlights the fundamental need for managers to understand how users' IT characteristics shape their preferences towards e-channel utilisation. Consistent with Wagner et al. [10], we emphasise that users' perceptions vary across different e-channels. It, therefore, becomes essential for business managers to consider users' IT characteristics in designing and managing e-channel strategies that optimise their experience. For instance, they can include innovative features in their e-channel offerings (e.g., gamification) to increase user engagement. Second, this study urges managers to focus on the long-term usage of their services and not just mere adoption. It specifically draws their attention towards the association between users' IT usage and their intentions for e-channel selection and continued use. In this sense, we believe industry practitioners can find utility in our model and gather insights to improve organisational performance.

References

1. Dwivedi, Y.K., Rana, N.P., Slade, E.L., Singh, N., Kizgin, H.: Editorial introduction: advances in theory and practice of digital marketing. J. Retail. Consum. Serv. **53**, 101909 (2020)
2. Singh, S., Swait, J.: Channels for search and purchase: does mobile internet matter? J. Retail. Consum. Serv. **39**, 123–134 (2017)
3. Statista. https://www.statista.com/statistics/1190270/number-of-devices-and-connections-per-person-worldwide/
4. Xu, X., Jackson, J.E.: Examining customer channel selection intention in the omni-channel retail environment. Int. J. Prod. Econ. **208**, 434–445 (2019)
5. Wang, C., Teo, T.S.H., Dwivedi, Y., Janssen, M.: Mobile services use and citizen satisfaction in government: integrating social benefits and uses and gratifications theory. Inf. Technol. People **34**(4), 1313–1337 (2021)
6. The Economic Times. https://economictimes.indiatimes.com/industry/media/entertainment/disneyhotstar-rejigs-pricing-strategy-to-offer-entire-content-library-to-all-paid-subscribers/articleshow/84787980.cms?from=mdr
7. Maity, M., Dass, M.: Consumer decision-making across modern and traditional channels: e-commerce, m-commerce, in-store. Decis. Support. Syst. **61**, 34–46 (2014)

8. Kim, E., Libaque-Saenz, C.F., Park, M.C.: Understanding shopping routes of offline purchasers: selection of search-channels (online vs. offline) and search platforms (mobile vs. PC) based on product types. Serv. Bus. **13**, 305–338 (2019)

9. Frasquet, M., Mollá, A., Ruiz, E.: Identifying patterns in channel usage across the search, purchase, and post-sales stages of shopping. Electron. Commer. Res. Appl. **14**, 654–665 (2015)

10. Wagner, G., Klein, H.S., Steinmann, S.: Online retailing across e-channel touchpoints: empirical studies of consumer behavior in the multichannel e-commerce environment. J. Bus. Res. **107**, 256–270 (2020)

11. Chen, J., Wang, H., Gao, W.: How do goal and product knowledge specificity influence online channel choice? A polynomial regression analysis. Electron. Commer. Res. Appl. **35**, 100846 (2019)

12. De Haan, E., Kannan, P.K., Verhoef, P.C., Wiesel, T.: Device switching in online purchasing: examining the strategic contingencies. J. Mark. **82**, 1–19 (2018)

13. Yan, M., Filieri, R., Gorton, M.: Continuance intention of online technologies: a systematic literature review. Int. J. Inf. Manag. **58**, 102315 (2021)

14. Palash, M.A.S., Talukder, M.S., Islam, A.K.M.N., Bao, Y.: Positive and negative valences, personal innovativeness and intention to use facial recognition for payments. Ind. Manag. Data Syst. **122**(4), 1081–1108 (2022)

15. Gupta, A., Yousaf, A., Mishra, A.: How pre-adoption expectancies shape post-adoption continuance intentions: an extended expectation-confirmation model. Int. J. Inf. Manage. **52**, 102094 (2020)

16. Wottrich, V.M., van Reijmersdal, E.A., Smit, E.G.: The privacy trade-off for mobile app downloads: the roles of app value, intrusiveness, and privacy concerns. Decis. Support. Syst. **106**, 44–52 (2018)

17. Goeke, R.J., Faley, R.H., Brandyberry, A.A., Dow, K.E.: How experience and expertise affect the use of a complex technology. Inf. Resour. Manag. J. **29**(2), 59–80 (2016)

18. Salim, T.A., Barachi, M.E., Onyia, O.P., Mathew, S.S.: Effects of smart city service channel- and user-characteristics on user satisfaction and continuance intention. Inf. Technol. People **34**(1), 147–177 (2021)

19. Bhattacherjee, A.: Understanding information systems continuance: an expectation-confirmation model. MIS Q. **25**(3), 351–370 (2001)

20. Gené Albesa, J.: Interaction channel choice in a multichannel environment, an empirical study. Int. J. Bank Mark. **25**(7), 490–506 (2007)

21. Konuş, U., Verhoef, P.C., Neslin, S.A.: Multichannel shopper segments and their covariates. J. Retail. **84**(4), 398–413 (2008)

22. Acquila-Natale, E., Iglesias-Pradas, S.: A matter of value? Predicting channel preference and multichannel behaviors in retail. Technol. Forecast. Soc. Change **162**, 120401 (2021)

23. Richard, J.E., Purnell, F.: Rethinking catalogue and online B2B buyer channel preferences in the education supplies market. J. Interact. Mark. **37**, 1–15 (2017)

24. Naegelein, P., Spann, M., Molitor, D.: The value of product presentation technologies on mobile vs. non-mobile devices: a randomised field experiment. Decis. Support Syst. **121**, 109–120 (2019)

25. Blázquez, M.: Fashion shopping in multichannel retail: the role of technology in enhancing the customer experience. Int. J. Electron. Commer. **18**(4), 97–116 (2014)

26. Foroughi, B., Iranmanesh, M., Hyun, S.S.: Understanding the determinants of mobile banking continuance usage intention. J. Enterp. Inf. Manag. **32**(6), 1015–1033 (2019)

27. Agarwal, R., Prasad, J.: A conceptual and operational definition of personal innovativeness in the domain of information technology. Inf. Syst. Res. **9**(2), 204–215 (1998)

28. Talukder, M.S., Chiong, R., Bao, Y., Hayat Malik, B.: Acceptance and use predictors of fitness wearable technology and intention to recommend: an empirical study. Ind. Manag. Data Syst. **119**(1), 170–188 (2019)

29. Lian, J.W., Lin, T.M.: Effects of consumer characteristics on their acceptance of online shopping: comparisons among different product types. Comput. Hum. Behav. **24**(1), 48–65 (2008)

30. Thakur, R., Srivastava, M.: Adoption readiness, personal innovativeness, perceived risk and usage intention across customer groups for mobile payment services in India. Internet Res. **24**(3), 369–392 (2014)

31. Compeau, D.R., Higgins, C.A.: Computer self-efficacy: development of a measure and initial test. MIS Q. **19**(2), 189–211 (1995)

32. Susanto, A., Chang, Y., Ha, Y.: Determinants of continuance intention to use the smartphone banking services: an extension to the expectation-confirmation model. Ind. Manag. Data Syst. **116**(3), 508–525 (2016)

33. Lu, H.P., Su, P.Y.J.: Factors affecting purchase intention on mobile shopping web sites. Internet Res. **19**(4), 442–458 (2009)

34. Chang, H.H., Wong, K.H., Li, S.Y.: Applying push-pull-mooring to investigate channel switching behaviors: m-shopping self-efficacy and switching costs as moderators. Electron. Commer. Res. Appl. **24**, 50–67 (2017)

35. Flavián, C., Guinalíu, M.: Consumer trust, perceived security and privacy policy: three basic elements of loyalty to a web site. Ind. Manag. Data Syst. **106**(5), 601–620 (2006)

36. Kim, C., Tao, W., Shin, N., Kim, K.S.: An empirical study of customers' perceptions of security and trust in e-payment systems. Electron. Commer. Res. Appl. **9**(1), 84–95 (2010)

37. O'Cass, A., Fenech, T.: Web retailing adoption: exploring the nature of internet users web retailing behaviour. J. Retail. Consum. Serv. **10**(2), 81–94 (2003)

38. Vijayasarathy, L.R.: Predicting consumer intentions to use online shopping: the case for an augmented technology acceptance model. Inf. Manag. **41**(6), 747–762 (2004)

39. Chan, E.Y., Saqib, N.U.: Privacy concerns can explain unwillingness to download and use contact tracing apps when covid-19 concerns are high. Comput. Hum. Behav. **119**, 106718 (2021)

40. Li, H., Wu, J., Gao, Y., Shi, Y.: Examining individuals' adoption of healthcare wearable devices: an empirical study from privacy calculus perspective. Int. J. Med. Inform. **88**, 8–17 (2016)

41. Norberg, P.A., Horne, D.R., Horne, D.A.: The privacy paradox: personal information disclosure intentions versus behaviors. J. Consum. Aff. **41**(1), 100–126 (2007)

42. Ryan, R.M., Deci, E.L.: Self-determination theory and the facilitation of intrinsic motivation, social development, and well-being. Am. Psychol. **55**(1), 68–78 (2000)

43. Ryan, R.M.. Deci, E.L.: Handbook of Self-Determination Research, 1st edn. University of Rochester Press, New York (2002)

44. Gao, W., Liu, Y., Liu, Z., Li, J.: How does presence influence purchase intention in online shopping markets? An explanation based on self-determination theory. Behav. Inf. Technol. **37**(8), 786–799 (2018)

45. Yoon, C., Rolland, E.: Knowledge-sharing in virtual communities: familiarity, anonymity and self-determination theory. Behav. Inf. Technol. **31**(11), 1133–1143 (2012)

46. Cheung, C.M., Lee, M.K.: Understanding consumer trust in internet shopping: a multidisciplinary approach. J. Am. Soc. Inf. Sci. Technol. **57**(4), 479–492 (2006)

47. Mahatanankoon, P., Wen, H.J., Lim, B.: Consumer-based m-commerce: exploring consumer perception of mobile applications. Comput. Stand. Interfaces **27**(4), 347–357 (2005)

48. Agarwal, H., Dixit, G.: Information technology usage and cognitive engagement: understanding effects on users' cognitive processes. In: International Working Conference on Transfer

and Diffusion of IT (TDIT), pp. 70–81. Springer International Publishing, Tiruchirappalli, India (2020)

49. Jackson, D.L.: Revisiting sample size and number of parameter estimates: some support for the N:q hypothesis. Struct. Equ. Modeling **10**(1), 128–141 (2003)

50. Hair, J.F., Black, W.C., Babin, B.J., Anderson, R.E.: Multivariate Data Analysis, 7th edn. Prentice Hall, New York (2010)

51. Bagozzi, R.P., Yi, Y.: Specification, evaluation, and interpretation of structural equation models. J. Acad. Mark. Sci. **40**, 8–34 (2012)

52. Kass, R.A., Tinsley, H.E.A.: Factor Analysis. J. Leis. Res. **11**(2), 120–138 (1979)

53. Reinartz, W., Haenlein, M., Henseler, J.: An empirical comparison of the efficacy of covariance-based and variance-based SEM. Int. J. Res. Mark. **26**(4), 332–344 (2009)

Blockchain Adoption Decision-Making Process in Business: An Empirical Study

Anastasiia Gurzhii$^{(\boxtimes)}$ (ID), Najmul Islam (ID), and Michael Tuape (ID)

LUT University, 53850 Lappeenranta, Finland
anastasiia.gurzhii@lut.fi

Abstract. Recent research has highlighted gaps between blockchain technology and its adoption decision-making process on the corporate level. This paper aims to resolve these gaps, exploring the issues and processes that need to be considered before utilizing blockchain-based solutions in various domains. We collected data using 10 semi-structured interviews among blockchain professionals that have already adopted blockchain in their companies or were involved in the adoption decision-making process. We analyzed the data using the Gioa approach and identified five dimensions that must be considered before blockchain utilization, namely infrastructure, business models, operational processes, management and environmental impact. Additionally, based on the collected data we provide questions to ask before considering blockchain and a final framework that includes 18 sub-themes of the identified dimensions. Our study extends prior frameworks that might help organizations utilize blockchain according to their business strategy. Based on our findings, we also put forward directions for future studies.

Keywords: Blockchain · decision-making framework · corporate domain

1 Introduction

Blockchain has recently been expanding from a niche technology to a viable solution for different domains [1]. For example, recent studies show the potential of blockchain in the supply chain [2], banking or financial industries [3], unified identification and verification systems [4], medical records keeping and pharmaceutical tracking [5], asset management [6], etc. Blockchain utilization in various business cases has far-reaching effects including transparent transactions, disintermediation in crucial processes and their automation, increased efficiency and confidence among stakeholders in an organizational ecosystem, etc. [7]. As organizations are focusing on operational efficiency and effectiveness improvement, adopting and using blockchain may address problems with inner processes and information exchange in traditional corporate management and external collaborations [7]. Nevertheless, even though the technology is gaining momentum and attracting more companies, there is still limited empirical research on developing a decision-making process framework that organizations can use when deciding on whether to adopt blockchain. In the existing literature, we identified the following

© IFIP International Federation for Information Processing 2023
Published by Springer Nature Switzerland AG 2023
M. Janssen et al. (Eds.): I3E 2023, LNCS 14316, pp. 166–182, 2023.
https://doi.org/10.1007/978-3-031-50040-4_13

research gaps. First, no unified framework considers the feasibility of using blockchain as a relevant solution for a particular use case. Second, the prior studies mostly cover factors that impact blockchain adoption or discuss various blockchain types and how to choose the right one (e.g., [8, 9]) without focusing on the decision-making process. Third, only a few studies covered blockchain adoption frameworks and provide constraints that influence the intention to utilize the technology [10, 11]. Hence, existing research is focused on various factors that lead to blockchain adoption in various domains, the applicability of various blockchain types and models on how the technology can benefit businesses (e.g., [12–16]) and there is still no clear understanding of the decision-making process from the practitioners perspective. To address these gaps, we investigate adoption factors, challenges, and decision-making steps involved in blockchain implementation and determine the following two research questions:

RQ1. What is the decision-making process in organizations in relation to blockchain?
RQ2. What are the most important dimensions to consider during the process of blockchain adoption and implementation in organizations?

To answer the research questions, we conducted a qualitative study with 10 semi-structured interviews with blockchain professionals. Compared to the current literature, this study contributes to the existing knowledge in several ways. First, while prior research focused mainly on three dimensions (e.g., technology, organization and environment), we included business models and management dimensions as well to broaden aspects that need to be considered before blockchain adoption on the corporate level. Second, we empirically tested existing findings. For example, we support that legal regulations, stakeholders' readiness, financial resources and infrastructure readiness [17, 18] are among the main dimensions to consider before blockchain adoption. Finally, this paper expands existing knowledge and proposes a new model of the decision-making process related to blockchain adoption.

The remaining paper is structured as follows. Section 2 covers the literature background related to blockchain adoption constants and adoption models. In Sect. 3 we explain the methodology used in the study and explain data analysis techniques. Results are described in Sect. 4 alongside the adoption process framework and potential questions to ask before blockchain utilization. Finally, in Sect. 5 we conclude the findings.

2 Literature Background

During the literature review, we have identified two major themes of research studies. The first theme identified various factors that lead to blockchain adoption decisions [9, 11, 17–20]. The second theme focused on the suitability of blockchain and the appropriate type of blockchain needed for a particular use case [8, 15]. Despite these important contributions, practitioners lack a framework that can guide them in the decision-making process when they consider adopting and implementing blockchain in their organizations. At the same time, the prior literature covers narrow solutions and provides frameworks for a single domain. For example, Sternberg et al. [35] and Sunmola et al. [11] cover blockchain adoption in the supply chain, focus on the challenges associated with the technology and provide essential constraints to consider before and during blockchain implementation. Azogu et al. [36] focus on the healthcare domain, Farahmand and Farahmand [20] give insights from the energy sector and Roth et al. [21] cover the public sector. Despite this valuable contribution, only a few studies focus on blockchain adoption in a cross-sector context. For example, Chhina et al. [10] focus on the stages and actors involved in the adoption process, while Gökalp et al. [17], Dehghani et al. [18] and Toufaily et al. [9] provide a detailed empirical investigation on factors that have an affect blockchain adoption.

Furthermore, authors in the prior literature claim that blockchain adoption research is linked with obstacles, potential barriers and benefits for various domains [22–24]. Any doubts are linked with blockchain-related challenges and the key ones identified in the literature include technical risks (e.g. scalability), infrastructure requirements, regulatory uncertainty, mistrust of early decision-makers, and lack of necessary competencies. Some authors remain sceptical about blockchain adoption and are urged to consider alternative solutions rather than follow hype trends (e.g., [25]). For example, Radanović and Likić [26] point out that blockchain integration in healthcare could lead to higher expenses, at least initially. This is due the cost of implementation can offset any savings achieved by reducing bureaucracy and increasing efficiency.

From a business models perspective blockchain technology offers new opportunities for decentralised communication and trust, potentially impacting corporate business models [27]. Scholars provide a number of research for blockchain integration models focused on the implementation of new and existing systems and proof-of-concept demonstrations (e.g. [28, 29]). Blockchain technology adoption can improve the profitability of various organizations, and improve the productivity and efficiency of businesses, prompting them to rethink their current business strategies [30, 31]. Nevertheless, because the technology is still in its early stages and research into the implications of various types of blockchain (public, private, and consortium) is limited, its relevance in business model innovation requires further research. Hence, before making a major investment in blockchain infrastructure, companies must carefully consider the potential benefits and dangers since the utilization of blockchain technology requires significant investment and skilled labour [30]. To conclude, the phenomenon of blockchain adoption requires multilevel, empirically tested research involving various interdependent parties to expand the existing knowledge.

3   Research Method

3.1   Data Collection

In this study, the data collection is divided into two steps. In the first step, we collected data through online semi-structured interviews with 10 participants from 10 different companies (see Table 1). The participants for the interviews were selected based on snowball sampling. When selecting the participants for the interviews, we ensured that they were willing to take part in the study voluntarily and had experience in implementing blockchain in their organizations. During interviews, we focused on three themes: the background of the organization, competitive advantages related to blockchain, and factors influencing blockchain adoption in the particular case. The interviews were recorded and transcribed for further analysis. In addition, notes were taken during the interviews. After analyzing the data, we identified a list of dimensions and sub-dimensions that the organizations considered when implementing blockchain. In step 2, we reached out to 5 interviewees who agreed for a second round of one-to-one interviews where we showed them the identified dimensions and requested them to prioritize the dimensions based on their importance. We have also asked them to justify their prioritization. These interview sessions were also recorded and transcribed. In addition, notes were taken by the researcher. After analyzing the collected data, we developed the final decision-making framework.

Table 1. Interview participants

Participants	Country	Position	Industry	Interview duration	Involved in the second round
Expert 1	Estonia	CEO	Consultancy	1:16	Yes
Expert 2	Kazakhstan/ Turkey	Consultant	Consultancy	0:54	Yes
Expert 3	Finland	Principal technology strategist	Banking	1:03	No
Expert 4	Belgium	CEO/co-founder	Supply chain	0:45	No
Expert 5	UAE	Senior Consultant	Consultancy	0:53	Yes
Expert 6	Switzerland	Co-founder	Supply chain	0:28	No
Expert 7	Finland	CEO	Information Technology and Services	1:17	Yes
Expert 8	USA	Senior tech specialist	Government official	1:42	Yes
Expert 9	Australia	CEO	Information Technology and Services	0:33	Yes
Expert 10	Netherlands	Co-Founder	Supply chain	0:41	No

3.2 Data Analysis

To analyze the collected data and classify issues, we used the Gioia method [32] which allows us to optimize the analysis process and extract all insights from interviews. The data analysis contained three main stages. First, we repeatedly looked over the collected empirical data and assigned codes to describe various content parts. Second, to create more abstract notions also referred to as second-order concepts, we classified the linked codes. Third, we combined the second-order ideas into four broader dimensions: infrastructure, business models, operational processes, management and environmental impact. Figure 1 shows the dimensions together with the related sub-dimensions.

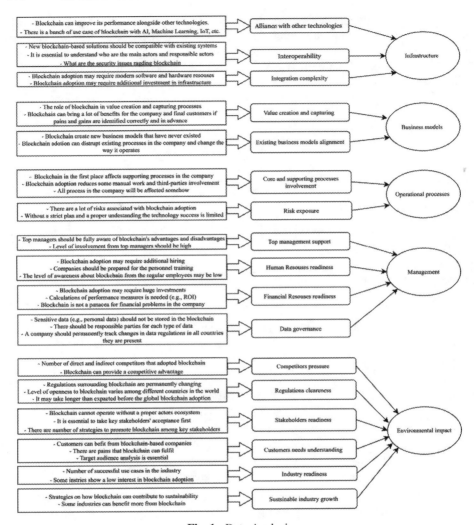

Fig. 1. Data Analysis

4   Results

From our interviews, we understood that every case is unique and the decision-making process significantly varies. Nevertheless, it is possible to identify and summarize the most important steps to consider before blockchain adoption. We also observed that organizations are most interested in permissioned solutions since there are too many insecurities and uncertainties around permissionless ones. Based on our empirical data, we identified 5 main dimensions that experts consider when making adoption decisions regarding blockchain. In Table 2 we summarize the identified dimensions with a short explanation and based on the collected data provide 27 potential questions companies should ask themselves before blockchain implementation. Next, we explain these dimensions in more detail.

4.1 Infrastructure

The resources and tools that enable blockchain-based systems to work effectively are blockchain infrastructure [12]. Blockchain is more than just computer code since it combines both hardware and software. Our interviewees mentioned that their organizations must pay upfront investments in terms of infrastructure and training before implementing blockchain. They have also mentioned the interoperability issues regarding blockchain and existing information systems that are used in organizations. They described that these are often heavy investments, which may result in looking for alternative solutions. For example, Expert 5 from the financial industry mentioned,

"After 2 years of trying, we decided to choose an alternative solution… blockchain requires additional investments in new infrastructure for interfaces, hardware, people… it is not so easy to link various systems together and now we are not looking for blockchain anymore".

Our interviewees also noted the complexities of changing existing infrastructure in comparison to establishing new infrastructure for newly established companies. For example, Expert 8 from the consultancy agency added that

"When a startup is established based on blockchain ideas the infrastructure is created for blockchain. For existing businesses, the situation is way complex and requires a detailed technical architecture analysis".

Our interviewees also discussed the fact that blockchain-based infrastructure development requires different skills. They also mentioned that if the infrastructure contains both blockchain and other solutions, skills from different areas would be necessary. Furthermore, the experts need to understand the interoperability issues among different systems. In order to highlight these issues, Expert 4 mentioned,

"It is important to note that existing knowledge of software project management is not sufficient for implementing blockchain… So we need to be sure that if there are multiple solutions in place, it will be possible to make them communicate with each other so the aspect of interoperability is also a challenge".

In line with the above, experts also mentioned that it is essential to consider what other technologies will be used (e.g. IoT or AI) when developing infrastructure for blockchain. Finally, a few experts argued that businesses do not want to use a blockchain as it would restrict their options for future external collaboration. They think the resources or infrastructure available for blockchain development are not enough, which is a potential obstacle or constraint to implementation.

Taken together, the frequent themes surrounding infrastructure that were highlighted during the interviews were interoperability, infrastructure readiness, and alliance with other technologies (IoT, AI). Consequently, we have included these sub-themes in the proposed decision-making framework.

4.2 Management

"When you start thinking about blockchain the question should be not about blockchain", Expert 10 claims. Several experts mentioned management and its support when making a decision about blockchain adoption. From the interviews we found that senior managers are more concerned with technical performance, perceived benefits and profitability and this finding is supported by the literature (e.g. [33]).

Our interviewees argued about strict requirements for additional education before adopting blockchain not only for regular employees but for business owners in particular. Experts from consulting agencies claimed that on the market, there is a huge potential for blockchain but without proper knowledge about the technology and surrounding environment, a lot of worthy projects fail. At the same time, 2 experts draw attention to the financial side of blockchain adoption and take into consideration all of the potential costs associated with the technology. For example, Expert 2 mentioned,

> *"For me, it is clear that there is a huge gap in education and awareness about blockchain itself... we can create a fully operational blockchain-based solution but they fail because of knowledge absence and because company owners decided just to follow hype... it is about people and may take months and a great deal of money to create a governance system for people".*

Hence, our interviewees are certain that to make the technology fully operational it is essential to have skilled employees, arrange additional training for the current staff member and open additional hiring if needed. To support this statement, Expert 4 mentioned that

> *"It is really hard to find the right balance between making people understand the benefits of blockchain, without necessity entering too many technical details that were not understandable by them".*

Additionally, most experts mentioned data governance must be considered before blockchain adoption since most companies view the disadvantage of public blockchains because of their excessive transparency. Our interviewees view data privacy, in terms of anonymity and transparency, as a contributing factor to the permissioned blockchain adoption focusing on the benefits and the controlled nature of such solutions. For example, Expert 8 mentioned,

> *"There is no pressure from governments in our case: the data access is limited, all parties involved are trustworthy, the ecosystem is private, sensitive data is stored on the cloud services ... but transparency and data immutability bring the whole industry* (supply chain) *to the next stage... there is strict control on who adds data, what type of data and who verifies it".*

Overall, the themes surrounding the management dimension include top management support, human resources readiness, financial resources readiness and data governance.

4.3 Business Models

In the business model domains we identified 2 themes and included them in the final framework: value creation and capture, and the existing company's business model alignment. Those themes were identified according to the expert's vision of blockchain adoption in organisations that can lead to a unique digital infrastructure that facilitates innovation in business models. Our interviewees mentioned that blockchain has the potential to transform companies' operations, offering new opportunities for growth, efficiency and sustainability in various spheres. For example, Expert 5's opinion on this matter is:

> *"Companies should consider adopting a new strategy and a completely different approach doing business… it is mostly about new business opportunities and value networks".*

Because our experts are more familiar with the kind of innovation that blockchain enables, they are looking for opportunities related to start-up creation. Additionally, they focused not only on the company level solution but also provided some examples of value that individuals can generate (e.g., an open market for everyone to start a business around blockchain, low competition among blockchain professionals, new work opportunities, etc.). For example, Expert 9 added that

> *"Proportionally, more money can be made in the blockchain technology market… The value is vivid for both companies and individuals",*

Additionally, our interviewees mentioned that among the main reasons why companies fail with blockchain implementation are the desire for independence and autonomy, regulation of industry and individuals, dependence on demand, duplication of projects, inability to control the project, desire to work with only one communication channel and new money-making tools. Nevertheless, Expert 2 added that

> *"Blockchain is transforming the entire digital culture and business models, it is unparalleled, and we should expect this technology to become fundamental in the world in the very near future. Activity is higher than you think".*

Overall, almost all experts are confident that the technology is trying to solve a problem that had not been solved by previous technologies and there are so few successful global cases that support the new way of doing business. But the main problem is explained by Expert 1,

> *"People who are very, very enthusiastic about the technology may fail…the point is that they don't look at the business and do not know how to look at the market… you would need to have an interdisciplinary approach…It's really important to understand the business you're trying to serve".*

4.4 Operational Processes

The operational process associated with blockchain adoption varies depending on the specific domain or sphere. All processes in a company can be classified as core and supporting [34]. The main difference between them is that the core ones are important for the fundamental value creation of the organisation, while the latter is important to the smooth running of the organisation as a whole. Our experts added that core operational processes directly impact the company's bottom line, while ancillary operational processes contribute indirectly to the organisation's success by providing the necessary infrastructure and assistance. Additionally, experts highlighted the importance of a detailed analysis of all processes in the company before considering blockchain adoption and understanding how blockchain can improve them in the short and long term. For instance, Expert 6 claimed,

> *"Understanding the core processes of the organization that will be affected by blockchain is among important steps to take... while the technology will change the supporting processes and improve the way the company operates".*

Additionally, our interviewees mentioned that there are scenarios for effective blockchain implementation in almost all areas of business but associated with a number of risks. We combined answers from experts 2, 5, 7 and 9 and linked them with 3 types of risks. 1. Systemic risks that include market risks, currency risks (standard currencies volatility), and random risks (unexpected economic crises or changes in the industry). 2. Non-systemic risks: user errors and lack of knowledge, fraud at the smart contract level, technical problems with protocols, poor management of companies leading to inability to meet the obligations, and high project leverage. 3. Regulatory risk: adoption of a law, the introduction of a package of by laws, formation of a broad judicial practice. Expert 2 added the following:

> *"The winners are not those with superficial knowledge of the field, but those who fundamentally develop in all areas, monitor the market and continually update their skills".*

Collectively, the themes included in the final framework surrounding operational processes include core and supporting process involvement and risk exposure.

4.5 Environmental Impact

Based on the conducted interviews, we identified 6 themes that can be taken into consideration in the analysis of the environmental impact: competitors' pressure, customer needs understanding, regulations clearness, stakeholders' readiness, industry readiness and sustainable industry growth. Our interviewees mentioned that the environmental impact of blockchain adoption on the corporate level has become a hot topic in recent years and competitors and consumers analysis is essential because it provides insights about market needs and preferences. Experts mentioned that with this knowledge a business can develop strategies to help it stand out from its competitors, attract and retain consumers, and succeed in the long term. In this case, Expert 6 mentioned:

"We are not the only one developing solution in that field... One of the problems with the blockchain is that it has a level of complexity, which is much bigger than others working on other technologies. So it's very important that when you are ready to launch it, it already includes all the elements that you and all involved members need".

In the case of laws, the blockchain itself is a new technology and there is still no clear vision from central authorities on how to regulate the industry and experts claim that the speed of blockchain adoption depends on clear regulations. Nevertheless, we found that experts are not positive about the current state of regulations and are waiting for debates surrounding blockchain. Our interviewees mentioned that regulation has to be adequate and understandable not only for companies but also for individuals. For example, Expert 9 mentioned:

"I do not share the optimism that there will be anything adequate in the next 2–3 years. We are going down the same road as 25 years ago when regulating the Internet".

At the same time, Expert 1 added: *"The legal body is not ready. Because as I said, the lowest or assuming is paradigm central planning and central control. Decentralization means the complete change in the current structure".*

Our interviewees also discussed the challenges surrounding readiness of the key stakeholders. Some experts were positive about the openness of their partners to transform business using blockchain, while others faced resistance and had to create a new promotion strategy among stakeholders. For instance, Expert 4 mentioned:

"At least for us we knew what blockchain was, and because one of the main problems was that everybody was associating blockchain with cryptocurrency. So it was not easy in the beginning to explain to them why we're using blockchain, it was something new for them".

Finally, experts slightly covered industry readiness and sustainability trends. In most cases, they agreed there is still a limited number of success stories around blockchain and all industries are not ready for blockchain adoption. While some businesses have embraced blockchain as a revolutionary technology, others are still hesitant to explore its advantages and disadvantages. Blockchain technology is most commonly adopted in sectors that rely heavily on transactions and data management, such as banking, supply chain management and healthcare. Nevertheless, our experts are confident that to achieve sustainable industry growth businesses must overcome regulatory obstacles including data privacy and security before they can fully utilize blockchain.

Table 2. Summary of decision-making factors and potential questions to ask

Definition	Description	Potential questions
Infrastructure for blockchain		
Interoperability	Blockchains' capacity to connect and interact with other systems in a coordinated manner	What requirements must a blockchain-based solution meet to operate successfully with existing systems?
Integration complexity	A set of all required resources to smoothly integrate blockchain	Do you consider all hardware and software resources? What are the maintenance and system updates requirements?
Alliance with other technologies	Blockchain can be considered alongside other technologies (e.g., AI). A clear understanding of what technologies will be connected with blockchain and why	How many technologies will be connected with blockchain? What infrastructure is needed?
Business models		
Value creation	What value can the company create for the final customer utilizing blockchain	How does your company create value and what is the role of blockchain in the process?
Value capturing	What value can the company generate and turn into profit utilizing blockchain	What benefits will you gain from blockchain adoption?
Existing business models' alignment	The way blockchain affects existing models in the company;	Does blockchain disrupt the current business models of your company or are slight adjustments needed?
Operational processes		
Core and supporting processes involvement	The number of core and supporting processes that will be affected by blockchain adoption	To what extent the blockchain adoption will influence the core processes? To what extent the blockchain adoption will influence the supporting processes?
Risk exposure	Evaluation of all potential risks related to blockchain adoption	How are you going to measure blockchain-related risks?
Management		

(*continued*)

Table 2. (*continued*)

Definition	Description	Potential questions
Top management support	The level of involvement and awareness about blockchain	Do top managers understand the whole nature of blockchain technology and the challenges associated?
Human resources readiness	Knowledge level about blockchain among employees, required training time, the relevance of additional hiring, etc	Do you have skilled employees that are aware of blockchain? Do you need additional training for personnel and how long will it take?
Financial resources readiness	The efficient number of financial resources to cover the whole blockchain adoption process	Do you have enough financial resources to adopt the technology? What is an expected ROI and how long will it take?
Data governance	Set of standards and requirements on how data is stored, processed and gathered; responsible actors	Is there a requirement to store a large amount of data? What governance strategies are the most appropriate for the case?
Environmental impact		
Competitors pressure	Assessment of competitors' readiness and openness to digital transformation trends; ability to provide unique solutions using emerging technologies	What are your direct and indirect competitors? What competitive strategies were crucial to blockchain commercial success in your sphere?
Regulations clearness	Set of rules to avoid legal and regulatory fragmentation during blockchain adoption and utilisation	What is the regulatory environment related to blockchain in the industry? What are the strategies to ensure that a company is able to respond to changes quickly after blockchain adoption?
Stakeholders readiness	The number of participants in the network for smooth operation; support from the key stakeholders	What are your strategies to promote the acceptance of blockchain among the main stakeholders?

(*continued*)

Table 2. (*continued*)

Definition	Description	Potential questions
Customers needs understanding	Ability to create a clear vision of user persona including current customers and new potential markets	How do you review your product development efforts related to blockchain to ensure be in line with what the customers want?
Sustainable industry growth	Set of activities on how blockchain can ensure sustainability in various domains	How can you ensure that you can contribute to sustainable growth in the industry?
Industry readiness	Set of frameworks, successful use cases and research in the particular domain	Are there any success stories and use cases of blockchain adoption in your industry?

4.6 Decision-Making Framework

From our analysis, we developed a process model for decision-making and important dimensions companies must consider before blockchain adoption (Fig. 2). To validate the model, five experts agreed to prioritize dimensions according to their experience and vision. The experts prioritized the dimensions into three levels. Experts assigned priority by considering a detailed analysis of the possible technology adoption effects, ensuring that both its advantages and disadvantages are considered. Priority levels also make sure that the technology is aligned with the organisation's goals and values. By determining which factors are most important, decision-makers can make more strategic decisions about whether a particular technology is right for their company.

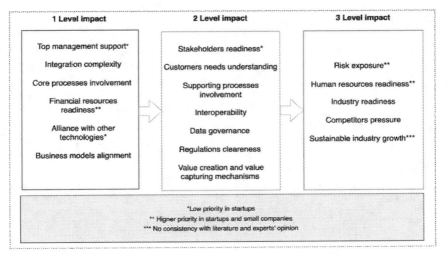

Fig. 2. Blockchain adoption decision-making framework

We found the importance of various factors depending on the size of the company, the experts' background and their position. For example, in startups that are created around blockchain, experts give less priority to stakeholders' readiness and top management support, since the decisions to adopt blockchain are made by business owners and *"stakeholders are never ready"*, according to Expert 1. At the same time, experts mentioned that for small companies and startups, it is highly important to control and understand all risks associated with blockchain adoption and prepare human and financial resources. There are a lot of discussions around blockchain and how it can contribute to sustainability. In that case, there are a lot of assumptions and speculations around this topic but more time is needed to notice a real contribution. Indeed, experts did not have a clear vision on this point and opinions were divided into completely different directions. Overall, our work provides a guideline on what dimensions alongside potential questions can be considered before adopting any emerging technology. Even though there are a lot of use cases discussing the applicability of blockchain, the technology still is not a panacea for most of them.

5   Discussion

5.1   Theoretical Implications

Our paper has two major theoretical implications. First, we found the major concepts related to blockchain adoption in companies. Under these concepts, we have identified five dimensions: infrastructure, business models, operational processes, management and environmental impact. Afterwards, we provide a detailed description of all dimensions and their prioritization according to experts' comments. We divide impact factors into 3 levels to explain the most crucial ones for practitioners. For example, we found that top management support and the technology integration complexity are considered highly important ones, while industry readiness and competitors' pressure do not hinder business people from blockchain adoption. Second, under the prior research, we identified that there is no clear answer when to use blockchain at the corporate level. Our results revealed that it is highly important to consider all dimensions in specific requirements, challenges, and potential benefits of blockchain adoption.

5.2   Practical Implications

Our study has several practical implications. First, during the interviews with our experts we revealed that global blockchain adoption is associated with a number of challenges and among the most important is a limited understanding of the technology itself. A lot of business people consider blockchain following hype without a proper analysis of other possible solutions. We provide a detailed framework of potential dimensions to consider with a 3 level of impact factors to guide decision-makers in various domains. Additionally, we found that the prioritization depends on the size of the company and awareness about blockchain among the main stakeholders. Second, the decision-making process of any emerging technology adoption is a complex procedure that requires a detailed analysis. We provide a summary of decision-making factors and potential questions to ask before blockchain utilization.

5.3 Limitations and Future Research Directions

The current study has several limitations. First, we conducted 10 interviews with experts from different countries during the research. Future research can expand our findings by considering a more extensive set of experts from various domains and countries. At the same time, the study can be limited to one country or a particular domain to provide a more comprehensive understanding of the challenges surrounding blockchain and the factors that lead to its adoption. Second, we provide an adoption framework based on the collected data from the experts and future validation through the case studies may broaden the findings. Third, future research can also focus on understanding the specific criteria that influence practitioners' intention to adopt blockchain in different use cases.

6 Conclusions

Blockchain technology has recently attracted a lot of attention. In this study, we identified the dimensions that business people take into consideration before blockchain adoption on the corporate level and developed the adoption decision-making framework to support the technology utilization process. The current research derived the following conclusions. First, we contributed to the existing knowledge with empirical findings and revealed the importance of looking at a broader perspective before blockchain adoption. Second, during the interviews data analysis using the Gioa method we identified 5 core dimensions and 18 sub-dimensions surrounding blockchain utilization. We validated the final framework by means of the second round of interviews with 5 experts and found that the decision-making process and priority of dimensions depends on various factors (e.g., size of the company or awareness level about blockchain). Third, the deeper insight into the business people's perspective reveals many directions for improvement.

References

1. Six, N., Herbaut, N., Salinesi, C.: Blockchain software patterns for the design of decentralized applications: a systematic literature review. Blockchain: Res. Appl. **3**, 100061 (2022)
2. Rejeb, A., Keogh, J.G., Zailani, S., Treiblmaier, H., Rejeb, K.: Blockchain technology in the food industry: a review of potentials, challenges and future research directions. Logistics. **4**, 27 (2020)
3. Ren, Y.-S., Ma, C.-Q., Chen, X.-Q., Lei, Y.-T., Wang, Y.-R.: Sustainable finance and blockchain: a systematic review and research agenda. Res. Int. Bus. Financ. **64**, 101871 (2023)
4. Elloh Adja, Y.C., Hammi, B., Serhrouchni, A., Zeadally, S.: A blockchain-based certificate revocation management and status verification system. Comput. Secur. **104**, 102209 (2021)
5. Andrew, J., Isravel, D.P., Sagayam, K.M., Bhushan, B., Sei, Y., Eunice, J.: Blockchain for healthcare systems: architecture, security challenges, trends and future directions. J. Netw. Comput. Appl. **215**, 103633 (2023)
6. Zhang, C., Xian, K., Wu, Q., Yang, H., Lang, J., Wang, X.: Blockchain-based power digital asset security management framework. Procedia Comput. Sci. **208**, 354–360 (2022)
7. Pan, X., Pan, X., Song, M., Ai, B., Ming, Y.: Blockchain technology and enterprise operational capabilities: an empirical test. Int. J. Inf. Manage. **52**, 101946 (2020)

8. Farshidi, S., Jansen, S., Espana, S., Verkleij, J.: Decision support for blockchain platform selection: three industry case studies. IEEE Trans. Eng. Manage. **67**, 1109–1128 (2020)
9. Toufaily, E., Zalan, T., Dhaou, S.B.: A framework of blockchain technology adoption: an investigation of challenges and expected value. Inf. Manage. **58**, 103444 (2021)
10. Chhina, S., Chadhar, M., Firmin, S., Tatnall, A.: Blockchain adoption framework using innovation translation approach - the preliminary study. In: ACIS 2021 Proceedings, 85
11. Sunmola, F.T., Burgess, P., Tan, A.: Building blocks for blockchain adoption in digital transformation of sustainable supply chains. Procedia Manuf. **55**, 513–520 (2021)
12. Upadhyay, N.: Demystifying blockchain: a critical analysis of challenges, applications and opportunities. Int. J. Inf. Manage. **54**, 102120 (2020)
13. Puthal, D., Mohanty, S.P., Kougianos, E., Das, G.: When do we need the blockchain? IEEE Consum. Electron. Mag. **10**, 53–56 (2021)
14. Krichen, M., Ammi, M., Mihoub, A., Almutiq, M.: Blockchain for modern applications: a survey. Sensors **22**, 5274 (2022)
15. Hassija, V., Zeadally, S., Jain, I., Tahiliani, A., Chamola, V., Gupta, S.: Framework for determining the suitability of blockchain: criteria and issues to consider. Trans. Emerg. Telecommun. Technol. **32** (2021)
16. Büyüközkan, G., Tüfekçi, G.: A decision-making framework for evaluating appropriate business blockchain platforms using multiple preference formats and VIKOR. Inf. Sci. **571**, 337–357 (2021)
17. Gökalp, E., Gökalp, M.O., Çoban, S.: Blockchain-based supply chain management: understanding the determinants of adoption in the context of organizations. Inf. Syst. Manag. **39**, 100–121 (2020)
18. Dehghani, M., William Kennedy, R., Mashatan, A., Rese, A., Karavidas, D.: High interest, low adoption. A mixed-method investigation into the factors influencing organisational adoption of blockchain technology. J. Bus. Res. **149**, 393–411 (2022)
19. Wust, K., Gervais, A.: Do you need a blockchain? In: 2018 Crypto Valley Conference on Blockchain Technology (CVCBT) (2018)
20. Farahmand, H., Farahmand, M.A.: Preparing for blockchain technology in the energy industry: how energy sector leaders can make informed decisions during the blockchain adoption process. In: Proceedings of the Annual Hawaii International Conference on System Sciences (2019)
21. Roth, T., Stohr, A., Amend, J., Fridgen, G., Rieger, A.: Blockchain as a driving force for federalism: a theory of cross-organizational task-technology fit. Int. J. Inf. Manage. **68**, 102476 (2023)
22. Marsal-Llacuna, M.-L.: Future living framework: is blockchain the next enabling network? Technol. Forecast. Soc. Chang. **128**, 226–234 (2018)
23. Zheng, X.R., Lu, Y.: Blockchain technology – recent research and future trend. Enterp. Inf. Syst. **16** (2021)
24. Bedin, A.R., Capretz, M., Mir, S.: Blockchain for collaborative businesses. Mobile Networks Appl. **26**, 277–284 (2020)
25. Chowdhury, M.J., Colman, A., Kabir, M.A., Han, J., Sarda, P.: Blockchain versus database: a critical analysis. In: 2018 17th IEEE International Conference on Trust, Security and Privacy in Computing and Communications/12th IEEE International Conference on Big Data Science and Engineering (TrustCom/BigDataSE) (2018)
26. Radanović, I., Likić, R.: Opportunities for use of blockchain technology in medicine. Appl. Health Econ. Health Policy **16**, 583–590 (2018)
27. Chong, A.Y., Lim, E.T., Hua, X., Zheng, S., Tan, C.-W.: Business on chain: a comparative case study of five blockchain-inspired business models. J. Assoc. Inf. Syst. **20**, 1308–1337 (2019)

28. Belhi, A., Gasmi, H., Bouras, A., Aouni, B., Khalil, I.: Integration of business applications with the blockchain: odoo and hyperledger fabric open source proof of concept. IFAC-PapersOnLine. **54**, 817–824 (2021)
29. Ciotta, V., Mariniello, G., Asprone, D., Botta, A., Manfredi, G.: Integration of blockchains and smart contracts into construction information flows: proof-of-concept. Autom. Constr. **132**, 103925 (2021)
30. Marikyan, D., Papagiannidis, S., Rana, O.F., Ranjan, R.: Blockchain: a business model innovation analysis. Digit. Bus. **2**, 100033 (2022)
31. Sjödin, D., Parida, V., Jovanovic, M., Visnjic, I.: Value creation and value capture alignment in business model innovation: a process view on outcome-based business models. J. Prod. Innov. Manag. **37**, 158–183 (2020)
32. Gioia, D.A., Corley, K.G., Hamilton, A.L.: Seeking qualitative rigor in inductive research: notes on the gioia methodology. Organ. Res. Methods **16**, 15–31 (2013)
33. Karamchandani, A., Srivastava, S.K., Srivastava, R.K.: Perception-based model for analyzing the impact of enterprise blockchain adoption on SCM in the Indian service industry. Int. J. Inf. Manage. **52**, 102019 (2020)
34. Kock, N., McQueen, R.: Knowledge and information communication in organizations: an analysis of core, support and improvement processes. Knowl. Process. Manag. **5**, 29–40 (1998)
35. Sternberg, H.S., Hofmann, E., Roeck, D.: The struggle is real: insights from a supply chain blockchain case. J. Bus. Logist. **42**, 71–87 (2020)
36. Azogu, I., Norta, A., Papper, I., Longo, J., Draheim, D.: A framework for the adoption of blockchain technology in healthcare information management systems. In: Proceedings of the 12th International Conference on Theory and Practice of Electronic Governance (2019)

Privacy Perceptions in Digital Games: A Study with Information Technology (IT) Undergraduates

Mônica da Silva[1,2]([✉]) [ID], Erica Mourão[1] [ID], Magaywer Moreira de Paiva[1] [ID], José Viterbo[1] [ID], and Luciana Salgado[1] [ID]

[1] Institute of Computing, Fluminense Federal University, Niterói, RJ, Brazil
{monica_silva,ericamourao,magaywermp}@id.uff.br,
{viterbo,luciana}@ic.uff.br
[2] Instituto Federal de Mato Grosso (IFMT), Sorriso, MT, Brazil

Abstract. This study explores the perceptions and practices of undergraduates in Information Technology (IT) regarding privacy issues in digital games. This topic becomes relevant in the current scenario where artificial intelligence (AI) is increasingly integrated into digital games, providing an enhanced experience for players. However, this integration poses security and privacy challenges, the understanding of which is crucial for both players and developers. The primary objective of this research is to comprehend the participants' perceptions and understandings of privacy in digital games. We employed a qualitative and quantitative methodology to address our research inquiries. Through an online form of data collection, we obtained 61 responses. Among the obtained information, we observed that 40% of the students are interested in pursuing a career in game development, and 50% would consider this possibility. Noteworthy among the identified issues is the necessity for companies to devise more effective means of communicating their privacy policies to players/users, adapting the language to their target audience. Participants reported attacks related to online multiplayer games and expressed concerns about the security of personal data.

Keywords: Privacy · Personal data · Game Development · Digital Game

1 Introduction

In the contemporary era, Artificial Intelligence (AI) has deeply infiltrated various technologies, including digital games. Modern games have incorporated technologies such as AI, machine learning, and data mining to enhance the player's experience [10, 19]. Experts anticipate that the convergence of games and AI will become more pronounced in the coming years, especially in titles destined for the Metaverse, where new technologies and integrations will add value to both the games and the pedagogical methods employed in serious games [4]. Experts estimate that by 2025, the serious games market will grow by 25%, an increase

Published by Springer Nature Switzerland AG 2023
M. Janssen et al. (Eds.): I3E 2023, LNCS 14316, pp. 183–194, 2023.
https://doi.org/10.1007/978-3-031-50040-4_14

driven by the influence of the Metaverse [7]. Simultaneously, projections indicate that the AI and video game markets will reach values of US\$ 126 billion and US\$ 268.81 million, respectively, by 2025 [4,10].

However, besides enhancing gameplay and immersion, the integration of AI can assist in protecting players from attacks and "cheaters", a growing necessity as many players feel insecure in online multiplayer game environments [4]. Renowned games like FIFA, Half-Life, The Last of Us, Minecraft, and Halo: Combat Evolved have proactively integrated AI into their frameworks [10]. Given this evolution, undergraduate programs focused on systems and game development must encourage students to create features that comply with regulations and safeguard user privacy [1,15].

In response to the escalating concerns about privacy in digital games, this study aims to explore first-year Information Technology (IT) students' perceptions and understandings of the practices and dilemmas related to privacy in this context.

The goal is to understand the privacy-related perspectives of future game developers who are currently beginners in an IT course. These views can significantly influence how games will be developed and utilized. We seek to answer the research question (RQ): **How do IT students perceive and interact with privacy features in digital games, and are there gender differences in intentions to become future game developers?**. This RQ is motivated by an initial investigation of how future developers perceive data privacy in games [12,18] and if there are divergences in the perspectives of men and women [13]. To this end, we devised a study with a quali-quantitative approach, outlined through the following research sub-questions (SQ):

SQ1 - *How do perceptions and intentions of becoming a game developer in the future differ between different gender identities?*

SQ2 - *How do future game developers perceive and regard the privacy of their personal data during the use of games?*

SQ3 - *What experiences of attacks on privacy or leakage of personal data are reported by participants?*

This study is an initial study, which was answered by 61 first-year students of an IT course at Fluminense Federal University (UFF) in Brazil. The team collected data through an online questionnaire. Among the collected data, it's crucial to note that companies need to adopt innovative methods of communicating their privacy policies to players/users, using vocabulary more suitable for their target audience. We also observed that 40% of participants are interested in working with game development, and 50% would consider this possibility.

The structure of this article is as follows: The subsequent section provides an overview of privacy issues in digital games. Section 3 details the methodology employed in the research. Next, Sect. 4 unveils the obtained results, while Sect. 5 fosters a brief discussion on the main identified points. Section 6 highlights the study's main limitations. Finally, Sect. 7 outlines our conclusions and proposes suggestions for future research.

2 Background

Privacy, a concept noted for its complexity and multifaceted nature, often emerges as a paradox due to the discrepancy between the concerns users express and the actions they undertake to protect their privacy [5,9]. This paradox is particularly prominent in the digital gaming industry, where the protection of personal data has garnered significant attention. This is underscored by recent lawsuits against companies like Epic Games for privacy violations, a trend also observed in cases involving games such as Silent Hill, Pokémon Go, and Ingress [8,9,16,18].

The industry is governed by a myriad of global legislations, including the General Data Protection Regulation (GDPR) in Europe, the General Data Protection Law (LGPD) in Brazil, the Personal Information Protection Law (PIPL) in China, and the California Consumer Privacy Act (CCPA) in the USA [1,6,14]. These legislations pose a considerable challenge for game developers, especially when incorporating Artificial Intelligence (AI) systems that significantly impact individual privacy [11].

Current research endeavors are focused on understanding players' perceptions of privacy, particularly within the realm of augmented and virtual reality games, which have raised significant concerns among players [9,12,16,18]. These studies aim to enhance players' privacy protection by involving them in the co-creation process, utilizing elements such as cards to foster reflection and discussion [2]. Moreover, there is a growing recognition of the need for further discourse concerning the challenges young system developers or ICT undergraduates face in complying with existing legislation, especially when navigating different laws across countries [1,15]. Furthermore, researchers have noted a correlation between women's gaming experiences and their propensity to pursue careers in game development [13].

3 Methodology

In this study, 70 students (were invited) from the first year of a TI course at UFF were invited via email by the course coordinator to respond to an online questionnaire (Gooble Forms) available from May-28-2023 to June-02-2023. The questionnaire, divided into five sections, explored demographic characteristics, attitudes towards privacy, specific aspects of privacy in digital games, and career intentions, in addition to offering space for final reflections. The research generated qualitative and quantitative data, utilizing responses structured in a five-point Likert scale, ranging from 1 - Strongly Disagree to 5 - Strongly Agree, and open-ended questions allowing detailed and personalized responses.

The research adhered to the ethical standards outlined in Resolutions 466/2012 and 510/2016 of the National Health Council of Brazil. Despite not undergoing review by an Ethics Committee, we requested participants to sign the Informed Consent Form to ensure the confidentiality and privacy of the collected data. To protect the students' anonymity, we chose not to disclose the full name of the course, referring to it simply as Information Technology course.

Participants received detailed information about the study objectives and the responsible researchers, with a clear indication that the utilization of the data would be for academic purposes only. Moreover, we guaranteed access to the study results in a suitable environment, implementing strategies to reduce fatigue and stress, without offering financial compensation. Participation was voluntary and free from any coercion.

4   Results

The study gathered responses from 61 first-year IT course students out of a sample of 70. The complete anonymized dataset, including responses from all 61 participants, can be accessed at either of these links: https://doi.org/10.5281/zenodo.8350533 or the alternative link: https://osf.io/z3ynp/.

The demographic distribution of the respondents included 12 women and 49 men, all of whom are enrolled in an undergraduate course in Information Systems. Predominantly a young group, the respondents are divided into two age brackets: 17 to 24 years old and 25 to 30 years old, with further details provided in Table 1. From the data gathered, it is evident that a significant number of individuals harbor concerns about safeguarding their personal information during gaming sessions. Yet, it emerges that a substantial 77.05% of them seldom refer to privacy policies before engaging with the games, thus highlighting the manifestation of the so-called "privacy paradox".

4.1   Engage in the Game Development Between Different Genders (SQ1)

When we inquired about the intention to work in the field of game development in the future, we noticed significant interest among participants, distributed similarly between men and women. In analyzing the question **SQ1 - How do perceptions and intentions of becoming a game developer in the future differ between different gender identities?**, we explored the current professional status of the participants and their past with personal data attacks. As detailed in Table 1, a significant portion (73.80%) of respondents are currently unemployed, which is more prevalent among women.

Additionally, it was recorded that 41.67% of women expressed interest in working in the game development area, while over 50% are considering this possibility. These data are more promising in our country compared to those presented in the study by Sigurðardóttir (2019) [13], where lower interest from women is observed in Iceland and Norway. This study also highlights the need to expand the dissemination of information and guidance about opportunities for women in the field of game development.

Regarding the participants' experiences with possible personal data violations, 22.95% confirmed they had been victims of some attack, the details of which can be consulted in Subsect. 4.3. In contrast, a significant majority (77.05%) stated they had not noticed or suffered any invasion of their digital privacy.

Table 1. Information about participants.

Question	Answer options	Gender		All participants
		Male	Female	
Age	17–24 years	98.88%	91.67%	93.40%
	25–30 years	6.12%	8.33%	6.6%
Current occupation	Works with IT	12.25%	0%	9.9%
	Works but is not IT	14.29%	16.67%	14.70%
	Don't work, just study	71.43%	83.33%	73.80%
	Others (scholarship holder, researcher, etc.)	2.04%	0%	1.60%
Interest in working with games in the future	Yes	40.82%	41.67%	40.00%
	No	10.20%	8.33%	10.00%
	Maybe	48.98%	50.00%	50.00%

4.2 Player Behavior Regarding Some Privacy Issues (SQ2)

Regarding **SQ2 - How do future game developers perceive and regard the privacy of their personal data during the use of games?**, we conducted an analysis to identify participants' behavior concerning certain privacy issues while engaging with digital games, as depicted in Fig. 1. The data were gathered based on both objective (Likert scale) and discursive questions. Initially, we noted that a significant number of participants do not peruse the privacy policies before commencing the game (question 1). On the flip side, as illustrated in question 2, we found that 16.40% and 32.80% of participants either fully or partially agree that they harbor privacy concerns, a finding that aligns with the privacy paradox phenomenon.

To gather participants' perceptions on certain points, we conducted the following inquiries using the Likert scale. The results are presented in Fig. 1.

Question 1 - Before playing a game I read the privacy policy.
Question 2 - I am concerned about my privacy when using Digital Games.
Question 3 - When I use a game, I block access permissions to my cell phone.
Question 4 - I think my privacy is well protected in the games I play.
Question 5 - When I use a game that asks for identification, I use my real name.
Question 6 - When I register in the game, I provide my real data (CPF, Phone, E-mail, etc.).
Question 7 - I deactivate permissions for sensors or folders after using the game on my smartphone.

One noteworthy finding from Fig. 1 relates to Question 6, where 54.1% of the participants reported providing their genuine data during game platform registration. However, 14.75% strongly disagreed with this statement, not providing their real data, and 16.39% mostly disagreed, not providing real data most of the time. Additionally, in Question 5 of the same figure, it can be observed that 27.87% do not use their real names during gameplay, and 18.03% rarely do so. Nevertheless, many players, totaling 34.39% (24.87% agree and 9.8% strongly agree), continue to use their real names for in-game identification.

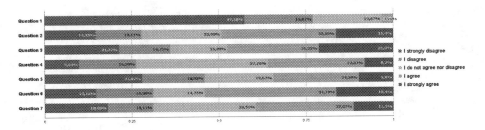

Fig. 1. Information from participants about how they perceive.

In the data analysis, utilizing the Shapiro-Wilk normality test, we observed that the p-value for the queries is less than 0.001, indicating that the values do not follow a normal distribution. This phenomenon might be attributed to the small size of the sample. Table 2 provides statistical information on the collected data, differentiating the data by gender and including details about the median, the standard deviation (SD), and the standard error (SE). From this table, we identified differences in the responses of males and females to questions 01 and 02. In the first question, women appear to pay more attention to the games' privacy policies than men. However, in the second question, they demonstrate lesser concern for privacy during gameplay.

We employed the Mann-Whitney test to evaluate the data, given that they originate from a Likert scale (ordinal qualitative). Simultaneously, we also applied a distribution to two independent groups (male and female) to examine the differences in the responses. Despite this, we concluded that there are no significant differences between the groups.

Considering this study is based on quali-quantitative data, we have structured some questions to capture the participants' perspectives more accurately. Concerning their views on privacy policies, we formulated the following question: **If you have tried to read the game's Privacy Policies, can you describe your experience?** Due to the similarity of the responses, we have chosen to present them in a structured manner.

1. **Lengthy and complex texts:** The majority of respondents expressed that privacy policies are often long and dense, making them arduous to read. This characteristic appears to discourage complete policy reading, with many respondents admitting to abandoning the reading before finishing due to the length and repetition of terms and phrases. For example, the response from P4 *"the texts are generally too verbose and overly lengthy"*.

2. **Difficulty in understanding the texts:** Furthermore, privacy policies seem to be complex for many users, especially due to the use of technical and

Table 2. Statistical information distributed by question and answers by gender.

	Gender	SE	Median	SD	Variance	Mann-Whitney - (p)
Question 1	Female	0.188	2	0.651	0.424	0.684
	Male	0.137	1	0.962	0.925	
Question 2	Female	0.358	3	1.240	1.538	0.550
	Male	0.188	4	1.319	1.741	
Question 3	Female	0.477	3	1.651	2.727	0.781
	Male	0.204		1.429	2.042	
Question 4	Female	0.271	3	0.937	0.879	0.349
	Male	0.160		1.118	1.250	
Question 5	Female	0.336	3	1.165	1.356	0.515
	Male	0.203		1.422	2.023	
Question 6	Female	0.417	4	1.443	2.083	0.686
	Male	0.187		1.307	1.708	
Question 7	Female	0.336	3.5	1.165	1.356	0.758
	Male	0.187	3	1.307	1.708	

legal terms. Some respondents mentioned that privacy policies contain "*I find the terms extremely difficult to read, with too many things to understand, and I believe that is intentional*" (P45) and "*...referring to various laws or regulations that, although easily accessible, are difficult to read.*" (P7).

3. **Disinterest and lack of access attempt:** Many participants expressed disinterest in reading the privacy policies or admitted never having tried to read. Some have justified this by considering the privacy policies as long-winded and tedious. Others choose to skip the text and jump right into the game.

4. **Concerns about privacy and transparency in access:** Some respondents expressed discomfort with the amount of data collected by games, as revealed by privacy policies. This indicates an underlying concern about privacy issues among some game users. On the other hand, several respondents reported that locating privacy policies is not a difficult task. Generally, privacy policies are easily accessible, appearing on the screen during the game registration or installation process.

5. **Trust in large game companies:** Some responses suggest a tendency to trust privacy policies from well-established game companies, as noted by one participant (P50), "*I usually play games that are well-established in the gaming scene, which automatically makes me trust their privacy policies*". This seems to occur even without careful reading of the policies, with users relying on the reputation of these companies, as indicated by another participant's response highlighting that "*It is a reading that is not at all intuitive, but in games from big companies, it is a clear read. It conveys trust*"(P57).

The data gathered underscores the necessity of devising innovative methods to communicate privacy policies effectively, particularly within the gaming industry, which encompasses highly creative groups. Modern games often require conveying privacy protocols to a broad spectrum of users, accentuating the demand for improved communication channels that encompass players and their guardians, especially concerning minors.

In an endeavor to delve deeper into the behavior surrounding privacy protection related to popular features in smartphone games, we solicited responses to the question: **If you have tried to disable privacy permissions/functionality in the game, such as sensors and found it difficult, can you describe the functionality and/or problems?** This query aimed to understand the players' experiences and perspectives regarding privacy controls within games.

From the responses to this question, it emerged that a significant segment of players have actively engaged in modifying game features to enhance their privacy and security. Participants acknowledged the ease and intuitiveness of the process, recounting experiences such as restricting access to phone folders and denying permissions to access contact lists or GPS, primarily to conserve battery life or bolster privacy. Conversely, some participants found the process complex and needing clarification, attributing their confusion to verbose and unclear permission descriptions.

Moreover, concerns were raised regarding the involuntary grant of permissions as certain games or applications failed to operate without specific accesses, consequently, compelling players to compromise their privacy preferences. This has been a source of frustration, with particular emphasis on issues related to disabling GPS functionalities, which hinder the gameplay experience. Furthermore, participants voiced fears over potential personal information misuse, including unauthorized profile creation or data sales to third parties. We also noted specific challenges reported in managing access to private features like photo galleries or microphones, indicating areas needing refinement and improvement.

4.3   Described Privacy and Security Attacks (SQ3)

To identify which negative experiences participants had already encountered regarding personal data issues, especially in digital games, we formulated the following: **SQ3 - What experiences of attacks on privacy or leakage of personal data are reported by participants?**, we observed in Table 1 that 22.95% of participants reported having experienced some form of attack involving personal data. Although the majority (77.05%) of the participants did not report suffering any attacks or data breaches, those who did did disbelieve the attacks suffered. The data collected was analyzed and grouped by thematic similarity of the attacks reported by the participants:

1. **Attacks related to or within online games:**
   - Invasion and password change of a League of Legends game account, which was later recovered.
   - Invasion in a game called Point Blank, account invasion by a hacker.
   - Game account hacking experiences, without specifying the games.
   - Constant game disruptions, possibly caused by hackers, leading to hacked accounts and loss of access.

2. **Social media account invasions:**
   - Harassment on social media for an extended period, with the harasser obtaining personal and residential information.
   - Attempted invasion on Facebook.
   - Multiple account hacks on platforms like YouTube, Instagram, Twitter, and League of Legends, with successful resolution of the situations.
3. **Financial data attack (credit card cloning):**
   - Instances of credit card cloning in different banks.
   - Information (credit card) theft and unauthorized online purchases.
4. **Other identified situations:**
   - Data leakage due to security vulnerabilities in digital platforms and websites, or the PC invasion through malware and victimization by phishing on a specific site (OLX).

The response that best exemplifies a privacy problem when third parties obtain personal data is from participant 13: "*A man harassed me on social media for 2 months and managed to find personal information about me, such as where I lived, where I studied, my school schedule, and other details*". This issue has been observed in other studies where women describe persecutions [18].

5   Discussions

This study aims to address a primary research question, which has been sub-divided into three sub-questions (SQ). From the data analysis, we emphasize that this research, albeit exploratory, is based on a limited sample from a single educational institution. As illustrated in Table 1, and considering SQ1, gender differences did not significantly influence the outcomes, although they might be affected by the participants' previous experiences [13]. The underrepresentation of women, however, signals a persistent male dominance in the sector. Enhancing the visibility of women as developers in the IT industry could encourage more young females to pursue careers in game development [13].

Addressing SQ2, which investigates the perceptions of first-year IT students regarding privacy features in digital games, we acknowledge that a significant portion of them effectively manage game permissions to access information on their devices. However, they encounter substantial challenges concerning the usability and functionality of games, particularly when certain permissions are disabled, thereby creating barriers to game progression. The implementation of extensive data collection techniques through sensors or player activities to optimize games using Artificial Intelligence (AI) solutions introduces an additional layer of complexity [11]. It is pertinent to note, as depicted in question 06 of Fig. 1, that a significant segment of participants admits to providing authentic data during the registration process on gaming platforms. Simultaneously, a considerable portion prefers to abstain from sharing real information, a decision often grounded in the player's valuation of this information and carefully considering whether privacy protection should prevail [17].

We identified that some participants have devised strategies to safeguard their privacy and prevent indiscriminate data collection by games. The difficulty in disabling sensors emerged as a significant concern, corroborating studies discussing challenges in disabling features like GPS [17]. It was mentioned that revoking permissions generally does not compromise the gaming experience, although some games restrict access when users disable specific permissions.

Our analysis unveils various experiences and viewpoints regarding privacy and security in digital games. This scenario underscores the urgent need for improvements in crafting privacy policies, which are often extensive and overlooked by users. Development companies need to demonstrate deeper engagement in protecting players' privacy and promoting more transparent privacy policies, especially in the face of rapid integration of AI, data mining, and machine learning tools [11,14].

As discussed in Subsect. 4.3 (SQ3), privacy breaches occur prominently during attacks in online multiplayer games. These attacks frequently target valuable information contained in credit cards, bank accounts, and social media profiles, among others. To mitigate these issues, the gaming industry has been utilizing AI to anticipate and prevent attacks, facilitating data extraction to initiate personalized attacks or extract personal information [3,11]. However, perpetrators also leverage AI technology to facilitate their illicit actions [4].

We note that many IT students are aware of privacy policies. Nonetheless, a significant portion opts not to engage with these documents, a trend corroborated by Thongmak's study [16], which found that 35% of veteran and new Pokémon GO players have never read the privacy policies. Players are cognizant of the potential to block sensors to prevent data collection. Yet, to fully enjoy the games, they consent to data collection practices that might compromise privacy in digital environments, which might be influenced by factors such as sensitivity, relevance, and convenience [17]. In light of this scenario, game developers must adopt a critical stance towards implementing AI technologies, discerning the ethical boundaries of its application and formulating robust strategies to ensure the protection of players [14].

6   Limitations of the Study

This study has several limitations that should be considered. Firstly, the sample consists only of individuals enrolled in an IT undergraduate program within a specific age range (17 to 30 years). Therefore, the results may only be representative of some of the population of digital gamers.

Secondly, the number of participants is small (61 individuals), which may limit the generalizability of the results and the detection of statistically significant differences. Additionally, there is a gender imbalance in the sample (49 males and 12 females).

Lastly, this study is based on self-reporting, which may be subject to social desirability bias and inaccurate memory. Some participants may have underestimated or overestimated their experiences of privacy breaches or the frequency with which they read privacy policies.

7   Final Considerations and Future Work

This study offers significant insights into the attitudes and behaviors of young IT students regarding privacy in digital games. Although most respondents expressed privacy concerns, many do not devote time to reading privacy policies, highlighting the privacy paradox present in the gaming universe. This phenomenon emphasizes the need for a proactive approach from the gaming industry to safeguard players' privacy.

The findings suggest that the complexity and length of privacy policy texts can create barriers to understanding, indicating that a more accessible and comprehensible presentation of these policies might be beneficial. Regarding involvement in the development of digital games, the study found no significant gender differences, indicating potential equitable participation between genders. However, further investigation is required to validate and expand this aspect.

Additionally, we recognize that fostering a deep understanding of effectively applying privacy strategies in game development remains a notable challenge. This challenge extends to understanding how perceptions about privacy influence game design and how to promote a "privacy by design" approach.

In the future, we plan to expand the research to include a broader spectrum of students and industry professionals, aiming to explore behavioral variations across different demographics and regions, utilizing additional multivariate tests. Additionally, we aim to discern how their privacy perceptions influence their approach to game design?. This supplementary aspect will enable us to devise more robust features, assisting developers in implementing effective privacy protection strategies.

Acknowledgements. This study was financed in part by Fundação de Amparo à Pesquisa do Estado do Rio de Janeiro (FAPERJ) and Coordenação de Aperfeiçoamento de Pessoal de Nível Superior Brazil (CAPES) Finance Code-001.

References

1. Alhazmi, A., AG Arachchilage, N.: A serious game design framework for software developers to put GDPR into practice. In: Proceedings of the 16th International Conference on Availability, Reliability and Security, pp. 1–6 (2021)
2. Bergen, E., Solberg, D.F., Sæthre, T.H., Divitini, M.: Supporting the co-design of games for privacy awareness. In: Auer, M.E., Tsiatsos, T. (eds.) ICL 2018. AISC, vol. 916, pp. 888–899. Springer, Cham (2020). https://doi.org/10.1007/978-3-030-11932-4_82
3. Chowdhury, T., Oredo, J.: Ethics in AI: a software developmental and philosophical perspective. In: Dennehy, D., Griva, A., Pouloudi, N., Dwivedi, Y.K., Pappas, I., Mäntymäki, M. (eds.) I3E 2021. LNCS, vol. 12896, pp. 233–241. Springer, Cham (2021). https://doi.org/10.1007/978-3-030-85447-8_21
4. Council, F.T.: How artificial intelligence can empower the future of the gaming industry. https://www.forbes.com/sites/forbestechcouncil/2022/07/13/how-artificial-intelligence-can-empower-the-future-of-the-gaming-industry/?sh=1063c3f54a9f. Accessed 5 June 2023

5. Friedewald, M., Pohoryles, R.J.: Technology and privacy (2013)
6. Frommel, J., Phillips, C., Mandryk, R.L.: Gathering self-report data in games through NPC dialogues: effects on data quality, data quantity, player experience, and information intimacy. In: Proceedings of the 2021 CHI Conference on Human Factors in Computing Systems, pp. 1–12 (2021)
7. Gartner: How artificial intelligence can empower the future of the gaming industry. https://www.gartner.com/en/newsroom/press-releases/2022-09-13-gartner-outlines-six-trends-driving-near-term-adoptio. Accessed 5 June 2023
8. Gugelmin, F.: Epic games vai ter que pagar us$ 520 milhões por violações de privacidade em fortnite. https://adrenaline.com.br/noticias/v/81153/epic-games-vai-ter-que-pagar-us-520-milhoes-por-violacoes-de-privacidade-em-fortnite. Accessed 12 March 2023
9. Harborth, D., Pape, S.: Privacy concerns and behavior of Pokémon go players in Germany. In: Hansen, M., Kosta, E., Nai-Fovino, I., Fischer-Hübner, S. (eds.) Privacy and Identity 2017. IAICT, vol. 526, pp. 314–329. Springer, Cham (2018). https://doi.org/10.1007/978-3-319-92925-5_21
10. Nagar, T.: AI in gaming: innovations changing the future of gaming. https://devtechnosys.com/insights/ai-in-gaming/. Accessed 7 June 2023
11. Ozmen Garibay, O., et al.: Six human-centered artificial intelligence grand challenges. Int. J. Hum.-Comput. Interact. **39**(3), 391–437 (2023)
12. Rauti, S., Laato, S.: Location-based games as interfaces for collecting user data. In: Rocha, Á., Adeli, H., Reis, L.P., Costanzo, S., Orovic, I., Moreira, F. (eds.) WorldCIST 2020. AISC, vol. 1160, pp. 631–642. Springer, Cham (2020). https://doi.org/10.1007/978-3-030-45691-7_59
13. Sigurðardóttir, H.D.Í.: Empowering women to seek careers in game development and creative IT studies. In: Pappas, I.O., Mikalef, P., Dwivedi, Y.K., Jaccheri, L., Krogstie, J., Mäntymäki, M. (eds.) I3E 2019. IAICT, vol. 573, pp. 103–115. Springer, Cham (2020). https://doi.org/10.1007/978-3-030-39634-3_10
14. da Silva, M., Viterbo, J., de Castro Salgado, L.C., Andrade, E.D.O.: Applying semiotic engineering in game pre-production to promote reflection on player privacy. In: Rocha, Á., Ferrás, C., Ibarra, W. (eds.) ICITS 2023. LNNS, vol. 691, pp. 159–169. Springer, Cham (2023). https://doi.org/10.1007/978-3-031-33258-6_15
15. da Silva, M., Viterbo, J., de Castro Salgado, L.C., Mourão, É.: Privacy orientation during online teaching-learning activities: practices adopted and lessons learned. J. Interact. Syst. **14**(1), 157–174 (2023)
16. Thongmak, M.: Protecting privacy in pokémon go: a multigroup analysis. Technol. Soc. **70**, 101999 (2022)
17. Williams, M., Nurse, J.R., Creese, S.: Smartwatch games: encouraging privacy-protective behaviour in a longitudinal study. Comput. Hum. Behav. **99**, 38–54 (2019)
18. Windleharth, T.W., Schmalz, M., Peterson, S., Lee, J.H.: Identity, safety, and information management within communities of practice in location-based augmented reality games: a case study of ingress (2020)
19. Yalalov, D.: AI in gaming: 3 innovation trends for the future of gaming. https://mpost.io/ai-in-gaming-3-innovation-trends-for-the-future-of-gaming/. Accessed 5 June 2023

Assessing Factors of User Participation in Social Media During Crisis Events: An Analysis of Features and Practices

Magaywer Moreira de Paiva[1]([⊠]) (ID), José Viterbo[1] (ID), Flavia Bernardini[1] (ID), Mônica da Silva[1] (ID), and Cristiano Maciel[2] (ID)

[1] Institute of Computing, Fluminense Federal University, Niterói, RJ, Brazil
{magaywermp,monica_silva}@id.uff.br, {viterbo,fcbernardini}@ic.uff.br
[2] Institute of Computing, Universidade Federal de Mato Grosso, Cuiabá, MT, Brazil
cristiano.maciel@ufmt.br

Abstract. The relevance of using social media in crisis scenarios has aroused the interest of researchers and teams responsible for crisis management. The aim of this study is to explore the experience and skills of social media users related to such events. To this end, we carried out an analysis of the social media functionalities used in this context, followed by a survey of social media users. The research involved the participation of 159 individuals and collected demographic data, data on the use of social networks, experience with crisis events, and aspects related to the production of alert messages. The results suggest that participants actively use social media and are inclined to share information about crisis events, as long as improvements are made to existing functionalities.

Keywords: Social Media · User Experience · Crisis Management · Mobile Technologies · Crowdsourcing

1 Introduction

Crisis events, characterized by natural disasters, accidents, or health and safety emergencies, have the potential to trigger dangerous situations and temporary disruptions for people nearby [10]. Climate change has exacerbated the frequency and intensity of such occurrences, leading to a worrying increase in natural disasters such as floods, wildfires, and earthquakes across the world [18]. The unpredictability of the affected locations and the unpredictability of the severity of the event make it difficult to develop preventive measures. Therefore, the disclosure of information during the event becomes vital to guarantee the safety and well-being of individuals, as access to information can avoid risks and save lives during serious events [2].

With technological advancements and increased connectivity, social media has emerged as a powerful platform for communication. These platforms provide a dynamic environment where users can transmit information, supported by

M. Janssen et al. (Eds.): I3E 2023, LNCS 14316, pp. 195–206, 2023.
https://doi.org/10.1007/978-3-031-50040-4_15

the information capture capabilities of mobile technologies [15]. This type of contribution allows the formation of a mass of data on crisis events. Thus, social media can be used to detect real-world events [7] and identify their locations [1]. Furthermore, the collaborative process, or Crowdsourcing, allows this data to be used to assess damage [12] or to extract the "Wisdom of the Crowd" to detect new crisis events [22]. These characteristics transform social media users into human sensors capable of collecting and sharing crucial information about the affected area and the severity of the crisis.

In the context of smart cities, social media data is extensively studied to help local governments make informed decisions during crisis events [20]. Social media can be used to extract details about events even before they are published in traditional media [14]. Advanced Artificial Intelligence techniques can be employed to process this data, assisting with crisis control and mitigation strategies aimed at increasing the resilience of cities [6]. In addition to enabling real-time monitoring of public sentiment, it also allows for rapid action in affected areas and immediate feedback and support to users [6].

The demand for rapid, automated identification of city-wide crisis events could spur the development of systems that make use of social media data. A notable investment has been directed towards improving machine learning algorithms for event detection [10]. However, even when messages are shared during events, an automatic system needs to deal with ambiguous or incomplete information [14]. Consequently, these systems can become complex, facing challenges related to semantic interpretation, temporal aspects, and geographic data [14]. For messages to be truly useful, it is imperative that users actively participate during the event by sharing event-related content, including location data. In the literature, we found, from the users' point of view, that social media platforms can be considered easy to use, beneficial, and crucial for disaster management [9]. Therefore, before moving forward with the development of automatic monitoring systems, a deeper analysis of users' experiences with these platforms during crisis events is essential.

This study aims to delve into the practices and knowledge of social media users, delineating their potential to contribute crucial information during crisis events. We propose a key question to evaluate how users participate on social media platforms during these events: What is the ability and interest of users to get involved in disseminating information related to crisis events? To gain insights into these questions, we designed a research methodology based on the Goal-Question-Metric (GQM) [5,19] with questions about user experience with social media platforms in relation to crisis events. We collected data from social media users in all regions of Brazil through online forms. Next, in Sect. 2, we delve deeper into the salient features necessary for posting messages on social media platforms. In Sect. 3 we describe the steps taken to collect data. In Sect. 4 we detail the results of respondents who completed the survey, while in Sect. 5 we present the discussion of these results. We conclude the study in Sect. 6, where we offer suggestions for future research.

2   Background

2.1   Using Social Media Tools

Social media platforms offer a plethora of tools that users can leverage in a variety of ways, affording multiple usage possibilities. The ability to share text messages enables users to express views, share relevant information, and report crisis events ahead of news channels [14]. Moreover, hashtags are used to categorize and index content, simplifying the search for specific information on various topics, such as natural disasters or emergencies [11]. The functionality of tagging or mentioning, others using the "@" symbol draws attention to private posts, thereby alerting authorities, emergency services, or individuals possessing pertinent knowledge in crisis situations [21].

Many social media platforms also offer location sharing [16]. This feature, usable in real-time, can be invaluable during crisis situations, informing those nearby of one's current location and facilitating appropriate assistance or rescue in emergencies. In addition, users can share the location of a specific place, such as an address or landmark, to inform others about crisis events at specific locations. The check-in feature, albeit not directly related to crisis events, can provide valuable information about people's movement in affected areas, aiding situation analysis and response coordination.

Social media platforms enable users to share videos and images, which play a crucial role in transmitting information during crisis events [17]. They allow users to document and share first-hand experiences, giving others a more profound understanding of the situation. Furthermore, the sharing feature of social media platforms promotes rapid and efficient content dissemination [13]. With a few clicks, users can share posts, photos, videos, and links with their network, reaching a potentially limitless audience.

2.2   Analysis of Tools for Crisis Events

La Rocca & Greco (2022) [11] analyzed the use of hashtags during the initial phase of the COVID-19 pandemic in three languages: Italian, Spanish, and French. Utilizing emotional text mining, the aim was to comprehend the representation of the pandemic, containment measures, and the perception of Europe within tweets containing the #Covid-19 hashtag. The study underscored the significance of hashtags as analysis tools in media events and crises, highlighting the prevailing attitudes towards Europe during times of crisis.

Scalia & Francalanci & Pernici (2022) [16] presented the CIME algorithm, a tool for geolocating pertinent social media posts for crisis mapping. This algorithm employs the context of posts, such as metadata and relationship networks, to filter and geolocate information. It was assessed during an emergency event and showed superior performance in terms of geolocated posts, accuracy, and relevance for rapid mapping.

Shang & Liou & Rao-Nicholson (2022) [17] investigated corporate communication on social media during the COVID-19 pandemic. They observed that businesses adopted functional and informative approaches initially during the various phases of the crisis, later seeking to increase customer engagement through the incorporation of videos and links. High media richness data formats received a higher rate of responses/retweets. The findings highlight the importance of strategic adaptation during an evolving crisis.

Atkinson & Lee (2023) [3] examined the use of Facebook by Australian emergency response agencies during a specific wildfire event. The results unveiled distinct agency approaches and their relationship with user engagement. Understanding user engagement with official social media content is essential in light of the increasing reliance on these platforms for crisis communication.

The research mentioned in this text provides an interesting insight into the different social media tools used in crisis situations. However, studies focus on analyzing posts and using text analysis tools and algorithms to extract valuable information. A new study that focuses on collecting user information could provide a deeper understanding of users' individual experiences and perceptions of social media in times of crisis. Furthermore, it is critical that a new study expands the scope to cover a variety of crises and emergency situations to develop more comprehensive recommendations and guidelines for interaction between users and social media tools.

3 Methodology

The survey was conducted through online questionnaires via Google Forms to facilitate access to participants. We adopt ethical measures based on the Informed Consent Form (ICF) [4] to guarantee the protection, well-being, and minimize risks to participants: presentation of the objective of the research and of those researched; anonymity of participants; non-identification of participants in the responses collected; free and uninfluenced participation; and, possibility of interrupting the research at any time if they wish. We adopted measures to mitigate possible weaknesses in the questionnaires that could hinder the investigation [4]: questions in a sequence from general to specific; closed questions with neutral options or alternatives such as "I don't know", "I don't want to answer" or "other"; and, instructions describing how to answer the questions. In addition, we established inclusion criteria, such as a minimum age of 18 years, and exclusion criteria, such as refusal of the ICF or non-compliance with the inclusion criteria. The minimum age of 18 is necessary to comply with legal and ethical requirements, ensuring informed consent and protecting the rights of participants. Combined with the acceptance of the ICF, it strengthens the integrity and validity of the results.

The research seeks to answer the research question: "What is the ability and interest of users to get involved in the dissemination of information related to crisis events?". We used the Goal-Question-Metric (GQM) paradigm to define the objectives, questions, and metrics used in the research [5, 19]. We can characterize the objective of this work as analyzing factors that can influence interactions and posts on social networks during a crisis event, with the aim of characterizing the participants' experience. Following Basili et al. (1992) [5], we can characterize the research with four Specific Objectives (SO). SO1 seeks to collect demographic information to contextualize the evaluation of the tool. SO2 seeks to characterize the use of social media by participants. SO3 seeks to characterize participants' experience with crisis events. Finally, SO4 seeks to characterize the perceptions related to the production of the alert message.

The objectives were refined into questions, moving from an abstract level to a more practical one [19]. All questions were objective and alternatives are presented in Sect. 4. To answer SO1, we use questions to recording age, gender, location and education. To answer SO2, we use questions to collect the frequency of use of social media and knowledge of existing features. To answer SO3, we use questions to gather whether participants witnessed any crisis events, whether they shared information about crisis events, and whether they consider it important to share this information on social media. To answer SO4, we used questions to determine whether participants would be willing to provide data to a tool that generates messages, whether they consider it important for the message to be temporary, and whether they prefer the message to be anonymous. Finally, metrics are a refinement of questions [19]. Metrics play a fundamental role in defining the information necessary to analyze the data collected. In the context of this research, the data collected underwent a quantitative analysis [8]. This analysis used basic and descriptive statistical methods with the aim of summarizing and synthesizing the data in a concise and understandable way.

4   Findings

The questionnaire was available for 5 days: between February 27th and March 3rd, 2023. We received 159 responses, all of which were submitted following acceptance of the Informed Consent Form (ICF). The questions were administered in the same way and order for all participants. The anonymized dataset is available at the following link: https://zenodo.org/records/10118628.

4.1   Demographic Data (SO1)

To achieve SO1, we present Questions to Characterize the Participants (QCP): age (QCP1), gender (QCP2), region of the country (QCP3), and level of education (QCP4). As per Table 1, a concentration of participants was observed in the younger first third of age, with 147 (92.5%) of participants aged between 18 and 35 years: 34% were under 24 years, 44.7% between 24 and 29 years, and 13.8% between 30 and 35 years. In addition, Table 2 (QCP2) shows that 61% of participants who identified as female (F), 38.4% identifying as male (M) e only 0.6% chose not to disclose their gender (N/A). Table 2 (QCP3) also presents the regions with the most participants, with the Southeast region standing out with 38.4%, followed by the North region with 31.4%, and the Midwest with 22%.

Table 3 presents the education level of the survey participants. We can divide the sample into two groups. In the first, 79 (49.7%) individuals who completed higher education: 34% have a completed higher education degree, and 15.7%

Table 1. Responses for Participants' Age (QCP1)

Question	QCP1								
Options	*18–24*	*24–29*	*30–35*	*36–41*	*42–47*	*48–53*	*54–59*	*>59*	*N/A*
Answers	54	71	22	3	5	1	1	1	1
Percent	34.0%	44.7%	13.8%	1.9%	3.1%	0.6%	0.6%	0.6%	0.6%

Table 2. Responses to the gender of participants (QCP2) and responses to the participants' region of residence (QCP3)

Question	QCP2			QCP3					
Options	*M*	*F*	*N/A*	*North*	*Southeast*	*Midwest*	*South*	*North East*	*N/A*
Answers	61	97	1	50	61	35	6	6	1
Percent	38.4%	61.0%	0.6%	31.4%	38.4%	22.0%	3.8%	3.8%	0.6%

have completed or are currently enrolled in postgraduate studies (Spec., M.Sc. or Ph.D.). In the second, 80 (50.3%) individuals have not yet completed higher education: 32.7% are higher education students, 15.1% are high school graduates, 1.9% have not completed high school, and 0.6% have completed primary education. There were no participants with incomplete primary education or who were illiterate.

Table 3. Answers regarding the level of education of the participants (QCP4) considering Complete (C) or Incomplete (IC)

Question	QCP4					
Options	*(C) primary education*	*(IC) high school*	*(C) high school*	*(IC) higher education*	*(C) higher education*	*(C or IC) Spec. M.Sc., Ph.D.*
Answers	1	3	24	52	54	25
Percent	0.6%	1.9%	15.1%	32.7%	34.0%	15.7%

4.2   Social Media Using (SO2)

To achieve the SO2 objective, we present Questions related to Social media Using (QSU): frequency of use of two type of social media platform (QSU1) and knowledge about the functionalities used to share information about crisis events (QSU2). Table 4 reveals that private messaging social media platforms were the most used. We asked participants to consider their use of WhatsApp. While public messaging platforms were the least used. We asked participants to consider their use of Facebook.

Table 4. Frequency of social media usage by participants (QSU1)

Question	QSU1 - Private message		QSU1 - Public message	
Options	*Frequent*	*Infrequent*	*Frequent*	*Infrequent*
Answers	153	6	60	99
Percent	96.2%	3.8%	37.7%	62.3%

The Table 5 presents the number of participants who know each feature of social networks that can be used to generate an alert message. Overall, the participants demonstrated a high level of knowledge concerning the presented tools. All participants (159) responded to the question, with a minimum of 120 of them (75.5%) confirming their familiarity with each of the options presented. It indicates that at least three-quarters of participants are familiar with all the features presented.

Table 5. Knowledge of social media functionalities by participants (QSU2)

Question	QSU2					
Options	*Text message*	*Index terms (#)*	*Mention account (@)*	*Real-time location*	*Location of specific place*	*Check-in at location*
Answers	157	121	152	143	130	120
Percent	98.7%	76.1%	95.6%	89.9%	81.8%	75.5%

4.3   Experience with Crisis Events (SO3)

To achieve SO3, we presented questions related to the Participant Experience (QPE): whether the participant has previously been present at a crisis event (QPE1), whether they have had any interactions with information about crisis events through social media (QPE2), and whether they consider it important for such information to circulate on social media platforms (QPE3). Upon analyzing the responses, we found that 145 (91.2%) of participants stated they had experienced at least one crisis event beyond the pandemic. Table 6 presents the percentage of participants who marked each presented crisis event. Among these events, the pandemic was the most frequently experienced, indicated by 153 (96.8%) participants. Overall, the participants reported experiencing other types of crisis events, such as traffic problems with 79.1%, flooding with 53.8%, and riots with 43.7%.

Table 6. Experience of crisis events by participants (QPE1)

Question	QPE1						
Options	Health (pandemic)	Water (flooding)	Fire (blaze)	Earth (slip)	People (riot)	Vehicle (accident)	Drought (water scarcity)
Answers	153	85	36	10	69	125	35
Percent	96.2%	53.5%	22.6%	6.3%	43.4%	78.6%	22.0%

Table 7 (QPE2) displays the percentage of participants who interact on social media with information about crisis events, whether through posting, commenting, or sharing: 66% confirmed having some form of interaction, 28% stated not engaging, and 6% were unsure or did not respond. Moreover, Table 7 (QPE3) presents the percentage of participants who consider the circulation of information about crisis events on social media important: 94% affirmed its importance, 3% expressed it as unimportant, and 3% were unsure or did not respond.

Table 7. Participants already had some kind of interaction on social media related to the crisis event (QPE2) and participants consider it important that information about crisis events circulate on social media (QPE3).

Question	QPE2			QPE3		
Options	Yes	Maybe	No	Yes	Maybe	No
Answers	104	10	45	149	5	5
Percent	65.4%	6.3%	28.3%	93.7%	3.1%	3.1%

4.4 Production of Alert Messages (SO4)

To achieve SO4, we addressed questions about Production of Alert messages (QPA): the intention of providing information to a tool that generates the message (QPA1), the need for the message to be temporary (QPA2) and the need for the message is anonymous (QPA3). Table 8 shows that, for QPA1, 82.8% of the participants evaluated that they would provide the information requested by a tool to generate the message. Furthermore, for QPA2, 47.1% of participants expressed that if the message was deleted after 24 h (temporary), they would post more often. Finally, regarding QPA3, 44.6% of the participants stated that they would publish more frequently if the publication did not include their name (anonymously).

Table 8. Participants would use a tool to generate the alert message (QPA1), Participants consider that the message needs to be temporary (QPA2) and Participants consider that the message needs to be anonymous (QPA3).

Question	QPA1			QPA2			QPA3		
Options	*Yes*	*Maybe*	*No*	*Yes*	*Maybe*	*No*	*Yes*	*Maybe*	*No*
Answers	130	18	11	74	53	32	70	49	40
Percent	81.8%	11.3%	6.9%	46.5%	33.3%	20.1%	44.0%	30.8%	25.2%

5 Discussion

This study comprised of 159 participants, predominantly between the ages of 18 to 35. Additionally, there were more female participants. It was conducted entirely online, thereby enabling a broader reach and diffusion of the research through sharing on social media platforms such as Facebook and WhatsApp. This strategy enabled data collection from cities across 14 different states, with the Southeast region having the most participants, followed by the North and Midwest regions. Researchers had some network of contacts in these regions, which may have introduced a bias to the research. None of the participants had an education level below completed high school or were illiterate, with the majority of the sample being composed of individuals who have completed or are pursuing higher education.

This study involved a group of individuals, where almost all of them make frequent use of some social media that allows the sending of private messages. Moreover, three-quarters or more of the participants are familiar with social media features that enable public crisis alerting. This reinforces the notion that social media is widely accessible and perceived as user-friendly [9]. On the other hand, within this same group, just over half of the participants make frequent use of social media that allow the sending of public messages. Although most participants are aware of the resources available to raise awareness of crisis events, it is of great importance that this is done quickly so that other people and crisis managers have access [14]. However, a small part of the participants may have contributed via private messages.

The survey revealed that the vast majority of participants have already experienced at least one type of crisis event, in addition to a health-related event: traffic problems, floods, or riots. They also considered the circulation of information about crisis events on social media as important. This reinforces the notion that social media is perceived as beneficial for communication during crisis events [9]. In addition, most participants claimed to have interactions with information about crisis events on social media, be it by posting, commenting, or sharing. However, despite having experienced such events and being familiar with most of the tools available to generate crisis alerts, the percentage of interaction was almost 28% points below the participation rate. It is possible that the majority of participants in this study experienced emotions related to crisis events, which may explain the importance they attach to sharing information about crisis events on social media. In this way, the difference between interest and participation may be associated with: the lack of specific tools for sharing alerts; the lack of greater interaction between government officials and crisis managers with citizens; or, the low circulation of related messages to encourage and serve as an example for participants to get involved in these online discussions.

By analyzing the features available on social media, we realized that there are tools that allow the production of data that facilitate the construction of solutions based on Crowdsourcing. One such solution is to identify and share crisis events [2]. In this context, a user can use these tools to notify both the relevant authorities and friends and family [21]. Hashtags can be used to index information about specific events or relevant locations [11]. In turn, crisis managers would receive complete information that would help them in rescue and control actions in crisis situations. While there are general tools, there isn't a specific option for writing about crisis events. Thus, more research is needed to investigate the factors that can influence the frequency of interactions when participants witness a crisis event. As well, the complexity of the user experience on social media during crisis events may requires a joint effort between users and platforms to improve communication and provide accurate and reliable information in critical situations.

Social media have technological support to provide tools that help the production of messages during crisis events [2]. For this, social media can use data available on users' devices, such as location and time. However, in settings with low participation, messages can be difficult to collect and with little useful information [14]. In this sense, social media themselves could offer tools to generate the message and establish a pattern of messages, depending only on the user's express willingness to participate. In our research, we observed that more than half of the participants would use a tool for this purpose. Moreover, they didn't show great concern about making this message temporary and anonymous. To encourage participation, the platform could offer additional features that assist in decision-making and guide users, such as targeted notifications for those close to a crisis event and the creation of an interface to view the points where an event was flagged. However, before investing in the production of such a tool, it is essential to adjust the characteristics and desires of the local communities that can use this tool. This must be done to check whether people are willing to adopt it in their daily lives. The receptiveness of local users can guarantee the effectiveness of a Crowdsourcing tool and support Smart Cities solutions.

6   Final Considerations

Aspects related to the experiences and skills of social media users are essential to gain a comprehensive understanding of usage during crisis events. The results of this research reveal that the participants are active users of social media, have already experienced a crisis event and have the necessary knowledge to share information. Although participants recognize the importance of this information to support communication, not everyone engages in discussions of this type on social media. During crisis events, users' interaction with social media can be affected by the negative effects of the crisis itself. In addition, the lack of a specific tool for crisis situations can make communication difficult during the event. Participants stated the need to improve existing resources, considering the user's context. Therefore, this study contributes to a deeper understanding of user interaction and need for information sharing during crisis events.

During our research, we faced challenges related to the validity of the study, such as the adequate representation of the questions under study and the lack of an instrument to verify the understanding of the participants. Obtaining a diverse sample was a challenge, and we recognize that the sample used may have limited the generalizability of the results. Furthermore, the lack of adequate statistical support and the predominance of descriptive statistical evaluations may have weakened our conclusions.

In future work, we consider the development and testing of a user-centered alert publishing tool for social networks. This tool can be designed with specific functionalities to facilitate communication during crisis events, allowing users to send important information about the type of event, location and time of crisis-related issues. In addition, we intend to conduct further research to understand the needs and expectations of local communities regarding the use of such tools. For this, the research may include interviews, focus groups or even conducting a pilot study with a specific group of users.

Acknowledgements. This study was financed in part by the Coordenação de Aperfeiçoamento de Pessoal de Nível Superior - Brasil (CAPES) - Finance Code 001.

References

1. Alkouz, B., Al Aghbari, Z.: SNSJam: road traffic analysis and prediction by fusing data from multiple social networks. Inf. Process. Manage. **57**(1), 102139 (2020)
2. Arapostathis, S.G.: A methodology for automatic acquisition of flood-event management information from social media: the flood in Messinia, south Greece, 2016. Inf. Syst. Front. **23**, 1127–1144 (2021)
3. Atkinson, S., Lee, J.Y.: Social media: connecting and sharing in a bushfire crisis. In: Media International Australia, p. 1329878X231163367 (2023)
4. Barbosa, S.D.J., Silva, B.S., Silveira, M.S., Gasparini, I., Darin, T., Barbosa, G.D.J.: Interação Humano-Computador e Experiência do Usuário. Autopublicação (2021)
5. Basili, V.R.: Software modeling and measurement: The goal/question/metric paradigm. University of Maryland at College Park, USA, Technical report (1992)
6. Dahou, A., Mabrouk, A., Ewees, A.A., Gaheen, M.A., Abd Elaziz, M.: A social media event detection framework based on transformers and swarm optimization for public notification of crises and emergency management. Technol. Forecast. Soc. Chang. **192**, 122546 (2023)
7. Erfanian, P.Y., Cami, B.R., Hassanpour, H.: An evolutionary event detection model using the matrix decomposition oriented Dirichlet process. Expert Syst. Appl. **189**, 116086 (2022)

8. Fontelles, M.J., Simões, M.G., Farias, S.H., Fontelles, R.G.S.: Metodologia da pesquisa científica: diretrizes para a elaboração de um protocolo de pesquisa. Revista paraense de medicina **23**(3), 1–8 (2009)
9. Kavota, J.K., Kamdjoug, J.R.K., Wamba, S.F.: Social media and disaster management: case of the north and South Kivu regions in the democratic republic of the Congo. Int. J. Inf. Manage. **52**, 102068 (2020)
10. Kruspe, A., Kersten, J., Klan, F.: Detection of actionable tweets in crisis events. Nat. Hazard. **21**(6), 1825–1845 (2021)
11. La Rocca, G., Greco, F.: # COVID-19: a hashtag for examining reactions towards Europe in times of crisis. An analysis of tweets in Italian, Spanish, and French. RES. Revista Española de Sociología **31**(4), 1 (2022)
12. Li, L., Bensi, M., Cui, Q., Baecher, G.B., Huang, Y.: Social media crowdsourcing for rapid damage assessment following a sudden-onset natural hazard event. Int. J. Inf. Manage. **60**, 102378 (2021)
13. Nesi, P., Pantaleo, G., Paoli, I., Zaza, I.: Assessing the retweet proneness of tweets: predictive models for retweeting. Multimedia Tools Appl. **77**, 26371–26396 (2018)
14. Paiva, M.M.D., Viterbo, J., Bernardini, F.: Assessing the suitability of social media data for identifying crisis events in smart cities: an exploratory study on flood situations. In: Janssen, M., et al. (eds.) EGOV 2022. LNCS, vol. 13391, pp. 147–162. Springer, Cham (2022). https://doi.org/10.1007/978-3-031-15086-9_10
15. Sadiq, R., Akhtar, Z., Imran, M., Ofli, F.: Integrating remote sensing and social sensing for flood mapping. Remote Sens. Appl. Soc. Environ. **25**, 100697 (2022)
16. Scalia, G., Francalanci, C., Pernici, B.: CIME: context-aware geolocation of emergency-related posts. GeoInformatica **26**(1), 125–157 (2022)
17. Shang, Y., Liou, R.S., Rao-Nicholson, R.: What to say and how to say it? corporate strategic communication through social media during the pandemic. Int. J. Strateg. Commun. **16**(4), 633–648 (2022)
18. UN Office for Disaster Risk Reduction - UNDRR: The human cost of disasters: an overview of the last 20 years (2000–2019) (2020)
19. Van Solingen, R., Berghout, E.W.: The Goal/Question/Metric Method: A Practical Guide for Quality Improvement of Software Development. McGraw-Hill, New York (1999)
20. Villegas, C.A., Martinez, M.J.: Lessons from Harvey: improving traditional damage estimates with social media sourced damage estimates. Cities **121**, 103500 (2022)
21. Wang, B., Zhuang, J.: Crisis information distribution on twitter: a content analysis of tweets during hurricane sandy. Nat. Hazards **89**, 161–181 (2017)
22. Zhang, Y., Zong, R., Wang, D.: A hybrid transfer learning approach to migratable disaster assessment in social media sensing. In: 2020 IEEE/ACM International Conference on Advances in Social Networks Analysis and Mining (ASONAM), pp. 131–138. IEEE (2020)

Investigating Social Commerce Factors: Motivation, Price Value, Habit, Risk and Attitude

Prianka Sarker[1]([⊠]), Yogesh K. Dwivedi[2,3], and Laurie Hughes[4]

[1] Department of Marketing, International Business and Tourism, Manchester Metropolitan University, Manchester M15 6BY, UK
p.sarker@mmu.ac.uk

[2] Digital Futures for Sustainable Business & Society Research Group School of Management, Swansea University, Bay Campus, Fabian Bay, Swansea SA1 8EN, Wales, UK
y.k.dwivedi@swansea.ac.uk

[3] Department of Management, Symbiosis Institute of Business Management, Pune & Symbiosis International (Deemed University), Pune, Maharashtra, India

[4] School of Business and Law, Edith Cowan University, Joondalup, WA, Australia
david.hughes@ecu.edu.au

Abstract. The popularity of social media as a useful tool for socialization and information exchange has resulted in a new type of electronic commerce known as social commerce. The rapid expansion of social media has generated significant interest from many e-retailers to enlarge their operations by taking advantage of social technology and services. Social commerce has gone mainstream among marketers, businesses, and scholars in recent years. Many countries, including the United Kingdom, United States, China, and South Korea, have already implemented the social shopping system. However, consumers in developing countries like Bangladesh are slower to accept social commerce. Despite the hype around this technology, no previous research has specifically studies consumer adoption of social commerce in the context of Bangladesh in a systematic manner. Consequently, this research aim to "develop and empirically validate a conceptual model for understanding factors influencing consumer behavioural intention of social commerce in the context of Bangladesh" utilizing the UTAUT2 model. This study utilized price value, hedonic motivation, habit, risk and attitude in order to investigate consumer behavioural intention. This study collected the data (n = 302) from social commerce users of Bangladesh using survey method in order to test and validate the research model. The results supported that price value and hedonic motivation have significant influence on consumer attitude while habit, risk and attitude have significant impact on consumer behavioural intention. This research contributes to the knowledge through adoption and validation of constructs that overlooked in social commerce studies.

Keywords: social commerce · Risk · Habit · Price value · behavioural intention · attitude · hedonic motivation

© IFIP International Federation for Information Processing 2023
Published by Springer Nature Switzerland AG 2023
M. Janssen et al. (Eds.): I3E 2023, LNCS 14316, pp. 207–223, 2023.
https://doi.org/10.1007/978-3-031-50040-4_16

1 Introduction

The development and adoption of technology has acted as an enabler for social commerce and has become mainstream following the success of social networking sites [1]. Although the term has been widely used within the literature, there is no universally accepted definition of the term 'social commerce'. It generally refers to the delivery of electronic commerce (e-commerce) activities and transactions conducted through social networking sites via Web 2.0 software [2]. According to Turban et al. [3], the combination of e-commerce, e-marketing, social media, web 2.0, and support theories creates a platform called social commerce. Within the last few years social commerce has become a key discussion point for many businesses. Not only businesses using this platform to be selling the goods, but also using this technology for understand consumer requirement, measuring consumer satisfaction, interaction with consumers and brand awareness. Many developed and developing countries are incorporating this technology to develop their business. Social commerce adoption is relatively higher in technologically developed countries such as USA, UK, South Korea and China. However, developing countries such as Bangladesh are far behind to adopt this technology.

In the last few years many scholars have attempted to investigate various influential factors of social commerce. Prior studies highlighted number of factors and models that repeatedly used in social commerce domain [4–13]. For examples, trust, social support and perceived usefulness and TAM, S-O-R model and social support theories are some frequently utilized models and constructs. However, there are many technology adoption constructs that have been overlooked for use in the social commerce research. Capturing the holistic literature review, this study found that consumer attitude has been overlooked despite its importance in many technology acceptance studies. For example, measuring consumer attitude can help businesses to understand an individual's behaviour, which helps company decision-making. A more positive attitude drives the consumer towards behavioural intention the technology [14]. Therefore, adopting a promising technology adoption model and empirically investigate and validating in the social commerce research is important. Thus, this study seeks to fill the gaps that theoretically enhance and contribute to the research as well practically implemented on social commerce system. This research conducts the empirical research on social commerce considering the users of Bangladesh.

The next sections will outline the theoretical foundation and conceptual model, drawing on relevant literature to select a promising model for this study. The methodology of the research will be discussed in Sect. 3, while Sect. 4 will present the results of the structural equation modelling (SEM). Following that, Sect. 5 will provide a discussion of the findings, along with contributions, limitations, and directions for future research.

2 Literature Review and Conceptual Model Development

Social commerce studies have shown that constructs such as perceived usefulness, perceived ease of use, trust and social support have been examined most frequently [15]. Constructs such as attitude, hedonic motivation, price value and habit have been overlooked in social commerce research despite being a significant predictor of many technology acceptance research. For examples, student perception using course management software [20]; Mobile commerce [21]; Mobile banking [22] and consumer behavioural intention of social commerce in the context of Saudi Arabia [6].

Few studies in social commerce research examined hedonic motivation, price value and habit as a part of UTAUT 2 model. For example, Sheikh et al. [6] examined UTAUT 2 in order to examined consumer behavioural intention of social commerce in the context of Saudi Arabia. Study found that hedonic motivation, habit and price saving orientation have significant influence on behavioural intention. Shoheib and Abu-Shanab [5] examined UTAUT 2 in the context of Qatar and found that the core constructs of the model have significant influence on behavioural intention. Additionally, there are limited studies that consider consumer attitude in the model despite being a significant predictor of behavioural intention. Additionally, negative factors such as risk has been utilized in limited studies. Scholars suggests that Risk factors can be change based on the geographical location and environment. Due to its novelty, there is a limited amount of literature available on social commerce considering the context of Bangladesh. Therefore, attitude, hedonic motivation, price value, habit and risk are needed further investigation in the context of Bangladesh.

2.1 Development of Conceptual Model

Although, UTAUT is a highly cited model within technology adoption research [18]. Few studies have utilized it for examining social commerce adoption. UTAUT contain four key constructs (independent variables) namely, performance expectancy, effort expectancy, social influence and facilitating conditions. UTAUT was proposed and validated for understanding IT/IS adoption at individual level in the organizational context. Afterwards, Venkatesh et al. [19] further extended this theory for consumer context by including three additional independent variables namely, price value, hedonic motivation, and habit for predicting behavioural intention to adopt technology. However, those constructs were rejected or cannot be validated in many contexts. Therefore, this study decided to examine those constructs utilizing attitude and behavioural intention in the context of Bangladesh.

Risk is another factor that is found to be negative in various aspects of technology acceptance research [24–26]. Internet usage for shopping causes additional uncertainty and risk perception due to its intangible nature [27]. Therefore, utilizing risk with will generate relevant information to understand consumer's behavioural intention in the social commerce domain. Therefore, the proposed conceptual model and hypothesis is structured below (see Fig. 1).

2.1.1 Hedonic Motivation (HM)

"Hedonic motivation can be defined as the fun or pleasure derived from using technology, and it has been shown to play an important role in determining technology acceptance and use [19]. In technology acceptance research, hedonic motivation has been found to be an influential factor in consumer's behavioural intention [19]. In social commerce studies, a few examinations of hedonic motivation have been conducted. For example, Shoheib and Abu-Shanab [5] found that hedonic motivation has a positive and significant influence on consumer behavioural intention in the context of Qatar. Additionally, Sheikh et al. [6]

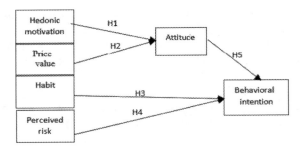

Fig. 1. Proposed Conceptual model (Adopted UTAUT2 by Venkatesh et al., 2012)

found that hedonic motivation has significant influence on behaviour in the context of Saudi Arabia. It is evident that hedonic motivation and behavioural intention have been examined in many existences. Therefore, hedonic motivation and consumer attitude would be beneficial to investigate in order to understand consumer's attitude toward social commerce. The following hypotheses is proposed:

H1: Hedonic motivation positively influences consumer attitude towards social commerce.

2.1.2 Price Value (PV)

Price value is another essential concept in UTAUT2. Consumers often incur the financial expense, and pricing structure may have a considerable impact on consumer technology adoption [19]. Price value is a significant consideration because social commerce does not incur any costs for technology use; instead, it gives consumers with a variety of benefits and cost-saving possibilities [6]. Furthermore, the UTAUT2 specific construct "price value" has been replaced with "price saving" because social commerce does not incur any costs for technology usage; instead, it gives consumers with a variety of benefits and cost-saving possibilities. Price value is an assessment of the value that a consumer will accrue and realize from utilizing a service or product, such as quality, functionality, after-sales service, and brand [5]. As a result, few studies in social commerce research have indicated that price value has a substantial influence on consumers' behavioural intention [5, 6]. This construct with attitude purpose was chosen and hypothesized in this investigation.

H2: Price value positively influences consumers' Attitude towards social commerce.

2.1.3 Habit (HT)

"Habit has been defined as the extent to which people tend to perform behaviour automatically because of learning" [19]. Many technology acceptance studies have found habit to be important and favourable [51]. A rise in habit, according to Limayem et al. [51], increases the inclination to utilize technology. In social commerce, habit has been employed sparingly; for example, Sheikh et al. [6] reported that habit has a considerable influence on consumer behavioural intention in the setting of Saudi Arabia. As a result, the following hypotheses is proposed:

H3: Habit positively influences consumer's behavioural intention towards social commerce.

2.1.4 Risk

Risk is one of the negative factors that inhibit consumer to use social commerce. Wu and Li [52] found that social commerce risk negatively and significantly influence consumer value in social commerce. Commerce risk decrease the intention to buy from the website and that perceived participation risk limits the intentions to post comments on social commerce forums. The result further reported that the influence of these risk assessments reduced when the degree of social identification with the website's community enhances [43]. Biucky et al., [53] found that privacy risk, functional risk, social risk, and time risk are negatively significant with intention to buy. Therefore, the less risk of psychological trauma generated from the unsuccessful buying. Risk concern increased when the perceived usefulness of e-service and usage intention reduce [54]. Thus, the proposes hypothesis is:

H4: Risk negatively influence consumer's behavioural intention towards social commerce.

2.1.5 Attitude (AT)

Attitude could be defined as the psychological path of evaluating an object with a positive or negative reaction [44]. Attitude is an individual's positive and negative feelings about performing the target behaviour [45]. Fishbein and Ajzen, [46] defined attitude as a belief that is sometimes influenced by socio-environmental pressure rather than personal behaviour. Venkatesh et al. [28] mentioned that enjoyment, interest, fun, and usefulness are essential factors that positively influence consumers' attitude. From a social commerce perspective, several studies found a significant positive relationship between attitude and intention to buy [16, 23, 47, 48, 55]. However, social commerce adoption in Bangladesh may be significantly influenced by customers' positive attitudes towards online shopping. Realizing that, this research utilizes the relationship between attitude and behavioural intention and proposes the following hypothesis:

H5: Attitude positively influence consumer's behavioural intention towards social commerce.

3 Methodology

After proposing a conceptual model, it is necessary to determine an appropriate method to validate the model. Thus, the methodological choices made in this study. The empirical part of this research was conducted in Bangladesh and its involved 500 Bangladeshi social media users. A self-administrated questionnaires was developed and distributed to the targeted participants. The survey method was used in this research to collect the data. It is evident that the survey approach allows for the measurement of a variety of unobservable variables, such as an individual's preferences, attitudes, beliefs, and behaviour [49]. This approach is ideal for collecting information about a population that is extensive to observe in person [49].

The measuring items of this research has been collected from various technology-based research [14, 16, 19]. A seven-point Likert scale was preferred to measure respondents' perception on survey questions. The survey questions were developed using google form and distributed through various social media sites such as Facebook, Instagram, WhatsApp, LinkedIn and twitter. To ensure an adequate level of reliability, a pilot study was conducted before the main survey. Reliability of the constructs were verified using 40 pilot samples. And found that all the constructs were the recommended threshold 0.70. SPSS v.28 and AMOS v.28 were selected as an appropriate exanimating tool to assist with data analysis.

4 Results

This study involved the collection of 500 samples using a survey method. After removing unengaged samples and outliers, a total of 302 samples remained for further analysis. The subsequent analysis was conducted in two stages. In the first stage, the results of the structural equation modelling (SEM) measurement model largely supported the level of goodness of fit. All the model fit indices demonstrated satisfactory values (refer to Table 1). The goodness of fit index showed AGFI = 0.93, CFI = 0.98, PNFI = 0.77, and RMSEA = 0.26. Similarly, the reliability of all constructs was found to be above 0.70, which is considered satisfactory. The composite reliability and average variance extracted are on the satisfactory level. For example, RISK (a = 0.93; CR = 0.94; AVE = 0.77); PV (a = 0.75; CR = 0.75; AVE = 0.51); HT (a = 0.84; CR = 0.84; AVE = 0.72); HM (a = 0.72; CR = 0.64; AVE = 0.47); AT (a = 0.72; CR = 0.72; AVE = 0.46); BI (a = 0.83; CR = 0.84; AVE = 0.51).

Table 1. Model fit indices

Model	χ^2/DF < 3.00	AGFI ≥ 0.80	CFI ≥ 0.90	PNFI > 0.50	RMSEA ≤ 0.06
Measurement model	1.26	0.93	0.98	0.77	0.026
Structural model	2.40	0.88	0.94	0.76	0.059

Once measurement model found to be satisfactory, this research conducted structural model analysis corelating the proposed hypothesis. The model fit indices found to be satisfactory in the structural model analysis without any further modifications in the model (Table 1). The goodness of fit index AGFI = 0.88; CFI = 0.94, PNFI = 0.76; RMSEA = 0.059. The analysis further found that all the hypotheses are significant.

The results also found that p-values for the structural model analysis are below the threshold value of 0.05 [58]. An examination of path coefficients reported that price value (γ = 0.37, p = 0.004) and Hedonic motivation (γ = 0.19, p = 0.001) positively and significantly influenced consumer's attitude to use social commerce. Additionally, Habit (γ = 0.21, p = 0.008), Attitude (γ = 0.20, p = 0.001) have positive and significant influence on consumer's behavioural intention to use social commerce. Finally, risk ($\gamma = -0.18$, p $= 0.05$) has a negative and significant influence on behavioural intention to use social commerce. Therefore, all five-hypothesis found to be supported (see Fig. 2).

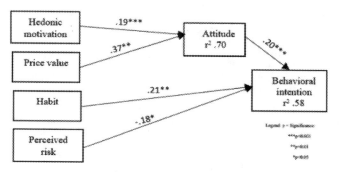

Fig. 2. Validated conceptual model

5 Discussion

The analysis of the structural model revealed the predictive power of the proposed model in examining social commerce adoption in this research. Based on the analysis of the structural model, this can conclude that the proposed model is highly predictive in investigating social commerce adoption. The results demonstrate that the validated model accounted for 70 percent of the variance in attitude and 58 percent of the variance in behavioural intention. For example, Patil et al. [31] reported the model explained 59 percent of the variance, Shin [47] found 23.80 percent of the variance, and Rashid et al. (2017) found 49.80 percent of the variance in attitude. Similarly, For instance, Rahman et al. (2020) investigated social commerce within Bangladesh, and the model explained 41.4 percent of the variance in behavioural intention. Abed [4] found 53 percent of the variance, Nadeem et al. [17] found 18.90 percent, and Wang and Yu [59] found 31 percent of the variance in behavioural intention, which are comparatively lower than the findings of the current research.

As discussed in the results, this study validated all five hypotheses. Two predictors price value and hedonic motivation found to be significant influence of consumer attitude. The relationship between price value and attitude in this study yielded better results compared to the relationship between hedonic motivation and attitude in many social commerce studies. In the context of Bangladesh, social commerce technology is relatively new for buying and selling products online. Many Bangladeshi consumers are unaware of this system and still rely on traditional outlets. Therefore, the user's perception towards price value plays a crucial role in creating a positive attitude, which leads to technology adoption. Price value is related to financial cost of using any new system like social commerce. When financial cost is more than the perceived benefit, consumers are not fully satisfied with the service [61]. Social commerce platform/manager should provide cost effective service to the consumer so that users can easily adopt this technology without concerning the cost. Consumers found to habitual to use social media specifically Facebook in Bangladesh which could turn to the customer of social commerce. Consumers already aware of various features of social media therefore, this is beneficials for social commerce vendors/managers to provide enjoyment and entertaining services so that users can easily adopt this technology. Consumer experience with new system could be impacted by the role of intrinsic motivation. Therefore, Social commerce could provide users with wide ranges of support and services that could motivate users to shape their attitude and eventually motivate to use social commerce. Entertaining apps, fun games could be accelerated users the feeling of pleasure and trigger the motivating factors to use the technology.

Three predictors (habit, risk and attitude) reported significant influence on consumer's behavioural intention while risk found to be negative factors that inhibit consumer to use social commerce. Consistent with the prior technology acceptance studies, risk has a negative and significant influence on consumer's behavioural intention to adopt social commerce. Bangladeshi consumers who are more comfortable using any technology are less likely to feel anxious using social commerce. The result reported that 76 percent of respondents prefer the cash-on- delivery method, which reduces financial anxiety amongst consumers. However, the negative and significant relationship between risk and behavioural intention clearly shows that there is still a sense of apprehension and fear among consumers while using social commerce. Risk levels might be higher for new social commerce users if they are comparatively new to technology adoption. Social commerce platforms should ensure the security and privacy of the users to minimize risk amongst consumers. Trustworthiness between the social commerce platform/seller and the consumer would reduce the risk, and eventually the consumer would adopt the social commerce technology without any hesitation. Users appear to be highly attached to social media, forming a habitual part of their daily lives, and becoming potential customers. This habitual behaviour on social media has the potential to transform into social commerce consumer.

Attitude, defined as a psychological evaluation of an object with a positive or negative response [44]. Attitude represents an individual's subjective evaluation of the social commerce technology. Attitude is crucial when studying consumer behaviour, as it helps businesses understand individual behaviour and make informed decisions. A positive attitude fosters an intention to use the technology and more positive attitude drives the consumer towards an intention to use the technology [14].

5.1 Research Contribution

As yet no study has explored social commerce considering the factors analysis and validated in study in the context of Bangladesh. Also, the literature review of social commerce found that price value, habit and hedonic motivation has been explore in very limited studies in the context of Qatar and Saudi Arabia. However, those studies cannot be applied to the Bangladesh due to cultural, political and environmental difference. Attitude is an another factor that is utilized in a limited number of studies. However, understanding the importance of attitude and validating the relationship with Price value and Hedonic motivation confirms that attitude can shape users' behaviours and further attitude, risk, and habit influence user's behaviour to adopt social commerce.

The Findings offer valuable and practical insights for both Bangladeshi consumers and business which engage social commerce. Managers are required to comprehend the validated model's constructs to implement it effectively. In terms of hedonic motivation and price value, it is recommended that managers incorporate entertaining, enjoyable content into their social commerce pages. This could include designing fun advertisements that have a positive impact on consumer attitudes towards adopting social commerce. Additionally, businesses should provide consumers with various cost-saving options, such as price and product comparison charts, free delivery choices, reasonable pricing, and assistance in finding the best prices on different websites. Habit and perceived risk have a direct influence on consumer behavioural intentions. Social shopping is not yet a habitual practice among Bangladeshi consumers due to a lack of technological advancement. However, businesses should acknowledge these challenges and offer user-friendly and easily learnable technology to encourage the development of habits around using their systems. Furthermore, perceived risk negatively affects consumer adoption of social commerce sites. Transaction-related issues, potential financial losses, lack of online safety and security, and insufficient post-purchase services are some of the risks associated with social commerce sites. Considering Bangladeshi consumers as risk-averse individuals with a tendency to be cautious when it comes to accepting or trusting new technology, managers need to provide enhanced safety and security measures, transparent transactions system, and financial assurances to instil confidence in consumers. This will facilitate the smooth adoption of social commerce technology without hesitation.

6 Conclusions

The development of social media platforms provides value to the customer through innovations such as creating a virtual marketplace, buying features, promotions, and advertisement options. Although Bangladeshi consumers are becoming innovative by adopting different technologies, people still feel hesitant about purchasing online, particularly via social commerce platforms, despite the platforms' efforts to offer value-added services. Therefore, the following section discusses limitations, future research, and recommendations for further enhancement of this technology. This research makes a valuable contribution to the existing literature by introducing and empirically validating several customer-centric constructs that are often overlooked or underrated, including price value, motivation, habit, attitude, and risk. The findings of this study reveal that both price value and hedonic motivation have a significant and positive impact on consumer attitude. Additionally, it was observed that consumer habit and attitude exert a significant influence on consumer behavioural intention. However, risk has a negative influence on consumer behavioural intention. Bangladesh as a developing country has a huge potential for new entrepreneurs and small businesses on social commerce platforms to grab the attention of the consumer. The appropriate implementation of the research model into the social commerce platform could significantly influence consumers to adopt this technology. For instance, offering price-saving options, enabling price comparisons between pages, incorporating fun and entertaining content, mitigating transaction and data-related risks, and fostering a habit of using the technology are recommended to use in this technology. Therefore, a proper implementation of the results presented can improve the social commerce system to a significant extent in the context of Bangladesh.

6.1 Limitation and Future Research

The first limitation of this research is the use of the non-probability-based convenient sampling method for data collection. The non-random sampling techniques are associated with less generalizability [50]. However, the research specifically included respondents who use and purchase through social commerce sites. Given that the non-probability sampling did not make a significant impact on this research. Future research could test the proposed model of this research with random samples to improve the generalizability of the findings. The quantitative method was adopted for this research due to the need to conduct statistical analysis to test the conceptual model and hypotheses. However, future research may use a qualitative method to explore more views of social commerce users and understand the technology adoption behaviour. Additionally, the data for this research is cross-sectional by nature. It is recommended that further research may use a longitudinal approach, which would enable researchers to explore the changes in the importance of antecedents over time. The model did not analyse demographic variables such as age and gender as a moderator. Moderators may be valuable but not universally applicable in all contexts. As a result, the majority of the existing research did not consider demographic variables in the models. However, future research may go beyond this by including the demographic variables as a moderator, which might help to obtain a more in-depth view of the social commerce research. Another limitation of this research is generalizability of the results. As previously mentioned, this research collected the data from social commerce users of Bangladesh. There is an economic, political, and cultural difference between one country and another, which limits the generalizability of the research model to other contrasting contexts. However, future studies could use this model with modification to examine social commerce adoption in other contexts.

Appendix

Research Questionnaires

Construct	Code	Item(s)	Source(s)
Hedonic motivation (HM)	HM1	Using social commerce sites for shopping online is fun	Venkatesh et al. (2012); Sheikh et al. (2017)
	HM2	Using social commerce sites for shopping online is enjoyable	
	HM3	Using social commerce sites for shopping online is very entertaining	

(continued)

(*continued*)

Construct	Code	Item(s)	Source(s)
Price value	PV1	Buying through social commerce sites is reasonably priced	Venkatesh et al. (2012); Sheikh et al. (2017)
	PV2	Buying through social commerce sites is a good value for the money	
	PV3	I can save money by examining the prices of products on different social media websites	
	PV4	I like to search for cheap products in different social media websites	
	PV5	Social media websites offer better value for money for online purchase	
Habit	HT1	Buying though social commerce sites has become a habit for me	Venkatesh et al. (2012); Sheikh et al. (2017)
	HT2	I am addicted to online buying though social commerce sites	
	HT3	I must use social commerce platforms for online shopping	
	HT4	Using social commerce sites for online shopping has become natural to me	
Perceived risk (PR)	PR1	Other people can know information about my transactions if I use social commerce sites	Gan and Wang (2017); Chiu et al. (2014); Farivar et al. (2017); William (2018)
	PR2	There is high potential for financial loss if I make purchases using social commerce sites	
	PR3	There is a significant risk in making purchases via social commerce sites	

(*continued*)

(continued)

Construct	Code	Item(s)	Source(s)
	PR4	Purchasing from social commerce sites would involve more product risks such as defective product	
	PR5	Purchasing from social commerce sites poses a risk that I will not be satisfied with the product, service or delivery	
	PR6	It is likely that shopping on social commerce sites will cause me to suffer a financial loss due to the lack of warranty in case of faults	
	PR7	It is likely that the online payment system required for social commerce is unsafe	
	PR8	It is likely that the customer services of post-purchase are not guaranteed	
Behavioural intention (BI)	BI1	I will always try to use social commerce sites for shopping online in my daily life	Venkatesh et al. (2012); Liang and Turban (2011); Hajli and Sims (2015); Gibreel et al. (2018)
	BI2	I plan to use social commerce sites for shopping online frequently	
	BI3	I am willing to provide my experiences and suggestions when my friends on the social commerce sites want my advice on buying something	
	BI4	I am willing to share my own shopping experience with my friends on social commerce sites	
	BI5	I will recommend others to purchase using social commerce sites	
Attitude (AT)	AT1	I would have positive feelings towards using social commerce sites for online shopping	Shin (2013); Patil et al. 2020)

(continued)

Construct	Code	Item(s)	Source(s)
	AT2	I think using social commerce sites for online shopping would make my life more interesting	
	AT3	It would be a good idea to make use of social commerce sites for shopping online	
	AT4	Using social commerce sites for online shopping is pleasant	
	AT5	Using social commerce sites for online shopping is beneficial	
	AT6	I like the idea of online buying through social commerce	
	AT7	Using social commerce sites for online shopping is a good idea	

References

1. Akman, I., Mishra, A.: Factors influencing consumer intention in social commerce adoption. Inf. Technol. People **30**(2), 356–370 (2017)
2. Liang, T.P., Ho, Y.T., Li, Y.W., Turban, E.: What drives social commerce: the role of social support and relationship quality. Int. J. Electron. Commer. **16**(2), 69–90 (2011)
3. Turban, E., King, D., Lee, J.K., Liang, T.-P., Turban, D.C.: Social commerce: foundations, social marketing, and advertising. In: Electronic Commerce. STBE, pp. 309–364. Springer, Cham (2015). https://doi.org/10.1007/978-3-319-10091-3_7
4. Abed, S.: An empirical examination of Instagram as an s-commerce channel. J. Adv. Manage. Res. **15**(2), 146–160 (2018)
5. Shoheib, Z., Abu-Shanab, E.A.: Adapting the UTAUT2 model for social commerce context. Int. J. e-Business Res. **18**(1), 1–20 (2022)
6. Sheikh, Z., Islam, T., Rana, S., Hameed, Z., Saeed, U.: Acceptance of social commerce framework in Saudi Arabia. Telematics Inform. **34**(8), 1693–1708 (2017)
7. Jadil, Y., Jeyaraj, A., Dwivedi, Y., Rana, N., Sarker, P.: A meta-analysis of the factors associated with s-commerce intention: Hofstede's cultural dimensions as moderators. Internet Res. **32**(7), 1066–2243 (2022). https://doi.org/10.1108/intr-10-2021-0768
8. Dwivedi, Y.K., Ismagilova, E., Sarker, P., Jeyaraj, A., Jadil, Y., Hughes, L.: A metaanalytic structural equation model for understanding social commerce adoption. Inf. Syst. Front. **25**, 1–17 (2021). https://doi.org/10.1007/s10796-021-10172-2
9. Jeyaraj, A., Ismagilova, E., Jadil, Y., Sarker, P., Rana, N., Hughes, L., Dwivedi, Y.K.: Mediating role of social commerce trust in behavioral intention and use. Inf. Syst. Manage. **40**, 1–17 (2022). https://doi.org/10.1080/10580530.2022.2140370

10. Sarker, P., Hughe, L., Dwivedi, Y.K., Rana, N.P.: Social commerce adoption predictors: a review and weight analysis. In: Hattingh, M., Matthee, M., Smuts, H., Pappas, I., Dwivedi, Y.K., Mäntymäki, M. (eds.) Responsible Design, Implementation and Use of Information and Communication Technology: 19th IFIP WG 6.11 Conference on e-Business, e-Services, and e-Society, I3E 2020, Skukuza, South Africa, April 6–8, 2020, Proceedings, Part I, pp. 176–191. Springer International Publishing, Cham (2020). https://doi.org/10.1007/978-3-030-44999-5_15

11. Sarker, P., Rana, N.P., Hughe, L., Dwivedi, Y.K.: A meta-analysis of social commerce adoption research. In: Sharma, S.K., Dwivedi, Y.K., Metri, B., Rana, N.P. (eds.) Re-imagining Diffusion and Adoption of Information Technology and Systems: A Continuing Conversation: IFIP WG 8.6 International Conference on Transfer and Diffusion of IT, TDIT 2020, Tiruchirappalli, India, December 18–19, 2020, Proceedings, Part II, pp. 404–418. Springer International Publishing, Cham (2020). https://doi.org/10.1007/978-3-030-64861-9_35

12. Sarker, P., Hughes, D.L., Dwivedi, Y.K.: Extension of META-UTAUT for examining consumer adoption of social commerce: Towards a conceptual model. In: Martínez-López, F.J., D'Alessandro, S. (eds.) Advances in Digital Marketing and eCommerce: First International Conference, 2020, pp. 122–129. Springer International Publishing, Cham (2020). https://doi.org/10.1007/978-3-030-47595-6_16

13. Sarker, P., Kizgin, H., Rana, N.P., Dwivedi, Y.K.: Review of theoretical models and limitations of social commerce adoption literature. In: Pappas, I.O., Mikalef, P., Dwivedi, Y.K., Jaccheri, L., Krogstie. J., Mäntymäki, M. (eds.) Digital Transformation for a Sustainable Society in the 21st Century: 18th IFIP WG 6.11 Conference on e-Business, e-Services, and e-Society, I3E 2019, Trondheim, Norway, September 18–20, 2019, Proceedings, pp. 3–12. Springer International Publishing, Cham (2019). https://doi.org/10.1007/978-3-030-29374-1_1

14. Dwivedi, Y.K., Rana, N.P., Tamilmani, K., Raman, R.: A meta-analysis based modified unified theory of acceptance and use of technology (meta-UTAUT): a review of emerging literature. Curr. Opin. Psychol. **36**, 13–18 (2020)

15. Makmor, N., Aziz Abd, N., Alam Shah, S.: Social commerce an extended technology acceptance model: the mediating effect of perceived ease of use and perceived usefulness. Malays. J. Consum. Fam. Econ. **22**, 119–136 (2019)

16. Rashid, N.A.A., Mokhlis, S., Yaakop, A.Y.: The antecedents of consumer behavioural intention in social commerce. Adv. Sci. Lett. **23**(4), 3111–3114 (2017)

17. Nadeem, W., Juntunen, M., Juntunen, J.: Consumer segments in social commerce: a latent class approach. J. Consum. Behav. **16**(3), 279–292 (2017)

18. Dwivedi, Y., Rana, N., Chen, H., Williams, M.: A meta-analysis of the unified theory of acceptance and use of technology (UTAUT). In: Proceedings of the Conference Governance and Sustainability in Information Systems, 155–170 (2011)

19. Venkatesh, V., Thong, J.Y., Xu, X.: Consumer acceptance and use of information technology: extending the unified theory of acceptance and use of technology. MIS Q. **36**(1), 157–178 (2012)

20. Marchewka, J.T., Kostiwa, K.: An application of the UTAUT model for understanding student perceptions using course management software. Commun. IIMA **7**(2), 10–25 (2007)

21. Min, Q., Ji, S., Qu, G.: Mobile commerce user acceptance study in China: a revised UTAUT model. Tsinghua Sci. Technol. **13**(3), 257–264 (2008)

22. Yu, C.S.: Factors affecting individuals to adopt mobile banking: empirical evidence from the UTAUT model. J. Electron. Commer. Res. **13**(2), 104–127 (2012)

23. Cho, E., Son, J.: The effect of social connectedness on consumer adoption of social commerce in apparel shopping. Fashion Text. **6**(1), 1–17 (2019)

24. Gan, C., Wang, W.: The influence of perceived value on purchase intention in social commerce context. Internet Res. **27**(4), 772–785 (2017)

25. Williams, M.D.: Social commerce and the mobile platform: payment and security perceptions of potential users. Comput. Hum. Behav. **115**, 105557 (2021)
26. Yin, X., Wang, H., Xia, Q., Gu, Q.: How social interaction affects purchase intention in social commerce: a cultural perspective. Sustainability **11**(8), 2423 (2019)
27. Kim, J., Forsythe, S.: Adoption of virtual try-on technology for online apparel shopping. J. Interact. Mark. **22**(2), 45–59 (2008)
28. Venkatesh, V., Morris, M.G., Davis, G.B., Davis, F.D.: User acceptance of information technology: toward a unified view. MIS Q. **27**(3), 425–478 (2003)
29. Ha, S., Stoel, L.: Consumer e-shopping acceptance: antecedents in a technology acceptance model. J. Bus. Res. **62**(5), 565–571 (2009)
30. Khurshid, M.M., Zakaria, N.H., Rashid, A., Ahmed, Y.A., Shafique, M.N.: Adoption of transactional service in electronic government–a case of Pak-identity service. In: The Proceedings of the Conference on e-Business, e-Services and e-Society, pp. 439–450 (2019)
31. Patil, P., Tamilmani, K., Rana, N.P., Raghavan, V.: Understanding consumer adoption of mobile payment in India: extending meta-UTAUT model with personal innovativeness, anxiety, trust, and grievance redressal. Int. J. Inform. Manage. **54**, 102144 (2020)
32. Rana, N.P., Dwivedi, Y.K., Lal, B., Williams, M.D., Clement, M.: Citizens' adoption of an electronic government system: towards a unified view. Inf. Syst. Front. **19**(3), 549–568 (2017)
33. Abu-Al-Aish, A., Love, S.: Factors influencing students' acceptance of m-learning: an investigation in higher education. Int. Rev. Res. Open Distrib. Learn. **14**(5), 83–107 (2013)
34. Engotoit, B., Kituyi, G.M., Moya, M.B.: Influence of performance expectancy on commercial farmers' intention to use mobile-based communication technologies for agricultural market information dissemination in Uganda. J. Syst. Inform. Technol. **18**(4), 346–363 (2016)
35. Friedrich, T., Schlauderer, S., Overhage, S.: Some things are just better rich: how social commerce feature richness affects consumers' buying intention via social factors. Electron. Markets **31**(1), 159–180 (2021)
36. Gatautis, R., Medziausiene, A.: Factors affecting social commerce acceptance in Lithuania. Procedia-Soc. Behav. Sci. **110**, 1235–1242 (2014)
37. Alam, M.Z., Hu, W., Kaium, M.A., Hoque, M.R., Alam, M.M.D.: Understanding the determinants of mHealth apps adoption in Bangladesh: a SEM-neural network approach. Technol. Soc. **61**, 101255 (2020)
38. Bervell, B.B., Kumar, J.A., Arkorful, V., Agyapong, E.M., Osman, S.: Remodelling the role of facilitating conditions for google classroom acceptance: a revision of UTAUT2. Australas. J. Educ. Technol. **38**(1), 115–135 (2021)
39. Fitrianie, S., Horsch, C., Beun, R.J., Griffioen-Both, F., Brinkman, W.P.: Factors affecting user's behavioural intention and use of a mobile-phone-delivered cognitive behavioural therapy for insomnia: a small-scale UTAUT analysis. J. Med. Syst. **45**(12), 1–18 (2021)
40. Weerakkody, V., El-Haddadeh, R., Al-Sobhi, F., Shareef, M.A., Dwivedi, Y.K.: Examining the influence of intermediaries in facilitating e-government adoption: an empirical investigation. Int. J. Inf. Manage. **33**(5), 716–725 (2013)
41. Prayoonphan, F., Xu, X.: Factors influencing the intention to use the common ticketing system (spider card) in Thailand. Behav. Sci. **9**(5), 46 (2019)
42. Yahia, I.B., Al-Neama, N., Kerbache, L.: Investigating the drivers for social commerce in social media platforms: importance of trust, social support and the platform perceived usage. J. Retail. Consum. Serv. **41**, 11–19 (2018)
43. Farivar, S., Turel, O., Yuan, Y.: Skewing users' rational risk considerations in social commerce: an empirical examination of the role of social identification. Inf. Manage. **55**(8), 1038–1048 (2018)
44. Eagly, A.H., Chaiken, S.: The advantages of an inclusive definition of attitude. Soc. Cognit. **25**(5), 582–602 (2007)

45. Davis, F.D.: Perceived usefulness, perceived ease of use, and user acceptance of information technology. MIS Q. **13**, 319–340 (1989)
46. Fishbein, M., Ajzen, I.: Belief, Attitude, Intention, and Behaviour: An Introduction to Theory and Research. Addison-Wesley, Reading, MA (1975)
47. Shin, D.H.: User experience in social commerce: in friends we trust. Behav. Inf. Technol. **32**(1), 52–67 (2013)
48. Shanmugam, M., Gheni, A.Y., Bin Yusof, A.F., Karunakaran, V.: The impact of social commerce determinants on social capital for energy sectors. J. Inf. Technol. Manage. **11**(1), 60–75 (2019)
49. Bhattacherjee, A.: Social Science Research: Principles, Methods, and Practices, USF Tampa Bay Open Access Textbooks
50. Slade, E., Williams, M., Dwivedi, Y., Piercy, N.: Exploring consumer adoption of proximity mobile payments. J. Strateg. Mark. **23**(3), 209–223 (2015)
51. Limayem, M., Hirt, S.G., Cheung, C.M.: How habit limits the predictive power of intention: the case of information systems continuance. MIS Q. **31**, 705–737 (2007)
52. Wu, Y.L., Li, E.Y.: Marketing mix, customer value, and customer loyalty in social commerce: a stimulus-organism-response perspective. Internet Res. **28**(1), 74–104 (2018)
53. Biucky, S.T., Harandi, S.R.: The effects of perceived risk on social commerce adoption based on tam model. Int. J. Electron. Commer. Stud. **8**(2), 173–196 (2017)
54. Featherman, M.S., Hajli, N.: Self-service technologies and e-services risks in social commerce era. J. Bus. Ethics **139**(2), 251–269 (2016)
55. Lin, C.S., Wu, S.: Exploring antecedents of online group-buying: social commerce perspective. Hum. Syst. Manage. **34**(2), 133–147 (2015)
56. Samarasinghe, S., Silva, K.: Social commerce acceptance: integrated model with collaboration theories and technology acceptance model. Am. Sci. Res. J. Eng., Technol., Sci. **62**(1), 39–53 (2019)
57. Hajli, N.: Social commerce constructs and consumer's intention to buy. Int. J. Inform. Manage. **35**(2), 183–191 (2015)
58. di Leo, G., Sardanelli, F.: Statistical significance: p value, 0.05 threshold, and applications to radiomics—reasons for a conservative approach. Eur. Radiol. Exp. **4**(1), 1–8 (2020)
59. Wang, Y., Yu, C.: Social interaction-based consumer decision-making model in social commerce: the role of word of mouth and observational learning. Int. J. Inf. Manage. **37**(3), 179–189 (2017)
60. Sair, S.A., Danish, R.Q.: Effect of performance expectancy and effort expectancy on the mobile commerce adoption intention through personal innovativeness among Pakistani consumers. Pak. J. Commer. Soc. Sci. **12**(2), 501–520 (2018)
61. Alalwan, A.A., Baabdullah, A.M., Rana, N.P., Dwivedi, Y.K., Kizgin, H.: Examining the influence of mobile store features on user e-satisfaction: extending UTAUT2 with personalization, responsiveness, and perceived security and privacy. In: Digital Transformation for a Sustainable Society in the 21st Century: 18th IFIP WG 6.11 Conference on e-Business, e-Services, and e-Society, I3E 2019, Trondheim, Norway, September 18–20 (2019)
62. Novela, S., Sihombing, Y.O., Caroline, E., Octavia, R.: The effects of hedonic and utilitarian motivation toward online purchase intention with attitude as intervening variable. In: 2020 International Conference on Information Management and Technology (ICIMTech), pp. 75–80 (2020)
63. Alsoud, M., Al-Muani, L., Alkhazali, Z.: Digital platform interactivity and Jordanian social commerce purchase intention. Int. J. Data Netw. Sci. **6**(2), 285–294 (2022)

64. Aladwani, A.M., Dwivedi, Y.K.: Towards a theory of sociocitizenry: quality anticipation, trust configuration, and approved adaptation of governmental social media. Int. J. Inf. Manage. **43**, 261–272 (2018)
65. Hughes, D.L., Dwivedi, Y.K., Rana, N.P., Simintiras, A.C.: Information systems project failure–analysis of causal links using interpretive structural modelling. Prod. Plann. Control **27**(16), 1313–1333 (2016)

Establishing a Health Data Marketplace: A Framework for Success

Magnus Erdvik[1,2], Kantasit Intaraphasuk[1,3], Ilias O. Pappas[1,4] (ID),
and Polyxeni Vassilakopoulou[1(✉)] (ID)

[1] University of Agder, 4639 Kristiansand, Norway
magnuse@egde.no, kantasit.intaraphasuk@sor.no, {ilias.pappas,
polyxeni.vasilakopoulou}@uia.no
[2] Egde, 4879 Grimstad, Norway
[3] Sparebanken Sør, 4610 Kristiansand, Norway
[4] Norwegian University of Science and Technology, 7491 Trondheim, Norway

Abstract. This study outlines essential elements needed to develop a Health Data Marketplace (HDM) by building upon an existing data platform in Norway. A comprehensive framework is proposed that accounts for technical, legal, financial, and additional considerations. The results highlight the pivotal roles of key HDM actors - Marketplace Operators, Marketplace Users, and Legal Authorities - and emphasize critical enablers such as Data Standardization, Interoperability, Integration, Security, Trust, and Legal Frameworks. Such a marketplace has the potential to catalyze the effective, secure, and ethical use of health data, contributing to enhanced healthcare outcomes, research, and innovation.

Keywords: Health Data Marketplace · Data Marketplace · Health Data · Data Sharing · Data Exchange · Gateway

1 Introduction

In Norway, reliable and good-quality health data are collected for patients. This is mainly attributable to the utilization of a singular, standardized personal identifier, which facilitates data combination and analysis [1–3]. Since 2017, the Norwegian eHealth Directorate has invested significant resources and collaborated closely with researchers and partners to enhance services for citizens, researchers, and patients across Norway. The primary focus of these development efforts lies in essential functions, including enabling quicker and more secure access to health data. The overarching objective is to stimulate research and innovation, improve public health, and support economic growth [4, 5].

Several innovative initiatives have emerged in the Norwegian e-health landscape, including Helseanalyseplatformen (Health Analysis Platform) and Helsedata.no. The Health Analysis Platform aimed to optimize health data usage, enhance understanding of diseases, and develop better medications and treatment methods, enabling researchers to interconnect and utilize data across stakeholders in Norway more effectively. Despite its promising and innovative premises, the initiative stopped in December 2021 due to

© IFIP International Federation for Information Processing 2023
Published by Springer Nature Switzerland AG 2023
M. Janssen et al. (Eds.): I3E 2023, LNCS 14316, pp. 224–235, 2023.
https://doi.org/10.1007/978-3-031-50040-4_17

legal and technical challenges related to adequately protecting the data [6, 7]. In contrast, Helsedata.no, a part of the health data program focusing on healthcare infrastructure and services, has successfully been established. This platform hosts different types of data and facilitates data access for research, quality improvement in health services, medical development, and other health-related aims. While the platform primarily targets research, healthcare services and commercial enterprises can also benefit. Although Helsedata.no is unique within Norway, operating with data from various sources, it has its limitations. The data sources belong only to specific categories such as central health registries, national medical quality registries, national health surveys, biobanks, and socio-economic data, while a complex and strict access request process is limiting its potential [5].

The observed limitations within present-day health data exchange systems inspired us to delve deeper into their potential. To do this, we performed a literature review, focusing on Data Marketplaces (DMs), Business Models, Gateway technologies, and the nuances of the Norwegian e-health context. Through this process, we identified critical gaps in our understanding of implementing a Health Data Marketplace (HDM) successfully. The literature highlights the importance of thorough case studies on DMs and their providers [8] and suggests the need for more research into novel marketplace solutions that tackle issues within data ecosystems [9–13]. Research areas that need to be further developed include privacy of sensitive data in DMs [14, 15], standardized data formats, and interoperability [16]. Also, there additional research is needed on data governance frameworks and their influence on DM dynamics [17]. The current study aims to address these complex issues through an exploratory case study. The study uses the Egde Health Gateway (EHG) as a case. EHG is a platform for data flow between health information systems and actors in line with the Norwegian target architecture for data sharing in the health and care sector. EHG is continuously expanded adding new connections to health record systems and application providers. The objective is to identify components required to establish a secure, efficient, and collaborative platform for health data exchange. The study is guided by two primary research questions (RQs):

RQ1: "What are the essential components for successfully implementing a Health Data Marketplace in Norway?".

RQ2: "How can a Health Data Marketplace be established using an existing data platform?".

The paper is organized as follows. Section 2 presents related literature. Section 3 presents the method employed. Section 4 presents the findings, and Sect. 5 provides a discussion along with implications and suggestions for future work.

2   Related Literature

This section presents key findings from our literature review. To facilitate structure, we have organized the content into four primary categories: Technology, Legal Hurdles, Financial, and Other Aspects in DMs. This literature is the background of our study.

Technology. IoT technology is vital for data gathering in and healthcare but there are challenges including scalability, data standardization, and AI integration [12]. Standardized protocols can improve wearable device data flows in healthcare [18]. Data sharing requires adherence to FAIR (Findable, Accessible, Interoperable, Reusable) principles and stable end-to-end systems [16, 19]. Health data interoperability involves both technology and human activity aspects [20, 21]. Storage arrangements can vary, with some DMs using cloud storage and others decentralized storage [8, 9]. Blockchain can enhance data trading trust and transparency [22].

Legal Hurdles. More and Alber [23] discuss the balance between gaining insights and maintaining privacy in DMs. Regulations like GDPR have specific provisions for data collection and retention [23, 24]. For instance, prior research discussed GDPR and HIPAA's impact on wearable health devices [18]. Furthermore, research by Spiekermann [25] outlines challenges related to trust, security, and the lack of established regulatory frameworks for data trading.

Financial Aspects. Prior research has suggested business model archetypes for DMs, useful across industries [8, 9]. Teece [26] underscores the role of dynamic capabilities and organizational design in business models. Specifically for healthcare, prior research [16] calls for more open solutions in health sensor industry. Furthermore, researcher identified essential properties for traded data, including compliance with FAIR principles [27] and emphasizes the role of metadata in data quality and trading [28].

Other Aspects in Data Marketplaces. Prior research explored non-economic benefits like knowledge transfer in open DMs [29]. Trust issues are common challenges in DMs [15, 23]. Decentralization and blockchain can address these by establishing trust and preventing market monopolies. Chowdhury, Ferdous [15] propose a trust framework for health data sharing. Nguyen and Ali [14] recommend a reputation system for transparent and trusted transactions. These insights set the stage for our study.

3   Research Method

To address the RQs, we opted for semi-structured interviews [30, 31]. The interviews were conducted based on a guide developed from the literature review and following a purposive sampling strategy [32]. The data collection method enabled the exploration of unanticipated themes and tailoring to different participant's background and expertise [33, 34]. Inherent in the study design are ethical considerations to safeguard the rights and information of the participants. This includes obtaining informed consent, adhering to data security measures following all Norwegian guidelines for research data [35]. We established a collaboration agreement with Egde, the developers of Egde Health Gateway (EHG), which provided us access to connections and resources within their ecosystem. As a result of this collaboration, we identified various interview participants that have roles as data providers, data users and consultants. Table 1 provides an overview of all study participants. The participants received the interview guide in advance and this allowed them to reflect on the questions before the interview. We recorded all interviews and transcribed them. The recordings enabled us to review the interviews multiple times, making them a more reliable data source.

Data analysis followed a systematic approach per Oates [31] and Miles, Huberman [36]. An inter-coder reliability approach was adopted to enhance the validity and reliability of the results [37]. Two authors individually coded the interview transcripts into

Table 1. Overview of study participants.

ID	Description	Category	Organization
HRE1	E-health Executive	Healthcare & Research	Egde Consulting
HRE2	Medical Researcher	Healthcare & Research	Academic Institution
HRE3	Healthcare Researcher	Healthcare & Research	Academic Institution 2
HRE4	Academic Researcher	Healthcare & Research	Academic Institution
TDS1	IT Consultant	Technology & Data	IT Consultancy firm 2
TDS2	Data Specialist	Technology & Data	Egde Consulting
TDS3	Data Consultant	Technology & Data	Egde Consulting
PMI1	Innovation Consultant	Project Management	Egde Consulting
PMI2	Project Manager	Project Management	Egde Consulting
PMI3	Innovation Consultant	Project Management	Egde Consulting
PHP1	C-Level Executive	Private Health Provider	Private Health Company
PHP2	C-Level Executive	Private Health Provider	Private Health Company

themes. We discerned patterns and trends in the data and synthesized the findings to respond to the RQs. We used NVivo to code the data into categories and grouped the codes into the themes identified in the literature.

4 Findings

4.1 Technical Findings

The operation of a Health Data Marketplace (HDM) hinges on the ability to address various technical aspects, including data standardization, integration, interoperability, and security. This section provides an overview of these findings.

Data Standardization and Interoperability. Both data standardization and interoperability were frequently discussed during the interviews. HRE1 highlighted the use of standardized data formats, like HL7's FHIR, noting that *"having intentional standardizations, the more people use it, the better it gets"*. PMI3 discussed the importance of terminology standards stating: *"...apart from how the data is structured and formatted. There is the whole terminology side of things..."*.

Integration and Collaboration. HRE1 mentioned the role of Egde Health Gateway (EHG) in enabling collaboration by providing an integration platform for secure sharing and interaction. PMI2 further noted: *"We see that customers communicate using the gateway [EHG], sharing services that can be complementary to each other."*

Data Storage and Access. Data sharing difficulties within healthcare were noted by PMI1, stating: *"There is quite a silo in this sector..."*. HRE4 identified an issue with how data are stored by vendors, stating: *"most of it (data) stored by the vendor that* *provides digital home follow up services, and if you as a hospital specialist want to have an insight into the data, you have to log in into a separate system for digital home follow up so you don't see these data from the EPR system".*

Potential of Emerging Technologies. Interviewees often mentioned the potential of emerging technologies like artificial intelligence (AI), machine learning (ML), and blockchain. TDS2 noted: *"When ML and AI are to be developed as services for end-users, for example, to provide recommendations, they need data input to be able to give good recommendations. This data can be tapped into and obtained from such a data marketplace".* However, uncertainty surrounds the applicability of new technologies. PMI3 discussed AI and ML's potential but showed skepticism regarding blockchain's immediate relevance saying, *"I am not too sure where blockchain is going to come in right now, to all of this".*

4.2 Legal Findings

Regulatory Compliance and Privacy. The interviews highlighted the pivotal role of the General Data Protection Regulation (GDPR) and privacy in operating an HDM. HRE1 stressed stricter privacy standards in the Nordics, saying, *"GDPR, laws, and privacy are the challenges that come to mind (…) We have strict rules that govern privacy in nordic countries."* Referencing the well-rounded security framework provided by *"Normen,"* PMI3 termed it as *"probably the most comprehensive security framework for health data in Europe".*

Ethical and Anonymization Challenges. Beyond mere legal compliance, participants drew attention to the considerable ethical issues coupled with the difficulties in anonymizing large population datasets. Consent was deemed crucial and also national ethical approvals as explained by HRE3 - *"…approval from the data owner at the service level… And you must have an overarching national ethical approval".*

Balancing Innovation and Overcoming Legal Barriers. The balancing act between fostering innovation and sticking to regulatory compliance posed a significant challenge. HRE4 expressed this as *"many times, instead of taking the risk, you decide to be cautious. So, you would rather not do too much instead of trying to manage the risk afterward".*

4.3 Financial Findings

Emerging Business Models and Collaboration. Interviewees often referred to the ongoing transition from traditional consultant services to subscription-based services, stimulating new business models. HRE1 noted, *"consultant services are being replaced by subscription-based services, with a connection fee."* and TDS3 proposed a consume-based service model where consumers pay for the data they use on the marketplace.

Data Marketplaces as a Source of Financial Benefits. Participants pointed out potential financial gains through DMs. HRE1 saw opportunities for entrepreneurs, stating, *"EHG, allows entrepreneurs to bypass the complexities of setting up different integrations with data providers."* PHP1 shared similar views, highlighting that HDMs could fill data gaps in organizations, thereby offering ready-made solutions for customers.

Financing and Financial Incentives. Participants pointed to important financial aspects. HRE2 emphasized the role of data storage costs, saying, *"We pay quite a large sum to (data storage provider)"*. PHP1 stressed the need for a just and transparent pricing model: "The pricing model should be fair and transparent to encourage widespread adoption. It should incentivize data providers to share their data while ensuring that researchers can access the data they need at an affordable price".

4.4   Other Findings

Trust Between Stakeholders. The critical role of trust among stakeholders was a dominant theme during the interviews. HRE2 highlighted the importance of trust in relation to the quality assurance of collected health data, stating. HRE4 cautioned about the difficulty of restoring faith following a breach of trust, *"Even one scandal can make it very difficult to regain trust subsequently"*.

Usability and Acceptability. The usability and acceptability of data solutions were brought up in several interviews. For instance, PHP1 stated: *"Data solutions must be transparent and user-friendly, offering clear data type descriptions ... Awareness of the data providers and price variations is critical"*.

Ongoing Projects and Initiatives. Various ongoing projects and initiatives related to HDMs were highlighted by the interviewees. For instance, Agder County efforts to improve mental health and reduce social inequality among children and young people were relayed by HRE3. Additionally, collaborations among partners like Kristiansand municipality, Siemens Healthineers, Fundable, and Zyberia were touched upon by PMI2, who works on EHG.

4.5   Synthesis – Proposed Set of Components

The investigation of the potential development of an HDM in Norway led to the identification of several key components, each of which can plays a vital role.

Data Standardization, Interoperability, and Integration (DSII). This component embodies the technical requirements for effective data exchange. Interoperability ensures that different systems and software applications can communicate and exchange data efficiently, whereas standardization promotes consistency and facilitates compatibility between different data sets. Integration and standardization ensure that data can be combined and used across various systems and institutions.

Data Security, Trust, and Legal Frameworks (DSTLF). The dual challenges of maintaining data security while also fostering trust between various stakeholders are encapsulated in this component. Building trust between stakeholders requires clear, consistent, and enforceable legal frameworks that protect data rights while facilitating cooperation and data sharing. Ensuring regulatory compliance is crucial.

Anonymization, Ethical, and Legal Considerations (AELC). Anonymizing personal health data is an ethical necessity, not just a legal requirement. Striking a balance between utilizing health data for benefit and protecting individuals' privacy is vital.

Overcoming Legal and Regulatory Barriers (OLRB). Navigating the complex legal and regulatory requirements is critical to successfully establishing an HDM. Identifying and overcoming legal hurdles merits dedicated attention. Innovation must be balanced with compliance, ensuring advancements do not violate laws or regulations.

Exploration of Emerging Technologies (EET). This component reflects the necessity of keeping abreast of cutting-edge technological developments. Utilizing emerging technologies such as AI and blockchain technologies could significantly enhance the functionality and capabilities of an HDM. However, it requires careful exploration and evaluation to determine the most appropriate and beneficial applications.

Business Model Development and Sustainability (BMDS). This component emphasizes the significance of having viable and sustainable business models. A collaborative approach is essential to drive innovation and ensure sustainability.

Financial Benefits and Incentives (FBI). The potential financial benefits derived from HDMs must be thoroughly assessed. Moreover, creating incentives to promote data sharing and exploring innovative financing methods for infrastructure and data storage is crucial to ensuring the marketplace's financial viability.

Collaboration and Innovative Solutions (CIS). This component underlines the importance of a cooperative approach, pooling resources, and leveraging existing projects to drive innovation in the marketplace. Collaboration saves resources and promotes a sense of shared ownership and responsibility, fostering innovation.

Usability and Acceptability of Data Solutions (UADS). A user-friendly, transparent, and acceptable system is essential for ensuring the efficient utilization of health data, thereby driving the marketplace's success.

A consolidated HDM framework including all components is provided in Fig. 1. The role of each component, as described above, aligns with its placement within this framework, demonstrating its influence and primary domain within the HDM.

5   Discussion

The synthesis of the literature and the empirical insights in our framework contribute to the existing body of knowledge on Data Marketplaces (DMs). The proposed framework aligns with past studies emphasizing the critical importance of privacy in handling sensitive data within DMs [14, 15]. The framework, focusing on secure data handling, anonymity, and compliance with regulations like GDPR, supports this. EHG supports standardized data formats like HL7 FHIR, HL7v2, CDA, ebXML, and KITH, and is compatible with various APIs, electronic message exchanges, and sensor data protocols. However, the practical implementation of these standards and the interoperability across health systems may pose challenges. Further research is required to in actual operational contexts.

Building on recent studies [17], our study also underscores the critical role of data governance frameworks for DMs. Our approach to data governance mainly focuses on data standardization, security, and compliance with regulations. Furthermore, the

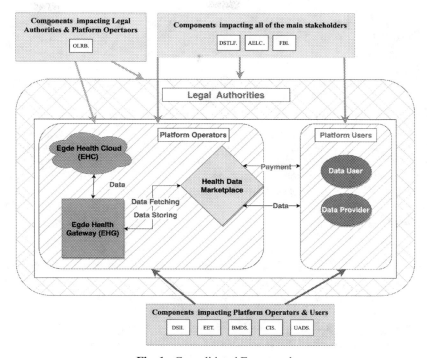

Fig. 1. Consolidated Framework

framework aligns with prior research on health data that points to the importance of arrangements for data quality assurance, data access (easing search and retrieval), and data crediting-rewarding (enabling tracing, attribution, and rewarding of data contributions) [38]. Additionally, the study provides a unique perspective on the role of HDMs in promoting sustainability. By reducing the resources needed for data acquisition, storage, and exchange, the framework suggests a new direction for research on sustainability and responsible data use in DMs, specifically HDMs [39]. Lastly, our research provides a novel view on democratizing health data by enabling various stakeholders, including citizens, to donate, sell and acquire data.

Implementing the framework can enhance data sharing and reduce data acquisition costs through a single, accessible platform, streamlining the process of obtaining and sharing data. Additionally, it allows for data donation and monetization, creating new revenue streams and encouraging participation in the health data ecosystem. This also promotes sustainability by mitigating the need for repetitive data collection, leading to more efficient resource usage. Furthermore, the availability of health data facilitates the development of AI models tailored to the needs of specific populations and bolsters healthcare research by offering a diverse and accessible data source. Implementing the framework can create an environment conducive to innovation and cross-sector collaboration with easy data access and sharing.

Despite the rigorous approach adopted in this study, its limitations must be acknowledged. Firstly, the study involved only twelve interviews, with uneven representation from each stakeholder group. While the selected participants provided valuable insights, more stakeholders in the ecosystem, such as patients or citizens who can donate/sell health data, were not interviewed. Additionally, the study lacked the perspectives of Legal Authorities, an important stakeholder group that remained unexplored. A notable future research direction would be addressing this study's methodological limitations by broadening stakeholder perspectives. Interviewing more stakeholders, including patients about their willingness to donate or sell health data can contribute to developing a more comprehensive understanding. Furthermore, as the regulatory landscape for health data continues to evolve, future research could explore the implications of these changes on marketplace dynamics. A more detailed economic analysis of the HDM ecosystem could also be valuable as pricing mechanisms and business models certainly require further research.

6   Conclusion

In addressing the first RQ *"What are the essential components for successfully implementing a Health Data Marketplace in Norway?"* our study identified several vital components, including Data Standardization, Interoperability, Integration (DSII), Data Security, Trust, Legal Frameworks (DSTLF), Anonymization, Ethical, Legal Considerations (AELC), Overcoming Legal and Regulatory Barriers (OLRB), Exploration of Emerging Technologies (EET), Business Model Development and Sustainability (BMDS), Financial Benefits and Incentives (FBI), Collaboration and Innovative Solutions (CIS), and Usability and Acceptability of Data Solutions (UADS).

In this context, we seek to highlight the roles of the identified components. Data Standardization, Interoperability, and Integration can ensure effective data exchange, and Data Security, Trust, Legal Frameworks can help in fostering trust while ensuring data security. Further, Anonymization, Ethical, Legal Considerations can balance privacy and public benefit, and by Overcoming Legal and Regulatory Barriers can ensure compliance with technological advancements. The Exploration of Emerging Technologies ensures that emerging tech, such as AI and blockchain, is part of new platform development, and through Business Model Development and Sustainability enables devising sustainable business models to drive innovation. Financial Benefits and Incentives can encourage data sharing and managing platforms' financial viability, Collaboration and Innovative Solutions can help promoting resource pooling and shared ownership, and finally, Usability and Acceptability of Data Solutions can help ensuring user-friendly and accepted data solutions.

Further, in addressing the second RQ: *"How can a Health Data Marketplace be established using an existing data platform?"*, our study outlined how the Egde Health Gateway (EHG) could extend its functionalities to accommodate a Health Data Marketplace. Leveraging on the EHG's infrastructure and addressing our identified key components, we propose a framework where the technical requirements of DSII, the regulatory aspects per OLRB, emerging technologies as per EET, financial benefits and incentives (FBI) aligned with business models, and usability and acceptability of data solutions (UADS), among others, are addressed.

By effectively surmounting the challenges identified and leveraging opportunities, we believe our work can contribute towards an ethical, secure, and efficient use of health data, consequently leading to improved healthcare outcomes, enhanced research, and stimulated innovation in Norway and beyond.

References

1. Bakken, I.J., Ariansen, A.M.S., Knudsen, G.P., Johansen, K.I., Vollset, S.E.: The Norwegian patient registry and the Norwegian registry for primary health care: research potential of two nationwide health-care registries. Scand. J. Public Health **48**(1), 49–55 (2020)
2. Direktoratet for e-helse. Helsedata (n.d.) https://www.ehelse.no/tema/helsedata. Accessed 30 May 2023
3. Saunes, I., Karanikolos, M., Sagan, A.: Norway: health system review. Health Syst. Transit. **22**(1) (2020)
4. Emberland, K.E., Rørtveit, G.: Norske helsedata - en utilgjengelig skatt. Tidsskr. Nor. Laegeforen. **136**(18), 1506 (2016)
5. Helsedata. Om helsedata.no. (n.d.). https://helsedata.no/no/om-helsedata/. Accessed 27 May 2023
6. Direktoratet for e-helse. Helseanalyseplattformen (2021). https://www.ehelse.no/progra mmer/helsedataprogrammet/helseanalyseplattformen. Accessed 27 May 2023
7. Direktoratet for e-helse. Setter arbeidet med Helseanalyseplattformen på pause (2021). https:// www.ehelse.no/aktuelt/setter-arbeidet-medhelseanalyseplattformen-pa-pause. Accessed 27 May 2023
8. Fruhwirth, M., Rachinger, M., Prlja, E.: Discovering business models of data marketplaces. In: 53rd Annual Hawaii International Conference on System Sciences, HICSS 2020. IEEE Computer Society (2020)
9. Bergman, R., Abbas, A.E., Jung, S., Werker, C., de Reuver, M.: Business model archetypes for data marketplaces in the automotive industry: contrasting business models of data marketplaces with varying ownership and orientation structures. Electron. Mark. **32**(2), 747–765 (2022)
10. Chakrabarti, A., Quix, C., Geisler, S., Pullmann, J., Khromov, A., Jarke, M.: Goaloriented modelling of relations and dependencies in data marketplaces. In: 11th International i* Workshop, iStar 2018. CEUR-WS (2018)
11. Ito, R.: ID-Link, an enabler for medical data marketplace. In: 16th IEEE International Conference on Data Mining Workshops, ICDMW 2016. IEEE Computer Society (2016)
12. Figueredo, K., Seed, D., Wang, C.: A scalable, standards-based approach for IoT data sharing and ecosystem monetization. IEEE Internet Things J. **9**(8), 5645–5652 (2022)
13. Rahmani, A.-M., et al.: Smart e-health gateway: bringing intelligence to Internet-of-Things based ubiquitous healthcare systems. IEEE (2015)
14. Nguyen, D.D. Ali, M.I.: Enabling on-demand decentralized IoT collectability marketplace using blockchain and crowdsensing. In: 3rd Global IoT Summit, GIoTS 2019. Institute of Electrical and Electronics Engineers Inc. (2019)
15. Chowdhury, M.J.M., et al.: Trust modeling for blockchain-based wearable data market. In: 2019 IEEE International Conference on Cloud Computing Technology and Science (CloudCom), Sydney, NSW, Australia, pp. 411–417 (2019)
16. Giordanengo, A., Bradway, M., Muzny, M., Woldaregay, A., Hartvigsen, G., Arsand, E.: Systems integrating self-collected health data by patients into EHRs: a state-of-the-art review (2018)
17. Paparova, D., Aanestad, M., Vassilakopoulou, P., Bahus, M.K.: Data governance spaces: the case of a national digital service for personal health data. Inf. Organ. **33**(1), 100451 (2023)

18. Muzny, M., et al.: Wearable sensors with possibilities for data exchange: analyzing status and needs of different actors in mobile health monitoring systems. Int. J. Med. Inform. **133**, 104017 (2020)

19. Pomp, A., Paulus, A., Burgdorf, A., Meisen, T.: A semantic data marketplace for easy data sharing within a smart city. In: 30th ACM International Conference on Information and Knowledge Management, CIKM 2021. Association for Computing Machinery (2021)

20. Vassilakopoulou, P., Aanestad, M.: Communal data work: data sharing and reuse in clinical genetics. Health Inform. J. **25**(3), 511–525 (2019)

21. Santos, J., Rodrigues, J.J.P.C., Silva, B.M.C., Casal, J., Saleem, K., Denisov, V.: An IoT-based mobile gateway for intelligent personal assistants on mobile health environments. J. Netw. Comput. Appl. **71**, 194–204 (2016)

22. Sharma, P., Lawrenz, S., Rausch, A.: Towards trustworthy and independent data marketplaces. In: 2nd International Conference on Blockchain Technology, ICBCT 2020. Association for Computing Machinery (2020)

23. More, S., Alber, L.: YOU SHALL NOT COMPUTE on my data: access policies for privacy-preserving data marketplaces and an implementation for a distributed market using MPC. In: 17th International Conference on Availability, Reliability and Security, ARES 2022. Association for Computing Machinery (2022)

24. Alvsvåg, R., Bokolo, A., Petersen, S.A.: The role of a data marketplace for innovation and value-added services in smart and sustainable cities. In: Phillipson, F., Eichler, G., Erfurth, C., Fahrnberger, G. (eds.) I4CS 2022. CCIS, vol. 1585, pp. 215–230. Springer, Cham (2022). https://doi.org/10.1007/978-3-031-06668-9_16

25. Spiekermann, M.: Data marketplaces: trends and monetisation of data goods. Intereconomics **54**(4), 208–216 (2019). https://doi.org/10.1007/s10272-019-0826-z

26. Teece, D.J.: Business models and dynamic capabilities. Long Range Plan. **51**(1), 40–49 (2018)

27. Demchenko, Y., Cushing, R., Los, W., Grosso, P., De Laat, C., Gommans, L.: Open data market architecture and functional components. In: 2019 International Conference on High Performance Computing and Simulation, HPCS 2019. Institute of Electrical and Electronics Engineers Inc. (2019)

28. Lawrenz, S., Sharma, P., Rausch, A.: The significant role of metadata for data marketplaces. In: 9th Dublin Core Metadata Initiative International Conference on Dublin Core and Metadata Applications, DCMI 2019. Dublin Core Metadata Initiative (2019)

29. Smith, G., Ofe, H.A., Sandberg, J.: Digital service innovation from open data: exploring the value proposition of an open data marketplace. In: 49th Annual Hawaii International Conference on System Sciences, HICSS 2016. IEEE Computer Society (2016)

30. DeCarlo, M.: 13.2: qualitative interview techniques. In: Scientific Inquiry in Social Work. Radford University (2021)

31. Oates, B.J.: Researching Information Systems and Computing. Sage Publications Ltd. (2006)

32. Palinkas, L.A., Horwitz, S.M., Green, C.A., Wisdom, J.P., Duan, N., Hoagwood, K.: Purposeful sampling for qualitative data collection and analysis in mixed method implementation research. Adm. Policy Ment. Health Ment. Health Serv. Res. **42**(5), 533–544 (2015)

33. Clifford, N., Cope, M., Gillespie, T., French, S.: Key Methods in Geography, 2nd edn. Sage Publications Ltd. (2016)

34. Kallio, H., Pietilä, A.M., Johnson, M., Kangasniemi, M.: Systematic methodological review: developing a framework for a qualitative semi-structured interview guide. J. Adv. Nurs. **72**(12), 2954–2965 (2016)

35. NSD - Norsk senter for forskningsdata. Vi sørger for at data om mennesker og samfunn kan hentes inn, bearbeides, lagres og deles trygt og lovlig, i dag og i fremtiden (n.d.) https://www.nsd.no/index.html. Accessed 30 May 2023

36. Miles, M.B., Huberman, A.M., Saldana, J.: Fundamentals of qualitative data analysis. In: Qualitative Data Analysis: A Methods Sourcebook, vol. 3 (2014)

37. Kurasaki, K.: Intercoder reliability for validating conclusions drawn from OpenEnded interview data. Field Methods - FIELD METHOD **12**, 179–194 (2000)
38. Vassilakopoulou, P., Skorve, E., Aanestad, M.: Enabling openness of valuable information resources: curbing data subtractability and exclusion. Inf. Syst. J. **29**(4), 768–786 (2019)
39. Pappas, I.O., Mikalef, P., Dwivedi, Y.K., Jaccheri, L., Krogstie, J.: Responsible digital transformation for a sustainable society. Inf. Syst. Front. (2023)

Industry 4.0 and Lean Manufacturing Contribute to the Development of the PDP and Market Performance? A Framework

Paulo Roberto Tardio⬚, Jones Luís Schaefer$^{(\boxtimes)}$ ⬚, Marcelo Carneiro Gonçalves⬚, and Elpidio Oscar Benitez Nara⬚

Industrial and Systems Engineering Graduate Program, Pontifical Catholic University, Curitiba, PR, Brazil
jones.schaefer@pucpr.br

Abstract. To improve production processes, manufacturing companies have made efforts to implement Industry 4.0 technologies and spread the use of Lean Manufacturing (LM) tools. Besides, in addition to the improvements in production processes, these efforts have also been reflected in other issues such as in the Product Development Process (PDP) and Market Performance. In this sense, the objective of this article is to elaborate a conceptual framework covering the constructs of Industry 4.0, LM, and PDP, and to evaluate the importance of these constructs on Market Performance in manufacturing companies in the South of Brazil. The conceptual framework, elaborated with the help of high-impact articles in the area, was evaluated by managers of 111 manufacturing companies in the southern Brazil. The research showed that the implementation of LM tools is more related to the PDP than Industry 4.0 and that large companies have had more positive effects in the implementation of both Industry 4.0 technologies and LM tools. This research can serve as a guide for manufacturing companies, showing the benefits, challenges and opportunities regarding the implementation of LM and Industry 4.0 tools and technologies aiming to improve PDP and Market Performance. It is possible to observe through a structured and systemic framework.

Keywords: Industry 4.0 · Smart Manufacturing · Lean Manufacturing · Product Development Process · Market Performance

1 Introduction

Product development involves following up on the product after launch to make it possible to make any necessary changes to specifications, plan for product discontinuation in the market, and incorporate lessons learned throughout the product lifecycle [1]. In this sense, continuous development and innovation that include the development of new products, or significant improvements to existing products, are necessary for organizational existence [2]. Thus, faced with intense global competition, business organizations have begun to shift their operations to smart business environments.

Published by Springer Nature Switzerland AG 2023
M. Janssen et al. (Eds.): I3E 2023, LNCS 14316, pp. 236–249, 2023.
https://doi.org/10.1007/978-3-031-50040-4_18

Lean Manufacturing is one of the optimization approaches that have been used in manufacturing processes to improve the management of shop floor operations [3], being an approach that provides a new production plan with a higher level of productivity [4].

Lean manufacturing is an integrated set of systems for optimizing production processes composed of interrelated elements whose main objective is to eliminate waste, reducing or minimizing the variability related to supply, processing time and demand [5]. In this way, the importance of implementing Lean in an integrated manner to improve production processes is highlighted [6]. The objective of Lean is to modify production processes seeking continuous improvement through the elimination of activities that do not add value to the product [7].

The use of hybrid approaches to improve production processes has shown good results in manufacturing environments [3].

Lean Product Development (LPD) can be defined as the application of lean principles to product development, aiming to develop new or improved products that are successful in the market [8].

The Aim of Industry 4.0 is to realize not only smart, intelligent, and cognitive manufacturing systems or factories but also to generate smart products and services. Therefore, also product development has to leave traditional ways coming closer to the development of Industry 4.0 [9].

Liker and Morgan [10] defined lean product development as: "a knowledge work job shop, which a company can continuously improve by using adapted tools used in repetitive manufacturing processes to eliminate waste and synchronize cross-functional activities".

Traditional products are becoming more and more multidisciplinary, intelligent, networked, and agile, and include product-related services. However, not only consumer goods (i.e. smartphones) but also industrial goods are becoming 'smart'. Thus, the engineering of these smart products will be of crucial importance for the competitiveness of industrial companies. There is a need for new Smart Engineering approaches, which also use the latest innovation [11].

Really understanding what drives a customer to purchase a product should be the main concern in product development [12].

Digitized product development processes allow us to face four major challenges: the need for multi-objective optimization, the need to enable multi-domain simulation, the need to explore different topological product families, and the need to deal with ever-changing environments [13].

Industry 4.0 is a way of promoting competitive advantages through the application and integration of new technologies, being also known for the diversification and power of its tools and techniques, such as Internet of Things (IoT), Big Data Analytics, Artificial Intelligence, Deep Learning, and others [14]. Industry 4.0 includes production processes, efficiency, data management, consumer relations, and competitiveness [15]. In Industry 4.0, technologies such as Big Data and Cloud Computing are integrated through IoT to enhance industrial performance [16].

Industry 4.0 and its technologies can potentially improve the market performance of companies in the age of digital transformation through the implementation of its technologies [17]. Reactivity to the market, flexibility and the development of smart products are some goals of companies within the context of Industry 4.0 [18]. The introduction of Industry 4.0 and its integration with Lean introduced the hybrid term 'Lean 4.0' [19].

Using these initial premises as a background, this article is motivated by the need to understand the phenomena and relationships between the Lean philosophy and the use of Industry 4.0 technologies, and how these relationships contribute to improvements in Product Development Plans, and consequently, impacting the performance of companies' markets.

This way, the objective of this research is to analyze and identify the concepts of Industry 4.0 related to the principles of Lean Manufacturing with the PDP (pre-development, in the development and post development of the product) and the effects of these relations with the market performance in the companies of general manufacturing. Alongside, a literature review will be conducted on the pillars of this research, identify industry 4.0 technologies and Lean Manufacturing tools that relate to the PDP, and carry out data collection through a survey.

This article has contributions in academic and managerial ways by presenting a systemic approach involving Lean Manufacturing, Industry 4.0 with PDP and Market Performance, where the search for all terms simultaneously in Scopus and WoS showed little or no results in the search for articles, so this article seeks to contribute to new literature and future related work. From the business point of view, companies face many difficulties when developing new products, mainly with project quality problems, long lead times and very high development costs. And it is in this scenario that a more efficient product development system with less waste becomes very strategic with the help of Industry 4.0 and Lean Manufacturing.

The remainder of the paper is organized as follows: Sect. 2 shows a theoretical background on the constructs of this research, Sect. 3 details the methodological procedures, Sect. 4 presents the results and discussion, and Sect. 5 presents the conclusions.

2 Theoretical Background

In this section, a theoretical background on the concepts, technologies, tools and implementation of Industry 4.0 and Lean Manufacturing, the Product Development Process and its impact on Market Performance will be presented.

2.1 Industry 4.0 – Resources, Innovation, and Implementation

In the current era, product life cycles are shortening and consumers are increasingly demanding products to be more complex and unique, which poses challenges for the manufacturing process [20]. Industry 4.0 is changing production – traditional processes previously controlled centrally are becoming decentralized and are based on self-regulation of products and work units that interact with each other [21]. This occur through the integration of technologies to provide connectivity, capturing and data processing in real time [22, 23]. The concept works on the principle that products manage their own production, during which virtual reality is intertwined with real [24].

From the point of view of competition, it is no longer enough to produce faster, cheaper and better, but it is also important and necessary to outline new innovative and digital strategies in the short term to guarantee a competitive advantage in the long term [9].

Digital innovation has become a key to the survival of all companies and by innovating digitally or producing innovative products, processes or business models using technology platforms, digital innovation helps transform industry and society to reach new levels of development and sustainability [25]. In this sense, the existence of a diversity of companies partners [26]will depend on the dominant innovation processes that this industry sector seeks [27].

Various technologies such as IoT, cloud computing, big data analytics, machine learning, and artificial intelligence are used to improve redundant and obsolete business models as well as the performance of existing organizational systems and "Smart factory" or "Smart manufacturing" has become the buzzword for organizations seeking to keep up with Industry 4.0 paradigms [28].

To thrive in the fourth industrial revolution (Industry 4.0), every company strives for smart production or manufacturing systems, efficient supply chains, improved customer services, and the development of innovative products, all of which can be accomplished through digital innovation [29].

2.2   Lean Manufacturing – Concepts, Tools, and Implementation

Lean production originates from the management system of Toyota Motor Corporation, also known as the Toyota Production System [30]. Inspired by the success of Toyota, the concept of Lean has spread all over the world and has been applied in various processes and sectors [31, 32].

Lean Manufacturing has as the first key objectives for Toyota were "the efficiency of production through the consistent and complete elimination of waste", Emiliani [33] states that Toyota later states that 'continuous improvements' and ' respect for people' are the main principles.

Lean Manufacturing is characterized by seven main types of waste and losses that need and must be eliminated [34]: the first of them is Overproduction: producing too much or too soon; Waiting: produces long idle periods of people, parts and information; Transport: motivated by excessive movement of people, information or parts; Overprocessing: as being thought of as using the wrong set of tools, systems or procedures; Inventory: the excessive storage and shortage of information or products; Handling: can cause disorganization of the work environment; Defective products: frequent problems with process charts, product quality issues, or poor delivery performance.

Value stream mapping (VSM), Kanban, Kaizen, Standard work, 5S, 8 wastes, Total Productive Maintenance (TPM), single minute exchange of dies (SMED), GEMBA, and failure mode effects analysis (FMEA) are some of the well-known techniques or too called tools available for manufacturing facilities nowadays [35].

Previous research has shown that Lean Manufacturing directly affects production processes, which improves the three pillars of sustainability: economic, social and business environment [36, 37]. For example, Lean improves cost reduction measures during the production process by reducing the number of non-value-added activities (activities that the customer does not want to pay for and that do not add value to the product), which leads to better economic performance [38].

2.3 Product Development Process and Market Performance

Many academic studies there is pressure to introduce new products into the market as soon as possible. Yet access to incubators, research facilities, and funding can often be limited, and the longer the time spent on New Product Development (NPD), the higher the cost and the higher the risk of failure [39]. However, faster is not always better [40]. Bringing a new product, albeit an innovative one, to market without carefully investigating the market's needs and the product quality exposes academic spin-offs to market failure [41].

In the context of NPD, speed, and quality are frequently discussed and regarded as key success strategies [42]. While extant research finds that both speed and quality define superior performance, few studies have investigated how both strategic orientations together impact market performance [43]. The literature has suggested for some time that introducing a new product faster than competitors has a positive effect on performance [44, 45]. Simultaneously, a strategic focus on product performance can be highlighted as important during NPD. Furthermore, product companies should prefer service customization over service standardization when facing environmental turbulence [46].

Collaborative cross-organizational NPD projects can potentially improve the design quality and market performance of a new product if external knowledge inputs are effectively integrated with internal knowledge to generate a significant increase in synergy [47]. Thus, successful new product development (NPD) projects, as a form of firm innovation, can generate and sustain competitive advantage across all industries.

3 Research Development

The development of this research took place in two stages: in the first stage, a conceptual framework was developed integrating the concepts of Industry 4.0, Lean Manufacturing, PDP, and Market Performance; while in the second stage a survey was carried out with managers of manufacturing companies in the South of Brazil to evaluate the implementation and use of these concepts in order to improve the market performance of these companies.

3.1 Conceptual Framework

Given the objective of this research to relate Industry 4.0, Lean Manufacturing, PDP and Market Performance, it was necessary to seek in these themes the main constructs that can be connected in a conceptual framework aimed at manufacturing companies. Under this approach, the most relevant technologies of Industry 4.0 are IoT, Automation, Artificial Intelligence, Cloud Computing [48], while the most relevant Lean Manufacturing tools are Kaizen, 5S, VSM, and Root Cause Analysis [49]. PDP consists of the

Pre-Development, Development and Post-Development stages [50]. The Market Performance constructs were defined as competitiveness [51], productivity [52] and innovation [53]. The framework's design integrates Industry 4.0 and Lean Manufacturing in parallel, with both concepts influencing the PDP. Afterwards, there is the connection with Market Performance (Fig. 1).

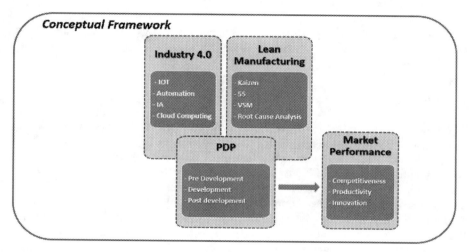

Fig. 1. Conceptual framework

From this framework, it is expected to obtain an assessment of how interactions occur between the application of Industry 4.0 concepts and technologies and Lean Manufacturing concepts and tools on the PDP stages. In addition, it is intended to verify the effects of these interactions on the competitiveness, productivity and innovation of small, medium and large manufacturing companies.

3.2 Survey

From the elaboration of the framework, the instrument was designed to capture the opinion of managers about the development degree of Industry 4.0 using questions about innovation practices, practices related to resources and practices for implementing Industry 4.0 technologies. Managers were also asked about the level of development of Lean Manufacturing and PDP practices in their companies. Questions were used to verify the applicability of Lean concepts, the use of Lean tools and on Lean implementation practices In all these questions the scale used was from 1 to 5: 1 - We hardly develop, 2 - Low development, 3 - We develop moderately, 4 - We develop a lot and 5 - We always/almost always develop. In addition, managers were consulted regarding questions that assess the degree of improvement in the companies' market performance. In these questions, the evaluation scale used was 1 - Very low, 2 - Low, 3 - Regular, 4 - High, and 5 - Very high.

Besides, to enable comparisons with respect to the different levels of approach and adoption of the concepts studied in this research, managers were also asked with regard to the time in the company, 7 had less than 1 year, 28 between 1 and 5 years, 16 between 6 and 10 before, 41 between 11 and 20 years, 14 between 21 and 30 years old and 5 had worked for the company for more than 30 years. Regarding the size of the companies, 14 respondents represented small companies (up to 100 employees), 42 respondents represented medium companies (between 101 and 500 employees and 56 respondents represented large companies (more than 500 employees).

The survey instrument was answered by 111 managers in the area of product development of manufacturing companies, such as managers, analysts, engineers and product development supervisors. Data collection took place over the internet between September and October 2022.

4   Results and Discussion

The survey results show that there is a considerable discrepancy between small and medium-sized companies in relation to large companies, both in relation to innovations, resources and implementation of 4.0 technologies, as well as in relation to the concepts and implementation of Lean Manufacturing tools [54]. In these areas, large companies are at a more advanced stage of development compared to small and medium-sized ones. The smallest difference in development is related to Industry 4.0 resources, where the degree of development of small and medium-sized companies is 0.611 lower than that of large companies. Meanwhile, the biggest difference is in the adoption of Lean concepts where the level of development of large companies is 0.876 higher than that of small and medium-sized companies.

Another interesting fact is that for both small and medium-sized and large companies, Industry 4.0 concepts are less developed than Lean Manufacturing concepts. Industry 4.0 innovations were the research point with the least development for companies, while the implementation of Lean has been the biggest concern for managers of these companies [55]. Table 1 shows the average results of the responses obtained.

Table 1. Evaluation of Industry 4.0 and Lean Manufacturing issues

	Small and Medium Companies	Large Companies	All Companies
I 4.0 Innovations	2,680	3,321	3,004
I 4.0 Resources	2,796	3,407	3,105
I 4.0 Implementation	3,142	3,814	3,481
Lean Concepts	3,153	4,029	3,595
Lean Tools	3,287	4,086	3,690
Lean Implementation	3,498	4,271	3,888

Regarding the stages of development of the PDP, there is also a difference related to the size of the companies in the levels of development between the companies. Large companies have a more advanced level of development in the three stages of the PDP than small and medium-sized companies.

Table 2. Evaluation of PDP stages development

	Small and Medium Companies	Large Companies	All Companies
Pre PDP	3,124	3,811	3,470
PDP	3,273	3,818	3,548
Post PDP	3,250	3,763	3,509

Still as a way to evaluate these research constructs, based on the data obtained from the survey, the dendrogram in Fig. 2 was created, where the levels of similarity between Industry 4.0, Lean and PDP are presented. In this figure, a red line was drawn so that it can be seen a higher level of similarity between Lean Manufacturing and PDP. This can be explained by the level of development that, as seen in Tables 1 and 2, is closer among these constructs in the surveyed companies, regardless of size [56].

Besides, in Fig. 2, it can be highlighted the greater similarity between the development of resources and innovations within Industry 4.0 itself compared to the implementation of these innovations in manufacturing companies [57]. Furthermore, there is a difference in similarity between the implementation of Lean concepts and tools within manufacturing companies [58]. This may indicate that there can be a certain difficulty in implementing new practices and technologies in manufacturing companies.

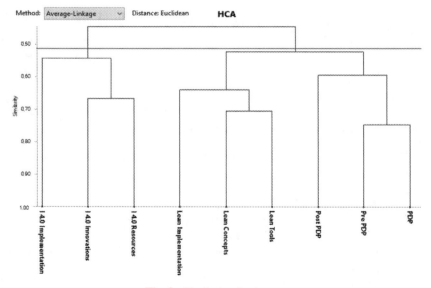

Fig. 2. Similarity dendogram

In Table 3, it can be highlighted that demand by product and productivity on average has increased more in large companies than in small and medium companies [59]. Similarly, profitability has increased and the market response has improved on average in large companies than in small and medium companies [60]. This may indicate, in both situations, that there can be particular difficulty in implementing new innovation and resources in small and medium manufacturing companies.

Table 3. Market performance evaluation

Performance indicators	Small and Medium Companies	Large Companies	All Companies
Profitability has increased	3,109	3,464	3,288
Market response has improved	3,000	3,625	3,315
Maintenance in the market	3,182	3,857	3,523
Customer loyalty has increased	3,255	3,679	3,468
Delivery time of our products has decreased	2,855	2,929	2,892
Demand has increased	3,145	3,911	3,532
Productivity has increased	3,273	3,679	3,477
Production methods have improved	3,291	3,625	3,459
Lead time has improved	3,018	3,464	3,243
The assertiveness of the production has improved	3,036	3,411	3,225

Companies, in general, seek to sustain themselves in the market in a competitive way. However, for decades, the focus of lean processes was focused only on manufacturing, extending to some support areas. At the same time, customers are constantly demanding new products, which results in an ever-shorter life cycle.

In this way, the market is volatile and demanding, configuring the permanent challenge of transforming ideas into sustainable projects that can help the organization to survive within its environment. Therefore, the PDP needs to be seen as a strategic element, not only for innovating or improving products in the customer's perception, but mainly for seeking a Lean essence that, in addition to making the production process customized, also makes product development itself more agile and, above all, effective.

With studies that technological innovations arising from the implementation of Industry 4.0 promote changes in line with the Lean approach that provide an evolution in the development of systems and production processes, consequently causing an improvement in profits for the company and greater satisfaction of customers.

The similarities found in the studies demonstrate that the Lean approach and Industry 4.0 seek to complement each other in what each production process requires. This reflects positively on companies, which thus seek to satisfy customer needs through greater possibilities provided by technological advances.

The implementation of Lean Manufacturing concepts is a great challenge for companies and the solutions provided by Industry 4.0 can corroborate the perspective of integration. Likewise, industries that have Lean Manufacturing as part of their cultures are better suited to explore the benefits of Industry 4.0 technologies.

Lean can be perceived as a fundamental agent in the implementation and consolidation of Industry 4.0, and Lean concepts such as standardization of work, organization and transparency are fundamental in supporting the implementation and consolidation of Industry 4.0.

Through this research, it can be observed that the interaction and alignment of perspectives between Lean Manufacturing, Industry 4.0 and the PDP can generate, for large companies, significant gains in productivity, consequently increasing their market performance and finally increases in profits, in the on which the existence of every competitive company is based.

5 Conclusion

This article concentrated efforts on elaborating a conceptual framework that encompasses the Industry 4.0, LM and PDP constructs, and evaluating the importance of the relationships between these constructs in the market performance of 111 manufacturing companies in southern Brazil. The development and implementation of Industry 4.0, LM and PDP concepts, technologies and tools were assessed. Market performance was evaluated from the perspective of competitiveness, innovation and profitability of manufacturing companies.

Among the implications of this article, it is important to mention the proximity found between the implementation of LM tools with the PDP stages, showing that, before there are investments in technological infrastructure, manufacturing companies usually implement LM concepts and tools such as Kaizen, 5S, Value Stream Mapping and Root Cause Analysis. While these tools are implemented, concerns arise with the implementation of 4.0 technologies, demonstrating that the surveyed companies seek, in a first moment, to improve the productive processes through the improvement of the existing processes without the execution of large investments. If the market's performance is still stagnant, in a second moment investments in technology are made.

The research was limited to investigating the level of development of manufacturing companies in relation to the presented constructs. For future research, it is intended to verify the existing mediating role between these constructs in order to improve market performance.

References

1. Amaral, D.C., Toledo, J.C., Silva, S.L., Alliprandini, D.H., Scalice, R.K.: Gestão de Desenvolvimento de Produto: uma referência para a melhoria do processo. Saraiva, São Paulo (2006)
2. Schaefer, J.L., Baierle, I.C., Sellitto, M.A., Siluk, J.C.M., Furtado, J.C., Nara, E.O.B.: Competitiveness scale as a basis for Brazilian small and medium-sized enterprises. EMJ - Eng. Manag. J. (2020). https://doi.org/10.1080/10429247.2020.1800385

3. Tripathi, V., et al.: Recent progression developments on process optimization approach for inherent issues in production shop floor management for industry 4.0. Processes **10**, 1587 (2022). https://doi.org/10.3390/PR10081587

4. Mathiyazhagan, K., Gnanavelbabu, A., Kumar, N.N., Agarwal, V.: A framework for implementing sustainable lean manufacturing in the electrical and electronics component manufacturing industry: an emerging economies country perspective. J. Clean. Prod. **334**, 130169 (2022). https://doi.org/10.1016/J.JCLEPRO.2021.130169

5. Shah, R., Ward, P.T.: Lean manufacturing: context, practice bundles, and performance. J. Oper. Manag. **21**, 129–149 (2003). https://doi.org/10.1016/S0272-6963(02)00108-0

6. Panwar, A., Jain, R., Rathore, A.P.S., Nepal, B., Lyons, A.C.: The impact of lean practices on operational performance – an empirical investigation of Indian process industries. Prod. Plann. Control **29**, 158–169 (2017). https://doi.org/10.1080/09537287.2017.1397788

7. Venugopal, V., Saleeshya, P.G.: Manufacturing system sustainability through lean and agile initiatives. Int. J. Sustain. Eng. **12**, 159–173 (2019). https://doi.org/10.1080/19397038.2019.1566411

8. Mynott, C.: Lean product development: a manager's guide (2012)

9. Rauch, E., Dallasega, P., Matt, D.T.: The way from lean product development (LPD) to smart product development (SPD). Procedia CIRP **50**, 26–31 (2016). https://doi.org/10.1016/J.PROCIR.2016.05.081

10. Liker, J.K., Morgan, J.M.: The Toyota way in services: the case of lean product development. Acad. Manage. Perspect. **20**, 5–20 (2006). https://doi.org/10.5465/AMP.2006.20591002

11. Abramovici, M., Göbel, J.C., Neges, M.: Smart engineering as enabler for the 4th industrial revolution. Integr. Syst. Innov. Appl. 163–170 (2015). https://doi.org/10.1007/978-3-319-15898-3_10/COVER

12. Fuchs, C., Gutmann, T.: How technical market segmentation can help build products your customers really need. IEEE Eng. Manag. Rev. **50**, 17–19 (2022). https://doi.org/10.1109/EMR.2022.3140715

13. Glönkler, V., Reick, B., Stetter, R., Till, M., Pfeil, M.: A contribution to sustainable product development using the example of battery electric vehicles. Sustainability **14**, 3729 (2022). https://doi.org/10.3390/SU14073729

14. Contreras, J.D., David, J., Pastrana, D.: Developing of industry 4.0 applications. Int. J. Online Eng. (2017). https://doi.org/10.3991/ijoe.v13i10.7331

15. Bittencourt, V.L., Alves, A.C., Leão, C.P.: Industry 4.0 triggered by lean thinking: insights from a systematic literature review. Int. J. Prod. Res. **59**, 1496–1510 (2020). https://doi.org/10.1080/00207543.2020.1832274

16. Dalenogare, L.S., Benitez, G.B., Ayala, N.F., Frank, A.G.: The expected contribution of industry 4.0 technologies for industrial performance. Int. J. Prod. Econ. **204**, 383–394 (2018). https://doi.org/10.1016/J.IJPE.2018.08.019

17. Baierle, I.C., et al.: Competitiveness of food industry in the era of digital transformation towards agriculture 4.0. Sustainability **14**, 11779 (2022). https://doi.org/10.3390/SU1418 11779

18. Dos Santos, L.M.A.L., et al.: Industry 4.0 collaborative networks for industrial performance. J. Manuf. Technol. Manag. **32**, 245–265 (2020). https://doi.org/10.1108/JMTM-04-2020-0156

19. Mayr, A., Weigelt, M., Kühl, A., Grimm, S., Erll, A., Cirp, M.P.: Lean 4.0-a conceptual conjunction of lean management and Industry 4.0. Procedia CIRP **72**, 622–628 (2018)

20. Ferreira, M.J., Moreira, F., Seruca, I.: Digital transformation towards a new context of labour: enterprise 4.0. Technol. Dev. Ind. 4.0 Bus. Appl. 26–49 (2019). https://doi.org/10.4018/978-1-5225-4936-9.CH002

21. Neri, A., Boggia, A., Kohnová, L., Salajová, N.: Re-thinking industry 4.0 effect on competitive forces: empirical study on innovation. Sustainability **15**, 2637 (2023). https://doi.org/10.3390/SU15032637

22. Brittes Benitez, G., José, M., Ferreira Lima, R., Lerman, L.V., Frank, A.G.: Understanding industry 4.0: definitions and insights from a cognitive map analysis. Braz. J. Oper. Prod. Manag. **16**, 192–200 (2019). https://doi.org/10.14488/BJOPM.2019.v16.n2.a3

23. Schaefer, J.L., Siluk, J.C.M., de Carvalho, P.S.: Critical success factors for the implementation and management of energy cloud environments. Int. J. Energy Res. **46**, 13752–13768 (2022). https://doi.org/10.1002/ER.8094

24. Pascual, D., Daponte, P., Kumar, U.: Handbook of Industry 4.0 and SMART Systems (2019)

25. Ciriello, R.F., Richter, A., Schwabe, G.: Digital innovation. Bus. Inf. Syst. Eng. **60**, 563–569 (2018). https://doi.org/10.1007/S12599-018-0559-8/METRICS

26. de Moraes, J., Schaefer, J.L., Schreiber, J.N.C., Thomas, J.D., Nara, E.O.B.: Algorithm applied: attracting MSEs to business associations. J. Bus. Ind. Mark. **35**, 13–22 (2019). https://doi.org/10.1108/JBIM-09-2018-0269

27. Frank, A.G., Benitez, G.B., Ferreira Lima, M., Bernardi, J.A.B.: Effects of open innovation breadth on industrial innovation input–output relationships. Eur. J. Innov. Manag. **25**, 975–996 (2022). https://doi.org/10.1108/EJIM-08-2020-0333/FULL/XML

28. Gupta, M., Jauhar, S.K.: Digital innovation: an essence for industry 4.0. Thunderbird Int. Bus. Rev. (2023). https://doi.org/10.1002/TIE.22337

29. Oesterreich, T.D., Teuteberg, F.: Understanding the implications of digitisation and automation in the context of industry 4.0: a triangulation approach and elements of a research agenda for the construction industry. Comput. Ind. **83**, 121–139 (2016). https://doi.org/10.1016/J.COMPIND.2016.09.006

30. Liker, J.K.: The Toyota Way: 14 Management Principles from the World's Greatest Manufacturer. McGraw-Hill Education (2004)

31. Marley, K.A., Ward, P.T.: Lean management as a countermeasure for "normal" disruptions. Oper. Manag. Res. **6**, 44–52 (2013). https://doi.org/10.1007/S12063-013-0077-2/METRICS

32. Bhutta, M.K.S., Egilmez, G., Chatha, K.A., Huq, F.: Survey of lean management practices in Pakistani industrial sectors. Int. J. Serv. Oper. Manag. **28**, 309–334 (2017). https://doi.org/10.1504/IJSOM.2017.087287

33. Emiliani, M.L.: Origins of lean management in America: the role of Connecticut businesses. J. Manag. Hist. **12**, 167–184 (2006). https://doi.org/10.1108/13552520610654069/FULL/XML

34. Kennedy, M.N.: The Toyota product development system. Mach. Des. **76**, 152 (2004). https://doi.org/10.4324/9781482293746/TOYOTA-PRODUCT-DEVELOPMENT-SYSTEM-JAMES-MORGAN-JEFFREY-LIKER

35. Shahriar, M.M., Parvez, M.S., Islam, M.A., Talapatra, S.: Implementation of 5S in a plastic bag manufacturing industry: a case study. Clean. Eng. Technol. **8**, 100488 (2022). https://doi.org/10.1016/J.CLET.2022.100488

36. Varela, L., Araújo, A., Ávila, P., Castro, H., Putnik, G.: Evaluation of the relation between lean manufacturing, industry 4.0, and sustainability. Sustainability **11**, 1439 (2019). https://doi.org/10.3390/SU11051439

37. Torielli, R.M., Abrahams, R.A., Smillie, R.W., Voigt, R.C.: Using lean methodologies for economically and environmentally sustainable foundries. China Foundry **8**, 74–88 (2010)

38. Todorut, A.V., Paliu-Popa, L., Tselentis, V.S., Cirnu, D.: Sustainable cost reduction by lean management in metallurgical processes. Metalurgija **55**, 846–848 (2016)

39. Barbalho, S.C.M.E., De Carvalho, M.M., Tavares, P.M., Llanos, C.H., Leite, G.A.: Exploring the relation among product complexity, team seniority, and project performance as a path for planning new product development projects: a predictive model applying the system dynamics theory. IEEE Trans. Eng. Manag. **69**, 1823–1836 (2022). https://doi.org/10.1109/TEM.2019.2936502

40. Cankurtaran, P., Langerak, F., Griffin, A.: Consequences of new product development speed: a meta-analysis. J. Prod. Innov. Manag. **30**, 465–486 (2013). https://doi.org/10.1111/JPIM.12011

41. Anand, K.S., Paç, M.F., Veeraraghavan, S.: Quality-speed conundrum: trade-offs in customer-intensive services. Manag. Sci. **57**, 40–56 (2010). https://doi.org/10.1287/MNSC.1100.1250
42. Jayaram, J., Narasimhan, R.: The influence of new product development competitive capabilities on project performance. IEEE Trans. Eng. Manag. **54**, 241–256 (2007). https://doi.org/10.1109/TEM.2007.893992
43. Yassine, A., Souweid, S.: Time-to-market and product performance tradeoff revisited. IEEE Trans. Eng. Manag. (2021). https://doi.org/10.1109/TEM.2021.3081987
44. Di Benedetto, C.A., DeSarbo, W.S., Song, M.: Strategic capabilities and radical innovation: an empirical study in three countries. IEEE Trans. Eng. Manag. **55**, 420–433 (2008). https://doi.org/10.1109/TEM.2008.922645
45. Moorman, C., Miner, A.S.: The impact of organizational memory on new product performance and creativity. J. Mark. Res. **34**, 91–106 (2018). https://doi.org/10.1177/002224379703400108
46. Frank, A.G., Mendes, G.H.D.S., Benitez, G.B., Ayala, N.F.: Service customization in turbulent environments: service business models and knowledge integration to create capability-based switching costs. Ind. Mark. Manag. **100**, 1–18 (2022). https://doi.org/10.1016/J.INDMARMAN.2021.10.010
47. Schmidt, C.G., Yan, T., Wagner, S.M., Lucianetti, L.: Performance implications of knowledge inputs in inter-organisational new product development projects: the moderating roles of technology interdependence. Int. J. Prod. Res. **60**, 6048–6071 (2021). https://doi.org/10.1080/00207543.2021.1978576
48. Da Costa, M.B., Dos Santos, L.M.A.L., Schaefer, J.L., Baierle, I.C., Nara, E.O.B.: Industry 4.0 technologies basic network identification. Scientometrics **121**, 977–994 (2019). https://doi.org/10.1007/s11192-019-03216-7
49. la Cruz-Felipe, C.P.D., Gómez-Cárdenas, M.F., Felipe-Bravo, G.M.: Implementación de herramientas de lean manufacturing en industrias manufactureras: una revisión de la literatura (2021). https://doi.org/10.18687/LACCEI2021.1.1.120
50. Rosenfeld, H., et al.: Gestão de desenvolvimento de produto - uma referência para melhoria dos processos. Saraiva, São Paulo (2010)
51. Nara, E.O.B., Schaefer, J.L., de Moraes, J., Tedesco, L.P.C., Furtado, J.C., Baierle, I.C.: Sourcing research papers on small- and medium-sized enterprises' competitiveness: an approach based on authors' networks. Rev. Esp. Doc. Cient. **42**, e230 (2019). https://doi.org/10.3989/redc.2019.2.1602
52. Porter, M.E.: Building the microeconomic foundations of prosperity: findings from the microeconomic competitiveness index (2004)
53. Sellitto, M.A., Camfield, C.G., Buzuku, S.: Green innovation and competitive advantages in a furniture industrial cluster: a survey and structural model. Sustain. Prod. Consum. **23**, 94–104 (2020). https://doi.org/10.1016/J.SPC.2020.04.007
54. Yu, F., Schweisfurth, T.: Industry 4.0 technology implementation in SMEs – a survey in the Danish-German border region. Int. J. Innov. Stud. **4**, 76–84 (2020). https://doi.org/10.1016/J.IJIS.2020.05.001
55. Sony, M.: Industry 4.0 and lean management: a proposed integration model and research propositions. Prod. Manuf. Res. **6**, 416–432 (2018). https://doi.org/10.1080/21693277.2018.1540949
56. Khan, M.S., et al.: Towards lean product and process development. Int. J. Comput. Integr. Manuf. **26**, 1105–1116 (2013). https://doi.org/10.1080/0951192X.2011.608723
57. Benitez, G.B., Ayala, N.F., Frank, A.G.: Industry 4.0 innovation ecosystems: an evolutionary perspective on value cocreation. Int. J. Prod. Econ. **228**, 107735 (2020). https://doi.org/10.1016/J.IJPE.2020.107735

58. Knapić, V., Rusjan, B., Božič, K.: Importance of first-line employees in lean implementation in SMEs: a systematic literature review. Int. J. Lean Six Sigma. **14**, 277–308 (2022). https://doi.org/10.1108/IJLSS-08-2021-0141/FULL/PDF

59. dos Reis Azevedo Botelho, M., de Fátima Sousa, G., de Castro Carrijo, M., Ferreira, J.B., da Silva, A.C.: Survival determinants for Brazilian companies, 1996 to 2016. J. Ind. Bus. Econ. **49**, 233–266 (2022). https://doi.org/10.1007/S40812-022-00217-1/TABLES/10

60. Pérez-Gómez, P., Arbelo-Pérez, M., Arbelo, A.: Profit efficiency and its determinants in small and medium-sized enterprises in Spain. BRQ Bus. Res. Q. **21**, 238–250 (2018). https://doi.org/10.1016/j.brq.2018.08.003

A Performance-Based Assessment Approach for Cloud Service Provider Selection

Raoul Hentschel[(✉)], Katja Bley, and Felix Lange

Business Information Systems, esp. IS in Trade and Industry, TU Dresden, Dresden, Germany
{raoul.hentschel,katja.bley}@tu-dresden.de

Abstract. More and more companies are increasingly using cloud services. Accordingly, the decision for a cloud service provider is crucial for the potentially added value of the cloud service to the company, which is why the selection should be subject to a well-planned process, and the final decision must be made carefully. Since cloud service providers make resources available via the internet, performance parameters are important for assessing cloud service providers and play an important role in the decision-making process. Therefore, this paper addresses the question of which network performance metrics are relevant for selecting a cloud service provider and how these metrics can be collected and evaluated. It provides and instantiates an assessment method that can be used as guidance for cloud service provider selection. Thereby, the results show the possibility of testing and evaluating technical instead of merely qualitative aspects of infrastructure provided by cloud service, which is a contribution to existing literature in the field.

Keywords: Cloud computing · cloud service provider selection · cloud performance · network connectivity

1 Introduction

Cloud computing (CC) plays an important role for digital transformation – promising organizations of all sizes new benefits such as consuming computing resources (e.g., networks, servers, storage, applications, and services) with low/minimal entry costs, pay-per-use options, and greater flexibility and scalability [1]. By using various cloud services, organizations are enabled to create higher efficiency in daily business operations [2]. The areas of application range from simple software-as-a-service (SaaS) applications, like e-mail and video conferencing tools, to complex infrastructure-as-a-service (IaaS) outsourcing scenarios with a multi-vendor strategy. To remain competitive, companies must balance two important considerations. First, they need to integrate their IT and business strategies to keep pace with evolving technologies, enabling them to venture into new digital markets and offer digital services. Secondly, they need to find the most appropriate service or application that aligns with their specific business model, whether it's through digital support for their IT infrastructure or the implementation and delivery of value propositions. Therefore, the selection of suitable cloud service providers (CSP)

Published by Springer Nature Switzerland AG 2023
M. Janssen et al. (Eds.): I3E 2023, LNCS 14316, pp. 250–264, 2023.
https://doi.org/10.1007/978-3-031-50040-4_19

as a prerequisite for the right cloud service should be made carefully and systematically. However, especially the pre-adoption phase of CC, which comprises the evaluation and selection of suitable cloud services, is a challenging and knowledge-intensive task for potential cloud service consumers (CSC), which requires experience [3] widespread participation, and ownership among heterogeneous stakeholder groups (e.g., business managers, IT departments, etc.) [4]. Even though various evaluation criteria (e.g., flexibility, cost, IT security & compliance, etc.) have already been considered in research (i.e., [5]) one crucial aspect is still neglected: the network performance, which allows the respective cloud service to operate.

Based on the strong relationship between the functionality of a cloud service and the CSP's performance, and thereby the crucial impact on the business performance of a CSC, this paper focuses on the selection process of CSPs based on network performance metrics. Since all cloud resources rely on their network or internet availability, the network connectivity from CSC to CSP should therefore be high-performance and liable to ensure high stability and good user experience and usability. This paper therefore addresses the following two research questions (RQs):

RQ1: Which network performance metrics can be identified in literature as being relevant for the selection of a CSP?

RQ2: How can these metrics be used to provide an adaptable assessment approach for CSP selection?

The results of our study show that network performance depends on the individual environmental factors and are influenced through incompatibilities (e.g., to a specific geographic location), which can be revealed by adequate measurement and then be considered when selecting a CSP. The remainder of the paper is structured as follows. First, we provide a brief overview of the fundamentals of CC and network technology as well as the conceptual research approach of the paper. Section 3 provides the literature review of measurement and assessment models for CSPs and presents the results. We then propose an assessment approach for the determined performance parameters in Sect. 4, which is applied in a case study in Sect. 5. Section 6 discusses the results and presents the contribution as well as directions for future research.

2 Theoretical Background

2.1 Cloud Computing (CC)

CC is an approach to IT sourcing that enables companies to access a shared pool of managed and scalable IT resources (e.g., networks, servers, storage, applications, and services) that are accessible via the internet on a pay-per-use basis without requiring long-term investments [6] or specific IT knowledge on the customer side [7]. CC represents a transformational shift in IT that is rapidly changing the way in which organizations manage and deliver IT services over the internet. In literature, the definition of the National Institute of Standards and Technology (NIST) is well accepted, which describes CC as "*a model for enabling ubiquitous, convenient, on-demand network access to a shared pool of configurable computing resources (e.g., networks, servers, storage, applications, and services) that can be rapidly provisioned and released with minimal management effort or service provider interaction*" [8]. The resources are to be made available with little administrative effort and require little or no provider interaction [8]. Thus, especially small companies gain access to state-of-the-art technologies and standards without providing development, maintenance, and operation [9].

Even though CC provides numerous technical and organizational advantages for organizations, CC is vulnerable to the same security issues as traditional web applications or data hosts. These include phishing attacks, downtime, data loss, weak passwords, and botnet-compromised hosts or a variety of security risks [10]. The multitude of security-relevant aspects becomes apparent, for instance, in the discussion of challenges on different abstraction levels, like the communication level (shared network infrastructure and virtual networks), architecture level (virtualization, storage, applications, and identity management), and a contractual level [11]. Due to this complex security environment, the concept of trust can be considered as a decisive factor in the initiation of the selection process [5, 12].

2.2 Network Technology

Internet-based communication between devices is enabled via standardized rules for syntax and semantics. Such protocols are typically stacked in a layer system and each layer holds a necessary function in communication. The most important reference in this context is the seven-layer ISO/OSI reference model by Zimmermann [13]. The public internet consists of many interconnected Autonomous Systems (AS). Each of these ASs has a unique number, which can be used to identify the respective AS. ASs, to which users are connected, are usually operated by internet service providers (ISP). A data packet, which is sent from a client to a server, usually passes through several ASs before reaching its destination. Due to the dynamic routing of ASs, these paths can change constantly. The number of connections between ASs varies. For example, either one's own ISP may have a direct connection to a destination AS, or several transit systems need to be passed. Furthermore, the performance of the connection between two ASs can vary, so that the quality of a connection depends on individual circumstances [14].

To measure the quality of such connections, various performance indicators have been established in practice. The *round-trip time (RTT)* describes the time required for a packet to get from source A to destination B and return to A, whereas a low RTT should be aimed [15]. An important variable related to RTT is its variance. This occurs because network packages do not always follow the same path due to redundant paths. This variance is called *Jitter* and should be as low as possible, especially for time-critical applications (e.g., Voice over IP telephony). Another performance indicator is the *throughp*ut. This specifies how much user data can be transferred in a given time [16]. The throughput is consequently specified for a specific layer in the OSI reference model. For end users, the throughput on layer four is usually of interest, as it shows which transfer rate can be effectively used for the protocols of the application layer. The *CPU load* during a network transfer can be an indicator, whether the hardware of a CSP supports offloading mechanisms or not. Offloading mechanisms assign functions to efficient hardware components that should be executed by the CPU and thus cause CPU load. For example, part of the *transmission control protocol (TCP)* processing is offloaded to the Network Interface Controller using the TCP offloading engine, resulting in a significant reduction in CPU load and significantly higher throughput rates [17].

Finally, packet loss can also occur due to a weak connection. This means, for example, that real-time applications such as voice-over-IP lose quality and TCP connections are interrupted. Therefore, the goal is to achieve a packet loss of zero.

2.3 Conceptual Research Approach

Trends like the digital transformation of companies encourage an ongoing dependence on the functionality of digital services like cloud services. Such services enable companies to digitally align their business models and daily business operations in order to stay competitive [3]. However, this dependence relies on the quality of the performance of the respective cloud service, which is why the selection process of the CSP in the first place becomes highly relevant. Therefore, on the one hand, this selection process should be considered from a practical perspective, as it is decisive for the competitive positioning of a CSC company in the future. On the other hand, the process should be considered from a theoretical perspective, as an abstracted assessment approach for the selection of a CSP based on network performance is able to address the problem class of network performance capabilities in companies. Our research approach focuses on the antecedents of cloud service applications as we address the ability of a CSC to evaluate the technical performance capabilities of CSPs, thus focusing on the IaaS level. Only by being able to assess the reliability of a CSP in terms of technical performance can a company be able to plan for the long time and defend its competitiveness in times of digital transformation. Thus, we argue that an assessment approach for the evaluation of CSP is needed to enable companies to not only identify the right cloud service but also to be aware of their own resources and thereby find a suitable CSP who will provide the required service with the suitable sourcing performance. Thus, we extend existing work in this field (i.e., [3, 18]) and provide further guidance in the complex setting of enabling CSCs in digitally transforming business processes.

3 Literature Review

To identify relevant literature addressing selection models for CSPs the databases IEEE, Xplore, Science Direct, and Wiley Online Library were selected due to their focus on computer science, information systems, and economics. As keywords we chose "cloud service provider", "selection model", and "selection framework". The initial search results were reduced regarding the publishing year (after 2015), exclusion criteria (PaaS, SaaS selection), and the availability (online access) to 386 papers. The remaining publications were analyzed for the topics of computer science and CC, IaaS, as well as a focus on the physical components of CC infrastructure, which are decisive for the deployment and operation of the services. Based on the abstracts we were further able to reduce the results to 23 relevant publications, which were then thoroughly analyzed for criteria in CSP selection models. We then analyzed the remaining eleven core papers for five main attributes. First, we determined whether they contain a model for automated selection of a CSP by a cloud broker (Table 1).

Such brokers provide the needed resources at runtime based on a CSC's requirements and dynamically select a suitable CSP for this service [19]. Otherwise, the CSC usually

Table 1. Results of the literature review

Paper	Aut. Sel.	Ranking algorithm	Criteria	Qual./Quant.	Specific Characteristics
Garg et al. [22]	yes	AHP	13 quantitative criteria	Quant.	- consideration of "service response time" instead of RTT and throughput
Ghosh et al. [20]	no	Level-based assessment	3 main criteria with sub-criteria: Trustworthiness, Competence, Risk	Quant. and qual.	- selection of a trustworthy and competent CSP for business outsourcing - assess trustworthiness and SLA interaction risk
Baranwal & Vidyarthi [23]	no	Improved ranked voting method (IRVM)	2 main criteria Application-related User-related	Quant. and qual.	- extension of SMI with additional metrics - consideration of "service response time" instead of RTT and throughput
Muhammad-Bello & Aritsugi [24]	no	Not specified	min. 5 QoS criteria: CPU, RAM, persistent memory, user feedback	Quant. and qual.	- performance parameter for the comparison of CSPs - network performance parameters not considered (but mentioned)
Hajlaoui et al. [25]	yes	Structure Matching and QoS ranking	2 main criteria with sub-criteria: Structure Matching QoS requirements	Quant.	- graph-based model for single cloud environments - user interface is populated with requirements - system automatically generates resources that match the user's requirements
Tripathi et al. [26]	no	Analytical network process (ANP)	16 QoS criteria divided into Provider-related, user-related and system-related	Quant. and qual.	- implementation and extension of SMICloud with ANP - detailed description of all criteria and their quantification as well as the ANP procedure - consideration of "service response time" instead of RTT and throughput

(continued)

Table 1. (*continued*)

Paper	Aut. Sel.	Ranking algorithm	Criteria	Qual./Quant.	Specific Characteristics
Farshidi et al. [27]	no	Multi-part decision support system/Weighted point evaluation	18 criteria	Quant. and qual.	- description of a DSS for multi criteria problems; application to CSP selection - complex method evaluation
Ghule & Gopal [21]	no	Weighted score	Economic, technological, organizational, and legal criteria	Quant.	- large collection of possible parameters - simple evaluation procedure
Chauhan et al. [28]	no	Utility Value Analysis (WSM), Analytic hierachy process (AHP), Revised AHP	10 main criteria based on SLAs	Quant.	- selection model with focus on criteria of redundant IaaS environments - values are not measured but determined by means of SLAs - several comparison algorithms yield the same result
Ramamurthy et al. [29]	yes	Linear optimization/TOPSIS	approx. 19 criteria	Quant. and qual.	- explicitly for multi-cloud environments - combination of VM selection and location selection
Liu et al. [30]	no	Evaluation of mixed data (EVAMIX)	14 criteria and Regret-Rejoice Function	Quant. and qual.	- reduction/avoidance of regret of a decision (avoidance psychology) - pairwise comparison of evaluation data prevent loss of original information

receives a ranked list of the compared CSPs, which is why we also analyzed for ranking algorithms. Furthermore, the criteria for comparing the CSPs are listed and further specified whether they are either quantitative (quant.) and/or qualitative (qual.) in nature. In addition, specific characteristics were mentioned if they required further explanation (Table 1).

The literature review revealed that CSP selection is a field that needs to be investigated from different perspectives. No uniform consensus of comparison algorithms could be determined, but rather a broad diversity (Table 1). For instance, Ghosh et al. [20] follow an approach in their work that determines "competence" based on quantitative characteristics of a CSP that are assured by service level agreements (SLAs). Even though these are not specified in detail, RTT and throughput are given as examples. Ghule & Gopal [21] provide a large number of metrics for IaaS environments in their work. Within each category, 3 to 16 evaluation criteria are mentioned superficially.

However, network performance parameters are only roughly summarized. Thus, each of the eleven models presented has unique capabilities (Table 1). While some models have a quantitative and qualitative focus, others are merely quantitatively oriented. Often, Quality of Service (QoS) parameters, such as CPU performance or disk performance, are measured based on SLAs or actual data logging using a benchmark for comparison. However, consistently across all papers it was revealed that very few to no network performance parameters are used. Even though RTT and throughput were mentioned they were not considered. In the following, we propose an assessment model which also focuses on CSP selection but based on different performance indicators.

4 Proposal of a New Assessment Approach

CC poses new technical challenges, since the quality indicators described are often no longer within the customers' scope of responsibility, and CSCs themselves are forced to maintain SLAs, e.g., due to contractual relationships with own customers. So far, possible performance indicators have been presented with which the network performance and thus the quality of the network connection to a cloud or to a CSP can be evaluated. However, the literature review revealed that these are used very little or not at all, due to a focus on rather complex and multi-characteristic models. The following section presents methods for collecting data that can be used to provide the network performance snapshot. From this data, a metric was developed that allows the CSC to include and consider network performance as indicator in the CSP selection process.

Initially, we defined a test scenario in which various constellations of locations and CSPs are collected. These scenarios are summarized in Table 2. They represent a collection of possible and common combinations for the case of having one on-premises location which needs to be connected to maximum two CSPs each in two available regions. We defined regions as data centers that differ in their geographical location. The aim was that the list should be extendable as well as adaptable to others than the given characteristics. The proposed scenarios are intended to cover the following cases:

- An organization wants to connect one CSP,
- An organization wants to connect two CSPs,
- An organization with an existing CSP wants to add another CSP.

To determine the final metric, it is necessary to define lower and upper thresholds, which must be met. Each user will define these limits individually since they depend on the individual scenario. A distinction is made between a soft and a hard limit. This is necessary to represent a desirable state in which an application is no longer expected to function and can therefore no longer be considered acceptable. Furthermore, a test period is defined in advance during which the data is collected. The data will be gathered at different times of the day and thus at different load conditions of the CSP and the public internet. From the data values collected, a single goal achievement level (GAL) is to be determined. For this purpose, a straight line is formed with the soft and hard limit value (LV) by means of linear interpolation. The points required for this are P_soft ($LVsoft$, 100) and P_hard ($LVhard$, 0). The measurement result (x) is then transferred to the straight line and the value achieved is calculated.

$$\text{GAL} = 100 - 100 \times \frac{x - \text{LV}_{\text{soft}}}{\text{LV}_{\text{hard}} - \text{LV}_{\text{soft}}}$$

A measurement result corresponding to the soft limit value, thus, fulfills the requirements 100%. If a better value is achieved, it results in a better evaluation. If a measurement result is determined that cannot meet the hard limit, it is given a rating of ≤ 0. This procedure can be used for all measurement values except the jitter. To calculate the degree of target jitter, the measurement points of the RTT whose distance from the mean value is within half the jitter value ($X0$) are set in relation to the total number of measurement points (X).

$$\text{GAL}_{\text{Jitter}} = \frac{\left| X' = \left\{ x \in \text{mean(RTT)} \pm \frac{\text{Jitter}}{2} \right\} \right|}{|X|}$$

Once all data has been gathered and the performance metrics have been evaluated individually, a weighted average of the n degrees of target achievement can be used for the overall evaluation. The weights ($\emptyset$) are also determined by the user, using.

$$\text{GAL}_{\text{Jitter}} = \frac{\left| X' = \left\{ x \in \text{mean(RTT)} \pm \frac{\text{Jitter}}{2} \right\} \right|}{|X|}.$$

5 Instantiation

5.1 Case Study Design

The proposed method was then applied in a case study. As a scenario we chose a company, which decides on the extension of an on-premises installation by comparing different CSPs. In a pre-selection, we already limited the set of CSPs to the two leading CSPs on the market (AWS and Azure) for creating a realistic setting. Our aim was further to verify, based on our developed model and the performance parameters, whether these CSPs can extend the existing network. For the use case we considered two locations: Germany and Ireland. Each location could have multiple regions that differ in their geographical location, which were operated by both CSPs. Table 2 provides an overview of the two locations with the geographical regions of each CSP.

A small virtual machine (VM) was used, based on the reference of 1 CPU core, 0.5 GB RAM, and Ubuntu 20.04 long term support, which is assumed to be the representative VM size for this case. The following values were set as thresholds for the performance parameters (Table 3).

The connections between the clouds and the on-premises location were each established with managed services of the CSP based on OpenVPN. The connections between the cloud services were also established with managed services, but IPsec is used as the VPN protocol here. The test period was defined as ranging from 10 a.m. - 6 p.m. CET to record a cross-section over one business day. During this period, the RTT of the scenarios mentioned in Table 2 was recorded with the tool "Ping" and saved in CSV files. At the

Table 2. Overview of the Considered Scenarios in the Case Study.

#	Location 1	Region 1	Location 2	Region 2	Connection
1	On-premise	1	Azure	2	P2S OpenVPN
2	On-premise	1	Azure	4	P2S OpenVPN
3	On-premise	1	AWS	3	P2S OpenVPN
4	On-premise	1	AWS	5	P2S OpenVPN
5	Azure	2	Azure	2	VNET/VPC
6	Azure	2	Azure	4	VNET/VPC
7	AWS	3	AWS	1	VNET/VPC
8	AWS	3	AWS	3	VNET/VPC
9	Azure	2	AWS	3	S2S IPsec VPN
10	Azure	2	AWS	5	S2S IPsec VPN
11	Azure	4	AWS	3	S2S IPsec VPN
12	Azure	4	AWS	5	S2S IPsec VPN

Regions: 1 = Germany, 2 = Germany West Central, 3 = Europe (Frankfurt), 4 = North Europe (Ireland), 5 = Europe (Ireland)

Table 3. Thresholds for the Case Study

Metrics	Threshold (soft)	Threshold (hard)
RTT near location	20 ms	80 ms
Jitter near location	20 ms	–
RTT distant location	50 ms	80 ms
Jitter distant location	20 ms	–
Network throughput	300 Mbit/s	50 Mbit/s
CPU load	1%	10%

same time, measurement points of the throughput were collected at 15-min intervals. To avoid the results being falsified by the fact that two throughput measurements are carried out simultaneously, they were each carried out offset by one minute. The measurement was done with the tool "iperf3", and the output was converted from JSON format to CSV format. However, the described procedure caused some upward outliers in the RTT measurement because the network adapter was partly fully utilized, and delays in the RTT measurement occurred correspondingly. These outliers were excluded by using only data within the 99th percentile. In addition, the measurements of the individual scenarios were split over two days and then combined.

5.2 Findings

The collected data were analyzed using the R programming language and plotted in Figs. 1, 2, and 3. Figure 1 shows that the RTT from the on-premises location in Germany to the datacenter region of Azure located in Germany is slightly higher than to the same region of AWS, but the remote location in Ireland is better connected by Azure.

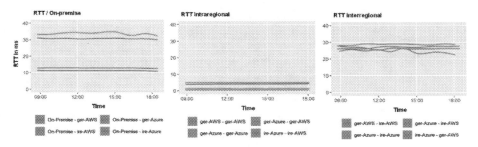

Fig. 1. RTT Results.

Here, the connection to AWS has a higher RTT and is associated with some fluctuations over the day. The reason for this could be that more transit ASs need to be passed to reach the network of AWS than that of Azure. The intra-region RTT is very low and stable. This indicates that the CSPs have a reliable internal network and have well established exchange points. Across geographical regions, RTTs are at a comparable level both within and between providers and are subject to only minor fluctuations, which may be due to distance. For the connection between the German and Irish locations of AWS, we could see that the RTT change visibly during the day. In contrast, the throughput shows a different result (Fig. 2). The connection to the on-premises location is stable but significantly lower than the CSP can provide. The throughput to the remote location in Ireland is mostly below what was previously expected to be a hard limit. The highest and most stable throughput was achieved by the Azure network. In both regional set ups and to the corresponding remote location, there is little to no fluctuation and the highest measured throughput. The intraregional throughput of AWS is also high, but with strong fluctuations.

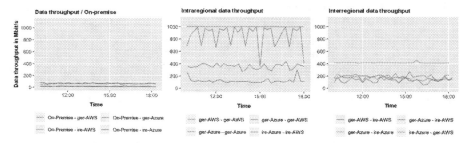

Fig. 2. Data Throughput Results.

As already shown by the measurements for RTT, the interconnection between the two CSP is very reliable. This is also reflected in high and relatively stable throughput rates, although these are significantly better at the location in Germany than in Ireland. Packet loss was not measured. Since throughput measurements were performed using TCP, lost segments were retransmitted. The tool only provides absolute numbers of retransmits and the total number of the sent TCP segments is missing, so that no ratio can be formed. However, the retransmits have a direct effect on the throughput and are therefore included in the evaluation. They reflect the partly large exclusions of the ger-AWS - ger-AWS connection, but otherwise do not allow any conclusion.

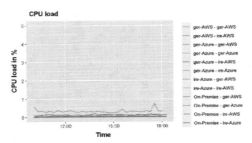

Fig. 3. CPU Results.

Figure 3 shows the measurement results of the CPU load that occurred at the receiver of the Iperf3 segments at the measurement time. Despite the low CPU performance of the VMs with only one core, all measurement points are in the low single-digit percentage range. It can therefore be assumed that efficient offloading mechanisms are used. However, in the case study, only comparatively low throughput rates were achieved. To test the relevance of this metric, a one-time measurement was performed on high-performance VMs at the CSP Azure. The VMs "Standard F8s v2" with 8 CPU cores and 16 GB RAM as well as Ubuntu 20.04 LTS were used for this purpose. A measurement with IPerf3 resulted in a TCP throughput of 4.73 GBit/s, whereby the target system had a CPU load of 12.98%. This shows that with higher throughput comes a significantly higher CPU load.

6 Discussion and Conclusion

Based on our developed metrics for the assessment of a CSP's service performance ability, we were able to demonstrate a sensitive performance difference in the provided infrastructure of the two leading IaaS providers AWS and Azure. For an exemplary use case scenario, we decided on a fictive weighting and the results showed that both CSPs are basically suitable for CSCs to extend the existing network from a network performance perspective. In this specific case, Azure was rated slightly above AWS, which is primarily due to the higher internal throughput and the slightly higher throughput to the on-premises location (Fig. 1 and 2). However, the weighted average results of the specific metrics revealed values of 0.78 (AWS) and 0.83 (Azure). Thus, for both CSPs, the location in Ireland does not fulfill ideal characteristics for potential CSCs. Since this occurs with both tested CSPs, it is likely to be caused by the on-premises location or the local ISP. The assessment approach is intended to uncover such incompatibilities in a specific constellation so that they can be considered in the final selection of a CSP. Our approach is thereby able to provide a possibility for companies to easily test and evaluate the technical aspects of IaaS provided by CSPs. Even though similar approaches exist in literature, they often consider quantitative performance parameters, like CPU and RAM [24], investigate merely SLA parameters [28], or service response time [22, 26]. Network parameters, like RTT or throughput are not yet considered. However, especially in IS research, such functional parameters are the missing link, when it comes to an overarching consideration of CSP selection and need to be considered rather than focusing on merely non-functional parameters, like trust [5, 12], flexibility and scalability [1], or efficiency [2]. Another remarkable result in literature was the partially high number of investigated parameters [26, 27, 29]. Although this complexity promises a fully comprehensive assessment basis, the actual applicability of approaches with more than 16 criteria might remain limited. Due to the missing accessibility to quantitative and qualitative criteria, CSCs' ability to select the most suitable CSPs may be limited, as well as the prediction of long-term effects of a selection decision (e.g., vendor lock-in) [31]. Thus, our presented approach, based on the network performance parameters as crucial prerequisite of the IaaS functionality, provides on the one hand an extension of existing assessment approaches (i.e., [3, 18, 24]), but on the other hand also an alternative and more feasible approach for companies, trying to identify the best CSP according to rather functional technical measurements.

The objective of this paper was to identify suitable network performance parameters and to quantitatively process them so that they can be integrated into a CSP selection approach. This is especially relevant in today's ongoing dependence on companies from CSPs as they often provide the infrastructure required for relevant business processes and even entire business models. To this end, a method was presented for quantitatively recording and evaluating the metrics so that a key figure is created that can subsequently be used. The literature review revealed that research had addressed the selection of a CSP from qualitative and quantitative perspectives and with various evaluation algorithms. However, network performance parameters had only minor importance in this context. Our approach focused on this research gap and elaborated an assessment approach applied in a case study. We revealed that throughput and RTT were the most critical performance metrics. Packet loss played a minor role, as it only indirectly influenced the evaluation in the tests used due to a reduction in throughput influence on the assessment. In addition, we show that the CPU load has little relevance at low throughput rates but that this becomes clearly measurable and thus comparable at considerably higher throughput rates. The case study showed that network performance depends on the individual environmental influences and that incompatibilities, e.g., to a specific location, can be revealed and considered when selecting a CSP.

Our research contributes to the body of knowledge in computer and information science in several ways. First, we provided insights in the academic literature in the field of IaaS assessment approaches and the evaluation of CSPs. Further, our presented assessment approach reveals the potentials of network performance parameters as guiding decisional criteria for the identification of the most suitable CSP. As a practical contribution, our research results provide guidance for CSCs that are forced to maintain and measure contracted services (SLAs), e.g., due to contractual relationships with their own customers. To improve the evaluation algorithms, proposals for defining the limits and weightings could be developed in future work. Furthermore, additional methods for collecting performance data should be evaluated. For instance, the influence of the throughput on the CPU load should be investigated, since above a certain throughput the CPU load increases significantly and, thus, becomes relevant for the assessment.

References

1. Schneider, S., Sunyaev, A.: Determinant factors of cloud-sourcing decisions: reflecting on the IT outsourcing literature in the era of cloud computing. J. Inf. Technol. 31, 1–31 (2016). https://doi.org/10.1057/jit.2014.25
2. Wulf, F., Westner, M., Schön, M., Strahringer, S., Loebbecke, C.: Preparing for a digital future: cloud strategy at continental AG. In: ICIS 2019 Proceedings, Munich (2019)
3. Hentschel, R., Bley, K., Schön, H.: Shifting micro-enterprises into the cloud: guidelines for cloud service providers. Presented at the Hawaii International Conference on System Sciences (2021). https://doi.org/10.24251/HICSS.2021.575
4. Winkler, T.J., Brown, C.V.: Horizontal allocation of decision rights for on-premise applications and software-as-a-service. J. Manag. Inf. Syst. 30, 13–48 (2013). https://doi.org/10.2753/MIS0742-1222300302
5. Hentschel, R., Leyh, C., Petznick, A.: Current cloud challenges in Germany: the perspective of cloud service providers. J. Cloud Comput. 7, 1–12 (2018). https://doi.org/10.1186/s13677-018-0107-6
6. Yang, H., Tate, M.: A descriptive literature review and classification of cloud computing research. Commun. Assoc. Inf. Syst. 31, 2 (2012)
7. Venters, W., Whitley, E.A.: A critical review of cloud computing: researching desires and realities. J. Inf. Technol. 27, 179–197 (2012). https://doi.org/10.1057/jit.2012.17
8. Mell, P., Grance, T.: The NIST definition of cloud computing. Natl. Inst. Stand. Technol. 53 (2011)
9. Mitra, A., O'Regan, N., Sarpong, D.: Cloud resource adaptation: a resource based perspective on value creation for corporate growth. Technol. Forecast. Soc. Chang. 130, 28–38 (2018). https://doi.org/10.1016/j.techfore.2017.08.012
10. Dillon, T., Wu, C., Chang, E.: Cloud computing: issues and challenges. In: 2010 24th IEEE International Conference on Advanced Information Networking and Applications, pp. 27–33. IEEE (2010). https://doi.org/10.1109/AINA.2010.187
11. Ali, M., Khan, S.U., Vasilakos, A.V.: Security in cloud computing: opportunities and challenges. Inf. Sci. 305, 357–383 (2015). https://doi.org/10.1016/j.ins.2015.01.025
12. Khan, K.M., Malluhi, Q.: Establishing trust in cloud computing. IT Prof. 12, 20–27 (2010). https://doi.org/10.1109/MITP.2010.128
13. Zimmermann, H.: OSI reference model - the ISO model of architecture for open systems interconnection. IEEE Trans. Commun. 28, 425–432 (1980). https://doi.org/10.1109/TCOM.1980.1094702
14. Tozal, M.E.: The internet: a system of interconnected autonomous systems. In: 2016 Annual IEEE Systems Conference (SysCon), pp. 1–8. IEEE (2016). https://doi.org/10.1109/SYSCON.2016.7490628

15. Sun, P., Yu, M., Freedman, M.J., Rexford, J.: Identifying performance bottlenecks in CDNs through TCP-level monitoring. In: Proceedings of the first ACM SIGCOMM Workshop on Measurements up the Stack - W-MUST 2011, p. 49. ACM Press, New York (2011). https://doi.org/10.1145/2018602.2018615

16. Constantine, B., Forget, G., Geib, R., Schrage, R.: Framework for TCP throughput testing (RFC Nr. 6349). (2011)

17. Chase, J.S., Gallatin, A.J., Yocum, K.G.: End system optimizations for high-speed TCP. IEEE Commun. Mag. **39**, 68–74 (2001). https://doi.org/10.1109/35.917506

18. Lang, M., Wiesche, M., Krcmar, H.: Criteria for selecting cloud service providers: a delphi study of quality-of-service attributes. Inf. Manage. **55**, 746–758 (2018). https://doi.org/10.1016/j.im.2018.03.004

19. Gutierrez-Garcia, J.O., Sim, K.M.: Agent-based cloud service composition. Appl. Intell. **38**, 436–464 (2013). https://doi.org/10.1007/s10489-012-0380-x

20. Ghosh, N., Ghosh, S.K., Das, S.K.: SelCSP: a framework to facilitate selection of cloud service providers. IEEE Trans. Cloud Comput. **3**, 66–79 (2015). https://doi.org/10.1109/TCC.2014.2328578

21. Ghule, D., Gopal, A.: Comparison parameters and evaluation technique to help selection of right IaaS cloud. In: 2018 5th IEEE Uttar Pradesh Section International Conference on Electrical, Electronics and Computer Engineering (UPCON), pp. 1–6. IEEE (2018). https://doi.org/10.1109/UPCON.2018.8597059

22. Garg, S.K., Versteeg, S., Buyya, R.: SMICloud: a framework for comparing and ranking cloud services. In: 2011 Fourth IEEE International Conference on Utility and Cloud Computing, pp. 210–218 (2011). https://doi.org/10.1109/UCC.2011.36

23. Baranwal, G., Vidyarthi, D.P.: A cloud service selection model using improved ranked voting method. Concurr. Comput.: Pract. Exp. **28**, 3540–3567 (2016). https://doi.org/10.1002/cpe.3740

24. Muhammad-Bello, B.L., Aritsugi, M.: TCloud: a transparent framework for public cloud service comparison. In: Proceedings of the 9th International Conference on Utility and Cloud Computing, pp. 228–233. ACM, New York (2016). https://doi.org/10.1145/2996890.3007864

25. Hajlaoui, J.E., Omri, M.N., Benslimane, D., Barhamgi, M.: QoS based framework for configurable IaaS cloud services discovery. In: 2017 IEEE International Conference on Web Services (ICWS), pp. 460–467. IEEE (2017). https://doi.org/10.1109/ICWS.2017.53

26. Tripathi, A., Pathak, I., Vidyarthi, D.P.: Integration of analytic network process with service measurement index framework for cloud service provider selection. Concurr. Comput.: Pract. Exp. **29**, e4144 (2017). https://doi.org/10.1002/cpe.4144

27. Farshidi, S., Jansen, S., de Jong, R., Brinkkemper, S.: A decision support system for cloud service provider selection problem in software producing organizations. In: 2018 IEEE 20th Conference on Business Informatics (CBI), pp. 139–148. IEEE (2018). https://doi.org/10.1109/CBI.2018.00024

28. Chauhan, N., Agarwal, R., Garg, K., Choudhury, T.: Redundant IaaS cloud selection with consideration of multi criteria decision analysis. Procedia Comput. Sci. **167**, 1325–1333 (2020). https://doi.org/10.1016/j.procs.2020.03.448

29. Ramamurthy, A., Saurabh, S., Gharote, M., Lodha, S.: Selection of cloud service providers for hosting web applications in a multi-cloud environment. In: 2020 IEEE International Conference on Services Computing (SCC), pp. 202–209. IEEE (2020). https://doi.org/10.1109/SCC49832.2020.00034

30. Liu, Z., Wang, D., Wang, W., Liu, P.: An integrated group decision-making framework for selecting cloud service providers based on regret theory and EVAMIX with hybrid information. Int. J. Intell. Syst. **37**, 3480–3513 (2022). https://doi.org/10.1002/int.22698

31. Silva, G.C., Rose, L.M., Calinescu, R.: A systematic review of cloud lock-in solutions. In: Proceedings of the 2013 IEEE International Conference on Cloud Computing Technology and Science, vol. 02, pp. 363–368. IEEE Computer Society, USA (2013). https://doi.org/10.1109/CloudCom.2013.130

Unveiling the Golden Thread: Unmasking the Power of Blockchain for Sustainable Consumption

Maryam Hina[1]([✉]) [iD], Najmul Islam[1] [iD], and Amandeep Dhir[2] [iD]

[1] Department of Software Engineering, LUT University, Lappeenranta, Finland
{Maryam.Hina,Najmul.Islam}@lut.fi
[2] Department of Management, University of Agder, Kristiansand, Norway
amandeep.dhir@uia.no

Abstract. There is limited empirical support for understanding how blockchain transparency shapes consumers' sustainable consumption. Therefore, this study investigates the impact of blockchain transparency on consumers' sustainable consumption choices. This study delves into the impact of blockchain transparency on consumers' intentions to purchase sustainable products, a topic of increasing relevance in contemporary markets. Employing a novel blockchain-based app scenario in the fashion apparel industry, we surveyed 282 European consumers. Robust data analysis using the partial least squares method reveals that blockchain transparency signals product sustainability trustworthiness and effectively satisfies consumer concerns, resulting in increased purchase intent and positive word of mouth. Notably, we uncover a moderating effect of information seeking on the trust-consumer satisfaction relationship. Our study contributes pivotal insights to the evolving discourse on blockchain and sustainable consumption, offering valuable implications for both academia and industry.

Keywords: Blockchain · Transparency · Sustainability · Consumer · Sustainable Consumption

1 Introduction

The growth of sustainability related concerns and consumers' demand for authentic sustainable products have encouraged sustainable consumption behavior [1]. While putting sustainability ideas into practice is essential for companies, it is also critical to effectively communicate this information to stakeholders, especially customers. The firms' disclosures of sustainability related information demonstrate their dedication to and credibility of sustainable activities, which influence consumers' decisions [2]. However, consumers face difficulties in validating sustainability promises made by the firms. Since producers have more information than consumers, they can decide on what information to share with stakeholders [3]. Moreover, due to the proliferation of digital technologies, consumers now have access to various information sources, making it much harder for them

© IFIP International Federation for Information Processing 2023
Published by Springer Nature Switzerland AG 2023
M. Janssen et al. (Eds.): I3E 2023, LNCS 14316, pp. 265–276, 2023.
https://doi.org/10.1007/978-3-031-50040-4_20

to determine the veracity of sustainable claims. It is also challenging for the companies to operate, communicate, and be transparent in the supply chain since the supply network connects multitiered companies at different geographical locations [4]. Together, these factors have caused information asymmetry, making it challenging for consumers to determine the sustainability of a product and to believe the information found on centralized systems or other numerous dispersed sources. Blockchain has recently emerged as a viable solution to supply chain transparency and lowering related risks [5].

The review of prior literature highlighted the dominance of previous investigations of blockchain applications for upstream supply chain aspects, such as tracking production processes and product components [5], and its technical usage in reducing carbon footprints, emission trading, avoiding fake products, and avoiding unethical behavior [6]. Despite the acknowledged benefits of blockchain for supply chain management and sustainability, outcomes of blockchain from consumers' standpoint have not been sufficiently manifested. We found that there has been relatively little prior scholarly work done to empirically identify the blockchain's influence on consumers' sustainable consumption behavior. For example, consumers' blockchain experience was acknowledged as strongly influencing impulsive buying in the context of green products [7]. While such findings offer insightful information on how blockchain affects consumer behavior, they fall short of offering a thorough understanding of the underlying mechanisms that influence consumers' purchase decisions for sustainable products from consumers' viewpoint. The current study extends this nascent research to examine how blockchain transparency shapes sustainable consumption behavior. Therefore, our study is an effort to address the following research questions (RQs).

RQ1: What effect do consumers perceive from blockchain transparency that influences their sustainable consumption behavior?

RQ2: Through what mechanism blockchain transparency shape sustainable consumption behavior?

Drawing upon signaling theory [8], we found blockchain transparency as a tool a company utilizes to indicate its reliability to consumers. The signaling of blockchain transparency can increase consumers' trust in product sustainability. This study contributes to the prior literature in two ways. Firstly, this study expands blockchain literature by explicitly exploring blockchain transparency with a market-focused approach and identifying its influence on consumers' sustainable purchasing decisions. Second, we delineate the mechanism through which the effect of blockchain technology is realized. We found that when companies transparently disclose information about their sustainable products using blockchain, consumers perceive them as trustworthy and satisfy their concerns about product sustainability. Which in return increases their intention to purchase sustainable products and the likelihood of spreading positive word of mouth. The adherence to signaling theory highlights the need for transparency to foster trust, shape consumers' responsible behavior, and encourage sustainable consumption habits.

2 Theoretical Background

2.1 Blockchain Transparency

Transparency is defined as the level of accessibility and visibility of information [9], generally referred to as an open flow of information amongst stakeholders [10]. Utilizing an advanced combination of consensus protocols, distributed architecture, and cryptography, blockchain technology unveils a revolutionary technique enabling transparent transactions to foster stakeholder trust [11]. Across the supply chain, blockchain has been recognized to improve product and process transparency by enabling information traceability and accessibility to the companies and end users involved in the supply chain [5]. Moreover, due to individuals' growing sensitivity to social and environmental issues, blockchain has arisen as a solution to sustainability issues such as sustainability in agrifood [12]. For example, referring to the ecological effect of sustainable fashion products, the information transparency provided by blockchain has been emphasized to induce an ideal environmental quality level of fashion products [13]. Such information (e.g., related to the sustainability of the product), when consumers find, lessens the uncertainty surrounding the likelihood that their needs and preferences will match the qualities of the product [14]. Blockchain's ability to trace product components can foster consumer trust in product's authenticity, quality, and ethical processing. These findings highlight the role of blockchain in protecting the consumer market by offering proof of authenticity and enabling customers to track and trace the product history. Prior research on the blockchain has mostly concentrated on the use of blockchain in the supply chain to measure its effects on sustainability. However, our study falls under the narrowly focused area of consumers' sustainable consumption decisions and quantifies the impact of blockchain transparency thereupon.

2.2 Signaling Theory

Signaling theory originated from an information economics study assuming that buyers and sellers have asymmetric information when they are involved in a market exchange [15]. This theory observes that signalers, aware of intangible values and qualities of the company, product, and individual, tend to transmit positive signals to the recipients [16]. In the digital realm, digital platform owners act as signalers and send signals using technology to attract and build trust with consumers. Our study adopted signaling theory to explain that consumers perceive signals transmitted by the blockchain and might draw conclusions about a product's sustainability by differentiating between high and low sustainability. In this way, blockchain transparency signaling trust effectively allays consumers' concerns about product sustainability by showcasing accurate sustainability related information [17]. In the prior literature, such blockchain signaling effect has been highlighted to be helpful in consumers' decision making [18]. Therefore, in the interaction of blockchain based information and sustainable consumption, signaling theory underpins the notion that a buyer's trust in product sustainability is associated with trustworthiness signals. Following the nascent literature that proposes blockchain as a trustworthy signal in supplier-buyer relationships [19], we extend this signaling effect to the context of blockchain transparency – sustainable consumption relationship and argue that the implementation of blockchain can signal the trustworthiness of sustainability related information about the product and ensuring its sustainability.

3 Hypothesis Development

Blockchain transparency, through a commitment to information sharing, serve as a signal of sellers' trust (i.e., product sustainability) [19]. The comprehensive information that many parties have compiled and disseminated via the blockchain includes information on the product's origins, the material used, the environmental effect of the product, and the impact of its life cycle [20]. Since blockchain is decentralized and all participants on the chain can view the information, it promotes trust in temper-proof information. Hence, in the quest for sustainable consumption, blockchain transparency enables consumers to trust the veracity and accuracy of numerous pieces of information provided [20]. Our study theoretically frames blockchain transparency as a signal of trust in product sustainability. Thus, we postulate:

H1: Blockchain transparency positively influences trust in product sustainability.

Tracing product sustainability has become significant as a means to encourage sustainable consumption by giving consumers a greater awareness of process sustainability and product life cycle [21]. The visibility of transactions and interactions on a blockchain contributes to its transparency [9], which increases consumers' confidence in the product [22]. Thus, the level of blockchain transparency confirmation affects consumer satisfaction [23]. Consumers find blockchain transparency satisfying them by solving their product sustainability related concerns. To examine this, we postulate:

H2: Blockchain transparency positively influences customer satisfaction.

Trust is the key element to determining how satisfied consumers are with a product's sustainability. Consumers are more satisfied, for instance, when they view blockchain as trustworthy [24]. It is assumed that trust and degree of satisfaction are associated. A transaction would not likely take place without a certain level of trust, let alone consumer satisfaction [25]. Trust is important as a crucial heuristic signal for consumers' satisfaction and meaningful decision making [24]. In the context of blockchain, a few studies have hypothesized blockchain based trust and consumers' satisfaction with sustainable products, suggesting that blockchain based trust is closely associated with consumers' satisfaction [26]. Similarly, we anticipate that blockchain based trust toward product sustainability is positively associated with consumers' satisfaction. Thus, we hypothesize:

H3: The presence of blockchain based trust positively influences consumer satisfaction with sustainable products.

Prior research suggests that consumer satisfaction significantly influences consumers' propensity to buy sustainable products. For example, consumers who are satisfied with sustainable brands do not plan to switch [27]. Accordingly, it may be assumed that consumers may continue to have the intention to purchase sustainable products if they are satisfied with product sustainability ensured by blockchain based trustworthy information. Consumer satisfaction with the sustainability of the product explains greater intention to purchase it [28]. Hence, we postulate:

H4: Consumer satisfaction positively influences consumers' purchase intention.

Prior scholars have acknowledged that satisfied consumers show the intention to recommend the company by good word of mouth [29]. Similarly, consumers are more inclined to accept and spread the word about firms' disclosures on product sustainability if they are satisfied with the information [30]. On the contrary, if they find it unsatisfactory, they will dissuade others from using it [31]. Consumer satisfaction is undoubtedly a key factor in influencing the propagation of positive word of mouth. Therefore, we hypothesize:

H5: Consumer satisfaction positively influences positive word of mouth.

People who believe in a product with high social value intend to seek information that enables them to assess the product benefits (i.e., sustainability) of making a purchase [32]. Consumers could be uninformed about sustainable products as a result of information asymmetry between producers and consumers [33]. For example, prior findings on consumers' perception of sustainable packaging have revealed a mismatch between what consumers believe about the qualities of sustainable packaging and how well it performs based on life cycle evaluation [34]. Therefore, consumers who are also information seekers may significantly seek information on sustainable products in order to engage in sustainable consumption [35]. To come to a decision or find a solution to the question, information seekers synthesize knowledge from several sources, which may strengthen their trust in the sustainability of the product. Consumer tendency to learn more about the sustainability of the product is important to understand the link between blockchain based trust and consumers' satisfaction with product sustainability. Thus, we posit:

H6a: Information seeking moderates the association between trust and consumers' satisfaction.

H6b: Information seeking moderates the association between blockchain transparency and consumers' satisfaction.

4 Methods

4.1 Study Design

To validate our research model, we conducted a scenario-based survey involving consumers of sustainable products, using vignettes to present plausible situations and gather responses through rating scales. Scenario based methods have been applied in information systems research on various topics. We selected the apparel fashion industry as our study context due to its significant sustainability challenges, such as contributing 4% global emission and 92 million tons of waste. Factors like high water usage, chemical pollution, and waste production amplify its environmental impact. A recent McKinsey report in 2022 highlighted low trust among 88% of Generation Z consumers in the United States regarding brands' sustainability claims, emphasizing the need for transparency and data backed evidence. The fashion apparel industry thus becomes the most pertinent setting for examining our research model.

To design our study scenario, we conducted two focus group discussions in April 2023 involving seven participants with a mix of genders. Participants were required to have a basic understanding of sustainability and blockchain. At least one participant from each group was chosen with a working knowledge of blockchain and sustainability.

Insights gained from this discussion informed the development of our study scenario and user interface (UI), aligned with the discussion's key themes.

4.2   Instrument Development

A multi-item scale was used to evaluate each construct. A five-point Likert scale was used to measure scale items, with 1 representing strongly disagree and 5 representing strongly agree. We adapted the validated study items from the prior studies. Three items were adapted for blockchain transparency [36], three items for trust [37], four items for consumer satisfaction [38], three items for consumers' purchase intention [39], and four items for information seeking [35].

4.3   Data Collection and Analysis

We collected data through the Academic Prolific platform to recruit study participants. Our sample was restricted to the Europe continent. The data pool consisted of 332 respondents in total. 39 of these collected responses were either not submitted at all or incomplete and therefore returned. After additional analysis, 14 responses that failed attention checks and did not match the screening criteria were removed from the remaining dataset. As a result, we received 282 valid responses. According to the descriptive analysis, there were 111 females (39.4%), 168 males (59.6%), and three other genders (1.1%) among the respondents. Respondents aged 21–30 years provided the majority of the responses (62.1%). We used partial least squares structural modelling (PLS-SEM) to analyze the empirical data.

5   Results

5.1   Measurement Model

The sample of 282 responses considered for analysis. First, we looked at item loadings that are required to be 0.70 or higher and are commonly used to assess the indicators' reliability. From this study's set of construct indicators, two items were found below this threshold and were eliminated. All the remaining item loading values were higher than the suggested threshold, as shown in Table 2. Next, we examined the constructs' convergent reliability and discriminant validity of the study model that includes six latent constructs such as blockchain transparency, trust, consumer satisfaction, consumers' purchase intention, positive word of mouth, and information seeking. To assess the constructs' internal consistency, we used Cronbach's alpha (CA) and composite reliability (CR) as alternative measurement. The reflective constructs in this research model met the prerequisite by having values greater than the cutoff values of CA = 0.50 and CR = 0.70. To verify the convergent validity of the constructs, the average variance extracted (AVE) values are more than the threshold value of 0.50. Since the values were higher than the thresholds, they satisfied the requirements of construct reliability and convergent validity (Table 1). The higher factor loading indicates higher internal consistency among proposed factors as a result showing higher value of CA and CR. However, these values are within the cutoff value prescribed by Hair et al. [40].

Table 1. The assessment of measurement model of constructs

Constructs	Indicators	Loadings	Mean	SD	CA(α)	CR	AVE
Transparency	TRNSP1	0.812	4.245	0.663	0.771	0.867	0.686
	TRNSP2	0.854	4.142	0.773			
	TRNSP3	0.818	4.110	0.794			
Trust	TRST1	0.924	3.940	0.729	0.904	0.94	0.838
	TRST2	0.916	3.858	0.791			
	TRST3	0.908	3.901	0.682			
Consumer satisfaction	CS1	0.902	3.862	0.728	0.849	0.909	0.77
	CS2	0.914	3.830	0.748			
	CS3	0.813	3.996	0.844			
Consumers' purchase intention	PI1	0.943	3.468	0.872	0.93	0.956	0.878
	PI2	0.953	3.429	0.881			
	PI3	0.915	3.557	0.870			
Positive word of mouth	WOM1	0.905	3.777	0.805	0.881	0.927	0.808
	WOM2	0.907	3.791	0.86			
	WOM3	0.885	3.433	0.909			
Information Seeking	IS1	0.793	3.734	0.909	0.827	0.897	0.745
	IS2	0.883	3.681	0.870			
	IS3	0.91	3.599	0.918			

The measurement model met the requirements for discriminant validity, as highlighted in Table 2, where the diagonal (bold) values denote the AVE square root of every construct, which is higher than the relevant correlation coefficient.

Table 2. Correlation matrix and the square root of AVEs

	1	2	3	4	5	6
1. Consumer satisfaction	**0.878**					
2. Consumers' purchase intention	0.639	**0.937**				
3. Information seeking	0.639	0.677	**0.863**			
4. Transparency	0.526	0.416	0.402	**0.828**		
5. Trust	0.629	0.428	0.421	0.539	**0.916**	
6. Positive word of mouth	0.752	0.766	0.626	0.396	0.520	**0.899**

5.2 Structural Model

The outcomes of the hypothesis testing are shown in Fig. 1. It shows that blockchain transparency is positively associated with trust ($\beta = 0.538$, $t = 9.351$, $p < 0.001$) and consumer satisfaction ($\beta = 0.159$, $t = 2.979$, $p < 0.01$) and supported H1 and H2 respectively. Trust is also seen to be positively related with consumer satisfaction ($\beta = 0.323$, $t = 6.232$, $p < 0.001$), supporting H3. Next, it is shown that consumer satisfaction is strongly associated with consumers' intention to purchase ($\beta = 0.581$, $t = 10.694$, $p < 0.001$) and positive word of mouth ($\beta = 0.752$, $t = 19.655$, $p < 0.0$), which supported H4 and H5 respectively. The study model is significant since it shows a variance of 28.9% in trust, 60.1% variance in consumer satisfaction, 41.8% variance in consumers' purchase intention, and 56.5% variance in positive word of mouth, which is above 26%. Moreover, information seeking does moderate the relationship between trust and consumer satisfaction ($\beta = 0.092$, $t = 1.997$, $p < 0.05$). The positive association between trust and consumer satisfaction is seen dampened by information seeking. Thus, our hypothesis H6a has been confirmed.

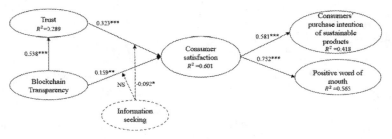

Fig. 1. Structural model results

6 Discussion

This study's results present several key findings. First, our study's findings highlight the considerable impact of blockchain transparency on consumer satisfaction, implying that disclosure of product sustainability related information on the blockchain increases consumer satisfaction. This result is consistent with prior literature which has validated the significant impact of blockchain transparency on consumer satisfaction [23]. This transparency fosters consumer satisfaction with the sustainability of the product which encourages them to adopt sustainable consumption behavior. Prior scholarly findings endorsed the causal nexus of transparency and satisfaction [22, 23]. This contrasts with the traditional environment without blockchain, where consumers would not use a product if they are not satisfied with its sustainability [28]. Such breakthroughs suggest that consumers value information offered through transparent and traceable systems.

Second, we delved deeper into the findings to investigate the signaling effect of blockchain technology through which it encourages sustainable consumption behavior. We found that the trust that consumers place in blockchain due to its transparency is aligned with the prior findings, suggesting the importance of overall transparency for establishing trust [20]. Since blockchain transparency signals trust, consumers can observe and verify the company's claim on sustainability. Such as this is realized through the verification of certificates that the third party granted to acknowledge the company's sustainable practices, for example, organic certifications [41]. This signaling impact becomes apparent when the problem of information asymmetry is resolved between consumers and producers, removing forgery suspicions. Consequently, consumers get satisfied with products' sustainability and eventually engage in sustainable consumption since they trust the information is indisputable. Hence, our study findings align with signaling theory [8], and prior findings [24], highlighting blockchain transparency as a trust building mechanism and promoting sustainable consumption.

Third, the study findings highlighted that the association between trust and consumer satisfaction is adversely moderated by information seeking behavior. We found this reasonable on the grounds of prior findings. First, many individuals lack digital information literacy, potentially leading to omitting vital details or retrieving inaccurate information through internet searches [42]. Second, the increased tendency of information seeking may result in information overload and conflicting information, such as 'reuse protects the environment' versus' reusable alternatives take more energy and generate greenhouse gas emissions', leaving the consumers perplexed. As a result, consumers overloaded with information are less confident, less satisfied, and more confused, dampening the relationship between trust and satisfaction.

7 Study Implications

7.1 Theoretical Implications

This study contributes in several ways. First, the study contributes to signaling theory highlighting the blockchain's signaling effect in terms of trustworthy information disclosure on product's sustainability. The results show that blockchain transparency signals the veracity of the company's sustainability claims. Second, prior literature has mainly covered blockchain for inbound supply chains. This study adds to the consumer research by exploring the individual consumers' perspective of blockchain, precisely when they are to make sustainable consumption decisions. The findings showed how consumers react to the blockchain based sustainability related product information and are likely to be satisfied when they believe blockchain is trustworthy. To decide on sustainable consumption, this study disclosed a mechanism through which blockchain facilitates consumers' decision making. This finding could lead to further intriguing exploration of signal effectiveness by examining the time and effort consumers will use to determine product sustainability through blockchain. Third, we identified that information seeking consumers might not be able to fully trust the mechanism owing to the conflicting information accessible from many sources, information overload, or lack of internet skills. This offers some observable prepositions on the consumers' sustainable beliefs in the event when they encounter insufficient or conflicting information from many other conventional sources as well as blockchain.

7.2 Practical Implications

Based on the study findings, this study presents some practical implications for managers and practitioners. First, it highlights that consumers trust blockchain based information due to its transparency. Managers can strategize the information disclosure using blockchain in a way that reduces information asymmetry between producer and consumer. Second, given that the consumers are exposed to a diversity of information from different sources, managers should consider the pertinent information available on other sources when maximizing the blockchain signaling effect. This will be beneficial in two ways: 1) they will be able to connect their sustainability claims with the sustainability policy framework, and 2) they could refute any contradicting information accessible from other sources to lessen its negative impact. As a result, the blockchain's signaling effect would be strengthened. Third, managers should coordinate with the designers to decide what sustainability related information should be presented in what way so that consumers can readily comprehend it and do not feel overloaded with the information. This will assist managers in considering and evaluating the relative observability and cost of blockchain signals to improve signal effectiveness.

8 Conclusion and Future Work

This study highlighted how blockchain signals work (i.e., the disclosure of trustworthy product sustainability-related information) to encourage sustainable consumption behavior (i.e., satisfying consumers' sustainability concerns leading to purchase intention). The findings emphasized the significance of blockchain signaling impact. In particular, blockchain transparency is the in-built mechanism that signifies the trustworthiness of product sustainability through transparent information disclosure and influencing consumers' decisions. However, we found that the tendency of information seeking might stifle the link between trust and sustainability. This could be due to information overload or a lack of information search skills.

Despite the nuanced findings, this study has some limitations that prospective research efforts could overcome. First, to examine the signaling effect, this study model only considered blockchain transparency and ignored other crucial aspects of blockchain, such as immutability and decentralization. Future scholars can consider other blockchain characteristics to validate the blockchain signaling effect. Next, given the early phases of blockchain development, this study undertook an exploratory step to assess how consumers perceive blockchain while making a decision. Future studies are encouraged to perform more systematic surveys with a bigger and wider population in order to generalize these findings.

References

1. White, K., Habib, R., Hardisty, D.J.: How to SHIFT consumer behaviors to be more sustainable: a literature review and guiding framework. J. Mark. **83**(3), 22–49 (2019)
2. Chen, Y.-S., Chang, C.-H.: Greenwash and green trust: the mediation effects of green consumer confusion and green perceived risk. J. Bus. Ethics **114**, 489–500 (2013)

3. Sodhi, M.S., Tang, C.S.: Research opportunities in supply chain transparency. Prod. Oper. Manag. **28**(12), 2946–2959 (2019)
4. Khan, S.A., Mubarik, M.S., Kusi-Sarpong, S., Gupta, H., Zaman, S.I., Mubarik, M.: Blockchain technologies as enablers of supply chain mapping for sustainable supply chains. Bus. Strateg. Environ. **31**(8), 3742–3756 (2022)
5. Hastig, G.M., Sodhi, M.S.: Blockchain for supply chain traceability: business requirements and critical success factors. Prod. Oper. Manag. **29**(4), 935–954 (2020)
6. Shen, B., Dong, C., Minner, S.: Combating copycats in the supply chain with permissioned blockchain technology. Prod. Oper. Manag. **31**(1), 138–154 (2022)
7. Liu, H., Ma, R., He, G., Lamrabet, A., Fu, S.: The impact of blockchain technology on the online purchase behavior of green agricultural products. J. Retail. Consum. Serv. **74**, 103387 (2023)
8. Spence, M.: Job market signaling: uncertainty in economics, pp. 281–306. Elsevier (1978)
9. Zhu, S., Song, M., Lim, M.K., Wang, J., Zhao, J.: The development of energy blockchain and its implications for China's energy sector. Resour. Policy **66**, 101595 (2020)
10. Herlihy, M., Moir, M.: Enhancing accountability and trust in distributed ledgers (2016). arXiv preprint arXiv:1606.07490
11. Yang, W., Aghasian, E., Garg, S., Herbert, D., Disiuta, L., Kang, B.: A survey on blockchain-based internet service architecture: requirements, challenges, trends, and future. IEEE Access **7**, 75845–75872 (2019)
12. Dal Mas, F., Massaro, M., Ndou, V., Raguseo, E.: Blockchain technologies for sustainability in the agrifood sector: a literature review of academic research and business perspectives. Technol. Forecast. Soc. Chang. **187**, 122155 (2023)
13. Guo, S., Sun, X., Lam, H.K.: Applications of blockchain technology in sustainable fashion supply chains: Operational transparency and environmental efforts. IEEE Trans. Eng. Manag. **70**(4), 1312–1328 (2020)
14. Sun, M., Tyagi, R.K.: Product fit uncertainty and information provision in a distribution channel. Prod. Oper. Manag. **29**(10), 2381–2402 (2020)
15. Michael, S.: Job market signaling. Q. J. Econ. **87**, 354–374 (1973)
16. Connelly, B.L., Certo, S.T., Ireland, R.D., Reutzel, C.R.: Signaling theory: a review and assessment. J. Manag. **37**(1), 39–67 (2011)
17. Ahmed, W.A., MacCarthy, B.L.: Blockchain-enabled supply chain traceability–How wide? How deep? Int. J. Prod. Econ. **263**, 108963 (2023)
18. Brach, S., Walsh, G., Shaw, D.: Sustainable consumption and third-party certification labels: consumers' perceptions and reactions. Eur. Manag. J. **36**(2), 254–265 (2018)
19. Xu, D., Dai, J., Paulraj, A., Chong, A.Y.-L.: Leveraging digital and relational governance mechanisms in developing trusting supply chain relationships: the interplay between blockchain and norm of solidarity. Int. J. Oper. Prod. Manag. **42**(12), 1878–1904 (2022)
20. Babich, V., Hilary, G.: OM Forum—Distributed ledgers and operations: what operations management researchers should know about blockchain technology. Manuf. Serv. Oper. Manag. **22**(2), 223–240 (2020)
21. Bai, C., Sarkis, J.: A supply chain transparency and sustainability technology appraisal model for blockchain technology. Int. J. Prod. Res. **58**(7), 2142–2162 (2020)
22. Kshetri, N.: 1 Blockchain's roles in meeting key supply chain management objectives. Int. J. Inf. Manag. **39**, 80–89 (2018)
23. Francisco, K., Swanson, D.: The supply chain has no clothes: technology adoption of blockchain for supply chain transparency. Logistics, **2**(1), 2 (2018)
24. Shin, D., Hwang, Y.: The effects of security and traceability of blockchain on digital affordance. Online Inf. Rev. **44**(4), 913–932 (2020)

25. Kim, D.J., Ferrin, D.L., Rao, H.R.: A study of the effect of consumer trust on consumer expectations and satisfaction: the Korean experience. In: Book A Study of the Effect of Consumer Trust on Consumer Expectations and Satisfaction: The Korean Experience, pp. 310–315 (2003). (2003, edn.)

26. Shin, D., Bianco, W.T.: In blockchain we trust: does blockchain itself generate trust? Soc. Sci. Q. **101**(7), 2522–2538 (2020)

27. Wu, H.-C., Wei, C.-F., Tseng, L.-Y., Cheng, C.-C.: What drives green brand switching behavior? Mark. Intell. Plan. **36**(6), 694–708 (2018)

28. Dhir, A., Talwar, S., Sadiq, M., Sakashita, M., Kaur, P.: Green apparel buying behaviour: a stimulus–organism–behaviour–consequence (SOBC) perspective on sustainability-oriented consumption in Japan. Bus. Strateg. Environ. **30**(8), 3589–3605 (2021)

29. Wang, J., Wang, S., Xue, H., Wang, Y., Li, J.: Green image and consumers' word-of-mouth intention in the green hotel industry: the moderating effect of Millennials. J. Clean. Prod. **181**, 426–436 (2018)

30. Karim, R.A., Rabiul, M.K.: The relationships of corporate sustainability, customer loyalty, and word of mouth: the mediating role of corporate image and customer satisfaction. J. Qual. Assurance Hosp. Tour. 1–21 (2022)

31. Chen, Y.-S., Lin, C.-L., Chang, C.-H.: The influence of greenwash on green word-of-mouth (green WOM): the mediation effects of green perceived quality and green satisfaction. Qual. Quant. **48**, 2411–2425 (2014)

32. Oliver, J.D., Lee, S.H.: Hybrid car purchase intentions: a cross-cultural analysis. J. Consum. Mark. **27**(2). 96–103 (2010)

33. Matthes, J., Wonneberger, A., Schmuck, D.: Consumers' green involvement and the persuasive effects of emotional versus functional ads. J. Bus. Res. **67**(9), 1885–1893 (2014)

34. Boesen, S., Bey, N., Niero, M.: Environmental sustainability of liquid food packaging: is there a gap between Danish consumers' perception and learnings from life cycle assessment? J. Clean. Prod. **210**, 1193–1206 (2019)

35. Lin, P.-C., Huang, Y.-H.: The influence factors on choice behavior regarding green products based on the theory of consumption values. J. Clean. Prod. **22**(1), 11–18 (2012)

36. Zelbst, P.J., Green, K.W., Sower, V.E., Bond, P.L.: The impact of RFID, IIoT, and Blockchain technologies on supply chain transparency. J. Manuf. Technol. Manag. **31**(3), 441–457 (2020)

37. Shin, D.-H.: The effects of trust, security and privacy in social networking: a security-based approach to understand the pattern of adoption. Interact. Comput. **22**(5), 428–438 (2010)

38. Park, E., Kim, K.J.: An integrated adoption model of mobile cloud services: exploration of key determinants and extension of technology acceptance model. Telemat. Inform. **31**(3), 376–385 (2014)

39. Michaelidou, N., Hassan, L.M.: The role of health consciousness, food safety concern and ethical identity on attitudes and intentions towards organic food. Int. J. Consum. Stud. **32**(2), 163–170 (2008)

40. Hair, J.F., Hult, G.T.M., Ringle, C.M., Sarstedt, M., Thiele, K.O.: Mirror, mirror on the wall: a comparative evaluation of composite-based structural equation modeling methods. J. Acad. Mark. Sci. **45**, 616–632 (2017)

41. Wang, Z., Li, M., Lu, J., Cheng, X.: Business Innovation based on artificial intelligence and Blockchain technology. Inf. Process. Manag. **59**(1), 102759 (2022)

42. Roscoe, R.D., Grebitus, C., O'Brian, J., Johnson, A.C., Kula, I.: Online information search and decision making: effects of web search stance. Comput. Hum. Behav. **56**, 103–118 (2016)

Understanding the Challenges Surrounding Decentralized Applications: An Empirical Study

Anastasiia Gurzhii[1]([✉]) [ID], Najmul Islam[1] [ID], and Venkata Marella[2] [ID]

[1] LUT University, 53850 Lappeenranta, Finland
anastasiia.gurzhii@lut.fi
[2] Open University, Heerlen, 6419 AT Heerlen, Limburg, The Netherlands

Abstract. As the Blockchain gains prominence as a disruptive technology, there has been a rapid growth in the number of decentralized applications (dApps) built on them. Despite the growing number and importance of dApps, we still know very little about the success factors surrounding such applications. While the existing research is primarily focused on the creation and development of dApps, very little research is dedicated to the challenges from dApps developers' perspective. We addressed these issues in the paper by collecting data by means of individual discussions with technical people. The purpose of this collection is to map, classify, and describe the challenges surrounding dApps to help organizations make adequate decisions regarding decentralized applications' development and promotion. We identified five dimensions of challenges and proposed a framework to describe dApps management and highlight how identified factors influence such applications' adoption.

Keywords: decentralized applications · dApps · developers · challenges

1 Introduction

Over recent years, the growth and rapid development of information and communication technologies disrupted existing business organizations. Blockchain, hailed as one of the most disruptive technologies of recent decades, promises organizations to transform from centralized governance to a decentralized approach [1]. After Satoshi Nakamoto introduced Bitcoin in 2008, the interest in blockchain technology rapidly increased both in industry and academia [2]. The main features of blockchain that attract organizations are decentralization, immutability, and transparency [3, 45]. As blockchain-based platforms gain momentum, decentralized applications (dApps) are becoming increasingly popular nowadays.

Existing research (e.g., [4–6, 43, 44]) in dApps is mostly focused on creating decentralised applications, providing development guidelines and strategies, or discussing such applications' benefits. However, there is little empirical evidence and understanding of the existing challenges and barriers related to dApps adoption from developers' perspective and only a few studies covered this dimension [7, 8]. To fill this gap, this

© IFIP International Federation for Information Processing 2023
Published by Springer Nature Switzerland AG 2023
M. Janssen et al. (Eds.): I3E 2023, LNCS 14316, pp. 277–293, 2023.
https://doi.org/10.1007/978-3-031-50040-4_21

study aims to contribute to the literature by identifying the most common challenges in dApps. Consequently, we address the following two research questions.

RQ1. What are the common challenges surrounding existing dApps adoption from the developers' perspective?

RQ2. How those obstacles should be overcome to increase the global adoption of dApps?

In order to answer the above research questions, we collected data from 14 decentralized applications developers. We analyzed the collected data using the GIOIA method [9]. The findings suggest that the dApps ecosystem is still in its infancy and widespread adoption is limited. Our paper contributes to the literature in two main dimensions. First, we empirically identify existing challenges surrounding existing dApps development and promotion by collecting data from developers. Second, we provide a conceptual framework for dApps management [10, 11] that can guide developers during the process of blockchain-based applications creation and future promotion on the market.

The remaining part of the paper is structured as follows: in Sect. 2, we shed light on the open blockchain platforms for dApps development and various types of decentralized applications. Section 3 focuses on the research methodology and data analysis. In Sect. 4, we summarize our findings that include observed challenges and a framework that unites various concepts which have an impact on further dApps development, followed by the discussion in Sect. 5. Finally, in Sect. 6, we provide conclusions of the study along with its limitations.

2   Background

Decentralized systems are mainly used to create fault-tolerant distributed computing systems where authority can be distributed without relying on a centralized system [12]. As the first application of blockchain, Bitcoin [2] contributed to the global popularity of the technology and made the world aware of its benefits. Blockchain can be described as a distributed system and a data structure that is arranged as a continuously growing chain of blocks [13]. It is open, allowing anyone to read the information. Various blockchain platforms have been developed over the last decade and since there are many technical features required to implement blockchain technology, choosing the right blockchain platform for a particular application can be a challenge [13]. For example, scalability, security, and cheap transaction costs are the most important issues to be considered. Gariga et al. [14] focused on the most popular public blockchains (e.g., Ethereum, Cardano) and their features namely cost, consistency, security, functionality, etc.

An application operating on a blockchain network is known as a decentralized application. Hence, dApps take advantage of the main blockchain characteristics: transparency, reliability, and data immutability [15]. Antal et al. [16] provided a detailed guideline for dApps application architecture design and implementation steps. Among the main features of such applications is the possibility to run on a distributed network, securely store information, and substantially protect the privacy of users. Decentralized programs, like mobile apps, generally have a user-friendly interface and nowadays the UX is straightforward. The application layer only handles user registration, transactions, queries, and other routine tasks [17]. The fundamental layer is made up of smart contracts created by developers and the code is written in special programming languages.

In other words, once developers have released their software into the public domain, no one can ever change the logic of the program [18, 44]. Pure decentralization can be achieved only if all the data is stored and all processes are handled in the blockchain and a dApp must be protected by a cryptographic token. This means that data and records must be publicly available and not operate under the control of a single person or group [15]. Nevertheless, modern dApps are far away from full decentralization. Wu et al. [19] described 3 types of architecture in DAPPs. The first type is a direct architecture where users interact directly with smart contracts and blockchain (e.g., NFT marketplaces). The second type of architecture has back-end services on a centralized server, and users communicate with smart contracts via the server (e.g., cryptocurrency hardware wallets). Finally, mixed architecture DApps are the combination of the previous 2 types, where users interact with smart contracts both directly and indirectly via a back-end server (e.g., GameFi domain).

At the same time, the prior literature is focused on the technical features of blockchain technology to take into consideration. The importance of providing safe management of personal clients' data creates a broad discussion about on-chain and off-chain data storage [20, 21]. On-chain storage involves storing data directly on the blockchain and has limitations such as finite capacity, scalability challenges, and increased transaction costs for large data volumes. While, off-chain storage utilizes external systems like centralized databases or cloud storage, offering scalability and efficiency advantages. Combining both storage methods is common, with critical data stored on-chain for trust and transparency, while larger or complex data is stored off-chain for scalability. Additionally, some research (e.g., [22, 23]) discusses the importance of business models in dApps. Unlike traditional centralized models, dApps leverage the decentralized nature of blockchain technology and create new models on the market that have never existed before. These applications offer diverse revenue streams, including tokenomics, subscription-based models, licensing fees, or transactional charges for accessing their services. Overall, the evolving landscape of business models in dApps showcases the potential for innovative and sustainable approaches that can disrupt traditional industries and create new economic paradigms.

3   Methodology

3.1   Data Collection and Participants

Our goal was to collect respondents that have development experience and can give comments from various perspectives regarding the technical side of blockchain and decentralized applications. To collect empirical data, we identified several active open groups on social networks (e.g., Twitter, Discord, and Telegram). Over there we found 14 current blockchain developers from various countries who are currently working on the creation or the decentralized applications testing. We interviewed these 14 blockchain experts. The interviews contained 3 major themes: 1. basic overview of the decentralized applications and the current situation on the market; 2. challenges associated with the development and adoption processes; 3. obstacles that hinder dApps global adoption. The background of some respondents is not only technical but additionally covers business, marketing and interface design domains.

3.2 Data Analysis

To analyze the collected data and classify issues we used the Gioia method [9]. The data analysis contained three main stages. First, we repeatedly looked over the collected empirical data and assigned codes to describe various content parts. Table 1 presents the codes that were produced at this point along with the relevant data quotations. Second, we classified the linked codes to create more abstract notions, also referred to as second-order concepts. Third, we combined the second-order ideas into five broader dimensions: infrastructure, limited resources of users, limited resources of developers, mechanics of a project, and governmental regulations. Figure 1 shows the dimensions together with the related sub-dimensions. In Table 1 we present 2nd and 1st-order concepts with example quotes.

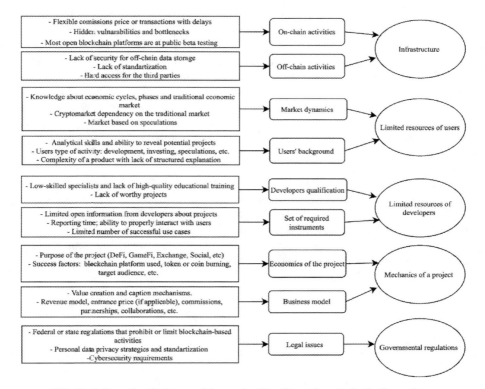

Fig. 1. Influencing factors on dApps adoption dimensions and sub-dimensions

At the same time, in Table 1 we present some quotes from experts that were extracted from the interview data and place them according to the dimensions identified earlier.

Table 1. Key concepts and associated codes with examples

2nd order concept	Example code/1st ordefr concept	Example quote
Scalability and stability challenges	Switching off transactions for a while; more than 24 h transactions delay	*"It is easy to suspend transactions in various blockchains. I missed a couple of good opportunities because of those limitations"* *"The network can be easily overloaded if the number of users increases. There are still complexities to achieve a perfect scalability level"*
Absence of additional services standards; on-chain and off-chain data storage	Personal data collection (e.g./e-mail address, locations), payment systems connection (e.g., bank transfers or card payments)	*"I've heard a lot of stories about the data and assets leak. It happens because of smart contacts' insecurities, manipulations from dishonest teams or a targeted attack on Access Control. A developer downloaded a new job invasion that was a virus file and this resulted in a millions dollar loss of assets for users... external solutions are full of vulnerabilities"* *"I have a secured e-mail address and a phone number that is not associated with me. Transactions in blockchain are visible to everyone, while sensitive data is stored on other servers and can be compromised one day"*

(*continued*)

Table 1. *(continued)*

2nd order concept	Example code/1st ordefr concept	Example quote
Easy access for the market for everyone	Potentially scam projects, the stolen ideas, lack of experience that can make an interesting project unnoticed, focus on financial products	*"I've been on the market since 2018 and have seen too many projects. The sphere gives a lot of opportunities but, at the same time, unscrupulous developers hold most of the market"* *"Most projects do not have a normal community and developers easily make changes in the product when something goes wrong, especially at the early stage"* *"The majority of projects are just for speculations. They are created in a rush just for money and with basic on-chain analysis skills you can easily detect this"*
Traditional market economics	Dependency on the leading market (the USA), a sphere with a high risk	*"I always support my experience with analytical reports and it's foolish to expect that during the economic crisis, everything will be smooth here" (in dApps)* *"Even though I can create a full working project, there is still a limited number of potential clients… the industry is claimed as a high-risk one and nowadays (2022–2023) it is too vivid"*

(continued)

Table 1. (*continued*)

2nd order concept	Example code/1st ordefr concept	Example quote
Knowledge about the market among potential users	Lack of awareness about the market, following hype projects rather than potential ones	*"I am on the market since 2018. Even though it's 2022, I still see people that say, "Hey, I got scammed, can you help me?". I understand that the level of education around blockchain is still low. I always tell people that knowledge and a "cold head" is a key to success"* *"There is a lot of information about blockchain in the internet... but the majority have too limited knowledge about the technology"*
Market share and tokenomics of the project	Projects purpose, inner mechanics, speculations on price by big players, absence of open documentation	*"From the developer's perspective, there is still a reluctance to add explanatory text for complete beginners or some guidance for a smooth experience"* *"Developers should create more value out of the product than they do now. The key is in the mechanism, which must work properly, avoiding chaos and dead loops."*

(*continued*)

Table 1. (*continued*)

2nd order concept	Example code/1st ordefr concept	Example quote
Financial side and project's viability	Ways to attract create a revenue stream, collaborations with other successful companies, strong community	*"It is very important to permanently evolve alongside the market and understand the reasons for all changes for a long-term and effective market collaboration"* *"Whitepaper is something I always follow in the first place. Of course, there are a lot of other factors that attract me to a project but well-structured open documentation gives me more trust and is proof that developers are scrupulous to details"*
Set of government-based challenges worldwide that limit dApps adoption	Unclear position about blockchain; strict limitations; lack of from authorities; no government-based programs	*"Some regulations and clear government positions can simplify things. Better than uncertainties"* *"If we want to see a global dApps adoption there should be cases from governments… People tend to follow the majority and without governments, it is likely possible in a global sense. Internet adoption is a good example"*

4   Results

From our interviews, we found that blockchain and dApps in particular are surrounded by numerous challenges. We identified 5 main categories as we discussed them next.

4.1   Infrastructure

Despite the growing number of blockchain platforms, there is still no well-functioning infrastructure for dApps. For example, it is still tough to choose the right blockchain platform: some of them have expensive transactions (e.g., Ethereum), while the new ones can cause problems when scaling dramatically, provide a lack of stability or lose popularity with essential liquidity. Due to source data, and the general principle of transparency, the public nature of dApps, an on-chain structure offers hackers a unique opportunity to find and exploit vulnerabilities that would otherwise go undetected [15]. In addition to on-chain activities that are linked with bridges between blockchains and smart contract execution results, dApps rely on off-chain infrastructure (e.g., web interface, and backend servers to index data from a blockchain used). Oracles give blockchains the ability to interact with the real world for the first time and transfer information securely from a blockchain platform to external services [24]. This opens up a huge range of new possibilities, as smart contracts can now work with data from the real world. But our experts mentioned that existing off-chain storage alternatives do not have equivalent security and immutability as on-chain data storage. It is essential to make transactions faster, not overload blockchain networks, hide some details about transactions when privacy is required (e.g., special use cases such as private data healthcare according to legal regulations for data protection – GDPR [25]), and provide an ability to delete or modify sensitive data outside blockchain [16]. The respondents mentioned that developers solve this problem independently since there is no unified and standardized model.

There are several key issues with existing data storage [26] hard access for third parties (e.g., auditors), risk of disclosure by a malicious team member, storage of a cryptographic proof to the blockchain that the data was not modified since the last access and in frequently modified repositories processing of such keys can be burdensome, lack of uniform response time from various sources, etc. Hence, the infrastructure dimension has a huge impact on the dApps future growth and it is included in the final framework.

4.2 Limited Resources for Developers

Since the market is at the early stage, non-homogenous and non-regulated, there are a lot of low-skilled developers with substandard projects. Hence, most people consider it as an opportunity for speculation. Respondents mentioned that dApp projects can be classified into cutting-edge and moderate. Cutting-edge projects can improve existing ecosystems with their ideas or even ground-breaking, while moderate ones do not provide innovative ideas, use open-source data of similar projects and may quickly lose popularity. At the same time, a lot of dApps lack good open documentation or even its absence. While brochures and other marketing materials can be flashy and include obvious sales pitches, a whitepaper [27] is designed to provide convincing and factual/technical evidence that a particular proposal is a superior method of solving a problem or challenge. Experts are sure that well-written open documentation with a roadmap can be among the most important features to take into consideration before using the app and showing the qualifications of a team. The respondents mentioned a lot of important elements of good documentation and we grouped them into 6 categories: 1. The project value from customers' perspective; 2. A relevant format with FAQ, guidelines, overviews, and analysis; 3. Writing style and literacy (preferably in English); 4. Readability and attractive design; 5. Sharing in various open resources (e.g., social networks). 6. Relevant information about the team, investors and other interested parties. In the technical documentation of the project, developers describe how their platform works, talk about the protocols used in the blockchain, and what problems their project solves.

Additionally, from the technical side, the smart contracts' immutability makes dApp design particularly difficult when the experience in the sphere is limited. Developers need to plan the whole process carefully from the beginning and ensure that future applications are consistent with decentralized applications. However, lack of knowledge about smart contracts' programming languages results in failures during the execution, security, and privacy issues that attract most hackers. Smart contracts audits show various errors at different levels and according to recent research [28], 40% of smart contract developers indicated the existence of vulnerabilities in the code. Overall, a lack of good educational programs or advanced training courses leads to low educational levels and unwillingness to improve skills.

In general, we found that the project can be easily listed without a proper audit and testing. This happens due to the costly audit process for small teams and code protection is not a paramount concern for the majority. Therefore, when the number of users grows, the load on each member of the team increases and negatively affects the project management at the company, individual and institutional levels (e.g., [10]). From the end user's perspective, dApps should not differ much from traditional applications from the usability side as well as problem resolving by the team.

4.3 Limited Resources for Users

Overall, respondents mentioned that most people consider all blockchain-related activities as a high-risk investment and a dependency on the traditional stock market. The main indicator of the crypto market is Bitcoin as the leading coin [29]. Currently, its correlation with stock indexes (especially S&P500 or NASDAQ) is a benchmark of market reaction. Additional factors include the exchange balance of the coin, transaction volume and the outflow of exchange capital [30]. Therefore, considering the most popular dApps categories, in the bearish market most people are less likely to use blockchain-based applications because of the market volatility, limited knowledge and concerns about the market potential. In the bullish market, the level of interest among potential users is high with fear of missing out on the high revenue and a lot of new projects emerge. Our interviewees mentioned that most new projects are gaining momentum for a short period and during our short-time analysis, we saw how some projects rose rapidly against the market and also lost their value instantly. Additionally, experts mentioned that the Defi sector offers a lot of possibilities and attracts users (e.g. P2P crypto exchange, coins staking, trading, mining, etc.). But as usual, manipulations by "big players" in every dApps category are significant which makes the whole industry more unpredictable rather than a traditional market.

At the same time, the more dApps developed, the more scams and high-risk projects emerged [1]. We noticed that a lot of users are not fully aware of blockchain technology, cannot analyse projects, and follow hype trends without a proper understanding of the inner mechanics. However, the market is dynamic and regular people are not able to follow all trends simultaneously without research. In this case, our experts strongly believe that individuals who have had unpleasant experiences with blockchain technology in the past would be hesitant to engage with any blockchain-based activities in the future, exercising an increased amount of caution.

An additional serious barrier for users is the complex procedure for account creation (e.g., wallet tools installation, data import, personal wallet creation with remembering seed phrases or private keys, gaining tokens for every particular blockchain (e.g., ETH for Ethereum) that requires knowledge and additional skills. Therefore our experts are sure that complex strategies are not very convenient for complete beginners, as most people are, while the ultimate goal of dApps should be an open, decentralized product that is available to everyone [31].

4.4 DApps Mechanics

Traditional apps are based on a robust business model where the companies develop them purposefully, emphasizing usability. But dApps tend to be developed by the community, lacking the essential resources (e.g., deep knowledge of the market, ability to create good project tokenomics, maintain stable transactions inside apps, collaborations with well-known and trusted brands, etc.) that traditional enterprise apps have. This means that the most popular business models are social or community-based, where success is determined by the activity of the users involved. Nevertheless, taking into consideration the GameFi sector, which holds more than half of active users [32], the business model can be described using a Ponzi scheme [33] or financial pyramid. The income system for members of the structure is created by constantly attracting funds from new members [3, 34].

Additionally, the main project token economics takes an important part in dApp mechanics. It describes the basic main features of various types of cryptocurrencies (e.g., demand or supply), studies the development mechanisms, and describes the rules that determine the development path of each currency's token [36]. The most valuable information includes token usage, launch with tokens model (inflationary or deflationary), distribution (how coins or tokens are mined, earned, and managed by the community), and supply schedule. This information can be used not only by active players but has a great impact on potential investors and speculators that may add value to the project.

4.5 Regulation Guidance

Last is regulation guidance and government involvement in the dApps market control. We revealed that countries are divided into four groups: 1. Loyal to the technology with governmental-level solutions, with low taxes (or without) on cryptocurrency transactions, with transparent laws and regulations of the industry and startups (e.g., Switzerland, Estonia, Japan, Germany, Sweden, etc.). 2. Less progressive than the first group but accept cryptocurrencies as a digital asset, have tax laws to regulate the sphere, less enthusiastic, trying to control somehow but do not prohibit any activities (e.g., Finland, France, Czech Republic, the USA, etc.). 3. Where blockchain is allowed only on the governmental level, strict regulations restrain and where regular citizens cannot easily access the market (e.g., China, Ecuador, Vietnam, Indonesia, Morocco, etc.). 4. Completely forbidden (e.g., North Macedonia, Iraq). Any uncertainties are because dApps offer significant opportunities alongside risks and concerns to regulators, investors, and financial markets. For example, because of their anonymity cryptocurrencies are widely used to make payments for criminal activities, such as money laundering, drug trafficking, and terrorist financing. Therefore, governments cannot agree on the international status of blockchain technology and blockchain-related activities. This, on the other hand, gives the industry an advantage over the developers of traditional applications.

Finally, taking into consideration low-quality projects, they can be easily identified since all transactions are stored on the blockchain [20, 21]. But experts are sure that this requires a lot of additional work such as on-chain data collection, processing, and visualization which cannot be easily done by individuals without proper knowledge. Therefore, with an absence of control and regulations, users with a lack of knowledge will suffer from information asymmetry, fraud, and self-trading (e.g., NFT collections on dApp marketplaces).

5 Discussion

5.1 Conceptual Framework

Our research supplemented existing literature, and according to the collected evidence, we developed a framework that contains factors that influence the adoption of dApps. We presented the factors that affect dApps management, business models, and long-term outcomes that have direct implications for the future of dApps (Fig. 2).

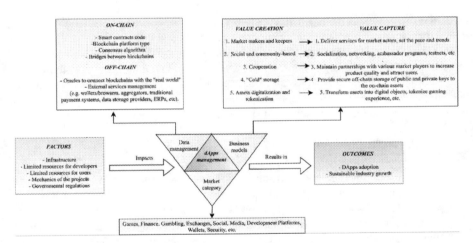

Fig. 2. Conceptual framework of dApps management

In the current study, we revealed 5 main challenges (Fig. 1) that affect the future of dApps adoption. Tallon et al. [35] describe such factors as antecedents and can be divided into external (e.g., regulations, infrastructure, limited resources for users) and internal (e.g., project mechanics and resources for developers). We found that all factors mentioned above have an impact on 16 market dApps categories (e.g., games, finance, wallets, etc.) [31]. For example, the mechanics of the project as an economic model contains the data on how tokens are distributed, in what proportions, the total supply of circulating coins, the price of the token on the launchpad, unlocks by rounds, etc. Hence, the capitalization of the project at the start should be low, it is calculated on the basis of the total sum of the project and the main emphasis with respect to the allocation of tokens should be the dominant area from which the project will work: the reserves and liquidity for DeFi, commissions for marketplaces, rewards for GameFi, etc. Resources for developers and users are limited in all categories and impact the further experience, while regulations are essential to reduce low-quality projects.

Data management in dApps depends on the complexity of the project, and the market category depends on the dApp architecture. Mixed and indirect types are divided into on-chain and off-chain, while direct includes only on-chain that relies on smart contracts [31]. The on-chain structure is most common for all dApps where the use of multiple blockchains with bridges can reduce the load on one network and provide faster transactions [24]. As it was mentioned before, sensitive data (e.g. phone numbers, e-mail addresses or even the customers' names) cannot be stored in blockchain. For this purpose, oracles were created to connect on-chain data with off-chain services. Some ideas from the developers' side include: *"If an oracle needs a reliable reputation, it can retrieve its data from multiple sources. In addition, when an on-chain contract makes a request, contracts are executed on several off-chain nodes as well"*. Connection with off-chain storages (external services) depends on the sphere and should be adapted according to the basic needs (e.g., traditional payment systems connection, extensions for browsers, data storage for personal clients' data)."*Among the options for how to move to blockchain is to connect existing systems with decentralized platforms. Nevertheless, there is no need to migrate the entire system to blockchain - only to identify areas where increased transaction speed, data protection and scalability are needed"*.

A lot of existing research is focused on business models in blockchain-based applications [10, 35, 37] but in the case of dApps, the data is limited. Business models that are mentioned in the current research are the basic methods that prevail in the majority of dApps. First, market makers and keepers may represent two types of dApps – innovators that set a trend in the sphere (e.g., CryptoKitties [34]) was the first blockchain-based game); and marketplaces with exchangers that act as an intermediary between market actors, systematize data, provide statistics, etc. Second, in "cold" storage value is created by connecting various blockchains to deliver completely decentralized access for users to their assets (e.g., SafePal wallet that helps to store assets and where the access can be restored only using a mnemonic phrase which is not available for any third parties). Third, the cooperation or partnership model is based on the shared experience with various projects to increase the number of active users (e.g., exchange platform Binance created a TrustWallet for "cold storage"). Nevertheless, the situation with partnerships is more ambiguous since those who are indicated in this role sometimes do not have any serious impact on the project. So, in low-grade projects, big projects (blockchains or marketplaces) can be indicated. Fourth, social and community-based as usual linked with other models and determines the success of a dApp on the market. The value is generated by active users that drive the industry forward by increasing the community size (e.g., Decentralend where users monetize their content and the project success is based on the number of active users). Fifth, assets digitalization and tokenization are linked with transferring physical property into digital objects (e.g., Brickken [38] dApp offers the infrastructure required for businesses to list their assets on the market, raise money on their own through securities offerings (STOs), and run DAOs in a compliant manner).

Currently, blockchain-related projects and dApps in particular evolve faster than standardization [11]. As a result, the industry evolves without the support of any international standards organization and complies individually with the regulations of various countries. For example, in Aave [39] management mechanism can be explained as follows: first, we can see that there is a precise distribution of responsibilities in the teams (e.g., CEO, the division into marketing, development, compliance, business, etc. departments) which leads to effective management where the area of responsibility corresponds to the area of employees' influence. The platform was created based on Ethereum which is among the most popular blockchains in the world and the POS consensus mechanism. Second, the project has huge and trusted investors, as well as collaborations with other successful projects from other market categories (e.g., Axie Infinity Game [40]). Third, for a better user experience, there is an active GitHub where important updates are provided regularly, the whole documentation is provided on the website and users can easily reach the team in a live chat with any possible issues. Finally, in the ranking of Coinmarketcap [41] in 2022, the Aave token ranks among the top 50. Therefore, since its launch in 2017, the project successfully covered institutional, company, and individual layers implementing the mechanisms mentioned earlier.

Finally, outcomes refer to the main consequences that are linked with dApps development and promotion. We identified 2 of them which are linked with long-term dApps performance. Adoption of blockchain and dApps in particular have a number of influencing factors such as social, organizational, user efficiency, technology characteristics, etc. [42]. Nevertheless, the research on this matter is essential in various industries, market categories, and counties as the result may vary across different domains. Sustainable industry growth leads to dApps promotion in various spheres since blockchain-based platforms can help to standardize and evaluate data, asset metrics and compliance (e.g., sustainability or ESG standards) [11]. A number of policies are needed to promote the development of blockchain-based solutions in a safe and fair manner.

5.2 Theoretical and Practical Implications

The paper has several theoretical contributions. First, even though there is a huge number of papers discussing challenges surrounding blockchain adoption [4–8, 43, 44] there is still limited feedback from the technical people's perspective surrounding dApps development and promotion. For example, Chiu and Meng [4] provided a detailed overview of a platform that can support the development of decentralized applications. Dao et al. [7] focused on challenges and strategies associated with decentralized applications development. Nevertheless, we found that prior research provides a broad overview of dApps. In research, we aim to fill the mentioned gaps and narrow the findings.

Second, we found up-to-date challenges surrounding the modern and rapidly growing industry from the developer's perspective. Under these concepts, we have identified five dimensions: infrastructure, limited resources for users, limited resources for developers, mechanics of the project and regulations guidance. We divide impact factors into 3 levels to explain the most crucial ones for practitioners to support future research. Third, under the prior research, we identified that there is no clear answer to how to create successful dApps and promote them. We collected and expanded the existing knowledge using the interview data with experts.

At the same time, we can identify 2 practical implications. First, as it was mentioned before the industry is at an early stage and companies that want to create dApps, make them fully operational and attract users should consider all potential challenges and overcome the most common obstacles. To support our findings, we conducted 14 interviews with experts from different countries during the research. Future research can expand our findings by considering a more extensive set of experts from various domains and countries. Second, we provide a conceptual framework based on the collected data from the experts and future validation through the case studies may broaden the findings.

6 Conclusions

The current research on existing dApps revealed the following conclusions. First, the existing sphere of decentralized applications or dApps is gaining momentum but still is not mature enough. Most people lack knowledge about blockchain technology, and scrupulous developers use this to create low-quality projects. Second, the lack of involvement from governments and the absence of standards creates a free area for low-quality projects. The current situation allows low-budget teams to show their potential and win market share in various categories. Third, uneven progress is still progress. The deeper insight into the market reveals that there are many directions for improvement, and we found a surprisingly small group of people involved in the development process of a quality product. Fourth, the level of maturity of dApps' UX is somewhere between "hostile to users" and "developer-centric", but not "user-centric" at all. It takes years for this area to reach full maturity and there are a lot of improvements.

Among the main limitations of the study is that we did not focus on the respondents' location since some of them do not permanently reside in one country and have a different experience with regulators. Additionally, we mostly focused on challenges and gaps rather than the benefits of the adoption. Further research can be linked with data privacy and frameworks that comply with existing legal regulations, ways how to increase awareness and acceptance levels among users, and some technical features of dApps (e.g., what are the main steps of blockchain-based applications development, how to keep synchronization on-chain and off-chain, how to increase the performance of such application or focus on frameworks both for private and public solutions). Additionally, more detailed and targeted research on business models in blockchain-based applications may complement the findings and expand the conclusions of this research. The results of the current study can be validated among users from one particular country.

References

1. Pinna, A., Baralla, G., Lallai, G., Marchesi, M., Tonelli, R.: Design of a sustainable blockchain-oriented software for building workers management. Front. Blockchain 3 (2020)
2. Nakamoto, S.: Bitcoin: a peer-to-peer electronic cash system. SSRN Electron. J. (2008)
3. Zheng, Z., Xie, S., Dai, H.N., Chen, X., Wang, H.: Blockchain challenges and opportunities: a survey. Int. J. Web Grid Serv. 14, 352 (2018)
4. Chiu, W.-Y., Meng, W.: DevLeChain - an open blockchain development platform for decentralized applications. In: 2022 IEEE International Conference on Blockchain (Blockchain) (2022)

5. Teisserenc, B., Sepasgozar, S.M.: Software architecture and non-fungible tokens for digital twin decentralized applications in the built environment. Buildings **12**, 1447 (2022)
6. Hainey, T., Baxter, G.: Selecting a software or games development life cycle methodology. Writing Successful Undergraduate Dissertations in Games Development and Computer Science, pp. 98–110 (2022)
7. Dao, T.C., Nguyen, B.M., Do, B.L.: Challenges and strategies for developing decentralized applications based on blockchain technology. In: Barolli, L., Takizawa, M., Xhafa, F., Enokido, T. (eds.) Advanced Information Networking and Applications. AINA 2019. AISC, vol. 926, pp. 952–962. Springer, Cham (2020). https://doi.org/10.1007/978-3-030-15032-7_80
8. Ray, P.P.: WEB3: a comprehensive review on background, technologies, applications, zero-trust architectures, challenges and future directions. Internet Things Cyber-Phys. Syst. **3**, 213–248 (2023)
9. Gioia, D.A., Corley, K.G., Hamilton, A.L.: Seeking qualitative rigor in inductive research: notes on the Gioia methodology. Organ. Res. Methods **16**, 15–31 (2013)
10. Rikken, O., Janssen, M., Kwee, Z.: Governance challenges of blockchain and decentralized autonomous organizations. Inf. Polity **24**, 397–417 (2019)
11. König, L., Korobeinikova, Y., Tjoa, S., Kieseberg, P.: Comparing blockchain standards and recommendations. Future Internet **12**, 222 (2020)
12. Di Francesco Maesa, D., Mori, P.: Blockchain 3.0 applications survey. J. Parallel Distrib. Comput. **138**, 99–114 (2020)
13. Shrivas, M.: The disruptive blockchain: types, platforms and applications. Texila Int. J. Acad. Res. 17–39 (2019)
14. Garriga, M., Arias, M., De Renzis, A.: Blockchain and cryptocurrency: a comparative framework of the main architectural drivers. In: Proceedings of Sample Conference (2018)
15. Min, T., Cai, W.: Portrait of decentralized application users: an overview based on large-scale ethereum data. CCF Trans. Pervasive Comput. Interact. **4**, 124–141 (2022)
16. Antal, C., Cioara, T., Anghel, I., Antal, M., Salomie, I.: Distributed ledger technology review and decentralized applications development guidelines. Future Internet **13**, 62 (2021)
17. Zeng, Y., Zhang, Y.: Review of research on blockchain application development method. J. Phys. Conf. Ser. **1187**, 052005 (2019)
18. Khan, S.N., Loukil, F., Ghedira-Guegan, C., Benkhelifa, E., Bani-Hani, A.: Blockchain smart contracts: applications, challenges, and future trends. Peer-to-Peer Netw. Appl. **14**, 2901–2925 (2021)
19. Wu, K., Ma, Y., Huang, G., Liu, X.: A first look at blockchain-based decentralized applications. Softw. Pract. Exp. **51**, 2033–2050 (2019)
20. Zheng, P., Zheng, Z., Wu, J., Dai, H.-N.: On-chain and off-chain blockchain data collection. Blockchain Intell. 15–39 (2021)
21. Singh, S.: An introduction to "on-chain" analysis. https://www.blockstar.ch/post/an-introduction-to-on-chain-analysis/. Accessed 26 Dec 2022
22. Soares, R., Araújo, A., Rodrigues, G., Alencar, C.: Streaming platforms based on blockchain technology a business model impact analysis. In: Latifi, S. (ed.) ITNG 2023 20th International Conference on Information Technology-New Generations. ITNG 2023. AISC, vol. 1445, pp. 143–149. Springer, Cham (2023). https://doi.org/10.1007/978-3-031-28332-1_17
23. Tang, X., Guo, H., Li, H., Yuan, Y., Wang, J., Cheng, J.: A DAPP business data storage model based on blockchain and IPFS. In: Sun, X., Zhang, X., Xia, Z., Bertino, E. (eds.) Artificial Intelligence and Security. ICAIS 2021. LNCS, vol. 12737, pp. 219–230. Springer, Cham (2021). https://doi.org/10.1007/978-3-030-78612-0_18
24. Hepp, T., Sharinghousen, M., Ehret, P., Schoenhals, A., Gipp, B.: On-chain vs. off-chain storage for supply- and blockchain integration. it – Inf. Technol. **60**, 283–291 (2018)

25. Pabst, M.: General Data Protection Regulation (GDPR) – Official Legal Text, General Data Protection Regulation (GDPR). https://gdpr-info.eu/. Accessed 26 Dec 2022

26. Lopez-Pimentel, J.C., Rojas, O., Monroy, R.: Blockchain and off-chain: a solution for audit issues in supply chain systems. In: 2020 IEEE International Conference on Blockchain (Blockchain) (2020)

27. Zhang, S., Aerts, W., Lu, L., Pan, H.: Readability of token whitepaper and ICO first-day return. Econ. Lett. **180**, 58–61 (2019)

28. Wan, Z., Xia, X., Lo, D., Chen, J., Luo, X., Yang, X.: Smart contract security: a practitioners' perspective. In: 2021 IEEE/ACM 43rd International Conference on Software Engineering (ICSE) (2021)

29. Dubey, P.: Short-run and long-run determinants of bitcoin returns: transnational evidence. Rev. Behav. Financ. **14**, 533–544 (2022)

30. Iconic Holding: Value drivers of leading cryptocurrencies. https://iconicholding.com/value-drivers-of-cryptocurrencies/. Accessed 17 Dec 2022

31. Wu, K.: An empirical study of blockchain-based decentralized applications. In: Proceedings of ACM Conference (Conference'17). ACM, New York (2019)

32. Kraken Intelligence Archives. https://blog.kraken.com/kraken-intelligence/. Accessed 25 Sep 2022

33. Moore, T., Han, J., Clayton, R.: The postmodern Ponzi scheme: empirical analysis of high-yield investment programs. In: Keromytis, A.D. (ed.) Financial Cryptography and Data Security. FC 2012. LNCS, vol. 7397, pp. 41–56. Springer, Berlin, Heidelberg (2012). https://doi.org/10.1007/978-3-642-32946-3_4

34. Jiang, X.-J., Liu, X.F.: Cryptokitties transaction network analysis: the rise and fall of the first blockchain game mania. Front. Phys. **9** (2021)

35. Tallon, P.P., Ramirez, R.V., Short, J.E.: The information artifact in IT governance: toward a theory of information governance. J. Manag. Inf. Syst. **30**, 141–178 (2013)

36. Voshmgir, S.: Token economy: how the web3 reinvents the internet. BLOCKCHAINHUB BERLIN, S.l. (2020)

37. Kramarenko, A., Kvitka, A., Diachek, V., Davydov, D.: Cryptocurrencies in the global space: factors and prospects of promotion. In: SHS Web of Conferences, vol. 67, p. 06031 (2019)

38. Brickken Whitepaper. https://brickken.com/whitepaper/. Accessed 26 Nov 2022

39. Messari.io. Aave overview. https://messari.io/asset/aave/profile/technology. Accessed 16 Aug 2022

40. Delic, A.J., Delfabbro, P.H.: Profiling the potential risks and benefits of emerging "play to earn" games: a qualitative analysis of players' experiences with Axie Infinity. Int. J. Ment. Health Addict. (2022)

41. Coinmarketcap. AAVE price today, AAVE to USD Live, marketcap and Chart. https://coinmarketcap.com/currencies/aave/. Accessed 26 Dec 2022

42. Alazab, M., Alhyari, S., Awajan, A., Abdallah, A.B.: Blockchain technology in supply chain management: an empirical study of the factors affecting user adoption/acceptance. Clust. Comput. **24**, 83–101 (2020)

43. Li, Y.: Emerging blockchain-based applications and techniques. Serv. Oriented Comput. Appl. **13**, 279–285 (2019)

44. Udokwu, C., Anyanka, H., Norta, A.: Evaluation of approaches for designing and developing decentralized applications on blockchain. In: Proceedings of the 2020 4th International Conference on Algorithms, Computing and Systems (2020)

45. Sanka, A.I., Irfan, M., Huang, I., Cheung, R.C.C.: A survey of breakthrough in blockchain technology: adoptions, applications, challenges and future research. Comput. Commun. **169**, 179–201 (2021)

Leveraging Enterprise Architecture Artifacts for Digital Transformation: Some Preliminary Findings

Hong Guo[1]([⊠]) [iD] and Shang Gao[2] [iD]

[1] Anhi University, No. 111 Jiulong Road, Hefei, People's Republic of China
homekuo@gmail.com
[2] School of Business, Örebro University, Örebro, Sweden
shang.gao@oru.se

Abstract. The global wave of Digital Transformation (DT) requires a large number of organizations to effectively respond to relevant challenges, plan and manage changes by aligning organizational elements. Enterprise Architecture (EA), which has a history of about 50 years, is considered to be a good alignment approach. But its application is mainly limited to developed countries and large enterprises, partly due to its high threshold. To benefit more organizations that are not yet familiar with EA, this study suggests EA beginners to firstly attempt to benefit from EA Artifacts (EAAs) without knowing/using EA Frameworks (EAFs). We conducted a survey with students in a Chinese university who participated in an EA course to verify the significance and feasibility of this proposal. The results showed that EA beginners recognized the value of EAAs and were willing to learn relevant knowledge and skills such as modeling languages and tools. It was also found that EAFs brought considerable complexity and its necessity was not directly perceived by participants. It should be noted that for EA beginners, even if they only attempt to benefit from EAAs, certain knowledge and practical skills are required. Some practical tips such as providing coaching style support are suggested accordingly.

Keywords: Digital Transformation · DT · Enterprise Architecture · EA · EA artifacts · EA frameworks

1 Introduction

Digital Transformation (DT) has become a global trend [1]. DT means significant changes [1] and requires organizations to better understand and align various elements to respond to such changes [1].

There are several types of such approaches like business analysis frameworks (e.g., Porter's Five Forces), Enterprise Modeling (EM), Digital Management Information Systems (MIS), and unstructured graphic & textual architectures. They present different benefits and shortcomings. Enterprise Architecture (EA), with a history of around 50 years,

M. Janssen et al. (Eds.): I3E 2023, LNCS 14316, pp. 294–307, 2023.
https://doi.org/10.1007/978-3-031-50040-4_22

synergy benefits of such approaches and has been acknowledged to be an effective align-ment approach for Strategy Alignment (StrA) [2], Business-Information Technology Alignment (BITA) [3], Stakeholder Alignment (StaA), and etc.

But EA's application is mainly used in developed countries [4] and large enterprises due to its high threshold and other challenges. To benefit more organizations that are not yet familiar with EA, we propose EA beginners may firstly attempt to apply EA Artifacts (EAAs) without knowing/using EA Frameworks (EAFs).

Traditionally, EAF is almost synonymous and discussed together with EA, and the former is usually developed within the scope defined by the latter. But EAF is not theoretically inevitable. Actually, empirical studies showed that many organizations announced EAF usage but in practice only produced a set of discrete EAAs [5]. In [6], it showed that studied EA practice hardly resembled established EAFs. We hereby further propose that EA beginners are able to benefit from EA Artifacts (EAAs) without referring to specific EA Frameworks (EAFs).

To verify the feasibility and significance of this proposal, we conducted a survey study with students in a Chinese university who participated in an EA course. The rest of this article is structured as follows. We introduce some background information in Sect. 2 including organization requirements caused by digital transformation, extant alignment approaches, EA basics, and challenges for EA beginners. We propose our research questions afterwards. Then in Sect. 3, we introduce the research method. The results are presented in Sect. 4 and discussed in Sect. 5. Lastly, we conclude the paper, discuss the limitations and point out future research work in Sect. 6.

2   Background

In this section, we introduce what digital transformation means to organizations, and how EA helps organizations align elements. Further, we introduce the challenges of large-scale application of EA and why lowering the threshold is important. We raise research questions afterwards.

2.1   Digital Transformation Requires Effective Alignment Approaches

DT as a global trend means significant changes [1] and requires organizations to better understand and coordinate various elements to respond to such changes. In order to man-age (plan, design, implement and manage) such changes brought by DT, organizations are required to be able to align organizational elements with proper approaches.

Various organizational elements might need to be aligned. Alignment is often referred to but not limited to Strategic Alignment (how to implement strategies), Stakeholder Alignment (how different stakeholders collaborate), Digital projects alignment (how digital projects collaboratively support business goals), and Business and Information Technology Alignment (BITA). To summarize, the content of alignment includes key elements such as strategy, institutions, members, and IT assets in different domains and at different levels related to enterprise composition and operation.

Alignment, as a series of mechanisms, covers organizational processes not only including thinking and expression, but also subsequent communication, decision-making, actions, and maintenance.

2.2 EA, EA Artifacts and EA Frameworks

EA, which has a history of about 50 years, is considered to be a good alignment approach [3].

EA is often called the blueprint of an enterprise, which describes the core logic of organizations' composition and operation. EA includes high-level strategic and business architecture documents, so it theoretically includes business analysis frameworks such as Porter's Five Forces model. Moreover, EA also includes lower-level architectures that support such high-level architectures [7], such as business architecture and Information Technology (IT) architecture. They are usually based on best practices. Therefore, EA has good **comprehensiveness** and **prominence**.

EA is usually presented in a graphic way, but is strictly defined using meta-models which describe which concepts and relations among such concepts are presented in EA models. Therefore, EA can present a user-friendly interface like enterprise models do, and can also be digitized to leverage computing advantages. Therefore, EA has good **user-friendliness** and **computer-friendliness**.

EA at the highest level, is a collection of diverse EA Artifacts (EAAs). Or, in another word, the smallest deliverable of EA is EAA. EAA is a single document describing specific aspects of EA, such as value chain, business process, organizational structure, and digital project roadmap. It can be textual but more often graphical.

EAAs can be used separately. But often, they are used in sets, which can ensure alignment among artifacts and makes all EA documents work as an integrated whole. For this purpose, EA Frameworks (EAFs) are further invented. An EAF typically includes a content framework and a process framework. Content frameworks usually divide EA aspects into layers according to the degree of abstraction, and into domains according to different elements of interest. For example, one of the earliest frameworks, the Zachman EAF, used a 5 × 5 framework to classify relevant EA documents. A process framework generally specifies how to develop and maintain models defined by the content framework. For example, the best-known framework TOGAF defines a nine-step process named Architecture Development Method (ADM).

EAFs can be designed and used not only for a general purpose, but also for specific purposes such as security [8] or specific domains such as smart cities [9]. Organizations can choose existing EAFs or develop their own EAFs as needed. Some EAFs are hosted by international organizations/communities and have gradually matured over years of development. They are even worked as international standards, such as TOGAF. The existence of such frameworks greatly expanded the popularity and promotion of the EA discipline. TOGAF is so well-known that it has even become a synonym for EA. From this perspective, EA can be **integrated well** with many other well-known and open platforms, standards, and documents.

2.3 Challenges and Our Proposal

Although EA brings many benefits, especially alignment [3], EA applications do not always succeed [10]. EA has not been adopted in large-scale either. Such a situation might be caused by EA **challenges** (e.g., high threshold, high cost, and the difficulty to assess the benefits).

To solve such challenges, practitioners and researchers explored different solutions such as Business Objects Driven EA (BODEA) [11], on demand informal EA process [12, 13], scenario-based metamodels, and softened EA model requirements of completeness and rigor [14]. Such approaches lowered the cost and made it easier to evaluate the benefits of EA. However, the threshold to apply EA is high to many organizations. To address this issue, the mechanisms that EA realizes its benefits/values are questioned and examined.

Traditionally, EA's learning and application are usually assumed to be based on frameworks, partly due to the successful promotion of the most well-known TOGAF framework [15]. However, the value of EAFs is questioned. As explained in [18], EAFs tend to evaluate all aspects of an enterprise. However, this might not be inevitable. Some empirical studies also showed that many organizations practically developed discrete EAAs only for specific purposes. Following this direction, we argue that EA beginners might benefit from EAAs without claiming the use of EAFs.

To validate the feasibility and significance from EA beginners' perspective, we propose the following Research Questions (RQs). It should be noted that EA domain covers a large number of concepts which are abstract and have complex relationships in between, such as *framework* and *meta-model* (usually as one type of framework). It is often difficult for beginners to clearly distinguish the meaning of EA, EAAs and EAFs. Therefore, we do not highlight such different concepts in RQs, but refer to them as EA in general. Nevertheless, with the answers to RQ3, RQ4, and RQ5, we will be able to determine what participants assume EA means (EAAs, or EAAs and EAFs).

- RQ1: Which organizations might benefit from applying EA/EAAs?
- RQ2: Which benefits can EA beginners expect from learning EA/EAAs?
- RQ3: Which knowledge and skills should EA beginners have to apply EA/EAAs?
- RQ4: Which challenges are EA beginners facing to apply EA/EAAs?
- RQ5: How to enable EA beginners to benefit from applying EA/EAAs?

3   Methods

We conducted a survey with first-year undergraduate students enrolled in an EA course to obtain responses to these questions. After a semester of study, these students from different majors had learned some basic enterprise management knowledge, EA knowledge including basic concepts, use cases, frameworks, as well as EA modeling techniques in ArchiMate.

We assume that these students can be qualified as EA beginners in terms of educational level, limited knowledge about management and EA. In addition, these students might have a keen perception of the trend and needs of digital transformation, as they are born in the digital era.

The survey was distributed to students as one part of the final assessment of the course. The survey questions were developed based on the proposed research questions and adapted based on the background of the students and the course, and were written in Chinese. The students were sufficiently briefed about the purpose of this survey study. The students were informed that they can answer them open-ended without affecting their grades. By doing so, it is good that almost all participants provided written responses to almost all questions, with details and rationale.

We extracted information from the responses. We analyzed the information using the qualitative analysis method by following the five steps of thematic analysis [16]: 1) extracting data, 2) coding data, 3) translating codes into themes, 4) creating a model of higher-order themes, and 5) assessing the trustworthiness of the synthesis. We answer the questions accordingly.

4   Results

In early 2023, we conducted a survey with first-year undergraduate students who enrolled in an EA course at a Chinese university. A total of 37 people from 5 different majors (e.g., computer science, e-commerce), participated in the survey and provided written responses.

4.1   RQ1: Which Organizations Might Benefit from Applying EA/EAAs?

Twelve students answered this question from the perspective of the scale and field of the enterprise. They believe that established enterprises (1), traditional manufacturing enterprises (1), and emerging field enterprises (1) are potential customers. 2 students provided example industries such as aerospace, government, semiconductor, automobile and Industrial Internet. It is worth noting that when talking about large enterprises (3), some students added the qualifier "ready to start Digital transformation". When referring to SMEs, almost all students added qualifiers such as "those with good momentum" (1), "those in the network industry" (2), or "those who have begun to explore Digital transformation and EA" (2).

More students answered this question from the perspective of the needs of enterprises. Enterprises with business problems, innovation and transformation needs (12), or that are not making good progress in digital transformation (12) may potentially need EA. **Business problems** include "poor management", "asset coordination issues", "poor coordination between business and information technology", and "unclear processes that need to be optimized". **The needs for innovation or transformation** include "the existence of huge problems", "stagnation of development", "lack of innovation", "active pursuit of change", "eagerness to change the status quo", and "the lack of appropriate methods, paths, and tools for transformation or innovation". The situations where **digital progress is not good** include "facing some transformation difficulties and unable to balance efficiency and innovation", or "innovation is effective, with higher scale and profit pursuit", or "hoping to improve efficiency, enhance resource integration, and enhance competitiveness".

One student indicated that organizations might need EA if high executives feel interested in EA. Two students did not provide specific answers to this question.

To summarize, EA is thought to be meaningful for organizations that need to change their operational logic for various reasons. These reasons seem to have no specific limitations, whether they are passively facing challenges, actively hoping for innovation, planning to start transformation, or the transformation failing to meet expectations. This means that **the number of potential EAA beneficiaries is very large**.

However, two **premises** were indicated here. First, specific meaning should be identified. Or, what kind of changes should EA be applied to deal with? Is this change complex enough that there is no alternative solution to EA available? **Goals to apply EA should be clarified**. Second, it needs to be **cost-effective**, or, the corresponding costs need to be affordable. This is why participants recognized the needs of large enterprises, but for small and medium-sized enterprises with limited resources, EA may need more preconditions to make sense.

4.2   RQ2: Which Benefits Can EA Beginners Expect from Learning EA/EAAs?

In overall, participants described their benefits from multiple perspectives. Interestingly, a considerable number of participants pointed out that the learning of EA is very helpful to their way of thinking. This may help them understand and work for enterprises, and it is also very helpful for their career growth. The overview of the answers is shown in Fig. 1.

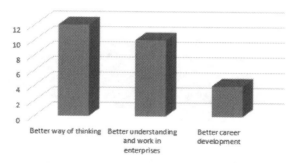

Fig. 1. Which benefits can EA beginners expect from learning EA/EAAs

As the figure shows, 12 students mentioned that learning EA improved their **way of thinking**. Such improvements might cover "macro coordination", "framework thinking", or "logic", "rationality", "rigor", "speculation", or "simplification" or "agile" thinking, or simply "enriching problem-solving thinking and perspectives". 4 other students believe that this is helpful for their cross-disciplinary growth (2), **career development** (1), or entrepreneurship (1).

10 students believe EA learning helped them to have a **full perspective on enterprises**. It helped them understand the different components of building an enterprise (5), understand the complexity of the enterprise (1), build an architecture suitable for the enterprise (1), realize digital transformation (5), adapt to changes in the times or maintain competitive advantage (3). EA learning can help them clarify their personal roles, improve their ability to collaborate with others and integrate themselves into the enterprise (1).

To summarize, in addition to the expected benefits to the organization, participants also clearly stated that learning EA would benefit their personal development, especially their thinking mode. We assume this will benefit organizations as well. On the one hand, for organizations, this is **how EA value starts to be realized**. Architects use EA to think first. Then they analyze, express, and further communicate and cooperate with other stakeholders with EA deliverables to realize changes and achieve expected benefits. On the other hand, this will establish positive EA reputation and enhance **the user base** of the organization's EA. It paves the way of EA understanding, EA knowledge and skills, improves organizations' ability to realize EA value, and the impression of EA. As user understanding [17] and engagement [18] has been thought as a significant issue corresponding to many EA failure projects. We assume that user base improvement is quite important.

4.3 RQ3: Which Knowledge and Skills Should EA Beginners Have to Apply EA/EAAs?

Compared to other research questions, responses to this one showed more concentrated opinions. As indicated in Fig. 2 and Fig. 3, 22 students believe that learning EAAs (5), EA languages (i.e., ArchiMate) (6), EA modeling (6), and EA tools (i.e., (5) are the most valuable knowledge and skills. These knowledge and skills have been introduced and practiced in the EA course around a series of EAA modeling exercises based on a case study.

In addition, students believe that learning EA composition (1), EA management methods (2), EA challenges(1), enterprise architects roles and responsibilities (1), IT strategic planning (1) are also valuable. It is worth noting that almost **no students mentioned EAFs**.

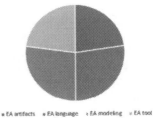

Fig. 2. What should be learned about EA

Fig. 3. What should be learned about EA modelling

To summarize, nearly 2/3 of the students pointed out that learning **EA modeling** knowledge and skills is the most important thing. This means that they can perceive the value of EA modeling work, and assume that the corresponding learning threshold can be overcome. Therefore, for EA beginners, **the threshold** for EA modeling, especially for EAAs modeling, might **not be quite high**. **The scope of learning** seems clear and direct, including EA language and EA tool knowledge, together with some general modeling techniques/skills. When talking about EAFs, their value seems indirect and is difficult to be perceived by beginners.

4.4 RQ4: Which Challenges Are EA Beginners Facing to Apply EA/EAAs?

Regarding the challenges encountered, 23 out of 37 participants indicated that understanding EA, especially EA relevant concepts, is challenging, as shown in Fig. 4 and

Fig. 5. On the one hand, they have never heard of EA before and everything is new to them (6). There are many concepts (4) which are cross domain (1), involving a wide range of things (2). On the other hand, these concepts are quite abstract (7), such as meta-model (1). Moreover, the relationships between concepts are complex (2) and prone to confusion (4).

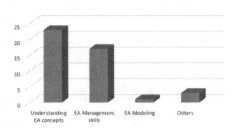

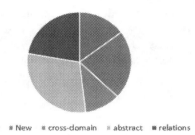

Fig. 4. What challenges do EA beginners have

Fig. 5. Why understanding EA concepts is challenging

Nearly half of the students thought that the flexible and practical part of EA is a great challenge (17/37). There is no standard answer (2), and EA needs to be "practices oriented", "combined with practical application" (1), and applied in a flexible way (1). Applying EA is not just an engineering task (1), but rather needs to consider the interests and needs of customers and other various people (3). It requires communication (2), coordination (1), decision-making (1), the use of management and political skills (2) and the "willingness of everyone to accept" (2).

In addition, few students pointed out that modeling skills (1), English requirements (1), especially the consistent translation of terms (1), and personal interest (1) are the main challenges they have faced.

When summarizing the answers to RQ4, it is interesting that although students think EA modeling is the most important part that they should learn, almost no student feels it challenging. Maybe this is because students feel modeling is tangible and concrete, based on concrete cases. They feel EA concepts are difficult to understand, not only because they are new, but also because there are "Many", "cross-domain", "related to each other", and "abstract". We assume frameworks might take responsibility for such challenges mostly, and such challenges might be greatly alleviated if we focus on modeling specific EAAs without considering EAFs.

4.5   RQ5: How to Enable EA Beginners to Benefit from Applying EA/EAAs?

As this question is quite open and exploratory, participants' responses varied significantly. 5 students did not provide clear answers, and 1 student mentioned that conversations with senior management is important. While in general, the students reviewed their learning experiences, pointing out works of four aspects might be helpful to the popularization and promotion of EA, providing rich clues for further work in this direction, as indicated in Fig. 6.

Firstly, 5 students mentioned the need to introduce the EA discipline in general, such as from top-level planning to specific work breakdown, or, from strategy to architecture and its implementation. 3 of them thought that it was useful to inspire architectural thinking and use blueprints for analogy in combination with discussing the environment of digital transformation. It should be noted that terminologies should be explained in plain language as much as possible and presented in graphical form as much as possible.

Second, compared with EA itself, 8 students pointed out that **the EA value to enterprises** should be clarified and emphasized. That is to say, in addition to introducing functions, benefits, general values and application prospects of EA, what kind of competitiveness can it bring to the enterprise, or how can it promote the development of the enterprise? For example, simplifying organizational structure, reducing costs, improving efficiency, sharing data, coordinating work, increasing profits, etc. should be discussed.

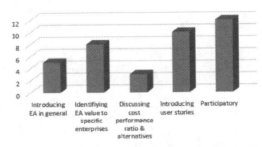

Fig. 6. How to enable EA beginners to benefit from applying EA/EAAs

In particular, 3 students pointed out that EA should be compared with other alternative approaches. Discussing its shortcomings and cost performance ratio helps to build dialectical thinking and understanding.

Third, 10 students mentioned the power of role models. They thought that other user stories should be introduced (3), about large enterprises or small and medium-sized enterprises in transition (2), "successful", "well-known", or excellent enterprises, especially domestic leading enterprises (1), such as Haier, Huawei, and Aviation (1).

Twelve students believe that experienced architects should further participate in EA activities and provide demonstrations. For example, they can demonstrate how and support beginners to find suitable EAAs (4) considering the enterprise's specific difficulties, goals, needs and expectations (3). They can provide EA services (5) on need to help the enterprise find areas for improvement by applying EA in practice, and evaluate the benefits afterwards.

To summarize, the response to RQ5 provided us much inspiration that is rarely discussed in traditional cognition. *Firstly*, compared to the advantages of EA, users are more concerned about **the value of EA to a specific organization**. *Secondly*, in addition to the value of EA, the discussion of **cost performance** and **EA alternatives** also matters. *Thirdly*, similar **use cases or customer stories** are important. This may be because learning about similar experiences in peers can alleviate the related pressure [19, 20], or it may be because people are accustomed to learning from examples. *Lastly*, beginners need **personal successful experience** to recognize and acknowledge EA's value. But personal experience often requires **practical support**, even if it is only about modeling relatively entry-level EAAs. Coaching-style support or participatory learning can be challenging and costly, but still may be a crucial step for beginners. This means that in each step of applying EA and realizing its value, timely and specific support may need to be provided for beginners, such as identifying potential beneficial scenarios, selecting potentially useful EAA types, using modeling languages and tools, and reflecting on the entire process and making improvements for the next iteration.

5 Discussion

In this section, we discuss benefits, implications of our proposal, as well as some related works.

5.1 Summary

According to the results of RQ1 and RQ2, the participants recognized the value of EA. To be noticed is that no participants mentioned EAF specific knowledge or skills when being asked what should be learned (RQ3). Without frameworks, EA is generally delivered as discrete artifacts. Therefore, we assume that participants recognized the significance of EAAs, without knowing EAFs. Furthermore, according to the results of RQ4, participants thought that the biggest challenges for beginners to benefit from applying EA are *understanding EA concepts* and *EA management skills*. Although these two challenges are related to both EAAs and EAFs, EAFs brought extra complexity and difficulty in addition to EAAs. Considering the suggestions indicated in RQ5 results, we find that realizing such suggestions will be much eaiser, if we assume EA means EAAs without using EAFs. To summarize, applying EA is challenging, even without frameworks. Participants are willing to learn and apply EA artifacts. They can be enabled in a smoother way if some practical tips can be employed.

5.2 Benefits

There are many potential benefits for beginners to benefit from EAAs without using/knowing EAFs. *Firstly*, it is much easier for beginners to understand and use EAAs than EAFs. The content of frameworks, namely content frameworks, meta-models, and development methods, are abstract and difficult for beginners to understand. While general-purpose oriented EAFs often present significant complexity, specific-purpose oriented or home-made EAFs require professional expertise which beginners can hardly manage. Beginners often do not have the essential qualifications to have a good under-standing of EAFs. *Secondly*, the workload is much lower. Without EAFs, beginners can focus on one or a limited set of EAAs, instead of a more comprehensive set of EAAs. In addition, much wasted work can be saved. Due to the existence of EAFs, EA modeling is often a pre-existing and separate process. This leads to unclear modeling scopes. When developing EA deliverables, the work tends to be an endless task. Therefore, focusing on business goals based on artifacts may significantly reduce unnecessary investment of EA modeling, as well as investment of related EA maintenance. *Thirdly*, the success rate has increased. On the one hand, direct outputs of EA development are artifacts, whether EA documents or models. On the other hand, EAAs are also the smallest units to assist in analysis, communication, and decision-making. It is easier for organizations to set business goals for EA development, to evaluate the inputs and benefits, to improve the experience, and to succeed in EA application.

It is worth noting that, making use of EAAs without knowing EAFs in the early stages does not hinder organizations to leverage frameworks in the future and boost more EA potentials [21]. It lays a good foundation and organizations can be more ready to leverage frameworks afterwards. There are three main reasons. Firstly, by leveraging EAAs in small cases, individuals and organizations can accumulate understanding of EA knowledge, as well as practical skills such as management, communication, and politics. Secondly, successful application of EA can accumulate EA reputation in organizations. Thirdly, EAAs are also accumulated. They can be integrated with appropriate frameworks when needed. It is technically feasible to derive meta-models based on existing discrete EAAs/repositories for further EA potential mining.

5.3 Implications

According to the results to the RQs, we validated that beginners felt EAAs useful and are willing to learn. Although EAFs brought much more complexity and difficulty than EAAs, their value does not appear appealing to beginners. Therefore, we draw the main conclusion that: For EA novices, individuals or organizations, it might be beneficial and feasible to learn to benefit from applying artifacts without frameworks. However, something still needs to be noticed:

- Such EAAs can come from some EAFs, suggested by experienced EA experts.
- Appropriate artifacts should be selected to generate value or business outcomes.

That means, although EA novices can try to learn EAAs and benefit from them. The success of EA application might still be challenging. Some empirical lessons can be helpful. We have collected some suggestions from our survey such as employing use stories and providing coach style support. We plan to further work on this part and test them in an industry environment.

5.4 Related Works

There are some related works regarding the EA adoption and EA success factors. In [22], a theoretical model was proposed based on literature reviews and interviews, and a survey of 133 EAM practitioners was conducted to test it. As a result, 'EAM product quality', 'EAM infrastructure quality', 'EAM service delivery quality', and 'EAM organizational anchoring' were confirmed as EAM success factors. And the construct 'EAM organizational anchoring' was thought to be a core focal concept that mediated the effect of success factors such as 'EAM infrastructure quality' and 'EAM service quality' on the success measures. Here 'EAM organizational Anchoring' consists of three dimensions: EAM top management commitment, EAM awareness, and EAM understanding.

Similarly, in [19] and [20], the researchers proposed a conceptual model based on the technology-organization-environment framework and organizational theory. The model was validated with data collected from 255 key informants from the public sector. The results showed that clear communication, coercive pressure, expected benefit, good governance, mimetic pressure, normative pressure, and organizational size have a significant influence on the adoption of EA by public sector organizations. [23] also pointed out that the main challenges to adopting EA was the lack of EA knowledge, leadership and involvement of senior management. Further, in [24], Performance Expectancy (PE) was found to be a significant predictor of EA use. In addition, training is also shown to enhance use of EA while also playing a mediating role within the relationship between PE and use of EA.

To summarize, most researchers recognized that how organizations are aware of EA and how well they understand EA is crucial to the EA adoption and success of EA application. Training is also thought to be important to improve the awareness and understanding of EA. However, few researchers provided more information about how to design such a training. In addition, previous research regarded EA as a whole and did not focus on how to enable beginners to gradually get involved in EA application. In our research, we propose that beginners can learn and try to benefit from applying EAAs without frameworks. During practices, they might progress to benefit from EAFs when they feel ready and necessary. We also provide some practical suggestions for references.

6 Conclusion

Traditionally, EA is often discussed tightly together with some general purpose frameworks such as well-known TOGAF. But according to previous research, enterprises often practically chose to use EAAs without EAFs. However, this might not be a must. Present research explores the possibility and practical way for EA beginners to benefit from EAAs without using/knowing EAFs.

We conducted a survey among students in a Chinese university. The results showed that EA beginners generally recognized the benefits/value of EAAs and were willing to learn necessary modeling techniques, as well as knowledge of languages and tools. These preliminary findings showed that, **by leveraging EAAs without frameworks, many potential organizations might gain enough benefits**. We assume EAAs can generate enough short-term benefits. More importantly, it increases the user base in the long run, and lays base for further exploring EA value.

However, the study also shows that for EA beginners, even just learning to leverage EAAs to gain value, **there is still a certain threshold and cost**. It is still necessary to carefully consider cost-effectiveness issues and alternative solutions. Careful operation and coaching style support might be necessary. Beginners may need experienced architects to provide necessary EA knowledge and skills, as well as to show how to find usage scenario, leverage appropriate artifacts, evaluate the benefit, and reflect on the process in practice.

The limitation of this study is that surveys were only conducted with college students. The future research plan is mainly to promote in actual enterprises, so as to further verify the possibility of EAAs promotion, best practices, and the possibility and necessity of developing to a higher maturity of EA application.

References

1. Vial, G.: Understanding digital transformation: a review and a research agenda. Manag. Digit. Transform. 13–66 (2021)
2. Bhattacharya, P.: Aligning enterprise systems capabilities with business strategy: an extension of the strategic alignment model (SAM) using enterprise architecture. Procedia Comput. Sci. **138**, 655–662 (2018)
3. Zhang, M., Chen, H., Luo, A.: A systematic review of business-IT alignment research with enterprise architecture. IEEE Access **6**, 18933–18944 (2018)
4. Ahmad, N.A., Drus, S.M., Bakar, N.A.A.: Enterprise architecture adoption issues and challenges: a systematic literature review. Indones. J. Electr. Eng. Comput. Sci. **15**(1), 399–408 (2019)
5. Kotusev, S.: Enterprise architecture and enterprise architecture artifacts: questioning the old concept in light of new findings. J. Inf. Technol. **34**(2), 102–128 (2019)
6. Kotusev, S.: TOGAF-based enterprise architecture practice: an exploratory case study. Commun. Assoc. Inf. Syst. **43**(1), 20 (2018)
7. Gampfer, F., et al.: Past, current and future trends in enterprise architecture—a view beyond the horizon. Comput. Ind. **100**, 70–84 (2018)
8. Diefenbach, T., Lucke, C., Lechner, U.: Towards an integration of information security management, risk management and enterprise architecture management - a literature review (2019)
9. Mamkaitis, A., Bezbradica, M., Helfert, M.: Urban enterprise: a review of Smart City frameworks from an enterprise architecture perspective (2016)
10. Santos, W.F., et al.: The State-of-the-art of enterprise architecture its definitions, contexts, frameworks, benefits, and challenges: a systematic mapping of literature. In: 2020 15th Iberian Conference on Information Systems and Technologies (CISTI). IEEE (2020)
11. Gartner Research. Stage Planning a Business-Outcome-Driven Enterprise Architecture. 2017 [cited 2020]. https://www.gartner.com/en/documents/3642517/stage-planning-a-bus iness-outcome-driven-enterprise-arch
12. Kotusev, S., Singh, M., Storey, I.: Consolidating enterprise architecture management research. In: 2015 48th Hawaii International Conference on System Sciences. IEEE (2015)
13. Löhe, J., Legner, C.: Overcoming implementation challenges in enterprise architecture management: a design theory for architecture-driven IT management (ADRIMA). Inf. Syst. e-Bus. Manag. **12**, 101–137 (2014)
14. Sandkuhl, K., et al.: From expert discipline to common practice: a vision and research agenda for extending the reach of enterprise modeling. Bus. Inf. Syst. Eng. **60**(1), 69–80 (2018)
15. Kotusev, S.: The critical scrutiny of TOGAF. British Computer Society (BCS) (2016). http://www.bcs.org/content/conWebDoc/55892
16. Cruzes, D.S., Dyba, T.: Recommended steps for thematic synthesis in software engineering. In: 2011 International Symposium on Empirical Software Engineering and Measurement. IEEE (2011)
17. Guo, H., Li, J., Gao, S.: Understanding challenges of applying enterprise architecture in public sectors: a technology acceptance perspective. In: 2019 IEEE 23rd International Enterprise Distributed Object Computing Workshop (EDOCW). IEEE (2019)
18. Kurnia, S., et al.: Stakeholder engagement in enterprise architecture practice: what inhibitors are there? Inf. Softw. Technol. **134**, 106536 (2021)
19. Ahmad, N.A., Drus, S.M., Kasim, H.: Factors that influence the adoption of enterprise architecture by public sector organizations: an empirical study. IEEE Access **8**, 98847–98873 (2020)

20. Ahmad, N.A., Mohd Drus, S., Kasim, H.: Factors of organizational adoption of enterprise architecture in Malaysian public sector: a multi group analysis. J. Syst. Inf. Technol. **24**(4), 331–360 (2022)
21. Guo, H., et al.: Boost the potential of EA: essential practices. In: Proceedings of the 23rd International Conference on Enterprise Information Systems - Volume 2: ICEIS. 2021, pp. 735–742 (2021)
22. Lange, M., Mendling, J., Recker, J.: An empirical analysis of the factors and measures of enterprise architecture management success. Eur. J. Inf. Syst. **25**(5), 411–431 (2016)
23. Jonnagaddala, J., et al.: Adoption of enterprise architecture for healthcare in AeHIN member countries. BMJ Health Care Inform. **27**(1) (2020)
24. Hazen, T.B., et al.: Performance expectancy and use of enterprise architecture: training as an intervention. J. Enterp. Inf. Manag. **27**(2), 180–196 (2014)

A Preliminary Digital Transformation Framework to Support Business Management Processes and Human Factors Impacts: Systematic Review and Gap Analysis

Camilla Buttura Chrusciak$^{(\boxtimes)}$ [ID], Anderson Luis Szejka [ID],
and Osiris Canciglieri Junior [ID]

Industrial and Systems Engineering Graduate Program (PPGEPS), Pontifical Catholic University of Parana (PUCPR), Curitiba, Brazil
camilla.chrusciak@pucpr.edu.br, {anderson.szejka,
osiris.canciglieri}@pucpr.br

Abstract. Digital Transformation (DT) integrates digital technologies like AI, IoT, and automation into organizations for efficiency and growth. It demands cultural change and an agile mindset alongside tech adoption. While DT enhances efficiency and decision-making through automation and real-time data, it impacts job roles, requiring new skills and attention to worker well-being. Digital Transformation's impact on work includes positive and negative effects on workers due to technology adoption and process automation. Negative impacts encompass skill inequality, information overload, multitasking strain, accelerated pace, and altered work relationships. These factors elevate cognitive load by overwhelming workers with excessive information, multitasking demands, interruptions, time pressures, and constant skill updates. In this way, this paper proposes to carry out a systematic literature review to identify contributions and limitations published on the topic of Digital Transformation, considering Ergonomics/Human Factors. Therefore, it was used the Scopus$^{©}$ and Web of Science™ database for the bibliometric literature review to achieve the research aim. As a result, it seeks to discover the gaps remaining in the literature and discover future research opportunities in this domain.

Keywords: Industry 4.0 · Digital Transformation · Ergonomics · Human Factors · Cognitive impacts

1 Introduction

The Digital Transformation (DT) is a process that involves integrating digital technologies into all areas and processes of an organization to drive efficiency, innovation, and growth [1]. This transformation is fueled by the rapid advancement of technologies such as artificial intelligence, big data, cloud computing, the Internet of Things (IoT), and automation [1].

© IFIP International Federation for Information Processing 2023
Published by Springer Nature Switzerland AG 2023
M. Janssen et al. (Eds.): I3E 2023, LNCS 14316, pp. 308–329, 2023.
https://doi.org/10.1007/978-3-031-50040-4_23

However, Digital Transformation is not just about adopting technology; it also encompasses cultural and organizational change. It requires an agile mindset, flexibility to adapt to changes, and the ability to leverage opportunities presented by emerging technologies [2].

Digital Transformation brings numerous benefits and opportunities to industries. Process automation enhances efficiency and productivity, reduces errors and operational costs, and enables more personalized and flexible production. Real-time data collection and analysis provide valuable insights for strategic decision-making and identifying improvement opportunities [3].

Process automation is a consequence of digitalization. While digitalization involves transforming analog workflows into electronic ones, automation refers to the application of technology to execute tasks automatically, reducing human intervention [4]. Digitalization provides the foundation for automation, allowing tasks to be accessed, manipulated, and shared more efficiently [4].

However, process automation significantly affects workers, impacting cognitive workload. With digitalization, many routine and repetitive tasks are automated, freeing up workers to focus on more strategic and cognitively challenging tasks [5]. This can be positive as workers can utilize their higher cognitive skills, such as abstract reasoning, creativity, and decision-making. However, it can also present challenges, requiring greater mental effort and specific skills to manage complex tasks [5].

Additionally, digitalization can change the nature of work, introducing new roles and replacing traditional occupations. This demands that workers acquire new skills and quickly adapt to the changing demands of the job market [6].

Therefore, understanding the impacts of digitalization on the cognitive workload of workers is crucial for adequately preparing for the changes and maximizing the benefits of Digital Transformation. This may involve developing training and empowerment programs, creating healthy work environments, and implementing strategies to ensure an equitable distribution of cognitive tasks and promote employee well-being [7, 8].

In this way, the research problem explored in this study is: "**How to achieve Digital Transformation in the administrative processes of companies using emerging technologies, while considering the cognitive impacts on workers?**".

2   Problem Statement

The Digital Transformation is causing a significant impact on the world of work. As companies adopt digital technologies and automate processes, workers are facing changes in their routines and responsibilities. These changes can have both positive and negative effects on workers and their cognitive capacity [9]. Some examples of negative impacts generated by Digital Transformation for workers are:

(i) Skill inequality: According to [10], Digital Transformation can exacerbate skill inequality among workers. Those with advanced digital skills are more likely to benefit from Digital Transformation, while those with less developed skills risk falling behind.

(ii) Information overload and multitasking: Digital transformation can lead to an increase in the amount of information that workers need to manage and process. Constant digital connectivity and the need for multitasking can lead to cognitive overload, stress, and decreased productivity [11].

(iii) Accelerated pace of work: Digitalization of processes often aims to increase efficiency and speed of operations. This can result in an accelerated pace of work, with shorter deadlines and urgent demands. Workers may face pressure to produce more in less time, leading to burnout and exhaustion [12].

(iv) Changes in work relationships: Digital transformation can also alter work relationships, such as the growing adoption of remote work. While this may bring flexibility for some workers, it can also lead to job insecurity, lack of benefits, and precarious work conditions [13].

Furthermore, these impacts can also affect workers' cognitive load, for example:

i) Information overload: With the advancement of Digital Transformation, workers are exposed to an increasingly large volume of information [13].

ii) Multitasking: Digitalization of work often requires workers to perform multiple tasks simultaneously, leading to cognitive overload. A study from Stanford University [14] found that multitaskers are less able to filter out irrelevant information and have difficulty maintaining focus. While many believe that multitasking can increase productivity it can have the opposite effect. Constantly switching between different tasks can lead to a loss of efficiency and quality of work, resulting in an overall reduction in productivity.

iii) Frequent interruptions: The presence of digital devices, such as smartphones and communication apps, increases work interruptions. According to research from the University of California [15], it takes an average of 23 min for a person to refocus on a task after an interruption.

iv) Time pressure and demand for speed: Digitalization accelerates the pace of work, requiring quick responses and agile decision-making. This can increase workers' cognitive load, leading to stress and mental fatigue. A study from the British Psychological Society [16] found that time demand and pressure to instantly respond to work messages contribute to mental exhaustion.

v) Constant need for skill updating: Digital transformation requires workers to constantly acquire new skills and knowledge to stay relevant. This need for continuous learning can increase cognitive load, especially for those who struggle to adapt to new technologies [17].

These data highlight how Digital Transformation can increase workers' cognitive load due to information overload, multitasking, frequent interruptions, time pressure, and the constant need for skill updating. It is essential for organizations to recognize these challenges and implement appropriate strategies to manage cognitive load, such as establishing communication policies, providing adequate training, and promoting a balanced work environment [18].

3   Research Methodology

This research carried out an extensive literature review based on two studies' guidelines: i) [19] which recommend the use of frequently cited bibliographies, and newspapers with a high impact factor to obtain a high-quality review, and ii) [20] which uses three main stages for literature review (1) literature review planning, (2) literature review conducting and (3) report (content analysis).

3.1   Literature Review Planning: Stage 1

The systematic literature review must be strictly planned to cover all the literature to identify the main contributions related to the research. In this way, for the literature review planning stage, three steps are necessary (i) identification for the need for a review; (ii) preparation of a proposal for a review and (iii) development of a review protocol.

(i) **Identification for the need for a review.** In this step, the authors propose conducting a scoping study to assess the relevance and size of the literature, and to delimit the subject area or topic. For this purpose, a scoping study was conducted on the four pillars of this review, which is aligned with the research objective: Digital Transformation/industry 4.0, Business Process Management (BPM), Emergent Technologies, and Ergonomics/Human Factors. An isolated search for each term was performed in the Scopus® database to identify related terms and define the research keywords. The relevant terms and keywords for each area were identified in the articles title, abstracts, and keywords sections. A similarity analysis was used to count and classified them according to the appearance frequency. The most frequent terms in the articles, that is, the most relevant terms to each research areas were elected as the search keywords for the next step and are shown in Table 1.

Table 1.   Selected keywords.

Digital Transformation/Industry 4.0	Business Process Management	Emergent Technologies	Ergonomics/Human Factors
Digitalization	Business Process Improvement	Artificial Intelligence	Human-Computer Interaction
Process Automation		IoT	Usability
Digital Twin			Industry 5.0

(ii) **Preparation of a proposal for a review.** Based on the previous step and the research objective, the focus of this systematic review was identified, and the following guiding questions were outlined:

- "Which articles address emerging technologies in management processes with a focus on Digital Transformation?"
- "Is there a framework/method/model/approach for the application of emerging technologies in management processes? Do any of them consider human factors or ergonomics?"
- "Which prominent authors and journals have published on the topic?"

(iii) **Development of a review protocol.** To obtain the answers to the guiding questions, a review protocol was developed. This protocol contains information about the specific questions addressed by the study, the search strategy to identify relevant studies, and the criteria for inclusion and exclusion of studies in the review.

Initially, a search was conducted in the Scopus® ad Web of Science™ databases using the following equation, considering only the main terms: *("Digital Transformation" OR "Industry 4.0") AND ("Business Process Management") AND ("Emergent Technologies") AND ("Ergonomics" OR "Human Factors")*. This search yielded no results.

Afterward, the search was revised to include related keywords as well: *("Digital Transformation" OR "Industry 4.0" OR "Digitalization" OR "Process Automation" OR "Digital Twin") AND ("Business Process Management" OR "Business Process Improvement") AND ("Emergent Technologies" OR "IoT" OR "Artificial Intelligence") AND ("Ergonomics" OR "Human Factors" OR "Human-Computer Interaction" OR "Usability" OR "Industry 5.0")*. As a result, 2 articles were found.

Subsequently, the four pillars of the research were related, first in trios and then in pairs. The correct relationship between the keywords ensures that a greater number of satisfactory results are achieved during the search for scientific literature related to the study topic, which also contributes to the optimization of the literature selection process.

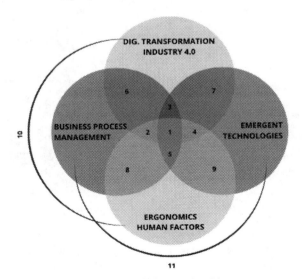

Fig. 1. Keywords relationship.

Thus, to obtain objective results in this research, the relationship presented in Fig. 1 was defined. Each number represents an equation used in Scopus® and Web of Science™ databases.

Afterward, inclusion and exclusion criteria were defined based on the research questions and the general characteristics of the articles found during the identification stage. The application of inclusion criteria selects articles from the pool gathered in the identification stage that have characteristics that might address the research questions.

On the other hand, exclusion criteria are used to eliminate works that do not cover relevant issues for the study or are duplicates. The articles that meet all the inclusion criteria are selected for further analysis. The inclusion and exclusion criteria were applied to the article's title, abstract, and keyword sections. The criteria are presented in Table 2.

Table 2. Inclusion and exclusion criteria

Inclusion criteria	Exclusion criteria
✓ English papers	✗ Duplicated papers
✓ Full-text available papers	✗ Non-English papers
✓ Last 10 years (>2012 until now)	✗ < 2012 papers
✓ Digital Transformation/ I4.0 keywords	✗ Does not approach Digital Transformation,
✓ BPM keywords	Industry 4.0 or BPM

3.2   Literature Review Conducting: Stage 2

This second stage consists of five phases. These phases correspond to (i) definition of the systematic review (keywords and search terms), (ii) filters and resulting articles, (iii) evaluation and selection of articles, and (iv) data extraction.

(i) **Definition of the systematic review.** The systematic search began with the identification of keywords and search terms, built from the scoping study. A comprehensive and unbiased search on the topic was conducted using the search equations presented in Table 2, which were generated based on the keyword's relationship (Fig. 1). All the equations are detailed in Annex I with their respective results (Table 3).

Table 3. Search equations.

#	Equations
1	("Digital Transformation" OR "Industry 4.0" OR "Digitalization" OR "Process Automation" OR "Digital Twin") AND ("Business Process Management" OR "Business Process Improvement") AND ("Emergent Technologies" OR "IoT" OR "Artificial Intelligence") AND ("Ergonomics" OR "Human Factors" OR "Human-Computer Interaction" OR "Usability" OR "Industry 5.0")
2	("Digital Transformation" OR "Industry 4.0" OR "Digitalization" OR "Process Automation" OR "Digital Twin") AND ("Business Process Management" OR "Business Process Improvement") AND ("Ergonomics" OR "Human Factors" OR "Human-Computer Interaction" OR "Usability" OR "Industry 5.0")
3	("Digital Transformation" OR "Industry 4.0" OR "Digitalization" OR "Process Automation" OR "Digital Twin") AND ("Business Process Management" OR "Business Process Improvement") AND ("Emergent Technologies" OR "IoT" OR "Artificial Intelligence")
4	("Digital Transformation" OR "Industry 4.0" OR "Digitalization" OR "Process Automation" OR "Digital Twin") AND ("Emergent Technologies" OR "IoT" OR "Artificial Intelligence") AND ("Ergonomics" OR "Human Factors" OR "Human-Computer Interaction" OR "Usability" OR "Industry 5.0")
5	("Business Process Management" OR "Business Process Improvement") AND ("Emergent Technologies" OR "IoT" OR "Artificial Intelligence") AND ("Ergonomics" OR "Human Factors" OR "Human-Computer Interaction" OR "Usability" OR "Industry 5.0")
6	("Digital Transformation" OR "Industry 4.0" OR "Digitalization" OR "Process Automation" OR "Digital Twin") AND ("Business Process Management" OR "Business Process Improvement")
7	("Digital Transformation" OR "Industry 4.0" OR "Digitalization" OR "Process Automation" OR "Digital Twin") AND ("Emergent Technologies" OR "IoT" OR "Artificial Intelligence")
8	("Business Process Management" OR "Business Process Improvement") AND ("Ergonomics" OR "Human Factors" OR "Human-Computer Interaction" OR "Usability" OR "Industry 5.0")
9	("Emergent Technologies" OR "IoT" OR "Artificial Intelligence") AND ("Ergonomics" OR "Human Factors" OR "Human-Computer Interaction" OR "Usability" OR "Industry 5.0")
10	("Digital Transformation" OR "Industry 4.0" OR "Digitalization" OR "Process Automation" OR "Digital Twin") AND ("Ergonomics" OR "Human Factors" OR "Human-Computer Interaction" OR "Usability" OR "Industry 5.0")
11	("Business Process Management" OR "Business Process Improvement") AND ("Emergent Technologies" OR "IoT" OR "Artificial Intelligence")

Also, the chosen databases for the research were Scopus® and Web of Science™. The selection of the Scopus® database is justified because it is considered the largest multidisciplinary database of abstracts, citations, and full-text scientific literature world-wide, launched by Elsevier in 2004 [19]. [20] states that Scopus® and Web of Science™, ranks among the largest multidisciplinary databases.

(ii) **Filters and resulting articles.** The results based on the search equation produced a comprehensive list of articles for the review. The search was conducted in June 2023 across the two selected databases. Filters were applied progressively, and the results of each step were recorded and are presented in Fig. 2.

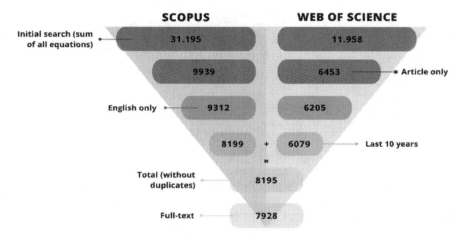

Fig. 2. Steps/filters for selecting articles.

The initial searches in the Scopus® and Web of Science™ databases yielded 13,195 and 11,958 articles, respectively. Then, for both cases, the "articles" filter was applied, as it was a bibliographic search, narrowing down the results to 9,939 and 6,453 articles. The second filter applied was the language filter, selecting only articles in English to ensure broader results, which led to 9,312 and 6,205 articles. Then, a temporal filter was applied, where only articles from the last completed 10 years were selected, resulting in 8,199 and 6,079 articles, respectively.

After that, the articles were added to the Mendeley© software, and the duplicates were removed from the base. Finally, the "full article" filter was applied, returning only articles published in their final stage, resulting in 7,928 articles.

(iii) **Evaluation and selection of articles.** To begin the selection of relevant articles, they were analyzed using the VOSviewer© software, which allowed the creation of a keyword network based on the keywords found in the articles, shown in Fig. 3.

All the keywords were identified and filtered based on their alignment with the research scope. Consequently, certain articles were excluded from the sample due to their lack of adherence to the defined inclusion criteria (e.g. words such as hydrogel, breast cancer, and ophthalmology were excluded). This selection narrowed down the results to 6,414 articles.

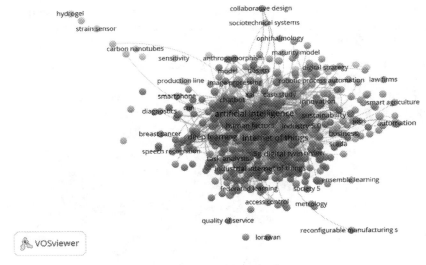

Fig. 3. Keywords network.

From the initial 6,414 articles, a thorough evaluation was conducted based on the titles and abstracts of each study. For this selection, new inclusion and exclusion criteria were established, and only articles that met all the defined inclusion criteria were considered. The defined criteria were as follows:

- Clearly addressing one of the areas of this research in the title or abstract;
- Discussing the application or proposal of a framework/method/model/approach in the theme.

As a result, only studies that fulfilled both inclusion criteria were incorporated into the review, resulting in a total of 145 articles for evaluation and selection based on full-text reading. Prior to the full-text reading, a pre-selection based on journal classification was performed, including only Q1 and Q2 journals according to the Scimago Journal Rankings (SJR) scale. Therefore, after this selection process, **108 articles** remained for full-text reading and extraction of relevant data for this research.

(iv) **Data extraction.** Data extraction from the 108 articles was conducted in a custom database using Microsoft Excel® software. The extracted information was divided into two parts: a) article characteristics, including publication year, authors, journal, country of publication, and title; and b) information related to the research variables and outcomes, such as the degree of alignment of the article with the research themes (DT, I4.0, BPM, and Technologies) (see an example in Table 4). Following the data classification and analysis, only articles that align with the main themes will be chosen as relevant for this research.

Table 4. Example of the classification of articles by adherence to the theme.

Title	Theme: BPM	Theme: Industry 4.0/DT	Theme: Emergent Technologies	Theme: Framework/Application
A business process and portfolio management approach for Industry 4.0 transformation	WELL-ADHERENT	WELL-ADHERENT	PARTIALLY ADHERENT	WELL-ADHERENT
A conceptual framework to support Digital Transformation in manufacturing using an integrated Business Process Management approach	WELL-ADHERENT	WELL-ADHERENT	WELL-ADHERENT	WELL-ADHERENT
Digital Transformation Models for the I4.0 Transition: Lessons from the Change Management Literature	WELL-ADHERENT	WELL-ADHERENT	WELL-ADHERENT	SLIGHTLY ADHERENT

After classifying the 108 articles, only 15 were selected and will be considered as the basis for future proposals in this research.

3.3   Content Analysis: Stage 3

The Content Analysis was performed based on the reading, interpretation, and comprehension of the selected research in the Systematic Literature Review. Initially, an examination of the articles' characteristics, such as publication countries, authors, journals, and more, was conducted.

This analysis was based on the complete reading of the 108 previously selected articles. The bibliometric analysis aims to explore the authors, the year of publication, the keywords, and the journals. From the 108 identified articles, about the most productive authors in the literature (Fig. 4), 15 authors wrote more than one article, while another 307 authors contributed only one.

Our findings on research productivity indicate that at least 74% of the articles were published during the past five years. These numbers indicate the research trend in these topics and show that research productivity increased from 2018 onward (Fig. 5).

The most frequent keywords among the articles are shown in the word cloud in Fig. 6. The most used keywords in the articles were "Industry 4.0", "Artificial Intelligence", "Digital Transformation", "Internet of Things", "Business Process", "Digitalization", and "Human Computer Interaction" (see Fig. 6).

And finally. The 108 articles were distributed in 52 different periodicals, concentrating on two journals: Business Process Management Journal and Sustainability (see Fig. 7). Only 11 journals had more than 1 article. The other 41 journals had 1 article each.

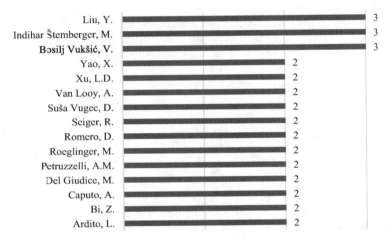

Fig. 4. Most productive researchers.

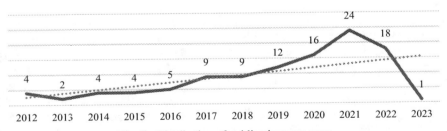

Fig. 5. Distribution of publications per year.

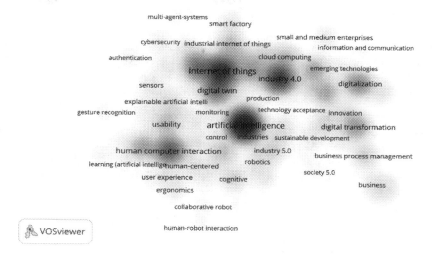

Fig. 6. Most used keywords.

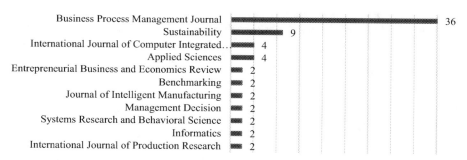

Fig. 7. Main journals.

The articles were classified to answer the research questions previously defined. Then, the purposes of each research were observed, and the contributions and limitations of each article were listed. The limitations shows the existing gaps in the theme and provided an opportunity to propose a preliminary framework to support Digital Transformation in the administrative processes of companies using emerging technologies, while considering the cognitive impacts on workers (Ergonomics/Human Factors). And the contributions helps to strengthen the suggested proposal.

The objectives, limitations, and contributions of the 15 articles selected as relevant to the scope of this research are detailed in Table 5.

4 Considerations and Future Research

This article aimed to report the main contributions, practical applications, and remaining limitations in Digital Transformation and Industry 4.0, considering BPM and Ergonomics/Human Factors, based on the literature. To this end, the study defined some guiding questions that helped achieve the proposed objective.

- *Which articles address emerging technologies in management processes with a focus on Digital Transformation?* 15 papers were selected within the study topic, addressing DT, Technologies, BPM and Ergonomics/Human Factors.
- *Which prominent authors and journals have published on the topic?* The three authors with the most publications were Indihar Stemberger, Bosilj Vukšić and Liu. Indihar is a Professor of Information Management from the University of Ljubljana, Bosilj Vukšić is a professor of Business Process Management, Simulation Modelling and Business Computing at the Faculty of Economics and Business from the University of Zagreb, and Liu is a Professor at the University of Electronic Science and Technology of China. The main journals that addressed the issue studied were Business Process Management Journal and Sustainability.
- Is *there a framework/method/model/approach for the application of emerging technologies in management processes? Do any of them consider human factors or ergonomics?* Some frameworks or models are related to the theme, but some have not been used or validated. All articles have a limitation, such as not considering or giving little consideration to one of the four pillars of this research.

Table 5. Limitations and contributions.

Title	Limitations	Contributions
A business process and portfolio management approach for Industry 4.0 transformation	Framework focused on the management of digital transformation projects and not on the actual application of technologies to achieve digital transformation. It is necessary to validate the method with other companies and portfolios with more projects to ensure the method's robustness. Do not consider human factors	The project portfolio management approach enables creating transparency and thus offers an existing framework less vulnerable to risks for companies wishing to implement an I4.0 transformation

(*continued*)

Table 5. (*continued*)

Title	Limitations	Contributions
A conceptual framework to support digital transformation in manufacturing using an integrated business process management approach	Directed only to manufacturing, but with expansion potential for any organization and sector. There was no actual application of the proposal and no validation. The framework proposed can help manufacturing organizations transition from traditional manufacturing to Industry 4.0. But the article deals with the organization and is not directed at administrative management processes	Presents a structured methodology that can be employed by manufacturing organizations to facilitate their transition towards Industry 4.0. it incorporates factors often overlooked in Industry 4.0 implementation, e.g., skills gap analysis, risk management, contingency planning, change management, and cost-benefit analysis. Shows the importance of KPIs to understand the requirements of the process. The authors show that one of the key challenges highlighted in the framework of Work 4.0 is Industry 4.0 and human-machine interaction. This raises serious concerns about job losses, the erosion of skills, and work intensification, to meet the technological demands of the business. Considering this challenge, they say it is imperative to invest in boosting skills and improving individual prospects for advancement at an early stage. The target for such a skills upgrade should not only be low-skilled workers or the people directly responsible for technical work, but the organization as a whole, to ensure that everyone can participate in value creation

(*continued*)

Table 5. (*continued*)

Title	Limitations	Contributions
Digital Transformation Models for the I4.0 Transition: Lessons from the Change Management Literature	It does not present its proposal. It only analyzes existing models and relates them to change management. The proposal did not specify or mention emerging technologies because it is a theoretical study	Investigates and analyze existing digital transformation models and roadmaps for the I4.0 transition. The authors suggest adopting a participatory and human-centric approach in managing a complex I4.0 transition. Adopting a participatory and human-centric approach means that the digital transformation must be carried out through with the active involvement of all the actors affected by the digital change in all the phases of the digital transformation process, from the definition of digital vision and strategy to the digital redesign of business processes. A participatory approach facilitates the identification of changes that are feasible and desirable from the perspectives of the actors affected by the change, thereby preventing resistance to change and reducing the change initiative's risk of failure
Digitalization Canvas - Towards Identifying Digitalization Use Cases and Projects	No practical application. They are focused on digitizing/digitalizing processes only. Do not focus on human factors	They conducted a study on the implementation of digitization in companies. Then, through a case study, the authors defined steps to implement digitization in canvas format

(*continued*)

Table 5. (*continued*)

Title	Limitations	Contributions
Industrie 4.0 process transformation: findings from a case study in automotive logistics	The article uses a single case study to attest to activities for transforming the processes toward Industry 4.0. However, the method could be further validated in a multiple case study covering different techniques and industries. It is a model that assesses maturity concerning Industry 4.0 and does not specify any emerging technology	The study provides guidelines for designing and managing Industry 4.0 compliant processes. It is a first version of a method for Industry 4.0 processes transformation. Consider human technology interaction in the framework
Managing business model innovation: an innovative approach towards designing a digital ecosystem and multi-sided platform	The article uses a single case study to attest to activities for transforming the processes toward Industry 4.0. However, the method could be further validated in a multiple case study covering diverse types of techniques and different industries. Only mentions human resources issues and not human factors	Demonstrates how different digital technologies and services can be implemented systematically and how added value is created through new offerings and collaborations within a business ecosystem
Methodology for Digital Transformation with Internet of Things and Cloud Computing: A Practical Guideline for Innovation in Small- and Medium-Sized Enterprises	The solution was developed for vertical plant walls so companies with similar needs can reference it. It had a focus only on IoT and Cloud Computing. Do not focus on human factors	The paper highlighted instructive principles for solution design to accelerate the digitalization process further and reduce the risk of failure
Process excellence the key for digitalization	The proposal did not specify or mention emerging technologies because it is a theoretical study. However, it could summarize the paths applied by the companies and establish a more efficient and evaluated single way. Do not consider human factors	The research compares the paths and summarizes the findings into a digitalization path model. It explains the digitalization of the studied organizations and serves as a guide for other organizations

(*continued*)

Table 5. (*continued*)

Title	Limitations	Contributions
Reviewing Literature on Digitalization, Business Model Innovation, and Sustainable Industry: Past Achievements and Future Promises	There was no actual application of the proposal and no validation. The research was focused on the sustainable industry	Contribute by developing a research agenda that communicates and sets the direction for future research by linking digitalization, business model innovation, and sustainability in industrial settings. The authors mention that an important criterion for value creation is that digital technology should not replace but rather complement human capabilities in the value-creation processes
A digital twin framework for online optimization of supply chain business processes	The framework was developed for the supply chain area. The authors described the steps and only exemplified how they would be in practice. There was no validation. Focus on simulation tools. Do not consider human factors	The research presented a framework for a supply chain business process digital twin, leveraging highly performant network modeling, simulation, and optimization packages. In addition, it gives a mathematical approach using discrete event simulation and mathematical programming as critical enablers
Industry 4.0 and the human factor: A systems framework and analysis methodology for successful development	The need for more research that can help teams understand the psychosocial impacts of their choices (e.g. the implementation of a specific I4.0 technology) on employees and, ultimately, system performance. Psychosocial stressors and their impact on work autonomy, motivation or job satisfaction in the context of I4.0 are still not fully understood and require further research	The framework developed can be used in research and development to systematically consider human factors in Industry 4.0 designs and implementations. It enables the analysis of changing demands for humans in Industry 4.0 environments and contributes towards a successful digital transformation that avoid the pitfalls of innovation performed without attention to human factors

(*continued*)

Table 5. (*continued*)

Title	Limitations	Contributions
Human-centered design of work systems in the transition to industry 4.0	The authors have tested the framework through one single case study, it might lack the necessary rigor to support the claim of its applications in all industrial settings	Proposes a framework for (re)designing industrial work systems in the transition towards Industry 4.0. The framework combines human factors and ergonomics, work system modeling, and strategy design
Augmented Workforce Canvas: a management tool for guiding human-centric, value-driven human-technology integration in industry	Besides exploring how Operator Assistance Systems have been successfully deployed in industry, it may be beneficial to review both industry use cases and related work for approaches specifically for technology-mediated learning and workforce training. The integration of human-technology systems addressing issues around technology mediated learning require some distinct considerations. It is expected that learning and education science are anticipated to become more relevant in future HTI research. Therefore, it appears promising to identify further requirements and develop managerial recommendations for technology-mediated learning on-the-job	The Canvas takes a value-driven, technology-neutral approach to Human-Technology Integration. The tool begins with an assessment by key stakeholder groups of the set of underlying problems and the required added value of the Human-Technology Integration. It can be used as a methodological framework for industrial researchers to identify their respective contributions to the overall context of Human-Technology Integration in industrial contexts

(*continued*)

Table 5. (*continued*)

Title	Limitations	Contributions
A framework to promote social sustainability in industry 4.0	In terms of applicability, one notable limitation is the small size of the sample, which could affect the generalizability of the findings. A statistically significant sample size is crucial to draw reliable conclusions and ensure that the results can be applied to a broader population	This study stems from the identification of the need to bring an update of the ergonomic analysis, going beyond the analogue tools used to assess the working conditions in production processes. The work presented focused on describing how a theoretical model can be used for the analysis of human posture and fatigue, can be integrated with technological devices and IoT algorithms to specify, analyse and support the assessment of working conditions, associated with specific variables
A framework for operator workstation interaction in Industry 4.0	The system is designed for a single operator in a single workstation. The proposed system is not equipped for cases in which more than one operator is interacting with the system, or in which the work is performed by a team of workers	The framework is general enough to allow a broad range of production types in a wide variety of work environments. The OWI 4.0's capabilities enable adaptive, ongoing interactions that enhance the operator's safety, well-being, performance, and satisfaction

In this context, we saw that the adoption of Industry 4.0 is no more a prolonged choice. It has become a necessity for businesses to succeed in the market. But, during the reading of the articles, it was revealed a wealth of information about how the adoption of new technologies and digital transformation impact business processes and human interaction in the workplace. It became evident that adequate consideration of human factors is crucial for the success of digital transformation initiatives [21].

An important conclusion is that the success of Digital Transformation goes beyond merely adopting innovative technologies; it is essential to understand how these technologies affect the people involved in business processes and how to ensure that the changes implemented improve employees' experience and performance.

To summarize, the impact of Digital Transformation on human factors presents a rich landscape for further study. The positive aspects, such as increased efficiency and flexibility, offer opportunities to enhance workplace productivity and employee well-being. However, the negative consequences, including skill inequality, information overload, accelerated work pace, changes in work relationships, and cognitive load, reveal significant gaps in our understanding of how to effectively navigate this digital landscape. Future research should focus on developing strategies to mitigate these negative effects, promote skill development for all, and create a balanced work environment that harnesses the benefits while addressing the challenges brought about by the Digital Transformation era. This evolving field presents an exciting avenue for exploration and innovation in optimizing the human experience in the digital age.

So, an opportunity for further research in this area is to investigate best practices for integrating human factors into the digital transformation process. This includes identifying effective strategies to engage and empower employees during the implementation of technological changes, ensuring that their perspectives and needs are considered from the outset.

Additionally, research could explore innovative approaches to measure the impact of Digital Transformation on employee satisfaction, productivity, and well-being. These metrics can help companies evaluate the success of their initiatives and identify areas that require ongoing improvements.

Furthermore, analyzing how emerging technologies such as Artificial Intelligence and Automation affect the work environment and how business processes can be redesigned to optimize human-machine collaboration is also relevant.

In summary, research in this area offers a valuable opportunity to enhance our understanding of how digital technologies shape business processes and workforce dynamics. By prioritizing human factors and creating more inclusive and empowering work environments, organizations can reap the benefits of Digital Transformation in a more sustainable and successful manner.

So finally, the upcoming stages of the research will entail conducting an in-depth analysis of the 15 selected articles to identify opportunities and gaps in the literature. This will serve as a basis for proposing a comprehensive framework that integrates emerging technologies for digital transformation in business processes while also accounting for Ergonomic/Human Factors considerations.

In future research, one step will be to extend the analysis of the identified gaps in the literature to provide a more comprehensive understanding of the research landscape. Another crucial step will be to propose and validate the framework mentioned in this study. The validation and application in real-world scenarios are essential to enhance the practical validity of these theoretical contributions. After the validation of the framework, it will be possible to define practical strategies for organizations to effectively incorporate human factors considerations during the digital transformation process.

As study limitations, it is considered that the exclusion criteria of the research may inadvertently eliminate studies that have useful information, innovative methodologies, or insights that could have been valuable for the review.

Acknowledgement. The authors especially thank the support of Pontifical Catholic University of Paraná (PUCPR) – Industrial and Systems Engineering Graduate Program (PPGEPS). This project is sponsored by the MAI/DAI Academic Master's and Doctoral Program for Innovation from Ministry of Science, Technology, Innovation and Communications and National Council for Scientific and Technological Development (CNPq).

References

1. Berman, S.: Digital transformation: opportunities to create new business models. Strategy Leadership **2**(40), 16–24 (2012). https://doi.org/10.1108/10878571211209314
2. Westerman, G., Bonnet, D., McAfee, A.: Leading Digital: Turning Technology into Business Transformation. Harvard Business Press, Massachusetts (2014)
3. Brynjolfsson, E., McAfee, A.: The Second Machine Age: Work, Progress, and Prosperity in a Time of Brilliant Technologies. W. W. Norton & Company, New York (2014)
4. Kovynyov, A., Mikut, R.: Digital technologies in airport ground operations. Netnomics Econ. Res. Electron. Netw. **20**(1–2), 1–19 (2019). https://doi.org/10.1007/s11066-019-09132-5
5. Stapel, J., Mullakkal-Babu, F.A., Happee, R.: Automated driving reduces perceived workload, but monitoring causes higher cognitive load than manual driving. Transp. Res. Part F: Traffic Psychol. Behav. **60**, 590–605 (2019). https://doi.org/10.1016/j.trf.2018.11.006
6. Wujarso, R.: Effect of digital transformation on company operational efficiency. Central Eur. Manag. J. **31**(2), 136–142 (2023). https://doi.org/10.57030/23364890.cemj.31.2.16
7. Li, Y., Fei, Y.: Network embeddedness, digital transformation, and enterprise performance—the moderating effect of top managerial cognition. Front. Psychol. **14**, 1098974 (2023). https://doi.org/10.3389/fpsyg.2023.1098974
8. Zhang, Y., et al.: Information technology investment and digital transformation: the roles of digital transformation strategy and top management. Bus. Process. Manag. J. **29**(1), 1–23 (2023). https://doi.org/10.1108/bpmj-06-2022-0254
9. Autor, D.H.: Why are there still so many jobs? the history and future of workplace automation. J. Econ. Perspect. **29**(3), 3–30 (2015). https://doi.org/10.1257/jep.29.3.3
10. Autor, D.H., Salomons, A.: Is automation labor-displacing? Prod. Growth, Employ. Labor Share. (2018). https://doi.org/10.3386/w24871
11. Richter, A., et al.: The impact of technostress on productivity: a systematic literature review. Inf. Syst. J. **26**(1), 35–76 (2016). https://doi.org/10.1111/isj.12082
12. Demerouti, E., et al.: Accelerated change and stress: a longitudinal test of the job demands-resources model in the context of organizational change. J. Occup. Health Psychol. **24**(1), 25–37 (2019). https://doi.org/10.1037/ocp0000113
13. Nijp, H.H., et al.: The impact of flexible working arrangements on workers' well-being and performance: a meta-analysis. Work Stress. **34**(1), 84–101 (2020). https://doi.org/10.1080/02678373.2019.1692425
14. Mark, G., Gudith, D., Klocke, U.: The cost of interrupted work: more speed and stress. In Proceedings of the SIGCHI Conference on Human Factors in Computing Systems (CHI 2008), pp. 107–110. Association for Computing Machinery, New York, NY, USA (2008). https://doi.org/10.1145/1357054.1357072
15. Ophir, E., Nass, C., Wagner, A.D.: Cognitive control in media multitaskers. Proc. Nat. Acad. Sci. **106**(37), 15583–15587 (2009). https://doi.org/10.1073/pnas.0903620106
16. McCormack, H.M., MacIntyre, T.E., O'Shea, D., Herring, M.P., Campbell, M.J.: The prevalence and cause(s) of burnout among applied psychologists: a systematic review. Front. Psychol. **16**(9), 1897 (2018). https://doi.org/10.3389/fpsyg.2018.01897
17. Bessen, J.: AI and jobs: the role of demand (2018). https://doi.org/10.3386/w24235
18. OECD. The future of work: OECD employment outlook 2019. OECD Publishing (2019). https://doi.org/10.1787/9ee00155-en
19. Sengers, F., Wieczorek, A. J., Raven, R.: Experimenting for sustainability transitions: a systematic literature review. Technol. Forecast. Soc. Change (2016)

20. Tranfield, D., Denyer, D., Smart, P.: Towards a methodology for developing evidence-informed management knowledge by means of systematic re-view. Br. J. Manag. **14**(1), 207–222 (2003)
21. Chrusciak, C.B., Poncini, C.R., Bitencourt, R.S., Canciglieri Junior, O.: Social responsibility in a university hospital: an application with a socio-technical focus. In: Leal Filho, W., Tortato, U., Frankenberger, F. (eds.) Integrating Social Responsibility and Sustainable Development. WSS, pp. 627–642. Springer, Cham (2021). https://doi.org/10.1007/978-3-030-59975-1_42

Data Use and Capacities Across the Global South: Implications for Open Data Policies and Practice

Luiz Pinheiro[1]([✉]), José Carlos Vaz[2], Renan Vieira[2], and Leticia Hora[2]

[1] Positivo University, Curitiba, Brazil
luiz.junior@up.edu.br
[2] University of Sao Paulo, Sao Paulo, Brazil

Abstract. This paper examines 17 case studies from the Open Data Research Network with the objective of identifying capacity of using open (government) data. The method used was a literature review of relevant concepts leading to the construction of a typology checklist to determine the capacity level of data use of each case. The findings are summarised in a stairs of open data capacity with nine of the case studies found to be in the *intermediate* category and the others in the *advanced* cluster. The findings have implications for identifying local capacity, capacity building needs, and areas for intervention.

Keywords: Open Data · Open Government Data · Capacity Building · Data Use · Typology

1 Introduction

The past five years has witnessed an increase in Open Data (OD), particularly Open Government Data (OGD) activity. This paper examines the data use and capacities in the 17 case study research exploring the emerging impacts of open data in developing countries (ODDC) to proffer a solution for OD capacity building across the global south. By examining the literature on OD practical initiatives, life cycle of usage, and capacity building level typology, the study proposes a model for organisational capacity building and situates each of the 17 case studies within this[1].

Recently, several international initiatives prompted milestones in the OD, Open Government (OG) and OGD discourse. The Obama Memorandum of Open Government and Transparency (Coglianese 2009; Obama 2009; Obama 2013), the Public Sector Information (PSI) European Directive (Cretu and Manolea 2013; Janssen 2011; Manolea and Cretu 2013), the Open Government Partnership (OGP) and the Tim Berners-Lee Open Data speech (Bizer et al. 2009) were some of those initiatives on the practical perspective. The most visibly seen results were the increasing number of Open Government Data Portals (OGDP) in different countries: 45 countries with OGDP since 2009 to 2014. Also, a "sibling" of the OG and OGD initiatives, Freedom of Information (FOI), can be included here. Since 1995, there are 102 countries with FOI Legislation, enabling citizens to ask about anything from their governments (Ackerman and Sandoval-Ballesteros 2006; Foerstel 1999).

On the other hand, the scientific literature reveals that since the boom of OGDP in the world there are 52 papers with the keywords Open Data and Open Government Data at Google Scholar but published on regular journals of the area (Scholl 2005). This shows us the increased relevance and importance of during the last 6 years around the OD and OGD subject. Of course it is possible to argue that FOI and transparency keywords could be inserted into this sum, however, this paper has the focus to only verify the OD and OGD concepts. Further on the governmental aspects and the scientific literature, civil society was also identified as using and improving the OGD arena (Matheus et al. 2020; Matheus and Janssen, 2015).

The Research Network of Open Data in Developing Countries (ODDC) initiative (Davies 2010; Davies et al. 2013), founded by International Development Research Centre (IDRC) and the Web Foundation during 2013, had 17 research case studies from across Africa, Asia and Latin America led by scholar institutions and non-governmental organizations (NGOs) (Mutuku and Mahihu). These case studies provide a wide variety in socio-political, economic, and technical context for OD discourse in the global south.

From this scenario, questions around the subject emerged and drove our objectives and research approach: "What type of data did the case investigate?", "What type and quality of data formats–5 stars of Open Linked Data - were found by the groups?", "What has been done with the data?" and "How have the institutions and organizations dealt with data".

The objective of this paper is to identify characteristics of data usage and capacity building of civil society organizations in the developing countries, using as database and object of study the 17 case study reports from the Research Network of the Open Data in Developing Countries initiative. The method used was based on a literature review of Open Data and Open Government Data concepts and the 17 case studies of ODDC to:

1. Verify determinants that enable and/or impede the open–or not–data usage in developing countries;
2. Develop a checklist of case studies characteristics found on the OGD Life Cycle from scientific literature and capacity level typology; and
3. Propose an Open Data capacity building level via a construction of typology.

2   Literature Review

International Practical Initiatives and Scientific Literature

Some international milestones on Open Data and Open Government Data helped to boost the number of practical initiatives and scientific literature in the world. With the Obama Memorandum of Open Government and Transparency, PSI European Directive, Tim Berners-Lee open Linked data speech and the Open Government Partnership, it was possible to identify that the number of OGDP started to rise significantly as the Fig. 1–Count of Countries with Open Government Data Portal reveals.

Coincidently, the jump of the OGDPs happened after the third milestone, that is, President Obama's Memorandum in 2009. However, this is not the only coincidence

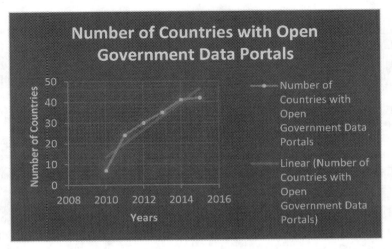

Fig. 1. Number of Countries with Open Government Data Portals

about OD and OGD. The number of scientific literature appearing in the top journals of the subject area also started to rise significantly only after 2009, as the Fig. 2–Count of Publications on Open Data and Open Government Data show us.

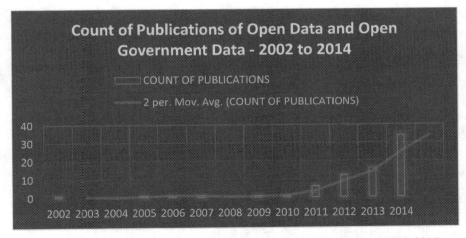

Fig. 2. Count of Publications of Open Data and Open Government Data (2002–2014)

From these numbers of governmental practice and scientific literature, we can conclude that despite the low numbers of OGD portals at the national level and the low number of top articles published, the quantities have risen fast over the past five years with a tendency to increase even exponentially due to the increased relevance of the subject. The results of the Open Data Barometer already showed the same trends including the accompanying improvement in the quality of those portals (Davies 2013) which this paper does not focus on.

On the scientific literature three mainstreams of publications were identified: **Guidelines of OD and OGD, New Theoretical frameworks** and **Case studies**, as the Fig. 3–Type of Publications shows. The concept of Guidelines of OD and OGD considered was literature that only presented guidelines on how to produce, treat or measure OD and OGD. The concept used for new theoretical frameworks came from the first type, Guidelines of OD and OGD, which are more practical than the in-depth studies found on the second type, theoretical frameworks. Normally the theoretical frameworks were published after the guidelines and improved small parts and methods previously published. The last type, case studies, only has the application of the first and second types. For example, case studies of opening data portals, or quality of opened datasets and usage of open data by institutions and organizations. The majority of the publications are on the last type, case studies with 29 publications. The new theoretical frameworks type has 18 publications and the Guidelines of OD and OGD has only 5 considered publications, on a total of 52 publications.

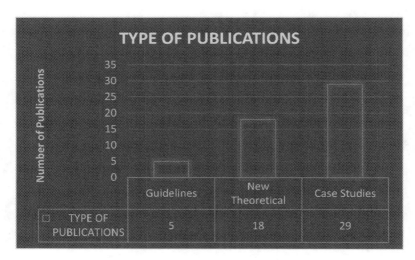

Fig. 3. Type of Publications

Life Cycle of Open Data Usage

To create the checklist for the 17 case studies it was necessary to create a theoretical background around the Life Cycle of open data usage. For this, the literature reveals that there are several cycles focusing on different aspects of open data usage such as infrastructure (Auer et al. 2012; Zuiderwijk and Janssen 2014c), the quality of the data (Davies and Frank 2013), maturity (Lee and Kwak 2012) and the flow of usage (Alexander and Hausenblas 2009; Fraunhofer 2013).

We decided to use the simpler Fraunhofer Institute model (Fraunhofer 2013), shown in Fig. 4, which is more directed toward open data usage for case studies. This life cycle takes into consideration linked data (Hendler et al. 2012; Höchtl and Reichstädter 2011; Janev et al. 2014) and semantic web technologies (Berners-Lee et al. 2006). The dimensions identified on this flow are:

1. **Identifying datasets on the City Content Management System (CMS):** the first part is the basic, which in this case is the recommended usage of the Comprehensive Knowledge Archive Network (CKAN) (Winn 2013; Matheus and Janssen, 2017) as environment to receive the data;
2. **Publishing Open Datasets from the owners:** the second part enables finding the place to store or just link the data, the Open Data Portal, via CMS. At this point it is possible to start sharing the open data from secretariats, municipalities, etc. (Bizer et al. 2009);
3. **Discovery of datasets by consumers to be used:** the third part of the flow is considering that the open data at the Open Data Portals is of interest to consumers (Hartig and Langegger 2010);
4. **Enriching data to create apps and citizen portals:** the last part happens when citizens start to access databases and create original analysis and applications with the open data (Matheus and Janssen 2013).

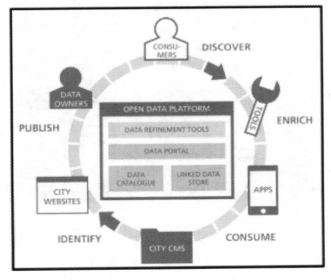

Fig. 4. Open Data Life Cycle

Capacity Building

Capacity building is conceptualized in this article as the way that institutions, in this case the scholar institutions and non-governmental organizations use open data to realize their objectives (to account and produce advocacy) to achieve measurable and sustainable results. It has become a topic of interest because capacity building started to enhance stakeholders' understanding of evaluation concepts and practices (Preskill and Boyle 2008a; Preskill and Boyle 2008f).

The asymmetry of information (Eisenhardt 1989; Laffont and Martimort 2009; Waterman and Meier 1998) between the agent and the principal (founders and organizations founded), was reduced through capacity building. Organizations have been implementing a variety of strategies to help their members learn from and about evaluation, and this paper makes an effort to create an evaluation checklist, and this is one of the biggest contribution of this article. Discovering ways to evaluate what is missing on the OD and OGD area.

For some authors (Berg 1993; Hawe et al. 1997; Jänicke and Weidner 1997; Preskill and Boyle 2008a; Preskill and Boyle 2008f), developing regions do not have organizations and institutions with the essential capacity building to achieve their objectives due to several reasons, summarized in the following three main dimensions:

- Access of infrastructure;
- Access of Human Resources and knowledge (know-how);
- Access of Data.

Open Data Capacity Building Level Typology

To identify answers to the issues raised by the types of case studies we considered two possible methodological tools: typology or taxonomy (Marradi 1990). Typologies were considered for this paper specially because of the simplicity to identify a form of theory building and fitting the need of the paper, an examination of actual 17 cases studies. Taxonomies are more generalist and requires rigorous meticulous work on the area (Rich 1992; Sokal 1962), and we considered it to be too ambitious a tool for the purposes of this paper.

Indeed our type of typology is an intentional classification identified on the scientific literature review and the practical observation of the authors on the field, all of the lecturers, consultants and activists in the area (Doty and Glick 1994). So, each class (dimension) defined in the typology, presented in Table 1–**Typology Dimensions of Open Data Capacity Building Level**, is the extension of the correspondent class concept. For the cluster analysis that we aimed for this paper, this tool fits very well. However, it is not the scope and the objective of the paper to create generality, which can be another future paper with the findings presented for the 17 case studies.

From the literature review about capacity building and the typology constructed, we decided to group, intentionally, on three main dimensions extended for more sub-dimensions as the Table 1 presents. The three main dimensions (or classes) of groups are: Access of Infrastructure; access of Human Resources (HR) and Knowledge (know-how); and, Access of Data.

It is important to highlight that for those dimensions, it is understood that every one of them need at least a minimal amount of funds to provide the needed resource. This list is not exhaustive and is expectedly, continuously growing, due to the flexible aspects of needs of some specific areas. Given again the type of the tool built - exploratory and intentionally grouped to form classes already known - based on scientific literature and practical perspective of authors, a description and reasons for inclusion of a sub-dimension, as well as the sources are presented in Table 1.

Table 1. Typology Dimensions of Open Data Capacity Building Level

Dimension	Sub-Dimensions	Description and Reason	Source
Access of Infrastructure	Hardware (Computers, Internet, printer)	At least basic hardware is needed to create analysis and reports for accountability and advocacy	(Berg 1993; Hawe et al. 1997; Jänicke and Weidner 1997; Preskill and Boyle 2008a; Preskill and Boyle 2008f)
	Office with adequate electricity, water, security, etc	Office is a need for meetings and space for work focused on the subject without any interference of anyone	(Berg 1993; Hawe et al. 1997; Jänicke and Weidner 1997; Preskill and Boyle 2008a; Preskill and Boyle 2008f)
Access of Human Resources (HR) and Knowledge (know-how)	Administrative and accountancy	Human resources that have knowledge of administrative and accountancy duties to provide for donors and founders. Knowledge from HR that can use properly the administrative and accountancy knowledge to provide for donors and founders	(Berg 1993; Hawe et al. 1997; Jänicke and Weidner 1997; Preskill and Boyle 2008a; Preskill and Boyle 2008f)
	Information Technology (IT) for network and hardware	Human resources that have knowledge of IT for network and hardware if the institution have any IT problem	(Fountain 2004; Fountain 2007; Mansell and Wehn 1998)

(*continued*)

Table 1. (*continued*)

Dimension	Sub-Dimensions	Description and Reason	Source
	Information Technology for programming and Analytical Software Usage (Statistical Programs, Business Intelligence)	Human resources that have knowledge of IT for programming and software usage if needed to create analysis. Knowledge from HR that can use properly the analytical software to produce analysis and reports. For languages programming to create specific programs for collecting, treating, analysing and visualizing data	(Fountain 2004; Fountain 2007; Mansell and Wehn 1998)
	Research development (survey, interviews, search, etc.)	Human resources that have knowledge of research development, to plan, implement and evaluate the research methods, implementation and results. Knowledge from HR that can use properly information from the political, cultural and social aspects of the object of study	(Fountain 2004; Fountain 2007; Mansell and Wehn 1998)
Access of Data	Open and Structured Databases	Open Data and structured databases are needed to better results of analysis	(Davies 2010; Davies 2013; Davies et al. 2013; Fraunhofer 2013)
	Updated Data	Data must be updated, otherwise is not possible to work for analysis	(Berners-Lee et al. 2006; Bizer et al. 2009)

(*continued*)

Table 1. (*continued*)

Dimension	Sub-Dimensions	Description and Reason	Source
	Data History	Data must have history, otherwise is not possible to compare and create analysis	(Höchtl and Reichstädter 2011; Janssen 2011; Matheus et al. 2012; Zuiderwijk and Janssen 2014a; Zuiderwijk and Janssen 2014c)
	Data Documentation	It is the manual of the data, with information about how deal with it	(Höchtl and Reichstädter 2011; Janssen 2011; Matheus et al. 2012; Zuiderwijk and Janssen 2014a; Zuiderwijk and Janssen 2014c)
	Application Programming Interface (Data in Real Time)	Data in real time is needed when the subject is ephemeral and change fast, such as traffic conditions	(Marienfeld et al. 2013; Matheus and Janssen 2013)
	Completeness	Data must be complete. Not complete data cannot be analysed	(Berners-Lee et al. 2006; Bizer et al. 2009)
	Online and Free	Data must be online and free to access	(Berners-Lee et al. 2006; Bizer et al. 2009)

3   Results and Findings

Organizational Capacity Building of Case Studies
After the creation of the **Typology Dimensions of Open Data Capacity Building Level**, described at Table 1, it was possible to do the checklist on the 17 case studies from the ODDC Research Network. The checklist results for each dimension and sub-dimension (classes) revealed that the analysis could be further than a "yes/no" to the dimensions. A cluster division, based on the same structured method of the typology, was designed based on the level achieved by the groups, as a ranking with detailed challenges of developments to go further or be downgraded. Three main levels were recognized as described in Table 2–**Clusters Maturity level of Open Data Capacity Level**.

The first dimension (class) identified is the Maturity of the group of case studies. In this case, the initiatives were catalogued as Advanced, Intermediate or Beginner as follows:

- *Advanced* are the institutions or organizations that have equipment, personnel and data, meeting all the sub-dimensions of the three catalogued groups of the typology.
- The second cluster identified is the *Intermediate*, considered when the organisation only meets some of the sub-dimensions of the three dimensions (personnel/know-how, data access and infrastructure/equipment).
- The last group considered on the typology of Maturity open data capacity level was the *Beginner*. The beginners do not present any of the dimensions at all. For example, no data, no people and not reasonable hardware. No case study group was identified in this cluster.

The lower the maturity of capacity building, the higher the probability of failures to accomplish the organizational objectives.

Table 2. Clusters Maturity level of Open Data Capacity Level of 17 Case Studies from ODDC

Maturity	Description
Advanced	All of the three dimensions on the checklist of typology 1 - **Dimensions of Open Data Capacity Building Level** are identified
Intermediate	Some of the three dimensions on the checklist of typology 1 - **Dimensions of Open Data Capacity Building Level** are identified
Beginner	None of the three dimensions of typology 1 - **Dimensions of Open Data Capacity Building Level** are identified

How each case study organisation fared is summarised in Table 3–**Clusters Maturity level of Open Data Capacity Level of the 17 ODDC Case Studies.** Eight organisations were found to be in the Advanced cluster while the remaining nine were in the Intermediate cluster and each cluster had a countries from each region–Africa, Asia and Latin America.

Table 3. Clusters Maturity level of Open Data Capacity Level of the 17 ODDC Case Studies

Maturity	Case study organisation	Country	Case study citation
Advanced	Step-Up Consulting	Philippines	M.P. Canares; J. de Guia; M. Narca; J. Arawiran (2014). Opening the Gates: Will Open Data Initiatives Make Local Governments in the Philippines More Transparent?

(continued)

Table 3. (*continued*)

Maturity	Case study organisation	Country	Case study citation
	Opening the Cities, Polis Institute	Brazil	Fumega, S., Mattheus, R., Scrollini, F. (2014). Opening The Cities:Open Government Data InLocalGovernments Of Argentina, BrazilAnd Uruguay
	University of Cape Town	South Africa	F. van Schalkwyk; M. Wilmers; L. Czerniewicz (2014) Case study: Open data in the governance of South African higher education
	GPoPAI, University of Sao Paulo	Brazil	Beghin, N., Zigoni, C., Craveiro, G., Tavares, M. (2014). Measuring open data's impact of Brazilian national and sub-national budget transparency websites and its impacts on people's rights
	University of Ilorin	Nigeria	Mejabi, O.V., Azeez, A.L., Adedoyin, A. and Oloyede, M.O. (2014). Case study report on Investigation of the use of the online national budget of Nigeria
	Hasgeek	India	S. Chattapadhyay (2014) Opening Government Data through Mediation: Exploring the Roles, Practices and Strategies of Data Intermediary Organisations in India
	Transparent Chennai	India	
	De La Salle University	Philippines	
Intermediate	i-Hub Research	Kenya	
	Freedom Forum	Nepal	Sapkota, K. (2014). Open Aid and Budget Data in Nepal: Experiences, perspectives and intentionalities
	The Energy and Resources Institute	India	

(*continued*)

Table 3. (*continued*)

Maturity	Case study organisation	Country	Case study citation
	INESC	Brazil	
	CIPPEC	Argentina	
	Jesuit Hakimani Centre	Kenya	Chiliswa, Z. (2014). Open Government Data for Effective Public Participation: Findings of a Case Study Research Investigating The Kenya's Open Data Initiative in Urban Slums and Rural Settlements
	Development Initiatives / Development Research and Training	Kenya / Uganda	Lwanga-Ntale, C., Mugambe, B., Sabiti, B., and Nganwa, P. (2014). Understanding how open data could impact resource allocation for poverty eradication in Kenya and Uganda
	Society for Democratic Initiatives	Sierra Leone	Emmanuel Saffa Abdulai (2014). Digital divides and open data definitions hinder the efficacy of open data in developing countries
	Sinerganta	Indonesia	Srimarga, I.C. (2014). Open Data Initiative of Ministry of Finance on National Budget Transparency in Indonesia
Beginner	No case study fell into this cluster		

Stairs of Open Data Organizational Maturity of Capacity Building Level

From the foregoing, the results demonstrate a model of maturity for capacity building which we propose as described in Fig. **5–Stairs of Open Data–ODDC Network**. This "stairs" contains all the 17 studied cases on the ODDC network and present how they can go further toward the Advanced degree or be downgraded if they do not maintain or achieve minimal expectations of capacity.

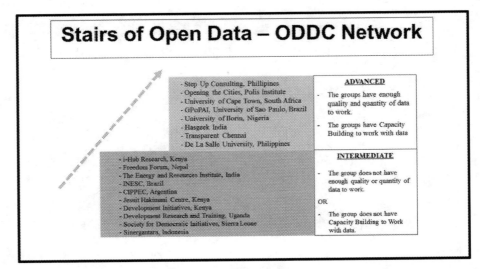

Fig. 5. Stairs of Open Data within the ODDC Network studies

4   Conclusions and Further Research

Having employed a typology checklist determined from the scientific literature on OD and OGD, we have established a three –cluster classification of organisations in the "stairs of open data capacity" in which not surprisingly, none of the 17 case studies were found in the *Beginners* cluster. Understandably, as all ratings are prone to be, summations falling around the boundaries may be sensitive to rating bias and this is a limitation of the methodology. To minimise this, conclusions based on only one set of ratings is to be avoided.

The findings have implications for identifying local capacity and capacity building needs, areas for intervention by funding agencies. The theory of open data and open government data via the literature review of the subject and for the practice, the identification of determinants found that enable and influence the organization to use OD and OGD, leading to the clustering of organizations according to their maturity and capacity level, is a major contribution of the paper. As an extension of the present study, we propose the distinction of the separate stakeholder groups across the different case studies and the application of taxonomy as a methodology.

End Notes. [1] Case study reports are available through each of the case studies on http://www. opendataresearch.org/emergingimpacts.

References

Ackerman, J.M., Sandoval-Ballesteros, I.E.: The global explosion of freedom of information laws. Admin. L. Rev. **58**, 85–130 (2006)

Alexander, K., Hausenblas, M.: Describing linked datasets-on the design and usage of void, the'vocabulary of interlinked datasets. In: Linked Data on the Web Workshop (LDOW 09), in Conjunction with 18th International World Wide Web Conference (WWW 09): Citeseer (2009)

Auer, S., et al.: Managing the life-cycle of linked data with the lod2 stack. In: Cudré-Mauroux, P., et al. (eds.) ISWC 2012. LNCS, vol. 7650, pp. 1–16. Springer, Heidelberg (2012). https://doi.org/10.1007/978-3-642-35173-0_1

Berg, E.J.: Rethinking Technical Cooperation: Reforms for Capacity Building in Africa. United Nations Development Programme (1993)

Berners-Lee, T., et al.: Tabulator: exploring and analyzing linked data on the semantic web. In: Proceedings of the 3rd International Semantic Web User Interaction Workshop: Athens, Georgia (2006)

Bizer, C., Heath, T., Berners-Lee, T.: Linked Data-the Story So Far (2009)

Coglianese, C.: The transparency president? The Obama administration and open government. Governance 22(4), 529–544 (2009)

Cretu, V., Manolea, B.: The Influence of the Open Government Partnership (Ogp) on the Open Data Discussions, Epsi, Topic Report (2013)

Davies, T.: Open Data, Democracy and Public Sector Reform. A look at open government data use from data. gov. uk) 2010

Davies, T.: Open Data Barometer: 2013 Global Report," World Wide Web Foundation and Open Data Institute (2013). http://www.opendataresearch.org/dl/odb2013/Open-Data-Barometer-2013-Global-Report.pdf

Davies, T., Frank, M.: There's no such thing as raw data': exploring the socio-technical life of a government dataset. In: Proceedings of the 5th Annual ACM Web Science Conference, pp. 75–78 ACM (2013)

Davies, T., Perini, F., Alonso, J.: Researching the emerging impacts of open data. World Wide Web foundation (2013). http://www.opendataresearch.org/sites/default/files/posts/Researching%20the%20emerging%20impacts%20of(20)

Doty, D.H., Glick, W.H.: Typologies as a unique form of theory building: toward improved understanding and modeling. Acad. Manag. Rev. 19(2), 230–251 (1994)

Eisenhardt, K.M.: Agency theory: an assessment and review. Acad. Manag. Rev. 14(1), 57–74 (1989)

Foerstel, H.N.: Freedom of Information and the Right to Know: The Origins and Applications of the Freedom of Information Act. Greenwood Publishing Group, Westport (1999)

Fountain, J.E.: Building the Virtual State: Information Technology and Institutional Change. Brookings Institution Press (2004)

Fountain, J.E.: Challenges to Organizational Change: Multi-Level Integrated Information Structures (Miis)," Governance and Information Technology: from Electronic Government to Information Government), pp. 63–83 (2007)

Fraunhofer. The Open Data Platform (2013). http://open-data.fokus.fraunhofer.de/en/platform/

Hartig, O., Langegger, A.: A database perspective on consuming linked data on the web. Datenbank-Spektrum 10(2), 57–66 (2010)

Hawe, P., Noort, M., King, L., Jordens, C.: Multiplying health gains: the critical role of capacity-building within health promotion programs. Health Policy 39(1), 29–42 (1997)

Hendler, J., Holm, J., Musialek, C., Thomas, G.: Us government linked open data: semantic. data. gov. IEEE Intell. Syst. 27(3), 0025–0031 (2012)

Höchtl, J., Reichstädter, P.: Linked open data-a means for public sector information management. In: Andersen, K.N., Francesconi, E., Grönlund, Å., van Engers, T.M. (eds.) Electronic Government and the Information Systems Perspective. EGOVIS 2011. LNCS, vol.6866, pp. 330–343 (2011). https://doi.org/10.1007/978-3-642-22961-9_26

Janev, V., Mijović, V., Paunović, D., Milošević, U.: Modeling, fusion and exploration of regional statistics and indicators with linked data tools. In: Kő, A., Francesconi, E. (eds.) EGOVIS 2014. LNCS, vol. 8650, pp. 208–221. Springer, Cham (2014). https://doi.org/10.1007/978-3-319-10178-1_17

Jänicke, M., Weidner, H.: National Environmental Policies: A Comparative Study of Capacity-Building. Springer, Heidelberg (1997)

Janssen, K.: The influence of the psi directive on open government data: an overview of recent developments. Gov. Inf. Q. 28(4), 446–456 (2011)

Laffont, J.-J., Martimort, D.: The Theory of Incentives: The Principal-Agent Model. Princeton University Press, Princeton (2009)

Lee, G., Kwak, Y.H.: An open government maturity model for social media-based public engagement. Gov. Inf. Q. 29(4), 492–503 (2012)

Manolea, B., Cretu, V.: Topic Report No. 2013/10: The Influence of the Open Government Partnership (Ogp) on the Open Data Discussions. European Public Sector Information Platform (2013). http://epsiplatform.eu/topicreports

Mansell, R., Wehn, U.: Knowledge Societies: Information Technology for Sustainable Development. United Nations Publications (1998)

Marienfeld, F., Schieferdecker, I., Lapi, E., and Tcholtchev, N.: Metadata aggregation at govdata. De: An Experience Report. In: Proceedings of the 9th International Symposium on Open Collaboration, p. 21 ACM (2013)

Marradi, A.: Classification, typology, taxonomy. Qual. Quant. 24(2), 129–157 (1990)

Matheus, R., and Janssen, M. 2013. "Transparency of Civil Society Websites: Towards a Model for Evaluation Websites Transparency," in: *Proceedings of the 7th International Conference on Theory and Practice of Electronic Governance*. Seoul, Republic of Korea: ACM, pp. 166–169

Matheus, R., Ribeiro, M.M., Vaz, J.C.: New perspectives for electronic government in Brazil: the adoption of open government data in national and subnational governments of brazil. In: Proceedings of the 6th International Conference on Theory and Practice of Electronic Governance, pp. 22–29. ACM (2012)

Matheus, R., Janssen, M.: Transparency dimensions of big and open linked data. In: Janssen, M., Mäntymäki, M., Hidders, J., Klievink, B., Lamersdorf, W., van Loenen, B., Zuiderwijk, A. (eds.) I3E 2015. LNCS, vol. 9373, pp. 236–246. Springer, Cham (2015). https://doi.org/10.1007/978-3-319-25013-7_19

Matheus, R., Janssen, M.: How to become a smart city?: Balancing ambidexterity in smart cities. In: Proceedings of the 10th International Conference on Theory and Practice of Electronic Governance. ACM (2017)

Matheus, R., Janssen, M., Maheshwari, D.: Data science empowering the public: Data-driven dashboards for transparent and accountable decision-making in smart cities. Gov. Inf. Q. 37(3), 101284 (2020)

Mutuku, L., Mahihu, C.M.: Open Data in Developing Countries

Obama, B.: Transparency and Open Government Memorandum for the heads of executive departments and agencies 2009

Obama, B.: Making Open and Machine Readable the New Default for Government Information. Washington DC, Executive Order (2013)

Preskill, H., Boyle, S.: Insights into evaluation capacity building: motivations, strategies, outcomes, and lessons learned. Can. J. Program Eval. 23(3), 147–174 (2008)

Preskill, H., Boyle, S.: A multidisciplinary model of evaluation capacity building. Am. J. Eval. 29(4), 443–459 (2008)

Rich, P.: The organizational taxonomy: definition and design. Acad. Manag. Rev. 17(4), 758–781 (1992)

Scholl, H.J.: Motives, strategic approach, objectives & focal areas in e-gov-induced change. Int. J. Electron. Gov. Res. (IJEGR) 1(1), 59–78 (2005)

Sokal, R.R.: Typology and empiricism in taxonomy. J. Theor. Biol. **3**(2), 230–267 (1962)

Waterman, R.W., Meier, K.J.: Principal-agent models: an expansion? J. Public Adm. Res. Theory **8**(2), 173–202 (1998)

Winn, J.: Open Data and the Academy: An Evaluation of Ckan for Research Data Management (2013)

Zuiderwijk, A., Janssen, M.: Barriers and development directions for the publication and usage of open data: a socio-technical view. In: Gascó-Hernández, M. (ed.) Open Government. PAIT, vol. 4, pp. 115–135. Springer, New York (2014). https://doi.org/10.1007/978-1-4614-9563-5_8

Zuiderwijk, A., Janssen, M.: Open data policies, their implementation and impact: a framework for comparison. Gov. Inf. Q. **31**(1), 17–29 (2014)

Sustainable Technologies and Smart Cities

What's in a Brand? Place Branding and Migration in Smart Cities

Ricardo Matheus[1], Naveen Naval[2], Nina Rizun[3], Charalampos Alexopoulos[4], Raphael Gouvea da Silva[5], Guilherme Wiedenhöft[5], and Stuti Saxena[6(✉)]

[1] TU Delft, Delft, The Netherlands
[2] Graphic Era University, Dehradun, India
[3] Gdansk University of Technology, Gdańsk, Poland
[4] University of the Aegean, Mitilini, Greece
[5] Federal University of Rio Grande, Rio Grande, Brazil
[6] Nainital, India
stutisaxenaogd.vishnu@gmail.com

Abstract. Among the reasons for migration, place branding is one important consideration. The present study seeks to present a gist of the reasons, possibilities and challenges for migration to Smart Cities which are 'branded' in terms of repute and specific unique aspects of the Smart City which pull and attract the migrants. Experts' opinion was considered as a viable research method for the purpose. It may be inferred from the experts' opinion that migrants prefer moving into 'branded' Smart Cities contingent upon the opportunities anticipated from moving into such Smart Cities apart from the avenues of a better quality of life in such 'branded' Smart Cities. As a first study aiming to understand the host of factors responsible for the migration in such Smart Cities, it is anticipated that a more nuanced understanding of the issues is attained.

Keywords: Migration · branding · smart city · experts' opinion · reasons · opportunities · challenges · barriers

1 Introduction

Branding of places is reflective of the identity espoused by the place such that the international standing is secured for the said place [1]. Given the increasing competition among the cities in the urbanized and globalized ecosystem, governments and the other stakeholders, including the private sector, invest heavily in the marketing of the places such that the uniqueness of the places is highlighted for retention of the existing populace and drawing the attention of the others from elsewhere [2]. Thus, owing to their anticipated economic value [3], such places are liable to draw the attention of the migrants-both domestic and international. Moreover, such places are liable to harbour cosmopolitan and urban outlook such that that the class, religious affiliations and ethnicity [4] are well-accommodated. Another aspect relates to the designing and implementation of policies

M. Janssen et al. (Eds.): I3E 2023, LNCS 14316, pp. 349–359, 2023.
https://doi.org/10.1007/978-3-031-50040-4_25

suited to the branded places [1, 5]. Furthermore, there is a strong correlation between place branding and decision-making of the target and potential individuals who may be influenced by place branding for some or the other reasons [6].

Given the impetus of the governments to refurbish the public service delivery formats, Smart Cities evolution has happened at a rapid pace over a period of time. Thus, the technological, economic and 'humane', i.e., quality of life, environment and societal inclusivity, dimensions of Smart Cities are being considered as the. metrics for their ranking [7]. As such, there is no unanimity regarding the definition of a Smart City but for the fact that there are user-friendly services being provisioned to the people with promises of advanced infrastructures, quality of life and a sustainable environment such that the invocation of digital innovations across a range of services facilitate or are initiated by the involvement of a range of stakeholders covering the public sector, private sector and the others concerned-all of these efforts result in the provision of agile and smart services resting on the state-of-the-art Information and Communications Technologies (ICTs) alongside the conservation and optimum deployment of natural resources [8–14]. Implicitly, the Smart Cities invokes Artificial Intelligence (AI) and advanced data analytics including Internet of Things (IoT) and Blockchain Technologies [15]. Incidentally, it has been attested that there is a linkage between migration and quality of life as well [16]. Extant research has also focused on the migration into Smart Cities alongside the issues related with migration movements (See, for instance, [17–21].

The study's objective is also in line with the assertion that the smart cities should be sustainable wherein the impetus is upon economic development and social inclusion apart from environmental protection [22] and these facets are spurs for migration propensities [23]. The research question for the study is: *"What is the role of place branding on the migration propensities in Smart Cities?"* In order to attend to this research question, expert opinion was sought from 15 academic professionals. Inferences drawn from the interviews were helpful in ascertaining the possibilities, challenges and barriers related with the place branding dimensions linked with migration in Smart Cities.

The rest of the paper is structured as follows: Sect. 2 provides a gist of the literature on place branding and migration in Smart Cities for deriving at the research question; Sect. 3 provides a brief on the research methodology; Sect. 4 enumerates the inferences from the interviews' responses and the final Section relates to the concluding remarks alongside the study limitations, implications for further research and implications for practitioners.

2 Related Research

2.1 Place Branding

Projecting an affirmative image of a place is important for ascertaining the commercial and non-commercial, i.e. personal and social, value in the eyes of the migrants [24, 25]. Place branding is pertinent not only for the local inhabitants but also for the outsiders [26]. Place branding is suggestive of the overarching aims and comprehensive identity of a place [27] such that the context in terms of the uniqueness is being projected upon in relation to its being a Smart City. It has been conceded that a Smart City has its own unique personality, tradition and attraction which maintains the emotional attachment of the people concerned [28]. One such parameter for branding relates to the potent quality of life based on the state-of-the-art ICT platforms. Similarly, another component of branding of Smart Cities relates to the aspects of being inclusive in terms of accommodating the diversely constituent migrants [29–31]. Furthermore, place branding is about self-image building such that the migrants are able to perceive belongingness and urban identity [32, 33] apart from clinching social networking and societal cohesion [34]. Place branding includes promotional campaigning highlighting the cultures, ethnicities and the inclusive and accommodative nature of the city apart from underscoring the ICT-edificed agile services and the opportunities of innovation and ingenuity by all alike [35, 36]. Place branding showcases the availability of the requisite amenities and the sophisticated accommodative and conducive lifestyles that are pertinent for its wholesome economic development [37]. On the opposite end of the spectrum is the assertion that place branding is a superficial ploy and does not have any bearing on the actual sound public policy objectives focused on the economic development or urban governance [38]. Place branding is reflective of the cultural diversity as well as the inherent civic pride apart from the distinctiveness and development of the place [39].

It may be pertinent to note that place branding incorporates the collaboration and involvement of a range of stakeholders like citizens, professionals, academic community, bureaucrats, and the like [40, 41]. The impact of place branding for Smart Cities may be evinced in the policy framing, objectives, vision and implementation strategies. In the specific context of Canada, it was clinched that immigrants were drawn to the country on account of the place branding initiatives rather less when compared with the other drivers like the availability of housing facilities or the conducive economic conditions [42]. A place's futuristic and progressive orientation in terms of the environmentally-conducive habitation, easy connectivity via transportation, availability of the required public space and the possibilities of unleashing one's creative potential are significant benchmarks of place branding which in the case of an Italian locale resulted in social cohesion and alliances on the one hand, and, divisive tendencies between the multiple ethnic identities, on the other hand [43]. Place branding helps in identifying a Smart City, as in the present case, with reference to its advanced technological infrastructure apart from the conducive features for individuals' drawing benefits from the economically developed agile city [13, 44]. Place branding is also reflective of the globalized and cosmopolitan outlook where the fulfilment of aspirations and dreams gets materialized optimally-case in point being dimensions like the entrepreneurial and innovative pursuits of the individuals which actualized in the branded cities [45].

2.2 Migration in Branded Cities, Including the Smart Cities

Given the impetus of Smart Cities on the two-fold impetus on envisioning sustainable ICT-backed futuristic economy and a knowledge and innovation economy [46], migration into the Smart Cities is determined by factors such as economy, mobility, environment, people, living and governance [19]. Immigration, especially of the labor class or the blue collar workers and other professionals, is important for refurbishing the economy of the destination country [47] given the fact that the immigrants are significant producers and consumers besides being involved in the factors of production [48]. Migration in Smart Cities is a factor of human capital formation such that the graduated migrants become a part of the workforce in the Smart Cities, and, hence, contributing towards the fast growth of the Smart Cities [21]. Thus, human capital management is furthered on account of migrants' movements [49]. This is also suggestive of the movement of the knowledge workers who are highly-skilled and well-educated [17]. Thus, it has been underscored how the migrants' creativity and ideation is conducive to the host country's affiliation organization, and, on the other hand, there are escalating costs to the host country's affiliation organization such that the retention policy of the concerned affiliation organization may want to provide increased perks and emoluments in contrast with the native workers [50]. Also, in the case of migration trends vis-a-vis the drive for seeking lifestyle accommodation and change promising better quality of life, individuals prefer places branded as global, borderless and international with accommodation for one and all [51].

2.3 Research Question

It is clear from the aforesaid that whilst place branding has been conceived as a potent reason for drawing the attention of the people towards moving into such sophisticated places, the specific case of the migration patterns in Smart Cities has not been discussed in the extant literature: the present study seeks to plug this gap by addressing the research question: *"What is the role of place branding on the migration propensities in Smart Cities?"*

3 Research Methodology

Given that extant research is silent regarding the research question addressed in the study, a qualitative research methodology was adopted wherein the semi-structured interviews were conducted with professionals in the academia [52–54]. Expert opinion is regarded as a significant research methodology wherein the experts help in understanding the intricacies entailed in an under-researched or neglected research theme. For the present study, perspectives were drawn from fifteen experts across myriad academic backgrounds with a focus on management, information and communications systems engineering, digital systems, and the like. Each of the experts have published extensively in the ICT (Information and Communication Technologies) domain with specific focus on Smart Cities and the societal ramifications.

The experts belonged to established varsities (Erasmus University, University of the Aegean, Gdansk University of Technology, TU Delft). Experts were contacted given the authors' familiarity with them as well as the propinquity with these experts. Authors contacted the experts personally via email wherein the study objectives were mentioned alongside the research question. In all, the authors contacted 21 academic professionals and 15 of them responded affirmatively. Semi-structured interviews were conducted via Google Meet, Skype or WhatsApp calls with the experts with an objective to derive insights regarding the issues and concerns of migration vis-a-vis the Smart Cities given the branding and visibility of the said cities. The academic experts were requested to deliberate upon the research context given their direct and/or indirect involvement in the Smart Cities- migration nexus. The entire interviewing process was done in February,

2023 through May, 2023 and each interview lasted for about 40–50 min. Thereafter, two of the authors sought to transcribe and validate the transcriptions. Furthermore, the interview responses were tape-recorded, transcribed and then coded manually by three of the authors individually and an open coding approach was being adopted [53]. Thereafter, the results were compared and any differences were resolved. The experts' profiles may be summarized in Table 1 and the generic questions posed to them are as below:

A) *How do you perceive the efficacy of the branding of Smart Cities for inviting the attention of the migrants?*
B) *What are the drivers for migrants' preferring such branded Smart Cities?*
C) *What are the hindrances for migrants' patterns into the branded Smart Cities?*
D) *Can branded Smart Cities be considered as possibilities of value creation and sustainability with the involvement of the migrants?*

Table 1. Experts' background

Expert's academic background/*country*/research interests→
• Technology, Policy and Management, *The Netherlands*, Digital transformation, Business intelligence, Data protection
• Business Analytics, *Poland*, Big Data, Computational and Linguistic Analytics, Smart Sustainable Cities
• Business-Society Management, *The Netherlands*, Policy and governance, Planning and decision-making in China, Transport infrastructures, Sustainable urban development
• Information and Communications Systems Engineering, *Greece*, Data mining, Computer security and reliability, Artificial Intelligence
• Information and Communications Systems Engineering, *Greece*, Cybersecurity, Data privacy, Digital forensics, Gamification strategies, Open and linked data ecosystems

4   Inferences Drawn from Experts' Opinions

Three cohorts of perspectives were drawn from the study:

4.1   Possibilities of Place Branding for Migration in Smart Cities

A country's image has been found to have direct and significant relationship to the migration decision [55]. Furthermore, destination branding and positioning in terms of its being a tourist attraction and the equitable imagery draws the migrant labors in the specific sector of hospitality and tourism, for instance, towards such places [50]. Even in the case of municipal planning, the migrants are involved in the policy sketching initiatives alongside the other stakeholders and this is suggestive of the inclusivity and engagement of the migrants in value co-creation pursuits [56–58]. Besides contributing towards value derivation and innovation pursuits, it is likely that the migrants shall be a significant asset for shaping the identity of the Smart City. As succinctly put by one of the experts:

"... Smart Cities are a haven for the entrepreneurs and professionals alike... You can perceive the influx of migrants in the Smart Cities where they raise their entrepreneurial ventures and earn names for themselves."

Therefore, the place branding must factor into account the aspirational needs of the migrants such that the opportunities of moving into the Smart Cities are being spelt out clearly. Place branding must incorporate the aspects of easy acclimatization and entertainment avenues such that a balanced quality of life is being laid out for them. Place branding would of Smart Cities should include the unique features of the Smart Cities with their focus on the efficacious service delivery based on the ICT formats such that the sustainable development is realized in the Smart Cities.

There are opportunities for the policy-makers and practitioners for place branding of Smart Cities for the migrants as well. For one, place branding would bring to the fore stakeholders across different socio-economic sectors such that enriched messages are being percolated among the locals and the prospective populace. Messages should be designed for ensuring that a mutually-understandable language is being used for impressing upon the migrants the advantages of moving to such Smart Cities. Novel technologies shall be used in the Smart Cities wherein the state-of-the-art technological solutions are being provisioned to the people and this would be an efficacious service delivery format. Therefore, the governments stand to gain from the robust place branding initiatives of the Smart Cities.

4.2   Challenges vis-a-vis Place Branding for Migration in Smart Cities

Three sets of challenges arise from the place branding initiatives for influencing the migrants to move into the Smart Cities. First, what may be a unique selling proposition (USP) for the place managers may not be conceived as a viable reason for moving into the Smart City. Thus, if ICT-backed public service delivery formats are considered as the reasons for the uniqueness of the Smart City, not all the migrants-to-be may be influenced by such a message because they may be more inclined towards specific distinctiveness of the Smart City contingent upon the target migrant populace-case in point being the people in their post-retirement phase or the ones in search for a better higher education varsity.

Second, the perceived identification and sense of belongingness of the people may vary such that the migrants might perceive threatened or vulnerable in terms of their personal security given the multitudinous online transactions being done by them on the ICT Platforms. Thus, the migrants would feel uncomfortable as far as the knowledge exchange or online commercial and non-commercial activities are concerned for want of anonymity and confidentiality. In the words of one of the experts:

"... Brand management and control mechanisms are such that the locals as well as the immigrants feel a sense of safety while conducting the online transactions. Therefore, their insecurity vis-a-vis the lack of robust ICT infrastructures might pose potential bottlenecks in influencing their decisions in terms of making the desired move to Smart Cities."

Finally, there are serious concerns regarding the management of place branding initiatives by the governments given the kind of international relations which the governments have with the other countries. There are also concerns regarding the management, execution and institutionalization of place branding initiatives by the government on account of the heavy expenditure being incurred in such pursuits wherein resources-human and technological-are required on an ongoing basis.

4.3   Barriers vis-a-vis Place Branding for Migration in Smart Cities

Primarily speaking, the barriers regarding place branding of Smart Cities catering to the needs and aspirations of the migrants relate to the lack of sustained political will and direction for instituting a brand management initiative. This includes the non-committal stance of the political leaders and bureaucrats for the allocation of resource allocation for the initiatives. Picking up the messages and customization of the messages for the migrants are challenges in themselves. Image-building is an important consideration for campaign designing for Smart Cities because the migrant communities are strongly influenced by the message content. Furthermore, the choice of the place branding initiatives-electronic or print-is a potent issue that merits attention. Government's disposition towards institutionalization of such brand management initiatives is likely to be determined by a host of factors like domestic economic standing, ICT Infrastructure, motivation of the personnel and leadership apart from the extraneous conditions involving the ties with the international leaders and coordination with the embassies.

5   Conclusion

The overall purport of the study was to ascertain the implications and role of place branding for influencing migrants' influx into the Smart Cities. Specifically, perspectives were drawn from 15 experts from the academia community regarding the research question, *"What is the role of place branding on the migration propensities in Smart Cities?"*. It was inferred that there are opportunities and challenges associated with place branding vis-a-vis the migrants' propensity towards moving into the Smart Cities. The study sought to underline the possibilities, challenges and barriers in the context of place branding of Smart Cities with a focus on the migrants. Besides individual factors, contextual factors also likely to impact the attitudinal disposition of the migrants. On the end of the policy-makers, the role of place branding of the Smart Cities vis-a-vis the migrants was also factored into account by the experts. Key inferences drawn from the expert opinion underline the need to strategize the brand management of the Smart Cities for securing the attention of migrants-current and prospective. Pitching forth the sustainable and entrepreneurial images of the Smart Cities wherein the aspirations of the migrants are realized in terms of improved quality of life and efficacious public service delivery formats, imagery of the Smart Cities needs to be customized accordingly. Finally, it was inferred from the perspectives of the interviewees that a sustained branding impetus needs to be led by the governments themselves which is directed towards encapsulating the knowledge capital in the Smart Cities which is contributory towards the economic growth, eventually.

As a contribution towards the extant literature on Smart Cities, the study furthers our understanding of the impinging role of branding of Smart Cities with its ramifications for the mobility of the individuals in the Smart Cities. However, the study is limited in its scope on account of the qualitative research approach including interviewees from a specific professional background, i.e., the academic community. It is anticipated that a broad-based focus group discussion or Delphi technique is undertaken to solicit responses from the practitioners as well.

The study leaves implications for further research. For one, an empirical research may be conducted to ascertain the manner in which the inferences drawn from the experts' opinion may be further validated with the actual or prospective migrants, on the one hand, and, the government representatives, on the other hand. Contextual influences as also the socio-demographic characteristics of the current migrants and the prospective ones are also significant determinants of the extent to which place branding of Smart Cities influences the individual decision-making. It is likely that there are disparities in terms of economic standing of the migrants thereby leading to differential impact on them as far as place branding is concerned-this is a potent research option in future. Finally, it is warranted that a more nuanced understanding of the relevance of place branding of Smart Cities is arrived at by drawing a comparison of the economic development of the Smart Cities across time and space.

There are practitioner implications as well. For one, there are lessons for the policy-makers and the designers of instruments related with place branding as to how to pitch the campaign messages which suit the interests of the migrants as much as they do for locale populace [57, 58]. Likewise, it is important for the governments to realize the importance of institutionalizing its place branding initiatives with a focus on the Smart Cities such that the influence on the locals and the migrants-current and prospective-is strategized accordingly. Thus, policy- making for the Smart Cities needs to factor into account the dimensions of urban development [59] for aligning them with brand management and migration management. Finally, the causal factors for the behavioral intention to migrate to Smart Cities need to be factored into consideration while framing the brand management strategies of the Smart Cities.

References

1. Hassen, I., Giovanardi, M.: The difference of 'being diverse': city branding and multiculturalism in the 'Leicester Model.' Cities **80**, 45–52 (2018)
2. Zenker, S., Martin, N.: Measuring success in place marketing and branding. Place Brand. Public Dipl. **7**, 32–41 (2011)
3. Glick Schiller, N., Çağlar, A.: Towards a comparative theory of locality in migration studies: migrant incorporation and city scale. J. Ethn. Migr. Stud. **35**(2), 177–202 (2009)
4. Foner, N., Rath, J., Duyvendak, J., van Reekum, R.: New York and Amsterdam: Immigration and the New Urban Landscape, vol. 22, pp. 13-42. NYO Press, New York (2014)
5. Eshuis, J., Klijn, E.: Branding in Governance and Public Management. Routledge, New York, London (2012)
6. Cleave, E.. Arku, G.: Putting a number on place: a systematic review of place branding influence. J. Place Manag. Dev. **10**(5), 425–446 (2017)

7. IMD. Smart City Index 2023. https://www.imd.org/smart-city-observatory/home/#:~: text=Index%20was%20published.-Smart%20City%20Index%202023,and%20Canberra% 20(3rd) (2023)
8. Albino, V., Beradi, U., Dangelico, R.M., Berardi, U., Dangelico, R.M.: Smart cities: definitions, dimensions, performance, and initiatives. J. Urban Technol. **22**, 3–21 (2015)
9. Allam, Z., Newman, P.: Redefining the smart city: culture, metabolism and governance. Smart Cities **1**, 2 (2018)
10. Kahn, M.E.: Sustainable and smart cities. In: World Bank Policy Research Working Paper, 6878 (2016). https://ssrn.com/abstract=2439699
11. Mouazen, A.M., Hernandez-Lara, A.B.: The role of sustainability in the relationship between migration and smart cities: a bibliometric review. Digit.Policy Regul. Gov. **23**(1), 77–94 (2021)
12. Pardo, N.: Conceptualizing smart city with dimension of technology, people and institutions. In: 12th Annual International Digital Government Research Conference: Digital Government Innovation in Challenging Times, Atlanta, GA, USA. (2011)
13. Valencia-Arias, A., Urrego-Marin, M., Bran-Piedrahita, L.: A methodological model to evaluate smart city sustainability. Sustainability **13**(20), 11214 (2021)
14. Yigitcanlar, T., Kankanamge, N., Vella, K.: How are smart city concepts and technologies perceived and utilized? A systematic geo-twitter analysis of smart cities in Australia. J. Urban Technol. 1–20. (2020)
15. Silva, B.N., Khan, M., Han, K.: Towards sustainable smart cities: a review of trends, architectures, components, and open challenges in smart cities. Sustain. Cities Soc. **38**, 697–713 (2018)
16. IMF.: Impact of migration on income levels in advanced economies (2016). https://www.imf. org/en/Publications/Spillover-Notes/Issues/2016/12/31/Impact-of-Migration-on-Income-Levels-in-Advanced-Economies-44343
17. Betz, M.R., Partridge, M.D., Fallah, B.: Smart cities and attracting knowledge workers: which cities attract highly-educated workers in the 21st century? Pap. Reg. Sci. **95**(4), 819–841 (2015)
18. Monachesi, P.: Shaping an alternative smart city discourse through Twitter: Amsterdam and the role of creative migrants. Cities **100**, 102664 (2020)
19. Tariq, M.A.U.R., Hussein, M., Mutti, N.: Smart city ranking system: a supporting tool to manage migration trends for Australian cities. Infrastructures **6**, 37 (2021)
20. Visvizi, A., Mazzucelli, C., Lytras, M.: Irregular migratory flows: towards an ICTs' enabled integrated framework for resilient urban systems. J. Sci. Technol. Policy Manage. **8**(2), 227–242 (2017)
21. Winters, J.V.: Why are smart cities growing? Who moves and who stays. Reg. Sci. **51**(2), 253–270 (2011)
22. United Nations. Transforming our world: The 2030 agenda for sustainable development, New York, US (2015)
23. Gil-Garcia, J.R., Chen, T., Gasco-Hernandez, M.: Smart city results and sustainability: current progress and emergent opportunities for future research. Sustainability **15**, 8082 (2023)
24. Belabas, W., George, B.: Do inclusive city branding and political othering affect migrants' identification? Experimental evidence. Cities **133**, 104119 (2023)
25. Govers, R.: From place marketing to place branding and back. Place Brand. Public Dipl. **7**, 227–231 (2011). https://doi.org/10.1057/pb.2011.28
26. Zenker, S., Petersen, S.: An integrative theoretical model for improving resident-city identification. Environ Plan A **46**(3), 715–729 (2014)
27. Kavaratzis, M.: From city marketing to city branding: an interdisciplinary analysis with reference to Amsterdam, Budapest and Athens. Groningen: Rijksuniversiteit Groningen. Unpublished PhD thesis (2008)

28. Batten, J.: Sustainable Cities Index 2015. Arcadis 2015 (2015). https://media.arcadis.com/-/media/project/arcadiscom/com/perspectives/global/sci/sustainable-cities-index-2015.pdf?rev=-1

29. Falcous, M., Silk, M.: Olympic bidding, multicultural nationalism, terror, and the epistemological violence of 'making Britain proud. Stud. Ethn. Natl. **10**(2), 167–186 (2010)

30. Hollands, R.G.: Will the real smart city please stand up? City **12**(3), 303–320 (2008)

31. Winter, A.: Race, multiculturalism and the 'progressive' politics of London 2012: passing the 'Boyle test.' Sociol. Res. Online **18**(2), 137–143 (2013)

32. Ashworth, G.: The instruments of place branding: how is it done? Eur. Spat. Res. Policy **16**(1), 9–22 (2009)

33. Belabas, W., Eshuis, J., Scholten, P.: Re-imagining the city: branding migration-related diversity. Eur. Plan. Stud. **28**(7), 1315–1332 (2020)

34. Mommaas, H.: City branding: the importance of socio-cultural goals. In: Hauben, T., Vermeulen, M., Patteeuw, V. (eds.), City Branding: Image Building and Building Images, pp. 34–44. NAI Uitgevers, Rotterdam, The Netherlands (2002)

35. Lucarelli, A.: The political dimension of place branding. (PhD Thesis) Stockholm University (2015)

36. Oliveira, E.: Place branding in strategic spatial planning. (Published PhD Thesis) University of Groningen, Groningen (2016)

37. Jackson, T.: Interregional place-branding concepts: the role of amenity migration in promoting place- and people-centred development. In: Zenker, S., Jacobsen, B.P. (eds.) Inter-Regional Place Branding, pp. 73–86. Springer, Cham (2015). https://doi.org/10.1007/978-3-319-15329-2_7

38. Cleave, E., Arku, G., Sadler, R., Gilliland, J.: Is it sound policy or fast policy? Practitioners' perspectives on the role of place branding in local economic development. Urban Geogr. **38**(8), 1133–1157 (2017)

39. Hall, C.M., Rath, J.: Tourism, Migration and Place Advantage in the Global Cultural Economy. Tourism, Ethnic Diversity and the City. London, Routledge (2006)

40. Andersson, I.: Green cities' going greener? Local environmental policy-making and place branding in the 'Greenest City in Europe. Eur. Plan. Stud. **24**(6), 1197–1215 (2016)

41. Boisen, M., Groote, P., Terlouw, K., Couwenberg, O.: Patterns of place promotion, place marketing and place branding in Dutch municipalities. J. Place Branding Public Diplomacy **14**(2), 78–88 (2018)

42. Cleave, E., Arku, G.: Immigrant attraction through place branding? Evidence of city-level effectiveness from Canada's London. Cities **97**, 102502 (2020)

43. Del Bono, A.: More than 'creative': analyzing place branding strategies and Chinese migration in the City of Prato Italy. Soc. Identities **28**(5), 643–657 (2022)

44. Riezebos, R.: Position paper Rotterdam 2014. Brand values and style characteristics regarding the marketing of the city of Rotterdam. Report by Municipality of Rotterdam (2014)

45. Gehrels, C., Van Munster, O., Pen, M., Prins, M., Thevenet, J.: Kiezen voor Amsterdam: Merk, concept en organisatie van de city marketing. Berenschot, Amsterdam (2003)

46. Angelidou, M.: Smart cities: a conjuncture of four forces. Cities **47**, 95–106 (2015)

47. Williams, A.: Tourism, migration and human capital: knowledge and skills at the intersection of flows. In: 9th Bi-annual Meeting of the International Academy for the Study of Tourism, Beijing (2005)

48. Jarman, N.: Migrant workers in Northern Ireland. Labour Market Bull. **18**, 51–59 (2004)

49. McLaughlin, D.: Immigration helps economy's performance. The Irish Times, 17th June, 2005, 5 (2005). https://www.irishtimes.com/business/immigration-helps-%20economy-s-performance-1.456875

50. Baum, T., Hearns, N., Devine, F.: Place branding and the representation of people at work: exploring issues of tourism imagery and migrant labour in the Republic of Ireland. Place Brand. Public Dipl. **4**, 45–60 (2008)
51. Torkington, K.: Place and lifestyle migration: The discursive construction of 'glocal' place-identity. Mobilities **7**(1), 71–92 (2012)
52. Doringer, S.: The problem-centered expert interview'. Combining qualitative interviewing approaches for investigating implicit expert knowledge. Int. J. Soc. Res. Meth. **24**(3), 265–278 (2021)
53. Maylor, H., Blackmon, K. Huemann, M.: Researching Business and Management. 2nd edn. McMillan Education, UK (2017)
54. Saunders, M., Lewis, P., Thornhill, A.: Research Methods for Business Students. Prentice Hall, Harlow (2007)
55. Nadeau, J., Olafsen, A.H.: Country image evaluations and migration intentions. Place Brand. Public Diplomacy **11**, 293–308 (2015). https://doi.org/10.1057/pb.2015.8
56. Jha, P.P., Iqbal, M.A.: A perspective on migration and community engagement in Smart Cities. In: Ahmed, S., Abbas, S.M., Zia, H. (eds.) Smart Cities—Opportunities and Challenges. LNCE, vol. 58, pp. 521–526. Springer, Singapore (2020). https://doi.org/10.1007/978-981-15-2545-2_43
57. Mapitsa, C.B.: Migration governance as place making: South African experiences. J. Place Manag. Dev. **12**(3), 391–407 (2019)
58. Kavaratzis, M., Hatch, M.J.: The dynamics of place brands: an identity-based approach to place branding. Theory Mark. Theory **13**(1), 69–86 (2013)
59. Sokolov, A., Veselitskaya, N., Carabias, V., Yildirim, O.: Scenario-based identification of key factors for smart cities development policies. Technol. Forecast. Soc. Chang. **148**, 119729 (2019)

Comparison of the Prediction of Anaerobic Digestion Through Different Architectures of Neural Networks

Leandro Correa Pykosz[1,2]([✉]), Alysson Nunes Diogenes[2],
and Maura Harumi Sugai-Guerios[2]

[1] Universidade do Estado de Santa Catarina, Florianópolis, Brazil
Leandro.pykosz@udesc.br
[2] Positivo University, Curitiba, Paraná, Brazil
{diogenes,maura.guerios}@up.edu.br

Abstract. In this work, multilayer perceptron and convolutional neural networks were trained in order to model the flow of biogas, from real data obtained from a treatment plant that uses anaerobic reactors for the treatment of domestic sewage using as input variables the physical- chemicals: sewage flow (L/s), COD (mg/L), TSS (mg/L) and SSV (mg/L). Based on these parameters, several simulations were performed in order to predict the biogas flow (Nm3/h). The simulations took place to identify which network would present the best performance, both used the same training criteria and the average of the results obtained with a 4–8-1, respectively were a regression coefficient $R2 = 0.90$ for the multilayer perceptron and for the convolutional $R2 = 0.93$ and an MSE error rate tending to zero.

Keywords: Modeling · Artificial Intelligence · Domestic wastewater

1 Introduction

The new Legal Framework for Sanitation approved in July 2020 in Brazil (Brazil, 2020) has as one of its goals to ensure that 90% of the population has access to sewage collection and treatment by 2033. Approximately 100 million Brazilians do not have access to sewage collection, indicating a trend of increasing load on Wastewater Treatment Plants (WWTPs) in the coming years. This indicates the potential of these plants in biogas production.

In Latin American countries, due to climate and economic factors, there is a leadership in the use of anaerobic technology in domestic wastewater treatment (CHERNICHARO, RIBEIRO, et al. 2018), (SPERLING, 2016) as they require fewer financial resources than aerobic reactors for implementation and maintenance. Anaerobic reactors are one of the most commonly used technologies for the biological degradation of organic matter in WWTPs, and biogas is one of the byproducts generated after treatment, consisting mainly of methane, a flammable, odorless, and colorless compound.

© IFIP International Federation for Information Processing 2023
Published by Springer Nature Switzerland AG 2023
M. Janssen et al. (Eds.): I3E 2023, LNCS 14316, pp. 360–371, 2023.
https://doi.org/10.1007/978-3-031-50040-4_26

The production of biogas depends mainly on the composition of the influent sewage, constant temperature, and operational characteristics of the biological reactor (Chernicharo, 2016).

Brazil has 1,373 WWTPs that use anaerobic reactors, representing the largest park of anaerobic reactors in the world (Brazil, 2020). However, in Brazil, the plants were not designed for biogas recovery for commercial purposes; typically, the gas is directed to open burners where it is partially destroyed. However, studies show that it is possible to utilize biogas for thermal or electrical energy generation (Bilotta and Ross, 2016), (Sperling, 2016) (Filho, Lima, et al. 2018). Currently, WWTPs that have infrastructure for biogas collection simply burn the gas to avoid health risks (Rosa, Lobato, et al. 2016) since methane is a greenhouse gas with a global warming potential 32 times higher than that of carbon dioxide generated after its combustion (Intergovernmental Panel on Climate Change (IPCC), 2023). It is necessary to consider sustainability in WWTPs, the energy utilization of the generated byproducts, so that with minimal investments, it is possible to promote economic and environmental equity within the plant, making the treatment process sustainable and environmentally friendly, creating a sustainable future.

With the world in the midst of the first global energy crisis triggered by the Russian invasion of Ukraine, the European Union intends to increase its participation in the construction of a "future-proof" energy system by investing in renewable energies such as biogas and hydrogen (International Energy Agency, 2022).

The European Union has been seeking ways to reduce its energy dependence on Russian imports and has supported the expansion of biogases, with a projected annual growth of 35%, with an estimate of producing over 1 billion cubic meters of low-emission gases such as hydrogen, biogases, and synthetic methane by 2050, which corresponds to almost one-third of the total gas fuel demand consumed (International Energy Agency, 2022).

Among the European Union countries, Germany leads in the potential for biogas generation. Approximately 40% of the WWTPs that receive population sewage utilize biogas to generate electricity and heat (Federal Ministry for Economic Affairs and Energy, 2018).

Most of the wastewater treatment plants in Brazil do not have electronic sensors that measure and monitor biogas production. This equipment is usually imported and expensive, and it is not enough to just acquire them; they need to be calibrated and frequently monitored. Therefore, considering the reality of WWTPs where investments are not always sufficient to equip them with electronic monitoring equipment, a computational model would allow greater control over the generated biogas so that it has a high calorific value, making its use viable. The computational model is an emerging alternative that brings prediction and optimization capabilities to anaerobic digestion systems (Kana, Oloke, et al. 2012).

Another recurring situation in the ETE's is that some of the dominant variables of the reactors that influence their performance, needed to control their control, are difficult to measure, such as BOD. To complete its analysis, it takes five days of sample incubation (Kim, Ko, et al. 2006), which makes it difficult to make a decision to interfere or not in real -time treatment, because when receiving the result of the material Analyzed, it is no longer in the season and biogas has already been produced, imposing the interference in that product already generated with attitudes such as changing the pH, temperature or even the amount of organic matter. Thus the manager cannot accurately evaluate if the byproduct that will be produced, such as biogas, will have an ideal composition, with high concentration of methane.

This research aims to make WWTPs sustainable by indicating the possibility of proactive control of biogas, a step towards sustainable WWTPs, where the plant byproduct, biogas, can be controlled and consequently commercialized or used within the plant to generate revenue, rather than just expenses, as is the current reality (Rosa, Lobato, et al. 2016).

The knowledge obtained by human experts has a degree of uncertainty that must be mapped in artificial intelligence tools, such as neural networks, which are gaining popularity in this modeling and in biological effluent treatment processes (Honga, Lee, et al. 2007).

As a result, ANNs have been frequently used for prediction in the environmental field, and in their structure, they can be divided into three parts: input layer, hidden or intermediate layer, and output layer. The first layer corresponds to the input variables of the system, and the last layer represents the expected output variable. The layers in between are the hidden layers (Lauwers, Appels, et al. 2013). When the network has one or more hidden layers between the input and output layer, it is considered a Multilayer Perceptron (MLP).

Neural networks are composed of artificial neurons capable of performing mathematical functions that are mostly nonlinear, suitable for adequately modeling biological processes, such as wastewater treatment, due to their complexity and nonlinear behavior. (Silva, Spatti, and Flauzino, 2010) define an artificial neuron as a simplified model of biological neurons, usually nonlinear, and they collect input values and produce a response considering their activation function.

The activation function is necessary to introduce nonlinearity to the network. Without this function, the hidden layers do not become as powerful. In the works addressed in this study, most authors used the sigmoid activation function, with variations such as tan-sigmoid. These activation functions are generally preferred over threshold activation functions because threshold functions are difficult to train due to the nonexistence or zero gradient, making it impossible to use backpropagation or more efficient methods (Kusiak and Wei, 2012). Multiple activation functions were used, and the best results for the activation function of the hidden layer, i.e., with the lowest validation errors, were the tan-sigmoid function. In his book (Haykin, 2009), confirms that the most common type of activation function applied is the sigmoid function. (Beltramo, Ranzan, and Hinrichs, 2016) affirm that the sigmoid function, when applied to the hidden layer, provides computational flexibility compared to linear regression methods, allowing for better performance and more accurate prediction of the desired variable.

The choice of neural networks was not arbitrary, as their use is widely found in the literature applied to nonlinear multivariate bioprocesses and environmental processes, such as anaerobic reactors, as they are powerful tools for predicting and optimizing biological processes (Waewsak, Nopharatana, and Chaiprasert, 2010) (Garlapati and Banerjee, 2010).

The objective of this article is to demonstrate that the anaerobic digestion process can be effectively modeled with convolutional neural networks and that its results are superior to multi-layer perceptron networks.

2 Materials and Methods

Ensuring efficient, parameterized, and high-performance sewage treatment is directly linked to the use of technology. It is not possible to guarantee total efficiency in the process by periodically collecting and analyzing samples in the laboratory. By the time this process is completed, the sewage has often already undergone treatment and been discharged into receiving bodies. However, with the application of technology, real-time control can be achieved, facilitating decision-making and necessary adjustments to maximize the treatment process.

The data for this study were collected at the Padilha Sul Wastewater Treatment Plant, located in Ganchinho neighborhood, Curitiba, Paraná, Brazil. The plant has been in operation since 2002 and currently operates at a flow rate of 319 L/s. It has a complete treatment system, including six Upflow Anaerobic Sludge Blanket (UASB) reactors, each with a nominal capacity of 70 L/s (Ross, 2015).

The implementation phase began with the formatting of the database, inserting the data relevant to this study. These data were based on pre-existing research by (Paula, 2019), who conducted tabulation in a laboratory under controlled conditions in their dissertation, and (Hernandez, 2019), who collected data from electronic sensors in a real scenario at the treatment plant in their thesis.

The database was formatted and normalized to allow the programming language to capture the information in a way that the data complied with a scaled interval, ranging between zero and one. This normalization process enabled the neural network to be trained and subsequently validated and tested using the obtained results.

Upon analyzing the database, the presence of periodic behavior in the observed data was identified, as shown in Fig. 1. It was observed that the biogas flow exhibited a similar behavior to the Chemical Oxygen Demand (COD) with an approximate 3-h delay. This behavior was also observed when comparing the sewage flow to the biogas flow, which exhibited a periodic behavior of 1 h, as shown in Fig. 2.

The periodic behavior observed in the relationships described indicates the presence of time series, which are collections of observations occurring over time and involving the relationship of at least one data point in the series with its preceding data points. In other words, there is a temporal relationship, where an element is related to its previous elements. Time-delay neural networks (TDNNs), also known as one-dimensional convolutional neural networks (CNNs), can capture these temporal relationships (Povey, Cheng, et al. 2018). The determination of the number of delays, i.e., how many previous data points impact the current data point, is flexible and should be adjusted for each dataset. In such systems, the data is no longer a set of independent samples but becomes functions of time.

According to (Haykin, 1998), incorporating time into a neural network can be achieved through an implicit representation. For example, the input signal is expressed in the same way, and the sequence of weights for each neuron connected to the input

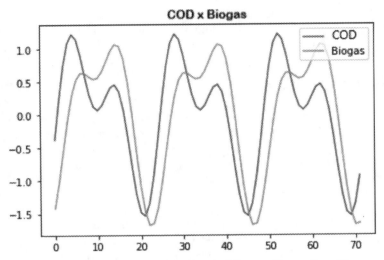

Fig. 1. Periodic behavior of COD (Chemical Oxygen Demand) vs. Biogas.

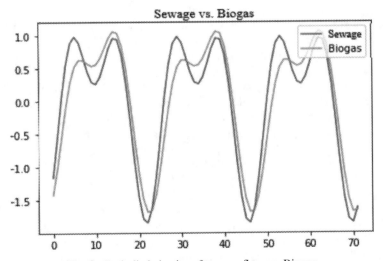

Fig. 2. Periodic behavior of sewage flow vs. Biogas.

layer is convolved with a different input sequence. This way, the temporal series of the signal is embedded in the network's structure.

Another relevant aspect is the presence of seasonal phenomena, which occur regularly at specific time intervals. In wastewater treatment plants, this phenomenon is closely related to population behavior, such as bathing times and the time it takes for material to reach the treatment plant from the sewer network, in addition to the configuration and structure of the pipes and networks (Hernandez, 2019).

To use temporal networks, it is necessary to consider the temporal information from the available past as part of the input data. This concept is referred to as memory. By doing this, the network becomes dynamic as it utilizes the output data from the neuron as input information. In other words, the network's output becomes a temporal function.

3 Training and Testing

Training and testing were conducted on a notebook with an Intel(R) Core(TM) i5-8250U CPU @ 1.60 GHz 1.80 GHz processor, 8 GB of RAM, and PyCharm version 2022.2.3.

The implementation of each algorithm began with reading and storing the data in matrices in memory. Subsequently, the data was normalized, and the training process was performed using the necessary parameters. One of the key parameters is the loss function, which was set to mean square error (MSE) for optimization in all topologies.

In all simulations, regardless of the topology, the network yielded the best results when using 80% of the data for training and 20% for testing. This ratio was standardized across all topologies, and the selection of training and testing data was done randomly and automatically using the training algorithm within the PyCharm programming language.

Due to the random nature of the input data for each training run, the output results also vary. To mitigate biases, the results presented in the tables are an average of 10 executions, providing greater reliability to the reported rates.

3.1 Training of the Multi-Layer Perceptron (MLP) Neural Network

The trained MLP neural network consists of an input layer with 4 inputs: sewage flow, COD, SST, and SSV. It also includes a hidden layer with a varying number of neurons, ranging from 2 to 16, and an output layer representing the sewage flow. During the training process, the number of neurons in the hidden layer was adjusted, starting from 2 and exponentially increasing up to 16 neurons.

The objective of the simulations was to find the model with the highest convergence and an error approaching zero, indicating the ability to estimate values close to the real data at all stages of training. The criteria for evaluation remained the same regardless of the number of neurons.

The results of the simulations are presented in Table 01, where it was observed that poor results were obtained with a small number of neurons, indicating underfitting. Conversely, when an excessive number of neurons was used, overfitting was observed (Table 1).

Table 1. The results of R2 (coefficient of determination) and MSE (mean squared error) for the training

	RNA (2)	RNA (4)	RNA (8)	RNA (16)
MSE	$2.26E^{-04}$	$3.11E^{-05}$	$\mathbf{4.88E^{-04}}$	$1.41E^{-04}$
Averange R^2	0.31	0.61	**0.90**	0.78

Considering the results from Table 01, the performances obtained by varying the number of neurons in the hidden layer, 8 neurons was the topology with the most satisfactory indices, showing a high correlation index ranging from 0.61 to 0.92, with an average R2 = 0.90 as a value approaching zero for MSE = 4.88E-04. The scatter plot presented in Fig. 3 shows points that are close to the line, indicating the approximation of the predicted data to the real data. These results are suitable for a neural network, as can also be observed in Fig. 4, which demonstrates point by point the real and predicted data.

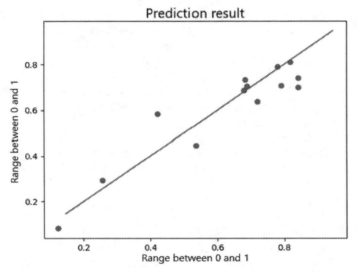

Fig. 3. Prediction of biogas flow for $R^2 = 0.87$.

By observing the best result with 8 neurons and in order to confirm it, the network was trained with 7 and 9 neurons to identify the exact point with the best relationship. However, the average result with 7 neurons was $R^2 = 0.62$ and MSE = 4.88E-04, while with 9 neurons, it obtained an average R^2 value of 0.86 and MSE = 1.59E-04, confirming the superiority of the configuration with 8 neurons.

3.2 Convolutional Neural Network Training–CNN

Applications with CNN dates from 1990, but they stayed many years "forgotten" when, in 2012, they resurfaced in the image-NET photographs competition, bringing spectacular results. This success caused a revolution in the area of computational vision, which can be observed to the present day and which was one of the motivations of this work, in the sense of the technology in the prediction of nonlinear behaviors of the biological reactor, because, besides the Temporal standards related to process seasonality, there is the time of hydraulic detention within the reactor, characteristic that can generate positive results in its application.

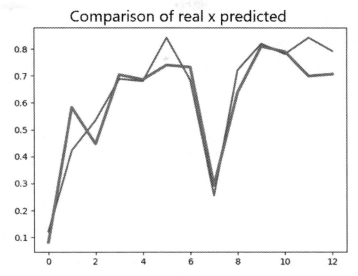

Fig. 4. Comparison of predicted results with actual data.

The choice of CNN is due to the fact that the periodic behavior of the COD and the flow of sewage has temporal characteristics, and it is an evolution of the MLP network, which has been successfully used in various AI applications, with consolidated implementation on the platforms of development, which guarantees ease of support to the code.

Due to the temporal aspect involved in the biological process of wastewater treatment, as shown in Fig. 1 and 2, where a periodic behavior of the data can be observed, the application of a neural network model capable of handling such situations was chosen, which motivated the testing using convolutional neural networks (CNN).

The CNN model, similar to the previous one for comparison purposes, had the number of neurons in the input layer set to four, which were: wastewater flow, COD, SST, and SSV. The remaining values of hidden layers and neurons remained the same for an equivalent comparison.

During the training phase, the number of neurons in the hidden layer was varied, starting from 2 and exponentially increasing up to 16 neurons. It was observed that the results were significantly worse compared to the MLP network, both with a small number of neurons, which could be characterized as underfitting, and with an excessive number of neurons, which led to overfitting.

The results of varying the number of neurons in the hidden layer are presented in Table 8, where it can be observed that the lowest error rate and the highest degree of correlation were achieved during training with 8 neurons in the hidden layer (Table 2).

It can be observed that the results obtained using convolutional neural networks (CNN) are superior compared to using the MLP neural network. Figure 5 presents the scatter plot of the CNN (8), which showed the best result among the performed simulations, achieving an R2 of 0.96 and a series of excellent results. In Fig. 5, the

Table 2. Results of R and MSE for the training stages of the CNN.

	CNN (2)	CNN (4)	CNN (8)	CNN (16)
MSE	$8.21E^{-04}$	$1.54E^{-03}$	**$2.08E^{-04}$**	$8.06E^{-06}$
Average R^2	0.77	0.82	**0.93**	0.32

points close to the line indicate the approximation of the predicted data to the real data. These results are suitable for a neural network, indicating the success of the application.

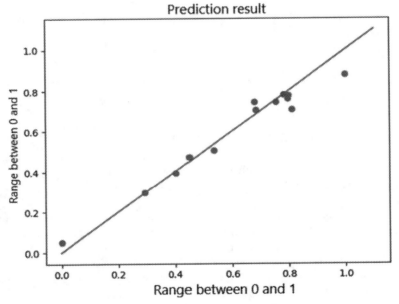

Fig. 5. Prediction of biogas flow for $R^2 = 0.93$.

In Fig. 18, it is possible to observe the proximity of the lines on the graph between the predicted and real data. The values are plotted in a non-normalized manner to facilitate the identification of real values that had greater disparity. When plotted in a normalized scale, the values are modified to fit the scale. By identifying the outlier points, an attempt was made to analyze the data to identify any abnormal behavior that could explain the lower accuracy of the prediction. It was found that peaks that deviate from the data pattern were cases of less accurate prediction (Fig. 6).

In order to determine if 8 neurons were indeed the best option, simulations were conducted with 7 and 9 neurons. The results obtained were as follows: for 7 neurons, the average R^2 was 0.54 and MSE was 7.32E-04, while for 9 neurons, the average R^2 was 0.73 and MSE was 1.49E-03. These results demonstrate that the simulation with 8 neurons had the best average performance.

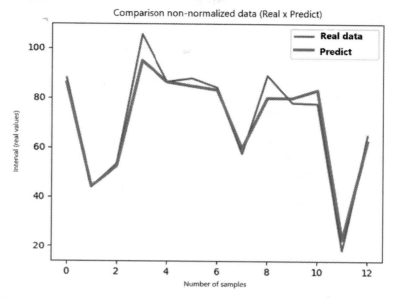

Fig. 6. Comparison of the predicted and actual values in a non-normalized scale.

4   Results and Discussion

The set of results obtained indicates that convolutional neural networks (CNN) outperform other simulations, making them an excellent topology and technology for predicting the biological behavior of treatment plants.

Among the results obtained in the simulations presented in this chapter, the highest efficiency was achieved by the CNN with 8 neurons, referred to as CNN (8). It obtained an MSE of $2.08E^{-04}$ and the best average R^2 value of 0.93. This indicates that for the four input variables applied, the best convergence of results and prediction occurred with 8 neurons. It is important to note that even in simulations without CNN, the best result was also obtained with 8 neurons in the hidden layer, with an MSE of $4.88E^{-04}$ and the best average R^2 value of 0.90. This suggests that this quantity best represents the abstractions of the model, ensuring that the predicted results closely approximate the real sample results.

Regarding the performance improvement in traditional MLP neural networks (RNA T), increasing the number of neurons exponentially resulted in the R^2 value doubling with each implementation until reaching a peak at 8 neurons, after which it started to decline. In contrast, with convolutional networks, the improvement was more gradual, with a close to 10% increase at each stage until reaching the best result with 8 neurons, at which point it started to decline.

5 Conclusions

This study aimed to apply computational models, compare and analyze the results. It is not possible to assert a well-defined pattern for the applicable models in solving the problem at hand, as models are constructed for various purposes and with different datasets and variables. Therefore, techniques that are suitable for one application may be inadequate for another, as evidenced throughout the study.

Secondly, this study aims to raise awareness among treatment plant managers regarding the usefulness of adopting artificial intelligence as a tool for supporting and developing sustainability and environmental management in sanitation. This study aligns with the objectives established in the sanitation framework in Brazil and can also assist in the development of treatment plants worldwide, promoting a sustainable and environmentally friendly business model. However, this requires the collection of experimental data from various regions of Brazil and potentially from other countries to construct models suitable for the respective climates and environments found in large countries like Brazil.

The implementation of prediction models in treatment plants can serve as a change in the biodigestion process, as it aids managers in decision-making and allows real-time intervention in the process, thereby increasing the efficiency of biogas production. Consequently, this promotes the use of biogas as an energy source in potential cogeneration systems implemented in the plants or its purification and commercialization.

References

Brasil: Presidência da República Federativa do Brasil, 15 July 2020. http://www.planalto.gov.br/ccivil_03/_ato2019-2022/2020/lei/l14026.htm. Accessed 21 July 2022

BRASIL: Atlas esgotos: atualização da base de dados de estações de tratamento de esgotos no Brasil, Brasília (2020)

Bilotta, P., Ross, B.Z.L.: Estimativa de geração de energia e emissão evitada de gás de efeito estufa na recuperação de biogás produzido em estação de tratamento de esgotos. Eng Sanit Ambient, pp. 275–282, junho (2016)

Sperling, M.V.: Urban Wastewater Treatment in Brazil Inter-American Development Bank (2016)

Filho, S., Lima, A.S., Mensah, J.H.R., Battiston, K.D.M., Matheus Siqueira Barros, I.F.S.D.S.: Dimensionamento de um reator UASB para tratamento de efluentes domésticos e recuperação do biogás para produção energética: Um estudo de caso em Pouso Alégre (MG), Revista Brasileira De Energias Renováveis, vol. 7, (2018)

Rosa, A.P., Lobato, L.C.d.S., Borges, J.M., Melo, G.C.B.d., Chernicharo, C.A.d.L.: Potencial energético e alternativas para o aproveitamento do biogás e lodo de reatores UASB: estudo de caso Estação de tratamento de efluentes Laboreaux (Itabira). Eng Sanit Ambient, vol. 21, n° 2, pp. 315–328 (2016)

Intergovernmental Panel on Climate Change (IPCC), AR6 Synthesis Report (SYR) (2023)

Chernicharo, C.A.d.L., Ribeiro, T.B., Pegorini, E.S., Possetti, G.R.C., Miki, M.K., Souza, S.N.d.: Contribuição para o aprimoramento de projeto, construção e operação de reatores UASB aplicados ao tratamento de esgoto sanitário – Parte 1: Tópicos de Interesse. DAE, vol. 66, n° 214, pp. 5–16 (2018)

Chernicharo, C.A.D.L.: Reatores Anaeróbios, Belo Horizonte: Editora UFMG (2016)

INTERNATIONAL ENERGY AGENCY: World Energy Outlook, 31 member countries (2022)

Federal Ministry for Economic Affairs and Energy: Development of Renewable Energy Sources in Germany 2017 (2018)

Kana, E.G., Oloke, J., Lateef, A., Adesiyan, M.: Modeling and optimization of biogas production on saw dust and other co-substrates using Artificial Neural network and Genetic Algorithm. Renew. Energy **46**, 276–281 2012

Hong, S.H., Lee, M.W., Lee, D.S., Park, J.M.: Monitoring of sequencing batch reactor for nitrogen and phosphorus removal using neural networks. Biochem. Eng. J. **35**(3), 365–370 (2007)

Lauwers, J., Appels, L., Thompson, I.P., Degrève, J., Van Impe, J.F., Dewil, R.: Mathematical modelling of anaerobic digestion of biomass and waste: Power and limitations. Prog. Energy Combust. Sci. **39**(4), 383–402 (2013)

Silva, I.N.d., Spatti, D.H., Flauzino, R.A.: Redes neurais artificiais para engenharia e ciências aplicadas - Curso pratico, São Paulo: Artliber (2010)

Kusiak, A., Wei, X.: A data-driven model for maximization of methane production in a wastewater treatment plant. Water Sci. Technol. **65**(6), 1116–1122 (2012)

Haykin, S.S.: Neural Networks and Learning Machines. Prentice Hall, USA (2009)

Beltramo, T., Ranzan, C., Hinrichs, J., Hitzmann, B.: Artificial neural network prediction of the biogas flow rate optimised with an ant colony algorithm. Biosyst. Eng. **143**, 68–78 (2016)

Waewsak, C., Nopharatana, A., Chaiprasert, P.: Neural-fuzzy control system application for monitoring process response and control of anaerobic hybrid reactor in wastewater treatment and biogas production. J. Environ. Sci. **22**(12), 1883–1890 (2010)

Garlapati, V.K., Banerjee, R.: Evolutionary and swarm intelligence-based approaches for optimization of lipase extraction from fermented broth. Eng. Life Sci. **10**(3), 265–273 (2010)

Ross, B.Z.L.: Escuma de reatores anaeróbios tratando esgotos domésticos em escala real: produção, caracterização e proposição de parâmetros para seu gerenciamento, UFPR, Curitiba (2015)

Paula, A.C.d.: Avaliação integrada do desempenho de reatores anaeróbios do tipo UASB. Dissertação, Curitiba (2019)

Hernandez, O.A.D.: Avaliação de sistemas de medição para controle de processo em tempo real numa Estação de Tratamento de Esgoto sanitário que utiliza reatores UASB, Curitiba (2019)

Povey, D., et al.: Semi-Orthogonal Low-Rank Matrix Factorization for Deep Neural Networks," em Interspeech (2018)

Haykin, S.O.: Neural Networks: A Comprehensive Foundation:, United States Edition: Pearson (1998)

Kim, J., et al.: Forecasting influent flow rate and composition with occasional data for supervisory management system by time series model. Water Sci. Technol. **53**(4–5), 185–192 (2006)

Factors Influencing Merchants' Adoption of Cashless Payment Systems in Sweden

Khando Khando$^{(\boxtimes)}$ ⓘ, M. Sirajul Islam ⓘ, and Shang Gao ⓘ

Department of Informatics, Örebro University School of Business, Örebro, Sweden
{khando.khando,sirajul.islam,shang.gao}@oru.se

Abstract. Sweden is practically becoming a cashless society and possesses a clear sign of future competitiveness in cashless payment which has a wider impact on businesses and society at large. However, according to the existing research, there is a lack of comprehensive understanding of how this cashless society has shaped up and how such competitiveness can be sustained over time. There has been much research on consumer adoption of cashless payment systems, but the research on adoption by merchants is scant. Thus, considering the critical role they play in the cashless payment ecosystem, this study aims to understand the factors influencing the adoption of cashless payment systems from Swedish merchants' perspective. The study used qualitative thematic analysis to identify seven factors: convenience, cost, trust, risks, norm, regulation, and customer preference. The findings contribute to limited knowledge of cashless payment systems in the context of Sweden and can be transferable to other countries.

Keywords: Cashless Payment Systems · Adoption Factors · Swedish Merchants · Thematic Analysis · Cashless Society

1 Introduction

The advent of financial technology and the widespread use of the internet have precipitated a paradigm shift in business transactions towards electronic-based operations. Over the past decade, there has been a significant decline in the utilization of cash as a payment method [1]. The concept of cashless societies is gaining traction, and we are witnessing an increasingly growing trend in cashless transactions [2]. A cashless payment is defined as any electronic or digital transaction conducted without the exchange of physical currency such as coins or paper money [3]. These cashless payment systems encompass the digital mediums or technologies employed by both the payer and payee to facilitate transactions [4]. These systems can be broadly classified into several categories including card payments, electronic payments, mobile payments [5], and cryptocurrencies [6].

The transition towards a cashless society is an emerging trend and plays a pivotal role in the global economy. The adoption of cashless payment systems yields numerous benefits, which are directly correlated with economic growth [7, 8]. The previous decade has witnessed an unprecedented growth rate in the volume of global cashless transactions. For instance, in 2018 and 2019, the number of global non-cash transactions increased by nearly 14%, reaching a total of 708.5 billion transactions. This growth rate is the highest recorded in the past decade [9]. Moreover, the COVID-19 pandemic has catalyzed a shift towards cashless transactions as countries sought to mitigate the risk of infection associated with handling cash [10].

Existing studies show that, apart from being convenient, fast and cost-effective, cashless payment systems help in reducing suspicious transactions of money, circulating fake currency, and combating money laundering to crack down on organized crime [11, 12]. Although the academic communities have paid increased attention to the adoption of cashless payment systems (e.g., cryptocurrencies, mobile payments) by consumers [6, 13–15], the research on adoption by merchants is scant [12, 16]. Arvidsson [1] emphasized that one aspect of payment research which has been largely ignored is merchant adoption. However, the cashless payment is crucial for the interactions between both merchants and consumers [17, 18]. Therefore, there is a strong need to understand the factors influencing the adoption of cashless payment systems from merchants' perspective.

Adoption is a concept defined as "making full use of a new idea as the best course of action available" [19]. The adoption process is a sequence of stages through which an individual or other decision-making unit passes from first knowledge of an innovation to forming an attitude towards the innovation, to a decision to adopt or reject, to implementation of the new idea, and confirmation of this decision [20]. In this study context, adoption is conceived as a concept related to the 'use' of cashless payment systems by merchants. The adoption of cashless payment systems varies in terms of maturity and penetration from country to country. In some countries, the adoption rates are marginal [21]. In the Scandinavian countries, cashless payment systems have become standard practice. Specifically, Sweden is spearheading the transition towards a cashless society[22, 23]. Merchants in Sweden have the right to not accept cash from customers and half of all merchants expect to stop cash by 2025 [1].

Given the above background, this study aims to explore the factors influencing the adoption of cashless payment systems by merchants in Sweden. Using in-depth semi-structured interviews and following a qualitative thematic analysis approach, the paper aims to address the research question: *What are the factors influencing merchants' adoption of cashless payment systems in Sweden?*

2 Related Research

Reviewing the literature on the adoption of cashless payment systems reveals that while many studies are concentrating on consumer acceptance, there are relatively few studies focusing on merchant adoption [16, 24]. Among the few studies, many focus on merchants' adoption of a particular payment system (e.g., *mobile payment systems* [24–29] instead of cashless payment systems. The studies identify factors e.g., cost, perceived risk, perceived ease of use, perceived usefulness, social influence, competition, and complexity etc. that influence merchants' adoption. Other related studies include investigation on card payments e.g., [30–32] and cryptocurrencies [33–35].

Recent years have witnessed a few more research on the adoption of cashless payment systems by retail merchants e.g., [36–40]. However, most of these studies follow a quantitative methodology. They use a pre-existing model, e.g., the Technology Acceptance Model (TAM) [41] (Davis, 1989) and Unified Theory of Adoption and Use of Technology (UTAUT) [42], to report adoption factors such as the technological, environmental, and business characteristics related to merchants and mostly highlight the intentions to use the system.

A small subset of research explored the adoption of mobile payment by merchants using qualitative methodology e.g., [18, 24]. They highlighted merchants' adoption factors such as payment processing time and cost, convenience, technology incompatibility, and cultural and infrastructural issues. However, they followed a deductive approach and used adoption factors taken from existing frameworks, e.g., Boateng [24] used the prerequisite framework of Mallat & Tuunainen [25] to study the drivers and barriers to adoption. However, their study was limited in capturing the novelty and complexity of a context-based payment system. Furthermore, a previous study on Swedish merchants [1] was also conducted using a quantitative survey. Therefore, this study has the potential to supplement previous findings by applying qualitative thematic analysis that allows for in-depth analysis of interview data which can reveal complex patterns and themes.

The prevalence of research on payment systems varies between developed and developing countries. Notably, most publications focus on developing countries like India and China because of the rapid growth in digital transactions [43]. This study aims to complement previous research by investigating the adoption of cashless payment systems from merchants' perspective in Sweden, one of the developed and digitalized countries in Europe.

3   Study Context

The context of this study is Sweden, one of the most digitalized countries in the world [44] which is on the verge of becoming the world's first cashless society and has the potential to serve as a role model for many other countries [23]. The Riksbank's (Sweden's Central Bank) survey on people's payment habits in 2022 shows that nine out of ten Swedes use the internet daily and three out of four identify themselves digitally using mobile e-ID [44]. The usage of cash is declining, and Sweden is among the countries with the lowest total value of banknotes and coins in circulation relative to gross national product. Most Swedish bank branches do not accept cash, thus there is a cash revolt known as "Kontantupppror" that calls for banks to take cash once again, particularly from lobby groups that represent the senior population and the cash-in-transit service industry [1]. In Sweden, merchants are not legally bound to accept cash and have the right to decide which payment systems to use. Therefore, many business stores are seen with 'cash-free' signs where only cashless payments are accepted [45].

One of the most widely used payment instruments by merchants is card payments (e.g., Visa and Mastercard) that are used in retail point of sales (POS) locations [1, 46]. As per the Riksbank, 59% of transactions were processed through card in the year 2021, out of which debit card accounts for 84%. Bank transfers make up almost 32% of all online transactions and constitute a larger proportion of monetary value. This is one of the preferred methods by merchants since bank transfers generally charge less fees than cards for merchants. The other most popular payment method is the Sweden-based mobile payment app called Swish. Furthermore, Buy Now Pay Later (BNPL) has become popular among merchants, as one of its largest companies (Klarna) was founded in Sweden in 2005. Other alternative payment methods commonly used in the Swedish market include digital wallets such as PayPal, Apple Pay, and Samsung Pay [47].

4 Methodology

This study was conducted by collecting empirical data from semi-structured interviews with Swedish merchants. A qualitative thematic analysis approach was used to analyse the collected data. This section presents the selection of participants, how the interviews were conducted and how the data was analysed.

4.1 Selection of Participants

Participants can be any retail merchants operating in the Swedish market, and there are many different sectors to choose from. The choice of participants is critical but should also be impartial because any merchant irrespective of size or sector can be chosen at random for this study. Thus, to select individuals who have the knowledge, experience, or characteristics necessary to provide in-depth insights into the contextual factors, a purposive sampling technique was adopted which is a typical technique in qualitative research [48]. We aim to focus on a single sector that is representative of merchants using cashless payment systems daily thereby providing us with rich and meaningful data that can be used to answer our research question. Hence, seven restaurant owners were selected for the interview based on the deeper knowledge they possess regarding their business, business decisions and payment solutions as well as their willingness to participate and share their experiences openly. Out of seven restaurant owners interviewed, five were males and two were females (ages between 35 and 50), with a minimum of 5 years' experience in running a restaurant business and were relatively knowledgeable about cashless payment systems in Sweden.

4.2 Data Collection

This study collected data from the restaurant owners by conducting semi-structured interviews. To determine what type of data to collect during the interview, we compiled literature of extant research and read online payment reports to gather theoretical data. After a comprehensive review of the assembled literature, we developed a general interview guide based on the existing key factors found in the literature. The interview guide comprises broad open-ended questions related to the most frequent themes: cost, trust, risk, convenience, and social influence. The interview guide can be found at the following web link: https://tinyurl.com/4n43j4yt.

Using semi-structured interviews provided more flexibility and allowed us to ask open-ended questions to gain in-depth insights into the feelings, views, and experiences of participants about their payment systems. The interview was conducted using the above interview guide, however, our focus was mainly on allowing participants to speak openly and freely during the interview, as a result, following an interview guide becomes less important. All seven interviews were conducted face-to-face which allowed for generating rich data as it enabled asking follow-up questions to their responses.

The interviews were conducted in central Sweden and audio recorded. Prior permission was sought with a written consent form signed by each participant. The interviewees were sufficiently briefed about the purpose of the research and reassured of the confidentiality of the recordings. Since all the interview participants are anonymous; we refer to them as e.g., Restaurant owner 1 as R1 in the results section. Out of the seven interviews, the first interview was used as a pilot interview, and necessary adjustments were made to the strategies and logical flows in the second interview to align with the research objectives. The interviews were conducted in English and each interview lasted for about an hour. The recorded audio was transcribed verbatim for data analysis and the transcript was further enriched by the field notes taken during the interview.

4.3 Data Analysis

The interview transcripts were analyzed by using qualitative Thematic Analysis (TA) following Braun and Clarke's [49] six-step guidelines. TA is an appropriate method for analyzing large amounts of data and offers an accessible and theoretically flexible approach to analyzing qualitative data [49].

As a first step, the interview transcripts were read and re-read to familiarize with the interview data which is 'a key phase of data analysis within interpretive qualitative methodology' [50]. Then, the initial list of ideas relevant to the research objectives was noted. Additionally, the field notes were linked to relevant points within the transcripts. The first author then coded the restaurant owners' verbatim and generated the initial codes using Quirkos (a software application for text analysis). The initial coding generated 17 sets of codes that represent the meaning and patterns in the data. The other two authors independently verified the codes and assessed the correctness of codes to minimize the level of bias when interpreting the results. We then reassessed and re-coded the 17 generated codes into 11 sub-themes in a more researcher-centric concept [51]. A thematic map was created to help organize and order the data in a meaningful and comprehensible manner, which in turn formed the basis of the thematic analysis.

The themes were reviewed to check if they were coherent and consistent with the research objectives [52]. This step involves the refinement of the candidate themes identified in the earlier step. For instance, the themes that were not supported with sufficient data extracts were discarded while others were collapsed into a single theme or combined to form another theme. For example, theme 'compatibility' and 'competition' were discarded because they were not supported by enough data extraction. All the collated data extracts from interviews were reviewed and checked that they form a coherent pattern. After that, the validity of individual themes concerning the restaurant owners' interview data set was ascertained and coded additional data under the themes that had been missed previously via an iterative process. This indicated that the thematic analysis was going in the right direction as this step provided a fairly good idea about different themes, how they fit together and the overall narrative of the data. This review process established a satisfactory set of seven refined candidate themes. After confirming the themes, they were named distinctively to set boundaries between the data. The 'essence' of what each theme was about and what aspect of the data each theme captured were defined.

Additionally, how the themes were related to the determining factors for adoption and how they fitted into the overall interview data had been considered. Upon establishing a satisfactory set of themes, a comprehensive report was compiled, substantiated by evidence drawn from the data. This evidence was presented in the form of illustrative quotes extracted from the interview [48]. A detailed exposition of these themes is provided in Sect. 5 below.

5 Findings

The thematic analysis of the interview data identified seven themes that represent the factors influencing Swedish merchants' adoption of cashless payment systems. The seven factors are convenience, cost, trust, risks, norms, regulation, and customer preference.

5.1 Convenience

'Convenience' is found as one of the common reasons for using cashless payments. The restaurant owners find it easy to operate and lessen the trouble of handling small cash changes at the counter.

> "The payment goes much faster when we don't deal with cash. We no longer collect coins and small changes at the counter." (R5)

> "I previously used to maintain big cash safe boxes to store money. We don't have the hassle of keeping those boxes now." (R1)

Restaurant owners also find the use of a cashless payment system convenient as it helps reduce queues at the counter.

> "…. Use of contactless payment system is faster. We have a 'tap and go' card terminal and 'swish' mobile payment as well. Our new payment systems speed up our payment process and we have less queuing at the counter during busy hours." (R3)

5.2 Cost

Restaurant owners are motivated by the fact that using cashless payment systems lowers the overall operating cost. They reported two types of cost: financial cost such as transaction fees and subscription fees, and technological cost which is incurred in either purchasing new payment system devices or renting and installing them at the store. They admitted that they are encouraged by lower fees charged by their service providers.

> "It is good to see that my payment service is getting better each year with decreased hire charge compared to previous years." (R6).

> "In Sweden, we don't have the hassle of going to the bank for cash deposits and withdrawals for our business, everything is cashless which saves operating costs." (R2)

5.3 Trust in Service Providers

The factor of 'trust' plays a major role in restaurant owners' adoption of cashless payment systems. The owners trust the payment service providers and regulatory bodies through which they think their sensitive data is protected and their privacy is guaranteed. They are also aware that the payments from the accepted accounts are duly credited to their account without alteration or leading to fraudulent activities. The restaurant owners consider cashless payments safe and have total faith in established service providers.

> *"I would confidently say that the use of cashless systems in Sweden has reached the maturity level. I fully trust the system here." (R3)*

> *"I've used the system without any complaint so far. So, I don't have any trust issues about the service provided." (R1)*

> *"I trust my payment service provider who keeps customers personal data because it is licensed and authorized by the government." (R4)*

The restaurant owners in general have a high level of confidence in cashless payment systems provided by the service providers. Owners also view that their customers have trust in the payment systems they use.

5.4 Risks

Cashless payment is highly dependent on internet connectivity and electricity power supply. Although it is unlikely to occur in countries like Sweden, the majority of restaurant owners often highlighted the possibility of greater risks of power outage and internet breakdown that could occur due to cyberattacks or disasters like earthquakes and storms etc. A moment of power blackout or system downtime causes a huge loss to them as they are unable to process payments.

> *"For me, the two biggest risks I foresee are the internet shutdown and an interruption in the electricity supply. I think these two are the potential dangers of cashless payment systems, imagine a day without a power supply or for that matter, a day without the internet. Things will stop working in Sweden." (R7)*

The restaurant owners mentioned that going cashless can prevent the risk of physical theft as one does not need to carry bulk cash in hand. However, they are anxious about identity theft - the risk of losing their system credentials and another person accessing their account.

> *"I log off my system immediately after I process payment from the customer because I worry about other people accessing my account like hackers taking control of my system using my password and username." (R4)*

Despite the existence of laws to improve the security of cashless payments and the verification and authentication of transactions, exposing user credentials can pose a risk.

> *"Security issue is a concern, although our systems are standardized and matured enough, we still need to take good care of our BankIDs which is the door key to our accounts." (R5)*

5.5 Norm

Most restaurant owners have the opinion that the wider use of cashless payment systems in Sweden is partly due to people's lifestyles. They consider going cashless in Sweden normal. As the use of cash for business and private purposes is declining, it is much more normal to see the sign 'cash-free' at the service counters. They reported that the cashless payment has successfully become part of their business lives effortlessly as it has become part of the society, they live in.

"I keep minimum of cash at the counter just in case someone needs to pay in cash. But people rarely come with cash. It's always cashless...either by card or mobile or other contactless mode." (R2)

"We live in the digital age. Nobody asks us to go digital and we can't live without it now. It is part of our lifestyle." (R6)

"My store is cash-free and I have no cash on me. It is the way of life now. Nobody carries cash." (R1)

5.6 Regulations

Most participants attributed the success of cashless payment systems to the transparent and well-established regulations. They indicated that for a payment system to be successful, it should be well-regulated, reliable, and safe for them to operate in the payment market without fear of losing money.

"I haven't experienced any fraudulent activities until now. The success of cashless payment in Sweden is mainly because of its transparency and having clear procedures in place." (R4)

"The payment services are bound by firstly the European financial laws and requirements, and then by the Riksbank directives. The service providers are well-regulated and certified entities...our job is only to record the transactions into the system, rest assured by the system." (R6)

Restaurant owners have consistently affirmed that the implementation of cashless payment systems enhances their ability to maintain transparency and ensures adherence to payment regulations.

"Since my payment system is connected with the tax system, I automatically fulfil my regulatory needs." (R3)

"I don't need to calculate VAT now, whereas dealing with cash was troublesome, I sometimes forget to enter the transaction into the system, particularly during busy hours and get into tax issues unnecessarily." (R7)

5.7 Customer Preference

The majority of restaurant owners reported using payment methods that are demanded by customers or frequently requested by their clients. They were interested in offering various payment methods that suit the needs of their customers. They were aware that offering a wider selection of payment options helped them to better serve a wide range of people.

"Most people pay by card or through swish. But there are a few people especially young customers who want to pay by other mobile apps such as Apple Pay, Paypal, and Google Pay. I make all options available to them." (R5).

The selection of payment methods by restaurant owners is largely influenced by shifts in customer behavior. They have observed that the COVID-19 pandemic has markedly altered the manner in which their customers interact with payment systems, indicating a change in customer preferences.

"The COVID pandemic had pushed people to use contactless payment due to health reasons. And now the trends seem to continue. Customers like to pay by contactless mode." (R7)

"People turned into a cashless mode during the pandemic especially many of our senior customers who used to pay cash, are now paying by cashless method, either by card or mobile." (R2)

6   Discussion

This study identified seven factors that determine Swedish merchants' adoption of cashless payment systems. The findings represent the experiences and perceptions of Swedish retail merchants who use cashless payment systems for their daily transactions. Some of the factors identified through this study fit in with the previously established factors, while others are inconsistent with the previous findings. For instance, two adoption factors identified in this study in the context of Swedish restaurant owners are 'convenience' and 'cost' related to the benefits of cashless payment systems. This is consistent with Boateng [24] and Moghavvemi [18] who previously found that merchants' adoption is influenced by the 'cost' factor since merchants are profit-oriented. They reported the adoption factors such as reducing operating cost and transaction processing fees, increasing sales, and improving customer satisfaction. Similarly, these studies argued 'convenience' as a determinant factor for merchants' adoption of cashless payment systems that are related to the means of decreased payment processing time and less queuing at the cash counter. This finding is particularly relevant to retail stores as they often face the difficulty of managing large crowds at their checkout counters. The use of cashless payment systems eases merchants' operating tasks at the counters by shortening the checkout process which in turn enhances the overall business efficiency. The finding is also in line with a study by Petrova and Wang [53] which concluded that the use of a cashless payment system has the potential to replace cash due to its efficiency and convenience factor.

On the contrary, the factors identified by the current study such as merchants' trust, risks, and norms are inconsistent with the findings revealed by the previous studies. For instance, the recent studies on merchants' adoption of cashless payment systems conducted by Kumar [54] and Altounjy [55] reported variables related to merchants' characteristics (e.g., perceived usefulness, perceived ease of use, willingness, capability, technology readiness etc.). These differences in findings can be attributed partly to the research traditions and methodology applied in the studies. They used a quantitative methodology, followed a deductive approach rooted in the positivist view, and used the pre-existing IS adoption theories to derive the factors influencing the merchants' adoption. Similarly, the findings of this study are also at odds with some of the recent studies.

For example, Mishra [12] and Moghavvemi [18] reported the merchants' adoption factors such as technology incompatibility and 'lack of critical mass', citing that merchants cannot rely on payment systems supplied by the service providers since they are not compatible with most of the customer devices. However, these factors do not concern Swedish merchants as the systems from service providers are regulated, matured, and trusted by the merchants [56], and going cashless to a large extent is determined by their lifestyle and the way they do business. Consequently, factors such as the 'lack of critical mass' are deemed irrelevant within the context of payment method selection by Swedish merchants. Previous studies [27, 56] also showed securing customer data and maintaining customers' 'trust' as the two main adoption factors which is in line with the current findings. However, the findings on how the merchants perceive trust and manage data security vary. For example, in the context of Malaysia [18], merchants' integrity and ethics play a critical role in protecting against customer data leaks and misuse, as the merchants themselves handle customers' data. In contrast, Swedish merchants exhibit minimal concern regarding customer data, as it is managed by certified service providers via secure network systems.

Through the thematic analysis, this study unearthed seven novel contextual adoption factors influencing Swedish merchants. The findings from this study can help policymakers (e.g., government and regulators) and practitioners (e.g., service providers) understand how the Swedish cashless ecosystem is progressing from merchants' perspective. This study also complements previous studies by exploring the adoption factors of cashless payment systems from merchants' perspective in Sweden. The insights generated can be transferable to other countries that aspire for a cashless society to have a wider impact on business and the nation at large.

7 Limitation

The Thematic Analysis methodology was employed to systematically code and identify latent themes, which were subsequently categorized as factors influencing merchants' adoption of cashless payment systems. These adoption factors were generated abductively, indicating a potential for the researchers' preconceived biases to influence the theme development and data interpretation. It is plausible that our personal beliefs and experiences may have shaped our interpretation of the data collected from restaurant owners. However, this study mitigates this limitation to a certain extent, as the coding process conducted by the first author was reviewed by two co-authors to minimize biases and validate the authenticity of the findings.

8 Conclusion

This study identified seven distinctive factors that play a key role in Swedish merchants' decision to adopt cashless payment systems: convenience, cost, trust, risks, norms, regulation, and customer preference. The findings from this study contribute towards providing a better understanding of the characteristics of a cashless society and insights on adoption factors, from Swedish merchants' perspective.

This study was conducted by collecting empirical data from seven semi-structured interviews with restaurant owners from central Sweden who were considered representative of retail merchants in Sweden. However, the findings can be further enriched by conducting more interviews with other sectors. Future research can focus on collecting more data from multiple sources for triangulation to increase the validity of the findings.

References

1. Arvidsson, N., Hedman, J., Segendorf, B.: Cashless society: when will merchants stop accepting cash in Sweden - a research model. In: Feuerriegel, S., Neumann, D. (eds.) FinanceCom 2016. LNBIP, vol. 276, pp. 105–113. Springer, Cham (2017). https://doi.org/10.1007/978-3-319-52764-2_8
2. Fabris, N.: Cashless society–the future of money or a utopia. J. Central Banking Theory Pract. 8(1), 53–66 (2019)
3. Bilińska-Reformat, K., Kieżel, M.: Retail banks and retail chains cooperation for the promotion of the cashless payments in Poland. In: Proceedings of 15th International Marketing Trends Conference, Venice (20160
4. Xena, P., Rahadi, R.A.: Adoption of e-payment to support small medium enterprise payment system: a conceptualised model. Int. J. Account. 4(18), 32–41 (2019)
5. Rahman, M., Ismail, I., Bahri, S.: Analysing consumer adoption of cashless payment in Malaysia. Digital Bus. 1(1), 100004 (2020)
6. García-Monleón, F., Erdmann, A., Arilla, R.: A value-based approach to the adoption of cryptocurrencies. J. Innov. Knowl. 8(2), 100342 (2023)
7. APEC. Fintech E-payment Readiness Index. Ecosystem Assessment and Status Report (2015). https://www.apec.org.au/apec-fintech-e-payment
8. Igudia, P.O.: A qualitative evaluation of the factors influencing the adoption of electronic payment systems (SMEs) by SMEs in Nigeria. Eur. Sci. J. ESJ 13(31), 472–502 (2017)
9. Capgemini. World Payments Report 2020 (2020). https://www.sogeti.com/explore/reports/world-payments-report-2020/
10. Jaafar, I.: A conceptual framework integration of UTAUT and HBM on evaluating the adoption of electronic payment system in Malaysia. Int. J. Soc. Polit. Econ. Res. 7(4), 1164–1176 (2020)
11. Arvidsson, N.: Building a Cashless Society: The Swedish Route to the Future of Cash Payments. Springerm, Cham (2019)
12. Mishra, V., Walsh, I., Srivastava, A.: Merchants' adoption of mobile payment in emerging economies: the case of unorganised retailers in India. Eur. J. Inf. Syst. 31(1), 74–90 (2022)
13. Khando, K., Islam, M.S., Gao, S.: The emerging technologies of digital payments and associated challenges: a systematic literature review. Future Internet 15(1), 21 (2023)
14. Singh, P., Dwivedi, Y.K., Kahlon, K.S., Rana, N.P., Patil, P.P., Sawhney, R.S.: Digital payment adoption in India: insights from Twitter analytics. In: Pappas, I.O., Mikalef, P., Dwivedi, Y.K., Jaccheri, L., Krogstie, J., Mäntymäki, M. (eds.) I3E 2019. LNCS, vol. 11701, pp. 425–436. Springer, Cham (2019). https://doi.org/10.1007/978-3-030-29374-1_35
15. Gao, S., et al.: An empirical study on users' continuous usage intention of QR code mobile payment services in China. Int. J. E-Adoption 10, 18–33 (2018)
16. Dahlberg, T., Guo, J., Ondrus, J.: A critical review of mobile payment research. Electron. Commer. Res. Appl. 14(5), 265–284 (2015)
17. Khando, K., Islam, M.S., Gao, S.: Factors shaping the cashless payment ecosystem: understanding the role of participating actors. In: 35th Bled eConference-Digital Restructuring and Human (Re) Action, Bled, Slovenia, June 26–29, 2022. University of Maribor University Press (2022)

18. Moghavvemi, S., et al.: Drivers and barriers of mobile payment adoption: Malaysian merchants' perspective. J. Retail. Consum. Serv. **59**, 12 (2021)
19. Rogers, E.M., Shoemaker, F.F.: Communication of Innovations; A Cross-Cultural Approach (1971)
20. Hua, Y., Liu, A.M.: An investigation of person-culture fit and person-task fit on ICT adoption in the Hong Kong construction industry. Architectural Eng. Des. Manag. **13**(6), 423–438 (2017)
21. Eelu, S., Nakakawa, A.: Framework towards enhancing adoption of electronic payment in a developing economy: a case of Uganda (2018)
22. Hedman, J.: Going Cashless: What Can We Learn from Sweden's Experience. Knowledge@ Wharton, Interviewer, & U. o. WHARTON, Editor (2018)
23. Fourtané, S.: Sweden: how to live in the world's first cashless society. Interesting Eng. **20** (2019)
24. Boateng, R., Afeti, E.Y., Afful-Dadzie, E.: Adoption of mobile payments in Ghana: a merchant perspective (2019)
25. Mallat, N., Tuunainen, V.K.: Exploring merchant adoption of mobile payment systems: an empirical study. E-service J. **6**(2), 24–57 (2008)
26. Liébana-Cabanillas, F., Lara-Rubio, J.: Predictive and explanatory modeling regarding adoption of mobile payment systems. Technol. Forecast. Soc. Chang. **120**, 32–40 (2017)
27. Stepcic, C., Salah, K.: The institutionalisation of mobile payment technologies in Kenya: retailers' pespective. In: Association for Information Systems, (ECIS 2016 Proceedings) (2016)
28. Esawe, A.T.: Exploring retailers' behavioural intentions towards using m-payment: extending UTAUT with perceived risk and trust. Paradigm **26**(1), 8–28 (2022)
29. Altwairesh, R., Aloud, M.: Mobile payments from merchants' perspective: an empirical study using the TAM Model in Saudi Arabia. Int. J. Comput. Sci. Netw. Secur. **21**(8), 317–326 (2021)
30. Ally, M.A., Toleman, M.: Towards a theoretical framework of determinants for the adoption and diffusion of buyer authenticated credit card payment programs: the online merchant's perspective. In: Proceedings. IEEE International Conference on e-Commerce Technology, 2004. CEC 2004. IEEE (2004)
31. Loke, Y.J.: Determinants of merchant participation in credit card payment schemes. Rev. Netw. Econ. **6**(4) 2007
32. Veljan, A.: Regulating the uncontrollable: the development of card scheme fees in payments markets in light of recent policy intervention, pp. 89–110 (2021)
33. Jonker, N.: What drives bitcoin adoption by retailers. De Nederlandsche Bank NV, Payments and Market Infrastructures Division, Working Paper No. 585 (2018)
34. Nuryyey, G., et al.: Factors of digital payment adoption in hospitality businesses: a conceptual approach. Eur. J. Tourism Res. **29**, 9 (2021)
35. Echchabi, A., Omar, M.M.S., Ayedh, A.M.: Factors influencing Bitcoin investment intention: the case of Oman. Int. J. Internet Technol. Secured Trans. **11**(1), 1–15 (2021)
36. Adhikary, A., et al.: How does the adoption of digital payment technologies influence unorganized retailers' performance? An investigation in an emerging market. J. Acad. Mark. Sci. **49**, 882–902 (2021)
37. Koul, S., Singh Jasrotia, S., Govind Mishra, H.: Acceptance of digital payments among rural retailers in India. J. Payments Strategy Syst. **15**(2), 201–213 (2021)
38. Jiang, Y., et al.: QR digital payment system adoption by retailers: the moderating role of COVID-19 knowledge. Inf. Res. Manage. J. (IRMJ) **34**(3), 41–63 (2021)
39. Ariffin, N.H.M., Ahmad, F., Haneef, U.M.: Acceptance of mobile payments by retailers using UTAUT model. Indonesian J. Electr. Eng. Comput. Sci. **19**(1), 149–155 (2020)
40. Ligon, E., et al.: What explains low adoption of digital payment technologies? Evidence from small-scale merchants in Jaipur, India. PLoS ONE **14**(7), 22 (2019)

41. Davis, F.D.: Perceived usefulness, perceived ease of use, and user acceptance of information technology. MIS Q. **13**, 319–340 (1989)
42. Venkatesh, V., et al.: User acceptance of information technology: toward a unified view. MIS Q. **27**(3), 425–478 (2003)
43. Abdullah, Naved Khan, M.: Determining mobile payment adoption: a systematic literature search and bibliometric analysis. Cogent Bus. Manage. **8**(1), 1893245 (2021)
44. Riksbank. Payments Report 2022 (2022). https://www.riksbank.se/en-gb/payments--cash/payments-in-sweden/payments-report-2022/trends-on-the-payment-market/
45. Peebles, G.: Banking on digital money: Swedish Cashlessness and the fraying currency tether. Cultural Anthropol. **36**(1), 1–24 (2021)
46. Riksbank. Payment Report 2021 (2021). https://www.riksbank.se/globalassets/media/rapporter/betalningsrapport/2021/engelska/payments-report-2021.pdf
47. Statista. Payment methods in Sweden. Statistics & Facts (2023). https://www.statista.com/topics/6286/payment-methods-in-sweden/#topicOverview
48. Silverman, D., Doing Qualitative Research: A Practical Handbook. in Doing Qualitative Research: A Practical Handbook. Sage Publications, London (2010)
49. Braun, V., Clarke, V.: Using thematic analysis in psychology. Qual. Res. Psychol. **3**(2), 77–101 (2006)
50. Bird, C.M.: How I stopped dreading and learned to love transcription. Qual. Inq. **11**(2), 226–248 (2005)
51. Gioia, D.A., Corley, K.G., Hamilton, A.L.: Seeking qualitative rigor in inductive research: notes on the Gioia methodology. Organ. Res. Methods **16**(1), 15–31 (2013)
52. Patton, M.Q.: In Qualitative research and evaluation methods. Thousand Oaks (2002)
53. Petrova, K., Wang, B.: Retailer adoption of mobile payment: a qualitative study. J. Electron. Commer. Organ. (JECO) **11**(4), 70–89 (2013)
54. Kumar, V., Nim, N., Sharma, A.: Driving growth of Mwallets in emerging markets: a retailer's perspective. J. Acad. Mark. Sci. **47**, 747–769 (2019)
55. Altounjy, R., et al.: Moving from bricks to clicks: Merchants' acceptance of the mobile payment in Malaysia (2020)
56. Yeboah, E., Boateng, R., Owusu, A., Afful-Dadzie, E., Ofori-Amanfo, J.: Assessing the role of trust in merchant adoption of mobile payments in Ghana. In: Hattingh, M., Matthee, M., Smuts, H., Pappas, I., Dwivedi, Y.K., Mäntymäki, M. (eds.) I3E 2020. LNCS, vol. 12066, pp. 204–215. Springer, Cham (2020). https://doi.org/10.1007/978-3-030-44999-5_17

Optimizing Dental Implant Distribution: A Strategic Approach for Supply Chain Management in the Beauty and Well-Being Industry

Marcelo Carneiro Gonçalves$^{(\boxtimes)}$ (ID), Ana Beatriz Pamplona,
Elpidio Oscar Benitez Nara(ID), and Izamara Cristina Palheta Dias(ID)

Pontifical Catholic University of Paraná, Curitiba, PR 80215-901, Brazil
{Carneiro.marcelo,elpidio.nara}@pucpr.br, {beatriz.pamplona,
izamara.dias}@pucpr.edu.br

Abstract. With the increasing demand for well-being and beauty, the dental industry has been strongly impacted in recent years. Consequently, companies in the dental implant production sector have needed to adjust their production volumes, sales, and product availability to meet market demand. Therefore, optimizing their product distribution network is essential to ensure timely delivery and customer satisfaction.

To achieve this performance, several aspects are taken into consideration, such as the strategic choice of the company's distribution center locations, the quantity of these centers, and the target clientele for each. This study proposed a new strategic point for the distribution of Neodent's products, based on the location of the company's candidate stores to become distribution centers. To this end, data on the distance and location of the company's stores, provided by Neodent, were compiled and implemented in the OpenSolver add-in for Excel, using the p-median mathematical model for facility location problems.

The results obtained through this tool proved to be valid, as they met both the overall and specific objectives of the study. They also demonstrated a significant cost-saving in the total road transport distance covered by the company's logistics department.

The aforementioned challenges are particularly relevant to supply chain management. As the dental industry continues to face increased demand, optimizing distribution strategies has become a central concern for companies. It is crucial for them to ensure customer satisfaction and keep up with the growing demand for their products.

Keywords: Dental Implants · Supply Chain Management · Beauty and Well-being Industry

1 Introduction

The COVID-19 pandemic has had varying impacts on different sectors of the economy, with some experiencing sharp declines, while others remained stable or even found opportunities to grow amid the crisis [1]. The well-being and beauty industry is a prime

M. Janssen et al. (Eds.): I3E 2023, LNCS 14316, pp. 385–397, 2023.
https://doi.org/10.1007/978-3-031-50040-4_28

example of a sector that maintained high growth rates, largely due to the increased focus on self-care during periods of social isolation. This trend towards self-care has also extended to other segments, such as dental aesthetics, which was traditionally centered on oral health.

The Brazilian Association of Medical, Dental, and Hospital Industry, approximately 2.4 million dental prosthesis procedures and 800 thousand dental implant procedures are performed in the country each year. These treatments offer dental patients the possibility of a healthy and visually harmonious smile. As the demand for dental implants continues to rise, the dental implant production sector faces the challenge of adjusting its production volumes, sales, and product availability to meet market demands [2].

Contrary to what some may believe, this exponential growth has not caused disruptions in the natural flow of the sector. On the contrary, it is expected that these numbers will continue to rise in the coming decades. In 2021, 1.28 million Brazilians acquired dental health plans, resulting in an increase in the number of dental patients and, consequently, a surge in dental treatments [2].

One of the significant challenges for companies adapting to increased market demand and production capacity is to ensure that the lead time, the total time each stage of the company's process takes for the product to reach the customer, is met within the financial limitations involving freight and operational costs [3]. Therefore, determining strategic points for the locations of inventory and product distribution services is essential to ensure efficient and effective delivery processes by optimizing variables such as time and cost [4].

The efficiency of customer order fulfillment, understood here as the level of service efficiency, is directly related to the time it takes for the company to deliver products to the customer's hands. Thus, various factors must be taken into consideration, such as geographical location, freight and operational costs, proximity, and delivery volumes [5].

In this context, the present work applies the p-median method to achieve its main objective of identifying among the "p" known facilities the point that minimizes the delivery costs of a specific demand to the "n" points. This involves calculating the sum of all distances traveled from each point "n" to the nearest "p" facility, resulting in the objective function value that needs to be minimized [6]. The primary question this study seeks to answer is: Which of the existing brand facilities in Brazil would best serve the other 16, minimizing freight and operational costs while meeting agreed delivery times? The overall objective is to apply the p-median method to locate a new distribution center for a dental implant company to reduce delivery time to customers. To achieve this objective, the following steps were taken: Mapping the process, proposing a facility location solution for the logistics process, gathering necessary data on the problem, analyzing the results obtained, and comparing the model's results with the current scenario.

2   Methodology

The initial step involved a stakeholder meeting to define the research problem collaboratively. Key personnel from the organization participated in a brainstorming session to identify a specific research focus that aligned with the organization's current needs.

This participatory approach ensured that all relevant ideas were considered, leading to a consensus on the most pertinent research topic.

To propose an effective facility location solution, a thorough literature review was conducted. This involved exploring various mathematical models known for addressing facility location problems. The research team relied on the Scopus database to gather relevant scholarly articles and studies, ensuring the proposed approach was in line with established methodologies and best practices.

To gain a comprehensive understanding of the distribution process at Neodent, the team performed process mapping and identified key issues. This involved analyzing the process flow and interrelationships among distribution sub-processes, utilizing the BPMN (Business Process Model and Notation) methodology to present the process clearly to the reader. Identifying bottlenecks and inefficiencies within the distribution process was essential to developing an optimized facility location solution.

The next step involved proposing a facility location model based on the findings from the literature review and process mapping. The classic combinatorial optimization model known as the p-median problem was chosen and adapted to suit the specific business context of Neodent. This model addressed the objective of proposing a facility location solution for the logistics process, focusing on minimizing costs and improving efficiency.

To ensure the effectiveness of the proposed model, comprehensive data collection was carried out. The research team engaged in meetings and exchanged emails with stakeholders to gather all necessary information for the application of the chosen mathematical model. The collected data was compiled and organized using Excel, creating a robust database for subsequent use in the model.

The proposed facility location model was then implemented using the collected data to optimize facility locations. The model considered factors such as geographical distribution, freight costs, and delivery volumes, aiming to enhance the efficiency of the distribution process.

To validate the model's effectiveness, a thorough comparison was made between the results obtained from the proposed facility location model and the initial problematic scenario at the company. This comparison allowed for a clear assessment of the model's impact on the distribution process, demonstrating its potential to address the identified issues effectively.

Throughout the research process, ethical considerations were of utmost importance. The research team ensured the confidentiality and data protection of sensitive information obtained from the company and stakeholders. Furthermore, the proposed facility location model aimed to optimize efficiency without compromising the well-being of employees or customers.

Finally, the research outcomes and implementation of the project were presented to stakeholders at various stages of the study. This ensured alignment with stakeholder needs and expectations and provided an opportunity for valuable feedback and validation, ensuring the final product of the research met the requirements and objectives of the stakeholders.

3 Theoretical Background

3.1 Supply Chain Management

Supply Chain Management (SCM) is a critical aspect of modern business operations, encompassing the planning, coordination, and control of the flow of goods, services, and information from the initial raw material sourcing to the final customer delivery [7]. In today's highly competitive and globalized marketplace, efficient and effective SCM plays a pivotal role in enhancing an organization's competitiveness, customer satisfaction, and overall profitability. By optimizing the entire supply chain, companies can streamline processes, reduce lead times, minimize inventory levels, and improve overall responsiveness to customer demands [8, 9].

Effective SCM involves the integration of various elements, including suppliers, manufacturers, distributors, retailers, and customers. This integration requires seamless information sharing and collaboration among all stakeholders, which can be facilitated through advanced technologies and communication systems. Key components of SCM include demand forecasting, inventory management, production planning, logistics, and distribution [10]. Implementing the right SCM strategies and methodologies enables companies to achieve cost savings, improve service levels, and gain a competitive advantage in the market [11].

For the well-being and beauty industry, particularly in the context of dental implant production and distribution, SCM plays a crucial role in ensuring timely and cost-effective delivery of products to meet the rising customer demand. As companies like Neodent expand their operations to cater to increasing market needs, optimizing their supply chain becomes imperative to remain competitive and deliver superior customer experiences. In this regard, the application of the p-median problem can provide valuable insights into strategically locating facilities to minimize distribution costs, reduce lead times, and enhance overall logistics efficiency.

3.2 The P-Median Problem

The p-median problem is a classical combinatorial optimization problem widely studied in operations research and facility location literature. The central objective of this problem is to identify "p" locations from a given set of facilities to serve "n" demand points in such a way that the total distance (or cost) between each demand point and its assigned facility is minimized. The p-median problem has diverse applications, including facility location decisions, network design, and supply chain optimization [12].

In the context of the dental implant production industry, solving the p-median problem can have significant implications for enhancing the efficiency of the distribution network. By strategically locating distribution centers (facilities) based on demand patterns, geographical coverage, and transportation costs, companies like Neodent can optimize their delivery processes and reduce overall logistics expenses. The p-median problem offers a powerful framework to allocate resources efficiently, streamline supply chain operations, and meet customer expectations promptly [6].

Various methodologies and algorithms have been developed to tackle the p-median problem, ranging from exact optimization techniques to heuristic and metaheuristic approaches. Researchers have explored mathematical programming models, such as linear programming and integer programming, as well as metaheuristic methods like genetic algorithms and simulated annealing. Each approach offers unique advantages in terms of computational efficiency and solution quality, and the choice of method depends on the problem size, complexity, and available computational resources [12].

By integrating the principles of Supply Chain Management with the solution methodologies of the p-median problem, companies in the dental implant production sector can gain a competitive edge by optimizing their distribution network [13]. The combination of efficient SCM practices and the strategic placement of facilities through the p-median problem can lead to reduced costs, faster delivery times, and enhanced customer satisfaction [14, 15]. As the industry continues to grow and evolve, leveraging these advanced optimization techniques becomes crucial for companies like Neodent to remain at the forefront of the market and fulfill the increasing demand for their products.

4 Application of the P-Median Mathematical Model

4.1 Process Mapping

Using the graphical BPMN tool, which is specifically designed for process flow visualization, a comprehensive mapping of the logistics process in the analyzed company, Neodent, was conducted regarding the national distribution of their products to their 17 sales points spread across Brazil. The following figure (Fig. 1) represents the process.

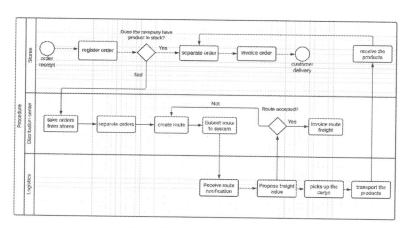

Fig. 1. Company current process.

As depicted in Fig. 1, the distribution process of the company involves four main stakeholders: the logistics department of the company located in the current Warehouse in Curitiba, Paraná; a secondary distribution center in São Paulo; the existing brand stores throughout Brazil (totaling 17); and the transportation companies.

In the case of Neodent, the transportation companies responsible for product transportation within Brazil are not fixed service providers. In other words, Neodent does not rely on a single, permanently outsourced service. Instead, a daily routing process is carried out, where all routes for the following day are planned based on the volumes allocated to each store. These routes, along with their characteristics, such as volume and stops, are then submitted to a system. Using this system, transportation companies can view the scheduled routes and submit proposals for providing the service. Once Neodent accepts a proposal, the chosen transportation company sends their designated means of transport - whether it is a truck, car, or motorcycle - to Neodent's Warehouse in Curitiba. There, the cargo is loaded, and the vehicle follows the pre-planned route set by the company. This way, the cargo is transported to the designated stores, where the products are received for sale to the end customers.

By employing this process, Neodent ensures an efficient and dynamic distribution network that meets the diverse demands of their sales points. By optimizing daily routes and engaging multiple transportation partners, the company achieves flexibility, cost-effectiveness, and timely delivery of products to their various outlets across the country. The use of the BPMN methodology offers a clear visualization of the distribution process, enabling the identification of potential areas for improvement and streamlining of the overall logistics operations within the organization.

4.2   Data Collection

The company currently operates 15 stores distributed throughout Brazil, in addition to 2 existing distribution centers. The cities where these 17 points are located are presented in Table 1 below:

Table 1. List of candidate cities for facility location.

Reference number	City
1	Fortaleza
2	Recife
3	Salvador
4	Cuiabá
5	Brasília
6	Goiânia
7	Belo Horizonte
8	Bauru
9	Campinas
10	São Paulo Showroom
11	São Paulo HUB
12	Rio de Janeiro
13	Maringá

(*continued*)

Table 1. (*continued*)

Reference number	City
14	Curitiba
15	Joinville
16	Florianópolis
17	Porto Alegre

The objective is to establish a new distribution center, in addition to the two existing ones. The current centers are located in the cities of Curitiba and São Paulo, which also have open stores at these locations. The selection of the new distribution center must consider the shortest distance to serve customers at the 15 stores.

For the purpose of naming the mathematical model, we will use the term "facilities" to refer to the candidate stores that could potentially become a new distribution center. Therefore, for a better understanding and analysis of the data provided by Neodent, it was necessary to tabulate the distances, in kilometers, between each potential city candidate to become a distribution center and the other stores. These distance-related data can be observed in Fig. 2 below. Currently, the total distance covered for supplying all points is 14,179 km.

								Stores									
Facilities	1	2	3	4	5	6	7	8	9	10	11	12	13	14	15	16	17
1	0	782	1.181	3.140	2.123	2.325	2.365	2.995	3.009	3.098	3.090	2.583	3.236	3.478	3.592	3.765	4.201
2	782	0	892	3.189	2.130	2.333	2.035	2.703	2.641	2.805	2.651	2.319	3.011	3.058	3.172	3.345	3.781
3	1.181	892	0	2.504	1.445	1.646	1.350	2.018	1.956	1.967	1.966	1.634	2.326	2.373	2.487	2.660	3.096
4	3.140	3.189	2.504	0	1.075	898	1.606	1.256	1.444	1.536	1.524	1.933	1.296	1.675	1.803	1.976	2.128
5	2.123	2.130	1.445	1.075	0	210	742	908	922	1.010	1.003	1.169	1.148	1.390	1.505	1.678	2.115
6	2.325	2.333	1.646	898	210	0	891	715	810	899	891	1.300	957	1.206	1.334	1.507	1.944
7	2.365	2.035	1.350	1.606	742	891	0	736	578	589	587	442	1.064	994	1.109	1.282	1.718
8	2.995	2.703	2.018	1.256	908	715	736	0	266	322	323	756	397	536	664	837	1.274
9	3.009	2.641	1.956	1.444	922	810	578	266	0	109	102	495	637	480	604	777	1.214
10	3.098	2.805	1.967	1.536	1.010	899	589	322	109	0	6	440	643	413	527	700	1.138
11	3.090	2.651	1.966	1.524	1.003	891	587	323	102	6	0	438	643	412	528	700	1.138
12	2.583	2.319	1.634	1.933	1.169	1.300	442	756	495	440	438	0	1.078	848	962	1.135	1.571
13	3.236	3.011	2.326	1.296	1.148	957	1.064	397	637	643	643	1.078	0	425	553	726	1.163
14	3.478	3.058	2.373	1.675	1.390	1.206	994	536	480	413	412	848	425	0	130	303	740
15	3.592	3.172	2.487	1.803	1.505	1.334	1.109	664	604	527	528	962	553	130	0	179	615
16	3.765	3.345	2.660	1.976	1.678	1.507	1.282	837	777	700	700	1.135	726	303	179	0	454
17	4.201	3.781	3.096	2.128	2.115	1.944	1.718	1.274	1.214	1.138	1.138	1.571	1.163	740	615	454	0

Fig. 2. List of candidate cities for facility location.

This data collection and tabulation process is crucial for the subsequent application of the mathematical model. By understanding the distances between each potential facility and the existing stores, the company can strategically determine the best location for the new distribution center. The objective is to minimize the total transportation distance and optimize the efficiency of the distribution network, ultimately resulting in cost savings and improved delivery times for the customers. The data presented in Table 1, Table 2, and Fig. 2 provide a comprehensive foundation for the subsequent analysis and application of the p-median problem to identify the most optimal facility location for Neodent's logistics operations.

4.3 The Model

In this study, we addressed the facility location problem by proposing a new distribution center for a Curitiba-based dental implant manufacturer using the p-median mathematical model. After structuring the model, we applied it to the dataset using OpenSolver in Excel. Our main objective was to assess the company's current distribution network and suggest an additional strategic point to reduce the total distance traveled, leading to decreased transportation costs and delivery time. Through careful analysis, considering geographical distribution and distances between potential facilities and existing stores, we aimed to find the optimal location for the new distribution center, ultimately enhancing Neodent's logistics operations, customer satisfaction, and overall competitive advantage.

The company provided the total number of physical points of sale nationwide (a set of stores) and specified that these same stores would be candidates for locating new distribution centers (facilities). Below, Table 2 illustrates the representation of the two sets:

Table 2. Model set and index.

Set	Set	Index
Stores	J	j
Facilities	I	i

The company's product distribution is carried out through road transportation, analyzed based on the distance measured in kilometers from the departure point (distribution center/facility) to its destination (store). Therefore, Table 3 represents the parameter of distances between facilities and stores, denoted as C_{ij}.

Table 3. Model Parameters.

Parameters	Description
C_{ij}	Distance from each facility (i) to each store (j)
$P = 3$	3 facilities that will open

The parameter P determines that 3 facilities will be opened from the set I described above. This is because, with 2 facilities already having distribution centers, Curitiba and São Paulo, these facilities are considered preselected candidates to have distribution centers. Thus, the model should only select one additional facility.

In Table 4 below, one can observe the two sets of decision variables for the model at hand:

Table 4. Model Variable Decisions.

Variables	Description
Yi	1 if facility "i" is open, 0 otherwise
Xij	1 if store "j" is serviced by facility "i", 0 otherwise

The variables Yi and Xij are both binary. Yi determines whether facility i will be opened or not, while Xij indicates whether store j will be served by facility i or not.

Given the sets, variables, and parameters of the model to be applied, the mathematical model is presented below:

$$min\, Z \;=\; \sum_{i \in I} \sum_{j \in J} C_{ij} X_{ij} \qquad (1)$$

Subject to:

$$\sum_{i \in I} X_{ij} = 1 \qquad \forall j \in J \qquad (2)$$

$$\sum_{i \in I} Y_i = p \qquad (3)$$

$$X_{ij} \leq\leq Y_i \qquad \forall i \in I, \; j \in J \qquad (4)$$

$$Y_i \in \{0, 1\} \qquad \forall i \in I \qquad (5)$$

$$X_{iJ} \in \{0, 1\} \qquad \forall i \in I, j \in J \qquad (6)$$

$$Yi = 1 \qquad i = 11, \, i = 14 \qquad (7)$$

As described above, the objective function (1) aims to minimize the sum of distances traveled from facilities "i" to locations "j." Eq. (2) ensures that each location "j" will be served by one and only one facility "i." Eq. (3) restricts the number of facilities to be opened and their respective locations based on the value of "p." Eq. (4) represents the facility opening, ensuring that a particular location will only be served by facility "i" if the facility is opened. Constraints (5) and (6) indicate the binary nature of the variables, allowing them to take only the values of zero or one. Finally, constraint (7) guarantees that facilities denoted by numbers 11 (São Paulo) and 14 (Curitiba) will be necessarily opened, as these cities already have distribution centers and should be considered as preselected candidates for having distribution centers

4.4 Results Analysis and Validation

To apply the proposed mathematical model, the Microsoft Excel tool was utilized with the assistance of the OpenSolver add-in. This add-in is widely used for testing hypotheses and solving combinatorial optimization problems. Unlike the standard Excel Solver, OpenSolver does not have a limit on the number of variables that can be used, allowing for finding an optimal (maximum or minimum) value for a given formula, subject to constraints on cell values in a worksheet.

The application of the model began with inputting all the problem data into an Excel worksheet (Fig. 3), including the sets, variables, and constraints presented in the work. OpenSolver was then used to find the optimal solution, ensuring that the chosen facility locations and assignments to stores adhere to the specified constraints. The comprehensive capabilities of OpenSolver facilitated an efficient and accurate solution to the facility location problem, ultimately leading to enhanced logistics efficiency and cost-effectiveness for the company.

Matrix C : cij
Distance (km)

Facilities	Stores																
	1	2	3	4	5	6	7	8	9	10	11	12	13	14	15	16	17
1	0	782	1.181	3.140	2.123	2.325	2.365	2.995	3.009	3.098	3.090	2.583	3.236	3.478	3.592	3.765	4.201
2	782	0	892	3.189	2.130	2.333	2.035	2.703	2.641	2.805	2.651	2.319	3.011	3.058	3.172	3.345	3.781
3	1.181	892	0	2.504	1.445	1.646	1.350	2.018	1.956	1.967	1.966	1.634	2.326	2.373	2.487	2.660	3.096
4	3.140	3.189	2.504	0	1.075	898	1.606	1.256	1.444	1.536	1.524	1.933	1.296	1.675	1.803	1.976	2.128
5	2.123	2.130	1.445	1.075	0	210	742	908	922	1.010	1.003	1.169	1.148	1.390	1.505	1.678	2.115
6	2.325	2.333	1.646	898	210	0	891	715	810	899	891	1.300	957	1.206	1.334	1.507	1.944
7	2.365	2.035	1.350	1.606	742	891	0	736	578	589	587	442	1.064	994	1.109	1.282	1.718
8	2.995	2.703	2.018	1.256	908	715	736	0	266	322	323	756	397	536	664	837	1.274
9	3.009	2.641	1.956	1.444	922	810	578	266	0	109	102	495	637	480	604	777	1.214
10	3.098	2.805	1.967	1.536	1.010	899	589	322	109	0	6	440	643	413	527	700	1.138
11	3.090	2.651	1.966	1.524	1.003	891	587	323	102	6	0	438	643	412	528	700	1.138
12	2.583	2.319	1.634	1.933	1.169	1.300	442	756	495	440	438	0	1.078	848	962	1.135	1.571
13	3.236	3.011	2.326	1.296	1.148	957	1.064	397	637	643	643	1.078	0	425	553	726	1.163
14	3.478	3.058	2.373	1.675	1.390	1.206	994	536	480	413	412	848	425	0	130	303	740
15	3.592	3.172	2.487	1.803	1.505	1.334	1.109	664	604	527	528	962	553	130	0	179	615
16	3.765	3.345	2.660	1.976	1.678	1.507	1.282	837	777	700	700	1.135	726	303	179	0	454
17	4.201	3.781	3.096	2.128	2.115	1.944	1.718	1.274	1.214	1.138	1.138	1.571	1.163	740	615	454	0

Fig. 3. Parameters.

In addition to inputting the problem data, spaces were created to accommodate the future results after the model's application (Fig. 4).

Facilities	1	2	3	4	5	6	7	8	9	10	11	12	13	14	15	16	17	Yi	Total Distance	P Value
1	0	0	0	0	0	0	0	0	0	0	0	0	0	0	0	0	0	0	0	1
2	0	0	0	0	0	0	0	0	0	0	0	0	0	0	0	0	0	0		HUBs opened
3	0	0	0	0	0	0	0	0	0	0	0	0	0	0	0	0	0	0		0
4	0	0	0	0	0	0	0	0	0	0	0	0	0	0	0	0	0	0		
5	0	0	0	0	0	0	0	0	0	0	0	0	0	0	0	0	0	0		
6	0	0	0	0	0	0	0	0	0	0	0	0	0	0	0	0	0	0		
7	0	0	0	0	0	0	0	0	0	0	0	0	0	0	0	0	0	0		
8	0	0	0	0	0	0	0	0	0	0	0	0	0	0	0	0	0	0		
9	0	0	0	0	0	0	0	0	0	0	0	0	0	0	0	0	0	0		
10	0	0	0	0	0	0	0	0	0	0	0	0	0	0	0	0	0	0		
11	0	0	0	0	0	0	0	0	0	0	0	0	0	0	0	0	0	0		
12	0	0	0	0	0	0	0	0	0	0	0	0	0	0	0	0	0	0		
13	0	0	0	0	0	0	0	0	0	0	0	0	0	0	0	0	0	0		
14	0	0	0	0	0	0	0	0	0	0	0	0	0	0	0	0	0	0		
15	0	0	0	0	0	0	0	0	0	0	0	0	0	0	0	0	0	0		
16	0	0	0	0	0	0	0	0	0	0	0	0	0	0	0	0	0	0		
17	0	0	0	0	0	0	0	0	0	0	0	0	0	0	0	0	0	0		
Sum																				

Fig. 4. Decision Variables.

The next step in the application process involved configuring the model's parameters within the OpenSolver add-in's tab. At this stage, the objective was set as a minimization function, the constraints were defined, and the resolution method chosen was LP Simplex. After solving the model with OpenSolver, the following results were obtained:

								Lojas										
Facilidades	1	2	3	4	5	6	7	8	9	10	11	12	13	14	15	16	17	Distância total
2	782	0	892	0	0	0	0	0	0	0	0	0	0	0	0	0	0	1.674
11	0	0	0	1.524	1.003	891	587	323	102	6	0	438	0	0	0	0	0	4.874
14	0	0	0	0	0	0	0	0	0	0	0	0	425	0	130	303	740	1.598
																		8.146

Fig. 5. Results obtained from set I.

The results shown in the Fig. 5 above indicate the proposed facility locations, where the openings in 11 (São Paulo) and 14 (Curitiba) were expected since they were pre-configured in the model. Therefore, the focus was on identifying the new facility, which in this case is represented by the number 2, located in Recife, to support the existing distribution centers in 11 and 14. It was possible to analyze which stores would be supplied by these three opened facilities (Recife, São Paulo, and Curitiba), aiming to optimize the distribution network's transportation. The minimum transportation distance achieved for the company's product distribution network is 8,146 km. The results obtained from the application of the proposed mathematical model in this study, when compared to the company's current transportation logistics network, are considered satisfactory as they reduced the total distance from 14,179 km to 8,146 km. This represents a 42.5% decrease in terms of road distance. The model suggests an optimized distribution strategy for supplying the brand's stores, achieved by opening a new distribution center in the northeast region of the country to serve the remaining stores in that area.

Upon presenting the solution to the stakeholders, the company's interested parties received the results with optimism, as the study met the company's need for initiating research for a future project of opening a new distribution center. The enthusiasm stemmed primarily from the significant cost-saving aspect, with over 40% reduction in distance traveled for store supply, leading to decreased lead time for final customer delivery, aligning with the company's customer-centric mission. To further enhance the results, the company suggests an additional research phase, wherein different values for kilometers traveled in various regions of the country would be considered. This approach would yield cost savings in monetary terms based on the proposed solution. Analyzing the economic investment required for opening a new center becomes crucial with this additional data, enabling the company to make informed decisions regarding the feasibility of the project.

5 Final Considerations

The general objective of this study aimed to "Apply the p-median method in locating a new distribution center for a dental implant company to reduce delivery time to customers," and this objective was achieved with the closest approximation to reality, as real data was used for the application of the chosen method.

The present study has certain limitations that should be considered when interpreting the results. Firstly, the impossibility of mapping the entire distribution chain of the company, as it operates in over 80 countries across 5 continents, with various transportation modes, thus, the analysis focused exclusively on the Brazilian territory. Additionally, the use of software for applying the chosen model, as there is no guarantee that the studied company has access to certain tools, hence the choice of Excel, a popular tool among companies. Another limitation is related to regulations and legal restrictions on data sharing, as precise data such as volume, demand, and economic values are considered confidential and could not be shared by the company. These recognized limitations offer opportunities for future studies to delve deeper into the field.

The work has the potential to bring positive impacts and significant external contributions to the applied company and the field of study. Firstly, by optimizing facility location search through the application of the p-median model in software, improvements in operational efficiency can be achieved, potentially resulting in reduced operational costs and resource savings. Moreover, the model's application provides an objective and quantitative basis for future decision-making within the company, facilitating the evaluation of different scenarios, comparing options, and identifying the best solutions based on specified criteria, such as distance. Additionally, from the results, the knowledge and insights gained can have an impact and influence in the academic realm, contributing to the advancement of the field of study and potentially benefiting society as a whole.

As a future suggestion, in alignment with the stakeholders of the company, implementing variables for transportation costs by region would allow for financial analysis of the study. Furthermore, it is suggested that the study initiated in this project be expanded to other countries where the company operates, encompassing all its points of sale, thus enabling significant financial savings and reduced delivery time to customers.

Acknowledgments. The authors would like to thank the Pontifical Catholic University of Paraná (PUCPR), PPGEPS-PUCPR and Neodent® Straumann Group.

References

1. Schaefer, J.L., Baierle, I.C., Sellitto, M.A., Furtado, J.C., Nara, E.O.B.: Competitiveness scale as a basis for brazilian small and medium-sized enterprises. EMJ – Eng. Manage. J. **33**(4), 255–271 (2021)
2. ABIMO. https://abimo.org.br/bid-brasil/. Accessed 18 July 2023
3. Nora, L.D.D., Siluk, J.C.M., Júnior, A.L.N., Nara, E.O.B., Furtado, J.C.: The performance measurement of innovation and competitiveness in the telecommunications services sector. Int. J. Bus. Excell. **9**(2), 210–224 (2016)
4. Baierle, I.C., Schaefer, J.L., Sellitto, M.A., Furtado, J.C., Nara, E.O.B.: MOONA software for survey classification and evaluation of criteria to support decision-making for properties portfolio. Int. J. Strat. Prop. Manage. **24**(2), 226–236 (2020)
5. Hamasaki, K., Gonçalves, M.C., Junior, O.C., Nara, E.O.B., Wollmann, R.R.G.: Robust linear programming application for the production planning problem. In: Deschamps, F., Pinheiro de Lima, E., Gouvêa da Costa, S.E., Trentin, M., (eds.) Proceedings of the 11th International Conference on Production Research – Americas, ICPR 2022, pp. 647–654. Springer, Cham (2023). https://doi.org/10.1007/978-3-031-36121-0_82
6. Hansen, P., Brimberg, J., Urošević, D., Mladenović, N.: Solving large p-median clustering problems by primal-dual variable neighborhood search. Data Min. Knowl. Discov. **19**(3), 351–375 (2009). https://doi.org/10.1007/s10618-009-0135-4
7. Aldrighetti, R., Battini, D., Ivanov, D., Zennaro, I.: Costs of resilience and disruptions in supply chain network design models: a review and future research directions. Int. J. Prod. Econ. **235**, 108103 (2021). https://doi.org/10.1016/j.ijpe.2021.108103
8. Goncalves, M., Sampaio, R., Wollmann, R., Nara, E.Dias, I.: Using robust approach concept to solve the production planning problem in manufacturing systems. In: International Joint Conference on Industrial Engineering and Operations Management, IJCIEOM 2022. Springer Proceedings in Mathematics and Statistics (2023)
9. Dias, I., Sampaio, R., Wollmann, R., Goncalves, M., Nara, E.: A decomposition scheme in production planning based on linear programming that incorporates the concept of a dynamic planning environment. In: International Joint Conference on Industrial Engineering and Operations Management, IJCIEOM 2022. Springer Proceedings in Mathematics and Statistics (2023)
10. Gonçalves, M.C, Wollmann, R. R. G., Sampaio, R.J.B.: Proposal of a numerical approximation theory to solve the robust convex problem of production planning. Int. J. Oper. Res. (2023). https://doi.org/10.1504/IJOR.2022.10049618
11. Allaoui, H., Guo, Y., Choudhary, A., Bloemhof, J.: Sustainable agro-food supply chain design using two-stage hybrid multi-objective decision-making approach. Comput. Oper. Res. **89**, 369–384 (2018). https://doi.org/10.1016/j.cor.2016.10.012
12. Masone, A., Sterle, C., Vasilyev, I., Ushakov, A.: A three-stage p-median based exact method for the optimal diversity management problem. Networks **74**(2), 174–189 (2019). https://doi.org/10.1002/net.21821
13. Gonçalves, M.C., Canciglieri, A.B., Strobel, K.M., Antunes, M.F., Zanellato, R.R.: Application of operational research in process optimization in the cement industry. J. Eng. Technol. Ind. Appl. **6**(24), 36–40 (2020). https://doi.org/10.5935/jetia.v6i24.677
14. De Faria, G.L., Gonçalves, M.C.: Proposition of a lean flow of processes based on the concept of process mapping for a bubalinocultura based dairy. J. Eng. Technol. Ind. Appl. **5**(18), 23–28 (2019). https://doi.org/10.5935/2447-0228.20190022
15. Junior, O.J.T., Gonçalves, M.C.: Application of quality and productivity improvement tools in a potato chips production line. J. Eng. Technol. Ind. Appl. **5**(18), 65–72 (2019). https://doi.org/10.5935/2447-0228.20190029

The Role of Citizen Engagement on Developing Smart Cities Under an Organizing Asymmetry Approach

Carolina Tavares Lopes[✉] and Edimara Mezzomo Luciano

Pontifical Catholic University of Rio Grande Do Sul, Porto Alegre, RS, Brazil
carolinatlop@gmail.com, eluciano@pucrs.br

Abstract. Urban areas worldwide are increasingly finding their way into the Smart Cities model. As an initiative that aims to enhance the quality of citizens' lives through the implementation of clever solutions, the success of Smart Cities relies on the involvement of academia, the public and private sectors, as well as society itself. Therefore, the quadruple-helix approach is considered relevant when discussing Smart Cities approaches. However, the society participation becomes a key challenge for these initiatives. The role of this actor, and its representativeness, still requires new studies to shed light on the potential of its contributions. The citizen represents an actor that, at the same time, can contribute to developing Smart Cities and being impacted by city changes. In this early-stage research paper, the society is approached as the citizen engagement. The authors argue that the shortage of citizen engagement and decision-making representativeness are influenced by organization asymmetry. The concept of organization asymmetry concerns the disparity in organizational struc- tures among the actors within the quadruple helix approach. Notably, three of the key actors, namely universities, government, and businesses, are represented by formal and well-structured organizations, while the societal component of the model lacks an equivalent level of organization, conse-quently resulting in a loss of representative- ness. This characterization aligns with the established concept of information asym- metry. Thus, we advocate for an app-roach that incorporates citizens as a pivotal actor within Smart City development plans, to promote meaningful and inclusive citizen involvement. This short paper aims to discuss the role of citizen engagement in the development of Smart Cities, providing a theoretical basis for describing the construct of organizing asymmetry.

Keywords: Smart City · Citizen Engagement · Organizing asymmetry

1 Introduction

Urban areas worldwide are increasingly finding their way into the Smart Cities approach. As an initiative that aims to enhance the quality of citizens' lives through the implemen-tation of intelligent solutions, smart cities are created through the interaction of physical and social infrastructure, in a social-technical perspective, as well as the use of data and information technology. Given that this movement aims to find new solutions to address the challenges of operating a city, it is crucial to consider the involvement of multiple actors [1].

© IFIP International Federation for Information Processing 2023
Published by Springer Nature Switzerland AG 2023
M. Janssen et al. (Eds.): I3E 2023, LNCS 14316, pp. 398–402, 2023.
https://doi.org/10.1007/978-3-031-50040-4_29

Hence, the quadruple-helix approach is verily relevant when discussing Smart Cities initiatives. This approach represents a comprehensive model of university- industry-government-society collaboration in driving innovation [2]. Most publications on smart cities have been addressing equal roles for these actors. However, the authors argue that society participation does not gather a seamless integration. The low citizen engagement and decision-making representativeness are influenced by organization asymmetry turning citizen participation a key challenge [3].

The concept of organization asymmetry concerns the disparity in organizational structures among the actors within the quadruple helix approach. Notably, three of the key actors, namely universities, government, and businesses, are represented by for- mal and well-structured organizations, while the societal component of the model lacks an equivalent level of organization, consequently resulting in a loss of representativeness. This characterization aligns with the established concept of information asymmetry.

The role of citizen, the latter being the focus of this research, still requires new studies to shed light on the potential contributions of its participation. The society represents an actor that, at the same time, can contribute to developing Smart Cities and being impacted by city changes, which reinforces they have a role in discussing Smart Cities. In this early-stage research paper, the society is approached as the citizen engagement.

Therefore, our proposal is based on accomplishing a new approach to undercover the importance of playing the role of citizen engagement in smart city development and how it should interact better with other actors. We advocate for the organization asymmetry approach, that incorporates citizens as pivotal actor within Smart City development plans, to promote meaningful and inclusive citizen involvement, thereby promoting democratic principles and enhancing the effectiveness of Smart City initiatives.

Thus, this short paper aims to discuss the role of citizen engagement in the development of Smart Cities, providing a theoretical basis for describing the construct of organizing asymmetry.

2 Citizen Engagement

In recent years, the study of Smart City development has encompassed a wide range of aspects, receiving substantial scholarly attention [4]. However, an area that has garnered relatively limited attention in this burgeoning field pertains to the examination of citizen engagement and the representation of their decision-making processes within the context of Smart Cities.

As an initiative that aims to enhance the quality of citizens' lives through the implementation of intelligent solutions, the cooperation between citizens and municipal authorities is a fundamental condition of reasonable management [5]. Moreover, the intrinsic success of Smart City endeavors hinges on the intrinsic cooperation between the architects and deliverers of services and the end-users of these services, under- scoring the significance of this multifaceted interaction [6].

The quadruple-helix approach, which emphasizes the involvement of academia, industry, government, and society, elucidates the pivotal role of society, with citizens being the focal point of interest. Citizens are perceived as the primary agents capable of identifying and defining urban opportunities, thereby ushering in the potential for social inclusion and fostering a culture of learning [7].

Given the paramount importance of citizen engagement, it becomes imperative to devise a comprehensive method of structuring the roles of citizens, offering a systematic approach to integrate their perspectives and contributions effectively. Such an approach not only fosters a sense of ownership and active participation among citizens but also catalyzes meaningful discussions on reshaping the city planning and management systems in pursuit of more sustainable and citizen-centric Smart Cities. Thus, the pressing question arises: How can we develop an inclusive and efficient tool for assessing the potential impact of citizens on Smart City development and monitoring the fruition of their inputs in real-time? Addressing this question holds significant promise for the evolution and refinement of Smart Cities, empowering citizens as active co-creators of their urban environment and advancing the collective vision of a more inclusive, technologically advanced, and socially equitable urban landscape.

3   Research Method and Preliminary Results

As the study lies in the examination of the complex interaction inherent in the process of smart city development, these initiatives necessitate the seamless integration of the multiple actors. Therefore, through a holistic and relational lens, the systemic- relational epistemological approach was adopted.

As a theoretical perspective focused on comprehending knowledge, it emphasizes the significance of relationships among multiple actors in the generation and dissemination of knowledge. The systemic-relational approach recognizes that knowledge is forged and shared through interactions among multiple actors involved in the process, enabling the identification of collaboration and innovation opportunities [6, 7].

Based on a preliminary analysis of the ongoing process, the initial stage underwent the following interventions:

- To validate the implementation of citizens-public-private-academic partnerships for the development of smart cities;
- To validate the role of citizen engagement for the development of smart cities;
- To identify the influence of citizen engagement in cities on the successful implementation of smart solutions;
- To understand the impact of citizen engagement promoting inclusion to stimulate the development of smart solutions;

Initially, the case of The Program for the 4th District (+4D) in Porto Alegre, Brazil is being studied. This city has been paying attention to the various agendas around smart cities, being the city that first applied participatory budgeting, in 1989.

More recently, the Sustainable Urban Regeneration Program for the 4th District (+4D) is being developed under a quadruple helix perspective supported by Pacto Alegre, a covenant among the Porto Alegre City Hall, the three main universities, private companies, and society representatives. The 4th District was the city's manufacturing district from 1800 to 1970; after that, companies started to move to other cities in the metropolitan region and the countryside. As the companies left, the inter- est of the people in living in the 4th District began to decline, and the region started to be degraded.

The + 4D program is focused on recovering the area, promoting the diversity of us- es and activities aimed at sustainable urban development, valuing its characteristics, history, and identity, and at the same time attracting new business to the region, creating jobs, and developing opportunities. During this initial phase of the study, our principal objective is to investigate and comprehend the organization asymmetry in the + 4D program.

The phenomenon of organizational asymmetry arises when a disparity in organizational structures is observed among the actors within the quadruple helix approach.

Therefore, we would note that the three actors, namely universities, government, and businesses, are represented by formal and well-structured organizations, while the societal component of the model lacks an equivalent level of organization due to its vague and imprecise nature as citizens, leading to a consequent loss of representativeness.

Consequently, we will note that the application of the quadruple helix concept in smart cities presents limitations due to this issue. It poses challenges in incorporating the societal component, as it treats society as an enigmatic entity.

In the context of innovation, the prevailing interpretation involves the three organizational actors coming together to conceive innovations that may be of interest to the fourth actor, which is society. However, in the context of cities, this approach is deemed insufficient; instead, society must play a more integral role in the solutions. Merely consulting or involving society is not enough; true engagement necessitates active co-creation of solutions with society. Smart cities are intended for people, and as such, they should provide a space for collective construction. Citizens should not merely vote on preconceived projects; instead, they should actively collaborate and participate in shaping these projects through meaningful engagement, co- collaboration, and co-implementation.

For this purpose, a research instrument for surveying important actors in the Program for the 4th District is being prepared. This survey is important to deeply understand what actors are being part of the whole steps of this program. The survey will be applied to persons involved in all thematic axes, the sets of actions in every axis, and the transversal projects. Aiming to support data analysis, statistical methods, including normality testing, homogeneity testing (Breusch-Pagan/Cook-Weisberg and White tests), correlation (Durbin-Watson), and multiple linear regression using IBM SPSS Statistics Version 2.0 software will be employed. The multiple linear regression techniques will demonstrate the impact of the citizen engagement on smart city development through the dependent and independent variables.

Qualitative analyses are also planned, focused on the discussions City Hall conducted with the actors of the quadruple Helix, having three sources of data:

a) Results from 39 events open to the community, aiming to discuss the ideas and the way the program was planned to be implemented;
b) Results from an online public consultation with the population, which received 116 valid responses;
c) The minutes from the private discussion by the Municipal Council for Urban and Environmental Development (CMDUA), which is a formal governance instance for discussing and approving acts related to the + 4D program.

Content analysis is the chosen technique for analyzing qualitative data.

Both quantitative and qualitative analyses will better achieve the goal of this research and support new research steps.

4 Further Work

In this ongoing/early-stage research, our aim is to systematically analyze the role of citizen engagement in the development of Smart Cities. Therefore, our research will develop the concept of organizational asymmetry until we arrive at testable propositions and examine its impact on the development of smart city initiatives.

By examining how these different actors interact with each other, we pursue to uncover important insights for the implementation of smart city development. Additionally, we seek to integrate the concept of organizational asymmetry into discussions about innovation to enhance the smartness of urban areas.

Furthermore, we aim to contribute to ongoing debates about citizens' decision- making representativeness, promoting democratic principles. Risks of gentrification are also on the agenda for further investigation. Our research aims to provide valuable knowledge and insights for urban planners and other stakeholders involved in the development of Smart Cities.

References

1. Albino, V., Berardi, U., Dangelico, R.M.: Smart cities: definitions, dimensions, performance and initiatives. J. Urban Technol. 22(1), 3–21 (2015)
2. STATISTA. Smart city revenue worldwide generated by startups 2020–2025 (2022). https://www.statista.com/statistics/1231469/worldwide-smart-city-market-revenue-startups/. Accessed 30 Nov 2022
3. Ansell, C., Gash, A.: Collaborative governance in theory and practice. J. Pub. Adm. Res. Theory 18(4), 543–571 (2008)
4. Coase, R.: The nature of the firm 1937. In: The Firm, the Market and the Law. University of Chicago Press, Chicago (1988)
5. Glueck, W.F.: Organization change in business and government. Acad. Manage. J. 12(4), 439–449 (1969)
6. Faria, F.A., Sympson, G.: Bridging the gap between business and IT: an information governance perspective in the banking industry. Data Gov.: Creat. Vaue Inf. Assets, 217 241 (2013)
7. Cunha, M. A.: Smart cities: transformação digital de cidades. Programa Gestão Pública e Cidadania - PGPC, São Paulo, p. 161 (2016)

Devising an Urban Learning Centre for Municipalities in Eastern Partnership Countries

Luiza Schuch de Azambuja[1,2(✉)] 🆔 and Ralf-Martin Soe[1,3] 🆔

[1] FinEst Centre for Smart Cities, Tallinn University of Technology, Tallinn, Estonia
{Luiza.Schuch,Ralf-Martin.Soe}@taltech.ee
[2] Ragnar Nurkse Department of Innovation and Governance, Tallinn University of Technology, Tallinn, Estonia
[3] Global Digital Governance Fellow 2023, Stanford University, Stanford, USA

Abstract. Municipalities worldwide face intricate challenges in promoting inclusive and sustainable development, often hampered by limited internal capacity. Trying to address these issues the Mayors for Economic Growth (M4EG) Facility, a joint initiative of the European Union (EU) and the United Nations Development Programme (UNDP), is devising an Urban Learning Center (ULC) seen as an ecosystem of learning programs, knowledge management, and stakeholder engagement to support municipalities in the Eastern Partnership (EaP) countries (Armenia, Azerbaijan, Georgia, Moldova and Ukraine). This research investigates how to foster capacity development in municipalities and discusses the learning needs of local authorities' members of the M4EG. An online survey was used to identify the learning needs and to define the learning programs to be developed and included in the ULC. The results of the survey reveal considerable interest in diverse learning domains, including project management, IT skills, funding, community engagement, and digital transformation. The ULC, an integral part of the M4EG Facility, seeks to foster collaboration, innovation, and foresight to address complex challenges and develop municipal capacity. By fostering innovation and collaboration, the ULC aims to drive positive transformations for a sustainable future. Future studies can be done to evaluate the ULC's effectiveness in strengthening public sector dynamic capabilities and promoting inclusive growth.

Keywords: Capacity Building · Capacity Development · Dynamic Capabilities · Smart Cities · Urban Learning Center · Knowledge Management

1 Introduction

Municipalities are constantly looking for ways to foster economic development in an inclusive and sustainable way. However, public authorities are facing complex challenges and are often lacking internal capacity to deal with them. A recent study stressed the need of strengthening the capacity of municipal systems to deal with diverse problems [1]. The

© IFIP International Federation for Information Processing 2023
Published by Springer Nature Switzerland AG 2023
M. Janssen et al. (Eds.): I3E 2023, LNCS 14316, pp. 403–417, 2023.
https://doi.org/10.1007/978-3-031-50040-4_30

lack of public sector capacity has been highlighted by the literature as a huge challenge for sustainable development [2–6]. This lack of capacity includes project management practices [7–9], lack of Information and Technology (IT) skills [10–12], among others. Furthermore, the so called "wicked problems" faced by public sector requires innovative approaches and the development of dynamic capabilities [13].

Considering this problem, the Mayors for Economic Growth (M4EG) Facility, a joint initiative of the European Union (EU) and United Nations Development Programme (UNDP) is devising an Urban Learning Center (ULC) seen as an ecosystem of learning programs, knowledge management and stakeholder engagement, supported by an online platform (https://www.sparkblue.org/urbanlearningcenter). The M4EG Facility was founded through a second phase of the M4EG initiative, launched and funded by the European Union in 2016/2017 to support Mayors and municipalities of the Eastern Partnership (EaP) countries (Armenia, Azerbaijan, Georgia, Moldova, and Ukraine), which represent post-soviet states that live in unstable economic, social, and political conditions. The M4EG Facility highlights that municipalities are at the forefront of crisis and opportunity, and these complex challenges require new models and modes of thinking, going beyond sector-specific or technical solutions [14].

In view of the need of developing capacity in the public sector and on the context of the M4EG project, this study aims to start the investigation on the following research questions:

- How to foster capacity development and continuous education in municipalities?
- What are the learning needs of local authorities' members of the M4EG?

The purpose of this article is to introduce the case of the Urban Learning Center as a way of fostering capacity development in municipalities and to discuss the learning needs of local authorities' members of the M4EG. The ULC is being developed as part of the UNDP M4EG Facility in partnership with Arup, EIT Climate-KIC and Tallinn University of Technology.

This paper is organized as follows. The next section contextualizes the research presenting the background of the M4EG Facility and a briefly conceptual overview of capacity development and capabilities in the public sector. Section 3 explains the methodology of this study and the process to devise the ULC, which includes a learning needs assessment survey sent to all local authorities' members of the M4EG Facility (350 members). The findings are presented in two subsections. Section 4.1 summarizes the results of the 166 responses obtained through the survey; and Sect. 4.2 introduces the Urban Learning Center. The last section brings final considerations, limitations of this research and suggestions of future studies.

2 Background

2.1 The M4EG Facility

The Mayors for Economic Growth Initiative was firstly launched in 2016, through the funds of the European Union (EU), but since 2021 the EU-funded M4EG has been managed by UNDP in close cooperation with the EU, local authorities, and other partners.

The first phase of the project was initially created as a four-year program of the European Neighbourhood Policy and Enlargement Negotiations (DG NEAR) to help local authorities in Armenia, Azerbaijan, Belarus, Georgia, Moldova, and Ukraine in their economic growth and job creation [15].

Although the first phase of the M4EG program has increased the knowledge of the local authorities to plan their initiatives for economic growth, they still need guidance and capacity development. Thus, a second phase of the M4EG initiative was created, originating the M4EG Facility, a joint initiative of the EU & UNDP which aims to encourage creative thinking about urban and local areas, with a focus on positive transformation and future readiness.

The focus of the M4EG is on sustainable local economic development (LED) with the ambition to "support Mayors and municipalities at local levels to become active facilitators for economic growth and job creation by developing their capacities and technical skills and working in partnership with their private sector and civil society". The project proposes to be a demonstration project of what new trajectories of growth may look like in the EaP, and how additional financing can be mobilized at the local level. Among the objectives of the M4EG is facilitating the network of the EaP local authorities to learn, test, connect, and mobilize new partnerships and funding opportunities; introducing new ways to help addressing complex challenges faced by municipalities as inequalities, energy transition, conflict and refugee, and test these through a learning and iterative journey of implementing seed-funds at the local level [16].

One of the projects under the Facility is the development of an Urban Learning Center, aiming to be a learning and exchange platform between different stakeholders. The ULC will act as an ecosystem of learning opportunities for municipality staff and their partners, including learning pathways for the new generation local economic development plans (LEDP), green and digital transition, and adaptive leadership, strategy and foresight [16]. The proposal is to have a ULC able to provide training programs, hands-on activities and making use of innovative methods (deep listening, leadership, sensemaking, strategic planning and foresight) [17].

2.2 Capacity Development

The concept of capacity development emerged around the 1980s and gained growing attention around the 1990s, but it is still complex to be grasped and operationalized [18]. Starting with basic definitions, what is capacity?

Capacity is the ability of people, organizations and society as a whole to manage their affairs successfully [19]. They can be grouped in *three levels*, namely *Individual* (improving individual skills, knowledge and performance through training, experiences, motivation, and incentives); *Organizational* (i.e., improving organizational performance through strategies, plans, rules and regulations, partnerships, leadership); and *Enabling Environment* (i.e., improving policy framework to address economic, political, environmental and social factors including economic growth, financing, among others) [19].

Those abilities or skills are often grouped into "*hard*" areas (tangible and visible) and "*soft*" (intangible and invisible, social, and relational, including leadership, values, behaviours, commitment, and accountability) areas. Furthermore, capacities can be classified according to their *types*, being *technical* capacities the ones related to one area as for instance health, education, etc., and *functional* capacities the cross sector ones, which usually refers to essential management skills that allow for planning, implementing and monitoring and evaluating initiatives for growth [19, 20].

Capacity building is "the process of developing and strengthening the skills, instincts, abilities, processes and resources that organizations and communities need to survive, adapt, and thrive in a fast-changing world" [21]. Nowadays, the term capacity development is used in preference to the traditional term capacity building aiming to give the idea of continuous improvement and not as something that is starting or being created from zero.

Another similar term found in the literature is *Capacity for development* defined as the availability of resources (human, financial and technical) and the efficiency and effectiveness with which societies deploy those resources to identify and pursue their development goals on a sustainable basis [22]. In a simple terms, "capacity is the means to plan and achieve and capacity development describes the ways to whose means" [20]. Developing capacity is considered a process of transformation and growth and the process is illustrated in Fig. 1.

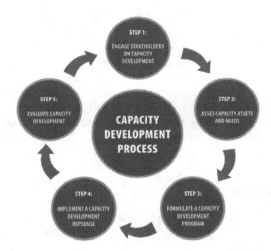

Fig. 1. The five steps of the capacity development cycle [20]

Developing capacity is a long-term process whereas outside partners can provide resources and facilitate the process, but it cannot be orchestrated externally, it must be embraced and guided by the individuals and organizations themselves [18, 23].

Another distinction to be made is the difference between capabilities and capacities, explained by Kattel and Mazzucato [13] as "Schumpeterian tradition of dynamic capabilities of the firm, and the Weberian tradition on public sector capacities to make policies". Talking about public sector capacity, it refers to the "set of skills, capabilities and resources necessary to perform policy functions – from the provision of public services to policy design and implementation" [24].

Dynamic capabilities are those which support dynamic actions, or the capabilities to anticipate, adapt and learn within and across organizations [24]. Public sector capacities revolve around the organizational structures within public institutions and dynamic capabilities focus on skills that enable changes [25]. Accordingly, public servants need skills and competencies that are able to face uncertainty as they often need to respond to rapidly changing environments [26, 27].

3 Methodology

This empirical research studies the case of the Urban Learning Center for municipalities of the Eastern Partnership under development as part of the UNDP M4EG Facility to foster capacity development among local authorities. The data of this study was collected from primary and secondary sources, including research and project deliverables, project reports, learning needs survey, and organizational websites.

The motivation behind the development of the ULC originated from the results of the first phase of the M4EG initiative and the need of new approaches for capacity development. As part of the project, the partners (UNDP, Arup, EIT Climate-KIC and Tallinn University of Technology) developed a survey to map the learning needs of the local authorities. The data collection instrument chosen was a written questionnaire, as this method is indicated when it is necessary to collect data from a large number of persons [28]. The purpose of the questionnaire was to map the needs and interests of the future users of the ULC; therefore, the results of the survey were used to define and prioritize the content to be included in the ULC and its delivery method. This follows the recommendation of the capacity development process suggested by UNDP [20] (see 2.2).

A first draft of the data collection instrument was developed in June 2022. After many discussions among the project partners, some adjustments were made to better match the profile of the respondents. The final version of the survey was translated in five languages (Armenian, Azerbaijani, Georgian, Romanian, Russian and Ukrainian). The survey was distributed by UNDP among all M4EG members in December 2022, the sample size included 350 local authorities. The list of questions can be found in Appendices, Appendix A1. In a broad way, the content and structure of the survey includes:

- Introductory text: what this survey is, what this will be used for and value in participation.
- General demographic questions.
- Existing learning opportunities and platforms.
- Expectations for new ULC – how to engage (quantitative select from list, plus qualitative final text box for additional comment).
- Learning needs and interests – what content (quantitative select from list, plus qualitative final text box for additional comment).

The survey data was collected between 7th of December 2022 to 13th of January 2023. The responses were translated to English and one of the project partners summarized the results and presented them during a collaborative project meeting. The data was used to define the expected learning objectives of the ULC courses and the learning methods to be used [22]. The learning programs were defined in a collaborative process online and offline. The project partners realized a two-days' workshop at the UNDP office in Istanbul, Turkey, in March 2023 to discuss and design the first structure of the learning programs. Afterwards, the project partners have had online workshops to refine the learning outcomes and the final structure of the courses. The course structure, modules and content were reviewed by UNDP experts.

4   Results

4.1   Main Findings of the Learning Needs Assessment Survey

The learning needs survey aimed to identify the learning needs of the local authorities' members of the M4EG. A total of 166 local authorities of the EaP answered the survey. The distribution according to the language of responses can be seen in Table 1.

Table 1. Survey Respondents according to the language.

Language	Count	Percentage
English	0	0%
Armenian	4	2%
Azerbaijani	4	2%
Georgian	24	14%
Romanian	21	13%
Russian	9	5%
Ukrainian	104	63%

Analysing the profile of the respondents, the majority are from a technical background including planning staff role (52%), followed by leadership or management (27%). The age range with more respondents are from 30–45 years (58.8%) and they can be considered as new in their role, as 50% of the respondents indicated that they are in their role from 1 to 5 years. Sixty percent of the participants are male and 40% female.

The results confirmed that there is a lack of project management knowledge, as highlighted by previous studies [7–9], as 67% of the respondents are interested in learning more about Project Management. Other high topics among the listed technical ones are Funding and Financing (63%), Community and Stakeholder Engagement (50%), Digital Transformation (46.7%) and City Planning (31.5%), as illustrated in Fig. 2 and 3.

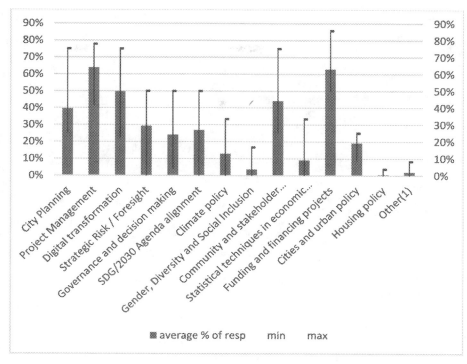

Fig. 2. Preferable technical topics.

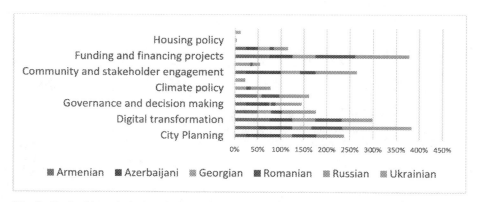

Fig. 3. Preferable technical topics (cumulative total of percentage of respondents per country).

In terms of soft and human skills, the topics that the municipalities are more interested in developing are Effective team collaboration (66%), Creativity and Innovation (64%), Strategic Leadership (43%) and Networking and City diplomacy (37%), as illustrated in Fig. 4 and Fig. 5.

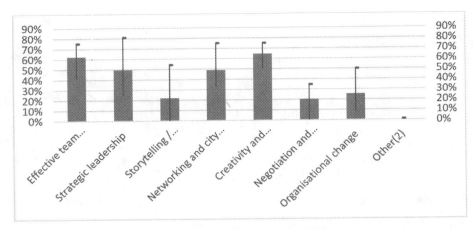

Fig. 4. Preferable soft/human skills.

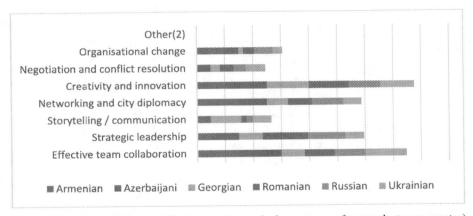

Fig. 5. Preferable soft/human skills (cumulative total of percentage of respondents per country).

Regarding the learning modules (question nine of the questionnaire) the respondents needed to score all modules indicating the relevance (1 not relevant, 2 relevant, 3 somewhat relevant and 4 very relevant). The results showed that they are interested in learning about attractive financing, core skills for economic development, alternative finance and crowdfunding, community engagement and inclusion and smarting your city, as illustrated in Fig. 6 and Fig. 7.

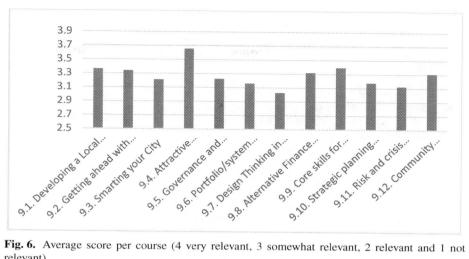

Fig. 6. Average score per course (4 very relevant, 3 somewhat relevant, 2 relevant and 1 not relevant).

Fig. 7. Average score per course per country.

In terms of sources of learning, the respondents showed a majority interest in online courses and in terms of duration, short courses are preferable, of three months (61.8%) or long ones (15.8% prefer courses of 12 months or more).

The results of the survey are being used to define the priorities in terms of content to be developed and added to the ULC. We are also analysing the best method to use in the capacity development, according to the preference of the respondents.

4.2 Urban Learning Center

The ULC part of the second phase of the M4EG initiative, is under development based on the lessons learned from the first phase of the M4EG project and on the insights gathered through the online survey. The ULC is created under the SparkBlue platform (https://www.sparkblue.org/urbanlearningcenter), which is a UNDP's digital platform for online engagement allowing collaboration across the international development landscape. The ULC under development:

- Provides a central point for the programme
- Repository of knowledge & information
- Delivers on-demand training packages (video presentation segments, guidance notes, further learning/reading, quizzes, evaluation feedback)
- Tracks learning activities and enables certification
- Signpost other learning
- Communicates activities and events (on & off-line)
- Enables peer-to-peer activities [29]

Figure 8 illustrate the components planned to be facilitated through the ULC.

Fig. 8. ULC ecosystem.

The ULC intends to introduce approaches beyond 'business as usual' with a range of tools and approaches with an 'urban makeover' intention, including foresight, social and community listening, sensemaking, adaptive and agile management, learning and monitoring effects, all with a strong focus on local solutions linked to the global objectives set out in the 2030 Agenda for Sustainable Development and its framework of SDGs [29].

The soft launch of the project happened in December 2022 and the launch of the first ULC course, namely Foundation for Future Readiness, happened on the 26th of July 2023. This course is a building block to a whole range of other courses that will be added under the ULC in the second half of 2023, including Smarter and Inclusive Cities, Green and Just Transition and Pathways for Economic Growth. The course content and videos are in English with translations to the Armenian, Azerbaijani, Georgian, Romanian, Russian and Ukrainian languages.

5   Final Considerations and Further Steps

This paper aimed to start the discussion on how to foster capacity development and continuous education in municipalities (research question one) and on the identification of the learning needs of the local authorities' members of the M4EG (research question two). The case study of the Urban Learning Center helped to answer the first question, as it is designed to be a learning ecosystem to foster capacity building and continuous education in cities, aiming to connect community members at different levels (see 4.2). The results of the survey (see 4.1) helped answering the second question of this study and serves as an initial step towards more comprehensive study in the future.

The main contribution of this paper is the provision of an empirical case study on capacity development in municipalities, which follows a different approach and create a network for knowledge sharing, aspects that were pointed by previous studies as a necessity. The ULC approach can be adapted and created in other regions. In addition, the method used for mapping the learning needs of the users can also be of help, as the questionnaire can be applied in other regions.

This research provides some practical insights and potential solutions for improving capacity development and to foster sustainable digitalization in municipalities, but we acknowledge some limitations of this study. First, the results of the survey could be complemented by focus groups or in-depth interviews with local authorities to gain a deeper understanding of their needs. However, this is not that simple considering the different languages spoken in the EaP. Another limitation of the study is that the respondents were in its huge majority from Ukraine (104 out of 166 respondents), but we considered the answers of all countries when analysing the data as the ULC is developed for all EaP countries and not just for Ukraine. Moreover, further investigation is suggested to provide more detailed insights, such as the examination of the learning needs of the local authorities based on different profiles (i.e., mayors and policy decision-makers, municipal leadership, municipal staff). In terms of theory, this study brought an overview of capacity development concepts and theories, but further studies could explore in a deeper way the theoretical basis of capabilities in the public sector and sustainability research, and on how the ULC case could, for instance, facilitate the development of dynamic capabilities.

In sum, considering the lack of capacity and the limited resources of local authorities, it is understood that conventional learning approaches are not enough. That is why the approach adopted by the M4EG ULC is based on continuous learning and co-creation of approaches. As the project is currently in place and the ULC launch just happened in the end of July 2023, it was not possible to analyse the concrete outcomes of the ULC in terms of capacity development. However, following the recommendation of performing a systematic learning on what is working and what need to be improved [23], a first round of feedback on the first ULC course was performed and it is possible to list some lessons learned to consider during the next phase of the project. For instance, online courses should use a simple language without long and complex sentences to avoid problems with the translation; key learning messages should be highlighted at the end of each chapter; it is important to bring examples to illustrate the statements; the course should be as interactive as possible providing spaces for discussions and reflections in each module.

As explained in 2.1 and 4.2, the ULC is part of an ecosystem and future studies could analyse other approaches used as part of the M4EG. In addition, we can suggest the investigation of other cases to understand how municipalities are investing in continuous learning, experimentation, and collaboration. It is important to learn from real cases of knowledge sharing among different municipalities that could benefit from similar solutions.

Acknowledgements. This research has been supported by the European Commission through the H2020 project Finest Twins (grant No. 856602).

Appendices

A.1 Survey Questions

0. Survey language
1. Which city, town, or local authority do you work in?
2. Which of these descriptions best describes your role?

- Options: Political role, policy and decision maker, leadership/management role, technical, including planning, other.

2.a If you selected Other, please specify: (open question).

3. How many years have you worked in this role?
4. What age range are you in?
5. What gender do you identify with?
6. What are the most pressing learning needs of your municipality? Please briefly specify.
7. Which of the following technical topics would be of interest for you and your colleagues? Please select your top 4.

- Options: City Planning, Project Management, Digital transformation, Strategic Risk/Foresight, Governance, and decision making, SDG/2030 Agenda alignment, Climate policy, Gender, Diversity and Social Inclusion, Community and stakeholder engagement, Statistical techniques in economic analysis, Funding and financing projects, Cities and urban policy, Housing policy, other.

7.a. If you selected Other, please specify: (open question).

8. Which of the following soft/human skills are of interest to you? Please select your top 3.

- Options: Effective team collaboration, Strategic leadership, Storytelling/communicationNetworking and city diplomacy, Creativity and innovation, Negotiation and conflict resolution, Organisational change, Other.

8.a. If you selected Other, please specify: (open question).

9. Which of the following learning modules would be of most interest for you and your colleagues?

9.1. Developing a Local Economic Development Plan

9.2. Getting ahead with Green Transition

9.3. Smarting your city

9.4. Attractive financing/resource mobilization for local authorities

9.5. Governance and organisational innovation for municipalities

9.6. Portfolio/system thinking in cities.

9.7. Design Thinking in cities

9.8. Alternative Finance and Crowdfunding

9.9. Core skills for Economic Development

9.10. Strategic planning for climate adaptation and resilience

9.11. Risk and crisis management

9.12. Community engagement and inclusion

10. When was your last training or learning opportunity?

11. What learning opportunities currently exist for you?

12. Which online tools, if any, do you use for knowledge exchange and learning purposes?

13. Please briefly comment on what you like and/or what you don't like about the current learning opportunities.

14. What learning functionality do you think you would benefit from the ULC platform?

14.1. Access to general online courses on various topics relevant to your municipality.

14.2. Access to skills-oriented masterclasses (e.g., developing business cases).

14.3. Possibility to find or interact with regional and global experts via discussion forums.

14.4. Possibility to find or interact with peers in a similar role via discussion forums.

14.5. Interaction with cities in your country.

14.6. Interaction with cities in the Eastern Partnerships region.

14.7. Would you like to be part of a cohort-based learning programme?

14.8. Co-creation tools and support for involvement of citizens.

14.9. A knowledge resource bank with downloadable documents and links e.g., policies, studies, strategy documents, guidance notes, etc.

14.10. Inspiration resources with downloadable documents and links e.g. case studies.

14.11. Lessons learned via various resources (i.e., a learning repository of train-the-trainers' videos, blogs, and tutorials).

14.12. Other expectations – please elaborate.

15. How important is it for you to have the content of the learning centre in your local language?

16. What is your preference for in-person vs. online learning?

17. How much time are you able to commit to learning within a month?

18. Is learning best scheduled within normal working times or outside normal working times? e.g., evenings or weekends.

19. Would you be willing to participate in a follow up meeting/workshop for helping the definition of the content to be included in the Urban Learning Centre?
20. I would like to get involved in the definition of the content.
21. I would like to receive updates on the progress of the ULC.
22. Do you have any important final comments to add that you feel has not been covered in the survey?

References

1. Kociuba, D., Sagan, M., Kociuba, W.: Toward the smart city ecosystem model. Energies 16(6), 2795 (2023). https://doi.org/10.3390/en16062795
2. Janowski, T.: Implementing sustainable development goals with digital government – aspiration-capacity gap. Gov. Inf. Q. 33(4), 603–613 (2016). https://doi.org/10.1016/j.giq.2016.12.001
3. Alawadhi, S., et al.: Building understanding of smart city initiatives. In: Scholl, H.J., Janssen, M., Wimmer, M.A., Moe, C.E., Flak, L.S. (eds.) EGOV 2012. LNCS, vol. 7443, pp. 40–53. Springer, Heidelberg (2012). https://doi.org/10.1007/978-3-642-33489-4_4
4. de Azambuja, L.S.: Drivers and barriers for the development of smart sustainable cities: In 14th International Conference on Theory and Practice of Electronic Governance, pp. 422–428. ACM, New York, NY, USA (2021). https://doi.org/10.1145/3494193.3494250
5. Ferraris, A., Santoro, G., Pellicelli, A.C.: "Openness" of public governments in smart cities: removing the barriers for innovation and entrepreneurship. Int. Entrepreneurship Manage. J. 16(4), 1259–1280 (2020). https://doi.org/10.1007/s11365-020-00651-4
6. Pereira, G.V., de Azambuja, L.S.: Smart sustainable city roadmap as a tool for addressing sustainability challenges and building governance capacity. Sustainability (Switzerland) 14(1), 1–22 (2022). https://doi.org/10.3390/su14010239
7. Joshi, S., Saxena, S., Godbole, T., Shreya.: Developing smart cities: an integrated framework. In Procedia Computer Science, vol. 93, pp. 902–909 (2016). https://doi.org/10.1016/j.procs.2016.07.258
8. Kramers, A., Wangel, J., Hojer, M.: Planning for smart sustainable cities: decisions in the planning process and actor networks. In: ICT for Sustainability 2014 (ICT4S-14). Atlantis Press (2014). https://doi.org/10.2991/ict4s-14.2014.36
9. Praharaj, S., Han, J.H., Hawken, S.: Urban innovation through policy integration: critical perspectives from 100 smart cities mission in India. City Cult. Soc. 12, 35–43 (2018). https://doi.org/10.1016/j.ccs.2017.06.004
10. Höjer, M., Wangel, J.: Smart sustainable cities: definition and challenges. In: Hilty, L.M., Aebischer, B. (eds.) ICT Innovations for Sustainability. AISC, vol. 310, pp. 333–349. Springer, Cham (2015). https://doi.org/10.1007/978-3-319-09228-7_20
11. Allam, Z., Dhunny, Z.A.: On big data, artificial intelligence and smart cities. Cities 89, 80–91 (2019). https://doi.org/10.1016/j.cities.2019.01.032
12. Yarime, M.: Facilitating data-intensive approaches to innovation for sustainability: opportunities and challenges in building smart cities. Sustain. Sci. 12(6), 881–885 (2017). https://doi.org/10.1007/s11625-017-0498-1
13. Kattel, R., Mazzucato, M.: Mission-oriented innovation policy and dynamic capabilities in the public sector. Ind. Corp. Chang. 27(5), 787–801 (2018). https://doi.org/10.1093/icc/dty032
14. M4EG. (n.d.). M4EG Overview. https://eum4eg.com/wp-content/uploads/2022/06/NEW mayors-for-economic-growth-facility1a10d3556e56580acebe8fc51e35cea980f81ea508a 0a9d2d04d8eb7a6d4baa8-2.pdf. Accessed 7 May 2023

15. World Bank Group. FINAL REPORT (TF072882): Mayors for Economic Growth (2020). https://documents1.worldbank.org/curated/en/788011616130496523/pdf/Mayors-for-Eco nomic-Growth-Final-Report.pdf
16. UNDP. (n.d.). Mayors for Economic Growth. https://www.undp.org/eurasia/projects/mayors-economic-growth-m4eg
17. UNDP. Inception Report (2021). https://info.undp.org/docs/pdc/Documents/SVK/Annex% 201%20-%20DOA%20Mayor%20for%20Economic%20Growth%202-cln.pdf
18. Lavergne, B.R., Saxby, J.: Capicity development: vision and implications. CIDA Policy Branch **3**(3), 1–11 (2001). https://www.researchgate.net/publication/242480268_Capacity_ Development_Vision_and_implications
19. UNDG. Capacity Development: UNDAF Companion Guidance (2017). https://unsdg.un.org/ resources/capacity-development-undaf-companion-guidance
20. UNDP. Capacity Development: A UNDP Primer. United Nations Development Programme (2015). https://www.undp.org/sites/g/files/zskgke326/files/publications/CDG_Pri merReport_final_web.pdf
21. United Nations. Capacity-Building—United Nations. United Nations (2020). https://www. un.org/en/academic-impact/capacity-building. Accessed 6 May 2023
22. Otoo, S., Agapitova, N., Behrens, J.: The Capacity Development Results Framework: A Strategic and Results-Oriented the Capacity Development Results Framework a Strategic and Results-Oriented. Washington D.C (2009). http://documents.worldbank.org/curated/ en/482971468188374127/The-capacity-development-results-framework-a-strategic-and-res ults-oriented-approach-to-learning-for-capacity-development
23. OECD. Supporting Partners to Develop their Capacity: 12 Lessons from DAC Peer Reviews (2012). https://www.oecd.org/dac/peer-reviews/12lessonscapdev.pdf
24. World Health Organization. Strengthening public sector capacity, budgets and dynamic capabilities towards Health for All (2022). https://cdn.who.int/media/docs/default-source/ council-on-the-economics-of-health-for-all/who_councileh4a_councilbrief4.pdf?sfvrsn= 275a7451_3&download=true
25. Karo, E., Kattel, R.: Innovation and the state: towards an evolutionary theory of policy capacity. In: Wu, X., Howlett, M., Ramesh, M. (eds.) Policy Capacity and Governance. SPEPP, pp. 123–150. Springer, Cham (2018). https://doi.org/10.1007/978-3-319-54675-9_6
26. Panagiotopoulos, P., Klievink, B., Cordella, A.: Public value creation in digital government. Gov. Inf. Quart. **36**(4), 101421 (2019). https://doi.org/10.1016/j.giq.2019.101421
27. Pang, M.-S., Lee, G., DeLone, W.H.: IT resources, organizational capabilities, and value creation in public-sector organizations: a public-value management perspective. J. Inf. Technol. **29**(3), 187–205 (2014). https://doi.org/10.1057/jit.2014.2
28. Van Thiel, S.: The survey. In: Research Methods in Public Administration and Public Management: An Introduction, pp. 74–85. Routledge, Milton Park (2014)
29. M4EG. (n.d.). Urban Learning Center Concept Note. https://eum4eg.com/wp-content/upl oads/2022/11/ULClaunchConceptNotefdedd47c35133378aa55b0e2542ef9dcf2dadb5d46c 1cf6f7e0b5f24667613b0.pdf

IoT and Big Data Analytics Enabling Public Communication Strategies of Smart Cities in Developing Countries

Luiz Pinheiro[1]([✉]), José Carlos Vaz[2], Renan Vieira[2], and Leticia Hora[2]

[1] Positivo University Brazil, Curitiba, Brazil
luiz.junior@up.edu.br
[2] University of Sao Paulo, São Paulo, Brazil

Abstract. Part of the recent effort of Brazilian municipalities had focus on the creation of smart cities. Through the collection of data from social media and sensors spread throughout the city, it was possible to excel the delivery of public services and information nearly in real-time. For this, the communication and exchange of information has been essential. This chapter aims to analyze how a developing country city used platforms and technical features from Internet of Things and Big Data Analytics in their smart city communication strategies. A case study about Center of Operations Rio de Janeiro (COR), in Brazil, was carried. Literature review in Portuguese was conducted to provide references to build a set of platforms and technical features recommended for social communication in the digital age. This recommended set of platforms and technical features were used to perform a structured visit in the COR´s portal and analyze how this set appears or identify new ones and their uses. The results bring a list of 7 platforms and 18 technical features. We believe that these platforms and features should be taken into account for the design of public communication strategies of smart cities of developing countries.

Keywords: Smart Cities · Communication · Technical Features · Big and Open Linked Data Analytics · Transparency

1 Introduction

A The Rio de Janeiro city hall has made an effort to become an intelligent city in the recent years. Its initiatives ensure it a leading position among Brazilian municipalities that have initiatives that can be classified as smart cities (Systems 2016). Literature (Nam and Pardo 2011, Cocchia 2014) pointed out that the concept of smart cities as the organization of the infrastructure and the local government for the delivery of public services in excellence level in several areas such as health, education, urban mobility etc.) through the intensive use of information and communication technologies (ICTs). Currently, part of this public service delivery quickly and effectively, cities have been organized based on the "Big Data Analytics" (BDA) approach.

© IFIP International Federation for Information Processing 2023
Published by Springer Nature Switzerland AG 2023
M. Janssen et al. (Eds.): I3E 2023, LNCS 14316, pp. 418–429, 2023.
https://doi.org/10.1007/978-3-031-50040-4_31

The BDA in smart cities can be divided in two main dimensions (Janssen et al. 2015). The first is the "big data" dimension, based in the collection of real data from users in the social media (Twitter, Facebook, etc.), smartphone applications (Waze, Moovit, etc.) as well from sensors spread over the city (traffic lights, speed traps, fines, etc.) currently powered via the Internet of things (IoT) (Riggins and Wamba 2015). The second dimension "analytics" is based in complex algorithms processing the big data collected aforementioned and exploiting in tables, graphs and maps.

The BDA approach helps public manager to improve the decision-making, the implementation and the evaluation of public policies (Chen et al. 2012). The BDA can also be used to support communication and transparency (Janssen et al. 2017) of public service delivery to citizens (Matheus and Janssen 2015). However, the smart cities approach for communication strategies is less explored by practitioners and scientific literature. Even considering the importance of this topic, the articles show a focus in strategies to create and sustain smart cities (Nam and Pardo 2011, Chourabi et al. 2012, Townsend 2013, Gil-Garcia et al. 2014) or technological technical features (Janssen et al. 2015, Rathore et al. 2016).

In Brazil, the focus of practical and scientific production is in the same situation that international showed. A structured literature review in the three main Brazilian scientific conferences in the field of public administration and technology applied in government (Enanpad, Enadi and Enapg) and in the main conference of practitioners of Brazilian public administration (Consad) give us few results of papers describing cases and theory about communication strategies in smart cities using BDA. The search of scientific articles about smart city communication strategy published in the three highest ranks of Brazilian system of scientific journals classification (Plataforma Sucupira, levels A1, A2 and B1) also returns to us an underdeveloped scenario.

This lack of attention given to the topic justify our object and scope in this work. Rio de Janeiro is a case of smart city that uses BDA and IoT further than simple public service delivery and started to use this data processed to provide relevant information services to citizens and to the government itself (Matheus et al. 2020). Information services are here understood as systematic provision of information that generates public value to be appropriated by the citizens as they use them to improve their infrastructure and urban services usage.

Rio adopted a structured strategy for communication centralized in a single platform and organization in charge, the Geoportal in the IBM Center Of Operations Rio de Janeiro (COR) (Matheus and Janssen 2017). To create impact not only in the public service delivery, Rio de Janeiro had to organize its civil servants to produce and select relevant BDA made at COR enabled by IoT. The production of analysis is naturally made every day, however, how select the "relevant ones" to the citizens? Taking this into consideration, the COR started to open channels to communicate with the citizens such as social media (Twitter, Facebook and Youtube), partnerships with smartphone applications and in the traditional media from TV, radio and newspapers.

This chapter aims to describe the communication strategies adopted by COR structured by platforms used and technical features selected to communicate with citizens information about the urban mobility (traffic jams) and tourism (events) during the Carnival 2017 in Rio de Janeiro (March, 20th to 27th, 2017). The scope for Carnival is justified considering Rio is a 6 million inhabitants city, attracting more than 1 million of tourists from all the world and boosting 1 billion of United States dollars in the local economy (RIOTUR 2017).

The research approach is based in a single case study, performed from a literature review on platforms and technical features recommended for communication in the Digital Era. The case study method was chosen considering to be a new area of study and the existence of a few publications about the topic. Further, the description of this case shows the existent technical features of an electronic portal and use of social media, identifying in an exploratory way new technical features not yet catalogued by scientific literature. Selecting Rio and COR as single case is also justified due its pioneer to bring communication to people and being awarded in Brazil and in the world as a top-level smart city, as well the high level of approval of its public service delivery by citizens.

Literature review provided references to build a set of platforms and technical features recommended for communication in the digital age. This recommended set of platforms and technical features was used to perform a structured visit in the COR´s portal (www.cor.rio) and analyze how recommended set list of platforms and technical features appear or identify new ones not considered in literature.

2 Literature Review - Public Information Service

The comprehensiveness and range of human communication are directly influenced by the channels used to perform the communication. As an example, the North-Americans newspapers experienced a boost since trains were built from New York (East Coast) to California (West Coast) (Canavilhas 2006). It happens because the trains were much more efficient than the old strategies of information dissemination, in that case the horses and carts. Every disruptive innovation brings new opportunities and threats. It was not different for communication, digital era and IoT. IoT enabled the creation of web journalism (Stovall 2003). Web journalism changed mass media modus-operandi. Newspapers, radio and TV started to lose the highest ranks as main channel to access information (Canavilhas 2003). However, it is important to highlight that Internet is still an "elite" channel to access information in Brazil. A study showed in 2015 that only 50% of Brazilians regularly access Internet and only 25% have experienced any public service delivery via web (CETIC.br 2015).

The web journalism followed the past models used in the previous technologies, as an example Internet pages are clearly inspired in the printed newspapers. After Internet popularization in the 90's, new strategies, platforms and technical features were created and adopted by web journalism. This context made the "inverted pyramid" technique (Scanlan 2003) obsolete, moving to the "lying pyramid" (Canavilhas 2006). While the inverted pyramid focuses in the provision of information in increasing order (more important -> less important), the lying pyramid does not use the usual chronological format of events, but organizing the news according to its ne news value, starting from the most impacting (relevant) information and thus reaching its audience more directly (Scanlan 2003).

Internet enabled web journalism to create news ad infinitum and ad aeternum, since it is possible to create how many web pages text or image based and keep them online forever (Canavilhas 2006). This is an advantage considering the limited space and time of newspapers, radio and TV. Internet also reduced the cost to produce and access information, being possible to be updated anytime by anyone anywhere. Furthermore, web pages can be linked to each other, generating infinite content access (Mielniczuk 2012). The Fig. 1 shows the informative potential enabled by Internet.

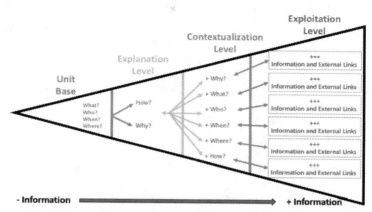

Fig. 1. Lying pyramid and the level of information depth from inverted pyramid. Source. Adapted from Canavilhas (2006)

Among the challenges to mass communication, while web journalism can lead many people to information, in real-time or close to real-time, reducing the barriers to access information has drastically dropped the price of advertising on all channels (Bakker 2012). By reducing barriers to create content and access to information, Internet enabled new content producers and niches of audience. Since 2000 is possible to notice a generation of new players in communication competing more and more with traditional media (TV, radio, newspapers). As example, the bloggers (small portals with daily and usually small entries), vloggers (small video daily produced, e.g. YouTube), microblogs and social networks such as Twitter, Facebook Instagram and others. Part of this boom happened due the called web 2.0, which already have been influencing touristic smart cities (Fernández-Cavia et al. 2010).

These new players are already influencing electoral results, as occurred in the United States of America, during the election of Trump (Oates and Moe 2016). In Brazil, during the general demonstrations in June 2013 against corruption and high expenses in World Cup 2014 and Olympics games 2016, the group Mídia Ninja became nationally known to stream in real-time the events around the country, using Internet, smartphones and microblogs for almost free (Krohling Peruzzo 2013).

It is important to highlight the opportunities brought to smart cities. First, they can create their own and new communication channels with citizens. Second, web journalism can be used as an ally in providing information to citizens, in real-time or close for a low cost, in order to facilitate citizen daily decision-making such as using the urban services and infrastructures (avoid traffic congestions or selecting best day based in the weather forecast to enjoy the sun in the Copacabana beach). BDA usage can generate informational products that will be absorbed by web journalism, which will "translate" in relevant content to reach the target citizens that will use this information. For this, it is necessary to create structured strategies based on platforms and technical features, topic of our next section.

2.1   Strategies, Platforms and Technical Features

There are two types of metaphors most commonly used in online news: document metaphor and broadsheet metaphor (Watters et al. 2000). It has changed the way we tell a story to the audience, leading to the so-called "data journalism" or data-driven journalism (Matheus et al. 2014). In this way, the strategies to broadcast information had changed. If newspapers used to have a specific audience, and are often captive for monthly fees, information is currently gaining its audience according to the access profiles and the participation of the readers (Barbosa 2005).

Creating news also occurs over (a shorter and shorter) time and influenced by later events (Fidalgo and Serra 2004). For example, to inform a car accident a journalist would use the "what", "who", "when", "where", "why" and "how" in a generic way (check Fig. 1) to attract the immediate and particular interest (Barbosa 2005). However, accidents can generate traffic congestions, and the interest is more and diffuse than the simple event that generated it. Thus, the news is structured based in the purpose to provide as much data and information as possible. This content can make readers to do the best possible decision-making based on their particular interests and the information accessed.

From the point of view of platforms, the ICTs ephemerality is natural. As an example, Orkut has already been one of the largest social networks in the world. Currently it has been discontinued and surpassed by other platforms like Facebook, Twitter and YouTube. The change of platforms was enabled in part by IoT, based in the spread of Internet and smartphones.

The technical features also followed the trends of the communication strategies and platforms. The first technical feature identified is the use of search and indexing the news and web sites in a structured way using the Search Engine Optimization (SEO) method to optimize the search results in search engines like Google, Bing and Yahoo (Palácios 2003).

SEO helps attract bigger and better selected audience, thereby generating more traffic, or better targeting the audience to the news. Most of this platform also uses databases in "user friendly" formats, such as eXtensible Markup Language (XML), allowing flexibility in the presentation of data according to user requirements (Barbosa 2005). Through XML, you can "transcode" news and web sites. It means creating content in different formats (text, maps, interactive pictures and videos) using the same data and potentially attracting different audiences and connecting platforms easily (Manovich 2001). Using the XML technical feature or structured databases is also possible to create metadata (Nadkarni 2011), which help the reader to acquire and understand the context more quickly, deepening the analysis of information for decision making.

Another feature identified in the literature is the ability to create memory at a low cost and tending to infinity of time and physical space (Manovich 2001). Fidalgo and Serra (2004)pointed out that Internet and its infinite capacity of memory and connections create the "Semantic Resolution". Semantic Resolution let writers (journalists) to go deeper into the news according to the audience that visits the pages. And if necessary, adding new links to relevant connections to the audience profile, and according to the collection of data and information (check Fig. 1). Finally, digital participation in social media such as Facebook, Twitter and YouTube allows readers themselves to supplement information and address readers' doubts, helping the role of communicators.

Next section analyses platforms and technical features that configured the communications strategy and information services of the city of Rio de Janeiro, implemented by the COR.

3 Results from Case Studies Analysis

The results point to a list of seven platforms and eighteen technical features. Below, the Fig. 2 presents, in numbers and red box, the communication strategies, platforms and technical features identified during the Carnival 2017 in Rio de Janeiro. Green circles present the interactive strategies of disseminating information on urban mobility and tourism, and the platforms presented in green frames:

A. Electronic portal;
B. Facebook;
C. Twitter;
D. YouTube;
E. Periscope;
F. Partnerships with smartphone applications; and,
G. Digital dashboard panel (video-wall).

Fig. 2. Platforms and technical features used by COR in Carnival 2017. Source. Elaborated by authors.

Eighteen technical features were identified in the literature review and in the case study. They are described in the Table 1 below.

Table 1. The 18 technical features observed in the Carnival 2017 in Rio de Janeiro

#	Name	Description	Source
1	**Audience tuning and customization**	Definition of the classification of the target audience will occur over time as information is collected and profiles of access and participation (young, elderly, etc.)	(Barbosa 2005)
2	**Generation of news in real-time**	Overlapping the immediate need to have information regarding the requirement of objectivity and verifiability	(Barbosa 2005)
3	**Immersive story (interactivity)**	Narrative ability to incorporate multimedia features (audio, video, links) allowing reader to "drill" into the news	Mielniczuk (2012)
4	**Classifications and Subtitles**	Classifications and captions that help readers to easily understand the content and make the best decision-make	(Barbosa 2005)
5	**Metadata**	Data that explains other data and helps readers to have context about the data used	Nadkarni (2011)
6	**Creating news over time**	News improvements over time and updated, complemented and corrected as the event needs. Example car accident that causes traffic congestions	Fidalgo and Serra (2004)
7	**Digital Participation**	If there is room for reader participation, the news can gain even more information and relevance	(Barbosa 2005)
8	**Semantic Resolution**	Plurality and diversity of online news contributes to improved understanding. Example of graphic resolution with increasing number of pixels per cm^2	Fidalgo and Serra (2004)

(*continued*)

Table 1. (*continued*)

#	Name	Description	Source
9	**Memory of contents**	Databases that can store publications *ad aeternum*	Manovich (2001)
10	**Transcoding**	Ability to transform the same content into different forms (text, video, map, figure, etc.)	Manovich (2001)
11	**Dynamic Languages (XML)**	Use of eXtensible Markup Language (XML), allowing flexibility in data presentation	(Barbosa 2005)
12	**Search and Indexing (SEO)**	Easy-to-understand and search content to attract greater public and traffic via search motor engines (e.g. Google)	Palácios (2003)
13	**Streaming Videos**	865 live camera and event memory. Helped by Periscope, blocks of carnivals and car accidents are streamed	Rio Case Study
14	**Interactivity via Social Media**	Posts on social media (Facebook, Twitter, Periscope and Youtube) with reader interactivity	Rio Case Study
15	**Partnerships with smartphone apps**	Partnership with applications most used by people, such as Waze and Moovit for urban mobility	Rio Case Study
16	**Partnership with Traditional Media**	Printed media, radio and television have a room within the COR and can access 100% of data from COR	Rio Case Study
17	**Weekly Bulletins**	Weekly bulletins are released in PDF with key information about weather, tourism and urban mobility	Rio Case Study
18	**Big Data Analytics**	The data collection from social media combined with internal data from COR allows to perform BDA	Janssen, Matheus et al. (2015)

Research data show that Rio de Janeiro adopted a strategy based on the joined use of several platforms, combined with a series of complementary technical features. This expanded possibility of informational services to reach users. So, they can be used by citizens and Rio de Janeiro visitors to make their decisions on mobility and touristic activities.

Articulation between the Rio de Janeiro BDA team (PENSA – www.pensa.rio) and the COR communication team played a fundamental role, since it allowed the integration of data and its dissemination in the various formats and platforms adopted. This strategy allowed Rio de Janeiro to produce an information services diversified portfolio to be offered to citizens, either directly or through the press and applications.

4 Final Considerations

The main contribution of this work was identifying platforms and technical features that allow to materialize smart cities strategies for public interest communication and information. In the case studied, the COR of Rio de Janeiro, it was possible to observe that the core of the strategy was the adoption of social media practices in articulation with big data analytics for information services provision to citizens (especially urban mobility and tourism in Carnival 2017).

Considering this work is a single case study, this chapter does not aim to explain patterns and correlations between cause and effect, nor to establish a definitive list of technical features to be adopted by any smart city. However, it was possible to construct a comprehensive list of strategies, platforms and technical features, produced from a combination of pre-existing knowledge of technical features in an established study area (social media in the digital age) with the collection of data from the structured inspection of the technical features present in the COR portal.

The inventory of strategies, platforms and technical features for smart cities social communication can contribute to further studies. Research about specific technical features adoption or their joint use can bring more knowledge about their impact on service performance. From a more practical point of view, this new list can serve as a starting point for smart cities initiatives to design or redesign their strategies, platforms and technical features for providing information services from collected data.

Literature review allowed to demonstrate the increasing importance of this type of service in smart cities portfolios. It was possible to understand the increasing approximation between the provision of information by the governments, the web journalism and the citizen participation. In some ways, it becomes more difficult to smart cities keep separated media activities from information services.

Changes in communication and interaction between governments and citizens practices also helps smart cities to increase information services delivery. High interactive technological resources and social practices associated to them put a stop to the so-called "broadcasting mode" of communication between government and citizens. This "broadcasting mode" become replaced by the multidirectional information flow (Vaz 2017). Information is publicized in a unidirectional way in the "broadcasting mode", in which there is a strong distinction between sender and receiver. Breaking this traditional flow of information means that roles are no longer univocal: journalists and citizens interfere in the content of government-published information, complementing and enriching this information, adding new levels of exploitation, as proposed in Canavilhas (2006) (see Fig. 1).

For smart cities that want to expand the scope of their action using BDA, using social media practices based on large volumes of data becomes a relevant alternative. Data and information generated from data analytics resources are an important asset to develop information services. Such practices require adoption of strategies based on various technological resources used jointly to facilitate and stimulate communication practices able to deliver informational services (generated from collected data processed by the BDA approach). These services can take on multiple configurations in terms of:

- Data Source: government data; sensor data; data from users obtained from applications; data from private companies; combinations of different sources.
- Origin of Main Content (initial publication): government; press (web journalism); private companies' applications.
- Level of Interactivity: information broadcast; automated on line updates; user interaction with each other or with government or the press.
- Platform to Share Content: services using a single platform; multi-platform services; integrated platforms and services.
- Technical Features: single features services; services that combine different technical features; integration of technical features into multiples of services.

Platforms to share content and technical features are decisive for smart cities information services strategies. They give materiality to the information service, whatever the configuration adopted. Therefore, service scope and reach depend on the choice of platforms and technical features suitable for the communication generated from the data analytics resources.

Technological developments stimulate the co-production of services, which depend not only on them, but also on business models appropriate to involve various stakeholders. Although it was not this work's focus to analyze business models and services production processes, it was possible to observe the importance of articulated actions between social communication and of big data analytics teams. It was also clear the relevancy of city government collaboration with web journalism and companies-owned applications based on interfaces with public infrastructures and services. It is hoped that these early results will serve as the basis for further, and comparative, studies to understand more appropriate characteristics for smart cities information services business models.

This chapter also did not aim to address deeply technologies used or their technical attributes. Further research in the technological field will be important to support IoT artefacts development. These efforts should help to create guidelines and methods for developing new services and expanding the reach of smart cities initiatives.

In the same way, this study did not turn to a deep understanding of the actors involved and the state capacities (technological resources, specific human resources skills, process structuring, governance tools, etc.) demanded by the production of COR informational services. Further studies on this subject are indispensable for the development of design and service management methods to extend the reach of the technological resources adopted by smart cities in the future.

References

Bakker, P.: Aggregation, content farms and Huffinization: the rise of low-pay and no-pay journalism. J. Pract. **6**(5–6), 627–637 (2012)

Barbosa, S.: Jornalismo digital e bases de dados: mapeando conceitos e funcionalidades. SOPCOM: Associação Portuguesa de Ciências da Comunicação 1310–1321 (2005)

Canavilhas, J.: Webjornalismo: considerações gerais sobre jornalismo na web (2003)

Canavilhas, J.: Webjornalismo: Da pirâmide invertida à pirâmide deitada. BOCC–Biblioteca Online de Ciências de Comunicação (2006)

CETIC.br: Pesquisa sobre o uso das tecnologias da informação e da comunicação no Brasil: TIC Domicílios e TIC Empresas 2009. São Paulo: Comitê Gestor da Internet no Brasil (2015)

Chen, H., et al.: Business intelligence and analytics: from big data to big impact. MIS Quart. **36**(4), 1165–1188 (2012)

Chourabi, H., et al.: Understanding smart cities: an integrative framework. In: 2012 45th Hawaii International Conference on System Science (HICSS). IEEE (2012)

Cocchia, A.: Smart and digital city: a systematic literature review. In: Dameri, R.P., Rosenthal-Sabroux, C. (eds.) Smart city. PI, pp. 13–43. Springer, Cham (2014). https://doi.org/10.1007/978-3-319-06160-3_2

Fernández-Cavia, J., et al.: Propuesta de diseño de una plantilla multidisciplinar para el análisis y evaluación de webs de destinos turísticos (2010)

Fidalgo, A., P. Serra.: Do poliedro à esfera: os campos de classificação. A resolução semântica no jornalismo online. Anais do II SBPJor. Salvador-BA/Brasil (2004)

Gil-Garcia, J.R., et al.: Being smart: Emerging technologies and innovation in the public sector. Gov. Inf. Q. **31**, I1–I8 (2014)

Janssen, M., et al.: Big and open linked data (BOLD) to create smart cities and citizens: insights from smart energy and mobility cases. In: Tambouris, E., et al. (eds.) EGOV 2015. LNCS, vol. 9248, pp. 79–90. Springer, Cham (2015). https://doi.org/10.1007/978-3-319-22479-4_6

Janssen, M., Matheus, R., Longo, J., Weerakkody, V.: Transparency-by-design as a foundation for open government. Transforming Gov. People Process Policy **11**(1), 2–8 (2017). https://doi.org/10.1108/TG-02-2017-0015

Krohling Peruzzo, C.M.: Movimentos sociais, redes virtuais e mídia alternativa no junho em que "o gigante acordou (?)". MATRIZes **7**(2), 73–93 (2013)

Manovich, L.: The Language of New Media. MIT Press, Cambridge (2001)

Matheus, R., et al.: Dados Abertos no Jornalismo: Os Limites e os Desafios das Estratégias de Uso e Criação de Cadeia de Valor Social incentivando a transparência e controle social na América Latina. OD4D, 2014 (2014)

Matheus, R., Janssen, M.: Transparency dimensions of big and open linked data. Janssen, M., et al. (eds.) Open and Big Data Management and Innovation. I3E 2015. LNCS, vol. 9373, pp. 236–246. Springer, Cham (2015)

Matheus, R., Janssen, M.: How to become a smart city? Balancing ambidexterity in smart cities. In: Proceedings of the 10th International Conference on Theory and Practice of Electronic Governance. ACM (2017)

Matheus, R., Janssen, M., Maheshwari, D.: Data science empowering the public: data-driven dashboards for transparent and accountable decision-making in smart cities. Gov. Inf. Q. **37**(3), 101284 (2020)

Mielniczuk, L.: Jornalismo na Web: uma contribuição para o estudo do formato da notícia na escrita hipertextual (2012)

Nadkarni, P.M.: What is Metadata? In: Metadata-Driven Software Systems in Biomedicine. Health Informatics, pp. 1–16. Springer, London (2011). https://doi.org/10.1007/978-0-85729-510-1_1

Nam, T., Pardo, T.A.: Conceptualizing smart city with dimensions of technology, people, and institutions. In: Proceedings of the 12th Annual International Digital Government Research Conference: Digital Government Innovation in Challenging Times. College Park, Maryland, USA, pp. 282–291. ACM (2011)

Oates, S., Moe, W.W.: Donald Trump and the 'Oxygen of Publicity': Branding, Social Media, and Mass Media in the 2016 Presidential Primary Elections (2016)

Palácios, M.: Ruptura, continuidade e potencialização no jornalismo on-line: o lugar da memória. Digital. MACHADO, Elias e PALÀCIOS, Marcos. Modelos de Jornalismo. Salvador: Edições GJOL e Ed. Calandra (2003)

Rathore, M.M., et al.: Urban planning and building smart cities based on the internet of things using big data analytics. Comput. Netw. **101**, 63–80 (2016)

Riggins, F.J., Wamba, S.F.: Research directions on the adoption, usage, and impact of the internet of things through the use of big data analytics. In: 2015 48th Hawaii International Conference on System Sciences (HICSS). IEEE (2015)

RIOTUR: Tourism Statistics in Rio de Janeiro (2017). http://www.rio.rj.gov.br/riotur

Scanlan, C.: Writing from the top down: Pros and cons of the inverted pyramid (2003). Accessed 15 June 2006

Stovall, J.G.: Web journalism: practice and promise of a new medium. Allyn & Bacon, Inc. (2003)

Systems, U.: Ranking connected smart cities (2016). http://www.urbansystems.com.br/reports/ler/ranking-connected-smart-cities-2016-foi-apresentado-no-rj

Townsend, A.M.: Smart Cities: Big Data, Civic Hackers, and the Quest for a New Utopia. WW Norton & Company, New York (2013)

Vaz, J.C.: Transformações tecnológicas e perspectivas para a gestão democrática das políticas culturais. Cadernos Gestão Pública e Cidadania **22**(71) (2017)

Watters, C.R., Shepherd, M.A., Chiasson, T., Manchester, L.: An evaluation of two metaphors for electronic news presentation. In: King, P., Munson, E.V. (eds.) PODDP 2000. LNCS, vol. 2023, pp. 223–241. Springer, Heidelberg (2004). https://doi.org/10.1007/978-3-540-39916-2_17

Author Index

© IFIP International Federation for Information Processing 2023
Published by Springer Nature Switzerland AG 2023
M. Janssen et al. (Eds.): I3E 2023, LNCS 14316, pp. 431–432, 2023.
https://doi.org/10.1007/978-3-031-50040-4

Printed in the United States
by Baker & Taylor Publisher Services